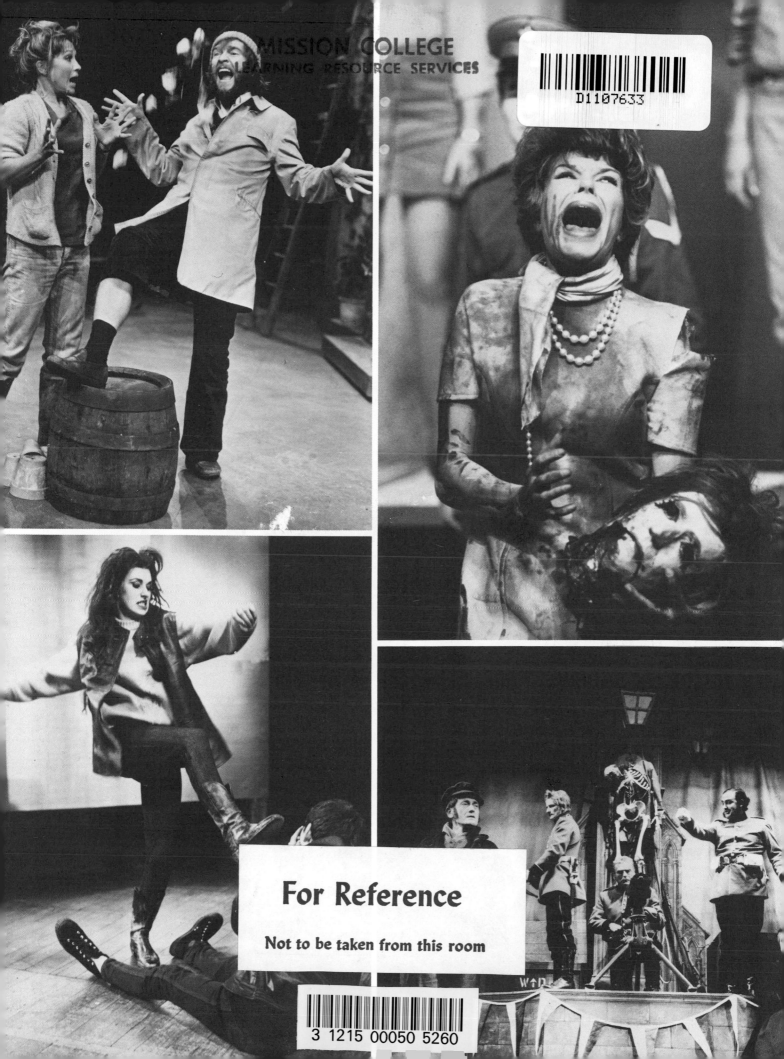

Dictionary of Literary Biography • Volume Thirteen

British Dramatists Since World War II

Part 1: A-L

Dictionary of Literary Biography

1: *The American Renaissance in New England*,
edited by Joel Myerson (1978)

2: *American Novelists Since World War II*,
edited by Jeffrey Helterman and Richard Layman (1978)

3: *Antebellum Writers in New York and the South*,
edited by Joel Myerson (1979)

4: *American Writers in Paris, 1920-1939*,
edited by Karen Lane Rood (1980)

5: *American Poets Since World War II*, 2 volumes,
edited by Donald J. Greiner (1980)

6: *American Novelists Since World War II*, Second Series,
edited by James E. Kibler, Jr. (1980)

7: *Twentieth-Century American Dramatists*, 2 volumes,
edited by John MacNicholas (1981)

8: *Twentieth-Century American Science-Fiction Writers*, 2 volumes,
edited by David Cowart and Thomas L. Wymer (1981)

9: *American Novelists, 1910-1945*, 3 volumes,
edited by James J. Martine (1981)

10: *Modern British Dramatists, 1900-1945*, 2 volumes,
edited by Stanley Weintraub (1982)

11: *American Humorists, 1800-1950*, 2 volumes,
edited by Stanley Trachtenberg (1982)

12: *American Realists and Naturalists*,
edited by Donald Pizer and Earl N. Harbert (1982)

13: *British Dramatists Since World War II*, 2 volumes,
edited by Stanley Weintraub (1982)

Yearbook: 1980,
edited by Karen L. Rood, Jean W. Ross, and Richard Ziegfeld (1981)

Yearbook: 1981,
edited by Karen L. Rood, Jean W. Ross, and Richard Ziegfeld (1982)

Documentary Series, volume 1,
edited by Margaret A. Van Antwerp (1982)

Documentary Series, volume 2,
edited by Margaret A. Van Antwerp (1982)

Dictionary of Literary Biography • Volume Thirteen

British Dramatists Since World War II

Part 1: A-L

Edited by
Stanley Weintraub
Pennsylvania State University

A Bruccoli Clark Book
Gale Research Company • Book Tower • Detroit, Michigan 48226
1982

Manufactured by Braun-Brumfield, Inc.
Ann Arbor, Michigan
Printed in the United States of America

Copyright © 1982
GALE RESEARCH COMPANY

Library of Congress Cataloging in Publication Data

Main entry under title:

British dramatists since World War II.

   (Dictionary of literary biography; v. 13)
   "A Bruccoli Clark Book."
   1. Dramatists, English—20th century—Biography.
I. Weintraub, Stanley, 1929- . II. Series.
PR106.B74   1982   822'.914'09 [B]   82-15724
ISBN 0-8103-0936-X

Contents

Contents

Foreword

"The theater world's Nirvana," the *Washington Post*'s emeritus drama critic, Richard Coe, now calls it, but in the autumn of 1945 London theatrical life was in as much of a shambles as its theaters, some damaged or destroyed in six years of war and others run down after years in which their physical condition was ignored. A fuel shortage made buildings feel colder than outdoors, and attending a performance was almost as much a strain as participating in the play: at least the performer could work up a sweat in a strenuous job of acting. American playwright S. N. Behrman, in London for the opening of one of his own works in the winter of 1945-1946, remembered that the fog and cold penetrated into hotel lobbies, galleries, and theaters. Mary Martin, starring in Noel Coward's *Pacific 1890*, a South Seas musical, told him how it felt to stand on the windy expanse of the Drury Lane stage, singing tropical ditties into the chill night: "You sing not at an audience but into a [cold] haze. You shiver and sing."

Fortunately for the personnel performing in most theaters, but less fortunate for theater itself, most plays in the first postwar years were revivals of classics or costume dramas, heavy on crinolines and floor-length gowns, and set in overfurnished drawing rooms hung with tapestried, voluminous drapes. In the late 1950s a theatergoer, looking about, would have seen little but a continuation of the dramatic life of the interwar years. Noel Coward and J. B. Priestley were back, as were Terence Rattigan and James Bridie. Sean O'Casey was still writing cantankerous plays which no one cared to produce, and Bernard Shaw, in his nineties, was turning out *Buoyant Billions* and *Far Fetched Fables*. Into mid-century, theater in London (and elsewhere in the Isles) was the same mixture as before.

As Kenneth Tynan would recall late in the 1950s, the British stage had been dominated, as one would have expected in the war years and after, by drawing-room comedy, barrack-room farce, and murder melodrama. Contemporary reality had failed to take hold, perhaps because it was too grim for an audience weary of postwar austerity after war years of privation. "Nightly, in dozens of theatres," Tynan wrote, "the curtain rose on the same set. French windows were its most prominent feature,

backed by a sky-cloth of brilliant and perpetual blue.... If we were not at Mark Trevannion's country house in Berkshire, we were probably at Hilary Egleston's flat in Knightsbridge, and wherever we were, we ran into the same crowd...."

That crowd, the staple of commercial theater for decades, included all the stereotypes, from the audacious ingenue to the "obligatory dragoness," from the porcine clubman ruddy with port wine to the tweedy complaisant husband, and, Tynan alleged, no one except a gardener was ever called Bert, while no one but a housemaid was ever named Myrtle. The language onstage "was of a rigid deformity," largely pseudo-upper-class. Anyone whose knowledge of England was informed by English commercial theater would have assumed, despite the bleakness of the late-1940s welfare state, that its life-style was comfortable and even opulent. "The poor were seldom with us, except when making antic contributions to broad farce or venturing, tongue-tied with embarrassment and clutching cloth caps, into the gracious salons of middle-class comedy, where they were expected to preface every remark with 'Beggin' yer pardon, Mum.' To become eligible for dramatic treatment, it was usually necessary either to have an income of more than three thousand pounds net [Tynan was writing when the pound was healthier and inflation milder] or to be murdered in the house of someone who did."

There had been an exception: the war years had included patriotic bows to the lower classes, and the depression of the 1930s had reminded a few playwrights, usually to the disgust of theater managers, that there was a life beyond Mayfair. Still, those who made their incomes from plays and their production had assumed for decades that the audiences who could afford tickets consisted of people who wanted their prejudices reinforced and their egos bolstered. Such a view of the world was shattered often enough by Bernard Shaw or one of his acknowledged or unacknowledged followers into the 1930s, but their commercial success—except for Shaw's—was too rare to encourage imitation, and imitation itself is in any case creatively sterile. As Max Beerbohm had complained in a *Saturday Re-*

view drama column as early as 1907, "If our dramatists will condescend to make our acquaintance. . . , they will find that we, too, the unmentioned by Debrett ['s *Peerage*], . . . have brains and hearts. They will find that we, too, are capable of great joys and griefs, and that such things come our way quite often really."

If any purely theatrical event rung down the curtain on the first phase of twentieth-century drama, it was one which occurred neatly at mid-century and at the end of the decade of war and its aftermath. Bernard Shaw, who had bestrode English drama since the 1890s, died at ninety-four on 2 November 1950. As playwright he left no obvious successors, and the winds of change he had blown through the stage on the surface seemed to have had little impact. His own repertory of plays remained a legacy of actable vigor, but the commercial theater he had attacked as a critic and undermined as a playwright had only retreated underground. When Shavian vitality ebbed, the traditional cliches of the theater emerged. The new underground became the theater of electric ideas and crisp characters which would return in new guises, even recalling the fantasy and extravaganza of his plays of the 1930s and 1940s. Shaw would not have been downcast at leaving no school. "It is my hope," he had written in 1921, when he was sixty-five, "that a hundred apter and more elegant parables by younger hands will soon leave mine as far behind as the religious pictures of the fifteenth century left behind the first attempts of the early Christians at iconography."

Change was gradual. Backers of plays and lessees of theaters are cautious souls. Even today any count of dramatic works onstage in London or New York will show a heavy preponderance of brainless comedies, forgettable melodramas, and musical entertainments with just enough plot to be classified as plays. But change is palpable in England when even the people who read the news on the telly no longer necessarily speak sophisticated BBC English. Onstage the variety of accents dramatizes the variety of life now viable by box-office measure, a metamorphosis which in recent legend occurred overnight.

The success of John Osborne's *Look Back in Anger* at the Royal Court Theatre in Sloane Square in May 1956 is the legendary opening shot in the playwriting fusillade which brought down the French doors and the drawing-room curtains of decades of English drama. Like most advances, it was prepared for by the unrewarded efforts of unsung writers, and by the changes in mood effected by years which had made the England of the com-

mercial stage of the past unrecognizable outside the theater. *Look Back in Anger* was no surprise to visiting Americans who remembered their own Clifford Odets of *Awake and Sing* in the 1930s; but there had been no Odets in England, although there had been an emigre O'Casey (who was poor box office). Theatergoers in London in 1956 would recall that some earlier shots had been fired by a stubborn but unsuccessful John Whiting, whose brilliant *Saint's Day* (1951), produced at the Arts Theatre Club for lack of a more commercial house, was dismissed by the *Times* as "having a badness that must be thought indescribable." Also, a Parisian Irishman, Samuel Beckett, had been able to produce a cryptic *Waiting for Godot* for a puzzled London in 1955, and a London novelist named Graham Greene had presented a deliberately drab *The Living Room* as early as 1953 to the huzzahs of audiences starved for ideas as well as for a breath of reality. And there were others, as this compendium will demonstrate, who prepared the way for the barriers to come down so dramatically in 1956-1958 for Harold Pinter, Brendan Behan, John Arden, Joan Littlewood, Arnold Wesker, Peter Shaffer, and others of the first wave of new drama.

Change had not come easily because even some of the brightest new names and most promising new plays at first looked back too much, and suggested directions which would prove wrong turnings. As T. S. Eliot had seemingly augured a new verse drama in the 1930s (and with *The Cocktail Party* would even continue his activities into the postwar theater), so Christopher Fry, with *The Lady's Not for Burning* (1945) and a few succeeding plays, would demonstrate that poetry and popularity were not necessarily alien to each other. Nevertheless, there would not be a new Elizabethan verse drama with a second Elizabeth any more than there would be a new drama of ideas on the Shaw model because Peter Ustinov appeared to point the way with *The Love of Four Colonels* (1951), or because Ronald Duncan had fashioned a Shavian *The Death of Satan* (1954). The new British drama had to find its own identity or identities, and it did.

In that sector of the Isles dominated by Dublin, a vigorous but largely regional drama remained, with bright exceptions, a backwater after the exile of O'Casey in 1926 and the death of Yeats in 1939. The opportunity for commercial success in London or New York for an Irish play had dwindled further with the 1939-1945 war, from which Ireland had stood aside. Irish playwrights would spend the following decades battling obscurity. International reputations for a flamboyant Brendan Behan and a few later successors would overshadow a flourishing but small-scale theatrical life, little touched at first by new influences and the new technology.

The view from London in the first postwar decade, on the other hand, was one of opportunity. Despite 1940s austerities and early 1950s frustrations with the tenacity of tradition, change was happening. The war had spurred a boom in radio, and television was rapidly becoming a new parallel theater. Usually quiescent British cinema was experiencing its most creative years. Each alternative dramatic medium was enlarging the potential audience for plays, the possible approaches to playwriting, and the market for playwrights. In the process, government more and more became partner to art. BBC radio, then television, fostered new schools of playwrights who not only cut their professional teeth on the electronic stage, but sustained themselves by such writing and then went on to the traditional (and untraditional) theaters or to films. Some writers had even been service veterans who had gone to college on government grants, thus having been sponsored by the public purse in more ways than one. Ironically, many of the playwrights nursed one way or another by the public sector would become harsh critics of their society, some turning out blistering agitprop plays aimed at converting, further leftward, audiences who seldom if ever went to a playhouse and who saw or heard the plays, if at all, via the public media of television and radio.

Some alternatives to the commercial theater—itself only a minority art—nevertheless did emerge, their models the "club" mechanisms which had evaded the Lord Chamberlain's official censorship, an anachronism which continued to emasculate drama until 1968, when the hypocrisy of half-regulating such taboos as four-letter words and nudity finally expired. Some playwrights took their brief agitprop plays to factories, convinced that they would "move the workers"; feminist writers often turned to workshop productions, which sometimes matured revolutionary vehicles into actable dramas creating commercial opportunities for their playwrights; lunch-hour theaters sprang up, where people in offices or shops, usually not in the habit of theatergoing, might acquire the taste; fringe theaters in urban centers and in seedy suburbs would attempt to compete with cinemas and the telly for their audiences. The result, even when many aspiring playwrights never made the big time and were forced for creative survival into a livelihood of BBC radio commissions, was a flowering of theatrical activity after 1956 which still continues. (A pallid American theater owes, annually, much of its most interesting fare to it.)

Even seemingly establishment venues, the stages of the Royal Shakespeare Company and the National Theatre, which represent the most striking changes in the postwar theatrical scene (they did not exist before the war), have been more than showplaces for the crown jewels of earlier drama or mere settings for self-praise of the system. Both national companies, one set in London in the huge Barbican complex north of St. Paul's (as well as in Stratford), the other situated on the South Bank below Waterloo Bridge, have proved their abilities to produce striking productions of Shakespeare, Sheridan, and Shaw as well as near-contemporary classics; however, they have also commissioned, and mounted, striking new plays, some of them explicitly as well as implicitly critical of their own societies, by such one-time fringe playwrights as Howard Brenton, Pam Gems, and David Edgar. Thus we will see in these pages evidences of a theatrical community able to absorb, creatively, its most talented practitioners, regardless of the political (or the box-office) popularity of their ideas. A writer such as Edgar can mature from a skimpy agitprop polemicist writing for a factory lunch-hour audience to the playwright of the Royal Shakespeare Company's sumptuous rendering of the no-less socially conscious *Nicholas Nickleby*.

An irony, given the revolutionary character of so much postwar drama, is its easy absorption into the theatrical mainstream, even to the bold works themselves being directed and performed by stage knights and dames. Some of the very heroes and heroines of the post-1945 drama are the professionals who have realized onstage the concepts of the playwrights who in another time would have been unperformable. To think of a Sir Peter Hall directing a Sir John Gielgud in a play by a radical Edward Bond suggests the qualities of English theater which reinforce its vigor—a vigor, one might add, given additional impetus by the one move which the establishment made in the postwar period to lessen its overt influence on theater—the ending of legal censorship. The intervention of the Lord Chamberlain's Office into the texts of British plays to be publicly performed would end only after decades of gradual erosion in the use of that office which reflected popular opinion that the time was long past when the stage should be denied the freedoms of the other electronic media. The price of a few shocked sensibilities would be a small one for the sense of intellectual release gained, and the years since have seen no burgeoning of blasphemy, obscenity, and sedition.

What is clear from the pages that follow is that drama—radio, television, film, and theater—has become the vehicle to which English writers with something to say naturally gravitate. It is *the* vital form of artistic expression in language, eclipsing the former preeminence of fiction and poetry. In part this is because television (and before it, radio) has become part of daily experience in every home. Besides, the voracious electronic media require regular feeding. Once, traditional theater and hallowed traditional values seemed to go hand in hand. Both have largely disappeared. Theater now dispenses with curtain and footlights and proscenium arch as often as it dispenses challenges to the old taboos. Theater exists, too, in an era when people seem no longer to read. If one wants to be heard, one writes plays.

One has no trouble *seeing* plays in Britain, either. Regional theater is lively, from The Traverse in Edinburgh south to Brighton. (In Ireland, Dublin is far more a theatrical center for the island; in England, Scotland, and Wales it is possible to have a regional reputation, even on television, without being well known in London.) When in London, however, one has a surfeit of plays and playhouses which beckon aspiring new playwrights as well as audiences. A walk—though hardly a straight line—from the tiny Half Moon (a converted East End church) to the venerable but renovated Lyric, Hammersmith, could include stops at the Royal Court, Sloane Square, and dozens of West End theaters as well as such fringe houses as the Round House, Chalk Farm (the "farm" is only a London Underground stop), the Donmar Warehouse, and the Tricycle, and the establishment Barbican and National. One could stretch a definition of London by including the Greenwich Theatre to the east and the Orange Tree Theatre, Richmond, to the west, but in either case the number of places where plays are performed runs, for the adventurous, to the many dozens, and suggests the opportunities magnetizing writers seeking audiences weaned on the tube and ready for the live stage.

The most significant, and the potentially most significant, playwrights of postwar Britain (including Ireland) are represented in the pages which follow. (For dramatists whose careers peaked before 1945 one should turn to *DLB 10, Modern British Dramatists, 1900-1945*.) Although biographies of playwrights and illustrations from their works fill, here, two substantial books, some gaps remain. Some once-promising playwrights who have never made it beyond the fringe are not covered, although in a few cases they are mentioned in connection with collaborative works involving writers treated here. A few one-act playwrights whose stars faded quickly

are missing from these pages, and readers can play the game of guessing who they are and which plays are unrepresented. Irish playwrights whose reputations have remained stubbornly and exclusively local have failed to make the cut. More significantly missing, perhaps, are the makers of plays largely for cinema and television (Frederic Raphael, for example) who have not written for the traditional stage, or the makers of major musical plays. The musical has been largely an American phenomenon; however one must make, at the least, a bow in the direction of Lionel Bart, who wrote the words and music for *Oliver!* and who was responsible, as well, for *Fings Ain't Wot They Used t'Be*, *Blitz!*, and *Lock Up Your Daughters*. And the musical stage has been even more transformed by Tim Rice and Andrew Lloyd Webber, the makers of *Jesus Christ Superstar* and *Evita*, among others. Perhaps it is an unreasonably purist definition of *dramatist* which eliminates them.

Most unfortunate of all is the necessary elimination of playwrights whose reputations only began to emerge as this book was being seen through production, such writers as Cecil Taylor, an Edinburgh playwright whose powerful political drama *Good*, a study of intellectual betrayal under the Nazis, opened three months before his death at age fifty-three in December 1981 and was the first of his works for the stage to succeed beyond a regional audience. On the other side of the chronological scale is the promising Paul Kember, author of the Royal Court Theatre comedy *Not Quite Jerusalem* (1982), a play which suggests a bright stage future but which only came to notice as this book was going into galley proof. Given the vitality of contemporary English drama, there are, or will be, others.

As in *Modern British Dramatists, 1900-1945*, this volume is a collaboration of younger theater scholars with veterans—British, European, American, and Asian. The writers contributing biographies here in some cases know the playwrights personally. Several have seen nearly every major play to have been staged in England since 1945, and many even earlier. Most of the researchers have discovered that few playwrights keep more than casual documentation of their plays and performances, and that even the published record lacks dependability. Nevertheless, *British Dramatists Since World War II* should be a mine of data about a vital and colorful era in theater still being enriched by the very makers of plays evoked in these pages. Even if the nation's proud place in the world has otherwise receded, in the theater the age of Elizabeth II has been truly Elizabethan.

–Stanley Weintraub

Permissions

The following people and institutions generously permitted the reproduction of photographs and other illustrative materials: Roger Mayne, pp. 3, 130, 255, 257, 259; Zoë Dominic, pp. 11, 53, 86, 127, 159, 190, 215, 256, 300, 314; Mark Gerson, pp. 15, 77, 84, 93, 101, 117, 119, 172, 199, 227, 235, 276; John Haynes, pp. 22, 41, 43, 62, 96, 103, 106, 122, 164, 176, 221, 224, 233, 238, 241; Jerry Bauer, p. 33; BBC Hulton Picture Library, pp. 36, 186, 209, 247, 249; *Evening Argus* (Brighton), p. 40; Peter Moyse, p. 47; Photo Bernard, p. 56; Photo Pic, p. 59; Ida Kar, p. 71; The Bettmann Archive, p. 75; Angus McBean, pp. 80, 212; Douglas H. Jeffrey, pp. 88, 229; Arnold Newman, p. 139; David Sim, p. 147; John Topham Picture Library, p. 157; Chris Davies, p. 163; Terence McDonal, p. 179; Joe Cocks, pp. 195, 197; Jennifer Beeston, p. 242; Reg Wilson, p. 253; Desmond Barrington, p. 284; Joy Chamberlin, p. 290; Basil Shackleton, p. 292; *Evening Standard* (London), p. 299; Romano Cagnoni, p. 301; Henry Grossman, p. 307; Christina Carr, p. 308; Gerald Murray, p. 309.

Acknowledgments

This book was produced by BC Research.

Karen L. Rood is senior editor for the *Dictionary of Literary Biography* series. Nadia Rasheed was the in-house editor.

The production staff included Judith S. Baughman, Mary Betts, Joseph Caldwell, Patricia Coate, Angela Dixon, Lynn Felder, Joyce Fowler, Robert H. Griffin, Patricia S. Hicks, Nancy L. Houghton, Sharon K. Kirkland, Cynthia D. Lybrand, Cheryl B. Martin, Shirley A. Ross, Walter W. Ross, Joycelyn R. Smith, Robin A. Sumner, Margaret A. Van Antwerp, Charles L. Wentworth, Carol J. Wilson, and Lynne C. Zeigler.

Anne Dixon did the library research with the assistance of the staff at the Thomas Cooper Library of the University of South Carolina, particularly Michael Freeman, Alexander Gilchrist, Michael Havener, David Lincove, Roger Mortimer, Donna Nance, Harriet Oglesbee, Jean Rhyne, Paula Swope, Jane Thesing, Ellen Tillett, and Beth Woodard. Special thanks are due to Anne-Marie Ehrlich, Keith Walters, and the staff of the Humanities Research Center, University of Texas, Austin. Photographic copy work for this volume was done by Pat Crawford of Imagery, Columbia, South Carolina.

Dictionary of Literary Biography • Volume Thirteen

British Dramatists Since World War II

Part 1: A-L

Dictionary of Literary Biography

John Arden
(26 October 1930-   )

Stanley Lourdeaux
College of William and Mary

PRODUCTIONS: *All Fall Down*, 1955, Edinburgh;
The Waters of Babylon, 20 October 1957, Royal Court Theatre, London; 1958, New York;
When Is a Door Not a Door?, 1958, Central School of Speech and Drama, London;
Live Like Pigs, 30 September 1958, Royal Court Theatre, London;
Serjeant Musgrave's Dance: An Unhistorical Parable, 22 October 1959, Royal Court Theatre, London; 8 March 1966, Theatre de Lys, New York, 135 [performances];
The Happy Haven, by Arden and Margaretta D'Arcy, 1960, Bristol; 14 September 1960, Royal Court Theatre, London; 1967, New York;
The Business of Good Government: A Christmas Play, by Arden and D'Arcy, December 1960, Church of St. Michael, Brent Knoll, Somerset;
The Workhouse Donkey: A Vulgar Melodrama, 8 July 1963, Chichester Festival Theatre, Sussex;
Ironhand, adapted from Goethe's *Goetz von Berlichingen*, 12 November 1963, Bristol Old Vic, Bristol;
Armstrong's Last Goodnight: An Exercise in Diplomacy, 5 May 1964, Glasgow Citizens' Theatre, Glasgow;
Ars Longa, Vita Brevis, by Arden and D'Arcy, 1964, Aldwych Theatre, London;
Fidelio, adapted from Joseph Sonnleithner and Friedrich Treitschke's libretto, music by Beethoven, 1965, London;
Left-Handed Liberty: A Play about Magna Carta, 14 June 1965, Mermaid Theatre, London;
Friday's Hiding, by Arden and D'Arcy, 1965, London;
Play Without Words, 1965, Glasgow;
The Royal Pardon; or, The Soldier Who Became an Actor,

by Arden and D'Arcy, 1 September 1966, Beaford Arts Centre, Devon, 21 December 1967; Arts Theatre, London;
The True History of Squire Jonathan and His Unfortunate Treasure, 17 June 1968, Ambiance Lunch Hour Theatre, London;

John Arden

Harold Muggins Is a Martyr, by Arden, D'Arcy, and Cartoon Archetypical Slogan Theatre, June 1968, Unity Theatre Club, London;

The Hero Rises Up: A Romantic Melodrama, by Arden and D'Arcy, 6 November 1968, Round House Theatre, London;

The Soldier's Tale, adapted from Ramuz's libretto, music by Igor Stravinsky, 1968, Bath;

Granny Welfare and the Wolf, by Arden, D'Arcy, and Muswell Hill Street Theatre, March 1971, Ducketts Common, Turnpike Lane, London;

My Old Man's a Tory, by Arden, D'Arcy, and Muswell Hill Street Theatre, March 1971, Wood Green, London;

Two Hundred Years of Labour History, by Arden, D'Arcy, and Socialist Labour League, April 1971, Alexandra Palace, London;

Rudi Dutschke Must Stay, by Arden, D'Arcy, and Writers Against Repression, Spring 1971, British Museum, London;

The Ballygombeen Bequest, by Arden and D'Arcy, May 1972, St. Mary and St. Joseph's College Drama Society, Belfast; 11 September 1972, Bush Theatre, London;

Serjeant Musgrave Dances On, by Arden and John McGrath, 1972, 7:84 Theatre Company, on tour;

The Island of the Mighty: A Play on a Traditional British Theme, by Arden and D'Arcy, 5 December 1972, Aldwych Theatre, London;

The Devil and the Parish Pump, by Arden, D'Arcy, and Corrandulla Arts Entertainment Club, April 1974, Gort Roe, Corrandulla, county Galway;

The Non-Stop Connolly Show, by Arden and D'Arcy, 29 March 1975, Liberty Hall, Dublin, 2; 17 May 1976, Ambiance Lunch Hour Theatre, London;

The Crown Strike Play, by Arden, D'Arcy, and Galway Theatre Workshop, December 1975, Eyre Square, Galway;

Sean O'Scrudu, by Arden, D'Arcy, and Galway Theatre Workshop, February 1976, Coachman Hotel, Galway;

The Mongrel Fox, by Arden, D'Arcy, and Galway Theatre Workshop, October 1976, Regional Technical College, Galway;

No Room at the Inn, by Arden, D'Arcy, and Galway Theatre Workshop, December 1976, Coachman Hotel, Galway;

Silence, by Arden, D'Arcy, and Galway Theatre Workshop, April 1977, Eyre Square, Galway;

Mary's Name, Arden, D'Arcy, and Galway Theatre Workshop, May 1977, University College, Galway;

Blow-in Chorus for Liam Cosgrave, by Arden, D'Arcy, and Galway Theatre Workshop, June 1977, Eyre Square, Galway;

Vandaleur's Folly, by Arden and D'Arcy, 1978, 7:84 Theatre Company, on tour.

BOOKS: *Serjeant Musgrave's Dance* (London: Methuen, 1960);

The Business of Good Government: A Christmas Play, by Arden and Margaretta D'Arcy (London: Methuen, 1963; New York: Grove, 1967);

Three Plays (Harmondsworth, U.K.: Penguin, 1964; Baltimore: Penguin, 1965)—includes *The Waters of Babylon*, *Live Like Pigs*, and *The Happy Haven*, by Arden and D'Arcy;

The Workhouse Donkey: A Vulgar Melodrama (London: Methuen, 1964; New York: Grove, 1967);

Ironhand, adapted from Goethe's *Goetz von Berlichingen* (London: Methuen, 1965);

Armstrong's Last Goodnight: An Exercise in Diplomacy (London: Methuen, 1965);

Ars Longa, Vita Brevis, by Arden and D'Arcy (London: Cassell, 1965);

Left-Handed Liberty: A Play about Magna Carta (London: Methuen, 1965; New York: Grove, 1966);

The Royal Pardon; or, The Soldier Who Became an Actor, by Arden and D'Arcy (London: Methuen, 1967);

Soldier, Soldier and Other Plays (London: Methuen, 1967)—includes *Soldier, Soldier: A Comic Song for Television; Wet Fish: A Professional Reminiscence for Television, When Is a Door Not a Door?*, and *Friday's Hiding*, by Arden and D'Arcy;

The Hero Rises Up: A Romantic Melodrama, by Arden and D'Arcy (London: Methuen, 1969);

Two Autobiographical Plays (London: Methuen, 1971)—includes *The True History of Squire Jonathan and His Unfortunate Treasure* and *The Bagman*;

The Island of the Mighty: A Play on a Traditional British Theme, by Arden and D'Arcy (London: Eyre Methuen, 1974);

To Present the Pretence (London: Eyre Methuen, 1977);

The Non-Stop Connolly Show, by Arden and D'Arcy (London: Pluto, 1978).

When in 1957 John Arden left his career as an architect for playwriting, critics hastily placed him with the other "angry young men" of the period. Recent critics have labeled Arden the British Brecht because of the generally Marxist politics in his recent social drama. But neither his present politics nor the "angry" nonconformity of his protagonists tells the story of why he gradually rejected the appearance of 1950s social realism for that of improvisation. Arden's first experiments scrutinized the basic social tension between aggressive survivors and the institutions meant to pacify them. Ironically, as these self-styled survivors would circumvent the established social order, their schemes for money and authority would take advantage of innocent bystanders; the underdogs quickly became the oppressors. When Arden began to collaborate more often with his wife, Irish actress and activist Margaretta D'Arcy, their plays grew increasingly closer to contemporary Anglo-Irish politics. The collaborative efforts allowed Arden to pursue the anti-realistic trend in his earlier work: a plot twisted by an inventive main character attempting to survive unexpected situations would provide for slapstick scenes resembling factious quarrels. Arden further challenged the theater establishment with his songs, doggerel verse, and detailed history. In recent years he has flaunted this impression of improvisation—based, as it is, on lengthy research and careful rewriting.

John Arden, the son of Charles Alwyn and Annie Elizabeth Layland Arden, was born in Barnsley, Yorkshire. Arden was graduated from King's College, Cambridge, in 1953 and received a diploma in architecture in 1955 from the Edinburgh College of Art, where his Victorian comedy *All Fall Down* was first performed in 1955. Earlier unperformed plays include a schoolboy piece "on the death of Hitler in the style of *Samson Agonistes*" and a pseudo-Elizabethan verse drama on the Gunpowder Plot. When Arden's radio play *The Life of Man* (1956) won the BBC Northern Region Prize in 1957, he was commissioned to write a piece for the Royal Court Theatre. His first submission, a play based on Arthurian legends, was rejected, but *The Waters of Babylon* was accepted and performed in October 1957 as a Sunday night production without decor. With this success and with the support of Margaretta D'Arcy, whom he had married on 1 May 1957, Arden quit his job as an architectural assistant in London to devote all his time to playwriting.

Sigismanfred Krankiewicz, the character who shapes the irregular plot in *The Waters of Babylon*, is a Polish immigrant working in London as an architectural assistant. He also runs an overcrowded boardinghouse and sets up prostitutes in business. Known in the evenings as Krank, he feels badgered by the London housing authorities because they object to the number of his boarders. As long as Arden does not present Krank as an exploiter of women and of other immigrants, the viewer enjoys his relaxed wit and inventive schemes for survival—especially in comparison to hollow idealogues like Henry Ginger, a British jingoist, and Krank's friend Paul, a Polish patriot. Trying to find money to pay Paul a debt rather than let him use the boardinghouse to build anarchist bombs, Krank becomes enmeshed in a public lottery sponsored by a naive black councilman named Caligula. In all Arden's works, as John Russell Taylor writes, "there seems to be brooding one basic principle: not exactly the obvious one that today there are no causes—that would be altogether too facile, and in any case just not true—but that there are too many." As Krank ruefully observes, "I was alone, and confident, and uninvolved. Now look at me." The audience hardly pities this clever schemer, though they have less heart for someone like Paul who would issue orders with no authority or someone like Caligula who has authority but can easily be manipulated.

Polish patriotism makes little sense to Krank in a world gone mad, as he explains when Paul almost shoots him after learning that he was a soldier in the German army at Buchenwald. Scenes of interrupted dialogue convey the madness Krank finds in life. In act 3, for example, all the characters come together for a rigged public lottery, though by accident the winner is chosen at random and Krank is revealed as the unlawful local landlord. When Paul then fatally shoots Krank by accident, the random results of the entire scene undermine Krank's clever individualism as well as social justice. The rhythm of realism is disrupted even earlier by Krank's clownlike changes of clothing, by his pantomimclike acting (as suggested in Arden's preface), and by his mixture of verse, song, and prose. Also, as Andrew Kennedy writes, Arden attempts "to regain touch with an all but lost pre industrial language in and for our own pan-industrial society, with all its urban complexities of speech." The final slapstick sound of cymbals at the lottery shatters whatever hope may have been held for a sensible resolution: the cymbals crash accidentally, the lights are turned out, and Krank is discovered on the floor trying to rig the drawing. Yet the accidental outcome does seem appropriate given the subplots spun so easily by Krank, the indefatigable opportunist. By the play's end viewers are at a loss for effective intentions or a social order. That is, after Krank's death they seem to be "down in t'cellar-hoyle /Wi't'muck-slaghts on t'windows" where they feel isolated, cold, and dirty because, as Krank sardonically observes, they cannot comprehend his death any more than he could the deaths at Buchenwald.

In Arden's next play, *When Is a Door Not a Door?* (1958), the architectural metaphor changes from Krank's construction of supple schemes, with any available material, to the literal repair of an office door by two workmen. Arden explores the tension between these men and aloof white-collar workers preoccupied with endless unsatisfying detail. The office workers regard the fixing of the broken door, and implicitly their own functions at work, as an inconsequential if necessary means of production; but the blue-collar workers regard the repair of the door as the product of human labor. Arden asks: when is a job not a satisfying job? Or, when is a play not an effective play? Arden no longer subordinates the development of secondary characters and their language to the development of the plot, as in realism. He favors the arbitrariness of life by placing minor characters in center stage; he lets his audience look through an open doorway at the work habits of mundane employees. For this reason, Arden allows one of the carpenters a gratuitous allusion to Hitler—a man who left "a botched job" because, like the office workers, he had no human sense of his work. To succeed on stage *When Is a Door Not a Door?* depends heavily on the actors' feel for farce and pantomime.

Like *The Waters of Babylon*, *Live Like Pigs* (1958) contains earthy and zestful language and depends greatly on performance. Arden presents the chaos of the gypsylike Sawney family who are forced out of their broken run-down tramcar and made to live in the local housing project. The Sawneys quickly manage to insult their new neighbors, the Jacksons, who eventually incite a vigilante group to run the unappreciative vulgar family out of the project. When the authorities finally intervene, a policeman breaks the eldest Sawney's leg with brutal carelessness. Though the audience has no sympathy for the vulgar selfishness of the Sawneys, they cannot help but wince to see such vitally alive characters brutalized; the insensitivity of the police and the neighbors is no less repulsive in Arden's slapstick farce than the petty cruelty of the Sawneys toward one another and the world.

In the preface to *Live Like Pigs*, Arden notes defensively that the piece "is in large part meant to be funny" and that the central contrast between the vagrant Sawneys and the middle-class Jacksons should be balanced: the play "is to be not so much a social drama as a study of different ways of life brought sharply into conflict and both losing their particular virtues under the stress of indolence and misunderstanding." What is more, "the apparent chaos of [the Sawneys'] lives becomes an ordered pattern when seen in terms of a wild empty countryside and a nomadic existence." Nevertheless, John Russell Taylor criticizes Arden for not taking sides in the fight between the two families, while Richard Gilman believes that Arden has failed because the Jacksons are nothing "more than a thin, conventional dramatic reality." In any case, the play initially confused and upset audiences. By the play's end all that is left is the Sawneys' fierce will to survive in an often hostile world where, as the old couple sings in the final scene, no help can be expected: "Nobody else nobody else nick nack noo." Comedy has a bitter note when adults are forced to behave like quarrelsome children to survive.

While *The Waters of Babylon* and *Live Like Pigs* show the struggle of unlikely central characters against institutions like the Housing Authority, *Serjeant Musgrave's Dance* (1959) offers a more likely hero who opposes all armies and wars. (As Robert Corrigan observes, "the central duality in all of Arden's work resides in the basic conflict between the institutionalized society of men under the aegis of law and order and a community based on the relations of service, loyalties, and affection among individuals. . . .") Because the serjeant deserts the army to protest war in general, the play has been Arden's most popular and embodies in one struggling man the contrasting elements in *Live Like Pigs*: lower-class insensitivity and vague middle-class idealism. Musgrave shows that he is insensitive to pain in others, as well as idealistic about the idea of suffering—a conflict which leads to his eventual execution by a less divided and practical public. He deserts the army along with three privates, one a murderer; they are fed up with a soldier's life and they want to commemorate the death of a young comrade, Billy Hicks, who was shot in the back by a sniper: they will return Billy's body to his hometown and hold the local authorities responsible for his death. When the four men arrive in town with a concealed Gatling gun, they discover that the local colliers are on strike and that, as soldiers, they are assumed to be either army recruiters or the militia come to suppress the strike; their intentions are misinterpreted because the townspeople understand them only in terms of the uniforms they wear. Before either the town or the audience learns of Musgrave's intention to display Billy's body, one private kills the other accidentally during a petty scuffle. While the tensions of the play are not immediately apparent, the individual characters—the soldiers, the mayor, the colliers, the barmaid—are intimate human portraits. As a result, the structural contrast between soldiers and civilians, or between

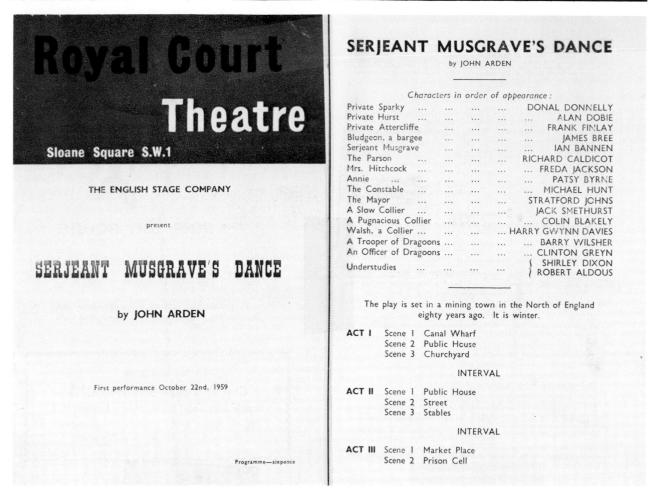

owners and employees, seems less important than each person's private concerns. Serjeant Musgrave, the one character with authority and decisiveness, becomes increasingly suspect once he describes his mission as God's own dance. What is worse, he considers Billy's death immaterial in comparison to his plan—first kill five men to avenge Billy's murder, then kill more citizens to avenge other deaths—to bring home the mad logic of war. Musgrave again shows his insensitivity for human life when he stubbornly rationalizes the deaths of the women and children who were killed by the British soldiers in their "search" for Billy's killer (an event based on a true story of the British army on Cyprus). As Musgrave increasingly identifies with God's power and authority, first the barmaid and then the colliers realize that he will only bring more bloodshed. His obsessive prayer—"our shining white word, let it dance!"—is more important than the individual lives of the townspeople; his resolute antiwar exhibition of Billy's skeleton in public at gunpoint

actually signifies the triumph of death. As Richard Gilman writes, "the dramatic vision is that of the horror of single-mindedness, of ends determining means and even more crucially of abstraction in moral life." When Musgrave finally awaits trial in jail, the audience is once again left in a cellarlike place without a secure protagonist—though each character's passion to survive remains with the viewers. Even though critics initially panned *Serjeant Musgrave's Dance*, it remains one of Arden's best-known works. In 1966 the play won the Vernon Rice Award.

Arden took a more middle-class slant on the misuse of authority when, as a 1959 Fellow in Playwriting at Bristol University, he wrote a comedy, *The Happy Haven* (1960), in collaboration with his wife. If *Live Like Pigs* could be misinterpreted as a grim social satire, *The Happy Haven* would be more explicit about its comic intentions: elderly patients wear masks in the tradition of the commedia dell'arte; an imaginary dog is transformed onstage into a puppy; adults in "the evening of their lives" act like and are treated like children. The comic plot begins when Doctor Copperwaite worries more about his research on a youth elixir and its potential market than about his word. After the patients uncover the authoritarian doctor's plan to test his secret serum on humans, they are overjoyed at the prospect of youth with wisdom, at least until Mrs. Phineus brushes aside their self-delusions:

> I'm an old old lady
> And I don't have long to live
> I am only strong enough to take
> Not to give. No time left to give.
> I want to drink, I want to eat,
> I want my shoes taken off my feet.
> I want to talk but not to walk
> Because if I walk, I have to know
> Where it is I want to go.
> I want to sleep but not to dream
> I want to play and win every game
> To live with love but not to love
> The world to move but me not move
> I want I want for ever and ever.
> The world to work, the world to be clever.
> Leave me be, but don't leave me alone.
> That's what I want. I'm a big round stone
> Sitting in the middle of a thunderstorm.
> There you are: that's true.
> That's me. Now: you.

In the end the inmates decide to give their overbearing director a touch of his own medicine: they inject him with his serum in the last scene and lead him offstage as a child. In contrast to the serious homeopathic effect of Serjeant Musgrave's Gatling gun, this comic twist of fate seems too facile—even as farce; the ironic attainment of justice in *The Happy Haven* arrives too abruptly and provides relief mainly from the increasingly tedious intrigues of the child-elders. Arden has limited himself for the first time to middle-class characters who lack the gutsy language and determined will which vividly personalized conflicts with authority in the earlier plays. Nevertheless, as Glenda Leeming writes, the masks "emphasize the character's 'type' or single ruling trait, so that individual nuances are effaced. . . . Experimenting with masks, Arden not only derived practical advantages—the non-realistic convention meant that young actors could be used and a brisk pace was possible—but increased the impact of *Happy Haven*: the masks underline the stereotyping of the old people as merely 'old' and not at all as 'people.'" Masks and slapstick are indeed required since the spoken word does not fix the character types on the stage.

Between the first productions of *The Happy Haven* in 1960 and *The Workhouse Donkey* in 1963, Arden wrote with his wife *The Business of Good Government* (1960), a nativity play for Christmas; *Ironhand* (1963), an adaptation of Goethe's *Goetz von Berlichingen*; and two plays for television. In *Soldier, Soldier: A Comic Song for Television* (1960), which won the Trieste Festival Award, Arden recycles the sardonic humor of *Live Like Pigs* when a lowland Scots soldier, home on leave, cheats the gullible parents of a young soldier stationed abroad. Once again the apparent contrast between vulgar lower-class characters and a contented middle-class couple dissolves. Mr. and Mrs. Scuffham maltreat their son's Irish wife, whom he married abruptly during his first leave. Like the barmaid who loved Billy Hicks and later offered to sleep with the soldier, Hurst, in *Serjeant Musgrave's Dance*, this Irish Mary wants to go to bed with the newly arrived soldier and yet she perceives his chicanery as well. In the end the Scotsman steals from the parents and deserts Mary only to spend the parents' savings on drink at the nearest pub; his opportunism is really no worse and no more self-rewarding than the lack of wisdom of the middle-class couple.

In *Wet Fish* (1961), Arden's next television play, he returns to an earlier, less cynical characterization of the opportunist, and he resurrects Sigismanfred Krankiewicz for the part. Now Krank is presented at his daytime job as an architect where he finds profit for himself when the owner of a small fish shop decides to remodel his shop. Because the fellow cannot afford the bungled repairs attempted by Krank's coworkers, Krank ends up buying the man's shop and then renting it back to him. Arden again satirizes insensitive management when the owner of Krank's firm, Gilbert Garnish, is closer to his pompous clients (churchmen who want architectural ornamentation) than he is to his workmen who understand their craft and who clearly have more in common with the small-time owner of the shop. With the exception of Krank, the characters can be divided into the craftsmen and the incompetent office workers of *When Is a Door Not a Door?*. In *Wet Fish*, however, the two groups of characters are not onstage at the same time but in alternating scenes. In his judgment of the characters' competence and loyalty to their work, Arden once again critiques the work ethic of his flawed idealistic heroes: to survive they acquire a greater authority over others but lose all sense of producing for others. As for Arden's own sense of craftsmanship, he increasingly stresses the playwright's responsibility to follow his work through to production—to assume to some degree the role of the director, which has only been a separate function since the nineteenth century.

The Workhouse Donkey is a more thorough treatment of a borderline figure like Krank who stands somewhere between the common worker and those in authority, all the while fatally grasping for more power himself. In *The Workhouse Donkey* Arden expands the characterization of Charlie Butterthwaite from his minor role in *The Waters of Babylon* as Krank's henchman, "the Napoleon of Local Government": the audience now learns that Charlie was born in a workhouse where he thought of himself as a stupid animal until one day he realized that he was "a naked human being," an insight which fired his ambition to become a union leader and eventually a town alderman. Charlie feels threatened when, at the play's beginning, a new chief of police named Colonel Feng arrives from London. Charlie hastily decides that Feng is only a stooge for Harold Sweetman, the town's wealthiest brewer and a foe of the unions. Feng, the epitome of adamantine British justice, soon irritates Charlie by enforcing the letter of the law—Charlie must leave a pub at the regular closing time. To get rid of Feng, Charlie tries to expose the police's tacit support of an illegal nightclub. But Charlie ends up robbing union funds to pay a debt, showing his complete disregard for law and order. Arden develops Charlie's character, drawing him closer to the audience, as Charlie revels in life as a competition in which one either deceives others or plays the dupe. As a result, Charlie regards any interference in his political intrigues as an attempt to put him back in the workhouse. Only at the play's end does he realize that Feng has his own standard of absolute British justice. Charlie has been fighting two foes all along, while he thought he had only Sweetman to contend with—a self-delusion which stems from his view of himself as a de facto lawmaker but not as a lawbreaker.

The arrival of Colonel Feng recalls the timely arrival of the Dragoons who stopped Musgrave's public demonstration in *Serjeant Musgrave's Dance* and of the police in *Live Like Pigs*: the police must eventually intervene when opportunists and the public are at one another's throats, if only to pacify the public. Feng is not himself the epitome of democratic justice since he views the public as "egalitarian garbage" and resigns his position in disgust when the town's officials all but prevent him from uncovering Charlie's half-baked robbery. In his commitment to an ideal immaterial justice, Feng is as self-deluded and out of touch with the townspeople as

Charlie, and he will never clear all the social garbage from the streets, as one cynical alderman notes. Society will always be a workhouse with authorities and obedient donkeys in it. In the end, Charlie and Feng show Arden's equal distrust of political opportunism and police idealism.

For Arden the human desire for authority and power is a rich source of comedy. As he remarks in the preface to *The Workhouse Donkey*, the play should be performed as "Comic Theatre" with the "old essential attributes of Dionysius: noise, disorder, drunkenness. . . ." In Charlie these Dionysian attributes (his drinking at the pub and his lurid laughter at the Copacabana) become apparent as he attempts to outmanuever Harold Sweetman and protect his authority in town. In this political satire Arden is conscious of the playwright's own authority over his audience. To avoid a theater of manipulation, he envisions a comedy with freedom of choices and speculates about a longer thirteen-hour version of *The Workhouse Donkey* in which the audience might come and go as they like, perhaps while enjoying an amusement park just outside the theater doors. This idea of comedy as an open form of entertainment is suggested further by his use of the nonverbal, the music and pantomime and slapstick, as well as by the hodgepodge of verbal forms in the play: songs, prose, and roughly rhymed verse. As George Wellwarth writes, "Arden has hit upon the correct way to integrate his songs and dances into the action: he makes no pretense at suspension of disbelief and has the whole play written half at the audience in the manner of vaudeville skits." Arden challenges not just Charlie's authority as a self-made alderman but his own authority over his script in order to reach the core of comedy in social drama.

In 1964 Arden finished *Armstrong's Last Goodnight*, a historical tragedy set in sixteenth-century Scotland which portrays the ambitious Scots outlaw James Armstrong of Gilnockie who, like Charlie Butterthwaite, emerges from lower-class obscurity to plague both those who are weaker and those with authority over him: Gilnockie conducts raids on English farmers across the border and thus disobeys his young Scots king James V, just as Butterthwaite cheated both the union and the local authorities. After a brief historical overview of the dilemma which Gilnockie creates for James V and the English king Henry VIII, the play opens with one of Gilnockie's typical acts of betrayal: he gains the trust of an enemy, James Johnstone of Wamphray, with sweet words and hospitality only to disarm Wamphray in his sleep. Within the hour Wamphray is speared by Gilnockie's men in order to settle a feud.

The betrayal displays Gilnockie's cunning as well as his personal philosophy: to trust another man is to become vulnerable and to secure a death sentence. To shape the irregular plot of multiple intrigues, Arden places a parallel scene of betrayal at the play's end, with James V as the deceiver and Gilnockie as the dupe. The king first changes Gilnockie's status from that of an outlaw to the king's lieutenant, and then sends Gilnockie a conciliatory letter which implies that Gilnockie is almost the king's brother and equal. In the end the opportunism of the rugged Scots leader makes him vulnerable to royal flattery; ambition blinds him to the repetition of his own earlier betrayal of Wamphray in royal guise: "Gif we canna destroy the mickle lords, we maun build up the lesser." Gilnockie's blindness is complicated further by his headstrong support for an itinerant Protestant evangelist whose theology helps explain disloyalty to the crown—"ilk ane of us is as it were ane God: but no yet manifest." Arden notes that, translated into politics, this priesthood of all believers would turn Scotland into a Switzerland—a country with many competing factions.

Arden prefers to delineate onstage a border between two countries for the Scots outlaw in order to dramatize the basic human desire both to escape authority and to oppress others. Likewise, Arden adopts the medieval staging of simultaneous mansions by putting several distant locations onstage at the same time as, for example, the king's palace and Gilnockie's castle. The audience is further presented with a borderlike position in dramatic language (and another improbable simultaneity) when Arden conflates the language of modern Scots with the language of poets David Lindsay, William Dunbar, and Robert Henryson to create his own "Babylonish dialect." (He cites Arthur Miller's adaptation of early American speech in *The Crucible* as his model.) The tension in this social drama includes that border area between modernity and the sixteenth century since Arden's tale is based not only on Scots history but also loosely on Conor Cruise O'Brien's book *To Katanga and Back* (1962): there is "a basic similarity of moral, rather than political, economic or racial problems," according to Arden. As Richard Gilman writes, the play "fully exhibits [Arden's] new species of post-political and post-ideological drama, resisting partisanship, disclaiming solutions, neither hortatory nor tendentious yet strenuously involved in actuality."

Although some of Arden's critics did not like *Armstrong's Last Goodnight* and would have preferred a return to the surface realism of *Serjeant Musgrave's Dance*, Arden did not pay much attention and continued to experiment with increasingly open forms of entertainment. For *Ars Longa, Vita Brevis* (1964), a short children's play written in collaboration with Margaretta D'Arcy, the playwrights observed children's games to adopt their rhythms. Planned with few set speeches, the play opens with the arrival of the school's new art master, Mr. Miltiades, who advocates "No free expression" (just the opposite of Arden's dramatic format). Mr. Miltiades runs his class as would a drill sergeant because he would in fact rather be a soldier and live according to "Hardihood and discipline, / Straight lines and repression." To his embarrassment, however, neither his pupils nor his own emotions live up to his strict code: when the headmaster visits the class unannounced, all the children are fighting while Mr. Miltiades yells at them, "Kill each other kill each other kill each other KILL!" Life for the children, as the play for the viewer, is too much fun to suppress spontaneity with morbid discipline.

In Arden's next major work, *Left-Handed Liberty* (1965), the vitality of a social contract depends on one's freedom to interpret it. Thus, Arden, as a craftsman of social drama, will not fix one meaning to a character or a scene. *Left-Handed Liberty* was commissioned by the City of London to commemorate the 750th anniversary of the Magna Carta. In notes made before writing the play, Arden said that the "complete failure of the Charter struck me as a more fruitful theme than the more obvious one of the events leading up to Runnymede." The agreement in which King John was forced to grant liberties to his barons in 1204 was a temporary reconciliation which neither party expected to last: in Arden's play the king promises to dismiss his Flemish mercenaries, while secretly keeping them in his pay; the barons in fact hope to strip the king of all his powers, with the aid of the French. Unlike Gilnockie in *Armstrong's Last Goodnight*, neither the king nor his barons forget that a "word is a word, you can turn it inside out like an old coat as many times as you want; but victory in war . . . is alone irreversible." Words in the end hold only as much authority as the action they invoke.

The authority of words and of the Magna Carta in particular gradually becomes a personal issue for King John. In act 1 he immediately distrusts the charter because its wording is vague enough to be used against him any time in the future. Likewise, the barons come to realize that the document not only serves their ambitions but can also undermine their campaign for power. Baron de Vesci, for example, is caught off guard when his self-willed, disobedient wife tells him that she has only the charter's "ambidextrous word" to defend herself—and will use it; de Vesci never thought of anyone besides himself and the other barons as wielding the charter. Lady de Vesci next points out to King John his double standard: he approves of her demand for her rights but not of the barons' demands, an inconsistency which he says lies in human nature as well as in the charter.

LADY DE VESCI: That should not have been relevant. You also condoned one or two adulteries on the part of your Queen.

JOHN: I was in love with her.

LADY DE VESCI: But you refused to condone the rebellion of your barons. So far as the doctrine of Authority—either in marriage or statecraft—was convenient to yourself, you insisted upon it: and where it was not, you ignored it.

JOHN: Exactly so! Inconsistent, irregular, unreasonable. And this is our uniqueness. Not in our capacity for damnation or salvation nor yet in our capacity for logical rationality—though both of them are glorious: and both of them, I fear, have distorted our

nature. Indeed I am inclined to think, that not only are you unsuited to be a married woman and I to be a king, but that none of us, ever, are suited to be either.

Social institutions and rationality are not really suited to human nature. King John has inherited a left-handed nature from his mother—a "beautiful, stubborn, and deceitful spirit"—which makes for a difficult kingship since the power to rule traditionally resides in the right hand. He feels deeply the conflict between his inconsistent human nature and his need for both rationality and institutions like kingship, a conflict summed up in the image of left-handed liberty.

In act 3 Arden stresses the ambidextrous nature of existence: the conflicts in the Magna Carta and in the king's personality will not be resolved. The deaths of King John and his mother frame Arden's play: she greets death as an undependable, tardy visitor; he dies after becoming trapped in a muddy tide as unexpected and uncontrollable as

Jack Shepherd (left) in a scene from the 1965 English Stage Company revival of Serjeant Musgrave's Dance

the charter. To break further the illusion that King John's is a tragic death with a fixed meaning, the house lights are turned up at the beginning of act 3 and King John explains that the charter, with its anti-Semitic passages, is hardly a perfect expression of political ideas—though it is more flexible, more open to varied interpretations, than the Church's codification of God. The dramatic effect, in Albert Hunt's words, is that the audience is "prepared to accept the Charter, not as an historic myth, nor as a prop in a play, but as a subject for consideration." Arden removes any remaining belief in King John as a representative man and as the playwright's spokesman by describing him not as Israel, as John sees himself, but as Pharoah. In sum the king has tried to conduct all the judicial trials throughout England himself by riding about the countryside to listen to every grievance. But in the end he succumbs to the judiciary, to the Magna Carta, and to death. Arden too must succumb to uncontrollable elements in plot and language; he must use an open dramatic form once he has dethroned his chief spokesman and left dramatic language, in an attempt to write with "the straightforwardness of medieval speech," open to numerous twists of interpretation. The relationship between Arden and his audience is, then, like that between King John and his barons: a temporary open contract.

In 1968 Arden became more openly intellectual and ambidextrous in two brief autobiographical allegories. *The True History of Squire Jonathan and His Unfortunate Treasure* (1968) is dedicated to "all those nosey-porkers who prefer / To know the poet's life and what he does / Rather than read his words upon the page / or listen to them spoken on the stage." This sparse, enigmatic allegory, based partly on Arden's personal experience, portrays Squire Jonathan secluded in his country tower with his gems and other treasures, safe from the primitive "dark men" who roam the surrounding countryside. From his elevated prospect, Jonathan spots "an enormous beautiful woman" as she falls by accident from her horse. After first refusing her entry, Jonathan lets the large blonde woman enjoy the warmth of his fireside where she strips to a chastity belt and then allows him to cover her with precious jewels; what he cannot keep outside his walls he will subjugate with extravagant presents. Soon Jonathan fears that his new treasure will desert him for the dark men, and he unwittingly plants the idea in her head. She takes the unconscious hint and jumps out the nearest window into waiting, grateful arms. In the preface Arden notes that the play is based loosely on his attachment, some eighteen

years earlier, to a "large blonde beautiful Scot" who did not understand why anyone would want to write plays. In *The Bagman*, first broadcast on radio in 1970, the main character survives alone in a threatening violent world where women are neither trusted companions nor idealized myths. The bagman, or the limited playwright, is capable only of watching the characters which strangers (or an audience's desires) put into his bag. Regardless of the poverty and misery he may discover in his cast of characters, the bagman says he can do nothing to help. Thus Arden judges other writers as self-serving if they hide behind the social realist's claim that characterization is largely uncontrollable ("All I can do is look at what I see"), though he himself had so far only approximated a more didactic, ideological drama.

Arden now became more radical in his experiments by stressing subject material per se and the actors' interactions rather than the well-shaped creation of a traditional director/writer. He began to present the appearance of improvisation in fragments of British history in six collaborations with D'Arcy from 1966 to 1972. The earthy metaphors of the Sawneys and Serjeant Musgrave are replaced by a fast-paced language which is twisted by the occurrence of unexpected events. In *The Royal Pardon* (1966), for example, an English acting troupe in the Renaissance goes to Paris to perform for the King of France only to be poisoned by jealous French actors. Recovering quickly and improvising their script, the English actors impress the king and eventually earn an appointment in England as the royal theater company. In the Paris scenes Arden attributes dull stagy acting to the French and uses the French king to pass judgment on directors: "But he is not an actor. He is a mechanical—a workman—he should not be here [in my presence] at all." In *The Hero Rises Up* (1968) Arden presents a historical figure, Admiral Horatio Nelson, who is such a multifaceted character that his varied interests and exploits stretch the plot into an apparently improvised shape. The seeds for such political improvisation were sown in the opportunism of Krankiewicz and the mad logic of Serjeant Musgrave. The preface of *The Hero Rises Up* makes clear that the plot should be subordinate to the characterization of Lord Nelson: "This play is about a man who was, by accident of birth and rearing, committed to a career governed by the old Roman 'rectilinear' principles. He himself was of asymmetrical 'curvilinear' temperament to an unusually passionate degree. But the English soon discovered how to handle him. He was *done properly*:

wasted his extraordinary energy, courage, and humanity upon having men killed (in the end himself killed): and then finally was installed as a National Monument." Arden then qualifies the simplistic dichotomy of rectilinear and curvilinear temperaments by adding that he wants "to present the audience with an experience akin to that of running up in a crowded wet street on a Saturday night against a drunken red-nosed man. . . . But you don't at once forget him: and although you know nothing about him and never will know anything about him, he has become some sort of *circumstance* in your life. You can't sit down and analyse him, because you haven't got the needful data: you can't ask him for his 'symbolism'—if he has any, you yourself will have provided it: and you can't go back and 're-evaluate' him, because the police will have moved him on. But there he was: and you saw him." Arden and D'Arcy would have the audience provide an interpretation from their instinctive response to the character, while the playwrights vivify biography and other facts of political history.

Since 1968 the Ardens have produced three major works which concentrate not so much on one character as on a vital stream of political events. *The Ballygombeen Bequest*, a play about an English absentee landlord who attempts to evict his caretakers from an Irish cottage kept by their family for generations, was first produced in 1972 in Falls Road, Belfast, at the height of political tension. The Ardens wanted to produce social drama in a political setting. *The Island of the Mighty: A Play on a Traditional British Theme*, also produced in 1972, harks back to the beginning of Arden's career with his submission of a play about King Arthur to the Royal Court Company, though his new version presents Arthur's fall in terms of a Marxist class struggle. Arden first wrote this new version as a trilogy for television and then, in collaboration with his wife, cut and reshaped much of the material after their trip in 1969 to India, where they lived with revolutionists and were very briefly jailed. By describing the economic breakdown of a tribal society, the Ardens translated their experience of parliamentary democracy's failure in India to respond to the improverished peasant majority. The final version presents the pallid gestures of Arthur's heroism against a backdrop of peasant poverty. Also, as Glenda Leeming notes, the play "gathers most of Arden's themes and techniques into one mighty plot." A controversy arose when the play was to be produced by the Royal Shakespeare Company at the Aldwych Theatre in London because the Ardens felt they had not been sufficiently allowed to

shape the final production, that is, to prevent a conventional realistic production; and so they took up pickets outside in the street. In the end some critics applauded the play but, the Ardens thought, for the wrong reasons and the wrong style of performance. In support of the playwrights' views, Albert Hunt notes that instead of the slapstick and farce intended by the playwrights, the play was a flat "post Stanislavski concentration on inner motivation."

The Ardens' even longer work, *The Non-Stop Connolly Show* (1975), is a "dramatic cycle of continuous struggle in six parts" which, the preface states, requires "*speed*—and close attention to *rhythm*." The cycle traces the life of James Connolly, a "revolutionary leader" in the international socialist movement, as he organizes trade unions in Ireland, America, and England. The epic cast of more than 100 characters includes historic figures like American Socialist Eugene Debs, Russian Communist leader Lenin, and Irish poet and dramatist William Butler Yeats, though the parts can be performed by a dozen actors whose approach, in the Ardens' opinion, "should be 'emblematic' rather than 'naturalistic.'" Thus the actors sometimes wear masks and sometimes sing popular political songs or speak in rhymed couplets. The "play will only work if the actors are more concerned with understanding the political arguments and implications of the story than with 'creating character' in the normal theatrical sense." In his own review of the first production, however, Arden praises Terry McGinity (who played the role of Connolly at the Dublin headquarters for the Irish Transport and General Workers Union) because he was "truly possessed by the dead hero's daimon"; McGinity seemed like Connolly himself in his political milieu. Despite Arden's use of the label "hero," the play is too long and the characters too numerous for viewers to focus exclusively on any one character or action in this complex political tapestry.

Arden began his career in theater as a trained architect who was guided by the basic foundation of social drama only to turn more and more to explicitly political material. Though at first interested in epic figures like Hitler and King Arthur, Arden tempered his taste to the smaller stature of men like Sigismanfred Krankiewicz and Serjeant Musgrave whose vivid speech and improvised actions supplanted the significance of seemingly realistic plots. With other fierce survivors like the Sawneys in *Live Like Pigs*, Arden seemed to have settled on contemporary social realism (at least until the historical figures of James Armstrong and King

John in his next plays pointed to a broader tragedy in inconsistent human nature). A second stage in Arden's career began with *The Happy Haven*, the first of many collaborations with D'Arcy in which characters are more middle-class and dramatic language less vividly suggestive of separate personalities than in earlier works. This change was a response to critics such as Laurence Kitchin who judged Arden severely for his occasionally doggerel verse and haphazard songs. At this time Arden discovered a forceful model for the appearance of improvisation—for apparently adaptable dramatic constructions which an audience would trust to be sturdy yet personal, like a well-designed public building. A third stage in his career began when he chose more explicitly political material in plots twisted not just by opportunists like Charlie Butterthwaite but by larger casts of secondary figures in longer works. Since Arden's 1969 trip to India, which radicalized his attitude toward realistic character and plot, he hopes that his social drama will provide moments of living history which impinge on today's politics. Although early in his career he expected his plays "to present the pretense" of an engaging and fluctuating realism of everyday modern life, he has turned now to epic characters and the fast-paced presentation of historical eras to make certain that his audience pauses to observe the pretense and its political content.

Television Scripts:
Soldier, Soldier: A Comic Song for Television, BBC, 1960;
Wet Fish: A Professional Reminiscence for Television, BBC, 1961;
Portrait of a Rebel, by Arden and Margaretta D'Arcy, Radio-Telefis Eireann, 1973.

Radio Scripts:
The Bagman, BBC Radio 3, 1970;
Keep Those People Moving, by Arden and Margaretta D'Arcy, BBC, 1972;
Pearl, BBC, 1978.

Periodical Publications:
"Telling a True Tale," *Encore*, (May-June 1960): 41-43;

"Delusions of Grandeur," *Twentieth Century*, 169 (February 1961): 200-206;
"Verse in the Theatre," *New Theatre Magazine*, 2 (April 1961): 200-206;
"Shakespeare—to a Young Dramatist," *Guardian*, 23 April 1964;
"Poetry and Theatre," *Times Literary Supplement*, 6 August 1964;
The Ballygombeen Bequest, by Arden and Margaretta D'Arcy, *Scripts*, 1 (September 1972).

Interviews:
Tom Milne and Clive Goodwin, "Building a Play (an interview)," *Encore*, 8 (July-August 1961): 22-41;
Frank Cox, "Arden of Chichester," *Plays and Players* (August 1963): 16-18;
Walter Wager and Simon Trussler, "Who's for a Revolution?," *Tulane Drama Review*, 11 (Winter 1966): 41-53;
Brendan Hennessy, "John Arden," *Times Educational Supplement*, 9 April 1971, p. 19.

References:
Michael Anderson, *Anger and Detachment: A Study of Arden, Osborne and Pinter* (London: Pitman, 1976), pp. 50-87;
Ronald Hayman, *John Arden* (London: Heinemann Educational Books, 1968);
Albert Hunt, *Arden: A Study of His Plays* (London: Eyre Methuen, 1974);
Andrew K. Kennedy, *Six Dramatists in Search of a Language: Studies in Dramatic Language* (Cambridge: Cambridge University Press, 1975), pp. 213-229;
Glenda Leeming, *John Arden*, edited by Ian Scott-Kilvert (Harlow: Longman, 1974);
John Russell Taylor, *Anger and After: A Guide to the New British Drama* (London: Methuen, 1962), pp. 72-86;
Marcus Tschudin, *A Writer's Theatre: George Devine and the English Stage Company at the Royal Court 1956-1965* (Bern: Lang, 1972);
Raymond Williams, *Drama from Ibsen to Brecht* (New York: Oxford University Press, 1969), pp. 325-328.

Alan Ayckbourn
(12 April 1939-   )

Albert E. Kalson
Purdue University

PRODUCTIONS: *The Square Cat*, as Roland Allen, Summer 1959, Library Theatre, Scarborough;

Love After All, as Roland Allen, 21 December 1959, Library Theatre, Scarborough;

Dad's Tale, as Roland Allen, 19 December 1960, Library Theatre, Scarborough;

Standing Room Only, as Roland Allen, 13 July 1961, Library Theatre, Scarborough;

Xmas v. Mastermind, December 1962, Victoria Theatre, Stoke on Trent;

Mr. Whatnot, 12 November 1963, Victoria Theatre, Stoke on Trent; revised and expanded version, 6 August 1964, Arts Theatre, London, 18 [performances];

Meet My Father, 8 July 1965, Library Theatre, Scarborough; produced again as *Relatively Speaking*, 29 March 1967, Duke of York's Theatre, London, 355;

The Sparrow, 10 July 1967, Library Theatre, Scarborough;

Countdown, in *We Who Are About To . . .* 6 February 1969, Hampstead Theatre Club, London; produced again in *Mixed Doubles: An Entertainment on Marriage* (a revised version of *We Who Are About To . . .*), 9 April 1969, Comedy Theatre, London;

How the Other Half Loves, 31 July 1969, Library Theatre, Scarborough; 5 August 1970, Lyric Theatre, London, 869;

The Story So Far, 20 August 1970, Library Theatre, Scarborough; revised as *Me Times Me Times Me*, 13 March 1972, on tour; produced again as *Family Circles*, 17 November 1978, Orange Tree Theatre, Richmond;

Ernie's Incredible Illucinations, 1971, London, 16;

Time and Time Again, 8 July 1971, Library Theatre, Scarborough; 16 August 1972, Comedy Theatre, London, 229;

Absurd Person Singular, 26 June 1972, Library Theatre, Scarborough; 4 July 1973, Criterion Theatre, London, 973;

Mother Figure, in *Mixed Blessings*, 1973, Capitol Theatre, Horsham, Sussex; produced again in *Confusions*, 30 September 1974, Library Theatre, Scarborough; 19 May 1976, Apollo Theatre, London, 269;

The Norman Conquests (*Table Manners, Living Together, Round and Round the Garden*), June 1973, Library Theatre, Scarborough; 1 August 1974, Globe Theatre (transferred 2 December 1975 to Apollo Theatre), London, 678;

Absent Friends, 17 June 1974, Library Theatre, Scarborough; 23 July 1975, Garrick Theatre, London, 317;

Confusions (*Mother Figure, Drinking Companion, Between Mouthfuls, Gosforth's Fête, A Talk in the Park*), 30 September 1974, Library Theatre, Scarborough; 19 May 1976, Apollo Theatre, London, 269;

Jeeves, adapted from P. G. Wodehouse's stories, book and lyrics by Ayckbourn, music by Andrew Lloyd Webber, 22 April 1975, Her

Alan Ayckbourn, 1981

Majesty's Theatre, London, 47;
Bedroom Farce, 16 June 1975, Library Theatre, Scarborough; 14 March 1977, Lyttelton Theatre (National Theatre) (transferred 6 November 1978 to Prince of Wales's Theatre), London;
Just Between Ourselves, 28 January 1976, Library Theatre, Scarborough; 20 April 1977, Queen's Theatre, London, 157;
Ten Times Table, 18 January 1977, Stephen Joseph Theatre-in-the-Round, Scarborough; 5 April 1978, Globe Theatre, London, 381;
Joking Apart, 11 January 1978, Stephen Joseph Theatre-in-the-Round, Scarborough; 7 March 1979, Globe Theatre, London, 142;
Men on Women on Men, music by Paul Todd, 17 June 1978, Stephen Joseph Theatre-in-the-Round, Scarborough;
Sisterly Feelings, 10 January 1979, Stephen Joseph Theatre-in-the-Round, Scarborough; 3 June 1980, Olivier Theatre (National Theatre), London;
Taking Steps, 27 September 1979, Stephen Joseph Theatre-in-the-Round, Scarborough; 2 September 1980, Lyric Theatre, London, 320;
Suburban Strains, music by Paul Todd, 20 January 1980, Stephen Joseph Theatre-in-the-Round, Scarborough; 2 February 1981, Round House Theatre, London, 36;
Season's Greetings, 24 September 1980, Stephen Joseph Theatre-in-the-Round, Scarborough; 14 October 1980, Round House Theatre, London, 15; revised version, 27 January 1982, Greenwich Theatre, Greenwich, 40; 27 March 1982, Apollo Theatre, London;
Way Upstream, October 1981, Stephen Joseph Theatre-in-the-Round, Scarborough; 18 August 1982, Lyttelton Theatre (National Theatre), London;
Making Tracks, music by Paul Todd, 16 December 1981, Stephen Joseph Theatre-in-the-Round, Scarborough;
Intimate Exchanges, 3 June 1982, Stephen Joseph Theatre-in-the-Round, Scarborough.

BOOKS: *Relatively Speaking* (London: Evans Plays, 1968; New York: French, 1968);
Ernie's Incredible Illucinations (London & New York: French, 1969);
How the Other Half Loves (New York: French, 1971; London: Evans Plays, 1972);
Time and Time Again (London & New York: French, 1973);
Absurd Person Singular (London & New York: French, 1974);
The Norman Conquests: Table Manners, Living Together, Round and Round the Garden (London & New York: French, 1975; London: Chatto & Windus, 1975; New York: Grove, 1979);
Absent Friends (London & New York: French, 1975);
Confusions (London & New York: French, 1977)— includes *Mother Figure, Drinking Companion, Between Mouthfuls, Gosforth's Fête, A Talk in the Park*;
Bedroom Farce (London & New York: French, 1977);
Three Plays (London: Chatto & Windus, 1977; New York: Grove, 1979)—includes *Absurd Person Singular, Absent Friends*, and *Bedroom Farce*;
Just Between Ourselves (London & New York: French, 1978);
Ten Times Table (London & New York: French, 1978);
Joking Apart (London & New York: French, 1979);
Joking Apart and Other Plays (London: Chatto & Windus, 1979)—includes *Joking Apart, Just Between Ourselves*, and *Ten Times Table*;
Sisterly Feelings and Taking Steps (London: Chatto & Windus, 1981).

Alan Ayckbourn, one of Britain's most prolific playwrights, is assuredly its most successful in terms of financial return. His plays, translated into twenty-six languages, earn him more than £100,000 a year; and hardly a year goes by without at least two of his works running concurrently in London with another in preparation at a small theater in Scarborough, the middle-class Yorkshire coastal resort where he has lived and worked for nearly all of his professional life. Yet Ayckbourn is a playwright in a quandary. His early works, delightful if occasionally mindless farces buoyed by his ability to explore the limits of staging, won him a devoted audience yet aroused the apprehensions of some critics who considered him little more than a facile trickster. Ayckbourn's own statement about his work, in fact, encouraged this critical view: "I'm far too fond of the theatre to take it too seriously."

Nonetheless, more discerning critics found him to be a committed dramatist early in his career. Beyond the easy jokes, the mistaken identities, the intricate staging, Ayckbourn was learning a craft that would enable him, always within the framework of bourgeois comedy, to illuminate the tedium, the pain, even the horror of daily life recognizable not only in England's Home Counties, where most of the plays are set, or in gruffer, heartier northern England, where most of them are initially performed, but all over the world.

Although he has been called "a left wing writer using a right wing form," Ayckbourn has made it clear that his "commitments are rather more general than to do with politics," which he finds boring. "I don't know much about . . . Marxist rallies," he says, and he does not believe that the theatergoing public knows much about them either: "They worry about their leaking roof, their central heating." Yet his success with domestic comedies at a time when aspiring British dramatists such as Edward Bond and Howard Brenton were devoting themselves to overtly political pieces in order to be taken seriously still surprises him.

Once the critics began to champion him for the underlying seriousness of his work, however, the audience became restive. They came to laugh but often left troubled. Ayckbourn's recent works have been attempts to win back the puzzled playgoer yet placate the demanding critic. If the task seems formidable, Ayckbourn has nonetheless frequently pleased them both. Whereas most of the audience has simply enjoyed a good night out, Ian Watson, for one, has noted in Ayckbourn's *Absurd Person Singular* (1972) "a total reversal in the professional pecking order [which] brings attendant shifts in social and personal relationships," and in other plays "the familiar totems of middle class life . . . their functions . . . twisted: competitive sports (in *Time and Time Again* and in *Joking Apart*, counter-pointing far more basic competitions on a personal level) . . . and do-it-yourself pursuits (the concern with manual mastery seen, in both *Bedroom Farce* and *Just Between Ourselves*, as a sublimation of a responsive and responsible marital relationship)." Praising *The Norman Conquests* (1973) extravagantly, Michael Billington was not alone in considering the entertaining comedy a work approaching profundity: "I defy anyone to sit through it all and not feel that he has been given a funny, serious, moving, and comprehensive account of the awfulness of middle-class family rituals un-fuelled by love or understanding."

Ayckbourn, whose maternal grandparents were music-hall performers, was attracted to the theater at an early age, and his mother recalls that "he started this acting lark by bullying other children to take part in plays which he put on in the garden shed." Ayckbourn was born in Hampstead, London. His mother, Irene Maud Worley Ayckbourn, a journalist in public relations, divorced his father, Horace Ayckbourn, the deputy leader of the London Symphony Orchestra, when Ayckbourn was five and remarried when he was eight. His stepfather, Cecil Pye, was a bank manager whose career took the family from one Sussex town to another: Billingshurst, Haywards Heath, Lewes, Uckfield. Ayckbourn's subsequent work is rooted in the Home Counties, his characters' speech patterns reflecting his upbringing.

In 1952 Ayckbourn won a bank scholarship to Haileybury School. He studied there until 1956, when, at seventeen, he left, determined to be an actor. His first professional job, which his French master helped him to obtain, was as assistant stage manager with Sir Donald Wolfit's company during an Edinburgh Festival. Next came a series of jobs as assistant stage manager, minor actor, and general factotum. He worked without salary in Worthing, supported by his mother, earned £12 a week in Leatherhead, and, having married Christine Roland when he was nineteen (the vicar required his mother's permission in writing), soon had a family to support. Informed of an opening in Scarborough in 1957, he applied, the most momentous decision of his life, although he did not even know where Scarborough was. What appealed to him was the prospect of a stage-managing job for a summer with no scenery to shift in the town's theater-in-the-round. The company there was founded and run by Stephen Joseph, first at the Library Theatre in Scarborough, briefly at the Victoria Theatre in Stoke on Trent, then back in Scarborough, where, after Joseph's death, Ayckbourn became director of production. Interrupted by a brief stint at the Oxford Playhouse in 1958 and a period from 1965 to 1969 when he was concurrently a radio producer with the BBC in Leeds, Ayckbourn's continuing association with the company eventually turned a minor actor into a major playwright.

Joseph, Hermione Gingold's son, a pioneer of in-the-round staging, took Ayckbourn under his wing. "He had that ability," Ayckbourn says, "to bring out talents people didn't know they had. . . . He introduced me to directing and writing. I think in his wisdom he saw that I wasn't going to make it as an actor, so it wasn't all that altruistic." When Ayckbourn complained about a bad play the company was rehearsing, his director dared him to write a better one. So Ayckbourn wrote *The Square Cat* (1959), not coincidentally supplying a good acting part for himself as a guitar-playing pop singer. He has described what followed this initial effort: "I wrote a second one for me in which I played four parts, and then I wrote a third one for me in which I played eight parts. But I was starting to write better than I could act, so I then wrote myself a super part and gave it to someone else. Then I gave up acting altogether." Among the plays, most of them written under the pseudonym Roland Allen, were *Love After All* (1959), an Edwardian farce; *Dad's Tale* (1960), described as "an ideal Christmas show"; *Standing Room Only* (1961), his first play to attract the attention of a London management; *Xmas v. Mastermind* (1962), a Christmas play for children; and *Mr. Whatnot* (1963), his first play to receive a London production. None of these has been published.

The most intriguing of the apprentice group is *Standing Room Only*, Ayckbourn's only absurdist work, which predates Jean-Luc Godard's 1968 film, *Weekend*. Set in the future, the play is a comic nightmare which details the lives of a family living on a London bus stranded in a twenty-year traffic jam on Shaftesbury Avenue. The masses of red tape embroiling the family struggling for a normal existence mirrors the bureaucracy in which contemporary man is mired. The mood, however, is lightened by pleasant jokes: informed that "the government are having what is known as Pause in Birth Increase," a character remarks, "A pregnant pause."

Mr. Whatnot, expanded from its original forty minutes for its London production in 1964, was "so prettied up that it was virtually destroyed" and lasted a mere two weeks. In the play, in which there is much miming by all the characters, Mint, a piano tuner who is mute, falls in love with Amanda, the daughter of Lord and Lady Slingsby-Craddock, when he is mistakenly accepted as a guest in their home. Although Cecil marries Amanda, it is Mint who beds her, foreshadowing *Taking Steps* (1979), written some sixteen years later. When Amanda's father and Cecil tell war stories and make gun noises, the audience actually begins to hear guns as all the guests take cover. Imagination becomes reality as in the later *Ernie's Incredible Illucinations* (1971). Most significantly, the play demonstrates early in Ayckbourn's career his reluctance to be limited by conventional staging techniques. Onstage car chases and intricate effects ("As the engine revs up, Pedestrian revolves on the end of the crank handle at great speed,") abound in *Mr. Whatnot*.

Calling the play "quite appallingly cute," Philip Hope-Wallace found *Mr. Whatnot* faintly Firbankian, but Ayckbourn's subsequent plays, by his own admission, would reveal his major influences to be William Congreve, Oscar Wilde, Georges Feydeau, Anton Chekhov and, among more recent dramatists, Noel Coward, Terence Rattigan, J. B. Priestley for his sense of theatrical time, and Harold Pinter (who once directed his own play *The Birthday Party* in Scarborough), from whom Ayckbourn

learned to distort "the everyday phrase, slightly bending it."

The failure of *Mr. Whatnot* led Ayckbourn to take a position with the BBC. Congratulating him on the new post, Joseph nevertheless asked him to find the time to write a play for the Scarborough company, the eventual success of which enabled Ayckbourn to return to Scarborough once and for all to settle into an unvarying routine.

Professing to hate the discipline of the writing process, Ayckbourn spends perhaps one week a year at providing the company, now housed in the Stephen Joseph Theatre-in-the-Round, with a new play. He requires a deadline, and constant reminders of the approach of that deadline, before he can force himself to work continuously for several nights in a room on the top floor of his home, a former vicarage once owned by Joseph which overlooks the bay at Scarborough. Frequently posters are printed, parts assigned, and tickets sold before Ayckbourn even begins to compose.

Ayckbourn does enjoy the challenge of writing for a particular company, a particular stage. He reminds himself, as director of the company, that he can afford to hire only six or eight actors at a time, and his efforts to please them all lead him to create, not star parts, but team plays, which take place in settings calling for the two doors which his in-the-round stage allows. Above all, he bears in mind the requirements of the Scarborough audience, many of them his neighbors, upon whom he depends for the testing of his work. He will neither insult nor shock them, respecting their desire to be entertained. He provides them with plays about the life he observes around him, sometimes even his own. Christine Ayckbourn, who now maintains a home in Leeds with their sons, Steven and Philip, asserts that "she would be among the richest women in the world if she claimed royalties for all the fodder she has provided for his bitter, biting domestic comedies."

According to the dramatist, the play which made all the difference to his career was *Relatively Speaking* (1967), originally performed as *Meet My Father* in Scarborough in 1965. Joseph had asked him "simply for a play which would make people laugh when their seaside summer holidays were spoiled by the rain and they came into the theatre to get dry before trudging back to their landladies." That seemed to Ayckbourn "as worthwhile a reason for writing a play as any," and he deliberately used the opportunity while still with the BBC to construct an old-fashioned, well-made play. After all, he believed, a playwright "cannot begin to shatter theatrical convention or break golden rules until he is reasonably sure in himself what they are and how they were arrived at." Thus began for Ayckbourn a learning experience which proved profitable as well, as he chose as a model one of the most perfect of all well-made comedies, Wilde's *The Importance of Being Earnest* (1895), and fashioned his first West End success.

Just as Algernon learns from the inscription on Jack's cigarette case the existence of Cecily and overhears her address—The Manor House, Woolton, Hertfordshire—Greg, suspicious that he may not be the only man in Ginny's life, finds an address penciled on a cigarette packet—The Willows, Lower Pendon, Bucks—and embarks on a Bunburying expedition of his own which leads to mistaken identities, suspicions of illegitimacy, and a denouement involving a handbag. Whereas Algernon leaves town for country to engage in a relationship, Ginny leaves London to break one off—her clandestine affair with an older man, her employer, Philip. Unfortunately arriving at Philip's country home after Greg does, just as Jack gets back to the manor house after Algernon's arrival there, Ginny forces Philip into the role of father, as Jack is forced into allowing Algernon to pose as his brother.

Both Wilde and Ayckbourn's plays could have become metaphysical explorations on the question of identity. Early in *Relatively Speaking* Greg claims to have a terror of losing his identity in the night—of being unsure who he is on awakening each morning. Yet both playwrights seem to have been guided by Gwendolen's assertion that metaphysical speculations have "very little reference at all to the actual facts of real life, as we know them." Both dramatists abandon metaphysics for incredible feats of legerdemain. Whereas Wilde dazzles with epigram and aphorism, Ayckbourn offers the serviceable joke: when Greg looks around to discover "No Ginny," Philip's wife Sheila responds, "No, I'm afraid not. There's some sherry, if you'd like." Asked what prize she won in school for Memory and Elocution, Sheila replies with a matter-of-fact "I've forgotten." Yet Ayckbourn keeps up what a publisher's blurb correctly called "this superbly constructed meringue" with the most extensive and astonishing use of comic quid pro quo of any recent play as each of the four engages every other character in cross-purpose dialogues. For Ayckbourn, the *pièce bien faite* proves an easy confection whose conflict, adultery involving couples of contrasting ages and social status, would reappear once the playwright began to shatter theatrical convention in earnest.

In the unpublished *The Sparrow*, a less derivative but still conventional comedy forgotten after its Scarborough production in 1967, Ayckbourn tried his hand with little success at writing about marital rifts at the lower end of the social scale. The forceful Tony, a car salesman, separated from his wife Julia, takes up with his bus-conductor friend Ed's pickup, Evie. He wants to prove to wife and friend, who have had a brief fling themselves, his continuing sexual authority. Eventually Tony and Julia are reunited in what will be a permanent, literal battle of the sexes, much to the consternation of Evie and Ed, whose view of marriage has been soured forever.

A young couple who brawl their way into the bedroom is one of three sets of husbands and wives in *How the Other Half Loves*. The highly inventive farce, produced in Scarborough in 1969 and a year later in London, is, without the crutch of a Wildean plot, a logical development of the skillfully juggled infidelities of the couples of *Relatively Speaking* and *The Sparrow*. Bob Phillips is involved in an affair with his employer's wife, Fiona Foster. Inventing a marital breakup for the socially backward Featherstones as an excuse for coming home in the middle of the night, he unwittingly sets off a chain of misunderstandings which nearly wreck three already unstable relationships. Before mate is reunited with proper mate, Teresa Phillips and Frank Foster learn the truth and forgive their wayward spouses, but hapless, innocent Mary and William Featherstone are not quite reconciled to what they may now perceive to be a sterile relationship.

A telling contrast of social and economic status made evident by the play's complicated but ingenious setting adds zest to the marital mix-up. It is Ayckbourn's masterstroke to place the living-dining area of both the tasteful Foster home and the cluttered, uncared-for Phillips home onstage together, not side by side as one might expect from a conventional playwright dealing with two locales, but actually superimposed. The expensive Foster period furniture shares a one-room stage with the modern, trendy Phillips pieces. (In the West End production the sofa was even sectioned into Foster cushions and Phillips cushions.) Yet, by means of clashing styles and colors, the audience has no difficulty in discerning which abode is which.

In the play's most remarkable innovation, which leads to one of the most hilarious scenes in the Ayckbourn canon, Thursday night at the Fosters

HOW
THE OTHER HALF
LOVES

C A S T

FRANK FOSTER	**ROBERT MORLEY**
FIONA FOSTER	**JOAN TETZEL**
BOB PHILLIPS	**DONALD BURTON**
TERRY PHILLIPS	**HEATHER SEARS**
WILLIAM FEATHERSTONE	**BRIAN MILLER**
MARY FEATHERSTONE	**ELIZABETH ASHTON**

Directed by
ROBIN MIDGLEY

FULLY LICENSED BARS IN ALL PARTS OF THE THEATRE

The living rooms of the Fosters and the Phillips

ACT ONE

Scene 1   **Thursday Morning**

Scene 2   **Thursday Evening
and Friday Evening**

ACT TWO

Scene 1   **Saturday Morning**

Scene 2   **Sunday Morning**

There will be one Interval of Fifteen Minutes

At the piano—**Clarry Ashton**

MISS JOAN TETZEL'S COSTUMES BY LACHASSE
"MODULA THEME" ARMCHAIR BY ERCOL FURNITURE LTD.
Theme music "Sidewinder" by Lee Morgan (Liberty Records Blue Note BLP 4157/84157.)
Scenery built by Brunskill & Loveday Ltd. & painted by Alick Johnstone Ltd.
Mr. Morley's sports clothing supplied by Lillywhites. The gold International wrist watch worn by Miss Joan Tetzel by courtesy of Watches of Switzerland, 16 New Bond Street, W.1. Telephones by Reliance Telephone Co. Ltd. Sound Equipment and effects by T.S.L. Vacuum Cleaner by Electrolux Ltd. Additional lighting by Theatre Projects (Lighting) Ltd. Transistor radio by courtesy of Sony (U.K.) Ltd. Tonic Water by Schhh . . . You-Know-Who. Double Diamond by Allied Breweries (U.K.) Ltd. Harvey's Duo-Cans from Cadbury Schweppes. Teabags by Tetley. Perfect Mashed Potatoes by Cadbury's "Smash". New Nescafe "The One Great Coffee Taste—Now Tastes Even Better". Lighters by Ronson. Wigs by Wig Creations Ltd. Silver and China by Lewis and Kaye.
COSTUME SUPERVISION BY HILARY VIRGO

FOR "HOW THE OTHER HALF LOVES" COMPANY

Production Manager	.. JOHN H. deLANNOY
Company and Stage Manager	LEONARD UPTON
Deputy Stage Manager	ANNE BICKERSTAFF
Assistant Stage Managers	ROGER FOUNTAYNE and HILARY CLAYPOLE
Secretary to Peter Bridge	DIANA STEEDMAN
Wardrobe Mistress	.. PAT DALTON
Press and Public Relations	**ROGER CLIFFORD LTD.**
(01-734 3117)

Cast list, scenes, and credits for the 1970 Lyric Theatre production of Ayckbourn's farce about infidelity and status

and Friday night at the Phillipses become the simultaneous action of two dinner parties at one extended dining table where the Featherstones are at once the guests for a properly served, elegant meal with linen napkins and crystal and a slopped-together casual supper with paper napkins and tumblers. The scene ends with poor William Featherstone wringing wet—hit with the soup which an enraged, drunken Teresa throws at Bob on Friday in the very spot where the Fosters' upstairs toilet suddenly leaks through the ceiling on Thursday.

The unique setting provides the play with a dimension beyond the visual. The audience is not kept in a state of apprehension as in a Feydeau farce wondering which character will next be revealed as doors open and close. The suspense in *How the Other Half Loves* transcends plot in involving the audience's appreciation of the characters as actors negotiating the onstage traffic jams to which they must seem to be oblivious. Depending more on per-

fect timing in performance than on plot or language, *How the Other Half Loves* is one of Ayckbourn's most felicitous concoctions.

Before fashioning another full-length play for the West End, Ayckbourn wrote two one-acts, one of them for children, and a two-act comedy which bogged down in its own gimmickry. *Ernie's Incredible Illucinations* concerns a young boy's daydreams which involve all those around him. When he imagines he has killed enemy soldiers surrounding his home, Mum and Dad actually have the job of disposing of the bodies. This amusing trifle reaches a climax when Ernie fails to convince a skeptical doctor that he can imagine a brass band into reality, but the play ends with the doctor as drum major leading his patients in a march.

In a different vein, darker than one might expect at this stage of his career, *Countdown* (1969) continues Ayckbourn's growing concern with the sterility of marriage. A husband and his wife of twenty years carry on a brief, desultory conversation over an after-supper cup of tea, while each reveals the hopeless rift between them in intersecting interior monologues. The work was included in *We Who Are About To . . .*, which was later revised as *Mixed Doubles: An Entertainment on Marriage*, comprised of several playlets by nine authors—Harold Pinter, John Bowen, and Alun Owen among them.

The Story So Far, produced in Scarborough in 1970, revised as *Me Times Me Times Me* in 1972, and retitled *Family Circles* in 1978, never got closer to the West End than its production at the Orange Tree in Richmond. More confusing than clever, the play involves three daughters and the men in their lives celebrating their parents' anniversary. To illustrate Ayckbourn's thesis that "depending on who you marry, you become slightly different," at some point in the play each of the girls is paired with each of the men for nine possible male-female relationships. To accentuate Ayckbourn's growing dissatisfaction with the institution of marriage, the tenth relationship, that of the parents, is not all it should be. Dad, it seems, may even be attempting to do away with Mum.

Time and Time Again, produced in Scarborough in 1971, marks a significant turning point in Ayckbourn's career. From this point, a new Ayckbourn work would be presented each year in the small Yorkshire theater, usually in the summer months, and then produced in London approximately a year later. Moreover, a new element emerges. Before *Time and Time Again*, Ayckbourn was primarily a farceur with aspirations as social observer, but in this play, a comedy of quiet desperation, he works in a gentler, sadder vein toward which *Countdown* had pointed, accenting character rather than situation. The sterility of middle-class suburbia is almost casually underscored as the childlike Leonard, an unemployed, inert schoolteacher in his late thirties, idles away his days in the home he shares with his sister Anna and her exasperated husband Graham. Partly out of loneliness and boredom, partly to annoy Graham, Leonard stealthily enters into a relationship with Joan, the fiancee of Peter, an obtuse sports enthusiast who works for Graham. To win time with Joan, to whom Graham also is attracted, Leonard allows himself to be lured into the seasonal rituals of cricket and football, at which he is as inept as he is in his personal relationships (he had been locked out of his home by his former wife). After Peter physically attacks Graham, mistakenly suspecting him to be the cause of the estrangement between himself and his fiancee, and Joan realizes that she may have been a pawn in Leonard's hands, all relationships

are off. The play ends as it began, with all of its characters a little sadder but no wiser.

With *Time and Time Again* it becomes apparent that no Ayckbourn play provides an audience with a wholly admirable, totally sympathetic character. An audience, however, can identify with characters marred by recognizable human weakness. One may side with Leonard against his fatuous brother-in-law; that he is himself, however, an agent of destruction cannot be ignored. Leonard may remain virtually unscathed, but anyone around him is subject to wounding. Deprived of his peace of mind, Graham is nearly choked to death, while Peter, deprived of a prospective bride, is hit in the knee and kicked in the ankle. Perhaps the play's ultimate failure can be traced to Ayckbourn's own ambivalence toward the protagonist. Though Leonard is appealing as an outsider not bound by convention, he lacks a moral center. He has no sense of responsibility toward friends, family, even self. Nonetheless, the play, with no gimmickry in its stagecraft, is significant in revealing Ayckbourn's widening range. He would return to a similar central character and further develop the secondary characters in a later commercial triumph, *The Norman Conquests*.

Absurd Person Singular (produced in Scarborough in 1972 and in London in 1973) represents Ayckbourn's most accomplished blending of farce and serious theme, combining as it does the pacing of *How the Other Half Loves* with the somber view of personal relationships of *Time and Time Again*. Frantically funny and incisively telling, the play achieves a painful sadness through laughter. Ayckbourn writes that he has always been aware of the British "preference for comedy. . . . At the same time . . . one can detect a faint sense of guilt. . . . It's to do with the mistaken belief that because it's funny, it can't be serious." In *Absurd Person Singular*, which received the *Evening Standard* Drama Award for the best comedy of the year, Ayckbourn proves that his view of the serious play is possible: "It can be funny, but let's make it truthful."

Three unhappily married couples entertain each other on three successive Christmas Eves. Calling it "my first offstage action play," Ayckbourn chooses as his setting not the sitting room or the drawing room but the kitchen—in the Hopcroft's small suburban house in act 1, in the Jackson's fourth-floor flat in act 2, in the Brewster-Wrights' old Victorian house in act 3—for its "greater comic possibilities." In act 1 the guests seek sanctuary in the kitchen to avoid the awful jokes of the hearty, unseen Potters; in act 2 they are held hostage by George, the Jacksons' large unseen dog, who has just bitten the still unseen Mr. Potter in the adjoining room; and in act 3 the Brewster-Wrights and the Jacksons hide unsuccessfully from the uninvited Hopcrofts, who have steadily risen from shopkeepers to building developers and now invade the home of their "friends." Each act represents simultaneously the battle of the sexes and class warfare.

Sidney Hopcroft—"Scratch mine, I'll scratch yours" is his credo—invites guests into his home who can be of use to him as he ascends the social scale: Ronald Brewster-Wright, bank manager, and Geoffrey Jackson, architect, along with their wives, Marion and Eva. His own wife Jane, who like Mary Featherstone of *How the Other Half Loves* is a chronic cleaner and duster, is a source of embarrassment to him as, single-handed, she turns the first act into a Feydeau-like farce by dashing in and out of doors dressed for the inclement weather in rain gear too large for her. They have run out of tonic, it seems. Ronald has spent the evening reading the instruction book for the stove while his equally bored wife admires the "apartheid" washing machine which separates "whites" from "coloureds." The evening, an obvious disaster, is judged to have come off "rather satisfactorily" by Sidney because "these people just weren't anybody."

In the first act Geoffrey and Eva make clear what has undermined their marriage. "As far as he's concerned, my existence ended the day he married me," she says; "I'm just an embarrassing smudge on a marriage license." Geoffrey tells the men, "She chooses to live with me, she lives by my rules." By act 2 Eva has been reduced to a zombie existing on pills. Unconcerned that guests are about to arrive, Eva, in her dressing gown, spends the evening attempting suicide. Finding her with her head in the oven, Jane assumes that she is attempting to clean it and happily takes over. Eva tries jumping to her death, stabbing herself, electrocuting herself, hanging, and overdosing. But everything fails as her guests, oblivious to her agony, shunt her from one corner of the kitchen to another, even use her suicide notes to draw plans for unclogging her sink and changing an electrical fixture. Before the evening ends, Sidney has been drenched under the sink, and Ronald has received a severe electrical shock. Through it all Eva remains unwillingly, unmercifully alive. Not having spoken a word in the entire act, she ends it by leading the others in a mad chorus of "On the first day of Christmas."

In act 3 Marion has confined herself to her bedroom, where she steadily, secretly drinks. Ronald admits to Eva and Geoffrey that he has never understood either of his two wives, their un-

accountable depressions and rages. By this time Geoffrey, responsible for the collapse of the ceiling of a shopping center (Ronald is sorry the deal "fell through"), needs Eva, less proud than he, to beg for work for him, even from Sidney, who now socializes with the most influential families in town yet still finds time for his old friends.

The play ends with a dance, not a harmonious return to order, mate paired with mate, but a *danse macabre* of individuals jumping, hopping, twirling grotesquely, as Sidney forces the others into a game of forfeits involving apples under the chin, oranges between the knees, pears on spoons in mouths, as he exhorts them hysterically to "Dance. Dance. Keep dancing. Dance...." In *Absurd Person Singular*, black farce at its best, life is a frantic game, badly played. One dances or dies.

The Norman Conquests, a trilogy comprising *Table Manners*, *Living Together*, and *Round and Round the Garden*, was performed in Scarborough in 1973 and in London the following year. Through a single set of characters in a house and its surroundings, Ayckbourn investigates the ultimate possibilities of offstage action. What happens onstage in any one of the plays becomes in effect the offstage action of the other two. The work is designed for performances on three successive nights with any one of the plays a

Felicity Kendal and Tom Courtenay in the London production of The Norman Conquests

possible starting point for any spectator, who may choose to see them all yet should find each one complete in itself. If *The Norman Conquests* is regarded as three plays, the monumental if trifling work represents the peak of Ayckbourn's commercial success, leading to a record five plays running simultaneously in the West End in 1975.

In a Victorian house in the country Annie awaits her brother Reg and his wife Sarah. They are to relieve her of caring for their bedridden and unseen mother so that Annie may take a well-deserved holiday. Unknown to the others, who suspect she may be going off with her neighbor Tom, the dull-witted local vet, Annie is in fact about to leave for East Grinstead for a "dirty weekend" with Norman, who is married to her sister Ruth. When an overeager Norman, a whimsically muddled, amoral assistant librarian, arrives on the scene too soon, complications multiply. Shocked upon learning the truth, Sarah forbids Annie to leave, summons Ruth, and takes over the household, forcing Reg, who is mainly interested in getting a square meal and trying out a game he has invented, to spy for her. Bewildered by the proceedings, Tom vaguely suspects that all the women have designs on his person, while Ruth, attempting without much success to retain her composure, sorts matters out. Through it all, exasperating, inept Norman remains a surprisingly irresistible shaggy dog whom all the women wish to cuddle. And all of them do—in a corner of the dining room, on a rug in the sitting room, or in the bushes of the garden. Norman offers happiness to each, for any woman holds the promise of happiness for Norman because for him, the conquest is all. Ultimately, however, the entire household is frustrated as they are trapped in the rituals of a summer weekend—eating, drinking, storytelling, game-playing, wooing. The male-female relationship with its dream of blissful happiness is reduced in *The Norman Conquests* to the comedy of furtive coupling and interrupted groping.

The characters of the trilogy owe much to the earlier and darker *Time and Time Again*. Since Norman is not quite as destructive as Leonard—both parts were effectively played in their West End productions by a shambling Tom Courtenay—he elicits more sympathy as he lives engagingly by his curiously self-indulgent code. By switching the sex of the outraged in-law Graham to the equally furious Sarah, the fun increases as anger metamorphoses into sexual arousal. *Time and Time Again*'s none-too-bright sportsman, Peter, grows even more obtuse in *The Norman Conquests* in the character of Tom, who is eager to box to defend his honor but

hesitant to declare his intentions concerning Annie, who plays Varya to his Lopakhin as communication breaks down between them, as in Chekhov's *The Cherry Orchard* (1904).

The three parts of *The Norman Conquests* enable the audience to know what every member of the household is up to at any given moment in any part of the house. When Sarah sends Reg from the dining room in *Table Manners* to fetch something from the sitting room in order to spy on Annie and Norman and he returns foolishly carrying a waste-paper basket, only to be berated by his wife, the audience is amused. In *Living Together* when Reg interrupts Annie and Norman in the sitting room and grabs the basket in embarrassed confusion, that part of the audience which has already seen *Table Manners* is implicated in an expanding joke. In order to bring off his prodigious feat, Ayckbourn wrote the plays crosswise: as he explains, he "started with Scene One of *Round and Round the Garden*, then the Scene One's of the other two plays and so on through the Scene Two's."

The three-part structure of *The Norman Conquests*, however, does not afford the characters added depth. Any one of the plays reveals all the audience needs to know of them. Neither characterization nor situation in the trilogy is intriguing enough to sustain interest in the whole of the outsized work. Seeing one play, the audience is diverted by a comedy of little substance; seeing a second play, the audience is appreciative of the extra rewards. By the third play, however, the audience is primarily conscious of an extraordinary craftsmanship which calls attention to itself in the repetition of incidents seen through altered perspectives and thus undermines rather than increases the comic effect. *The Norman Conquests*, nonetheless, remains Ayckbourn's best-known, most widely performed work. In 1974 both the *Evening Standard* and *Plays and Players* named *The Norman Conquests* best play of the year.

The mood darkens perceptibly in *Absent Friends* which Ayckbourn, at the time of its first production in Scarborough in 1974, considered a "terrifying risk," for he had "never pitched anything in quite such a low key before." In *The Norman Conquests* an unseen, sick old woman made her presence felt throughout her household. *Time and Time Again* had opened immediately following the funeral of Leonard's indulgent mother. In *Absent Friends*, however, the hovering spirit is a perfect young woman cut off in the prime of life by drowning. When Colin returns to visit some friends who had never met his deceased fiancee, Carol, the reality of three longstanding male-female relationships is contrasted with a fond if perhaps imperfect memory of a romance of fourteen months.

Diana thinks Colin, whom she has not seen in years, needs cheering up, so she invites him to come round for what proves a disastrous afternoon tea. After all, she thinks, Colin and Paul were once inseparable friends—they even came courting Diana and her sister Barbara together. Paul's recollections of his past acquaintance with Colin are markedly different, and who was courting whom seems subject to Pinterish shifts of memory as the three reminisce about old times. That Diana has also invited John, a salesman who depends on the more successful Paul for business, and his hostile, nearly silent wife Evelyn, who has recently had a decidedly unromantic encounter with Paul in the back seat of his car, adds to the tension of the situation. Also present is Marge, whose pampered husband George, an accident-prone fire prevention officer, is sick in bed at home, and keeps telephoning to report the latest calamity—the medicine has spilled all over the bed, the hot water bottle has burst.

Cautioning each other to refrain from reopening Colin's wounds by speaking of Carol, the others are astounded when Colin, who produces an album of her photos, will speak of nothing else. Before the continuous action of the two-act play ends—its time span of a single afternoon, according to Ayckbourn, "had the intended consequence of making the play far more claustrophobic, almost oppressive"—Diana pours a jug of cream over her husband's head, recalls wanting to join the Canadian Royal Mounted Police as a child in a madly comic parody of Mary Tyrone's final speech in Eugene O'Neill's *Long Day's Journey Into Night* (1956), begins a series of short, staccato screams and has a nervous breakdown at center stage. A perfect relationship, Ayckbourn suggests, is one that need not stand the test of time. Death has made Colin a happy man.

"There's nothing like telling your audience an old joke to make them laugh," Ayckbourn says. But telling old jokes cannot extend a writer's craft. He has admitted that a play such as *Absent Friends* represents a conscious attempt to test dangerous territory: "One of the areas I wanted to write about . . . was not about death itself but about people's attitudes to death. . . . I'm dealing in topics which I suppose in themselves are quite serious, but viewing them, I hope, in a sympathetically comic way." If he has failed to provide as much sympathy as he intends in what seems a coldly detached view of the contemporary mores of a hypocritical society, he

has supplied a bitchy, witty dialogue which carries the audience past its initial distaste for the subject matter. *Absent Friends*, an overlooked, underrated play, is a skillful comic blending of unlikely materials.

Confusions (1974), a group of five slight one-acts which can be performed separately but are held together by some cursory links, deals with Ayckbourn's characteristic themes of loneliness, adultery, and marriage gone sour. The brightest and perhaps saddest moment occurs in *Gosforth's Fête* when a faulty loudspeaker system suddenly broadcasts the news of the village spinster's pregnancy, which is intended only for the ears of the publican responsible for her condition, across four acres of field at a charity bazaar. In *Between Mouthfuls*, like Ayckbourn's television play *Service Not Included*, which was transmitted in 1974, the same year as the Scarborough production of *Confusions*, two couples in a restaurant inadvertently reveal their adulterous secret to an impervious waiter.

In 1975, a year before the West End production of *Confusions*, Ayckbourn was involved as author of the book and lyrics for a short-lived musical adaptation with a score by Andrew Lloyd Webber of P. G. Wodehouse's *Jeeves* stories. Without the benefit of a Scarborough run, the elaborate and costly production opened prematurely in London to one of the severest critical drubbings ever suffered by either the author or the composer. The experience reinforced Ayckbourn's faith and dependence upon his Scarborough theater where a playwright has the opportunity to revise, and an entire production can be mounted for £3,000. However, Ayckbourn's first attempt at a musical would not be his last.

His return to Scarborough in the summer of 1975 led, two years later, to another commercial success and to the distinction of his first production at the National Theatre, where in 1977 he co-directed his *Bedroom Farce* with Peter Hall. A comedy of manners about disappointed expectations, the play offers neither the titillation nor the frenzy its title suggests, thus disappointing that portion of its audience which entered the theater anticipating a bed-hopping sex farce. The discrepancy between the title and the play itself, which is set simultaneously in three bedrooms side by side on stage, suggests Ayckbourn's theme: one must accept life as it is and not as one romantically imagines it ought to be. Its most farcical moment, having nothing at all to do with sex, involves a brief telephone conversation in which a father discovers that the son he is speaking with is not his own—the wrong party is at

Front cover and credits for Ayckbourn's 1975 play that ran for one and a half years at the National Theatre before it was transferred to the Prince of Wales's Theatre for a run of 376 performances

the other end of the line. Its funniest scene involving two people actually in bed together concerns an elderly couple topping off what has been a disappointing anniversary dinner by savoring pilchards on toast. Ayckbourn himself suggests that *Bedroom Farce* has elements of both *Absurd Person Singular* and *Absent Friends*: "It has its moments of near farce and yet still contains elements of the claustrophobic."

Dithering Trevor and his neurotic wife Susannah, who spends her offstage moments having breakdowns in the bathrooms of her friends and in-laws, disrupt the lives of everyone they know as they attempt a reconciliation. Trevor is not quite as destructive as he imagines himself to be, despite his accidentally wrecking the assemble-it-yourself

dressing table which his friend Malcolm has worked on all night as a surprise gift for his wife Kate. Trevor may cause Nick some temporary mental anguish when he explains that he is no longer involved in a relationship with Nick's wife Jan, but he is not the cause of the back problem which keeps Nick, like the offstage George of *Absent Friends*, bedridden (Nick is visible throughout the play). Trevor may cause his parents Delia and Ernest the usual anxieties, but his mother and father have made an accommodation to life, and to one another, the same accommodation which a more optimistic Ayckbourn here suggests is perhaps a possibility in every relationship. The play even ends with Trevor asleep in Susannah's arms, albeit in Malcolm and Kate's bed.

With Malcolm and Kate's bedroom in the middle, Ernest and Delia's at stage right and Nick and Jan's at stage left, Ayckbourn manipulates a visual as well as an emotional split and reunion for his disturbed young couple. Trevor and Susannah battle at Malcolm and Kate's, go their separate ways—Susannah to stage right to her in-laws, Trevor to stage left to his friends. Keeping up the symmetry of the pattern, Ayckbourn even manages to get Susannah into Delia's bed and Trevor into Nick's before the two reaffirm their love for one another at the very center of the stage. The arrangement allows Ayckbourn a cinematic crosscutting which gives the play, in his words, "an added rhythm over and above what the dialogue normally provides," a rhythm necessary to pace a work which lacks the incisive observation, the biting wit, and intriguing situation of some earlier Ayckbourn plays. Yet a sign of a further step in the playwright's development is that here, more than ever before, he has "allowed the characters to progress, develop and resolve very much in their own way. Perhaps," he writes, " . . . none of them finds instant happiness or sudden self-insight. But at least they retain the dignity of their own destinies."

The guarded optimism of *Bedroom Farce*, which achieved a run of 376 performances when it transferred to the Prince of Wales's Theatre after a year and a half in repertory at the National Theatre, proved a temporary respite in Ayckbourn's darkening view of human relationships. *Just Between Ourselves* (produced in Scarborough in 1976 and in London in 1977) is comedy at its bleakest, more satisfying for critics in search of psychosocial profundities than for bewildered audiences eager to be entertained who discover to their embarrassment that they are laughing in the wrong places. Ayckbourn calls *Just Between Ourselves* "the first of my winter plays." Unlike his earlier work which was "written in late spring for performance during the Scarborough summer season," it was composed in December 1975 for performance in January as his company, in preparation for its change from a summer repertory policy and its move from the makeshift Library Theatre to a new year-round home, sought "permanency within the town" by encouraging and developing a "much needed winter audience." Because of the proposed move, Ayckbourn for the first time was relieved of the pressure of producing a play "suited primarily to a holiday audience." He started *Just Between Ourselves* at night, his customary practice, but this time as "North Sea storms hurtled round the house . . . and metal chimney cowlings were bounced off parked cars below my window, rebounding hither and thither like demented pinballs. Not surprisingly," he writes, "the result was a rather sad (some say a rather savage) play with themes concerned with total lack of understanding, with growing old and with spiritual and mental collapse."

"I never sit down to write a grim play," Ayckbourn has stated. "Vera in *Just Between* took me by surprise. I was going to write about a man who was awfully nice and friendly and whom everyone loathed. . . . But out of the corner of my eye I saw this wife . . . and she was *crumbling away*. And I thought, hang on, what's happening to *her?*"

What happens to Vera has happened in Ayckbourn plays to many female characters at the end of their rope, unable to make contact with their more assured, even arrogant and uncomprehending husbands. But for Vera the nervous collapse is complete and irreversible. Constantly at odds with her live-in mother-in-law, she has no one to turn to. She has no friends, only embarrassed acquaintances, Neil and Pam, who are themselves at the point of giving up on a loveless marriage. All the while Dennis spends his leisure hours puttering about a garage (the play's setting) as hopelessly messy as his life, ineffectually tinkering with faulty appliances. Typically, he is trying to sell a car he cannot get out of the garage due to the malfunctioning of its "up-and-over" door. His method of coping is to laugh away his problems—the door, the car, even a wife drifting unnoticed into catatonia. Vera cannot penetrate his cheery oblivion. It is left to Pam to express to him the affliction of the middle-class, middle-aged prototypical Ayckbourn female: "I feel old, Dennis—old, unfulfilled, frustrated, unattractive, dull, washed out, undesirable—you name it. And I've got absolutely nothing to look forward to." That each scene is set on the birthday of one of the characters contributes to the mortality all of them feel.

In resisting the temptation to provide a happy ending, to allow Vera a miraculous cure, Ayckbourn felt he was taking "a large stride towards maturity as a playwright. It continued my small progress . . . towards my unattainable goal: to write a totally effortless, totally truthful, unforced comedy shaped like a flawless diamond in which one can see a million reflections, both one's own and other people's." Despite its winning the *Evening Standard* Drama Award for best play of the year, *Just Between Ourselves* is far from that goal. It is comedy in the Chekhovian manner without Chekhovian humanity. By not providing any of the five characters with a single redeeming quality, Ayckbourn alienates the audience to the point of indifference. A man coming out of the theater commented to the author on the scene in act 1 in which Vera has a breakdown at the tea table: "If I'd known what I was laughing at at the time, I wouldn't have laughed." Ayckbourn prides himself on such an ambiguous response, but his predominantly dark plays like *Absent Friends* and *Just Between Ourselves* have had disappointing runs and may have affected audience response to his later work.

After *Just Between Ourselves* the mood lightened. Ayckbourn describes *Ten Times Table* (produced in Scarborough in 1977 and in London in 1978) as "a predominantly sedentary farce with faintly allegorical overtones. . . . Certainly, if in *Just Between Ourselves* I moved towards maturity, in *Ten Times Table* I reverted, happily, to my playwright's childhood." The idea came to him in 1976 as he was forced to attend "an interminable series of repetitive . . . committee meetings to finance and facilitate" the company's move from the Scarborough Library to the old Boys' Grammar School.

Ten Times Table, Ayckbourn's farcical "study of the committee person," takes him from his "usual domestic setting" to "the more public surroundings of the ballroom of the quite awful Swan Hotel." A civic committee meets there over several months to plan a pageant based on a questionable historic event which occurred two centuries earlier, the Massacre of the Pendon Twelve, in which a local farmer, John Cockle, had so vigorously protested against unfair taxation that the militia summoned to quell the disturbance mortally wounded the agitator and several of his followers. In the last scene of the play, which takes place on Festival Day, the Marxist schoolteacher who would turn the pageant into a political rally meets his match in a Fascist dog-breeder who sees it as a breeding ground for an inevitable class war. In the end, the pageant becomes a shambles, yet a good time is had by all, with some of the committee already beginning to contemplate next year's event—a battle between Romans and ancient Britons.

Ayckbourn's efforts to find comedy within the tedium of the committee room result in tedium for the audience. The mild joke cannot sustain a full-length play. *Ten Times Table* is less clever than the one-act which it resembles, *Gosforth's Fête*, which is also set in the typical provincial English town which Ayckbourn dubs Pendon, to which he will return in *Sisterly Feelings* (1979). Better at exploring personal relationships than public ones, Ayckbourn fails with material more capably handled before him by J. B. Priestley in the political farce, *Bees on the Boat Deck*

(1936) and the comic novels, *Let the People Sing* (1939) and *Festival at Farbridge* (1951). Later, in *Way Upstream* (1981) Ayckbourn would demonstrate a firmer control in his second play with political implications.

Ayckbourn returns to home ground in *Joking Apart* (produced in Scarborough in 1978 and in London in 1979), which its author believes combines "the truth of *Just Between Ourselves* with some of the fun of *Ten Times Table*." It was written as the thirty-eight-year-old Ayckbourn, confronted by his "suddenly adult" eighteen-year-old son, began, like his characters, to feel his age. The play, unusual in its time span in covering twelve years, is unique in Ayckbourn's canon in centering on a perfect male-female relationship. Yet Ayckbourn is even more interested in revealing its disastrous effects on the friends and business associates of the charmed couple than he is in exploring the basis of the longstanding relationship.

What sets Richard and Anthea apart from their conventional friends as well as all the conventional couples of Ayckbourn's plays is the fact that they are blissfully unmarried yet seem to function as ideal mates, even ideal parents for Anthea's two children by the husband she divorced. Sven, a Finn and Richard's partner in Scandinavian Craftware Co. Ltd., is certain he has a better head for business, yet it is Richard's instinctive decisions made without Sven's knowledge which keep the firm solvent. And despite his claim to having once been the Finnish Junior Tennis Champion, Sven can only win when Richard throws the game by playing left-handed. Even worse for Sven than losing might have been, however, is the discovery of his associate's insulting duplicity on the court.

For Brian, who works for the firm, the occasional weekend visits to the couple's country home are particularly painful in light of his unrequited love for Anthea, aggravated by the fact that the girlfriends who accompany him generally find Richard devastatingly attractive. (All three of Brian's girlfriends, as well as Anthea's daughter Debbie, Brian's last hope for an Anthea substitute, are played by the same actress.) Even the next-door neighbors fall prey to the spell. Hugh, the local vicar, must measure his failure as husband and father against Richard's success, while his timid wife Louise tries to mask her jealousy. While Richard and Anthea age gracefully over a dozen years, the rest merely age, with Sven developing a serious heart condition and Louise drifting closer to the inevitable breakdown.

The play, set on various holidays and special

family occasions, takes place in a garden in which half a tennis court can be seen, necessitating some frantic comic action on the part of the visible player which frequently counterpoints a moment of desperation for one of the others. Sven, who verbalizes a growing resentment, and Olive, the wife who lives in his shadow, are admirably drawn. On the other hand, Richard and Anthea remain ciphers except as their friends react to them. They do not convince an audience that their lack of a marriage license has increased their chance for happiness, and Ayckbourn has failed to supply any other basis for their seemingly faultless union.

Between his first National Theatre production, *Bedroom Farce*, in which his characters resolve their destinies, and his return there with *Sisterly Feelings* in 1980 (first produced in Scarborough in 1979), Ayckbourn seems to have come to believe that man's fate is fixed. Neither chance nor choice can alter it. To illustrate his theory of comic determinism, Ayckbourn has devised his most elaborate theatrical trick. Whereas audiences may devote three evenings in the theater to appreciate fully the machinations of Norman at his conquests, they ought in theory to attend four performances of *Sisterly Feelings*, Ayckbourn's seemingly inverted life cycle from death to birth. Two evenings, however, enable one to construct for himself the combinations he has not seen played, for by then he may have seen all the scenes which together make up *Sisterly Feelings*. But chance or choice plays upon the audience as well. One may choose a performance in which the toss of a coin at one point and an actress's whim at another dictate what is to follow—these performances are billed as "Chances"—or one may choose to attend performances at which the result of the toss and the actress's decision have been predetermined.

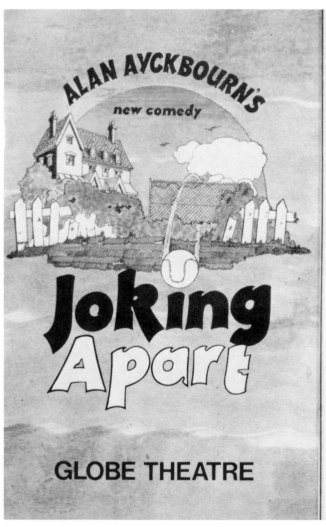

GLOBE THEATRE
Shaftesbury Avenue, London W1

Proprietors: Chairman:
ATP (London) Ltd   LORD GRADE
Managing Director: Deputy Chairman:
TOBY ROWLAND   LOUIS BENJAMIN

Manager: S. BAILEY
Box Office: 01-437 1592/3

MICHAEL CODRON

presents

**ALISON   CHRISTOPHER
STEADMAN   CAZENOVE**

in

ALAN AYCKBOURN'S

new comedy

JOKING APART

with

JULIAN FELLOWES

**JOHN   JENNIFER
PRICE   PIERCEY**

**DIANE   MARCIA
BULL   WARREN**

and

ROBERT AUSTIN

Directed by ALAN AYCKBOURN
Designed by ALAN TAGG
Lighting by RICHARD PILBROW
Costumes by LINDY HEMMING

First performance at the Globe Theatre, Wednesday 7th March 1979

Program cover and credits for the first production of Ayckbourn's 1978 play, which grew out of his realization that his eighteen-year-old son was "suddenly adult"

Alison Steadman and Christopher Cazenove in a scene from the Globe Theatre production of Joking Apart

As an aid to an audience obviously unaccustomed to an arbitrary performance, the theater program provides a cast list in the form of a genealogy and a map suggesting the alternative routes this unique comic vehicle may travel. The genealogical table and the map underscore Ayckbourn's indisputable ingenuity, further proclaimed by his subtitle, "A Related Comedy," a pun, like *Relatively Speaking*, encompassing content, form, and theme. Nearly all the characters of *Sisterly Feelings* are or are about to be members of a single family; the incidents are intertwined; and, since variable scenes obviously exist, any one version suggests for the central characters only a relative truth.

Every version of *Sisterly Feelings* begins with a scene entitled "A Funeral." On the day of his wife's interment, Dr. Matthews takes his family to the spot where years before he had proposed to her on Pendon Common, the play's single setting, on which many of life's rituals from courtship to burial take place. The setting itself, which serves variously as a site for the town's annual foot race, a family picnic ground, even a campground for lovers, metaphorically suggests life's pitfalls: "There is no firm ground. We are standing in a marsh."

The doctor has three children: Abigail, whose husband Patrick is a pompous businessman; Dorcas, a local radio newscaster involved with Stafford,

an unemployable, shaggy poet; and Melvin, engaged to Brenda. The sisters both find themselves attracted to Brenda's brother, narcissistic, muscular Simon, who is home from Africa. When Patrick drives off early to attend a board meeting, one place is left in another car once the rest of the party, which includes the doctor's brother-in-law Len, a policeman, and Len's wife Rita, are accommodated. The sisters, flipping a coin for the remaining seat, are actually vying for the opportunity to remain behind to walk home with Simon. The one who stays establishes a relationship with him, thus incurring not only her sister's jealousy but the displeasure of either Patrick or Stafford, one or the other of whom disrupts the next family outing a few months later in the play's second scene, which, depending on the coin toss, is either "Abigail's Picnic" or "Dorcas' Picnic."

When a rainstorm abruptly ends the picnic, the sister (or rather the actress playing the role) who has ensnared Simon, has the choice of prolonging her affair with him or giving him up to her rival, thus initiating the third scene, either "A Day at the Races" or "A Night under Canvas." If Dorcas is with Simon after the picnic, she becomes a steward for the cross-country race which, Stafford's attempts at sabotage failing, Simon wins. If Abigail is with Simon after the picnic, the two go camping and endure interruptions from Len, then Patrick.

The variable scenes, initiated by chance—a coin toss—or choice—a performer's spur-of-the-moment decision—do not determine the outcome. *Sisterly Feelings* always ends with the same fourth scene, "A Wedding," in which the bride is neither Abigail, who resumes a conventional life with Patrick, nor Dorcas, who resumes her nursemaiding of unconventional, childlike Stafford, but bossy Brenda, now pregnant, who is having her way with docile Melvin. Neither chance nor choice has seriously interrupted life's flow. As Dorcas says, "The important thing is for us to *feel* we've made decisions."

The reaction of American critic Mel Gussow, who witnessed two versions of *Sisterly Feelings*, is perhaps typical: "Two is one more than the average theatergoer need encounter. The first made me look forward to the second; the second made me realize that one had been enough." Agreeing with his British counterparts that the Abigail scenes are the more amusing, he found the play's funniest moment in "Abigail's Picnic." The scene in which lugubrious Uncle Len is repeatedly passed over as the sandwiches are distributed led Gussow to identify the writer's two equally strong suits in his observation that Ayckbourn "is a social behaviorist and a champion theatrical gamesman." If the unique combination leads Ayckbourn to overextend himself on occasion, it sometimes enables him to prop up his diverting comic observations with delightfully unpredictable theatrical high jinks as in *Sisterly Feelings*, or to support his frenetic activity with some sobering truths as in his next play, *Taking Steps* (produced in Scarborough in 1979 and in London in 1980).

Whereas the Abigail scenes of *Sisterly Feelings* may be richer in comic invention, it is the Dorcas scenes which provide a germ of an idea other than the role of fate in our lives. Dorcas is unsure whether she wants to take charge of her life, or whether she might prefer being cared for, under the safe control of another, as brother Melvin will be in the capable hands of businesslike Brenda. To boss or to be bossed is a question which Ayckbourn raises in *Sisterly Feelings*. It becomes the slender thread which leads him to *Taking Steps*, a farce in which the aggressive characters who habitually take matters into their own hands are finally outmaneuvered by the meek, who, for once, may inherit the earth.

The tone of *Taking Steps*, is immediately indicated by its dedication to dramatist Ben Travers—the honor might just as well have gone to Feydeau

were the protagonist Roland, the bucket king, not so overwhelmingly a Colonel Blimp type, thus unmistakably British. The work is described by its author as "an attic, a bedroom, a lounge, a wife in a quandary and a fiancee in a cupboard, a devious builder, a nervous solicitor, a ponderous personnel officer and a drunken manufacturer all embroiled in a tale of love, confusion and freedom." When Elizabeth decides to leave Roland, the blustering, self-assured husband who rules her life, her brother Mark brings his fiancee Kitty, arrested for soliciting on Haverstock Hill, to the decaying Tudor house (another metaphorical setting) which Roland has leased and is considering for purchase. The house was once a brothel, and Scarlet Lucy, murdered there, is said to haunt it still, or so Tristram, Roland's shy, tongue-tied solicitor is informed. Upset that Elizabeth has left him, Roland is unwilling to sleep in the master bedroom, partly because his wife's orthopedic mattress is "about as comfortable as sleeping on the fast lane of the M1." He installs Tristram there instead. When Roland moves himself into the attic room which has become Kitty's haven, she hides in a tiny closet, but is trapped inside when the manufacturer, to avoid the dripping rain, moves his bed across the closet door. Late that night Elizabeth, having changed her mind, returns home, flings her red dress at the figure in her bed and jumps in, much to Tristram's initial horror but growing rapture.

Further complications ensue, such as the reading of what may or may not be suicide notes; and before the night is over, Tristram has bedded not only Elizabeth but Kitty as well. By the end Tristram, Kitty, and Elizabeth are all fed up with having their lives organized by others. Tristram and Kitty leave together, and Elizabeth will make up her own mind, once and for all, as to whether or not she will remain as Roland's wife.

The title *Taking Steps*, with Ayckbourn's usual verbal dexterity, refers here to more than theme, suggesting a matter of staging on which much of the farce depends. Having written the work originally for the single-level stage of Scarborough's theater-in-the-round, Ayckbourn makes frequent use of flights of stairs for slapstick pratfalls, somersaults, and general frenzy. But the stairs are flattened, merely indicated, so that three levels supposedly exist on a single stage floor, which means that characters rushing about the attic or the first floor actually move in close proximity to those on the ground floor. The device, reminiscent of the superimposition of two households in *How the Other Half Loves*, makes perfect sense in the theater for which it was designed. On a proscenium stage which can accommodate various levels, however, it is reduced to pure gimmickry, assuring laughter without providing the telling counterpoint of the earlier production. But *Taking Steps*, unabashedly frivolous, is irresistibly entertaining for audiences wary of Ayckbourn's mounting significance, albeit dismaying to some of his critics.

Ayckbourn's practice had been to test a play with one cast in Scarborough and then release it to an established West End management which would recast it and mount a new production for a conventional proscenium stage. However, in October 1980 Ayckbourn gave evidence of his gratitude to the loyal actors of his Scarborough company by affording them the opportunity to appear before a London audience in the limited, brief engagement of *Season's Greetings* at the Round House, a theater outside the West End which, as its name indicates, is easily converted to in-the-round staging. The new comedy, while providing Londoners the chance to see what an Ayckbourn play looks like in Scarborough, was perhaps not a fair test for the provincial actors, who were in fact more warmly greeted by the London critics than was the play itself, for *Season's Greetings* presents overly familiar Ayckbourn material without a fresh perspective. John Russell Taylor describes it as "a solid, rather old-fashioned three-act play about the horrors of suburban family life in the allegedly festive season." Neville putters in the shed ignoring his wife Belinda; childless Phyllis finds solace in drink as her husband Bernard puts on puppet shows to which no one cares to be subjected; and Eddie and his pregnant wife Pattie are equally unhappy. Into this menagerie comes a writer, the guest of the unmarried thirty-eight-year-old sister, who must "cope with illiterate advice from all sides."

Undaunted by the mild reception of *Season's Greetings*, Ayckbourn repeated the experiment with a return engagement of the Scarborough company in a play with music a few months later at the Round House, but this time he limited the seating to 300 to duplicate the intimacy of the Stephen Joseph Theatre. When *Suburban Strains* opened on 5 February 1981, it was the fourth new Ayckbourn work to be seen in London in a period of eight months. On the same night *Sisterly Feelings* was performed for the last time in the repertory of the National Theatre.

In 1978, three years after the failure of *Jeeves* and two years before the Scarborough premiere of *Suburban Strains*, Ayckbourn had returned to the musical with *Men on Women on Men*, "a late-night

revue" performed on a tiny stage in the bar of Scarborough's Stephen Joseph Theatre-in-the-Round by a cast of four, women in cocktail dress, men in black-tie. Their bickering led them into sprightly songs composed by Paul Todd with Ayckbourn's lyrics about, not surprisingly, the breakdown in the male-female relationship: "Marriage was designed by women. / Marriage is a trap. / Wedding veils and plastic blossoms. / Sentimental crap." A London critic who made the trip to Scarborough, finding in the revue "fresh evidence of his versatility," was especially pleased that Ayckbourn was "able to be both frank and funny about matters at which . . . Coward could only hint broadly," giving "the show an edge which its predecessors in the 1930s often lacked." Significantly, the piece gave Ayckbourn, comfortable with Todd as collaborator, the confidence to explore further the musical form. Subsequently, the two followed *Men on Women on Men* with two brief "lunchtime" pieces for the theater, *First Course* and *Second Helping*.

To Ayckbourn the primary appeal of the book musical and the musical play is that the song becomes the "equivalent of the soliloquy," allowing the lyricist to move beyond naturalism: "no need for a boring old drunk scene to make characters say what they feel. If you suddenly bring in a shaft of music from somewhere, they can actually play the subtext."

Performed on two concentric revolving stages with the actors usually in the inner circle with props and furnishings gliding into position on the outer, *Suburban Strains* centers on Caroline, whom Ayckbourn describes as a "lovely, silly girl. . . . She's 32 and a teacher, more or less untroubled by a personal life, and then along comes this actor. . . ." Afterwards, along comes a tyrannical doctor. Caroline explores the two intimate relationships, occasionally juxtaposing them in her head.

For most critics Ayckbourn's book for *Suburban Strains* seemed a concoction of leftover bits and pieces, the songs mere embellishments, an occasional lyric suggesting that one of Britain's most energetic playwrights was showing signs of strain: "Happiness is something / That is never yours by right. / Why not settle for today / And cuddle up tonight?" Reviewing the Scarborough premiere of the musical play for the *Observer*, however, Robert Cushman noted a new thematic element: "He has tended before to show us relationships so far gone in decay that the participants are too tired to shift or too blind to notice. Here we see the rot starting, the characters struggling. There are even love-scenes."

Ayckbourn may yet expand that element. And

should there be a formula for a successful large-scale British musical about a bewildered middle class casually yet joyfully inflicting pain on kith and kin, it may well be he who finds it. Meanwhile, his audience will be content with Ayckbourn's annual intricately staged domestic comedy with a half-dozen intertwined characters who reflect the audience's own unattainable dreams and disappointments while moving them to laughter with at least a suggestion of a tear—in other words, the mixture as before, which John Peter, critic for the *Sunday Times*, has described as plays "about families or small communities engaged in the great tribal rituals of Christmas party, cricket, tennis, selling the car, funeral, picnic—scenes in which he observes the English Middle Class in the bizarre activity it calls Life."

Television Script:
Service Not Included, BBC, 1974.

Other:
Countdown, in *Mixed Doubles* (London: Methuen, 1970).

References:

Michael Billington, "Ayckbourn is a Left-Wing Writer Using a Right-Wing Form," *Guardian*, 14 August 1974, p. 11;

Brian Connell, "Playing for Laughs to a Lady Typist: A Times Profile," *Times*, 5 January 1976, p. 5;

Michael Coveney, "Scarborough Fare," *Plays and Players*, September 1975, pp. 15-19;

John Elsom, *Post-War British Theatre* (London: Routledge & Kegan Paul, 1976);

Ronald Hayman, *British Theatre Since 1955* (London: Oxford University Press, 1979);

John Heilpern, "Striking Sparks off Suburbia," *Observer*, 13 February 1977, p. 14;

Stephen Joseph, *Theatre in the Round* (London: Barrie & Rockcliff, 1967);

Oleg Kerensky, *The New British Drama* (London: Hamish Hamilton, 1977);

Anthony Masters, "The Essentially Ambiguous Response," *Times*, 4 February 1981, p. 8;

Russell Miller, "The Hit-Man from Scarborough," *Sunday Times Magazine*, 20 February 1977, pp. 22-24, 26;

Philip Oakes, "Lines and Deadlines," *Sunday Times*, 3 June 1973, p. 36;

"Q: Mr. Ayckbourn, is Sex Fun? A: It Depends. With Me it's Hilarious," *New York Times*, 20 October 1974, II;

John Russell Taylor, *The Second Wave* (London: Methuen, 1971);

Robin Thornber, "A Farceur, Relatively Speaking," *Guardian*, 7 August 1970, p. 8;

Ian Watson, *Alan Ayckbourn: Bibliography, Biography, Playography, Theatre Checklist, No. 21* (London: T. Q. Publications, 1980);

Watson, "Ayckbourn of Scarborough," *Municipal Entertainment*, May 1978;

Watson, *Conversations with Ayckbourn* (London: Macdonald Futura, 1981);

Janet Watts, "Absurd Persons, Plural and Suburban," *Observer*, 4 March 1979, p. 39.

Enid Bagnold

(27 October 1889-31 March 1981)

Richard B. Gidez
Pennsylvania State University

PRODUCTIONS: *Lottie Dundass*, 21 July 1943, Vaudeville Theatre, London, 147 [performances];

National Velvet, adapted from Bagnold's novel, 23 April 1946, Embassy Theatre, London;

Poor Judas, 18 July 1951, Arts Theatre, London;

Gertie, 30 January 1952, Plymouth Theatre, New York, 5; produced again as *Little Idiot*, 10 November 1953, Q Theatre, London;

The Chalk Garden, 26 October 1955, Ethel Barrymore Theatre, New York, 182; 11 April 1956, Haymarket Theatre, London, 658;

The Last Joke, 28 September 1960, Phoenix Theatre, London, 61;

The Chinese Prime Minister, 2 January 1964, Royale Theatre, New York, 108; 20 May 1965, Globe Theatre, London, 108;

Call Me Jacky, 27 February 1968, Oxford Playhouse, Oxford; revised as *A Matter of Gravity*, 3 February 1976, Broadhurst Theatre, New York, 79.

BOOKS: *The Sailing Ships and Other Poems* (London: Heinemann, 1917);

A Diary Without Dates (London: Heinemann, 1918; Boston: Luce, 1918);

The Happy Foreigner (London: Heinemann, 1920; New York: Century, 1920);

Serena Blandish; or, the Difficulty of Getting Married (London: Heinemann, 1924; New York: Doran, 1925);

Alice and Thomas and Jane (London: Heinemann, 1930; New York: Knopf, 1931);

National Velvet (London: Heinemann, 1935; New York: Morrow, 1935);

The Squire (London: Heinemann, 1938); republished as *The Door of Life* (New York: Morrow, 1938);

Lottie Dundass (London: Heinemann, 1941);

The Loved and Envied (London: Heinemann, 1951; Garden City: Doubleday, 1951);

Two Plays (London: Heinemann, 1951); republished as *Theatre* (Garden City: Doubleday, 1951)—includes *Lottie Dundass* and *Poor Judas*;

The Girl's Journey (London: Heinemann, 1954; Garden City: Doubleday, 1954)—includes *The*

Happy Foreigner and *The Squire*;

The Chalk Garden (London: Heinemann, 1956; New York: Random House, 1956);

The Chinese Prime Minister (London: French, 1964; New York: Random House, 1964);

Autobiography: From 1889 (London: Heinemann, 1969); republished as *Enid Bagnold's Autobiography* (Boston: Little, Brown, 1970);

Four Plays (London: Heinemann, 1970; Boston: Little, Brown, 1971)—includes *The Chalk Garden*, *The Last Joke*, *The Chinese Prime Minister*, and *Call Me Jacky*;

A Matter of Gravity (London: Heinemann, 1978; New York: French, 1978).

When Enid Bagnold's first play, *Lottie Dundass*, opened at the Vaudeville Theatre in London in the summer of 1943, its author was fifty-three with a twenty-five-year career as novelist behind her. The next twenty-three years she would devote to the theater, returning to the novel but once. In all, she

Enid Bagnold

wrote eight plays, one of which, *The Chalk Garden* (1955), verbally dazzling, has the mark of permanency about it.

Born in Rochester, Kent, England, Enid Bagnold was the daughter of A. H. and Ethel Alger Bagnold. She spent part of her childhood in Jamaica where her father was in command of the Royal Engineers. When she was twelve, she returned to England to an exclusive girls' school, Prior's Field, run by Aldous Huxley's mother. At seventeen she attended finishing schools in Germany and Switzerland before coming back to England and making her debut at age eighteen. As a young woman, she lived a bohemian existence in London as suffragette, artist's model, and artist, studying painting with Walter Sickert when she was nineteen. But she also moved in the world of the international set. During World War I she served in an English hospital and then in 1918 as an ambulance driver in France. In 1920 she married Sir Roderick Jones, owner and director of Reuters News Agency; the marriage lasted until his death in 1962; the couple had four children. As Lady Jones she led a busy social life. As Enid Bagnold she had an active and distinguished career as a writer. On 31 March 1981 she died at the age of ninety-one at her home in North London.

Published in 1918, *A Diary Without Dates*, about her days as a nurse's aide before and during the war, led to Bagnold's expulsion from the hospital. *The Sailing Ships and Other Poems* had been published the previous year (she had been writing poetry since she was nine). Her first two novels were published under the pseudonym A Lady of Quality out of deference to her father who did not care much for fiction. *The Happy Foreigner* (1920) is a love story set against the backdrop of France after the time of the armistice. *Serena Blandish; or, the Difficulty of Getting Married* (1924), a satiric tale of a young girl who tries unsuccessfully to be better than she is, was considered shocking in its day. The social world of the novel is similar to the world of high society from which Mrs. St. Maugham retires in *The Chalk Garden*. S. N. Behrman dramatized *Serena Blandish* in 1928. *National Velvet*, her best-known work, appeared in 1935, with illustrations by her thirteen-year-old daughter. This is the story of Velvet Brown, the butcher's daughter, who rides her piebald to victory in the Grand National. Since its publication, it has been dramatized for the stage by its author, and adapted by others for the motion pictures and for television. She wrote two other novels. *The Squire* (1938)—called *The Door of Life* in the United States—deals with the problems and

traumas that accompany a woman in a late pregnancy. *The Loved and Envied* (1951) returns to the world of *Serena Blandish*. Lady MacLean, a society beauty, recalls the social triumphs of her past. Its theme is the same as that of the 1964 play *The Chinese Prime Minister*: life and old age are not mutually exclusive. In addition to novels, Bagnold wrote a children's story, *Alice and Thomas and Jane* (1930), translated Princess Marthe Bibesco's *Alexander of Asia* (1935), and wrote her *Autobiography* (1969), which contains savage passages of her theatrical failures and those persons responsible.

Her first play came about accidentally during World War II. She had been asked to substitute for Juliet Duff, who had fallen ill, by reading a prologue at the opening of a new play being done in Brighton as a money raiser for a war charity. The idea of appearing on stage thrilled her, and she spent all night learning the lines, only to be disappointed when Duff got up from a sickbed and replaced her. Frustrated, she told her friend, novelist and playwright Maurice Baring, that she could kill Duff. He suggested, instead, that she make a play of the incident. Published in 1941, *Lottie Dundass* was not produced until 1943, when it was staged in London's West End.

Lottie, a stagestruck girl with an all-consuming ego, is the granddaughter of a distinguished actor and the daughter of a less successful one, now committed to an asylum for a bloody, senseless murder. Which one will Lottie take after? When a touring company of *Evelyn Innes* (the dramatization of George Moore's 1898 novel) finds itself without its leading lady or understudy, the management, rather than cancel the performance, calls on Lottie, who knows the role but has no stage experience, to save the day. Minutes before curtain time, the understudy shows up. Rather than lose her big chance, Lottie strangles the actress, hides the body, and makes her debut to acclaim. The excitement, however, proves too much for Lottie, who suffers from heart disease, and she has an attack. Her mother, always protective of her and aware of the crime, allows Lottie to die by withholding her medicine.

This psychological melodrama starts slowly as Bagnold builds up the character of the dominating, ambitious monster, Lottie. But once the scene shifts to the theater, the pace picks up. With its strong reliance on incident, *Lottie Dundass* is not typical of her later plays, although elements of Lottie's character can be found in Laurel in *The Chalk Garden*. Although critic Desmond MacCarthy found the play moving, he feared its "pathological aspect" would limit its appeal.

In her *Autobiography* Bagnold refers to *Lottie Dundass* as a modest hit (it ran for five months), and she calls *Gertie* her second play and a flop. *Gertie* was indeed a failure both in New York in 1952 and in 1953 in London, where it was called *Little Idiot*, but it was her fourth, not her second play. The oversight may be either a lapse of memory or a critical judgment on her second and third plays. *National Velvet*, a dramatization of her 1935 novel, was her second play, produced in 1946. For a play about horses and racing in which there are no horses on stage and the running of the Grand National horse race is conveyed by means of a radio report, it comes off fairly well. Bagnold wisely discarded the element of fantasy that is in the novel, but did preserve the warmth of the characters, especially the sensitive, horse-crazy Velvet with her dream of winning the Grand National. Unfortunately, the dialogue, in this her most realistic play, does not sound natural; it needs to be sharper. Although the play does generate an air of excitement, the material works better as either novel or film. *Time and Tide*'s critic was succinct in his comments on the play: "It plods."

Poor Judas, her third play, was awarded the Arts Theatre Prize in 1951 for a new play of "contemporary significance." This murky drama, however, appears to be devoid of both life and significance. As its title implies, the play is about betrayal and treachery. Set in Dieppe in the early days of World War II, the drama focuses upon Edward Mission Walker, an English author who plans to give up his own career to write up the notes of Jules Pasdeloupe Calas, a Czech scholar, for Calas's multivolume *History of Political Wickedness*. After much talk, Calas entrusts his material to Walker, who departs for England, promising to complete the history. When Calas unexpectedly shows up four years later, the viewer learns that Walker has not even untied the string around the notes. Nor does he have the excuse that he has been working on his own book. He has certainly betrayed Calas and, one might think, himself as writer. But he feels no chagrin, no guilt.

The treachery of one artist to another may symbolize the treachery of one nation to another. That may be the "contemporary significance" of the play. But as T. C. Worsley points out, one cannot be sure: "*Poor Judas* is evidently a symbolic play, but I must confess from the start to being by no means confident that I have grasped the whole significance of its symbolism." *Time and Tide* echoed that view, feeling that Bagnold "loses herself and her play in a maze."

It is difficult to take Walker seriously as a writer or to find him interesting as a character. Moreover, he is so unpleasant that it is hard to understand the devotion of others to him. Another failing of the play is that the subplot dealing with Walker's daughter and her first love has nothing to do with anything else in the play. After a three-week limited engagement in 1951, *Poor Judas* has not been produced again.

Gertie, less pretentious than *Poor Judas*, is no more successful. It is the story of an eccentric widower whose future and that of his children are quite dim. When a scriptwriter from Hollywood and a producer from Broadway arrive on the scene, Gertie, the cleverest of the children, arranges matters so that she and her sister will have the opportunity to go to America, the promised land. The play is so lightweight that the narrative does not hold the interest of the audience. Although the dialogue is amusing, the play never develops any tension. It managed no more than a week in either New York or London. Bagnold wrote an amusing account of her experiences with the play in "Flop," an article published in 1952 in the *Atlantic Monthly*.

For a time it seemed as if *The Chalk Garden*, Bagnold's next play, would go unproduced. London managements had turned the script down, but Irene Mayer Selznick, producer of Tennessee Williams's *A Streetcar Named Desire* (1947), expressed interest in doing the play in New York, on her own terms. Bagnold described her resulting "collaboration" with Selznick as "two tigresses growling over moving words." According to Bagnold, for two years Selznick "lived with one end—to put on this play. She flew, she cabled, she battled. She 'cast.' In casting she would have ransacked the Shades. More imperious than I on my behalf she was filled towards the play with an unfaltering magnificence of loyalty." When the first director, George Cukor, departed, Albert Marre took over, even though, according to Bagnold, he found the script "oblique" and "continued to dislike it, disliked me, disliked Irene, and loathed the words." But the words make this play a triumphant achievement. As Noel Coward said, the play was "for those who love *words*." What rivets the audience's attention are not the twists of plot but the dialogue, rich in its use of the resources of language.

In *The Chalk Garden* Mrs. St. Maugham, a worldly woman, once a brilliant ornament in society, has failed both with her estranged daughter, Olivia, and her wayward granddaughter, Laurel, whom she is trying to bring up in her own image. A neurotic, undisciplined child, like Lottie Dundass, Laurel lives in a world of fantasy, believing her

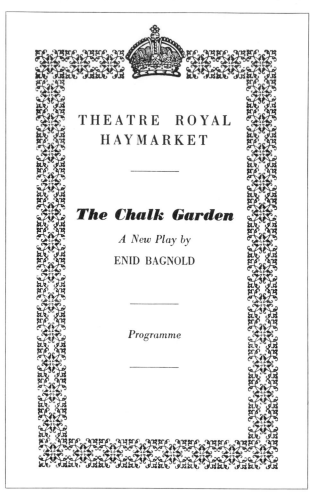

Program cover for the first London production of Bagnold's best-known play

At the close of the play, Laurel has gone with Olivia, and Pinkbell has died in a pique of exasperation over Miss Madrigal's double success. She will remain to comfort the grandmother in her declining years and to tend the garden.

The behavior of the characters is striking, their problems gripping. The theme is serious—the need to save Laurel from the aridity of an irresponsible life—but the treatment is witty and the play is often funny. Whether Bagnold sees the significance of the play as extending to the state of England after the war or to the state of mankind in general or to no more than the state of Mrs. St. Maugham's chalk garden is not entirely clear.

The Chalk Garden was the best received, critically and popularly, of Bagnold's plays. Kenneth Tynan believed it "may well be the finest artificial comedy to have flowed from an English (as opposed to an Irish) pen since the death of Congreve." Brooks Atkinson also recalled Congreve in characterizing the play as witty. He found it "always verged on the point of saying more than it did." He traced the obscurities in the play to Bagnold's disdain of easy solutions. For this play Bagnold won the Award of Merit Medal of the American Academy of Arts

Dame Edith Evans and Judith Stott in the Haymarket Theatre production of The Chalk Garden

mother does not love her. Upstairs in Mrs. St. Maugham's manor house lies Pinkbell, her butler, who has suffered a stroke. A voice heard but not seen, Pinkbell presides over both household and the chalk garden. For Mrs. St. Maugham has failed with her garden as well as Laurel. Sterile soil is destroying the one, sterile atmosphere the other. Like Madame Ranevski's cherry orchard in Anton Chekhov's play, Mrs. St. Maugham's chalk garden is both reality and a symbol of life within the house.

Into this barren household enters Miss Madrigal as Laurel's governess, aloof and reserved in manner. Recently released from prison for a murder she may or may not be guilty of, she is committed to "the astonishment of living." She recognizes in Laurel what she once was. Under her ministrations the garden blossoms and Laurel, given the freedom to grow, is made to see that she both needs and loves her mother and that her mother loves her.

and Letters for distinguished Achievement in the Art of Drama. The play was included in the Burns Mantle *Best Plays of 1955-1956*. When it was produced in London in 1956, it ran one month short of two years.

The Last Joke (1960) is a falling off. Though based on an actual event and real people—the suicide of Prince Emmanuel Bibesco, brother to Bagnold's close friend, Antoine Bibesco, Rumanian diplomat and friend of Marcel Proust—the play curiously has little life to it. Part philosophical study of a man with a "rage for death" so that he can meet God and part mystery (complete with a secret panel, a character in disguise, and a missing portrait), the play is euphuistic in style, cryptic in meaning, and uncertain as to direction. Moreover, the characters are far less believable than those in her other plays.

On the basis of its distinguished cast—John Gielgud and Ralph Richardson—*The Last Joke* managed eight weeks in London. Bagnold felt the failure was in part owing to Gielgud's insistence that his character shoot himself at play's end rather than take poison, depriving him of the deathbed speech and the parallels to Socrates, both of which she desired. Further, she felt Richardson was miscast and unattentive to direction. "My knights," she writes, "turned author on their way to London. They [the dialogue] were my words, but sorted out and re-jammed together." The failure, however, ultimately lies with the play. Underneath its urbane language, it is very thin. "Aimless," "capricious," and "disappointing" were adjectives critics applied to the play. *The Spectator* was especially critical of the play. "It is just possible," wrote its critic, Alan Brien, "to trace the connection between one event in the play and the next if you nerve yourself to the task, but as with so many thrillers the more the actions are explained, the less plausible and the more tedious they become." In the final analysis, wrote *New Statesman and Nation* critic Jeremy Brook, the play has not got "a breath of meaning, cohesion, or dramatic excitement."

"Why," the aging actress in *The Chinese Prime Minister* asks, "does no one write *real* plays—about the fascination and disaster of being old!" *The Chinese Prime Minister* is such a play, a comedy of manners on the meaning and expectations of old age. A seventy-year-old actress, known only as She, retires from the stage but not from life. Old age, she believes, should be as it once was for the elder Chinese prime ministers, the most fulfilling time of life, "and not a prison." These elder statesmen made a triumph of retirement. Wishing to find a man, old and wise, who will give her wisdom, she

mistakes her long estranged husband for such a man. She discovers, however, that she is meant to be a single woman: "It is *I* who am the Chinese Prime Minister." Her materialistic husband, another representative of old age, is too busy with his oil wells in Arabia. Her sons are preoccupied with their marital difficulties. Like Miss Madrigal, she will "continue to explore—the astonishment of living," but alone.

Old age, needing a foil, is played off against youth—She's sons and their wives. But they are lightweights, not worthy sparring partners. They are prosaic, lacking the element of the fantastic that characterizes She. They do not strike sparks. Bagnold has more success with the character Bent, the third example of old age in the play. This decrepit, lecherous family retainer, She's guardian angel, is as faithful as Firs in Chekhov's *The Cherry Orchard*, but unlike his Russian counterpart, Bent does not let life slip by as if he has never lived. Twice in the play he literally dies—"you'll find it's nothing"— only to come back to life.

What the play lacks in dramatic involvement is provided by the dialogue, most of which is spirited and literate, though some exchanges are obtuse and directionless. The artificial flavor of some conver-

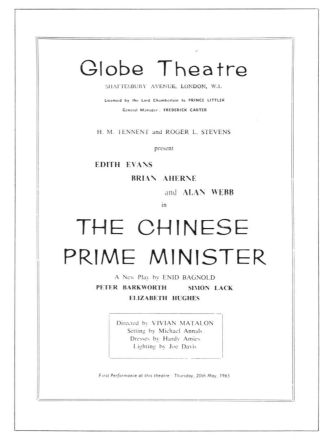

Program title page for the first London production of Bagnold's comedy of manners about old age

Alan Webb and Dame Edith Evans in the Globe Theatre production of The Chinese Prime Minister

sations reflects Bagnold's conscious striving for the aphoristic and the epigrammatic in style. The play, finally, is more tenuous and less viable than *The Chalk Garden*.

Often at odds with her actors, directors, producers, and designers, Bagnold felt that Joseph Anthony, director of the New York production, who professed to love the play, did not understand it. In the Globe Theatre production, Edith Evans as She made one of Bent's death scenes an occasion for tears and sentiment, finding pity where there was none. As presented in London, it was not the play Bagnold had written. Although he found little dramatic involvement in the play, Henry Hewes felt there would be those "who would enjoy the pleasure of Miss Bagnold's very special company." Howard Taubman felt the play short of action—"little is happening and a lot is being said about it"—but believed "the stimulation of the good talk of spirited minds" was recompense.

Although the materials of *A Matter of Gravity* (1976) are familiar—wealthy old lady, eccentric servant, younger generation, the element of the fantastic—they needed more honing. As it is, the play is a rewrite of an earlier work, *Call Me Jacky*, which closed in Oxford in 1968, a victim of devas-

tating reviews, before it could open in London. Bagnold felt the play needed more rehearsal time for director and actors to discover "its barely indicated, shrugged-off implications below its frivolity." However, in both versions not only is frivolity absent, but also the implications lie buried under the stilted dialogue.

In a decaying country home lives Mrs. Basil, an elderly lady clinging tenaciously to life, attended by her drunken housemaid, Jacky DuBois, a lesbian, who levitates in the confines of the kitchen. Contemporary society invades Mrs. Basil's home in the persons of Nicky, her adored grandson, and his weekend guests: a left-wing philosopher and her girl friend, Elizabeth, who is part black; and Herbert, an Oxford don, "old-time Left," and his suicidal boyfriend. Nicky proposes marriage to Elizabeth who accepts, not out of love but from a desire to inherit Mrs. Basil's estate. They go off to Jamaica, have two children, one white, one black, and eight years later return. Mrs. Basil turns the estate over to them. A materialist, she does not believe in God, but she has witnessed a miracle, Jacky's rising in the air. Caught between what she sees—the miracle in the kitchen—and what she knows—the crazy world of Nicky and his friends—

she takes refuge in an asylum. Civilized life, like her house, is coming apart, what with communism, homosexuality, and interracial marriage, all of which she tolerates to a degree. Life in an asylum can be no crazier than what she has experienced over the years. *A Matter of Gravity* is a tiring and tired play, the writing lumpish and slack, the characters unpleasant, the meaning vague. Clive Barnes summed up criticial opinion: "Too much matter, not enough wit."

Bagnold's plays have attracted illustrious actors such as Sybil Thorndike, Ann Todd, Glynis Johns, Siobhan McKenna, Gladys Cooper, Peggy Ashcroft, Edith Evans, Margaret Leighton, Katharine Hepburn, John Gielgud, Ralph Richardson, Fritz Weaver, Alan Webb, George Rose, and John Williams. But with the exception of *The Chalk Garden* they have not always attracted audiences. If theatergoers came to *A Matter of Gravity*, it was more likely to see Katharine Hepburn than the play. One reason for the superiority of *The Chalk Garden* among Bagnold's works is the interplay of its characters. One person's ideas do not dominate the play. By contrast, in *The Chinese Prime Minister* and *A Matter of Gravity*, Bagnold indulges the views of She and Mrs. Basil to the virtual exclusion of other valid points of view. There are no effective counters among the other characters in these plays to balance the views of the leading character.

The frequent lack of action in the plays and the obfuscation of plot line and meaning did not win for her popular success or much critical success. From her first play to her last, critics, among them Walter Kerr and Brooks Atkinson, have suggested that Bagnold was more at ease with fiction than with drama.

Yet what are weak elements in the poor plays are not so in the better ones. The plot of *Lottie Dundass* is no more improbable than that of *The Chinese Prime Minister*, but the latter does not pre-tend to be a realistic play. The language of *Poor Judas* is no more allusive or elliptical than that of *The Chalk Garden*, but it lacks the precision and coruscating wit of the later play. Her best work excites through arresting characters and richly suggestive language. In *The Chalk Garden* she writes in a sympathetic and scintillating way about the complexities of human relationships and the need for hope and affirmation. In *The Chinese Prime Minister* she gracefully depicts old age as a special time. These plays may be short on action and may not reflect the rules of traditional dramaturgy, but they do offer stimulating conversation, exciting ideas, and mature understanding.

Other:

National Velvet [play], in *Embassy Successes II 1945-46* (London: Low, Marston, 1946).

Translation:

Princess Marthe Bibesco, *Alexander of Asia* (London: Heinemann, 1935).

Letters:

Letters to Frank Harris, & other friends, edited by R. P. Lister (Andoversford, Gloucestershire: Whittington Press/Heinemann, 1980).

References:

Henry Hewes, "The Accents of Truth," *Saturday Review*, 38 (12 November 1955): 24;

Hewes, "The Talk Garden," *Saturday Review*, 47 (18 January 1964): 22;

Harold Hobson, *The Theatre Now* (London: Longmans Green, 1953), pp. 99-100;

Kenneth Tynan, *Curtains* (New York: Atheneum, 1961), pp. 127-128;

Gerald Weales, "The Madrigal in the Garden," *Drama Review*, 3 (December 1958): 42-50.

Howard Barker
(28 June 1946-   )

Andrew Parkin
University of British Columbia

PRODUCTIONS: *Cheek*, 10 September 1970, Royal Court Theatre Upstairs, London;

No One Was Saved, 19 November 1970, Royal Court Theatre Upstairs, London, 30 [performances];

Edward: The Final Days and *Faceache*, 15 February 1972, Open Space Theatre, London;

Alpha Alpha, 17 September 1972, Open Space Theatre, London;

Private Parts, 1972, Edinburgh;

Rule Britannia, 9 January 1973, Open Space Theatre, London;

My Sister and I and *Skipper*, 12 March 1973, Bush Theatre, London, 18;

Bang, 23 May 1973, Open Space Theatre, London;

Claw, 30 January 1975, Open Space Theatre, London;

Stripwell, 14 October 1975, Royal Court Theatre, London;

Wax, 1976, Edinburgh; 1976, London;

Fair Slaughter, 13 June 1977, Royal Court Theatre, London;

That Good Between Us, 28 July 1977, Warehouse Theatre, London;

The Hang of the Gaol, 15 December 1978, Warehouse Theatre, London;

The Love of a Good Man, November 1979, Oxford Playhouse, Oxford; 14 January 1980, Royal Court Theatre, London;

The Loud Boy's Life, 27 February 1980, Warehouse Theatre, London;

Birth on a Hard Shoulder, 1980, Stockholm National Theatre, Stockholm;

No End of Blame, February 1981, Oxford Playhouse, Oxford; June 1981, Royal Court Theatre, London;

The Poor Man's Friend, 1981, Colway Theatre, Colfox School.

BOOKS: *Cheek* (London: Methuen, 1971);

Stripwell and Claw (London: Calder & Boyars, 1977);

Fair Slaughter (London: Calder & Boyars, 1978; New York: Riverrun, 1978);

That Good Between Us and Credentials of a Sympathizer (London: Calder & Boyars, 1980; New York: Riverrun, 1980);

The Love of a Good Man and All Bleeding (London: Calder & Boyars, 1980; New York: Riverrun, 1980);

No End of Blame (London: Calder & Boyars, 1981);

The Hang of the Gaol (London: Calder & Boyars, 1981; New York: Riverrun, 1981);

Two Plays for the Right (London: Calder & Boyars, 1981)—includes *The Loud Boy's Life* and *Birth on a Hard Shoulder*.

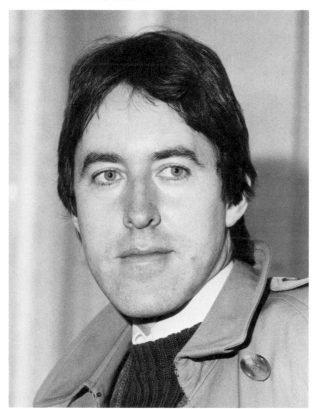

Howard Barker

Howard Barker, the son of Sydney Charles and Georgina Irene Carter Barker, was born in Dulwich, London. Between 1958 and 1964 he attended Battersea Grammar School, before going to Sussex University where he took an M.A. in history in 1968. Four years later he married Sandra Mary Law.

Cheek (1970), Barker's first play, was performed when he was twenty-four. The work is set in

Tom Chadbon, Kenneth Cranham, Liz Edmiston, and Cheryl Hall in the 1970 Royal Court Theatre production of Cheek, *Barker's first play*

suburbia and is concerned with the gap between reality and the adolescent fantasies of its hero, Laurie. Clearly derivative, the play is reminiscent of not only the works of Edward Bond, Donald Howarth, Keith Waterhouse and Willis Hall but also of Shakespeare's *Hamlet*. *Times* critic Michael Billington noted, "The play is as full of echoes as a whispering gallery," taking Barker to task also for sentimentality when Laurie switches from fiercely berating his dying father to cradling him in his arms. Laurie's adolescent sexuality, mother fixation, and misogyny combine with selfishness to make him a decidedly unappealing character, and the play leaves no doubt that the moral consequences for such a person are loneliness and abandonment by mistress, mother, and crony. Yet Barker's main point is that the cheek of avoiding work is, like crime or political protest, a valid expression of working-class resentment. In an interview with Catherine Itzin, Barker said, "If you're

cheeky enough you can get by doing very little in life, succeeding by exploiting other people. Capitalism is, basically, a great swindle. An immense cheek."

Barker's talents for neat ordering of material through cartoonlike structure, for harsh comedy, and for verbal abuse are demonstrated in *Cheek*. His instinct for strong situation, verbal flights, and sometimes grotesque comedy has developed in subsequent plays. Throughout his career he has been concerned with a political context of continuous class conflict in a declining Britain. Social strife fuels Barker's dramatic conflicts. Radio and television plays, as well as short plays for the theater such as *Edward: the Final Days* (1972), a satirical squib on a Tory prime minister, and *My Sister and I* (1973), a satire aimed at royalty, are no less firmly rooted in class conflict and resentment than are the larger stage works.

Another working-class aspect of Barker's

writing is his use of popular culture. The opening scene of *Stripwell* (1975), for example, builds on the ironic use of American rock artist Stevie Wonder's song "Higher Ground," but Barker does not merely accept popular art as a working-class addiction. His allusiveness now serves a dramatic function. The "whispering gallery" of *Cheek* is deserted for a more purposeful allusiveness as early as *No One Was Saved* (1970). This work, Barker's second play to be staged, takes its title from the Lennon/McCartney song "Eleanor Rigby" and also refers to Edward Bond's *Saved* (1965). Yet it attempts to go beyond both these works, for Barker portrays the Lennon figure in his play as exploiting Eleanor's lonely life as fodder for songwriting, and, though referring in his title to Bond's play and repeating in his play the episode of the death of the baby in *Saved*, Barker strives for a more articulate kind of working-class speech than comic illiteracies and expletives. Barker sometimes gives us an idiom as acute as early Pinter. A *Sunday Times* reviewer praised Barker for infusing the play with the "aching sense of solitariness which is so haunting in the Beatles' song" and providing a role in which "Maureen Lipman's inarticulate Eleanor grows in beauty as she grows in sadness."

In 1971 Barker received an Arts Council bursary. The following year he had finished *Alpha Alpha* (1972), produced at the Open Space Theatre, where he would serve as resident dramatist in 1974-1975. The play presents episodes from the careers of criminal twins (based upon the infamous brothers Kray) who seem to a naive hippie reporter to be genuine urban freedom fighters. To a demented homosexual sadomasochistic peer, the incestuous twins are sexual fodder as well as political tools when they can counter the troublemakers in Northern Ireland by kidnapping, torturing, and murdering an obstreperous woman like Bernadette Devlin. A searching review from Martin Esslin in *Plays and Players* found that "The theme has indeed immense potential for satire . . . ," but "satire needs an intellectual edge, a depth of real insight which seems absent here . . . the genuine satirical possibilities lie in the exploration of the relationship between violence and society, violence and social action." When the female activist pleads for her life in Marxist jargon, Barker opts simply for laughs in a way which misses the scene's potential for, in Esslin's view, "Swiftian impact," that is, satire of the greatest intensity. The humor and the outrages of the dapper duo at the center of *Alpha Alpha* made for amusement and provocation with Barker emerging as a playwright reputed for political comedy and

verbal exuberance fired by class rancor.

The cartoon as a prominent feature of mass culture has influenced Barker's style with its terse dialogue and short, vivid scenes. Indeed, a cartoonist becomes the hero of one of his most recent plays, *No End of Blame* (1981). The tense cut-to-the-bone interchange between the judge and his killer in the last seconds of *Stripwell* suggests the final frames of a strip cartoon. Another such effect appears in the television play, *Heroes of Labour* (1976), where Dockerill, a revolutionary in his late seventies, is bound and about to be blown up by his own cache of hand grenades through the wiles of an evil capitalist. When the explosion fails, the old man vents his relief in the rhetoric of cartoon-bubble remarks: "It didn't go off! Capitalist rubbish! Junk from slave factories! Vomit spewed up from the bowels of a system in decline! *He laughs hysterically*."

Barker's plays are "comics" of class conflict, probing the bowels of national decline. A fairly constant feature is the aging revolutionary or Communist betrayed by a postwar Labour party unable or unwilling to create a truly Socialist Britain. Corrupt and self-serving politicians, as in *The Hang of the Gaol* (1978), vie with entrepreneurs and criminals for the fruits of the rotting system. Capitalist, criminal, and revolutionary violence reflect one another in *Alpha Alpha* and some of the plays which follow it. Reviewing *Bang* (1973), Frank Lipsius noted that "Starting from a position close to Marx's notion of society as the embodiment of class violence, Howard Barker projects a world view of all social and personal relations being at bottom violent." However, the anarchists in *Bang* fail to present social relationships in a way that reveals the roots of violence within living characters. While caricature may be the basis of the cartoon, it may not always be effective on the stage.

The analysis of state power becomes more acute and varied in *Claw* (1975), *Stripwell*, *That Good Between Us* (1977), and *The Hang of the Gaol*, which with *Fair Slaughter* (1977) and *No End of Blame* represent Barker's most striking work so far. These plays reveal more of Barker's strengths as a dramatist and provide additional insight into the nature of his dramatic imagination. *Claw* charts the rise and fall of Noel Biledew, bastard wartime baby, pimp, and would-be agent of political scandal. In adolescence Noel reaches a moment of choice: to be a "good citizen" or a "criminal." Mrs. Biledew's ex-POW husband, betrayed by her adultery, speaks for the first time to Noel: "Don't pour away your precious anger, Noel. Use it. (Pause) For the workers." Noel claims that pimping under the criminal alias

Claw will be "political action" for he will be "carrying anthrax into their [the middle class's] woolly nests!" Yet Claw's actions are as much self-serving exploitative cheek and an immediate desire for the "bright lights" as they are a political plan. Claw has noncapitalist victims, such as Nora and Christine, his whores. The involvement of Claw with the home secretary and his chorus-girl wife is a measure of worldly success as much as politically motivated infiltration by crime into the very ministry designed to control it. When Clapcott, the home secretary, prepares to throw him back into the gutter, Claw dives for a revolver, inspired by Mr. Biledew's rendition of the Socialist song, "The Red Flag." Ambiguity persists, though, for Claw has just confessed that he loved Clapcott's wife; personal and political motivations coexist. Clapcott eludes Claw and, in act 3, has him drowned like a troublesome kitten by two male "nurses" in a Soviet-style mental hospital, the death being covered up in Parliament as just another statistic. Act 3 was criticized by *New York Times* critic Mel Gussow in a 1976 review of Stephen Pascal's New York production at the Manhattan Theatre Club as "too long and too verbose" though having the "germ of an interesting idea: About how society selects its hangmen and its victims." But act 3 makes further significant points: state assassins prove to be deadlier than either Claw himself or the gangster punishment squad at the end of act 1: Claw's final monologue shows him through desperation at last feeling and thinking politically in his vision of bourgeois state power as also a "great claw, slashing us, splitting our people up, their great claw ripping our faces and tearing up our streets." This speech does not convince his jailers, who silently drown him in his bath.

Claw's confrontation with authority when he wields a revolver is repeated with the criminal who actually succeeds in shooting his trial judge in the final scene of *Stripwell*, Barker's first play to achieve production on a major London stage, the Royal Court Theatre. Again, the plausible representative of the state, Judge Stripwell, gives the gunman pause, but this time the criminal bounds back, crying "No!" to compromise and well-considered action. Ironically, he then shoots a man who not only charms the audience but has already given up being a judge. State power is distinctly flabby in the person of the liberal Stripwell. Yet the churlish ice-cream vendor, representative of the man-in-the-street's morality, wallops Stripwell for taking up with a girl young enough to be his daughter. In *Stripwell* Barker's satirical use of contradictions works well, providing comic unmaskings: the judge wants to

Constance Cummings and Tim Woodward in the 1975 Royal Court Theatre production of Stripwell

drop his wife for a young stripper; the stripper is really a woman writer; the judge's Socialist wife cherishes memories of copulating on the floor of the House with a Tory member of Parliament; her son, raised as a Socialist, plans capitalist success by smuggling massive amounts of heroin in the massive vaginas of elephants. These humorous contradictions, and the more painful ones—Stripwell betraying his son to the police, or a privileged child becoming a criminal—are to Barker the symptoms of a social decay leading to a depressing conclusion: "the only alternative we seem to have before us— either to accept a perpetually treacherous social democratic Labour Party (which simply cannot deliver the goods), and to live with that hypocrisy—or to destroy it. I am not certain which gives the greater pain." Aesthetically, though, Barker revealed in this play his growing power as a dramatist; he made Stripwell, who belongs to the upper middle class—the wrong class for Barker's politics—an engaging and sometimes sympathetic character well suited to Michael Hordern, who created the role. Class hatred and prejudice are as damaging to society as racism, and Barker is interested enough in

Stripwell as a human being to shape him as more than a mere target for sniping in a class quarrel.

The treachery of a possible Socialist Britain is depicted in *That Good Between Us*. Whereas in *Stripwell*, after the opening scene in court, state power is not overtly presented on the stage, it is here brought to the center of the action through the activities of the special branch of the police, the home secretary, and the army. The crimes of officialdom outlined in *Claw*'s last act are now the major concern. Jeremy Treglown's review of this "gripping but uneven new play" praised the rapid "series of vivid and grotesque images of impoverishment, degeneracy and ruthlessness." Socialist Britain is shown slipping into the grip of totalitarian methods. In McPhee, a singing Glaswegian homosexual spy for and victim of the authorities, Barker creates another acting role as interesting as that of Stripwell. McPhee is, according to Treglown, "so inescapably degraded by the society that exploits him, and yet so capable of warmth and courage. Ian McDiarmid's performance was remorselessly unsentimental, triumphantly ugly, breathtakingly self-contradictory and vivacious."

Replying to a charge of nihilism, Barker rightly asserted that McPhee's repeated use of "I" when he emerges from the sea after an attempt to drown him at the play's end is "an affirmation of the spirit of survival . . . Godber [another agent] and Rhoda [daughter of the Labour home secretary], unmotivated products of a motiveless world, are swept aside." The viewer may accept the obvious contrast Barker makes between the humanity of McPhee and the kinds of nastiness found in the others, while rejecting the idea of a motiveless world, a concept which seems impossible. However, the play succeeds in dramatizing a quotation from Matthew Arnold's "Stanzas from the Grande Chartreuse" (1855) which heads the text: "Wandering between two worlds, one dead, / The other powerless to be born." Arnold's narrator in the poem mourns the loss of faith in the modern world. Barker mourns the lost faith of British socialism. When McPhee emerges gasping from the sea at the end of the play, he is not reborn into a brave new world, but merely arrives on a beach at night (an allusion to Arnold's poem "Dover Beach," 1867) illuminated only by the five-second flash of a distant lighthouse. Reminiscent of a popular culture image, the film cliche of a patrol car's light flashing in some bleak dockside slum, the lighthouse effect is also literary, suggesting an ironic reference to Virginia Woolf's novel *To the Lighthouse* (1927). The Bloomsbury group of writers with their genteel aestheticism and belief in the importance of human relationships are a long way from the world Barker constructs. In a letter to the *Tribune*, Barker wrote: "What both *That Good Between Us* and my other recent play *Fair Slaughter* show, I think, is that without political change, human nature deteriorates. And England is not changing."

England has declined and therefore changed very rapidly some observers would say. That Barker chronicles decline while denying change may mean that the dramatist cannot detect the kind of changes he wants. This contradiction in Barker's generalizations confirms the impression that the plays are vivid but often shallow in their social analyses. *The Love of a Good Man* (1979), an irreverent play about World War I, fails to convince. Everyone is a target for satire, but the worst kind of class prejudice and callowness appears in Barker when he makes fun of a fond mother searching for her son's corpse amid the blood-sodden mud of Passchendaele in a futile attempt to get the body back to England. Had she been of a different class or nation would she have been less irrational or more heroic? Furthermore, the language of the play at times falls into self-indulgent reliance on extravagant swearing, though in general Barker's style is effective. *Times* critic Ned Chaillet's review praised the "manipulation of offensive materials into a play that succeeds in holding attention, not simply by its boldness, but by its regular offering of the unexpected in language." But Barker, despite his training in history, writes better when he exposes contemporary hypocrisies, as when he depicts the cover-up after a prison fire in *The Hang of the Gaol*, or better still when he juxtaposes past with present, as in *Fair Slaughter*.

Fair Slaughter presents Old Gocher, most memorable of Barker's decrepit Communists, a leftover from the expeditionary force sent to counter the Soviet revolution in Russia, where he was converted to socialism. Having the great good fortune to get a grip on the severed hand of Trotsky's engine driver, he keeps this grim talisman of the cause with him in a bottle like some holy relic, using it to bolster his faith and to bludgeon his foes. In a series of short scenes the audience encounters Gocher as the oldest murderer in jail, as young soldier, as postwar busker, as music-hall artist (managed by Stavely, his erstwhile officer and capitalist art collector), as factory steward and fireman, as would-be murderer of Stavely during the blitzkrieg, and, with horrifying pathos, as would-be indoctrinator of his young daughter. She inevitably reacts against his bitterly hysterical ravings. However, Gocher converts Leary, the prison guard, and

COSTUMES OF VARIOUS PERIODS, e.g. BENTLEY and　　　1

OPENING SCENE　　　ELLIS are modern, FIST in eighteenth-century.

THE HANGED PEOPLE'S PARTY　　AN ORGY OF SELF-JUSTIFICATION

THE AUDITORIUM IS PEOPLED BY HANGED PERSONS IN SHROUDS, WEARING SHORT NOOSES ROUND THEIR NECKS. THEY STAND IN SALIENT POSITIONS HECTORING THE AUDIENCE AS THEY ENTER, OR MERELY MINGLE WITH THE CROWD. AT CERTAIN POINTS THEY SHOUT ONE ANOTHER DOWN. THE ATMOSPHERE IS NOT ANGRY BUT RAUCOUS AND COMIC, FULL OF SELF-JUSTIFICATION AND ARGUMENT. THE GHOSTS ARE OF ALL AGES AND INCLUDE A FEW BLACKS FROM ENGLISH COLONIES. THEY ARE RARELY MELANCHOLY, BUT DEFIANTLY ARGUMENTATIVE, DESPERATELY KEEN TO GO OVER THEIR HISTORY. SOME WEAR PARTY HATS, BLOW PAPER TRUMPETS, ETC. IT IS IMPORTANT THAT A NUMBER SHOULD BE TALKING AT THE SAME TIME, AND THAT THE AUDIENCE IS ENCOURAGED TO WANDER FROM SPEAKER TO SPEAKER.

SLADE: I saw a sheep, all right? This sheep, this great pig of a sheep, was sitting in a field, in the corner of a field and it looked ill, all right, it looked sick as sick, it was on its last legs, well, it wasn't on its legs, it was too sick to be on its legs, but it would 'ave been on its last legs if it could 'ave been, it was that ill, and I thought, I thought to myself, being a merciful man, being a lover of the dumb beasts of the field and 'edgerow - I AM SPEAKING CAN I FINISH, DO YOU MIND?

BISTO: Do you know Bond Street? I was near Bond Street, in the great city of London, in the metropolis, in the flog and fetchit quarter, I was loiterin', I was on this corner doin' nothin' very much and what should slip off of the counter but this 'andkerchief, a very nice and lovely 'andkerchief, worth what, worth two an' six the serjeant says, I say no, I say more like one an' tenpence, never mind that, I never quarrelled with the cost of it, I never said - I DIDN'T ARGUE, DID I? Thank you, saw it there an' thought, I thought - I ADMIT TO PREVIOUS OFFENCES OF A SIMILAR DESCRIPTION! And it fell off, caught by the wind, or the jacket of a gentleman 'ad flicked it, I dunno - I DON'T KNOW - I DON'T KNOW - well, let me speak, will yer?

KNOCKER: The Magistrate disliked my face.

SLADE: That sheep will die, will definitely perish of its own accord, will never trot across a field again, this much was very obvious, it was a carcass in its final throes, you don't think I would TOUCH A SHEEP IF IT WAS 'EALTHY DO YOU? No, of course not, SWIPE AN 'EALTHY SHEEP? NOTHING WAS FURTHER FROM MY MIND!

BENTLEY: The thing is, I am barmy. No, no, don't go away, don't go away, I am telling you what the thing is, aren't I? I am barmy, I am really very very lunatic -

BISTO: The fact remains, I don't care what you say, this 'andkerchief had come into contact with the ground, 'ad of its own will volition quit the draper's stall - I'm sorry that is the point, that is th whole point THE WHOLE POINT AND NOTHING BUT THE POINT -

KNOCKER: My face did not appeal to 'im. FACT.

POSSER: I would 'ave got off, I would 'ave got off only. Who was the witness for the prospecution, then? Who was? Ask yerself, who was? It was, yes, it was. So I would 'ave got off, only. On a technicality, of course! A techni- ask yerself. No, no. It stands to reason - would 'ave got off. I'm not complaining. All right, I am. I am complaining. OF COURSE I AM COMPLAINING. No, not with the sentence. Not with the gentle man. The magistrate. A gent, a real gent. yes, I loved the way he - his manner were - I am not complaing of the judge because I would have got off only.

BENTLEY: stop going away, stop going away I got something to tell you. About my being barmy, because what I did, I had a blackout, I was in the dark, a great black hood descended on me, probably from God, I say God, maybe the devil, descended on me and PUT OUT MY LIGHT. So what I did I knew not.

MCMIN: A noo consider masel' a wicked wooman, noo, I doo nae, I do nae carry sin wi' me, I do nae -

KNOCKER: Killed yer baby!

MCMIN: I did na noo such thing, on ma life -

KNOCKER: Take no notice of 'er! The magistrate disliked my face.

MCMIN: Noo stackin' surprise 'e did!

BISTO: Don't listen to 'em! Don't bother with 'em! Listen to me! The 'andkerchief was on the pavement, in the dust it was, I thought, I'll pick this up, I'll take it to the constable -

KNOCKER: Why not put it on the counter, then?

BISTO: This was my error.

KNOCKER: Lyin' 'ypocrite.

BISTO: This was my error, this was it. My error. My terrible error.

LILO/BROWN/MACKINDOE: (THE BLACKS) So we sez what we done ain't murder

Opening page from the typescript for The Poor Man's Friend

they abscond, with Gocher, like the dying Tolstoy, waiting at a railway station and later wandering on the downs near Dover, site of Lear's end and symbol of embattled Britain. But Barker brilliantly transforms, through Gocher's senility, the London borough Wandsworth into Germany and Dover into the Russian city Murmansk. Mental decay links the Russian revolution, fifty years of failed British communism, and the present state of the nation. Yet the play is stronger on bizarre biography than social analysis. Again Barker provides the actor with a powerful role, one designed for Max Wall. As W. Stephen Gilbert observed, "Wall makes the character his own—indeed, some of the lines clearly *are* his own—and the result is authentic and often moving."

Like Beckett, Barker snatches some humanity from the terror, bitterness, and squalor. This humanity flowers in the gap between Young Gocher's hysterical bloodlust and, in the following and final scene, Old Gocher's dismay that Leary is determined to kill Stavely: "Christ, do not lose sight of your humanity! You have so much good in you!" But Gocher's cry brings sentimentality with it. Leary's goodness has not been demonstrated, and Gocher's grandiose dying vision of Soviet heaven is embarrassing. The confrontation between Leary's murderous desire and Gocher's unaccommodated humanity is cut short, left undeveloped, and the final stage picture is the degenerate Stavely drooling over Picasso's decadent art.

In *No End of Blame*, a play written for television but banned, and so presented for the stage, Barker once again juxtaposes the protagonist's past with his present. On a battlefield during World War I Grigor, Hungarian soldier and artist, draws a peasant girl, naked save for one stocking. Bela, his friend, undresses and tries to rape her. Grigor attacks, falls, and then draws Bela. Soldiers appear, arrest and prepare to execute the pair as homosexuals, but Communist rebels rescue the condemned duo. Luckily the absurdities of the opening give way to an account of the life of Bela, a cartoonist first in postrevolutionary Russia and then in London during and after World War II. In Russia, when Bela produces work satirical of Lenin, a polite committee of fellow artists gently taps his wrist; in England, as a wartime newspaper cartoonist like the famous Vicky or Zec, Bela is again critical of the establishment and has to appear before a committee of politicians and bureaucrats who ferociously rebuke him. The scenes make a neat contrast, but for those who value works of real genius by artists most

cruelly suppressed by the Soviets, Barker's point is at best silly, at worst dishonest, especially when one remembers that Barker's own education and writing have been subsidized by the very society whose freedoms he treats as largely illusory.

Barker seems unimpressed by the hard-won free elections still enjoyed in democracies. He reduces the problem of artistic freedom to partisan dishonesties which arise from his ability to excuse Soviet contempt for civil rights as merely a consequence of bureaucracy: "The real tragedy of England is the fact that the population subscribes to a myth of freedom, a notion that freedom is about universal suffrage and the parliamentary system, and they are aided and abetted in this by the capitalist press. Freedom is something different. In communist and East European countries freedom means freedom from unemployment, racial prejudice, exploitation, bad health and housing—all the things we have here. But this is accompanied by a stultifying bureaucratic repression. Here freedom means ballot-boxing. We are still lumbered with nineteenth-century concepts. And they are stiff with materialism. Neither is right. Neither is adequate." It is possible to agree with Barker's last two sentences yet assert that British freedoms were attained through the parliamentary process and will be better protected and even further developed through social democracy than through the political ideas dramatized in Barker's work.

Barker's theater gives vivid, fragmented images of the state of the nation: class conflicts, crime, government corruption and cover-ups, the loss of humane values. At his best, in *Stripwell*, *Claw*, and *Fair Slaughter*, his dramatic structure is sharp and bony, dialogue highly charged and tense, characterization bold and intriguing, and there are high moments of acidic comedy. His faults are grotesque unfairness and class prejudice which hinder insight, too sketchy a treatment of women in the plays, perhaps because men usually dominate British politics, and a failure to develop more fully genuinely significant themes such as artistic freedom, the brutal slaughter of modern warfare, the nature of crime, and the possibility of a truly integral society. At his worst, agitprop simplification impedes a genuine talent for playwriting.

Barker's apprenticeship is over. Work of real power has begun to emerge. So far he has been preaching largely to the converted left-wing fringe. To keep writing and to reach a larger audience he will need to dramatize conflicts revealed by deeper, less doctrinaire analysis, develop more complex relationships among his characters, and discover more humanity to balance his political hatred.

Screenplay:
Aces High, E. M. I., 1976.

Periodical Publication:
Heroes of Labour, Gambit, 8, no. 29 (1976): 49-76.

Reference:
Catherine Itzin, *Stages in the Revolution: Political Theatre in Britain Since 1968* (London: Eyre Methuen, 1980), pp. 249-258.

Peter Barnes
(10 January 1931-   )

Bernard F. Dukore
University of Hawaii at Manoa

PRODUCTIONS: *The Time of the Barracudas*, 1963, San Francisco;

Sclerosis, 20 June 1965, Traverse Theatre, Edinburgh; 27 June 1965, Aldwych Theatre, London;

The Ruling Class, 6 November 1968, Nottingham Playhouse, Nottingham; 26 February 1969, Piccadilly Theatre, London;

Leonardo's Last Supper and *Noonday Demons*, 4 December 1969, Open Space Theatre, London;

The Alchemist, edited version of Ben Jonson's play, 9 February 1970, Old Vic, London; revised version, 23 May 1977, Other Place Theatre, Stratford-upon-Avon; 14 December 1977, Aldwych Theatre, London;

Lulu, adapted from Frank Wedekind's *Earth Spirit* and *Pandora's Box*, 7 October 1970, Nottingham Playhouse, Nottingham; 8 December 1970, Royal Court Theatre, London;

The Devil is an Ass, adapted from Jonson's play, 14 March 1973, Nottingham Playhouse, Nottingham; revised version, October 1976, Edinburgh Festival, Edinburgh; 2 May 1977, Lyttelton Theatre, London;

The Bewitched, 7 May 1974, Aldwych Theatre, London;

For All Those Who Get Despondent, adapted from Bertolt Brecht and Wedekind's poems and songs, March 1976, Royal Court Theatre Upstairs, London; revised as *The Two Hangmen: Brecht and Wedekind*, 20 December 1978, BBC Radio, London;

The Frontiers of Farce, adapted from Wedekind's *The Singer* and Georges Feydeau's *The Purging*, 11

October 1976, Old Vic Theatre, London;

Antonio, adapted from John Marston's *Antonio and Mellida* and *Antonio's Revenge*, 1977, BBC Radio, London; revised version, 20 September 1979, Nottingham Playhouse, Nottingham;

Laughter!, 25 January 1978, Royal Court Theatre, London;

Bartholomew Fair, edited version of Jonson's play, 3 August 1978, Round House Theatre, London;

The Devil Himself, adapted from Wedekind's songs and sketches, 28 April 1980, Lyric Theatre, Hammersmith, London;

Sommersaults (revue), October 1981, Haymarket Theatre, Leicester.

BOOKS: *The Ruling Class* (London: Heinemann, 1969; New York: Grove, 1972);

Leonardo's Last Supper and Noonday Demons (London: Heinemann, 1970);

Lulu, adapted from Frank Wedekind's *Earth Spirit* and *Pandora's Box* (London: Heinemann, 1971);

The Bewitched (London: Heinemann, 1974);

The Frontiers of Farce, adapted from Wedekind's *The Singer* and Georges Feydeau's *The Purging* (London: Heinemann, 1977);

Laughter! (London: Heinemann, 1978);

Collected Plays (London: Heinemann, 1981).

Ranking among the most distinctive contemporary British dramas, Peter Barnes's mordantly comic satires blend neo-Jacobean language, modern gags, invented words, literary allusions, and such aspects of popular culture as songs and movie references. Opposed to naturalism, Barnes opts for bold theatricality. Lightly, swiftly, and within the same scene, he transforms theatrical styles: from archaic diction to contemporary slang to expressionism to formal rhetoric to lyricism to classical music to modern song to ritual to slapstick.

The son of Frederick and Martha Miller Barnes, he was born in London's East End, within the sound of the bells of Bow Church—certification, he points out with pride, that he is an authentic cockney. Before World War II, the family moved to the seaside resort Clacton-on-Sea, where Barnes's parents ran an amusement stall on the pier. At age seventeen, he left school for a job with the Greater London Council and soon began contributing film reviews to the in-house magazine. In the early 1950s, he became a free-lance movie reviewer and in 1956 a story editor for Warwick Films, where he read novels and movie scripts, synopsized them, and recommended purchase of film rights. On 14 October 1961, he married Charlotte Beck. The following year, he began to compose, on assignment, screenplays and television plays.

Because the stage offered him greater control of the performed text, Barnes turned to the theater. His first play, *The Time of the Barracudas* (1963), about a man and woman who kill their spouses for money, had a California production starring Laurence Harvey and Elaine Stritch. However, the work failed to reach Broadway. The Traverse Theatre in Edinburgh presented *Sclerosis* (1965), a one-act satire on the Cypriot struggle for independence from England. An unproduced work, "Clap Hands, Here Comes Charlie," written in 1966, contrasts its anarchic title character with repressed conformists. Barnes now refuses to permit the publication or production of these apprentice works.

A major artistic breakthrough, *The Ruling Class* opened in Nottingham on 6 November 1968 and transferred to London on 26 February 1969. Its title indicates the chief target of this savage satire which, like Barnes's other original works, combines farce and verbal wit. Exemplifying the insanity of a society based on class stratification, the aristocratic protagonist thinks he is God. Cured of this delusion when confronted with a rival self-proclaimed Messiah, he falls into another self-delusion. Believing he is Jack the Ripper, he murders women and, in an expressionistic scene, he assumes his place in a cobwebbed House of Lords filled with skeletons and goitered freaks who applaud his speech demanding that the death penalty and flogging be restored. In a comically bizarre manner, characters quote and misquote the classics (including John of Gaunt's apostrophe to "This royal throne of kings" in Shakespeare's *Richard II*, distorted to eulogize England's class structure) and they burst into song (for example, "Dry Bones," which Jack the Ripper urges be *disconnected* rather than *connected*, as in the American song). The reception of *The Ruling Class* was mixed. Whereas an admirer maintained it put Barnes in the company of Samuel Beckett and Harold Pinter, a detractor dismissed it as shallow. Barnes's critical supporters had the day. For this play, he shared the John Whiting Award with Edward Bond (who was honored for *Narrow Road to the Deep North*) and in 1969 won the *Evening Standard* Award for most promising playwright.

His next work, a double bill, opened in London on 4 December 1969. *Leonardo's Last Supper* contrasts the artist-intellectual da Vinci with a rapacious, money-grubbing family. Ruthless commer-

Scene from the first London production of The Ruling Class

cial interests destroy the artist. In the companion piece, *Noonday Demons*, two fourth-century hermits argue about whom God truly addresses. Unable to persuade one another, they fight. Ostensibly in the name of Christ, one kills the other. In both plays, which superbly employ an invented language that combines archaisms and modern slang, self-interest debases religion.

In addition to writing original works, Barnes has adapted and edited works by others. He edited Ben Jonson's *The Alchemist* for production in 1970 (a revised version was produced in 1977), and his adaptation of Jonson's *The Devil is an Ass* was staged in 1973 (a revised version was produced in 1976 by the Birmingham Repertory Company at the Edinburgh Festival and in 1977 at the Lyttelton Theatre). Also produced in 1970 was his adaptation *Lulu*, combining Frank Wedekind's *Earth Spirit* (*Erdgeist*) and *Pandora's Box* (*Die Büchse der Pandora*). He wrote the screenplays of his own plays *The Ruling Class* (1971), starring Peter O'Toole, and

Leonardo's Last Supper (1977), which he directed. In 1973, the BBC broadcast *Eastward Ho!*, Barnes's radio adaptation of Jonson, George Chapman, and John Marston's play.

On 7 May 1974, in London, the Royal Shakespeare Company premiered his full-length play *The Bewitched*, a dazzling satire that, even more than *The Ruling Class*, demonstrates Barnes's mastery of language and of the resources of the physical theater. In *The Bewitched*, familiar elements—the power of a ruling class, authority and submission, the profit motive, murder in the name of God, and theatrical entertainment—received new treatment. Both rulers and ruled are bewitched by authority, personified by Spain's Carlos II, whose inability to beget an heir resulted in the War of the Spanish Succession, which devastated western Europe, leaving millions dead and wounded. The Church and aristocracy support the regime of the last of the Hapsburgs, a stuttering, vomiting, pants-wetting, spastic, epileptic, impotent cretin. In a theatrical

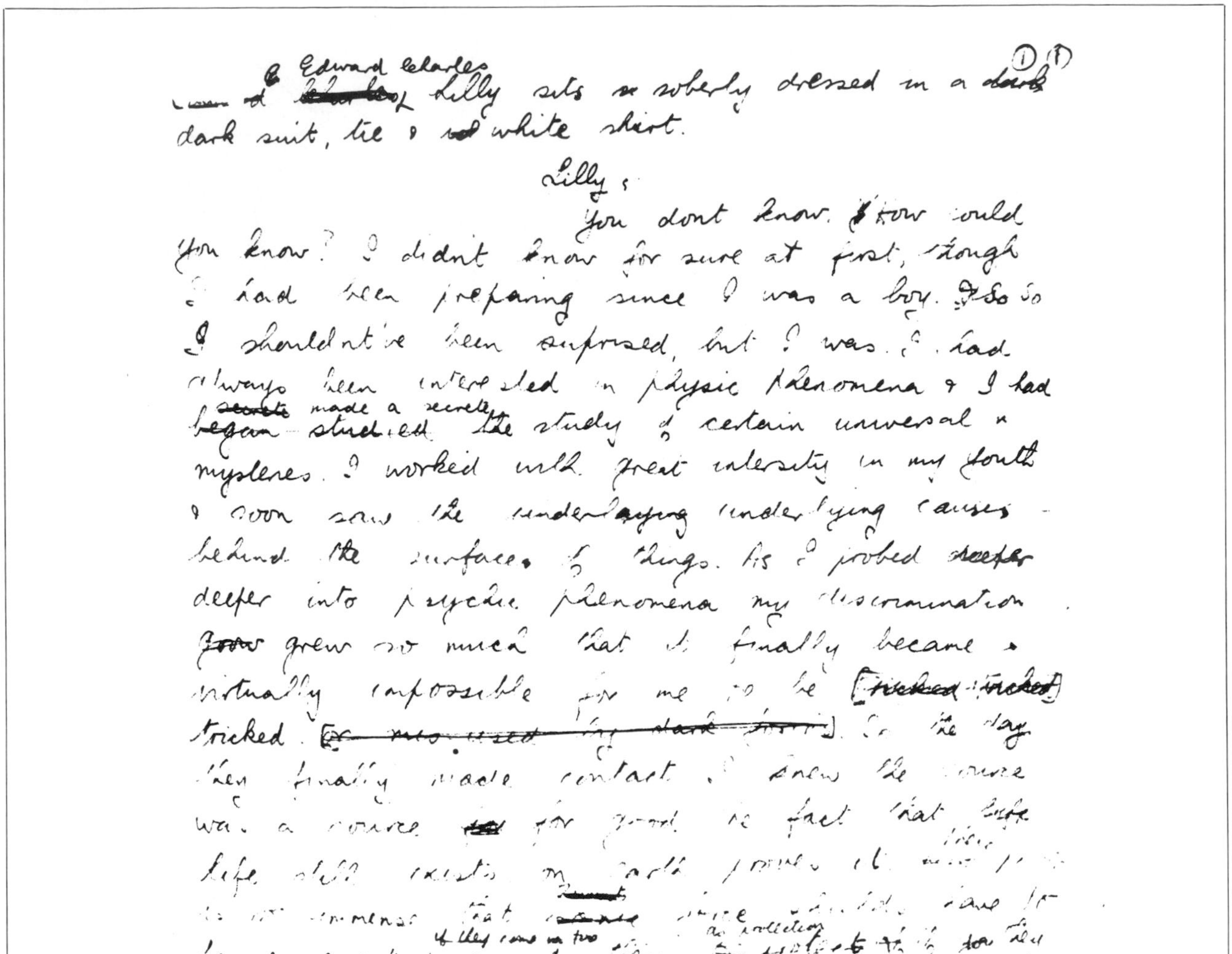
Edward Charles Lilly sits soberly dressed in a dark suit, tie & white shirt.

Lilly:

You dont know. How could you know? I didnt know for sure at first, though I had been preparing since I was a boy. So I shouldnt've been surprised, but I was. I had always been interested in physic phenomena & I had made a secret study of the study of certain universal mysteries. I worked with great intensity in my youth & soon saw the underlying causes behind the surfaces of things. As I probed deeper into psychic phenomena my discrimination grew so much that it finally became virtually impossible for me to be tricked. So the day they finally made contact I knew the source was a source for good. The fact that life still exists on earth proves it [illegible] is so immense that [illegible] if they came in too close [illegible] round them [illegible] Fortunately I was in that elevated state which [illegible] when they first called [illegible] which is an absolute requirement if you are to have mental rapport with them. I was designated "Primary Terrestrial Mental Receiver & Communicator: Num III Mark I."

I had had an earlier warning that something extraordinary was going to happen & that I might be asked to help when a famous Hindu Yeti Master, Bun-la Singh, who by mastering the disciplines of Raja, Jnani & Kundalini Yoga, attained a state of

Page from the manuscript for Confessions of a Primary Terrestrial Mental Receiver & Communicator: Num III Mark I, *a monologue performed by Sir Alec Guinness and included in Barnes's* Collected Plays

tour de force, a choir sings a hymn, victims burn at the stake, and vendors hawk their wares while, sexually aroused by the slaughter, Carlos sprouts an eight-foot phallus that impales his queen. As before, archaic, poetic language mixes with modern vernacular, literary quotations pepper the dialogue, and characters burst into parodies of popular songs, such as "Lucky in Love," which the royal couple is not. As before, critical opinion was divided. Whereas some perceived *The Bewitched* to be a work of genius, those who were offended called it meretricious and tasteless.

In 1976, Barnes's adaptation of songs and poems by Wedekind and Bertolt Brecht was produced under the title *For All Those Who Get Despondent*, broadcast over radio by the BBC in 1978 as *The Two Hangmen: Brecht and Wedekind*. *The Frontiers of Farce*, which he directed in 1976, consists of his adaptations of Wedekind's *The Singer* (*Der Kammersänger*) and Georges Feydeau's *The Purging* (*On purge bébé!*). In 1977, the BBC broadcast his radio adaptation *Antonio*, composed of Marston's *Antonio and Mellida* and *Antonio's Revenge*. In 1978, he directed his edited version of Jonson's *Bartholomew Fair*.

On 25 January 1978, *Laughter!* opened in London. In a prologue, a character called Author denies the theory that comedy is a social corrective. Rather, he contends, comedy diverts audiences from evils, deflects their hatred, and thereby perpetuates what it condemns. Two related one-act plays follow. *Tsar* employs operatic music, Russian dancing, and modern gags, also wrests laughter from the tortures inflicted by Ivan the Terrible; *Auschwitz* combines vaudeville patter and expressionistic horror, attacks the audience by first making them identify with civil servants who successfully and comically vie with a Nazi, then making the audience recognize the culpability of the civil servants, who unlike the Nazi shut their eyes to Auschwitz's atrocities, for which they disclaim responsibility. As one might expect of the response to a play that boldly condemns spectators, the critics were more hostile than friendly to *Laughter!*

"Red Noses, Black Death," written in 1978 but not yet performed, is set in the fourteenth century, when the plague ravaged Europe. It further develops the Author's theme in *Laughter!* The Red Noses is a religious order of entertainers, founded to divert the populace from the horrors of the Black Death. Although the entertainers join revolutionists to make people change rather than bear their lot, they do so too late and are killed by the combined forces of Church and State. Like the earlier plays, but with still greater virtuosity, "Red Noses, Black Death" employs theatricality, an archaic idiom, modern gags, literary allusions, popular songs, and, for the first time, original songs. Unlike the earlier plays, it not only satirizes the status quo, but it also points toward a nonrepressive, egalitarian society that might replace it.

In 1979, the BBC broadcast Thomas Middleton's *A Chaste Maid in Cheapside*, which Barnes edited for radio, and he directed his stage version of *Antonio*. The same year, he adapted Christian Dietrich Grabbe's *Don Juan and Faust*, though it has not yet been produced. In 1980, BBC radio produced his adaptation of Synesius of Cyrene's *Eulogy of Baldness*, and the Lyric Theatre, Hammersmith, produced *The Devil Himself*, consisting of songs and sketches Barnes adapted from Wedekind's works. In 1981, BBC Radio produced seven original monologues, *Barnes' People: Confessions of a Primary Terrestrial Mental Receiver and Communicator: NUM III Mark I*, *The Jumping Mimuses of Byzantium*, *The Theory and Practice of Belly-Dancing*, *The End of the World–and After*, *Yesterday's News*, *Glory*, and *Rosa*. The second monologue received the Giles Cooper Award as one of the best radio plays of 1981.

Larger than life, Peter Barnes's controversial satiric comedies employ flamboyant techniques that include expressionism and theatrical self-consciousness (that is, characters refer to the stage, the audience, and in *Noonday Demons*, that play's title and author). He has been influenced by Brecht and Antonin Artaud, as his plays both employ and parody techniques of Brecht's epic theater and Artaud's theater of cruelty. He has also been influenced by English music halls and American movies, particularly comedies and musicals. Yet he has a unique artistic signature, a transformational technique that juxtaposes comedy, shock effects, music, social commentary, popular culture, and literary allusions to produce a gaudy theatrical extravaganza.

Screenplays:
Ring of Spies, by Barnes and Frank Launder, British Lion, 1964; released in the United States as *Ring of Treason*, 1964;
Not With My Wife You Don't, by Barnes, Norman Panama, and Larry Gelbart, Warner Brothers, 1966;
The Ruling Class, Keep Films, 1971.

Television Script:
The Man with a Feather in His Hat, British ABC, 1960.

Radio Scripts:

Eastward Ho!, adapted from Ben Jonson, George Chapman, and John Marston's play, BBC, 1973;

My Ben Jonson, BBC, 1973;

Lulu, adapted from Frank Wedekind's *Earth Spirit* and *Pandora's Box*, BBC, 1975;

Antonio, adapted from Marston's *Antonio and Mellida* and *Antonio's Revenge*, BBC, 1977;

A Chaste Maid in Cheapside, edited version of Thomas Middleton's play, BBC, 1979;

Eulogy on Baldness, adapted from Synesius of Cyrene's essay, BBC, 1980;

The Soldier's Fortune, adapted from Thomas Otway's play, BBC, 1981;

The Atheist, adapted from Otway's play, BBC, 1981;

Barnes' People (*Confessions of a Primary Terrestrial and Mental Receiver and Communicator: NUM III Mark I*, *The Jumping Mimuses of Byzantium*, *The Theory and Practice of Belly-Dancing*, *The End of the World–and After*, *Yesterday's News*, *Glory*, and *Rosa*), BBC, 1981;

The Dutch Courtesan, adapted from Middleton's play, BBC, 1982.

Other:

"Staging Jonson," in *Shakespeare and Jonson: Papers from the Humanities Research Centre* [Canberra, Australia], edited by Ian Donaldson (London: Macmillan, 1982).

Periodical Publications:

"Ben Jonson and the Modern Stage," by Barnes and others, *Gambit*, 6, no. 22 (1972): 5-30;

"Hands Off the Classics—Asses and Devilry," by Barnes and others, *Listener*, 99 (5 January 1978): 17-19.

Interviews:

"Liberating Laughter," *Plays and Players*, 25 (March 1978): 14-17;

"The Playwright Who Can't Find a Stage," *Guardian*, 18 September 1979, p. 10.

References:

Bernard F. Dukore, "Peter Barnes," in *Contemporary British Drama*, edited by Albert Wertheim and Hedwig Bock (Ismanning/München: Max Hueber Verlag, 1981);

Dukore, *The Theatre of Peter Barnes* (London: Heinemann, 1981);

John Elsom, *Post-War British Theatre* (London: Routledge & Kegan Paul, 1976), pp. 180-181;

Martin Esslin, "The Bewitched," *Plays and Players*, 21 (June 1974): 36-37;

Arnold Hinchliffe, *British Theatre 1950-70* (Oxford: Basil Blackwell, 1974), pp. 169-170;

John Russell Taylor, *The Second Wave* (New York: Hill & Wang, 1971), pp. 206-208;

Katharine J. Worth, *Revolutions in Modern English Drama* (London: Bell, 1972), pp. 156-160.

Samuel Beckett
(13 April 1906-   )

Deirdre Bair
University of Pennsylvania

PRODUCTIONS: *Le Kid*, parody of Corneille's *Le Cid*, 1931, French Group of the Modern Language Society of Trinity College, Dublin;

En attendant Godot, 5 January 1953, Theatre de Babylone, Paris; produced in English as *Waiting for Godot*, 3 August 1955, Arts Theatre Club (transferred 12 September 1955 to Criterion Theatre), London; 3 January 1956, Coconut Grove Playhouse, Miami; 19 April 1956, John Golden Theatre, New York, 59 [performances];

Fin de partie, produced with *Acte sans paroles I*, 3 April 1957, Royal Court Theatre, London; 26 April 1957, Studio des Champs Elysées, Paris; produced in English as *Endgame*, 28 January 1958, Cherry Lane Theatre, New York, 104; produced with *Krapp's Last Tape*, 28 October 1958, Royal Court Theatre, London;

Acte sans paroles I, produced with *Fin de partie*, 3 April 1957, Royal Court Theatre, London; 27 April 1957, Studio des Champs Elysées, Paris;

Krapp's Last Tape, produced with *Endgame*, 28 October 1958, Royal Court Theatre, London; produced in French as *La Dernière Bande*, translation by Beckett and Pierre Leyris, 22 March 1960, Théâtre Recamier, Paris; produced again as *Krapp's Last Tape*, 14 January 1960, Provincetown Playhouse, New York, 582;

Acte sans paroles II, 25 January 1960, Institute of Contemporary Arts, London;

Happy Days, 17 September 1961, Cherry Lane Theatre, New York, 29; 1 November 1962, Royal Court Theatre, London; produced in French as *Oh les beaux jours*, 29 October 1963, Odéon-Théâtre de France, Paris;

Spiel, translated into German by Elmar Tophoven, 14 June 1963, Ulmer Theater, Ulm-Donau, Germany; produced in English as *Play*, 4 January 1964, Cherry Lane Theatre, New York; 7 April 1964, Old Vic Theatre, London; produced in French as *Comedie*, 14 June 1964, Pavillon de Marsan, Paris;

Va et vient, 14 January 1966, Schiller Theater, Berlin; 28 February 1966, Odeon-Theatre de France, Paris; produced in English as *Come and Go*, 28 February 1968, Peacock Theatre, Dublin;

Breath, 8 March 1970, Oxford Playhouse, Oxford;

Not I, 7 December 1972, Lincoln Center, New York; 16 January 1973, Royal Court Theatre, London; produced in French as *Pas Moi*, 3 April 1975, D'Orsay Petite Salle, Paris;

The Lost Ones, 7 April 1975, Theatre for the New City, New York;

That Time, 20 May 1976, Royal Court Theatre, London;

Footfalls, 20 May 1976, Royal Court Theatre, London;

A Piece of Monologue, 14 December 1979, La Mama Experimental Theatre Club, New York, 7;

Texts for Nothing, 24 February 1981, Public Theatre, New York;

Rockaby, 8 April 1981, State University of New York at Buffalo, Buffalo; 14 October 1981, Centre Georges Pompidou, Paris;

Ohio Impromptu, 7 May 1981, Ohio State University, Columbus, 2.

BOOKS: *Whoroscope* (Paris: Hours Press, 1930);

Proust (London: Chatto & Windus, 1931; New York: Grove, 1957);

More Pricks Than Kicks (London: Chatto & Windus, 1934);

Echo's Bones and Other Precipitates (Paris: Europa Press, 1935);

Murphy (London: Routledge, 1938; New York: Grove, 1957); French translation by Beckett (Paris: Bordas, 1947);

Molloy (Paris: Editions de Minuit, 1951); English translation by Beckett and Patrick Bowles (Paris: Olympia Press, 1955; New York: Grove, 1955; London: Calder & Boyars, 1966);

Malone meurt (Paris: Editions de Minuit, 1951); published in English as *Malone Dies*, translation by Beckett (New York: Grove, 1956; London: Calder, 1958);

En attendant Godot (Paris: Editions de Minuit, 1952); published in English as *Waiting for Godot*, translation by Beckett (New York: Grove, 1954; London: Faber & Faber, 1956);

L'Innommable (Paris: Editions de Minuit, 1953); published in English as *The Unnamable*, translation by Beckett (New York: Grove, 1958; London: Calder & Boyars, 1975);

Watt (Paris: Olympia Press, 1953; New York: Grove, 1959; London: Calder, 1963); French translation by Beckett, Ludovic Janvier, and Agnès Janvier (Paris: Editions de Minuit, 1968);

Nouvelles et Textes pour rien (Paris: Editions de Minuit, 1955); published in English as *Stories & Texts for Nothing*, translation by Beckett (New York: Grove, 1967);

Fin de partie, suivi de Acte sans paroles [I] (Paris: Edi-

Samuel Beckett

tions de Minuit, 1957); published in English as *Endgame, Followed by Act Without Words* [I], translation by Beckett (New York: Grove, 1958; London: Faber & Faber, 1958);

All That Fall (New York: Grove, 1957; London: Faber & Faber, 1957); published in French as *Tous ceux qui tombent*, translation by Beckett and Robert Pinget (Paris: Editions de Minuit, 1957);

From an Abandoned Work (London: Faber & Faber, 1958); published in French as *D'un ouvrage abandonné*, translation by Beckett and Ludovic Janvier (Paris: Editions de Minuit, 1967);

Waiting for Godot, All That Fall, Endgame, From An Abandoned Work, Krapp's Last Tape, and Embers (London: Faber & Faber, 1959);

La Dernière Bande, suivi de Cendres, French versions of *Krapp's Last Tape* and *Embers*, translation by Beckett and Pierre Leyris (Paris: Editions de Minuit, 1960);

Krapp's Last Tape and Other Dramatic Pieces (New York: Grove, 1960)—includes *Krapp's Last Tape, All That Fall, Embers, Act Without Words I*, and *Act Without Words II*;

Comment c'est (Paris: Editions de Minuit, 1961); published in English as *How It Is*, translation by Beckett (New York: Grove, 1964; London: Calder, 1964);

Happy Days (New York: Grove, 1961; London: Faber & Faber, 1962); published in French as *Oh les beaux jours*, translation by Beckett (Paris: Editions de Minuit, 1963);

Poems in English (London: Calder, 1961; New York: Grove, 1963);

Play and Two Short Pieces for Radio (London: Faber & Faber, 1964)—includes *Play, Words and Music*, and *Cascando*;

Imagination morte imaginez (Paris: Editions de Minuit, 1965); published in English as *Imagination Dead Imagine*, translation by Beckett (London: Calder & Boyars, 1965);

Assez (Paris: Editions de Minuit, 1966);

Bing (Paris: Editions de Minuit, 1966);

Comedie et actes divers, French translations by Beckett (Paris: Editions de Minuit, 1966)—includes *Comédie, Va et vient (Come and Go), Parole et Music (Words and Music), Dis Joe (Eh Joe)*, and *Acte sans paroles II (Act Without Words II)*;

Eh Joe and Other Writings (London: Faber & Faber, 1967)—includes *Eh Joe, Act Without Words II*, and *Film*;

Come and Go (London: Calder & Boyars, 1967);

No's Knife: Collected Shorter Prose 1945-1966 (London: Calder & Boyars, 1967);

Poèmes (Paris: Editions de Minuit, 1968);

Cascando and Other Short Dramatic Pieces (New York: Grove, 1969)—includes *Cascando, Words and Music, Eh Joe, Play, Come and Go*, and *Film*;

Sans (Paris: Editions de Minuit, 1969); published in English as *Lessness*, translation by Beckett (London: Caldar & Boyars, 1970);

Le Dépeupleur (Paris: Editions de Minuit, 1970); published in English as *The Lost Ones*, translation by Beckett (London: Calder & Boyars, 1972; New York: Grove, 1972);

Mercier et Camier (Paris: Editions de Minuit, 1970); published in English as *Mercier and Camier*, translation by Beckett (London: Calder & Boyars, 1974; New York: Grove, 1975);

Premier amour (Paris: Editions de Minuit, 1970); published in English as *First Love*, translation by Beckett (London: Calder & Boyars, 1973);

Breath and Other Shorts (London: Faber & Faber, 1972)—includes *Breath, Come and Go, Act Without Words I, Act Without Words II*, and *From an Abandoned Work*;

Film, suivi de Souffle, translation by Beckett (Paris: Editions de Minuit, 1972);

Not I (London: Faber & Faber, 1973);

First Love and Other Shorts (New York: Grove, 1974)—includes *First Love, From an Abandoned Work, Enough, Imagination Dead Imagine, Ping, Not I*, and *Breath*;

Oh les beaux jours, suivi de Pas moi, translation by Beckett (Paris: Editions de Minuit, 1975);

I Can't Go On, I'll Go On: A Selection from Samuel Beckett's Work, edited by Richard W. Seaver (New York: Grove, 1976);

That Time (London: Faber & Faber, 1976);

Fizzles (New York: Grove, 1976);

Foirade: Fizzles, bilingual edition, with French translations by Beckett (London & New York: Petersburg / Paris: Fequet & Baudier, 1976);

Footfalls (London: Faber & Faber, 1976);

Ends and Odds (New York: Grove, 1976)—includes *Not I, That Time, Footfalls, Ghost Trio, Theatre I, Theatre II, Radio I*, and *Radio II*;

Pour finir encore et autres foirades, translation by Beckett (Paris: Editions de Minuit, 1976);

Companie (Paris: Editions de Minuit, 1979); published in English as *Company*, translation by Beckett (New York: Grove, 1980);

Rockaby and Other Short Pieces (New York: Grove, 1981)—includes *Rockaby, Ohio Impromptu, All Strange Away*, and *A Piece of Monologue*.

COLLECTION: *The Collected Works of Samuel Beckett*, 19 volumes (New York: Grove, 1971-   ).

Samuel Beckett, whose play *Waiting for Godot* has influenced several generations of contemporary playwrights throughout the world, is a dramatist who considers himself a much better novelist. He thinks of his plays as diversions undertaken at times when work on his fiction has brought him to a creative impasse, but since *Waiting for Godot* was first performed (as *En attendant Godot*) in Paris on 5 January 1953, the greater part of his literary career has resulted in some form of writing for the theater.

An Irishman who has lived in Paris since 1938, Beckett writes in French and is a one-time follower of the other great Irish writer in exile, James Joyce. He has been lumped loosely at various times with groups ranging from the French *nouveau roman* to the existentialists, and his plays place him in the center of the theater of the absurd, one of the major movements in modern drama since the end of World War II. He has been labeled Proustian, Joycean, Sartrean, Jungian, and even a Christian writer, but while he does exhibit characteristics of each, it would be reductive to limit him to any single one. In recent years, both his drama and fiction have taken an intensely personal turn, and critics who had viewed Beckett as a disinterested theoretician, impersonal philosopher of negation, or abstract mathematician obsessed by permutation and combination have begun to recognize the extensive biographical underpinnings which are the foundation of his theoretical musings. Katharine Worth writes that "Beckett can only be surely placed as a man of many facets, the writer above all who has sensed the deep movements of the modern imagination and found spellbinding images to express them."

Samuel Barclay Beckett was born in the Stillorgan district of Dublin on Good Friday, 13 April 1906, a date to which he has imparted significance in some of his dramatic writings and a date which has had an almost mystical significance to him in his personal life. Both the Christian belief in Good Friday as the date of the death of Christ and the attendant theory that one of the two thieves who was to have been crucified with him was saved while the other was damned are ideas which Beckett has used in various forms throughout his writings. Also, he sometimes uses the date and place of his birth as a possible explanation of his introspective personality. His parents were comfortably situated members of the Anglo-Irish professional class, descendants of Huguenots who had fled from France to Ireland in the late seventeenth century to avoid religious persecution. In Ireland, Beckett's ancestors found the freedom to practice their successful professions in the linen trade. William Frank Beckett, Jr., Samuel Beckett's father, was a robust man and jovial sportsman who had no affinity for intellectual endeavor and who left school at the age of fifteen to build a significant reputation and sizable fortune in the exacting profession of quantity surveying (the business of estimating from architects' drawings the amount of material necessary to construct a building). Beckett's mother was born Mary Jones Roe in Leixlip, county Kildare, and her father listed his profession as "gentleman," meaning that he lived off the income of his family's milling business and had no profession of his own. Mary Roe Beckett, called May, was strong-willed and independent, and, at a time when young women of good family were not expected to work, she trained as a nurse and worked in a Dublin hospital before her marriage. Of the two parents, she was the more rigid and demanding, and her role in Beckett's life has led to conflicting and mostly troubled representations of her in his writings.

The Beckett sons grew up in the architect-designed house commissioned by Bill Beckett and named by his wife Cooldrinagh, after her family home in Leixlip.

Beckett followed his brother (Frank Edward, born 26 July 1902) to schools throughout his education: first to Miss Ida Elsner's Academy in Stillorgan, then to Earlsfort House School in Dublin, and, in 1919 when he was thirteen, to the Portora Royal School in Enniskillen, County Fermanagh, in Northern Ireland. Both boys were excellent athletes and by the end of his first term, Samuel Beckett had won a place on the varsity cricket team. It was the beginning of his lifelong interest in the sport, and he holds the distinction of being the only Nobel Prize winner to be listed in *Wisden*, the cricketeer's annual. He also boxed and swam and was one of the leaders of his class. Despite his apparent success at games and his popularity with classmates, Beckett had grown into an aloof young man, reserved in bearing and unwilling to take an easy pleasure in the activities of his school.

It was taken for granted that he would follow his brother to Trinity College, and he entered in 1923, telling his tutor, Dr. Arthur Aston Luce, that he wanted to study law and become a chartered accountant so that he could enter the family firm. His first two years were academically dismal, but he discovered modern languages in his third year and became the star pupil of Dr. Thomas B. Rudmose-Brown, Trinity's professor of French, an authority on Racine and Corneille and one of the first to introduce contemporary French poetry to Ireland.

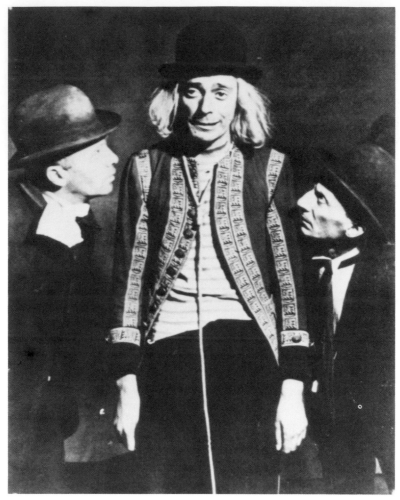

Pierre Latour, Jean Martin, and Lucien Raimbourg in the Paris 1953 first production of En attendant Godot (Waiting for Godot)

Beckett's grades improved so dramatically that at the end of his third year he won the coveted Foundation Scholarship in Modern Languages, and he spent the summer of 1926, before his senior year at Trinity, in France.

Beckett received his B.A. degree from Trinity College on 8 December 1927, standing first in his class in modern languages. He received the large gold medal given for outstanding scholarship and an award of £50 toward his expenses at the Ecole Normale Supérieure in Paris, where he had been named to the post of exchange *lecteur* for the years 1928-1930. Since Beckett's appointment did not begin until October 1928, he spent the first nine months of that year teaching in Campbell College, a secondary school in Belfast.

On his way to Paris, he traveled first to Germany to visit his father's sister, who had moved to Kassel with her husband. William and Frances (Cis-sie) Beckett Sinclair were artists and writers living with their five children a casual sort of bohemian life quite different from the elegant formality of Cooldrinagh. Beckett was quite taken with the Sinclair family, and, for the few remaining years that they lived in Kassel, he visited them frequently. He became fond of his cousin Peggy, and it is generally believed that she was the original for the green-eyed heroines who occur in his writing.

In Paris, Beckett made two friendships which were to have enormous importance in his life. The first was with the English *lecteur* whom he was to replace at Ecole Normale Supérieure, Thomas McGreevy, an Irishman who was also a graduate of Trinity College, but who, unlike Beckett, was a Catholic from a poor family in the west of Ireland. McGreevy, outgoing, witty, and brash, knew the other Irishmen in Paris, and he took Beckett to meet James Joyce.

The bond between Beckett and Joyce was a curious one, on Beckett's part forged at first because of great respect for Joyce's writing and then out of complex and still not completely understood psychological attitudes. Joyce became for Beckett both a surrogate father and a model of artistic integrity. Joyce's eyesight was very bad, and Beckett soon became the most eager and willing of all his young Irish helpers, tracking down obscure references, collecting arcane information, taking dictation when Joyce could not see to write, and even running errands for the Joyce family. Beckett marveled at Joyce's ability to write every day despite the trials of his personal life or the pain of his eyes, and later in his life Beckett would speak of the "moral effect" Joyce had on him, making him "realize artistic integrity."

Very soon after they met, Joyce asked Beckett to contribute an essay to the volume which became *Our Exagmination Round His Factification for Incamination of Work in Progress*, published by Sylvia Beach's Shakespeare and Company in 1929. Beckett's essay, "Dante...Bruno.Vico..Joyce," was his first published writing, one which shows his unbounded admiration for Joyce but which also demonstrates his ability to manipulate language, extract the essence of a writer's thought, and then use it to elucidate a critical theory.

By the start of his second year in Paris he had begun to explore philosophy, reading parts of Schopenhauer and all of Descartes. He was expected to return to Trinity College with a thesis on the poet and novelist Pierre-Jean Jouve, but instead his interest in Descartes led him to the Belgian philosopher Arnold Geulincx. Geulincx's theory, that the thinking man must realize that the only area in which he can achieve total independence is his own mind and therefore he should strive to control his own mental state rather than the exterior world, has had a lasting effect upon Beckett's literary thinking. Geulincx's dictum, *Ubi nihil vales, ibi nihil velis* ("Where you are worth nothing, there you should want nothing"), became a central thesis in Beckett's novel, *Murphy* (1938; French version, 1947), and has been expressed many times in his plays.

But Beckett's major interest at this time was poetry, possibly because of the influence of McGreevy and also because of the other, better-known poets he was meeting in Paris. Besides Richard Aldington, there was Ezra Pound (whom Beckett met only once and briefly), the Irish poets Brian Coffey, Denis Devlin, and George Reavey, and the American poet and translator Samuel Put-

nam, who was then editing *The European Caravan* (1931), an anthology of writings by French, Spanish, English, and Irish writers. Beckett prepared translations and reviews for several of the small literary magazines that proliferated in Paris at this time, but the culmination of these two years was his first separately published book, *Whoroscope* (1930), which he wrote in one night, 15 June, and which won the Hours Press competition sponsored by Aldington and Nancy Cunard, the owner of the press.

Ostensibly, the subject of entries in the competition was time, but time is present in Beckett's poem primarily in the title, a pun on the Greek word *horo* ("hour") that alludes to Descartes's superstitious refusal to tell the date of his birth so that no astrologer could use it to create his horoscope and thus predict the date of his death. It follows closely the life of Descartes written by Adrien Baillet and is more a prose monologue than a poem. It is strongly influenced by Joyce and the symbolist poets, and is filled with overtones of what John Fletcher identifies as Beckett's future themes, especially his preoccupation with the revolting.

Whoroscope led to Beckett's third published work, the essay *Proust* (1931), a study of *A la recherche du temps perdu* commissioned by London publishers Chatto and Windus for its Dolphin series probably because Aldington and McGreevy were friends of the editor, Charles Prentice, and had brought *Whoroscope* to his attention.

Beckett wrote the essay in the summer of 1930 in Paris. It shows his critical mind at its finest, and it also shows how much his writing was influenced by Proust's multilayered fiction. The essay is generally believed to be Beckett's first attempt to form a literary credo of his own. His literary thought is seen in its formative phase, when the ideas, such as habit and memory, that shape his mature writings were still some twenty years in his future.

Beckett was pleased to have the commission because he had not written the thesis on Jouve, and since he would soon return to Trinity College, it made his homecoming easier. As he had suspected two years earlier at Campbell College and had confirmed now that he was back, he was temperamentally unsuited to the profession of teaching. He disliked academic research, was ill at ease in the classroom, and was increasingly unhappy about his restrictive life in Dublin after the personal freedom he had enjoyed in Paris.

By November 1931 he had become seriously depressed and was unable to leave the bed in his darkened room. His parents consulted physicians, who decided that only a change of scene was needed, and so it was agreed that he should go to the Sinclairs in Kassel. He went there when the term ended in December and, shortly after his arrival, wired his resignation.

His depression persisted, but it was not as serious as it had been in Dublin. He stayed in Kassel for the first six months of 1932 trying to decide what to do. He was afraid to return to Paris because he had had a painful break with Joyce over his daughter, Lucia. She was then in the early stages of severe schizophrenia and had imagined herself in love with Beckett, who did not reciprocate. For real or imagined slights, Joyce refused to see Beckett, and Beckett's regard for Joyce was such that he felt he could not even try to live in the same city.

Beckett recovered enough to realize that he could not stay on in Kassel doing nothing. So he saved the small allowance that came to him from home each month until he had enough to make several exploratory trips to Paris, where he avoided Joyce. Beckett discovered that he was able to place the few stories, poems, reviews, and miscellaneous pieces he had written in the little magazines even though payment was nonexistent. He realized that he needed to earn money if he wanted to live in Paris and set to work to complete a collection of short stories to accompany the ones he had already written, thinking to offer them all to Chatto and Windus. He also thought he could supplement his writing with translation. By late May 1932 he was domiciled in a Paris hotel. He began to write what became the unpublished novel "Dream of Fair to Middling Women," portions of which he used later in the collection of short stories, *More Pricks than Kicks* (1934). He finished the novel in a few weeks only to discover that it was too long for magazines, unsuited to serialization, of little interest to French publishers, and impossible to publish in English because it contained material that would be objectionable to the censors.

This brief stay in Paris came to an unforeseen close: the president of the Third Republic, Paul Doumer, was assassinated and the French Police were deporting all aliens who did not have valid papers. This included Beckett, who rushed to Edward Titus, publisher of the little magazine *This Quarter*, and offered to translate Rimbaud's *Le Bateau Ivre* for enough money to live in London while he hunted a publisher for the novel. Titus paid him enough money for passage to London but not enough to live there, so Beckett was forced to return to Dublin to face his family's disapproval. Thus began several years of unhappiness and mis-

understanding while Beckett lived at home on a small allowance doled out by his parents, they unhappy because he would not find an occupation and he unable to write the commercially successful works he needed in order to leave.

Beckett was rewriting stories and trying to amass enough poetry for George Reavey (now in London where he had founded the Europa Press and begun acting as Beckett's informal literary agent) when his father died suddenly on 26 June 1933 from a second massive heart attack after an illness of one week. Six months later, following a second and even more severe mental breakdown, Beckett left Dublin for London. His mother had agreed to subsidize him for six months so that he could begin psychoanalysis and establish himself as a writer. Thus he began two years with Dr. W. R. Bion, later an authority on group psychology, but then practicing at the Tavistock Clinic.

Beckett had known for many years that he was not happy in the comfortable world of his parents or the achievement-oriented world of his Dublin peers. This was an era when many artists and writers, especially those he knew in Paris, were strongly influenced by Sigmund Freud and Carl Jung, and many of them had already been in analysis. Beckett had read Freud in a haphazard manner and was familiar with Jung's essay "Psychology and Poetry," which had been published in *transition* in 1930. Still, the idea of psychoanalysis for himself would probably not have entered his mind had it not been for the crippling instances of physical and mental debilitation he had suffered since his father's death.

Just as he was beginning psychoanalysis, the publication of several of his works made him think he could combine analysis with living and working in London. There were nineteen translations of prose and poetry for *Negro Anthology* (1934), edited by Nancy Cunard; an acrostic poem, "Home Olga," written for Joyce's birthday in 1932, appeared in the American magazine, *Contempo*, in February 1934; his collection of ten short stories, *More Pricks than Kicks*, appeared in May 1934.

The stories in *More Pricks than Kicks* received some critical attention but did not sell, and Beckett was forced by economic necessity to write reviews, criticism, and literary journalism. He was not successful at any of these, and since he had not been able to write fiction while in analysis, he decided to accept George Reavey's offer to publish a collection of poems. In order to subsidize the book, *Echo's Bones and Other Precipitates* (a requirement, as Reavey had no money for authors other than what they earned in royalties once they had paid for the printing costs), Beckett was forced to return to Cooldrinagh, where he remained from August through September 1934. His mother was determined that his stay should be permanent, but he was just as determined to leave. In September, he found a room in the World's End district of London, which became the setting for the novel *Murphy*. For the next three years Beckett found himself dabbling in poetry, writing an occasional book review, and trying to get on with *Murphy*, coping through false starts and hopeless stalls.

His analysis dragged on, and he chafed at the lack of positive results. If there was any one thing about it that could be considered positive, it was Bion's insistence that Beckett attend the third of a series of lectures given by Jung in October 1935 which have come to be known as the Tavistock Lectures. Jung's thesis was that the unity of consciousness is an illusion and when the unknown number of complex or fragmentary personalities in each person is gradually channeled into a fascination with the unconscious, the increase of energy in that section of the mind grows so strong that the person "sinks into the unconscious altogether and becomes completely victimized by it. He is the victim of a new autonomous activity that does not start from his ego but starts from the dark sphere." This is an idea which has had enormous resonance in Beckett's mature writings.

In the meantime, his mother's insistence that he return to live in the family home created a period of hostile uncertainty which was characterized by excessive peregrination. Beckett went back and forth between London and Dublin, each time returning to London in a state of rage, anxiety, or frustration at his inability to be what his mother wanted and his unwillingness to live in Dublin permanently. He was miserable in London, a city he described many years later as one he hated then. In November 1935 *Echo's Bones* was published. By December he was well along with *Murphy* and decided that the writing was progressing so smoothly that it did not matter where he lived, as he could finish it anywhere, and he went back to Dublin. Actually, his financial situation was so bleak that he had no other choice.

He abruptly ended the analysis, over Bion's concerned objections that it was incomplete. As his doctor predicted, Beckett's personal life in Dublin soon became intolerable. Very shortly, he had another breakdown of sorts, this time resulting in prolonged inactivity, physical dissolution and dishevelment, excessive drinking, and wandering around Dublin. He concluded that if he did not write his way out of Dublin, he would be there forever.

While *Murphy* was being refused in London by publisher after publisher, Beckett spent his time in Dublin reading, in his own word, "wildly." From Goethe to Grillparzer to Guarini, he finally settled into a single-minded concentration upon the life and work of Samuel Johnson. He began to collect information about Johnson in the same manner as he had studied Descartes, filling page after page in a large three-ring notebook with miscellaneous facts and quotations. Quite possibly this exercise was a means to keep his mind off *Murphy*, which had recently been refused by the twenty-fifth publisher to see it, but also it represented a means to engage in a form of agreeable activity that counterbalanced his unpleasant circumstances.

During this time, Beckett began to be seen on the fringes of various dramatic groups in Dublin. He saw productions by the Dramiks, a local group

Roger Blin in the first production of Fin de partie (Endgame)

which included playwright Denis Johnston and which performed German expressionist plays and, to a lesser extent, contemporary French drama. He went to performances by the Drama League, the real center of theatrical activity in Dublin, run by Mrs. William Butler Yeats and Lennox Robinson and with a company of actors who also performed at the Abbey Theatre and the Gate Theatre. He also mingled with the amateur Dun Laoghaire Theatre Group, which brought a high level of enthusiasm to performances of contemporary plays. Still, Beckett's involvement was peripheral: he was simply going about Dublin trying to find a group of young intellectuals which would be as congenial as his friends in Paris, and it just happened that the people he saw in Dublin were engaged in the theater. He was not a serious student of drama, nor was he eager to become actively involved in productions by any of these groups. In fact, his interest in the movies, first developed during his student days at Trinity College, was even more marked during this period, and he went more often to films than to the theater.

Nevertheless, something convinced Beckett that he must turn all the material he had collected about Dr. Johnson into a play, and by early summer 1936, he was calling it his "Johnson Fantasy." He claimed to have the entire play outlined in his head and that he only needed to commit it to paper. His original idea was to write a long four-act play to be called "Human Wishes," after Johnson's poem, "The Vanity of Human Wishes." He intended the play to concentrate on the mature Johnson's relationship with Hester Thrale and the obsessive, unspoken love Johnson felt for her. Each act was to be devoted to one of the four years between the death of her husband, Henry Thrale, and Mrs. Thrale's marriage to Italian music master Gabriel Piozzi, after which the enraged Johnson swore that he would never hear her name mentioned again.

Beckett wrote a ten-page scene of the play, but the rest of the material remains unwritten and the notes are unedited. His work was halted by the realization that he could not accurately capture the eighteenth-century English language as Johnson and his contemporaries spoke it. A way around this problem seemed to lie in having Johnson speak only those words found in James Boswell's account of his life, but that approach proved too complicated to work out for the other characters. Beckett also found it impossible to remove from the work his own twentieth-century sensitivities, which he felt veering from gentle irony to open sarcasm, and despite his struggle, he could not remove aspects of

himself from the personalities he created for the characters in the drama. Finally, the four-act play would have required at various times a divided stage, many changes of scenery, elaborate stage directions, and even a live cat who would have had to perform on cue and then move off and on the stage according to Beckett's direction. All this proved insurmountable and the burgeoning playwright was defeated. However mismatched Beckett and his medium were at this time, there are a number of instances, such as the brevity of the lines, the one-line exchanges of dialogue, the all-important directions (especially "silence"), that hint of the synthesis to come in his later writings for the stage.

Beckett thought so little of this first attempt at dramatic writing that he did not mention it to Raymond Federman and John Fletcher, his official bibliographers, and when an American scholar asked him for the manuscript as well as the notebook containing the information he had collected, he was glad to give it all away. In recent years, because of Beckett's continuing interest in Johnson, the manuscript has become of interest to scholars and critics.

At the time he was concentrating his energies on the "Johnson Fantasy," his personal situation had deteriorated to the point where he felt he was better off living somewhere else in poverty than remaining in Ireland. His only refuge seemed to be reading Schopenhauer, whose philosophy later became one of the important foundations of his novels and plays. By the last week in October 1937 he had gone to Paris. Soon after, Beckett received news that *Murphy* was finally accepted for publication by Routledge, the forty-second publisher who had seen it.

A celebrated but brief affair with American heiress Peggy Guggenheim marked the beginning of 1938. Around this time, Beckett was stabbed by a stranger while walking home late one night. He was hospitalized for a serious wound that penetrated his lung and just missed his heart, but his recovery was without complications. Shortly after he was released from the hospital he began a relationship with Suzanne Deschevaux-Dumesnil, a French pianist with whom he has lived ever since, and whom he married on 25 March 1961 in England for the same legal reasons that Joyce had married Nora Barnacle after they had lived together as man and wife for many years.

As 1938 progressed, he became once again integrated into the expatriate literary life of Paris and planned to write articles and reviews. Jack Kahane, owner of the Obelisk Press, asked him to translate Sade's *Les Cent-vingt Jours de Sodom*, but Beckett refused because he preferred to let *Murphy* provide him with a literary reputation and because he did not want to be associated with what he considered pornography. Beckett spent the rest of the year trying to translate *Murphy* into French with Alfred Péron. From early 1938 until the outbreak of war in 1939 he wrote short pieces to augment his income, as well as twelve untitled poems which were not published until 1946 as a cycle in *Les Temps*

been infiltrated and betrayed, and he and Suzanne Deschevaux-Dumesnil left their apartment as if they were going for a walk and never went back. For the next two months they moved from one safe place to another until they were smuggled across German lines into Unoccupied France. In 1945, when the war ended and Beckett returned to Paris, he received the *Croix de Guerre* and the *Médaille de la Résistance*.

Beckett spent the years 1942-1945 in south-

Hume Cronyn in the 1972 Royal Court Theatre revival of Krapp's Last Tape

Modernes. Despite this brief flurry of literary journalism and the other publications, the decade of the 1930s is best characterized by the personal upheaval of Beckett's life rather than by a consistent development of literary activity.

Beckett tried to write during the early years of World War II, but all around him friends were disappearing, and he decided that he could not remain in Paris and be as uninvolved as his Irish citizenship required. He officially abandoned his neutrality by the end of October 1940, when he became a member of one of the earliest French Resistance groups. By August 1942 his group had

east France in Roussillon, Vaucluse, hiding from the Germans and writing the novel *Watt*, probably the least appealing of all his fictions and the one that has drawn the scantiest critical appraisal. When the war ended, he took it to George Reavey, who was unable to place it, and the book languished for the next nine years as Beckett turned to other things. It was finally published in 1953, not because of the sudden fame of *Waiting for Godot*, but because a group of young people who formed the editorial board of *Merlin* magazine liked it. Beckett has always maintained that *Watt* has its place in his canon and is an important bridge from the prewar to the

Beckett rehearsing Billie Whitelaw at the Royal Court Theatre. Beckett claims to have heard her voice speaking the woman's roles as he wrote Not I.

postwar writings, but critics have neglected it until recently.

The first two years after the war ended were filled with the same sort of unsettled movement that had characterized Beckett's life in the 1930s. There were trips back and forth to Dublin. He sought writing assignments and even attempted to take private pupils for English language lessons while he was preparing a French translation of *Murphy* and working on his first original novel in French, *Mercier et Camier* (written in 1945 but unpublished until 1970), for expected publication by the publishing house of Bordas. Bordas declined to publish both books, and with their financial situation in crisis and the feeling of helplessness at not being able to organize his prose into something publishable and profitable, his wife, a gifted seamstress, became instrumental in their support, and Beckett turned once again to drama as a means of escape from the realities of his life.

In 1972, Beckett spoke of how he came to write "Eleuthéria," his first complete play: "I turned to writing plays to relieve myself of the awful depression the prose led me into. Life at that time was too demanding, too terrible, and I thought theatre would be a diversion." "Eleuthéria" is still Beckett's longest and most complex dramatic writing, with three acts, seventeen characters, and three sets. Like "Human Wishes," it also uses a divided stage (during acts 1 and 2) and requires rigorously executed spotlighting to focus the audience's attention upon the action. The title is the Greek word for freedom and the plot mainly concerns the efforts of a young man called Victor Krap to free himself from the constraints of his bourgeois family. Half of the divided set is the overcluttered living room of the Krap family and the other half is the shabby and spare hotel room in which Victor has gone to live. Beckett meant the set to symbolize two ways of life: Victor's family's exaggerated sense of propriety and his inactivity and indecisiveness amid squalor. The action takes place on three successive winter afternoons, and most of act 1 is on the half of the stage comprising the family living room, while act 2 is in Victor's room, and the third act has Victor's room filling the stage, while his family's living room is entirely absent.

Besides the length of the play and the complication of the set, the play is also atypical of Beckett's other plays in that there are none of the detailed instructions or precise directions that make directorial license or acting interpretation utterly impossible in his later works. Here, Beckett writes only that the text concerns the principal action of the play and that any marginal action is the concern of the actor. Still, there are hints of the mature playwright: Beckett's characters in "Eleuthéria" have names like Krap, Piouk ("puke"), Skunk, and Meck ("Mec" is French for pimp); Victor's father has difficulty with urination as does Vladimir in *Waiting for Godot*, and to a lesser extent, Krapp of *Krapp's Last Tape* (1958); Victor's conversations in the second act are similar to those between the boy and Vladimir in *Waiting for Godot*; the boredom of the female characters and the tenor of their conversation is strikingly similar to that in *Play* (1964; produced in German as *Spiel* the previous year). Indeed, the central character of the play, Victor Krap, is a man on a bed in a room, and there is comment throughout that this is a play within a play, as at one point a cry comes from the audience demanding to know who is the author of this play, with the response given as "Becquet," a French variant of Beckett's name. Both situations are characteristic of the rest of Beckett's canon.

Although Beckett has often allowed other plays that he feels are not worthy of production to be published years after he actually wrote them, and, even though he sent "Eleuthéria" to producers at the same time he sent *Waiting for Godot*, he remains firm in his resolve that it will never be published to insure that it will never be performed.

"Eleuthéria" followed the aborted *Mercier et Camier* and "Quatre Nouvelles" just as *Waiting for Godot* followed the novels *Molloy* and *Malone Meurt* (1951; published in English as *Malone Dies*, 1956). Beckett began a pattern of creation at this time that he has followed ever since: when he cannot write fiction for whatever reason, when he is blocked or, in his own words, "at an impasse," he turns from the rigors of that form to what he considers the more accessible form of drama. For example, *Molloy* and *Malone Dies* were to be a continuation of the fictional heroes begun with Murphy, Watt, and the others, and their tales were to be a continuation and a

development of the earlier ones. The development, as he envisioned it, would make the various fictional techniques of distancing that he had first used in *Murphy* and *Watt* unnecessary now. With these novels, Beckett uses for the first time a first-person narrator and allows his characters, all perhaps variants of the same character and containing variants of Beckett himself, to confront the reader without the description or detail the third-person narrator had previously required. Authorial commentary necessitated by third-person narration ranged from sarcastic involvement to apathetic unconcern, but with the fictional "I" Beckett created beings of no fixed abode, discernable universe, or specific time. They involve the reader in what are often harrowing personal journeys through the desperate spirals of their existence.

Malone Dies was supposed to be the last "of the series" that began with *Murphy* and continued through *Watt*, *Mercier et Camier*, and *Molloy*. As he finished this work that had been so satisfyingly autobiographical during its creation but so devastating to reread when finished, he was once again a victim of the periodic blocks that threatened to disrupt his writing. A brief holiday did nothing to dispel his inability to work. Though the impetus to write was there, continuation of the fiction was impossible. At first as an exercise, then with increasing absorption, he began to write the play that made him famous and changed the nature of drama in the last half of the present century, *Waiting for Godot*.

He wrote it quickly, from 9 October 1948 to 29 January 1949, and the writing became "a marvelous liberating diversion." Because Beckett's earlier attempts at writing drama left him with no real experience at writing for the stage, it now became a game to move the characters and plot the speeches of this play. "Eleuthéria" had gotten out of control with its elaborate setting and large number of characters, so in *Waiting for Godot* Beckett began by giving the framework of the play the same attention as he would have given to a game of chess. This play was much simpler than his earlier work: it contained two acts in which two men, Vladimir and Estragon, both down-and-out, wait for someone named Godot who is supposed to keep an appointment with them. They are joined by a man and his servant, Pozzo and Lucky, who stay with them briefly, then continue on their unspecified way. A boy comes at the end of the first act to tell Vladimir and Estragon that Mr. Godot will not come that day, but most surely the next. A tree which has been bare of leaves is the only setting, and a moon rises to signify that day has ended and night has come as the first act ends. In the second act, the tree miraculously sprouts a few leaves but nothing else has changed for Vladimir and Estragon. Pozzo and Lucky return and then leave; the boy comes again and repeats the same information. Vladimir and Estragon are disappointed and consider suicide but agree that they have done the best they could—they have kept their appointment. They speak of leaving but do not. The moon comes up again, and the curtain falls as the two men stand silently facing the audience in attitudes of solemn dignity, displaying both resignation and dejection.

Beckett refined the play several times before he sent it to producers, but almost three years passed before it would be performed. During this period Beckett gave up hope many times, but his wife, acting as his agent, persisted and took the manuscript to various producers until she came to Roger Blin, the play's first director. Even then arranging for production was difficult—money had to be raised, theaters they had hoped to use became unavailable, and actors came and went. Nonetheless, Beckett's meeting with Blin was a fortunate one, for although Beckett had firmly in his mind the idea of what he wanted the play to represent, Blin's acute theatrical vision was responsible for much that brought the drama to life. Blin had already had a long career in the French theater as actor, producer, and director, and he was able to bring technical knowledge as well as artistic vision to Beckett's play. In fact, it was Blin who was responsible for the costumes the four characters wore as well as for much of the decor and a great deal of the stage business in the first production. Beckett wanted to present a circus/vaudeville atmosphere in which his characters would speak in language much as anyone engaged in conversation would use. This marked a striking departure from the formal language, both eloquent and resonant, which was dominant in French theater at that time. The play retains the impersonal aspects of Beckett's fiction—characters with no past, no future, and very little present; no concern for the realities of life such as occupation, abode, relationships; and deliberate unconcern for the subject matter of ordinary discourse. But it also incorporated, just as the fiction did, much from Beckett's own life. His characters sing a German round song that first appeared in a letter Beckett wrote to a friend several years earlier; there are conversations that his friends and family felt were directly transposed from those that Beckett had with his wife in the presence of family and friends; and the line from Saint Augustine concerning one of the thieves being saved and the other damned

was found in Beckett's correspondence as early as 1935 and had come to be one that Beckett used routinely for situations he defined as "either/or."

Beckett returned to fiction after completing *Waiting for Godot* and wrote *L'Innommable* (1953), which became the third work in a novel trilogy with *Molloy* and *Malone Dies* and which was translated into English as *The Unnamable* (1958). Finally, all the circumstances became propitious for the production of *Waiting for Godot* on 5 January 1953. *Le tout Paris* came to see this play in which, to use Vivian Mercier's words, "nothing happens twice." Critical attitudes toward the play were positive from the premiere, when Sylvain Zegel wrote in the very first review that "The audience understood this much: Paris had just recognized in Samuel Beckett one of today's best playwrights." Armand Salacrou wrote "An author has appeared who has taken us by the hand to lead us into his universe." More than a decade later, Martin Esslin described the "*succes de scandale*" the play had become: "Was it not an outrage that people could be asked to come and see a play that could not be anything but a hoax, a play in which nothing whatever happened! People went to see the play just to be able to see that scandalous impertinence with their own eyes and to be in a position to say at the next party that they had actually been the victims of that outrage." At the age of forty-seven, Beckett suddenly found himself an overnight sensation.

Still, it was not until 1955 that the play was translated by Beckett and performed in England, where in 1955 it won the *Evening Standard* Drama Award for most controversial play, and not until the next year that the first American production was staged. Disastrously advertised as the "laugh sensation of two continents," it closed almost as soon as it opened at the Coconut Grove Playhouse in Miami. Since then the play has been performed, written about, analyzed, and categorized in numerous languages and according to many points of view. It has been called a parable of Christian salvation, an illustration of Schopenhauer's metaphysics, an exercise in the meaninglessness of existentialism, an allegory of French resistance to German occupation or the English occupation of Ireland, and so many other meanings that a sizable catalogue could be compiled of them with very little effort, and it has spawned a host of lesser plays written in direct imitation. Beckett expresses surprise over the effect this play has had on world drama, generally dismissing the work as a diversion or exercise, and even in several instances calling it a "bad" play, although he has never elaborated upon this remark.

Nevertheless, it is the one manuscript he still retains in his possession and adamantly refuses to sell or give away.

His next full-length play, *Fin de partie* (1957; produced as *Endgame*, 1958), remains one of his two favorite writings (the other is *Malone Dies*). Unlike *Waiting for Godot*, which was written through accidental circumstances, *Fin de partie* was deliberately conceived as a conscious intellectual exercise in which Beckett hoped to draw upon whatever he had learned of theatrical technique from his involvement with the several productions of the earlier play. *Fin de partie* marked the beginning of his preoccupation with dramatic exactitude and is replete with adverbial admonitions for anything the actor or director might wish to do. Once again Beckett has chosen a couple, Hamm and Clov, as the focus of the drama. Clov is perhaps younger and some of his behavior makes him seem at times a servant but at other times he is independent and distanced. To one side of the stage are Hamm's parents, Nagg and Nell, who live in two trash cans side by side simply because Beckett could think of no other dramatic device that would let them speak their lines on cue and then disappear from the audience's view as swiftly as he wanted.

The governing metaphor of the play is a chess game. Assisting with a 1967 Berlin production, Beckett said "Hamm is a king in this chess game lost from the start. From the start, he knows he is making loud senseless moves. That he will make no progress at all with the gaff. Now at the last he makes a few senseless moves as only a bad player would. A good one would have given up long ago. He is only trying to delay the inevitable end. Each of his gestures is one of the last useless moves which puts off the end. He's a bad player." Beckett has also stated that there "are no accidents in this play," and that, as with *Waiting for Godot*, "everything is based on analogy and repetition." Although, as with the earlier play, many interpretations have been attached to it, Beckett insists that one of the most important speeches in the play and one that should govern the entire performance is "nothing is funnier than unhappiness."

In a letter to his American director, Alan Schneider, Beckett made a strong objection to those who wanted elucidation of mysteries of interpretation that he said he had not made and insisted, "Hamm as stated, and Clov as stated. . . ." However, this play remains fertile exegetical ground for scholars and theatergoers alike, and they are all probably correct to insist on a more subtle and complex interpretation than Beckett seems at times to

want. It moved Harold Hobson, writing in 1973, to comment: "In recent years there has been some danger of Mr. Beckett being sentimentalized. Self-defensively we are driven to persuade ourselves that his plays are not really filled with terror and horror, but are, at bottom, jolly good fun. Well, they are not jolly good fun. They are amongst the most frightening prophecies of, and longing for, doom ever written."

Both these plays were written first in French, just as "Eleuthéria" had been, and one of the ironies that surrounds much of Beckett's dramatic writings concerns the first production of *Fin de partie*. No theater owner in Paris wanted to risk losing money by renting the theater to Beckett and Blin for the second play, despite the dramatic stir caused by *Waiting for Godot*. Beckett regretfully withdrew it from French consideration and began to translate it for production at the Royal Court Theatre in London, then under the artistic direction of George Devine. Beckett was unable to complete it as quickly or as well as he wanted. When the date for rehearsal drew near and Beckett was still not finished, Devine agreed that since he could not present an English *Endgame*, he would invite the French company to London to perform *Fin de partie*.

Thus, the French play received its world premiere in England and so outraged French patriotism that the management of the Studio des Champs Elysées Theatre, attracted by the commotion and hoping to profit from it, agreed to mount the play. Both productions of *Fin de partie* were accompanied by the mime *Acte sans parole I* (1957; produced as *Act Without Words I*, 1957), written to round out the evening because *Fin de partie* was deemed too short for production without a companion piece.

Beckett never liked this combination and wanted to substitute another short play instead of the mime. Thus he began to write *Krapp's Last Tape* (produced in French as *Le Dernière Bande*, 1960), which became too long for his original intention and which marked a new development in his dramatic writing. His first postwar play written in English, it deals with biographical information much more gently than the three novels that preceded it. The emotion in this play is recollected in a tranquillity of sorts, as an old exhausted Krapp sits in his room and listens to his tapes. Krapp's reflections include a summer day on the shores of the Baltic, where Beckett went with his Sinclair cousins, and the green-eyed girl in the boat whom he loves is generally assumed to be Peggy Sinclair. A character named Fanny, one of Beckett's aunt's nicknames, may represent Cissie Sinclair, and the woman who

Page from the manuscript for Beckett's French translation of A Piece of Monologue

sang songs in the evening was probably a variant of the Englishwoman who hid during the war in the same village as Beckett. These, of course, are only some of the most obvious examples and do not capture the sensitivity of the use Beckett makes of them.

Dublin journalist Alec Reid has described the play as "total theatre," saying, "It is not the words, the movements, the sights severally which produce the impact; it is the new experience, evoked through their combination on stage. This process involving eye, ear, intellect, emotion, all at once, we shall call total theatre."

Beckett claims that he had never seen a tape recorder before he wrote this play, but that it seemed a good way to allow a man to recapture his memories. It is quite likely that Beckett wrote the play in English because he was so taken by the voice of the English actor, Patrick Magee. Beckett said that when he heard the lines he had written spoken inside his head, it was as if Magee's voice had been speaking them. Years later when he first heard the actress Billie Whitelaw, who was a member of a 1964 Royal Court production of *Play*, he said that it was her voice he heard speaking his woman's roles and he wrote *Not I* (1972; produced in French as *Pas Moi*, 1975).

Although it is difficult to make any statement regarding the exact chronology of Beckett's dramatic writing, it is generally believed that the latest two-act play he has written is *Happy Days*, completed sometime in 1961 and given its first performance in New York shortly after. The work was produced in French as *Oh les beaux jours* in 1963. It was deliberately written first in English to accomplish several things that had become important to Beckett. He was sensitive to the fact that none of his plays had been instant commercial successes, and he wanted public acclaim to go along with the critical approval that was building with each new production. Two subjects had also become important to Beckett to express dramatically, namely the Catholic church and the British government, both from the Ireland of his youth. He knew subjects like these would suffer if expressed in French so he wrote in English. However, many of the long passages denouncing Church domination of the Irish and what he considered to be British misrule were excised by Beckett from the final manuscript.

Happy Days is the story of a woman named Winnie, buried in sand up to her waist in the first act. She amuses herself with possessions, occasionally calling to her husband, Willie, who lives behind her mound and spends his time reading the newspaper and looking at a postcard. A bell governs Winnie's waking and sleeping, and she passes the time between the harsh clangs, which signify the beginning and end of her day, by talking. Occasionally she breaks down, but always she regains her composure. In the second act, she is buried to her neck and cannot even turn to her possessions for respite but must while away the hours by inventing stories. Willie appears toward the end of this act, "dressed to kill," as Beckett writes, and tries to crawl up the mound. The ending is ambiguous as Willie's hand is outstretched toward Winnie, but also toward "Brownie," the little revolver she had amused herself with in the first act. She sings the waltz from Franz Lehár's *The Merry Widow*, and the curtain falls on this unsettling note. Ruth White won an Obie Award for her New York performance as Winnie despite Walter Kerr's objection to the play. *Happy Days* did not achieve the commercial success Beckett had wanted, but public reaction was generally favorable.

By the time he finished *Happy Days* Beckett was moving freely between writing in French or English. At first he agreed with Herbert Blau's statement that by writing in French he had been able to achieve the right "weakening" effect, that is, to rid his language of any affectation so that content and language were united in a simplicity of form that often belied the complexity of the statement he made. He moved from language to language with the same ease that he wrote mimes, radio plays, dramatic monologues, or whatever else he was inspired to try at the time.

In the same year that *Happy Days* was produced, Beckett had published *Comment c'est* (1961; published in English as *How It Is*, 1964), an elliptical text divided into three sections in which a speaker crawls through the mud dragging his few possessions with him in a sack pressed to his naked belly. It continues Beckett's preoccupations with identity and his obsession with words and things—both natural objects and phenomena. The nameless narrator might just as well have been an addendum to *The Unnamable* as he is a prefiguration of future writings, such as *Assez* (*Enough*, 1966), *Sans* (1969; published in English as *Lessness*, 1970); and *Le Dépeupleur* (1970; published in English as *The Lost Ones*, 1972).

The brevity of this prose also signaled the beginning of brevity in Beckett's plays as well. *Breath* (1970) is 120 words and lasts thirty-five seconds; *Not I* should be played in no more than sixteen minutes; and *That Time* (1976) should last between twenty-four and thirty minutes. Beckett continued to write

A body. Where none. No mind. Where none. That at least.
A place. Where none. For the body. To be in. Move in. Out
of. Back into. No. No out. In only. Stay in. On in. Nothing
more. Nothing sweet blest all.

All before. Nothing else ever. Ever tried. Ever failed.
No matter. Same again. Try again. Fail again. Fail better.

First the body. No. The place. No. Together. Now either.
Now the other. Sick of either try the other. Sick of it back
sick of the either. So on. Till sick of both. Throw up
and go. Where neither. Till sick of there. Then again. A body
again. Where none. A place again. Where none. Fail again. Better
again. Or better worse. Fail worse again. Still worse again.
Till sick for good. Throw up for good. Go for good. Where neither
for good. Good and all.

It stands. What? Yes. Must up in the end and stand. Yes. No
choice in the end but up and stand. Say the bones. Say for
example the bones. The ground. Say for example the ground or
whatever ironhard. No mind and pain? Say yes that the bones may
pain till it must stand. Up somehow and stand. Or a minimum. Say
a minimum of mind where none to permit of pain. Here that the bones
may pain till they must up somehow and stand. Somehow stand. Either.
Providing pain. Here of bones. Other examples to come. Of pain.
Relief from pain. Temporary relief from pain. Change of pain.

Another. Here again. Supine on a water mattress in the light
of a night-light. Ceiling or whatever just visible. Seeing it all.
Straining to see it all. Dimly all. Dim scraps. On and off. On the
ceiling. Muttering it all as it comes. On and off the ceiling or
whatever. Or in the void. Sick of lids. Try the void. No ceiling.
None visible. Dim scraps in the void. For the moment in the void.
On and off in the void. Another listening. Another other. Here again.
Straining to catch. Somewhere there straining to catch. In the light
of the night-light. All that before. Nothing else ever. But never so
ill. With care never so ill. Worse failed. With care never worse
failed.

Too much. Water-mattress too much. Any mattress too much. Night-
light too much. Simply supine. Somehow supine. Faint light source
unknown. Know the minimum. Know nothing no. Not here. Not yet. At
most the minimum. Mere minimum. Bare minimum.

Long since it stood and no choice but stand. Up somehow and stand.
Somehow stand. That or cry out. The cry so long on its way. Of pain.
No. No or. No cry. Not here. Not yet. Simply up. Somehow off the
ground or whatever ironhard. A time when the various stages. The way
finally first if lying to begin it somehow stands sits. In detail.
So on from there. Till the impossible achieved. Not now. Fail better
worse now.

Revised typescript for a work in progress

fiction with *Fizzles*, which Paul Gray called "slight to the point of frippery."

There has been much speculation as to what Beckett's intention is in these ever-diminishing writings. Opinions range from the purely psychological—now that his fictional voices are integrated, all of his tellers of tales have become unified to the point where the tale no longer needs to be told and so it decreases—to the literary—having perfected his artistic vision, Beckett no longer needs long-winded narrators who ramble on interminably because he can make all his fictional points with a precision so sharp as to leave audiences and readers breathless with the end which comes so abruptly soon after the beginning.

In the mid-1970s, however, Beckett surprised publishers and scholars alike by announcing that he was hard at work on another novel which marked a complete departure from his previously published work. He said this one was to be a "romance," a novel of 300-400 pages written in the traditional manner and which would tell the story of himself and his wife. Instead, he produced in 1979 *Companie* (published as *Company* in 1980), just sixty-three pages long, strongly autobiographical, and resembling *Comment c'est* in style.

All this speculation only compounds the mystery of Beckett's vision and the chronology of the writing. Beckett surrounds his work with secrecy, privacy, and the occasional tantalizing clue as to a work's provenance and literary history. Many works which he calls "trunk manuscripts" are suddenly given for publication with Beckett unable to remember how or when he came to write them, or even if they might or might not be variants of other works. He never knows when his creative impulses will grow fallow, and he refuses to discuss his writing or his intention. His work becomes a Chinese box puzzle which continues to fascinate readers and theatergoers alike.

The years from 1965 to the present have been marked by Beckett's almost constant presence in a theater where his work was in production even though he still maintains that fiction is his most important writing. He acquired an increasing sense of self-confidence as the years passed, and the early dependence on Roger Blin in France and George Devine in London gave way to a sure sense of command of his material. Public acceptance of his work gave him the freedom to insist upon it being presented as he had written and envisioned it, and he soon grew independent enough to insist upon full charge of many productions. He who had been so insecure and unhappy about meeting people that he had to allow his wife to take his first plays to producers now became so confident that he stopped being only an adviser or spectator and became if not the director in name, certainly in spirit.

The years of his collaboration with Devine at the Royal Court were felicitous. Besides Blin, Beckett worked with varying degrees of satisfaction with Jean Louis Barrault and Madeleine Renaud in France. In 1964, he made his only visit to the United States to be present for the filming of *Film*, his only known writing for the cinema. *Film* won several awards including the Prix Filmcritice (1965) and the Tours Film Prize (1966). He was uncomfortable in New York despite his high regard for Alan Schneider, who usually directs American performances of Beckett's plays, and Barney Rosset, his publisher at Grove Press.

It is in Germany that he seems most at home in the theater. He has worked on an almost annual basis with the Schiller Theater in Berlin and has gone with the same frequency to Stuttgart, to assist or direct productions for radio and television. He directed the Schiller Theater actors in the definitive German production of *Waiting for Godot* in 1977 and again in 1978 and allowed the company to tour in London and in Brooklyn the following year. In 1979, he directed a festival of his work at the Royal Court Theatre and since then has made several more trips to Germany and London for recordings of radio plays. He has even begun to write dramatic pieces on request. In 1980 David Warrilow performed *A Piece of Monologue* in New York, and in 1981 Beckett wrote a short piece called *Ohio Impromptu* for presentation at a symposium at Ohio State University in honor of his seventy-fifth birthday.

Although all his plays have attracted respectable audiences, Beckett has become well known more because of *Waiting for Godot* than any of his other works. *Waiting for Godot* has been published in numerous languages and in so many editions that Beckett has lost count. Editions of all the other plays combined do not come close to this achievement. With his novels, total sales in France are less than 50,000 copies, and the figure is not much higher in all English language editions.

Beckett continues to live quietly in Paris in the apartment he bought in the early 1960s and the small house in the country just east of Paris that he calls "The house that *Godot* built." He keeps to a schedule that would defeat most younger men, writing, translating, collaborating, and overseeing productions, and still finding time for an extensive social life. The rumor that he has been a recluse skulking about the back alleys of Paris is one he would like particularly to lay to rest.

It is probably not an exaggeration to say that his involvement with the theater has been responsible in great part for his prolific output during the years between 1960 and 1980. All this activity which required his involvement with people also led to a kind of personal harmony that had hitherto eluded him.

In 1969, Beckett received the Nobel Prize, an honor for which he did not actively campaign but one which he did not (as Jean-Paul Sartre had done) refuse. He had been nominated as early as 1957 by Maurice Nadeau and then by a succession of American professors who championed him. He seemed effectively out of consideration when Erik Wahlund, drama critic of *Svenska Dagbladet*, wrote that Beckett had written only a "single first-rank work," *Waiting for Godot*, and that none of his other writings had ever approached its depth of thought or structure. Thus, there was genuine surprise when the prize was given to Beckett for "a body of work that, in new forms of fiction and the theatre, has transmuted the destitution of modern man into his exaltation." This comment is probably the most accurate description of Beckett's writing, as in its succinctness it takes into account his prose, his plays, his achievement, his life.

Screenplay:

Film, New York Film Festival, 1965.

Television Script:

Eh Joe, BBC, 1966; broadcast in French as *Dis Joe*, Official Radio Television Français, 1968.

Radio Scripts:

All That Fall, BBC Third Programme, 1957; broadcast in French as *Tous ceux qui tombent*, translation by Beckett and Robert Pinget, Official Radio Television Français, 1959;

From an Abandoned Work, BBC Third Programme, 1957;

Embers, BBC Third Programme, 1959; broadcast in French as *Cendres*, Official Radio Television Français, 1966;

Words and Music, BBC Third Programme, 1962;

Cascando, Official Radio Television Français, 1963;

BBC Third Programme, 1964;

Lessness, BBC Third Programme, 1971;

Radio II, BBC Third Programme, 1976;

Ghost Trio, BBC, 1976.

Bibliographies:

Raymond Federman and John Fletcher, *Samuel Beckett: His Work and His Critics* (Berkeley: University of California Press, 1970);

Robin J. Davis, *Samuel Beckett: Checklist and index of his published works* (Stirling, Scotland: Privately printed, 1979).

Biography:

Deirdre Bair, *Samuel Beckett: A Biography* (New York: Harcourt Brace Jovanovich, 1978).

References:

Bell Gale Chevigny, ed., *Twentieth Century Interpretations of Endgame* (Englewood Cliffs: Prentice-Hall, 1969);

Ruby Cohn, *Back to Beckett* (Princeton: Princeton University Press, 1973);

Cohn, ed., *Casebook on Waiting for Godot* (New York: Grove, 1967);

Colin Duckworth, *Angels of Darkness* (London: Allen & Unwin, 1972);

Beryl Fletcher and others, *A Student's Guide to the Plays of Samuel Beckett* (London: Faber & Faber, 1978);

John Fletcher, *Samuel Beckett's Art* (London: Chatto & Windus, 1967);

Fletcher and John Spurling, *Beckett: A Study of His Plays* (New York: Hill & Wang, 1972);

Pierre Mélèse, *Beckett* (Paris: Seghers, 1966);

Alec Reid, *All I Can Manage, More Than I Could* (New York: Grove, 1968);

Eugene Webb, *The Plays of Samuel Beckett* (Seattle: University of Washington Press, 1974).

Papers:

Portions of Beckett's manuscripts are housed in the Humanities Research Center, University of Texas, Austin; Baker Library of Dartmouth College; Ohio State University Libraries, Columbus; and the Beineke Library of Yale University. In England, there is a Samuel Beckett Archive at the University of Reading, and a small number of manuscripts are housed in Trinity College Library, Dublin.

Brendan Behan

(9 February 1923-20 March 1964)

Patrick A. McCarthy
University of Miami

PRODUCTIONS: *The Quare Fellow*, 19 November 1954, Pike Theatre Club, Dublin; Theatre Workshop version, 24 May 1956, Theatre Royal, Stratford, London;

The Big House, Spring 1957, BBC Radio Third Programme, London; 6 May 1958, Pike Theatre Club, Dublin;

The New House, 6 May 1958, Pike Theatre Club, Dublin;

An Giall, June 1958, An Damer, Dublin; translated and revised as *The Hostage*, 14 October 1958, Theatre Royal, Stratford, London;

Richard's Cork Leg, 14 March 1972, Peacock Theatre, Dublin.

BOOKS: *The Quare Fellow* (London: Methuen, 1956; New York: Grove Press, 1957);

Borstal Boy (London: Hutchinson, 1958; New York: Knopf, 1959);

An Giall (Dublin: An Chomhairle Náisiúnta Drámaíochta, 1958?); translated and revised as *The Hostage* (London: Methuen, 1958; New York: Grove Press, 1959);

Brendan Behan's Island: An Irish Sketchbook (New York: Bernard Geis, 1962; London: Hutchinson, 1962);

Hold Your Hour and Have Another (London: Hutchinson, 1963; Boston: Little, Brown, 1964);

The Scarperer (Garden City: Doubleday, 1964; London: Hutchinson, 1966);

Brendan Behan's New York (New York: Bernard Geis, 1964; London: Hutchinson, 1964);

Confessions of an Irish Rebel (New York: Bernard Geis, 1965; London: Hutchinson, 1965);

Moving Out and A Garden Party: Two Plays, edited by Robert Hogan (Dixon, Cal.: Proscenium Press, 1967);

Richard's Cork Leg (London: Eyre Methuen, 1973; New York: Grove Press, 1974);

The Complete Plays (New York: Grove Press, 1978; London: Eyre Methuen, 1978);

Poems and Stories (Dublin: Liffey Press, 1978).

Brendan Behan was the most important new Irish dramatist of the 1950s. Writing without the support of the theatrical establishment (the Abbey

Brendan Behan

Theatre rejected his early efforts), Behan developed an original style that combined bawdy humor, genuine pathos, and social insight. If he had a model for his role as dramatist, it was probably Sean O'Casey, whom Behan admired both as a playwright and as an opponent of censorship. The major influence on his plays, however, was Joan Littlewood's Theatre Workshop, which emphasized improvisational effects, songs, and contemporary allusions which are supposed to make the play more immediately relevant to an audience. Unfortunately, Behan's dependence on these methods led to such loose structuring of his plays that in his unfinished play, *Richard's Cork Leg* (1972), songs and joke sequences are substituted for the de-

Program cover and cast list for the first production of Behan's work in London

velopment of plot, character, and theme. Disappointed at his inability to repeat the success of *The Quare Fellow* (1954) and *The Hostage* (1958), Behan retreated more and more often into alcoholic binges until his death in March 1964.

It is evident from his plays and other writings that one of the major factors in Behan's life was his involvement with the Irish Republican cause. He inherited his Republican sympathies from his intensely patriotic working-class family: when Brendan was born, his father Stephen Behan, a house painter, labor leader, and soldier, was serving a jail term for IRA activities during the Irish Civil War; his mother, Kathleen Kearney Behan, boasted of her ability to sing rebel songs; his uncle, Peadar Kearney, wrote the Irish national anthem; and at the age of seventy-seven, his stepgrandmother was arrested and sentenced to three years in an English prison for terrorist activities. Educated from 1928 to 1937 at Irish Catholic schools and employed as an

apprentice house painter from 1937 until 1939, Behan himself was imprisoned in 1939 when he was arrested in Liverpool for possession of explosives. After serving two years in a Borstal institution (an English reform school), Behan returned to Dublin but was soon involved in a drunken shoot-out with police that led to a sentence of fourteen years in prison. His sentence was commuted in 1946, but Behan remained at liberty only a few months before being arrested in Manchester, where he had gone to help an Irish prisoner escape. The four-month sentence he served for this adventure was his last major term of imprisonment for Republican activities, but in 1948 he was sentenced to a month in jail for being drunk and disorderly. In the remaining sixteen years of his life he would serve many more such terms for drunkenness, not only in Ireland but in several other countries as well.

One of Behan's favorite books was Irish revolutionist and journalist John Mitchel's *Jail Journal*

(1856). That book, and other accounts of prison experiences, might have suggested to Behan the idea for his finest nondramatic work, *Borstal Boy* (1958), a sensitive, often ironic description of his two years in reform school. The four years he spent in Irish prisons may have had an even greater effect on his career, for it was during this time that Behan had his first significant article published, wrote his first play, "The Landlady" (based on the life of his eccentric paternal grandmother), and determined to make his way as a writer. While he was in Dublin's Mountjoy Jail he knew Bernard Kirwan, who was hanged for the murder of his own brother, and in 1946 Behan began work on a play about Kirwan's execution, which he called "The Twisting of Another Rope." Eight years later, after the play was rejected by the Abbey Theatre, he rewrote it and, at the suggestion of director Alan Simpson, who wanted to save space in newspaper advertisements, retitled it *The Quare Fellow*.

During the years between the initial conception that led to *The Quare Fellow* and the first performance of the play in Dublin in 1954, Behan was involved in a number of occupations: painting houses in Dublin, soliciting customers for prostitutes in Paris, writing a column for the *Irish Press*, singing songs for a radio program. The broadcasting experience proved important in 1952 when Micheál Ó hAodha asked Behan to write a series of comedy shows for Radio Eireann. Behan wrote only two radio plays, *Moving Out* (1952) and *A Garden Party* (1952), for this series, but these short domestic comedies (later combined into a stage version, *The New House*, produced in 1958 and included in *Best Short Plays of the World Theatre 1958-1967*) showed that Behan had considerable talent in characterization and in developing comic situations. A later radio play, *The Big House* (1957), was less successful although its satiric treatment of the conflict of the Anglo-Irish and Irish peasant classes is often very funny.

While these apprentice works are interesting, Behan's reputation as a dramatist rests on his two major plays, *The Quare Fellow* and *The Hostage*. The

[The Quare Fellow

Warden Regan—DUDLEY FOSTER   *Neighbour*—GERARD DYNEVOR
Dunlavin—MAXWELL SHAW

Cartoon by Ronald Searle that appeared in the 8 January 1956 issue of Punch

Quare Fellow is particularly impressive for its development of the audience's sympathy for a character who is never seen on stage: the "quare fellow" or condemned man who is scheduled to be "topped" in the morning for killing his brother. The *raisonneur* of the play is the prison guard, Regan, a sensitive man who despises hangings and sees past the hypocrisy of the judicial system but nevertheless considers his work "a soft job . . . between hangings," when he is not forced to see himself as part of the brutal prison system. Regan is a man caught between his conscience and his "duty" to keep order and to make preparations for hangings, but other representatives of the system are viewed less sympathetically. The governor of the prison is concerned only with appearances and formalities: he objects to jokes about hanging but not to the death sentence itself. The other warders are generally concerned only with advancing their careers while doing as little work as possible, and some of the prisoners are less interested in the fate of the quare fellow than in getting a cigarette or a drink or in maintaining their status within the prison's pecking order. The major exception is Prisoner C, a Gaelic-speaking youth from Kerry, whose honesty and innocence stand in contrast to the hardened attitude of the English executioner and most of the Irish prisoners.

It is tempting to view *The Quare Fellow* simply as a protest against capital punishment, but Behan never confined any of his plays to so narrow a target. Actually the death penalty is seen in the play mainly as the most obvious example of the brutality built into a system that punishes men for the very brutality that the system engenders. Behan's relentless attacks on the absurdity of the penal system, and the larger social system that it represents, are effective because the play's black humor builds in the audience a sense of horror even as the audience laughs at joke after joke. In *The Quare Fellow* one can observe what was to become the main technique of *The Hostage*: the revelation of serious thematic concerns through such apparently trivial elements as jokes and songs. In this respect, Behan bears at least a passing resemblance to such dramatists as Samuel Beckett and Bertolt Brecht.

If the years 1954-1958 were the most productive of Behan's career, part of the credit for his success during this period may undoubtedly be attributed to his 1955 marriage to painter Beatrice ffrench-Salkeld, an understanding and long-suffering woman who recognized her husband's weaknesses and tried to help him. Despite several arrests for public drunkenness, Behan accomplished a great deal during these years. In 1956 *The Quare Fellow* was presented in London by Joan Lit-

A scene from the 1958 Theatre Royal production of The Hostage

tlewood's Theatre Workshop. Meanwhile Behan worked on *Borstal Boy*, which was published in 1958, and on a Gaelic play, *An Giall*, which was first produced in Dublin in June 1958. Reserving the right to "translate" the play into English, he actually introduced new characters, dialogue, songs, and dances; other material was added by Theatre Workshop during rehearsals for the 1958 London production. The result was *The Hostage*, a controversial play that is often deemed inferior to *An Giall* but is nonetheless a successful amalgam of farce and social commentary.

Behan had begun to see that the political aims of the Irish Republican Army might conflict at times with fundamental human values. As an artist, he was bound to portray the conflict of values, not merely to act as a propagandist for the IRA. *The Hostage*, which is about the kidnapping and execution of a British soldier by the IRA, reflects this new complexity in Behan's attitude toward the IRA. Pat, who comes as close as anyone to being Behan's spokesman in the play, is a cynical critic of the Republican cause, yet he joyfully sings a song in celebration of a victory over the British troops, the Black and Tans; the IRA is constantly depicted as a group of demented revolutionaries—like the Marx Brothers with guns and explosives—yet throughout the play Behan emphasizes the justice of Irish complaints against Britain. Small wonder that on one of his trips to America, Behan said that the IRA was uncertain "whether to accept a charity performance of *The Hostage* or bomb the theatre."

Always uncertain of his talent, unable to cope with his success, Behan was soon to turn into a caricature of himself. For instance, he was barred from participating in the 1961 St. Patrick's Day parade in New York City because parade sponsors felt he gave the Irish a bad image. The legend of Behan the drunk was in fact superseding the reputation of the playwright. He was not to find freedom from the public image of himself that he created, nor was he able to marshal the creative energies necessary for another play on the level of *The Quare Fellow* or *The Hostage*. His final theatrical effort was *Richard's Cork Leg* (originally written in Gaelic under the title "La Breagh San Reilg," or "A Fine Day in the Graveyard"), which, like the books *Brendan Behan's Island* (1962), *Brendan Behan's New York* (1964), and *Confessions of an Irish Rebel* (1965), was composed largely by dictation into a tape recorder. That method of composition was unfortunate since it resulted in rambling works that resemble pub talk more than professional writing. *Richard's Cork Leg* has several flashes of brilliant dialogue; Behan's use

Brendan Behan in London, 1959

of Irish speech had long been an arresting feature of his plays, as various critics have noted. But this final play as a whole is a failure. Like Dylan Thomas and Malcolm Lowry, Behan spent his last few years haunted by creative triumphs that he was never to repeat.

Although he wrote only two notable plays, even that achievement entitles Behan to a place of some significance in the modern Irish theater. At a time when the only substantial Irish playwrights were emigres Sean O'Casey and Samuel Beckett, Behan helped to revitalize the theater in Ireland, largely by producing two plays that have more than a parochial interest, and by using realistic speech in combination with Brechtian music-hall effects. His public rebelliousness, combined with the consistently antiestablishment tone of his plays, has earned him comparison with John Osborne. Other critics have seen a relationship between Behan's method and the absurdist plays of Jean Genet, Eugene Ionesco, and Beckett. However, Behan might best be compared to John Millington Synge and O'Casey, who experimented boldly, offended Irish nationalists with their irreverence, and gave Ireland plays that later generations were to recognize as masterpieces. When Behan died in March 1964, only a few months after the birth of his daughter Blanaid, his outrageous public image made it difficult for the public to view him as more than a self-destructive exhibitionist. He was certainly that, but as the awards for *The Hostage* (the Obie Award and the Paris Festival Award, both 1958, and the French Critics' Award, 1962) and the inclusion of both *The Hostage* and *The Quare Fellow* in *Drury's Guide to Best Plays*, indicate, he was also a talented dramatist. Behan's iconoclastic interpretation of the modern Irish scene, related in the tough language of the Dublin slums yet informed by a warm human vision, represents a substantial addition to the modern Irish theater.

Radio Scripts:
Moving Out, Radio Eireann, 1952;
A Garden Party, Radio Eireann, 1952;
The Big House, BBC Radio Third Programme, 1957.

Periodical Publication:
The Big House, Evergreen Review, 5 (September-October 1961): 40-63.

Biographies:
Dominic Behan, *My Brother Brendan* (London: Leslie Frewin, 1965);
Rae Jeffs, *Brendan Behan, Man and Showman* (London: Hutchinson, 1966);
Sean McCann, ed., *The World of Brendan Behan* (New York: Twayne, 1966);
Ulick O'Connor, *Brendan* (Englewood Cliffs, N.J.: Prentice-Hall, 1970);
Seamus de Burca, *Brendan Behan: A Memoir* (Newark, Del.: Proscenium Press, 1971);
Beatrice Behan, Des Hickey, and Gus Smith, *My Life with Brendan* (London: Leslie Frewin, 1973);
Peter Arthurs, *With Brendan Behan: A Personal Mem-*

oir (New York: St. Martin's Press, 1981).

References:
Ted E. Boyle, *Brendan Behan* (New York: Twayne, 1969);
Anthony Burgess, "The Writer as Drunk," in his *Urgent Copy: Literary Studies* (New York: Norton, 1968);
Peter René Gerdes, *The Major Works of Brendan Behan* (Bern: Herbert Lang, 1973);
Howard Goorney, *The Theatre Workshop Story* (New York & London: Eyre Methuen, 1981), pp. 110-116, 155-157;
Johan Hendricks, "The 'Theatre of Fun': In Defence of Brendan Behan's *The Hostage*," *Anglo-Irish Studies*, 3 (1977): 85-95;
Colbert Kearney, *The Writings of Brendan Behan* (New York: St. Martin's Press, 1977);
Benedict Kiely, "That Old Triangle: A Memory of Brendan Behan," *Hollins Critic*, 2 (February 1965): 1-12;
Johannes Kleinstuck, "Brendan Behan's 'The Hostage,'" *Essays and Studies by Members of the English Association*, 24 (1971): 69-83;
Patrick A. McCarthy, "Triviality and Dramatic Achievement in Two Plays by Brendan Behan," *Modern British Literature*, 3 (Fall 1978): 113-121;
Sean McMahon, "The Quare Fellow," *Eire-Ireland*, 4 (Winter 1969): 143-157;
E. H. Mikhail, ed., *The Art of Brendan Behan* (Totowa, N.J.: Barnes & Noble, 1979);
Mikhail, *Brendan Behan: An Annotated Bibliography of Criticism* (Totowa, N.J.: Barnes & Noble, 1980);
Raymond J. Porter, *Brendan Behan* (New York: Columbia University Press, 1973);
Alan Simpson, *Beckett and Behan and a Theatre in Dublin* (London: Routledge & Kegan Paul, 1962);
Richard Wall, "*An Giall* and *The Hostage* Compared," *Modern Drama*, 18 (1975): 165-172;
Gordon M. Wickstrom, "The Heroic Dimension in Brendan Behan's *The Hostage*," *Educational Theatre Journal*, 22 (1970): 406-411.

Robert Bolt
(15 August 1924-   )

John R. Kaiser
Pennsylvania State University

PRODUCTIONS: *A Man for All Seasons*, July 1954, BBC Radio, London; January 1957, BBC Television, London; 1 July 1960, Globe Theatre, London; 22 November 1961, ANTA Theatre, New York, 640 [performances];

The Last of the Wine, 1955, BBC Radio, London; 1956, Theatre in the Round, London;

The Critic and the Heart, 1 April 1957, Oxford Playhouse, Oxford; revised as *Brother and Sister*, 1967, Brighton Festival, Brighton; revised again, 1968, Bristol Old Vic, Bristol;

Flowering Cherry, 21 November 1957, Haymarket Theatre, London, 435; 21 October, 1959, Lyceum Theatre, New York, 5;

The Tiger and the Horse, 24 August 1960, Queen's Theatre, London;

Gentle Jack, 28 November 1963, Queen's Theatre, London, 75;

The Thwarting of Baron Bolligrew, 11 December 1965, Aldwych Theatre, London;

Vivat! Vivat Regina!, 20 May 1970, Chichester Festival Theatre, Chichester; 8 October 1970, Piccadilly Theatre, London; 20 January 1972, Broadhurst Theatre, New York, 116;

State of Revolution, 1977, Birmingham Repertory Theatre, Birmingham; 18 May 1977, Lyttelton Theatre (National Theatre), London.

BOOKS: *Flowering Cherry* (London: Heinemann, 1958);

A Man for All Seasons (London: Heinemann, 1961; New York: Random House, 1962);

The Tiger and the Horse (London: Heinemann, 1961);

Gentle Jack (London: French, 1964; New York: Random House, 1965);

The Thwarting of Baron Bolligrew (London: Heinemann, 1966; New York: Theatre Arts, 1967);

Doctor Zhivago: The Screenplay Based on the Novel by Boris Pasternak (London: Harvill, 1966; New York: Random House, 1966);

Vivat! Vivat Regina! (London: Heinemann, 1971; New York: Random House, 1972);

State of Revolution (London: Heinemann, 1977; New York: French, 1977).

Robert Bolt has been characterized by critic John Russell Taylor as a "good, traditional playwright." Unlike his contemporaries during the late 1950s—Harold Pinter, John Osborne, John Arden, and Arnold Wesker—who followed formulas of the theaters of cruelty and of the absurd, Bolt wrote more in the manner of Terence Rattigan. That is to say, he wrote "sensitive, competent acting vehicles" for "a largely middle-class, West-End, theatre-going audience." His distinctiveness is the concern for elegance of language and structure.

Born in the small Lancashire town of Sale, near Manchester, Robert Oxton Bolt is the younger of two sons of Ralph and Leah Binnion Bolt. Bolt's mother taught in a primary school, and his father ran a small shop, where he sold mostly china, glass, and furniture. Bolt has described his early years as a time of "northern nonconformity . . . much emphasis on education, social responsibility and progressive politics; a good deal of Chapel and Sunday

Robert Bolt, 1976

77

School in early years . . . the *Manchester Guardian* and no alcohol . . . and all much better fun than it sounds because of the vigour and seriousness."

Bolt was graduated from the Manchester Grammar School in 1940. Not being qualified to enter a university, he took a job as office boy in the Sun Life Assurance Company of Manchester in 1942. Bolt detested his work of running errands, stoking the furnace, and filing letters. He was, however, delivered from this drudgery by a special wartime arrangement waiving the customary entrance requirement to a university. In 1943 at Manchester University he studied history and became a Marxist and a member of the Communist party.

Bolt went into the Royal Air Force before the end of 1943. After a time Bolt abandoned his attempt to become a pilot and transferred to the army. He entered an officer training program at Sandhurst and subsequently served with the Royal West African Frontier Force in Ghana. Demobilized in 1946 with the rank of lieutenant, Bolt went back to Manchester University. He was graduated with an honors degree in history in 1949 and then went to Exeter University where he received his teaching diploma in 1950. In 1949 he married Celia Ann Roberts, a painter; before they were divorced in 1967, the couple had three children, Sally, Benedict, and Joanna. From 1950 until 1958, Bolt taught English, first for two years at a village school in Bishopsteignton in Devon, and then at Millfield School in Street, Somerset. It was during this period that Bolt began to write plays, first for radio and then for the stage.

Bolt had written stories since his childhood, but he did not seriously consider drama until he was asked in 1950 to write a nativity play for the school. This event was for Bolt "an astonishing turning point . . ." because, as he recalls, he realized "this was what I was going to do and that I was going to succeed or fail by this." Bolt's first radio play was *The Master*, a tale of wandering scholars in the Middle Ages; this was broadcast on 15 February 1953. *Fifty Pigs* was also broadcast in 1953, and an early version of *A Man for All Seasons*, Bolt's first attempt to portray the life of Sir Thomas More, was broadcast in July 1954. Bolt wrote a television version of *A Man for All Seasons*, which was presented by the BBC in January 1957. Among other radio plays by Bolt are *Ladies and Gentlemen* (1954), *Mr. Sampson's Sundays* (1955), *The Last of the Wine* (1955), *The Window* (1958), *The Drunken Sailor* (1958), and *The Banana Tree* (1961). By 1958 the BBC had broadcast fifteen of his radio plays—eight written for adults and seven for children. Most of the children's plays were

about the comings and goings of the dim-witted knight named Sir Oblong Fitz-Oblong who battled with dragons and various wicked barons.

Bolt's first work produced in the legitimate theater was his stage adaptation of his 1955 radio play, *The Last of the Wine*. This play, "a stylised examination of society's helplessness in the face of the atomic threat," was presented in London at the Theatre in the Round in 1956. His next play, *The Critic and the Heart*, produced at the Oxford Playhouse in April 1957, featured Michael Redgrave and his daughter, Vanessa. The work was later rewritten as *Brother and Sister* and produced in Brighton in 1967 and again at Bristol in 1968 in another revised version. One critic found it to be "a well-made and orthodox play," and in Bolt's own words the play was "utterly naturalistic," that is, it is a play detailing the lives of ordinary people in a very orthodox style. It deals with the sacrifices that a dying painter imposes upon his sister and others. Bolt modeled the play on the form of W. Somerset Maugham's *The Circle* (1921), even to the point of having the same act lengths. Bolt's imitation of Maugham is doubtless the flaw in the play. The plot is so tightly knit and moves so swiftly that it does not allow Bolt time to develop fully the characters in the play.

In his next play, *Flowering Cherry*, Bolt wished to escape the criticism of writing well-made plays with simplified characters, although eventually he "criticized the play as being uneasily straddled between naturalism and non-naturalism." Produced in 1957 in London's West End, the play had Ralph Richardson and Celia Johnson in the principal roles and ran for 435 performances. The central character, Jim Cherry, is an unsuccessful insurance salesman who dreams of returning one day to the rural Somerset of his childhood to plant a cherry orchard. However, when an inheritance would enable him to realize his dream, he rejects the opportunity to return to a rural life. The play was a critical and popular success in London, and Bolt received the *Evening Standard* Drama Award in 1957 for Most Promising British playwright. The six-character play has a strong unity of time and place and with "its extremely conventional and operatic conclusion with Cherry's death and his wife's departure, the play is a model of competent but extremely conservative dramatic structure." One critic called the play "a provocative, honest and mature drama." The popular success of *Flowering Cherry* enabled Bolt to devote full time to his writing. The play's success in London, however, was not matched by its reception two years later in New York, where the critics found that the play "lacked vitality and creativity."

Undoubtedly the best and most successful of Bolt's works is *A Man for All Seasons*. The play opened in London in July 1960 at the Globe Theatre, where it ran for over nine months before embarking on an even longer run in New York, where it opened in November 1961 and ran for a year and a half. The play won the Tony Award of the American Theatre Wing for best play in 1962 and the New York Drama Critics Circle Award for best foreign play the same year. The 1966 film version of the play won an Academy Award for best motion picture and Bolt received an Oscar for his adaptation. Paul Scofield appeared in both the stage and film versions. In the play Bolt dramatizes the well-known story of the martyrdom of Sir Thomas More who, torn between his loyalty to king and Catholicism, finds that he values his principles more than his life, and because he cannot pledge his allegiance to the king he is executed. Bolt described

his Thomas More as "a man with an adamantine sense of his own self. He knew where he began and left off, what area of himself he could yield to the encroachments of his enemies, and what to the encroachments of those he loved."

A Man for All Seasons shows two major changes in Bolt's work. First, the setting is historical rather than contemporary, and second, Bolt uses an open stage not cluttered by realistic sets, or as he describes it, a mise-en-scene "most recently associated with Bertolt Brecht." One critic said that "Robert Bolt has had the boldness and skill here to successfully carry Brecht's own theoretical pronouncements on Epic Theatre further than Brecht ever carried them himself in his major plays." Gone is the fourth-wall style of staging, and the characters in the play candidly acknowledge that they are indeed actors in a historical play.

Bolt's next play to reach the stage was *The Tiger and the Horse*, which opened in London on 24 Au-

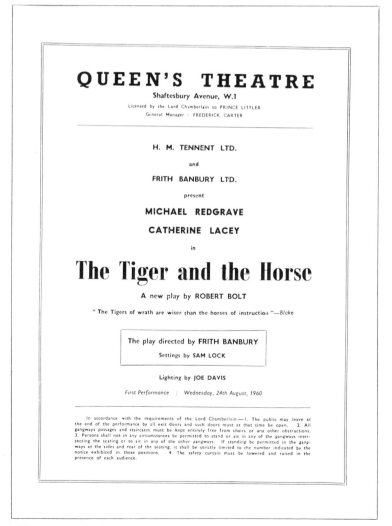

Program title page for the first production of Bolt's dramatization of a modern moral dilemma

gust 1960. Although it had been written before *A Man for All Seasons*, it opened a month after that play. Like Sir Thomas More in *A Man for All Seasons*, the central character of *The Tiger and the Horse* faces an important moral choice. Jack Dean has been asked to sign a ban-the-bomb petition. If he does, he will lose the chance to become the vice chancellor of the university; if he does not, he will lose his self-respect. Dean's wife, Gwendoline, also wants to sign the petition but knows that her signing will deny her husband his opportunity for advancement. Finally Dean decides in favor of signing because "The tygers of wrath are wiser than the horses of instruction." Bolt alludes to William Blake's "The Tyger" to show that an emotional judgment may be preferable to one based on reason. Bolt himself was a member of the Campaign for Nuclear Disarmament and went to prison for a brief period in 1961 for taking part in a demonstration. *The Tiger and the Horse* is an orthodox, well-made play with realistic dialogue displaying more Bolt's characteristic genius for West-End craftsmanship than the re-

pudiation of naturalism that Bolt was seeking.

As a screenwriter Bolt has achieved many successes. *Lawrence of Arabia*, which Bolt adapted from the writings of T. E. Lawrence, won an Academy Award for best motion picture of 1962, and Bolt's scenario was awarded a special trophy by the British Film Academy. For the film adaptation of Boris Pasternak's novel *Doctor Zhivago* (1965), Bolt won an Academy Award as he would in 1966 for *A Man for All Seasons*. Bolt has also written *Ryan's Daughter* (1970) and *Lady Caroline Lamb* (1972), in which his second wife, Sarah Miles (whom he married in 1969), appeared and which Bolt himself directed.

In 1963, returning to the theater, Bolt wrote *Gentle Jack*, which opened in November in London with Edith Evans and Kenneth Williams. The play, which can be looked upon as an adult fairy tale or an allegorical fantasy—reminiscent in theme of some of Bolt's radio plays—tells how Jack-in-the-Green (based on the god Pan) turns over his magical powers to the hero, Jacko. In his attempt to resolve the various conflicts around him through love, Jacko is

Jennifer Wright and Kynaston Reeves in the 1960 Queen's Theatre production of The Tiger and the Horse

thwarted by the destructive forces in man. One critic observed, "I have no doubt though that in writing about the polarity between gentleness and destructiveness, Bolt has found a theme which is capable of involving him far more deeply as a writer than any of his previous themes." Another critic saw the play as "a clash of the immoral world of monopoly capitalism with the amoral world of the ancient Jack-of-the-Green." However it is considered, the play is undoubtedly one of Bolt's most original works in structure, style, and content. Using the same form as he did for *A Man for All Seasons*, Bolt, like Brecht, did not try to create a realistic impression with his adult fairy tale set in modern times. His attempt to include both satire and fantasy with a "complicated plot that involves several shifts between two subjects and two areas of action" was new. Bolt described the play as an attempt "to combine all the elements of ritual, dance, and music in a specific modern context." The public, however, refused to accept Bolt's marked departure from the orthodox tradition of the well-

made, realistic plays with which he had become associated during his career. *Gentle Jack* ran for only seventy-five performances.

Bolt's next West End production was a children's play, *The Thwarting of Baron Bolligrew*, which was produced by the Royal Shakespeare Company in December 1965 and again in 1966 as a Christmas show. As in *Gentle Jack*, Bolt writes of the conflict of contrasting value systems. The play is a fairy tale about a dragon-slaying duke named Sir Oblong Fitz-Oblong and his clash with the evil Baron Bolligrew. One critic said that "Bolt's talent for larger-than-life figures is well-suited to children's plays. This one is oft performed and one of the best written this century."

With *Vivat! Vivat Regina!*, produced in 1970, first at the Chichester Festival and then at the Piccadilly Theatre in London, Bolt returned to adult drama. Presenting the tragic conflict between Queen Elizabeth and Mary, Queen of Scots, the play has been described as "something of a historical pageant, a brilliantly contrived mosaic of short

---

VIVAT! VIVAT REGINA!

Characters in order of speaking:

1st Court Lady	Isabel Metliss
2nd Court Lady	Angela Easton
Claud Nau	David Bird
Mary, Queen of Scots	Judy Parfitt
William Cecil	Mark Dignam
Elizabeth I of England	Margaret Tyzack
Robert Dudley	Norman Eshley
John Knox	Leonard Maguire
Bagpiper	Willie Cochrane
David Rizzio	Kenneth Caswell
Lord Morton	Archie Duncan
Lord Bothwell	David McKail
Lord Bishop of Durham	Brian Hawksley
A Cleric	Howard Benbrook
Sir Francis Walsingham	Edgar Wreford
de Quadra	Edward Atienza
Davison	Eilian Wyn
Henry Stuart, Lord Darnley	Dallas Adams
Ruthven	Glyn Grain
Lindsey	Alexander John
Scots Archbishop	Maurice Jones
Lord Mor	Brian Hawksley
Ormiston	Jonathan Mallard
Tala	Malcolm Rogers
A Doctor	Ken Grant
A Prisoner	Malcolm Rogers

Philip, King of Spain	Alastair Meldrum
The Pope	Kenneth Caswell
Jailers	Adrian Reynolds
	Ken Grant
Brewer	Adrian Reynolds
Courtiers, Lairds, Clerks, Servants, etc.	Glyn Grain, Ken Grant, Maurice Jones, Alastair Meldrum, Adrian Reynolds Stuart Knee

The action of the play takes place in France, England and Scotland.

FOR H. M. TENNENT LTD.
General Manager . BERNARD GORDON
Assistant to
Managing Director . . . Anthony Howell
Company and
Stage Manager . . . . . Robert Nelson
Deputy Stage Managers . . . . Jenny Bos
David Saxon
Assistant Stage Managers . . . Ken Grant
Stuart Knee
Production Manager . . . . Ian Dow
Lighting Designer . . . . . . Joe Davis
Chief Costume Supervisor . . Lily Taylor
Press Representative . . David Fairweather
(486 0681)

FOR CHICHESTER FESTIVAL PRODUCTION
General Manager . . . . Doreen Dixon
Production Manager . . . . Robert Selbie
Press Representative . David Fairweather

Costumes by
M. Berman Ltd.

Settings and furniture built by Ray Addison Ltd. Painted by Harkers' Studios. Properties made by Hester Rowbottom. Lighting equipment by Rank Strand Electric Ltd. Sound by Stage Sound. Headdresses and jewellery by Hugh Skillen. Shoes by Gamba. Make up by Stanley Hall. Wigs by Wig Creations. Wardrobe care by Fairy Snow. Fairy Toilet Soap supplied for the production by Proctor & Gamble Ltd.

This Theatre is fully air-conditioned for your greater comfort.

XERO-COPYING FOR THIS THEATRE BY RANK XEROX

FOR PICCADILLY THEATRE
General Manager . . . IAN B. ALBERY
Manager . . . . DAVID LEACH
Master Carpenter . . . . . . Harry Pegg
Chief Electrician . . . . Stanley Coppin
Box Office Manager . . . . John Hulbert
Assistants . . . . Howard Thomas
Anne Lytton
Open 10 am to 8 pm   01-437 4506/7

CATERING DEPARTMENT (01-836 9074)
General Manager . . . . VIVIAN BURNS

Additional lighting, stage and sound equipment for the Piccadilly Theatre supplied by Donmar Productions Ltd. Display of Photographs in the Foyer by courtesy of The Raymond Mander and Joe Mitchenson Theatre Collection.

The Management reserve the right to refuse admission, and to alter this programme, or to make any alteration in the cast which may be rendered necessary by illness or other unavoidable causes.

Patrons are reminded that it is strictly forbidden to take photographs or use any form or recording apparatus in the Theatre.

Outside performance hours this theatre is available for conferences or similar gatherings.

In accordance with the requirements of the G.L.C. 1.—The public may leave at the end of the performance by all exit doors and such doors must at that time be open. 2.—All gangways, passages and staircases must be kept entirely free from chairs or any other obstructions 3.—Persons shall not in any circumstances be permitted to stand or sit in any of the gangways intersecting the seating or to sit in any of the other gangways. If standing be permitted in the gangways at the sides and rear of the seating it shall be strictly limited to the number indicated in the notices exhibited in those positions. 4.—The safety curtain must be lowered and raised in the presence of each audience.

Cast list and credits for the first London production of Bolt's contemporary treatment of the conflict between Mary, Queen of Scots, and Elizabeth I of England

Archie Duncan, Judy Parfitt, and Barry Jackson in a scene from the 1970 London production of Vivat! Vivat Regina!

scenes." Again, as with *A Man for All Seasons*, "the historical distance afforded by the 16th century and the dramaturgical freedom associated with the theatre theatrical" admirably suits Bolt in developing a theme which runs throughout his work in interesting variations—that of the conflict between the natural man and the society within which he lives. In the case of *Vivat! Vivat Regina!*, one critic said that "In a suitably contemporary and frank treatment of the sex life of both monarchs Bolt demonstrates how that sexuality is deformed by state office," another that Elizabeth and Mary share the inability "to enter into normal family relationships," and another that the two women are "equal mirror-images of each other. Mary fails as a queen to succeed as a woman, Elizabeth as a woman to triumph as a queen." *Vivat! Vivat Regina!* points up Bolt's strengths and weaknesses as a playwright: again he has written a meticulous play in terms of structure and dialogue; again in so doing he did not go deeply enough into the rich materials of his text.

Not until seven years later did Bolt produce another play. A political drama set in the twentieth century, *State of Revolution* was staged first at the Birmingham Repertory Theatre and subsequently at the National Theatre in 1977. According to an acting edition, the play is about "the Russian Revolution and its chief personalities through the life of Lenin, opening at Gorky's villa on Capri in 1910 and ending just after Lenin's death with the suppression of his 'Testament' recommending the dismissal of Stalin." Bolt explained why he had chosen a modern event: "I'm a political animal. The Russian Revolution is the formative political event of this century. If you're politically interested you've got to be interested in the Russian Revolution and in Lenin." The critics' reactions to the play were mixed. It was called mighty and profound by some, lacking in passion by others; the equivocal compliments of "best-crafted" and "well-made" carried the implication that Bolt did not allow himself room to develop fully either characters or themes. However, no one questioned the seriousness of his themes: the place of sympathy, compassion, and tolerance in revolutionary action and the relationship between history and the hero—which creates which?

Throughout the years, Bolt's work has been taken more seriously by audiences than by critics, and Bolt's popularity with the public has been enhanced by his screenplays. Many critics, smitten by the theater of the absurd, have found Bolt's work old-fashioned but meticulously structured and realistic. But not all are unmindful of his importance and one critic frankly declared: "There is much to be said for playwrights who possess such skills, for it is they, finally, who preserve whatever life there is on the contemporary stage."

Screenplays:
Lawrence of Arabia, adapted from T. E. Lawrence's writings, Columbia, 1962;
Doctor Zhivago, adapted from Boris Pasternak's novel, MGM, 1965;
A Man for All Seasons, Columbia, 1966;
Ryan's Daughter, MGM, 1970;
Lady Caroline Lamb, United Artists, 1972.

Television Script:
A Man for All Seasons, BBC, 1957.

Radio Scripts:
The Master, BBC, 1953;
Fifty Pigs, BBC, 1953;
Ladies and Gentlemen, BBC, 1954;
A Man for All Seasons, BBC, 1954;
Mr. Sampson's Sundays, BBC, 1955;

The Last of the Wine, BBC, 1955;
The Window, BBC, 1958;
The Drunken Sailor, BBC, 1958;
The Banana Tree, BBC, 1961.

Other:
"English Theatre Today: The Importance of Shape," in *International Theatre Annual, III*, edited by Harold Hobson (London: Calder, 1958), pp. 140-145;
Cecil Woolf and John Bagguley, eds., *Authors Take Sides on Vietnam*, includes a contribution by Bolt (London: Peter Owen, 1967).

References:
Sally Emerson, "Playing the game: Robert Bolt and William Douglas Home," *Plays and Players*, 24 (June 1977): 10-15;
Ronald Hayman, "Like a Woman They Keep Going Back To," *Drama*, no. 98 (Autumn 1970): 57-64;
Hayman, *Robert Bolt* (London: Heinemann, 1969);
Myron Matlaw, *Modern World Drama* (New York: Dutton, 1972), pp. 96-97;
Barry Pree, "Robert Bolt," in *Behind the Scenes: Theater and Film Interviews from the 'Transatlantic Review'* (New York: Holt, Rinehart & Winston, 1971), pp. 199-204;
John Russell Taylor, *The Angry Theatre* (New York: Hill & Wang, 1969), p. 367.

Edward Bond
(18 July 1934-   )

Max Le Blond
National University of Singapore

PRODUCTIONS: *The Pope's Wedding*, 9 December 1962, Royal Court Theatre, London;
Saved, 3 November 1965, Royal Court Theatre, London;
A Chaste Maid in Cheapside, adapted from Thomas Middleton's play, 13 January 1966, Royal Court Theatre, London;
The Three Sisters, translated by Bond with Richard Cottrell from Anton Chekhov's play, 18 April 1967, Royal Court Theatre, London;
Early Morning, 31 March 1968, Royal Court Theatre, London;

Narrow Road to the Deep North, 24 June 1968, Belgrade Theatre, Coventry; 19 February 1969, Royal Court Theatre, London;
Black Mass, 22 March 1970, Lyceum Theatre, London;
Passion, 11 April 1971, Alexandra Park Racecourse, London;
Lear, 29 September 1971, Royal Court Theatre, London;
The Sea, 22 May 1973, Royal Court Theatre, London;
Bingo: Scenes of Money and Death, 14 November 1973,

Northcott Theatre, Exeter, Devon;

Spring Awakening, translated from Frank Wedekind's play, 28 May 1974, National Theatre, London;

The Fool: Scenes of Bread and Love, 18 November 1975, Royal Court Theatre, London;

Stone, 8 June 1976, Institute of Contemporary Arts Theatre, London;

The White Devil, adapted from John Webster's play, 12 July 1976, Old Vic Theatre, London;

We Come to the River, 12 June 1976, Royal Opera House, Covent Garden, London;

A-A-America! (*Grandma Faust: A Burlesque* and *The Swing: A Documentary*), 25 October 1976, Almost Free Theatre, London;

The Bundle, or, New Narrow Road to the Deep North, 13 January 1978, Warehouse Theatre, London;

The Woman: Scenes of War and Freedom, 10 August 1978, Olivier Theatre (National Theatre), London;

The Worlds, 8 March 1979, Newcastle Playhouse, Newcastle upon Tyne; 16 June 1981, New Half Moon Theatre, London;

Restoration, 21 July 1981, Royal Court Theatre, London;

Summer, 27 January 1982, Cottesloe Theatre, London.

BOOKS: *Saved* (London: Methuen, 1966; New York: Hill & Wang, 1966);

Early Morning (London: Calder & Boyars, 1968; New York: Hill & Wang, 1969; revised edition, London: Methuen, 1977);

Narrow Road to the Deep North (London: Methuen, 1968; New York: Hill & Wang, 1969);

The Pope's Wedding (London: Methuen, 1971; revised, 1977)—includes *The Pope's Wedding* and *Black Mass*;

Lear (London: Methuen, 1972; New York: Hill & Wang, 1972; revised edition, London: Methuen, 1978);

The Sea (London: Methuen, 1973; revised, 1978);

Bingo: Scenes of Money and Death (London: Methuen, 1974)—includes *Bingo: Scenes of Money and Death* and *Passion*;

The Fool and We Come to the River (London: Methuen, 1976);

We Come to the River: Libretto (Mainz: B. Schott's Söhne, 1976);

A-A-America! and Stone (London: Methuen, 1976; revised, 1981);

Plays: One: Saved, Early Morning, The Pope's Wedding (London: Methuen, 1977);

The Bundle, or, New Narrow Road to the Deep North (London: Methuen, 1978);

The Woman: Scenes of War and Freedom (London: Methuen, 1978; New York: Hill & Wang, 1979);

Plays: Two: Lear, The Sea, Narrow Road to the Deep North, Black Mass, Passion (London: Methuen, 1978);

Theatre Poems and Songs (London: Methuen, 1978);

Spring Awakening, translated from Frank Wedekind's play (London: Methuen, 1980);

The Worlds (London: Methuen, 1980)—includes *The Activist Papers*;

Restoration (London: Methuen, 1981); revised version, in *Restoration and The Cat* (London: Methuen, 1982);

Summer (London: Methuen, 1982).

Edward Bond was born of working-class parents in the North London suburb of Holloway. He attended state schools till the age of fourteen, left school without completing the eleven-plus examination to qualify for grammar school, and subsequently fulfilled his national service obligations in the British army. Among the honors Bond has received are the George Devine Award for *Early Morning* (1968) and the John Whiting Award for *Narrow Road to the Deep North* (1968), the latter shared with Peter Barnes. Although little is known of Bond's personal life, the most significant consideration is that he belongs to that generation of British playwrights which includes John Osborne, Arnold Wesker, and Harold Pinter. As individuals, they came to maturity in the decade immediately succeeding World War II; as dramatists, they have been integrally associated with the postwar renaissance of British drama. Bond's work warrants special attention in any consideration of the achievement of this period: stylistically an eclectic, he has demonstrated his skills in the realistic mode and is also a gifted exponent of the predominantly Continental antirealistic traditions of dramatic writing. Like Osborne and Wesker, Bond is essentially a social satirist whose works document the evils of modern British society and of contemporary Western civilization. He utilizes both realist as well as symbolist dramatic methods in his plays and has provided contemporary British theater with some of its most compelling images of a corrupt and decaying society.

Throughout his career, Bond has structured his works around social and public, rather than private and personal themes. Perhaps the most misunderstood of his concerns has been his preoccupation with violence, a preoccupation which often has brought him the catcalls and vilification of both the general public and the critical establishment. Bond's plays are indeed crowded with vividly particularized images of macabre, gruesome violence. The most notorious of these is the stoning of the baby in *Saved* (1965), which is arguably the most horrifying episode in postwar British drama. In *The Sea* (1973), the body of a man drowned at sea is washed miles inland by floodwaters and finally snags on the branches of an apple tree in his own garden; the man's wife and children, themselves stranded on the roof of their house by the flood, are for three days confronted with the sight of his putrefying body.

Yet, such images do not amount to a morbid and gratuitous indulgence in violence for its own sake. Bond himself has noted: "I write about violence as naturally as Jane Austen wrote about manners. Violence shapes and obsesses our society, and if we do not stop being violent we have no future. People who do not want writers to write about violence want to stop them writing about us and our time. It would be immoral not to write about vio-

lence." Violence, as this comment suggests, functions as a controlling element of the vision dramatized in Bond's plays. At the heart of Bond's response to society is the powerful conviction that industrial capitalist civilization, the whole system of political and economic arrangements on which British society is based, is fundamentally unjust and dehumanizing. The social, political, and economic structures of capitalism, Bond believes, create aggression and violence in men by insidiously encouraging the lust for profit, cutthroat competition, and by forcing men into patterns of work which result in the loss of a sense of individuality and in physical and emotional deprivation. Modern men live in "urban, crowded regimented groups, working like machines (mostly for the benefit of other men)" and possess negligible control over their own lives. Through the perpetuation of this injustice and exploitation of humanity, society breeds the aggression and violence which threaten to destroy it.

Throughout Bond's work, therefore, is a preoccupation with the problem of violence as a social phenomenon and with the search for a more humane society. These concerns are already present in the earliest of Bond's plays to be produced, *The Pope's Wedding*, staged at London's Royal Court Theatre in 1962. Bond had in fact written some fifteen plays before this but none has been published or produced, and he has not made them available for study. *The Pope's Wedding*, which deals with the haunting, obsessive relationship between Scopey, a young East Anglian farm worker, and Alen, a recluse, contains an early and not altogether coherent statement of the theme of violence. Scopey's growing obsession with Alen causes him to isolate himself from his friends and from Pat, his wife, and ultimately results in Scopey's murdering Alen. But the basis of the relationship and the act of violence are never fleshed out by a solid context of motivation, and the result is a play that hovers uneasily between a grimly naturalistic depiction of squalor and poverty in the English rural working class and a Pinteresque dramatic landscape in which the desire to find a rational basis for human action is consistently thwarted by insufficient details of character, motive, and event.

In *Saved*, produced in 1965 at the Royal Court Theatre, Bond transferred his attention from a rural setting to an urban South London working-class environment and shaped his concern with social violence into a controlling theatrical symbol— the stoning of a baby in a pram—which generated

Scene from the 1965 Royal Court Theatre production of Saved

one of the great theatrical controversies of the 1960s. *Saved* treats the lives of a group of young working-class characters and evokes a powerful and bitter portrait of individuals condemned to a state of utter cultural, educational, spiritual, and emotional deprivation, individuals condemned to crawl like lice on the underbelly of the welfare state. The central figure in the play is Len, a young man as much a part of the working-class milieu of South London as the rest of the characters, but set apart from his girl friend Pam and from the "yobbos" such as Pete, Mike, Barry, and Colin, by his enduring, pathetically inarticulate struggle to affirm human values of tolerance, compassion, and affection in a dehumanized environment. The central scene of the play takes place in a London park, when Pam's baby—it is a testament to the dehumanization of this environment that the identity of the infant's father is uncertain—is set upon, tortured, and finally stoned to death by the yobbos in an orgiastic release of aggressive instincts. The shock and pain generated by that scene should not deceive viewers into dismissing it as a clever piece of theatrical sensationalism. The act is meaningful, even if hideous,

for it is essentially an act of repudiation, of aggression against a society which has failed to provide an environment embodying the values to which it pays lip service. The stoning scene is a brilliant dramatic symbol which indicts the welfare state for its failure to care, for perpetuating or ignoring conditions of social and cultural deprivation which dehumanize individuals and thereby create the aggression and violence that society purports to abhor.

Len is the lone figure standing against this violence; at the end of the play, despite Pam's disloyalty as a friend and infidelity as a lover, he retains his capacity for tenderness and concern for the well-being of others. Around him, Pam and her family resume the bovine rhythms of their existence, largely ignoring him as he mends a chair. The image of the mending of a chair with which the play closes suggests the idea of reconstruction, and Bond himself has described the play as "almost irresponsibly optimistic." Whatever hope there is, however, rests with the isolated individual, rather than with the general run of humanity. *Saved* is a dramatic masterpiece which has survived the "slaughter" of its early critical reception and come to be recognized as the "first great dramatic self-indictment of the welfare state."

Bond's next play at the Royal Court Theatre was *Early Morning*, produced in 1968. Earlier that year, *Early Morning* earned him the distinction of being the author of the last play to be banned by the Lord Chamberlain before the powers of theatrical censorship invested in his office were abolished. Like *Saved*, *Early Morning* is one of the major works of Bond's dramatic career, breaking away from the realistic depiction of working-class life in the earlier play and utilizing expressionist and surrealist techniques such as deliberate distortions of chronological and historical perspective and outrageous patterns of grotesque image and symbol to create a nightmare vision of a doomed and tottering capitalist Britain. The play's action is set in nineteenth-century England, a period which represents for Bond the zenith of industrialism and capitalism, and he selects as a dominant symbol the figure of Queen Victoria, who presided over a nation that is portrayed in the full flower of its imperialist and capitalist energies. Britain is presented as aggressive, militarist, exploitative, violent, and bent upon its own destruction as well as the destruction of others. Victoria, depicted in the play as involved in a lesbian relationship with Florence Nightingale, comes to symbolize the destructive forces of capitalist civilization as well as the prudishness and hypocrisy of Victorian values. To stress the persistence of these evils in contemporary historical reality there are deliberate anachronisms and manipulations of historical detail, such as references to Hitler and Einstein, to the English football club, Manchester United, and to the Radio One Service of the BBC. The other characters include Victoria's consort, Prince Albert, the politicians Disraeli and Gladstone, and the twenty-year-old princes, Arthur and George, the latter being Prince of Wales. The intensely convoluted plot is centered upon the political intrigues which involve the throne, and there are rapid shifts and countershifts of allegiance. Through the depiction of these intrigues, Bond develops a vision of self-hating humanity, of a civilization riven by hatred and shaped ultimately by a profound death wish. This theme of a destructive, self-hating society is reinforced through the macabre symbolic motif of cannibalism which informs *Early Morning*. Len, a working-class character, kills a man for breaking into a cinema queue, proceeds to eat him, and is joined by the crowd. Later in the play, after the intrigues have climaxed in the total destruction of the conspirators, the action switches to the after-life with the closing scenes set in Heaven. Here too, cannibalism is rife, while on earth, Florence Nightingale has opened a brothel and numbers Disraeli and Gladstone among her customers.

Like Len in *Saved*, Prince Arthur in this play functions as the lone character who questions the brutality of the social system in which he finds himself. Arthur is in fact a Siamese twin to Prince George, that relationship functioning for Bond as a symbolic equivalent for the situation of the individual dimly aware of the injustice of his society, but at the same time confused and deceived by the process of socialization into accepting the evils of the system. Thus society inculcates the values of freedom, justice, and democracy and uses these values to justify the exploitation of foreign nations. George represents the socialized version of Arthur and thus serves to confuse Arthur in his attempts to confront the evils of his society. In the closing scenes of the play, Arthur acquires a fuller understanding of the evils of Victoria's society, but as in *Saved*, the rebel fails to change his society. Arthur is killed and the civilization of Victoria reigns supreme in heaven. As the various details of plot, character, and symbolism suggest, *Early Morning* is indeed a bizarre piece of dramatic writing, demanding a great deal from audience and reader alike; in the theater however, it is a compelling experience, its convolutions of plot and structures of image and symbol functioning to evoke a nightmarish dramatic vision of society in crisis which is unique in its satiric force. Early critical responses were often hostile, and the first production was attacked as an "incoherent, innocuous farrago" and as a "theatrical strip cartoon." But the work has survived because, as Ronald Bryden noted in an early review, it is "serious and passionately moral" and also because ultimately, as John Russell Taylor observes, "the strength of Bond's own obsession bludgeons us into suspending disbelief."

If *Early Morning* and *Saved* are explorations in dramatic terms of Bond's conviction of society as radically corrupt and violent, succeeding works represent development of his vision in that they examine in greater detail the means by which those in power legitimize the evils of an exploitative social system, or they even go on to consider the possibilities and dilemmas of revolutionary change. For example, in *Narrow Road to the Deep North*, set in Japan in "about the seventeenth, eighteenth or nineteenth centuries," Bond mocks the civilized pretensions of British imperialism. He also satirizes the role of Christian missionaries in Japan and, by implication, elsewhere in British imperial territories: the representatives of the Church are seen essentially in terms of a Marxist conception of religion as a superstructure which functions to legitimize the interests of the capitalist and imperialist power. Through the contrast between the Japanese ruler Shogo on the one hand and characters such as the Commodore and the missionary figure Georgina on the other, Bond sets up an opposition between two forms of tyranny, two modes of social control and subjugation of a populace. Shogo practices rule by despotism, the exercise of political control in which order is maintained by the threat of bloody and violent repression. The British imperialists on the other hand practice a more subtle form of political subjugation. Georgina tells the Japanese poet-priest Basho: "instead of atrocity I use morality." She adds that "the missions and

churches and bishops and magistrates and politicians and papers will tell people they are sin and must be kept in order. If sin didn't exist it would be necessary to invent it." Bond here indicts the British political and religious establishments, who force-feed the common people an ideology of human depravity, thereby making it easier to inflict upon them the yoke of authoritarian rule and to make them serve the interests of the ruling clique. The play's satiric points are efficiently, eloquently made, but *Narrow Road to the Deep North* ultimately lacks the imaginative power and sheer theatrical panache of *Early Morning*.

Bond's *Lear* (1971), set in Britain in the year of the world 3100, contains episodes of terrifying violence, including the torture of Lord Warrington

Gillian Martell and Kenneth Cranham in a scene from the 1969 Royal Court Theatre production of Narrow Road to the Deep North

and the scrupulously scientific—and anachronistic—removal of the eyes of the old King himself. A prisoner, charged with the task of removing Lear's eyes, says during the process: "Note how the eye passes into the lower chamber and is received into a soothing solution of formaldehyde crystals." This play, however, is not a mere restatement of the themes of earlier works. Going back to Shakespeare's own historical sources for the story of Lear, Bond reworks the narrative of the deposed monarch, stripped of power by his daughters Bodice and Fontanelle, and stresses the despotism of the old king's rule. Lear's overthrow, however, does not result in an enlightened new social order, for Bodice and Fontanelle are infected by the same lust for power as Lear and by the same capacity for maintaining power through cruelty and violent repression which was the hallmark of their father's rule. Ultimately, Bodice and Fontanelle themselves become victims of rebellions. In the action of the play, one ruling clique replaces another only to be replaced in its turn. It is arguable that Bond was offering *Lear* as a parable of political violence in the twentieth century. As in *Early Morning*, there are anachronistic references to electric bulbs and honours lists to suggest the continuity of past and present, and the fundamental lesson which Bond would draw for the modern period is that those implicated in revolutionary violence and the construction by force of a new social order are often infected by the same capacity for brutally repressive political rule which characterized their enemies. At the end of the play, Lear sees the great wall which he had dedicated his career to building as the symbol of a social order based on the denial of a basic human need. Thus he pleads with the latest revolutionary leader, ironically named Cordelia (in Shakespeare's play Cordelia is the daughter who remains loyal to her father): "Our lives are awkward and fragile and we have only one thing to keep us sane: pity, and the man without pity is mad." Lear is killed trying, in a pathetic, noble gesture, to dig up his great wall.

Among the plays immediately following *Lear* are two works focused not on a character made famous by creative genius, but rather on literary creators themselves. The subjects of *Bingo: Scenes of Money and Death* (1973) and *The Fool: Scenes of Bread and Love* (1975) are the lives of William Shakespeare and John Clare respectively. Both works articulate a conception of the problematic and even destructive relationship between an author and his society. Bond's dramatic exploration of the life of Shakespeare stresses the contradiction between the profound compassion and humanity of Shakespeare's vision of man and his role as a property owner in society which, in Bond's view, led the dramatist to elevate his own selfish material interests above the cause of social justice. Bond contends that as a property owner Shakespeare led an existence closer to Goneril (one of the two evil daughters of King Lear) than to Lear. "He supported and benefited from the Goneril-society—with its prisons, workhouses, whipping, starvation, mutilation, pulpit-hysteria and all the rest of it."

The Shakespeare of Bond's *Bingo* acquiesced in the enclosure of common land which led to the poor being deprived of land and livelihood. *The Fool*, a play about the life of poet John Clare, is also concerned with the enclosures and the consequent suffering of the peasantry. As the common fen is drained and converted into private property to fatten the purses of already wealthy landowners, Clare and his friends are forced into a life of scavenging and theft in order to survive. Both *Bingo* and *The Fool* thus dramatize the rapacious materialism of a society which creates the conditions of a dehumanized environment and then punishes individuals for behaving in a manner consonant with such conditions. In *The Fool*, John Clare finally suffers a breakdown, the victim of a society which condemns him to neglect and poverty because it finds the truths concerning social injustice embodied in his poems dangerously subversive. Clare however achieves a victory in that he refuses to compromise his poetic integrity and write verse acceptable to the authorities. Clare thus tells the establishment figure Lord Milton: "I've eaten my portion of the universe an' I shall die of it. It was bitter fruit. But I had more out of the stones in your field than you had out of the harvest."

Bond's work since *Bingo* and *The Fool*, and since the slightly earlier play *The Sea*, a somewhat portentously atmospheric piece returning to the theme of modern civilization's death wish, reveals a sustained commitment to the themes of violence in society, the possible justifications of revolutionary violence, and the destructiveness of industrial capitalism. Bond himself has provided a useful summary of the central thematic concern of *The Bundle, or, New Narrow Road to the Deep North* (1978), a play which returns to the scenario of *Narrow Road to the Deep North*: "The people in *The Bundle* live by a river. Directly or indirectly they all live from it. From time to time it floods and destroys them. If, as the play invites, you substitute factories and offices—all industrialism—for the river, then my purpose is plain." In *The Woman: Scenes of War and Freedom* (1978), first performed in the Olivier au-

Programme note for The Fool. Draft. Page 4   20.9.75

But the gap between the initial triumphs of technology and its final
apotheosis in Utopia may be so great, that technolgy will simply enable the
irrationality of a society that changes only slowly to panic so much that it
destroys the species. Technology cannot therefore produce Utopia out of the
hat like a white rabbit. Culture must be fought out on its own ground as well.
And that cultural struggle, while of course it cant exist in a vacuum, cannot
all the same be reduced to something else. Without technological invention
and activity there could be no abundance, no destruction of myth, no Utopia.
But without a cultural struggle technology can remain allied to irrationalism
and therefore be destructive. Brecht said: First bread, then morals. That is
true - as far as it goes. But morals dont follow bread like a dog sniffing
after its dinner. Nor are morals the smile on the face of a well-fed man.
Morals exist only in a culture: wihout that they can by shibboleths - as in
primitive societies - or hypocrasy - as in Western democracy. So culture must
be articulated in its own terms.

So what is culture ? Culture is the only possibility for rationality by the
only species capable of rationality, human beings. It is the only possibility
of assuring the continuatiop of xxxxx the only species free from instinctual
captivity, the human species. Culture is the implimentation of rationality
in all human activities - economic, xxitxxxi social, political, industrial,
domestic and so on. It is the rational ordering of human existence. It can
co-exist with myths - but not in Plato's sense, because it must not take the
myths as truth. There can no longer be any noble lies. Its myths will by
hypothesis. To achieve a culture various things are necessary: an efficient
technocracy (an technocracy that could only get water out of a well by
poisoning it would not be efficient), a self-perpetuating ecology, a social
structure which does not need to lie about human nature in order to justify
the force it needs to maintain itself - lies in the historical sequence:
some men are slaves, all men are sinners till they are saved, all men are
violent behind the policeman's back (presumably policeman are an exception in
human nature). That culture is an ideal state not yet achieved. Our present
social organisation specifically requires that we live in ignorance. Culture
is a state of knowledge. Our society tries to maintain itself, and to sweeten
its violence, by consumer affluence. What of consumer affluence ?

Capitalism destroys itself by advertising. Advertising destroys its social base.
Capitalism depends on trade unions being acquiesent and business aggressive.
The worker must know his place. He is, in any case, lazier than the entrepre-ne
ur. (If this is so, would it ever be possible to prevent strikes or malinger-
ing ? Capitalism seems, when it criticizes the workshy shiftless etc., to
be objecting to the axiom on which it bases its xpningxx) philosophy.) But
advertising tells the worker, as consumer, to demand everything, to want
everything, to need everything: the consumer is the master, and he is entitled
to the latest gadgets, adult toys, the newest life-style and so forth. So
capitalism depends on the worker being schizophrenic: a placid worker, a
rampaging, selfish, egocentic consumer. Advertising incites strikes. It goads
workers into demanding, needing, more. Advertising therefore destroys the
social basis of capitalism. Capitalism must advertise agressively to provoke
consumption - and in doing this it destroys its social base. The consumer
cannot accept the role assigned to him as a worker. Not only this, but
because the consumer-worker is goaded into an ultimately unrewarding consumptio
, the many of the foundations of a culture are destroyed by neglect. If the
nation's money must be spent on consuming erzats satisfactions of affluence
there is less and less money to spend on health, education, city care, the
socialization of the young. So "consumer affluence" progressively impoverishes
a community. The necessities, and the decencies, of life are neglected - in
favour of a trivializing and ultimately impoverishing consumption. And it rema
ins true that while some of the rich get richer all of the poor get poorer.
So just a technology by itself cannot make a culture, nor can affluence.
It is obviously important to be aware of this in an age of science.
And in an age of consumerism we have to remember that their can be no culture
without ideas. We are a rational species - and when we are not rational we
are in a state of aggressive decay, as I've said - so the idea of a culture
of drugged hedonism, perpetual sensual stimulation, lights and smells, is
false. The bright people would murder one another on the street.

And so we must answer the question what is culture. The role of technology is
clear: to be inventive and active, and to provide work for people as long
as it is needed. What is the role of the artist ? I've said that the artist
is needed to help to build culture and that his role cant be reduced to any
other. What is the artists role - or, because that stresses specialism too
much - what is the role of art in creating culture ?

Draft of Bond's program note for The Fool

ditorium of the National Theatre on London's South Bank (with Bond directing), the dramatist turns his imagination to Greek history and mythology to create a long and difficult play which is set in the Aegean in the time of the Trojan War and focuses upon themes such as the horror and absurdity of war and the evils of religious superstition. Bond's most recent work for the stage includes *The Worlds*, which returns to a modern British setting. *The Worlds* was premiered at the Newcastle Playhouse on 8 March 1979 and treats the subject of revolutionary violence and its usefulness as a response to the corruptions of contemporary society. *Restoration*, first performed at the Royal Court Theatre on 21 July 1981, is a satiric comedy set in eighteenth-century England. The play focuses on the intrigues of the aristocrat Lord Are, who kills his wife, whom he married for money, and then places the blame for the killing on an illiterate footman. The play engages themes such as social injustice, the complexities of the English class system, and the abuses of aristocratic privilege. *Summer*, premiered at the Cottesloe Theatre, London, on 27 January 1982, is set in an unnamed European country, and returns to the contemporary world to deal with a set of characters seeking to confront or come to terms with their past and its legacy of anxieties and bitterness.

Impressive as these recent achievements have been, none of Bond's works of the late 1970s has generated the critical excitement of early works such as *Saved* and *Early Morning*, an indication, perhaps, that his public, while willing to be respectful, may be more difficult to excite and compel than in the early years of his playwriting career.

Despite such considerations, however, Bond's achievement in the theater to date possesses a solidity and an artistic integrity matched by few writers of his generation. It has often been charged against Bond that his pronouncements on society are long-winded and intellectually naive, that he has a pronounced tendency to think in terms of simplistic abstractions: good versus bad, us versus them. Indeed, Bond has never satisfactorily resolved the problem of how society is originally infected by evil, given the fact that it is men who make up society and that, by his own account, men are born essentially noble and good. These considerations, however, are fundamentally irrelevant in that they pertain to Bond as social theorist and not as a man of the theater. Bond's strength lies not in a capacity for intellectual abstraction but in his great gift for the

creation of theatrical images which express with force, resonance, and complexity a vision of modern society in crisis. His place in the front ranks of postwar British dramatists seems assured.

Screenplays:

Blow-Up, by Bond, Michelangelo Antonioni, and Tonino Guerra, adapted from Julio Cortazar's story, 1967;

Laughter in the Dark, adapted by Bond and others from Vladimir Nabokov's novel, United Artists, 1969;

Michael Kohlhaas, by Bond and others, Columbia, 1969;

Walkabout, by Bond and others, Twentieth Century-Fox, 1971.

Periodical Publications:

"When Violence is Meant to Shock," *Guardian*, 12 November 1965, p. 12;

"Beating Barbarism," *Sunday Times Weekly Review*, 25 November 1973, p. 37;

"Work in Hand," *Guardian*, 13 January 1978, p. 8.

Interviews:

"Edward Bond: An Interview by Giles Gordon," *Transatlantic Review*, no. 22 (Autumn 1966): 7-15;

Ronald Bryden, "Society Makes Men Animals," *Observer Review*, 9 February 1969, p. 27;

John Calder, Harold Hobson, Jane Howell, and Irving Wardle, "A Discussion with Edward Bond," *Gambit*, 5, no. 17 (1970): 5-38;

Karl-Heinz Stoll, "Interviews with Edward Bond and Arnold Wesker," *Twentieth Century Literature*, 22 (December 1976): 411-432.

References:

Tony Coult, *The Plays of Edward Bond* (London: Methuen, 1977);

Malcolm Hay and Philip Roberts, *Bond: A Study of His Plays* (London: Methuen, 1980);

Hay and Roberts, *Edward Bond: A Companion to the Plays* (London: Theatre Quarterly Publications, 1978);

Richard Scharine, *The Plays of Edward Bond* (London: Associated University Presses, 1976);

John Russell Taylor, "British Dramatists: The New Arrivals, no. 5: Edward Bond," *Plays and Players*, 17 (August 1970): 16-18;

Simon Trussler, *Edward Bond* (Harlow: Longman, 1976).

John Bowen

(5 November 1924-   )

Betsy Greenleaf Yarrison
Rutgers University

PRODUCTIONS: *I Love You, Mrs. Patterson*, 1964, Cambridge; 1964, London;

The Corsican Brothers, 1965, televised; 17 March 1970, Greenwich Theatre, London;

After the Rain, adapted from Bowen's novel, 1 September 1966, Hampstead Theatre Club, London;

Silver Wedding, 1967, televised; produced again in *We Who Are About To . . .* , 6 February 1969, Hampstead Theatre Club, London; produced again in *Mixed Doubles: An Entertainment on Marriage* (a revised version of *We Who Are About To . . .*), 9 April 1969, Comedy Theatre, London;

Fall and Redemption of Man, 5 December 1967, London Academy of Music and Dramatic Art Theatre, London; produced again as *Fall and Redemption*, 1974, New York;

Little Boxes (*The Coffee Lace* and *Trevor*), 26 February 1968, Hampstead Theatre Club, London;

The Disorderly Women, adapted from Euripides' *Bacchae*, 19 February 1969, Stables Theatre Club, Manchester; 5 November 1970, Hampstead Theatre Club, London;

The Waiting Room, 7 July 1970, Soho Theatre, London;

Robin Redbreast, 10 December 1970, BBC Television, London; 1974, Guildford;

Heil Caesar, 1973, televised; 25 April 1974, Midland Arts Theatre, Birmingham;

Diversions, 1973, London;

Roger, in *Mixed Blessings*, 1973, Capitol Theatre, Horsham, Sussex;

Miss Nightingale, 1974, televised; revised as *Florence Nightingale*, 1975, Canterbury;

Which Way Are You Facing?, 1976, Bristol;

Singles, 23 June 1977, Greenwich Theatre, London;

The Fortunate Conspiracy, adapted from Pierre de Marivaux's play, 1977, London;

Bondage, 10 April 1978, Soho Theatre, London.

SELECTED BOOKS: *The Truth Will Not Help Us: Embroidery on an Historical Theme* (London: Chatto & Windus, 1956);

After the Rain [novel] (London: Faber & Faber, 1958; New York: Ballantine, 1959);

The Centre of the Green (London: Faber & Faber, 1959; New York: McDowell Obolensky, 1960);

Storyboard (London: Faber & Faber, 1960);

The Birdcage (London: Faber & Faber, 1962; New York: Harper & Row, 1962);

The Essay Prize, with a Holiday Abroad and The Candidate: Plays for Television (London: Faber & Faber, 1962);

I Love You, Mrs. Patterson (London: Evans, 1964);

A World Elsewhere (London: Faber & Faber, 1966; New York: Coward-McCann, 1967);

After the Rain [play] (London: Faber & Faber, 1967; New York: Random House, 1968; revised edition, London: Faber & Faber, 1972);

Fall and Redemption of Man (London: Faber & Faber, 1968); republished as *Fall and Redemption* (London: Faber & Faber, 1969);

The Disorderly Women, adapted from Euripides' *Bacchae* (London: Methuen, 1969);

Little Boxes (London: Methuen, 1968; New York: French, 1970);

The Corsican Brothers (London: Methuen, 1970);

The Waiting Room (London: French, 1971; New York: French, 1971);

Heil Caesar (London: French, 1974).

John Bowen belongs to that small group of playwrights who, since the 1950s, have undertaken to write serious original dramas intended for performance on television. Since Bowen shifted his attention from the novel to the play in the 1960s, he has divided his efforts more or less equally between the theater and television, writing some plays specifically for the stage and others specifically for television, then adapting some of his television plays for subsequent performance in the theater.

John Griffith Bowen was born in Calcutta, India, and at the age of six was brought to England, where he attended British boarding schools and spent his holidays shuttled among grandparents and other close relatives. He returned to India during World War II, serving as a captain in the Mahratha Light Infantry from 1943 to 1947. Admitted to Pembroke College, Oxford, in 1947, he

was obliged to delay his entrance until a space was available for him, so he taught school for a year and entered Oxford in 1948. There he read history, contemplated a career as an actor, and dabbled at writing. After receiving a B.A. in 1951, he was awarded the Frere Exhibition in Indian studies, so he remained at St. Anthony's College, Oxford, for graduate work in history. During the academic year 1952-1953 he taught English at Ohio State University, spending the summer of 1953 hitchhiking across the United States before returning to England in the fall. He was awarded an M. A. in 1953 from Oxford, but was unable to complete his doctorate because the British government withdrew his scholarship. He became an assistant editor, and later a senior editor, at the *Sketch* magazine, where he worked for three years. In 1956, his first novel,

The Truth Will Not Help Us, was published, and he left the *Sketch* to become an advertising copywriter. He produced two more novels in quick succession then, in 1960, abandoned his position as copy chief at a major London advertising agency to devote himself exclusively to writing. It was at this point in his career that his association with television began; he was asked to become a script consultant for Associated Television, and since the early 1960s he has written more than twenty plays for television and dozens of episodes for television series, including the ambitious and controversial political serial, *The Guardians* (1971).

Bowen's earliest television plays—*A Holiday Abroad* (1960), *The Essay Prize* (1960), *The Jackpot Question* (1961), and *The Candidate* (1961)—were all conscientious attempts to explore serious moral issues through storylines that would be readily accessible to the average television viewer. As he explains in the introduction to a 1962 collection of three of these early plays: "If you believe, as I do, that a writer is not just making something, but communicating something, is trying to share a kind of insight, a way of looking at life, an enjoyment of the complexity of human motives, the ambivalence of human behaviour, and if you believe that this sharing, the making an act of communication and the response to it, is what one means by 'art,' and that the sharing of artistic experience is important to man, then you will not want to be cut off from those many people who do not have the habit of reading books. . . . If you are a person, as I am, who believes that democracy doesn't work if one begins by assuming that three-quarters of the people can be written off as 'consumers', as those to whom one feeds prepackaged moral attitudes and stereotypes of human behaviour, if you believe that all men are born with the capacities for moral choice and the exercise of reason, but that those capacities will atrophy if they are not used, then also you will want to write seriously for television and to try to communicate your own moral vision within the form of the television play."

While the dominant influence on this line of thinking appears to have been Bowen's recently terminated career in advertising, one can see quite clearly in his first plays, all written for television, the emergence of themes and issues that would preoccupy Bowen and dominate his work for the next twenty years: the manipulation of one human being by another, the struggle between rational man and instinctive man, the loneliness and isolation of people not at peace with their surroundings, the hunger for power at odds with the hunger for values, the failure of individuals to form lasting emotional bonds with one another, and the prevalence of self-deception in modern life. According to Bowen, in both his novels and his plays "there is a statement of the need for Ibsen's 'Life Lie' even when one knows it to be a lie, and Forster's 'Only connect' becomes 'Only accept' in my work."

A Holiday Abroad, *The Essay Prize*, and *The Candidate* are all concerned with disillusionment and with the discovery through disillusionment of the extent of one's self-deception. In *A Holiday Abroad*, an English schoolboy is invited by the wealthy father of his closest friend to spend a week at their home on the continent; not surprisingly, the experience makes him something of a snob, and it is only after he has railed at his widowed mother for allowing him to go and thus to become disenchanted with their poverty-governed life that he learns why he was actually invited. His friend's father has smuggled a diamond necklace into England by concealing it in young Tom's luggage, which was unlikely to be opened at customs and inspected for contraband. In *The Essay Prize*, a father is forced by his son to confront his own failure, his intellectual arrogance, his pretentious overrepresentation of himself as a writer, and his corrosive jealousy of his son's superior literary talent. In *The Candidate*, successful provincial businessman James Glover learns from his wife and son that, much to his surprise, he is possessed of an ambition so powerful that he is willing to sacrifice his business career and, if need be, his marriage to obtain a parliamentary seat. With characteristic dramatic irony, Bowen grounds his character's self-discovery in new knowledge that he has acquired from others: Glover has no reason to question his motives until it is pointed out to him that the local party is very lukewarm in its support of his candidacy and that the qualities which make him such an effective businessman will likely make him a mediocre and miserable politician. Such reversal is typical of Bowen's work. He generally does not devise highly original plots, but he does provide more-or-less predictable plots with unexpected twists and small, pleasant departures from convention.

Bowen's early television plays are in the realistic tradition; he has said more than once that he was initially attracted to television because he admired naturalistic acting but not naturalistic staging. His first stage play, *I Love You, Mrs. Patterson* (1964), was also conventionally realistic. The play, which treats the love affair between a schoolboy and the wife of one of his teachers, was labeled Ibsenesque by Bowen and has been aptly described by Ronald Hayman as "well carpentered." But in the mid-1960s, Bowen began to depart from realism and to experiment with writing adaptations as well as original plays. His 1965 television play *The Corsican Brothers*, which he revised and expanded for the stage in 1970, is emblematic of both new directions in his work: the play is a diffuse and semiserious costume epic loosely based on Dion Boucicault's dramatization of a story by Alexandre Dumas. Bowen, always conscious of his models, called the play Stendhalian, and it does seem so in its odd blend of witty, urbane dialogue and grand opera plot. But Bowen's theatricalization is actually somewhat Brechtian; in particular, he has added nineteenth-century songs, masks, and toy properties representing their real-life counterparts to the melodramatic scenario. Identical twin brothers fall in love with the same girl. When one brother is killed in a duel, the other must take up the sword to avenge his murder only moments after he has lectured his villagers on the pernicious futility of the vendetta. Perhaps because of its curious splicing of elements of tragedy with elements of farce, the play was not a success either in its television or stage versions.

Brechtian theatrical innovation worked better for Bowen when he successfully adapted his novel *After the Rain* (1958) for the stage in 1966. (He had written a stage version of *After the Rain* in 1960 for Bryan Bailey of the Belgrade Theatre, Coventry, but had withdrawn the play after Bailey's death.) *After the Rain*, which enjoyed modestly successful runs in both London and New York, is a philosophical satire that takes as its opening premise the destruction of the world by flood and the creation by its six survivors of a new society based on totalitarian socialism. The play concerns the survivors' mythic voyage through Chaos to Enlightenment—a trip marked by murder, mutiny, jealousy, lust, and greed. Bowen credited Brecht, Pirandello, and the Chinese theater with providing ideas for the dramatization of *After the Rain*, but the play more immediately recalls Peter Weiss's *Marat/Sade*, which had been staged in England in 1964. Stage-managed by an imperious lecturer, who narrates the play and gives commands to the actors, *After the Rain* uses an antirealistic mise-en-scene, including masks, imaginary properties, placards, and other trappings of the epic theater, well suited to its self-consciously archetypal plot and one-dimensional characters. As in *Marat/Sade*, the story of the voyage is entirely reenacted 200 years later for students in a university lecture hall by actors who are hypnotized criminals from a local prison. At the end, one of the actors breaks out of his hypnotized state (referred to in the play as a case of "advanced individualism") and protests his being forced to live the life of the character. When the lecturer is unsympathetic to his "disobedience" and assures him that he will be returned to medical care, he lets one of the other actors actually kill him.

After the Rain is an ambitious play: the survivors create a religion and a political system in the course of their voyage, and the drama makes some incisive comments on the political values of contemporary society. But Bowen seems to need the amplitude of the novel to do justice to the themes. The play is really a pageant, lacking energy because it is so stylized. Moreover, the characters are, finally, unsympathetic, a quality which is uncharacteristic for a Bowen play. Usually he creates characters who

are likeable even when they behave stupidly or cruelly, and perhaps it is the characters' failure to engage the audience's compassion that has kept the play from living up to its intellectual promise.

Bowen's next play was *Fall and Redemption of Man*, produced in London in 1967. The work exhibits a far more felicitous union of Bowen's movement away from realism, his interest in myth, and his flair for adaptation. The play, originally composed as an acting exercise for students at the London Academy of Music and Dramatic Art, conflates material from the Chester, Coventry, Lincoln, Norwich, Wakefield, and York cycles into a single mystery play, written in highly rhythmic and slightly archaic English which in its careful simplicity looks back to Anglo-Saxon rather than to Norman French. Bowen is not a notable poet, but the play stages well and was well received by critics when Bowen directed it at LAMDA. His first attempt at direction marked the beginning of a long association with LAMDA born of his increasing disenchantment with television as a medium for artistic expression and coincident with the expiration of his contract with ATV in 1967.

Bowen followed *Fall and Redemption of Man* with *Little Boxes* (1968), an original work written for the stage, his first such piece since *I Love You, Mrs. Patterson* and, like the earlier work, a well-made play. *Little Boxes* is a pair of one-acts—*The Coffee Lace* and *Trevor*—intended as companion pieces concerned with the lives of isolated and trapped city dwellers. *The Coffee Lace*, an elegant, acidic, slice-of-life drama, depicts the plight of three pairs of ex-vaudevillians caught in the cycle of poverty and old age; *Trevor* examines the self-imposed prison of two young women who lack the courage to tell their families that they are lovers and who are inadvertently caught in their own elaborate charade. The plays provide the perfect vehicle for Bowen to exercise his talent for writing realistic dialogue, but realistic theater was not in vogue in 1968, and these plays, remarkable for their verisimilitude, were lambasted by several reviewers as insufficiently experimental. In particular, the critics seem to have been discomfited by *Trevor*, which begins as a bedroom farce and ends as a plea for tolerance. In the play two lesbians, Jane Kempton and Sarah Lawrence, hire a young actor to play the role of Jane's imaginary fiance, Trevor, for the benefit of her parents. When both sets of parents appear unexpectedly, he has to pretend to be each girl's fiance, and is forced to dash back and forth from room to room in a series of calamitous encounters reminiscent of Feydeau. The young women's unmasking and subsequent arrival at self-awareness is typical of Bowen—in the end, they must admit their hypocrisy, face the fact that they have used Trevor, and confront the possibility that their motives may have been selfish ones after all. Still, the play ends on a rather chilling note when, instead of being sobered by their discovery that they are flawed and only human, Jane and Sarah entreat the viewer to respect their right to live as homosexuals. Because it is a legitimate one, their impassioned plea seems not to belong in a play which up to that point has focused on their comic discomfiture and imminent exposure. Despite this criticism, *Little Boxes* proved popular with audiences and helped to establish Bowen's reputation as a dramatist for the stage as well as for television.

In 1969, still concentrating his creative efforts on the legitimate stage, Bowen produced his second political parable in the form of myth—*The Disorderly Women*, a version of Euripides' *The Bacchae*—and directed its first professional production at the Stables Theatre Club, Manchester. *The Disorderly Women* drew praise from critics; in fact, it is considered by many to be Bowen's finest play. Clearly, Bowen found in the highly theatrical neo-Greek drama a form that would not trivialize the momen-

Rachel Roberts in The Disorderly Women

tous issues that *The Disorderly Women* addresses, would allow him to include both high tragedy and low comedy, both Shavian discussions and choral odes, and would give him room to explore more fully the ancient struggle between Apollonian and Dionysian impulses in mankind that appears as a theme in nearly all of his plays. In *The Disorderly Women* Bowen sought to demonstrate the interplay among the hunger for power, the need for justice, and the irrational desire for violence within all humans. The play is an appeal for balance; Bowen explains in his introduction to the 1969 published version of the play that Pentheus is destroyed because of "his refusal to accept the imperfectability of man, his denial both in himself and others of what is instinctive, irrational, irresponsible, selfish, and destructive." But in Pentheus's failure, Bowen also sees the failure of modern man and of modern political thought. Discussing the play with a newspaper reporter immediately before its opening, Bowen described its political core: "My generation was brought up with a belief in perfectable man, which reached its most ludicrous determinist view in Marxism—man perfectable in our time. We thought that by improving the environment we would be able to create a society in which men grew more like men, less like animals. We believed in planning." The failure of so idealistic a philosophy is also at the thematic center of *After the Rain*, but in *The Disorderly Women* Bowen finally dramatized it with theatrical grandeur.

The Disorderly Women has been Bowen's most extravagant work for the theater. *The Disorderly Women* is stately and discursive, but Bowen's next stage play, *The Waiting Room* (1970), is modest and tightly crafted, much like *The Coffee Lace*. Another of Bowen's directorial efforts, the one-act play treats the brief encounter between the ex-wife and the young ex-lover of a middle-aged man who has finally abandoned them both. The ex-wife and young man meet in the waiting room of what turns out in the end to be the morgue, cautiously sharing their life stories and gaining increasing intimacy as they recount to one another the pain they both experienced in trying to live with the unnamed man's bisexuality and his infidelity. Like *The Coffee Lace*, *The Waiting Room* is a character study rather than a problem play; it is a humane and engrossing drama whose dialogue is witty, realistic, and consistently on-key.

Bowen has produced over a dozen television plays since 1970; two of these, both of which have been adapted for the stage, deserve special mention. The first, *Robin Redbreast* (1970), is another of

Bowen's myth-dramas disguised as a murder mystery: Norah Palmer, the heroine of Bowen's novel *The Birdcage* (1962), retreats to a country cottage after the dissolution of an eight-year love affair. Surrounded by mysterious and menacing townspeople, she takes a local youth as her lover, becomes pregnant, fears that she will become a sacrificial victim, and finally learns that it is the young man who is destined for ritual murder to ensure good crops. Bowen had used the myth of society's resurrection after the death of a god before, in both *After the Rain* and *The Disorderly Women*, but here it is presented within a story readily accessible to television viewers—so accessible, in fact, that the play was rejected as irreligious by the BBC Series Department, which had commissioned it as a suspense play, and was broadcast instead by the BBC Drama Department, whose programs are subject to less rigorous scrutiny by censors.

The second of Bowen's significant television plays of the 1970s was *Heil Caesar* (1973), a contemporary political drama loosely modeled on Shakespeare's *Julius Caesar*. The play was commissioned by producer Ronald Smedley as an experiment to see if the political values underpinning the behavior of Shakespeare's characters could be made comprehensible to a twentieth-century audience if the play were stripped of its ornate language. *Heil Caesar* is, however, only partially *Julius Caesar* in modern dress; it is close in spirit to Bowen's ruthless explorations of the behavior and motivations of politicians in *The Candidate*, *The Disorderly Women*, and *The Guardians*. Unfortunately, since Bowen was not completely free either to create his own characters or to write his own dialogue, he produced in *Heil Caesar* a play that is bloodless, neither good Shakespeare nor good Bowen.

Heil Caesar is not Bowen's best work. It is probably his realistic plays, particularly the one-acts, that will mark his most important contribution to the twentieth-century theater, for though they are not innovative, they are well written, and Bowen's more inventive efforts such as *After the Rain* have tended to be artistic failures. Bowen is too derivative a playwright to be a seminal figure in modern drama, but he is noteworthy for his sound craftsmanship, his gift for writing dialogue that is both realistic and theatrically effective, and above all for his discerning portraiture of ordinary human beings struggling to be good in a corrupt modern world—confusing ambition and morality, equivocating and rationalizing, failing consistently to see their own strengths and letting their weaknesses defeat them. Bowen calls his characters "defiant": as he once

(+b)

The living-room of the two-roomed flat in which SOPHIE [lives]. It has a kitchen above. SOPHIE [sits] at the kitchen table. Before interviewing the respondents to her advertisement, she has prepared a questionnaire, and photo-stated copies: a pile of even completed questionnaires lies on the table. She is interviewing the eighth and last respondent, BRIAN. ~~They are both in their mid-twenties.~~ SOPHIE is a mature 25-year-old; BRIAN is ~~27~~ 26.

S: Father living?
B: Yes.
S: Age?
B: About ~~48~~ 50. I think.
S: Mother?
B: About 48
S: Very suitable. Father's father? (EXPLAINS) Your grandfather on your father's side?
B: What about him?
S: Is he living?
B: Yes. And in good health.
S: Mother's father?
B: No.
S: Ah! What did he die of?
B: A torpedo. He went down with all hands on the North Atlantic.
S: (DOUBTFUL) Yes.. You don't happen to know if he was suffering from any serious illness at the time.

Pause. He is looking at her.

B: I wasn't born.
S: Well, never mind: it don't matter. (MAKES A NOTE) Father's mother? (EXPLAINS) Your grandmother on your —

A page from the manuscript for the opening scene of Singles

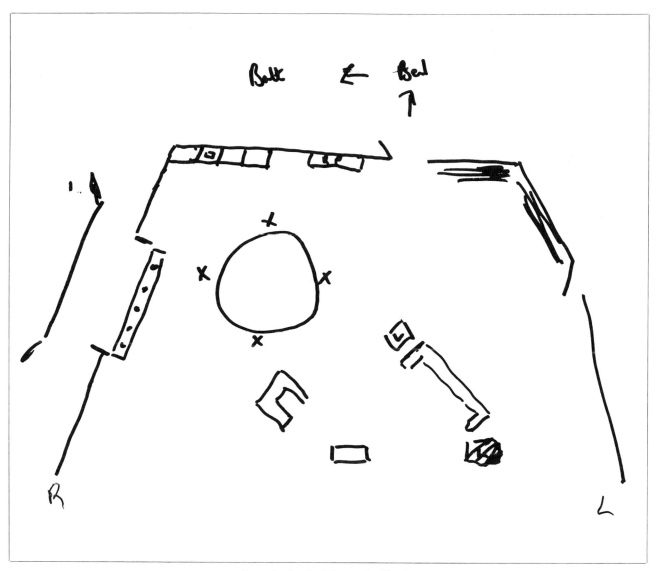

Bowen's sketch of the set for Singles

explained to critic Hugh Herbert, "If you are logical you will always be defeated by the belief that other people work by logic. . . . People don't fit in with statistical tables. It isn't reasonable for a woman on National Assistance to spend it all on cream cakes—and bad cakes with artificial cream—but that may be exactly what she does. You become used not just to idiosyncratic behaviour but to defiant behaviour."

In the 1970s, as Bowen's work has become less philosophical and mythic and more pragmatically political, it is the defiant characters who have begun to dominate. Though stricken with glaucoma in 1969, he has continued to produce approximately one play per year; about half have been written for the stage and half for television. Most have addressed some aspect of the search for power—its lure, its abuse, its corrosive effects on those who cherish it. Not only the stage plays, but the television plays as well have grappled seriously with issues of power and morality. As Bowen himself has expressed it, "I say nowadays that I write television plays in order to buy time to write in other ways, but nobody writes only for money, and nobody would fret so about getting it right if money were the only consideration. There is still the possibility of excellence, and even if a television play ends up as a truffle in the stew . . . someone out there may yet know a truffle when he sees it, and savour it, and be glad."

Other:
"The Viewfinder," in *Writers on Themselves* (London: BBC Publications, 1964), pp. 53-66;
Silver Wedding, in *Mixed Doubles* (London: Methuen, 1970);
Robin Redbreast, in *The Television Dramatist*, edited by Robert Muller (London: Elek, 1973).

Periodical Publications:
"Author/Director," *London Magazine*, 11 (December 1971-January 1972): 81-88;
"The Guardians: A Post Mortem," in *Plays and Players*, 19 (January 1972): 60-62;
Roger, *London Magazine*, 16 (October/November 1976): 83-93.

References:
Ronald Hayman, "Like a Woman They Keep Going Back To," *Drama*, no. 98 (Autumn 1970): 57-64;
Hugh Herbert, "Bowen on the Box," *Guardian*, 6 August 1971, p. 8.
Sheridan Morley, "Mr. Eyes-and-Pen," *Times*, 21 June 1977;
Robin Thornber, "The Man Behind *The Disorderly Women*," *Guardian*, 19 February 1969, p. 8.

Papers:
Bowen's manuscripts are housed at the Mugar Memorial Library, Boston University, and television plays are on deposit in the Rare Book Department, Temple University, Philadelphia.

Howard Brenton
(13 December 1942-)

Roger Cornish
Pennsylvania State University

PRODUCTIONS: *Ladder of Fools*, 1965, Cambridge University, Cambridge;
Winter, Daddykins, 1965, Dublin;
It's My Criminal, 21 August 1966, Royal Court Theatre, London;
A Sky Blue Life, adapted from Maksim Gorki's stories, 1966, London;
Gargantua, 1969, Brighton Combination, Brighton;
Gum and Goo, January 1969, Brighton Combination, Brighton;
Revenge, 2 September 1969, Royal Court Theatre Upstairs, London;
Heads, June 1969, Bradford University, Bradford;
The Education of Skinny Spew, June 1969, Bradford University, Bradford;
Christie in Love, 23 November 1969, Portable Theatre, London; 10 March 1970, Royal Court Theatre Upstairs, London;
Wesley, 27 February 1970, Eastbrook Hall Methodist Church, Bradford;
Cheek, 10 September 1970, Royal Court Theatre Upstairs, London;
Fruit, 28 September 1970, Royal Court Theatre Upstairs, London;

Scott of the Antarctic: What God Didn't See, 1971, Bradford Festival, Bradford;
Lay By, by Brenton, Brian Clark, Trevor Griffiths, David Hare, Steven Poliakoff, Hugh Stoddart, and Snoo Wilson, 24 August 1971, Traverse Theatre, Edinburgh; 26 September 1971, Royal Court Theatre, London;
Hitler Dances, 20 January 1972, Traverse Theatre, Edinburgh; 13 June 1972, Royal Court Theatre Upstairs, London;
How Beautiful with Badges, 2 May 1972, Open Space Theatre, London;
Measure for Measure, adapted from Shakespeare's play, 25 September 1972, Northcott Theatre, Exeter;
England's Ireland, by Brenton, David Edgar, Tony Bicat, Clark, Francis Fuchs, Hare, and Wilson, September 1972, Mickery Theatre, Amsterdam; 2 October 1972, Round House Theatre, London;
A Fart for Europe, by Brenton and Edgar, 18 January 1973, Royal Court Theatre Upstairs, London;
The Screens, adapted from Jean Genet's play, 1973, Bristol;

Howard Brenton, 1977

Mug, 9 June 1973, Inter-Cities Conference, Manchester;

Magnificence, 28 June 1973, Royal Court Theatre, London;

Brassneck, by Brenton and Hare, 10 September 1973, Nottingham Playhouse, Nottingham;

The Churchill Play, 8 May 1974, Nottingham Playhouse, Nottingham; 1979, Warehouse Theatre, London;

The Saliva Milkshake, adapted from Joseph Conrad's *Under Western Eyes*, 23 June 1975, Soho Poly Theatre, London; 1978, Theatre at St. Clements, New York;

Weapons of Happiness, 14 July 1976, Lyttelton Theatre (National Theatre), London;

Government Property, 1976, Aarhus, Denmark;

Epsom Downs, 4 August 1977, Round House, London;

Deeds, by Brenton, Griffiths, Ken Campbell, and Hare, 8 March 1978, Nottingham Playhouse, Nottingham;

Sore Throats, 1979, Warehouse Theatre, London;

A Short Sharp Shock, by Brenton and Tony Howard, 21 June 1980, Theatre Royal, Stratford; 16 July 1980, Royal Court Theatre, London;

The Romans in Britain, October 1980, Olivier Theatre (National Theatre), London;

Thirteenth Night, 2 July 1981, Warehouse Theatre, London.

BOOKS: *Notes from a Psychotic Journal and Other Poems* (Brighton: Privately printed, 1969);

Revenge (London: Eyre Methuen, 1970);

Christie in Love and Other Plays (London: Eyre Methuen, 1970)—includes *Christie in Love*, *Heads*, and *The Education of Skinny Spew*;

Plays for Public Places (London: Eyre Methuen, 1972)—includes *Gum and Goo*, *Wesley*, and *Scott of the Antarctic*;

Lay By, by Brenton, Brian Clark, Trevor Griffiths, David Hare, Steven Poliakoff, Hugh Stoddart, and Snoo Wilson (London: Calder & Boyars, 1972);

Magnificence (London: Eyre Methuen, 1973);

Brassneck, by Brenton and Hare (London: Eyre Methuen, 1974);

The Churchill Play (London: Eyre Methuen, 1974);

Weapons of Happiness (London: Eyre Methuen, 1976);

The Saliva Milkshake (London & Los Angeles: T. Q. Publications, 1977);

Epsom Downs (London: Eyre Methuen, 1977);

Sore Throats and Sonnets of Love and Opposition (London: Eyre Methuen, 1979);

The Romans in Britain (London: Eyre Methuen, 1981);

Thirteenth Night and A Short Sharp Shock, the latter by Brenton and Tony Howard (London: Eyre Methuen, 1981);

Plays for the Poor Theatre (London: Eyre Methuen, 1980)—includes *The Saliva Milkshake*, *Christie in Love*, *Heads*, *The Education of Skinny Spew*, and *Gum and Goo*.

Howard Brenton has been described by critic Peter Roberts as "the most solid talent to emerge from the lunch hour theatre scene," a manifestation of London's fringe theater. Brenton is a leader among the so-called second generation of English dramatists, the generation which is succeeding Arnold Wesker, John Osborne, and Harold Pinter. Within this large group of younger playwrights of the 1970s, which includes Tom Stoppard, David Storey, and Christopher Hampton, Brenton is closely associated with a smaller group that critic John Peter names the "wild bunch": Brenton, Snoo Wilson, Howard Barker, and David Hare, the last closely associated with Brenton as writing collaborator and director of many of Brenton's plays.

Born in Portsmouth, Hampshire, Brenton is the son of Donald Henry and Rose Lilian Lewis Brenton. A "blitz baby," as an infant he spent many hours in an air–raid shelter. Before becoming a Methodist minister, his father had served twenty-five years on the police force, a role which would inform most of Brenton's major plays. That his father was also an amateur actor and theater director insures that all discussions of Brenton's career will include some speculation on parental influence. Brenton was educated at Chichester High School before he attended St. Catherine's College, Cambridge. In 1965 he was graduated with honors in English from Cambridge. Brenton claims to have detested Cambridge, although he admired Professor George Steiner, author of *The Death of Tragedy* (1960), who lectured there on Marx and Freud, and though his first play, *Ladder of Fools* (1965), was produced there in his final year. After graduation, he worked as a theater stage manager and occasional actor, and began to have plays produced by semiprofessional and fringe groups.

All discussions of Brenton begin with the fact that he is an avowedly political playwright, in the words of Malcolm Hay and Philip Roberts, "the most radical writer of his generation." Believing that all drama is political, Brenton declares that his plays are written "unreservedly in the cause of socialism." But his plays are not prescriptive in the Brechtian way. Instead, they indict numerous facets of British society, presenting his view of British decay and capitalist abuse by means of highly theatrical images full of shock value, verbal and visual jokes, and language that is both elevated and crude.

For his main targets, Brenton chooses England's upper classes, her political leaders, her ineffectual radicals who revolt to no good result, and the material greed which he posits as the universal cancer of British life. But no target receives more of his attention than the keepers of the law, the police and policelike servants of the state, whom Brenton portrays as ignorant, brutal, venal, and poised for sadistic repression. Every major play is marked by the presence of a criminal policeman.

In 1969, Brenton's career as a playwright began in earnest as six of his plays premiered. The four which were produced outside of London had little impact, but the two produced in London are formidable plays. His first London play was *Revenge*, a two-act seriocomic vaudeville in which an ancient professional criminal, Adam Hepple, seeks to destroy his nemesis, MacLeish of Scotland Yard. Both men are driven by ideals, Hepple by a mob-

ster's code, MacLeish by Calvinist fervor. But their motives are confusingly (and purposely) mixed: Hepple seeks to preserve a sense of traditional values; MacLeish models his toughness on American gangster Al Capone. At the finish, all characters die, narrating their deaths and biting blood bags, one of several theatricalisms which set the tone for Brenton's later work. Although all the characters in the play, lawbreakers and lawmen alike, are corrupt and violent, the play is without anger and is filled with good-natured high jinks larded with obscene slang and underworld argot.

During *Revenge*'s production at the Royal Court Theatre, Brenton met David Hare. (Brenton claims to have been the entire audience at a performance by Hare's Portable Theatre). Through Hare, the Portable Theatre commissioned *Christie in Love*, a one-act play which is nevertheless a major theater work, for which Brenton won in 1970 the John Whiting Award and, in 1971, bursary awards from the Arts Council of Great Britain. *Christie in Love* is a surrealistic treatment of John Reginald Christie, London's most famous postwar criminal, a middle-class mass murderer and rapist. In this three-actor play, Christie is investigated, grilled, and finally hanged by a constable and an inspector who prove to be as unpredictable and violent as Christie himself. The inspector, who represents middle-class morality, sees Christie's worst crime as anarchy: "What would happen if we all went right ahead, according to desire, fucking all? Bleeding anarchy, Reg." He has Christie hanged and calls it "a blow struck for married life."

As in many of his plays to come, the morality of the law seems as perverse as Christie, who represents not only violence but middle-class banality and British inability to choose between attraction to and repulsion by women. A dummy represents all the female victims in this highly conventionalized play; Brenton would later say that he could not create female characters before his marriage to Jane Margaret Fry in 1970. *Christie in Love* combines Grand Guignol, scatological imagery, and some of the most obscene limericks ever to be spoken on the stage in a way that foreshadows clearly Brenton's difficulties in moving beyond critical applause to acceptance from the broad theater audience, something he has not achieved to date.

During the early 1970s, Brenton remained a fringe playwright whose work was seen primarily in provincial experimental theaters or on small London stages like the Royal Court Theatre Upstairs. The work of this period, all highly theatrical, bears the stamp of rapid, almost improvisational writing.

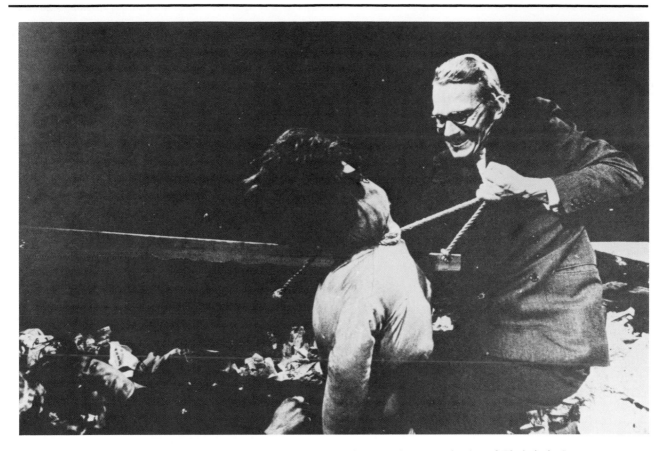

Brian Croucher and William Hoyland in the 1970 Royal Court Theatre production of Christie in Love

Nevertheless, many of the plays hold up very well. For the Bradford Festival, he created *Wesley* (1970), a transformation play which takes a serious look at the founder of the Methodist church and, indeed, premiered in a church. In this rich mix of Brechtian narration, choir singing, and complex pantomime, Wesley escapes his dark night of the soul by jettisoning fears of his own sinfulness in favor of a God-given state of grace. Brenton handles Wesley's Atlantic crossing much as American dramatist Paul Foster handled Paine's in *Tom Paine* (1967). The dozen-member cast of *Wesley* is called upon to create ship, storm, and crew through pantomime. In *Scott of the Antarctic: What God Didn't See* (1971), first performed on a Bradford ice rink, Brenton parodied British imperialism and its heroes. Scott is a frightfully keen public-school cheerleader who never says die but leads his men to death by his amateur enthusiasm. In the final scene, a pantheon of English hero-explorers, including Captain James Cook, Sir Francis Drake, and, in an Anglo-Saxon world embrace, American astronaut Neil Armstrong, devours the bodies of Scott and his men.

With six other men, Brenton shares authorial credit for *Lay By* (1971), a riveting study of a legal system which chews up three underclass Britons involved stupidly but guiltlessly in a sex crime. Despite its communal authorship, the play is very much of a piece and bears unmistakable signs of a Brenton play in its theme, theatricality, and apparent intent to offend the squeamish with sexual explicitness—a courtroom scene features simulated fellatio with a dildo. The final cannibal imagery echoes *Scott of the Antarctic*.

In 1972-1973, Brenton was resident playwright at the Royal Court Theatre and embarked on the series of full-length plays which he calls *epic*: *Magnificence* (1973), *Brassneck* (1973), *The Churchill Play* (1974), *Weapons of Happiness* (1976), and *Epsom Downs* (1977). Brenton, who considers himself anti-Brechtian, has stated that by epic he means a play that consists of many short scenes or "windows" which, taken together, construct an argument. The message, he says, comes first.

Magnificence was the first Brenton play produced on an important London main stage, the Royal Court. The work concerns a group of young radicals who clumsily attempt to impress their revolutionary message on British society, first by staging a tenement sit-in, and then by assassinating a cabinet officer. The core of the play seems to be the futility of their efforts. The only effect of the seizure of the building is Mary's accidental abortion and Jed's jailing. The planned assassination aborts when the gelignite face mask, which Jed forces over the head of the cabinet minister, a homosexual called Alice, misfires due to a bad fuse. Then, moments before the final curtain, Jed blows up both Alice and himself by accident. Waste is the final image and the final word. As in his other work, Brenton's reactionaries are depicted harshly—the police figures are brutal and ignorant, the politicians painted queens. While loosely constructed, the play has fewer expressionistic or theatricalist touches than most of Brenton's works.

Magnificence, which critic Oleg Kerensky faults for failing to make its point, had only a short run. But his next plays, *Brassneck* and *The Churchill Play*, solidly established Brenton with the critical community. *Brassneck* was written with David Hare in a collaboration described by the writers as so close that "the work is indivisible." It is a mammoth three-act play whose technical requirements—multiple locales and thirty acting parts—may have prevented it from moving to London despite its Nottingham success. *Brassneck* (which is Midlands slang for criminal nerve) traces the thirty-year career of the Bagley family as it rises, falls, and rises again through the corruption of postwar Britain. The elder Bagley gets his start by murdering his wife during the blitzkrieg so that he can become a slumlord on her insurance money. Roderick, Bagley's nephew, prospers by obtaining building contracts through bribery and then goes to jail because he stupidly keeps records of the bribes. The third generation Bagley, Roderick's son, becomes a nightclub owner and heroin entrepreneur. Throughout, the business community and upper class connive at Bagley success because of fear or greed. As the Bagleys' lawyer puts it, "I could take all my clothes off . . . greed would be blazoned across my bum." The decay of Britain dominates the play. Worse than criminality is incompetence—Roderick Bagley is prosecuted when his prefab building stress system cracks in the rain. None of the characters are even half-good, least of all the two laborite politicians who sell out socialism for establishment perks. One of them, Browne, who had been a leftist postal worker in the 1940s, says, "I was a communist in my youth. Now I'm looking for revenge . . . on everything I believed in." Although the play did not move to London, its impact was

undeniable. Michael Coveny called it a watershed event because it proved the public appeal of the group of dramatists to which Hare and Brenton belonged.

Ronald Hayman has called *The Churchill Play*, which also premiered at Nottingham, Brenton's best because Brenton had begun to sympathize with right-wing as well as left-wing characters. The play is set in an Orwellian 1984 turned upside down—the extreme right has seized power and turned England into a chain of gulags, in one of which left-wing political prisoners entertain visiting bureaucrats by putting on a play about Winston Churchill. Churchill is excoriated as a queen ("Give us a kiss, Jolly Jack Tar") and a twister of the truth. The play climaxes with an escape that fails because the prisoners, like the radicals of *Magnificence*, can act on impulse but can make no practical plans. Brenton's favorite themes are strongly stated, especially his fixation on the police. In *The Churchill Play*, authority has gone berserk and, poisoned by the experience of Ulster, comes to regard the common British people as its enemies, to be interned, brutalized, exploited, and "dumped." While rejecting its message, Harold Hobson called *The Churchill Play* "a work of great aesthetic and intellectual power." Though the play languished after its Nottingham production, it was finally revived at Stratford-upon-Avon in 1978, and that production later moved to London's Warehouse Theatre in 1979. In response to the revival, John Peter called *The Churchill Play* "one of the best English plays of the last ten years."

Though *Brassneck* and *The Churchill Play* were undeservedly short-lived, they led to a major breakthrough for Brenton, who was commissioned to write the first play to be premiered at the National Theatre's new Lyttelton Theatre. The play was *Weapons of Happiness*, the title taken from a phrase that the young radicals of *Magnificence* painted on the walls of the flat they seized. Its hero, Josef Frank, is an expatriate Czech Communist who, though purged by Stalinists like the hero of Arthur Koestler's novel *Darkness at Noon* (1941), has remained loyal to his socialist ideals. He is contrasted to young English workers whose shallowmindedness and general ignorance he tries to overcome during a badly planned sit-down strike at the plant where they all work. Before he dies from the lingering effects of his mistreatment by the Stalinists, Frank sends the young workers off to try a new, free existence. In this bleak play both Communists and capitalists are corrupt. Neither workers nor bosses have vision; Frank alone clings to a socialist ideal. Brenton describes the play as "anti-Stalinist and pro-communist," but it presents no hopeful image of the possibilities of communism. With Brenton's usual free theatricality, the play flashes backward in time to the Prague uprisings. Stalin appears, laughing at Frank's attempt to stop a Soviet tank during the Russian invasion. As he had previously done with *Christie in Love* and other Brenton works, David Hare directed this production, which inspired Harold Hobson to review the play twice and call it "a vision of revolution that is quite extraordinary in its creative ambiguity, . . ." The play won the *Evening Standard* Drama Award for best play of 1976.

The last play in Brenton's epic series was *Epsom Downs*, a play which, although it continued the pattern of sweeping, large-cast theatricality, broke completely away from the dark views of life that dominated his preceding work. A kaleidoscopic celebration of life rather in the manner of a Brueghel canvas, *Epsom Downs* fills the stage with punters, bookies, jockeys, horse owners, evangelists, even a horse that refuses to race without his groupie, a goat. In the most important of the play's several miniplots, a poor young couple wages its entire fortune on the Derby and wins, a happy conclusion completely at variance with Brenton's previous work. This is not to say that *Epsom Downs* does not reflect Brenton's basic concerns. One of the play's characters is the ghost of Emily Davison, who martyred herself for the Irish cause at the 1913 Derby by plunging under the hooves of the king's horse. In the final moments of the play, Sandy, the young wife who has won £2,000, communes with Emily's ghost and finds her winnings meaningless. The last image is four lunatics being introduced to clean up the mess on the Downs, which obviously can be taken to stand for England. Nevertheless, *Epsom Downs* is, as critics have recognized, Brenton's sunniest play, rich in racetrack detail, working-class slang, and a very effective climax in which the Derby is run to the narration of an actor who plays the Spirit of the Race.

As he achieved recognition in the mid-1970s, Brenton began to be offered opportunities in television and responded with *The Saliva Milkshake* in 1975 and *The Paradise Run* in 1976. The former achieved a transition to the stage, being produced in London by Soho Poly, a lunchtime theater group, and marking Brenton's New York debut at the Theatre at St. Clements in 1978. Based on Joseph Conrad's *Under Western Eyes* (1911), *The Saliva Milkshake* examines terrorism in a manner that for Brenton is quite dispassionate. A don, Martin, is forced to deal with an old lover, Joan, who has assassinated the home secretary. In the Yeatsian way, he is a good modern man who can find no certainty by which to make decisions. Thus he at first helps Joan, fails by chance to manage her escape, and then betrays her, and finally pays for that betrayal by confessing to her compatriots and accepting their punishment. In his liberal indecision he reflects the ineffectiveness that plagues all of Brenton's political characters. Both Mel Gussow in New York and Harold Hobson in London praised the play for its sober investigation of political commitment.

In 1979, *Sore Throats* was produced at the Royal Shakespeare Company's Warehouse Theatre. It marked a complete departure from Brenton's epic series in that he confined himself to three characters, one room, and action that is almost wholly realistic. In theme, however, *Sore Throats* fits comfortably into his canon. Jack, a forty-five-year-old police inspector, viciously beats his ex-wife, Judy, until she signs over to him the money from the sale of their home that he needs for his migration to Canada. In her turn, Judy seeks meaning in life by joining her new roommate, Sally, in a year-long round of boy chasing, drink, and drugs—the sort of dissipation that used to be associated only with men. The women fail to achieve any sense of meaning by their rebellion, and by the play's finish, Jack has returned, having lost his new woman, their child, and the money in Canada, to beg Judy's sympathy and support. At the curtain, Judy is poised to burn the last few bank notes they possess; nothing has really changed.

Having set aside his usual mechanical theater devices in this play, Brenton goes as far as he can with language, which is ripe almost to the point of rottenness. Describing a teenage lover from head to toe, Judy concludes with "little sausages of dirt between his toes." Brenton's preoccupation with police barbarism reaches a new height in this play when Jack, clad in a Scotland Yard inspector's uniform, kicks Judy repeatedly in the stomach. Few plays in the language have made life seem as truly empty as this one.

In the summer of 1980, Stratford Theatre Royal presented *A Short Sharp Shock*, in which Brenton and collaborator Tony Howard mounted an all-out attack on the current Tory government and, particularly, its prime minister, Margaret Thatcher, whose photo was featured on the program cover, her head being simultaneously bashed by a hammer and cut off by a sickle. In a series of cruel vignettes depicting actual events, the play chronicles Thatcher's rise to power and presents her as a boring middle-class matron surrounded by weak, sycophantic aides. In his usual fashion, Brenton employs a wide variety of theatrical devices, including current rock songs, masks, and variety-hall turns.

Before the year was out, the prolific Brenton had his second National Theatre premiere when *The Romans in Britain* opened on the Olivier stage. Political as any Brenton work, the play marked a departure by incorporating ancient history as a central motif. Brenton explores the mixed curse of imperialism by depicting Julius Caesar's English raid of 54 B.C., the aftermath of the Roman departure of A.D. 515, and current parallels in the English-Irish struggles in Ulster. As one would expect, he portrays violently the cruelty of imperialist power. At the same time, however, he maintains his usual divided stance; the victims of ancient Roman and modern English imperialism commit murder

and mayhem with no less gusto than their conquerors. Oswyn Murray praised Brenton's power and purpose but condemned the raw language, explicit sex, and violence as mere shock devices.

Other critics found *The Romans in Britain* totally offensive, and it became the subject of England's greatest theater storm since the opening of *Hair* in 1968. Director Michael Bogdanov was charged under the Sexual Offenses Act of 1956, and, in the Greater London Council, voices were raised to threaten the subsidy of the National Theatre. The controversy earned Brenton his greatest notice in the United States by prompting Yale's *Theater* to publish three articles about him in its spring 1981 issue.

In July 1981, Brenton returned to the Warehouse Theatre, where the Royal Shakespeare Company performed his *Thirteenth Night*, a political fantasy modeled on Shakespeare's *Macbeth*. Brenton's thane, Jack Beaty, is a minister in a future

Frank Finlay and Julie Covington in a scene from the 1976 London production of Weapons of Happiness

Socialist government who, having been tempted by three female radicals to dreams of perfected revolution, assassinates Prime Minister Dunn because the latter is in the thrall of the United States. Like Macbeth, Beaty sinks into a swamp of murder and turns Britain into a terror state. At the play's finish, Stalin's ghost prowls the ruins of Beaty's Whitehall bunker. In *Thirteenth Night*, Brenton reverses the political vision of *The Churchill Play*, raising the specter of socialism, turning it against the people. It might be argued that *Thirteenth Night* stands as a retort to recent plays by Edward Bond, in particular *The Bundle* (1978), which seem to demonstrate that the vision of a better future society justifies, even requires, apparently barbaric acts. In *Thirteenth Night*, the three temptresses tell Beaty, "The road from Evil to Good is worse than Evil. But what decent man or woman dares not go down the road to Good?" However, when Beaty acts on this justification of murder, the road leads to the gulag instead of the workers' paradise. Once again, Brenton reveals an ambivalence at the core of his political vision.

Though the controversy over *The Romans in Britain* drew full houses to the Olivier, Brenton remains in many ways a fringe playwright, one who is yet to make his mark in the West End. However, given Brenton's conscious struggle against the values of the English establishment, this is perhaps quite as it should be. He has said that "the theatre is a bourgeois institution: you have to live and work against that." The qualities that may keep his work from broad acceptance are several. First, to the extent that plot requires causally related events, his plays tend to be weakly plotted. Instead of neatly polished plots, Brenton offers explosive language and vivid theatrical imagery in service of assaultive themes. These themes have earned him critical praise, but the ordinary audience may have little taste for language that is powerfully sexual, scatological, or otherwise unsettling, as in *The Churchill Play*, where word pictures—dead men rotting on the wires; scratching an itch till the skin tears back—call to mind the decadence of John Webster. In the same way, Brenton bombards the audience with visual images—the rotten corpses that appear in *Christie in Love*, *The Churchill Play*, and *Lay By*, for instance—that may repel as many people as they appeal to. His constant attacks on English values are hardly calculated to win friends among the theatergoing middle class. Brenton has spoken of his wish to agitate the audience; *aggro* (for aggression) is his favorite term for the audience-jarring techniques

he uses. It is hardly surprising that he remains a coterie playwright.

Nevertheless, he is a leader among the politically minded dramatists, like Bond and Hare, who matured in the 1970s. More easily comprehended than Bond and more visceral than Hare, he may finally command a large audience, but to do so he may need to solve his problems of closure. Brenton plays tend to be more satisfying in their explosive moments than in their final effects. That his characters are not finally explicable is reasonable; he has taken the position that character is not to be understood, only observed in action. But the actions of his characters often lead nowhere. His plays are full of revolt that produces little change. In *Weapons of Happiness*, after Frank's death, the young strikers, who avoided arrest with Frank's help, putter aimlessly about a deserted farm and debate whether to return to the dismal factory life they know or try to become farmers. One of them, Janice, shows a spark of enlightenment when she explains that Frank was a Communist, but the rest show barely a flicker of understanding. It seems unlikely that the new generation will change the world. *Epsom Downs* builds for two hours toward a cheery conclusion and at the last moment casts the lucky happiness of the leading couple into question as if Brenton were uncomfortable with the political implications of a happy ending. In *The Romans in Britain*, Brenton sets a firm tone of condemnation for all forms of imperialism. But at the play's climax the modern Irish rebels who execute a captured English officer demonstrate no sense of the moral complexity of their position— they promise only a continuity of bloodshed. There is as yet in Brenton's work no clearly positive picture of the socialist political future he professes to espouse. In contrast to Bond, Brenton draws back from this final optimism, his hopes apparently muffled by fears of Stalinism or suspicions that English society is too far gone in corruption to be saved. Perhaps Brenton should be viewed as an anomaly, a politically committed dramatist who cannot believe in change for the better.

Television Scripts:
The Saliva Milkshake, adapted from Joseph Conrad's *Under Western Eyes*, BBC, 1975;
The Paradise Run, Thames Television, 1976.

Other:
The Saliva Milkshake [television script], *Performing Arts Journal*, 3 (Winter 1979).

Interviews:

Catherine Itzin and Simon Trussler, "Petrol Bombs Through the Proscenium Arch," *Theatre Quarterly*, 5 (March 1975): 4-20;

Malcolm Hay and Philip Roberts, "Interview: Howard Brenton," *Performing Arts Journal*, 3 (Winter 1979): 134-141.

References:

Richard Beacham, "Brenton Invades Britain: The *Romans in Britain* Controversy," *Theater*, 12 (Spring 1981): 34-37;

Edward Bond, "The Romans and the Establishment's Fig Leaf," *Theater*, 12 (Spring 1981): 39-42;

Ben Cameron, "Howard Brenton: The Privilege of Revolt," *Theater*, 12 (Spring 1981): 28-33;

Michael Coveny, "Beyond the Fringe," *Sunday Times Magazine*, 26 November 1978, p. 73;

Ronald Hayman, *British Theatre Since 1955* (London: Oxford University Press, 1979), pp. 92-97;

Albert Hunt, "Theatre of Violence," *New Society* (4 November 1976): 261-262;

Oleg Kerensky, *The New British Drama* (New York: Taplinger, 1977), pp. 206-225;

Paul Merchant, "The Theatre Poems of Bertholt Brecht, Edward Bond, and Howard Brenton," *Theatre Quarterly*, 9 (Summer 1979): 49-51;

Sheridan Morley, "The Man Behind the Lyttelton's First New Play," *Times*, 10 July 1976, p. 9.

Wynyard Browne
(6 October 1911-19 February 1964)

J. C. Trewin

PRODUCTIONS: *Dark Summer*, 1947, St. Martin's Theatre, London;

The Holly and the Ivy, 1950, Lyric Theatre, Hammersmith; 10 May 1950, Duchess Theatre, London, 412 [performances];

A Question of Fact, October 1953, Piccadilly Theatre, London;

The Ring of Truth, 16 July 1959, Savoy Theatre, London, 250.

BOOKS: *Queenie Molson* (London: Cobden-Sanderson, 1934);

Sheldon's Way (London: Cobden-Sanderson, 1935; New York & London: Appleton-Century, 1936);

The Fire and the Fiddle (London: Cobden-Sanderson, 1937);

Dark Summer (London: Evans, 1950);

The Holly and the Ivy (London: Evans, 1951);

A Question of Fact (London: Evans, 1955).

Though Wynyard Browne wrote only four plays that were produced, he will be remembered as a gentle, civilized dramatist with a gift for potent dialogue and an affection for his characters that, with the aid of good casts, he could transmit to an audience. The son of Eleanor Muriel Verena Malcolmson Browne and Barry Mathew Charles Sleater Browne, a clergyman, Wynyard Barry Browne was born in London. Educated at Marlborough and Christ's College, Cambridge, he had been a journalist and novelist before turning to the theater.

His first writing success came early, with his 1934 novel *Queenie Molson*, a portrait of a Communist undergraduate of that period, accomplished with wry humor and a sharp eye for character. After the publication of his novels *Sheldon's Way* (1935) and *The Fire and the Fiddle* (1937), it appeared that he was on his way to becoming a major novelist; however, he remained a working journalist. He did not turn to the theater until 1945, giving up journalism in 1950. He had always been strongly attracted to the stage, having read all Henrik Ibsen's works by the time he was fourteen. But he would be far from Ibsenian in nature; where Ibsen drew scathing portraits of the clergy, Browne was attracted to the schoolmasters and clergymen in his own background, and they became central to his plays.

His first play would be unlike the ones which followed, and perhaps more indebted to Ibsen. In *Dark Summer*, which tried out at the Lyric Theatre,

Hammersmith, before opening in the West End in 1947, Browne limited his cast to five, a blind sailor who regains his sight in the third act; the two devoted women between whom he must choose; his possessive mother; and a twittering spinster who is a paying guest. Four of these people have truth and character; they are personages. The fifth, the blind man, is neurotic and difficult, not a strong figure for the core of the play. If Browne had been less economical and peopled his single set more freely, the piece would have gained in effect; as it is, it lags toward the end, though this is not vastly important. Browne was adept at writing dialogue; he never allowed his creations to stand about in the manner of cartoon puppets, verbal balloons trailing from every mouth. The principal women who move around the blind man in *Dark Summer* are most carefully observed. One is a fading Viennese Jewess who has suffered in the concentration camps and who is seen honestly and sympathetically. The second is a girl of cosmopolitan upbringing to whom the sailor was engaged in Cairo before his blindness but whom he hardly knows. A third figure is the mother who ties her children to her with a silver cord. There is nothing showy about the play, but in 1947 it pleased connoisseurs, and critics warned Browne not to confine his cast so rigidly next time to a hand of five.

Browne heeded their advice. Three years later, his second and best play, *The Holly and the Ivy* (1950), had a company of eight and a more mature and detailed construction. It also had good luck. Trying out on tour, with a cast that included Herbert Lomas, Jane Baxter, and Daphne Arthur, the production limped along until Brighton, where, despite good notices in two local papers, the box office was so poor that the management despaired of its London chances. However, the final week prior to the West End opening, *The Holly and the Ivy* was staged at the Lyric Theatre in Hammersmith—remote in location but nevertheless a London theater—and generated a wave of enthusiasm which carried over to London critics as well as to the production at the Duchess Theatre. Daphne Arthur won the Clarence Derwent Award for her acting as one of the vicar's daughters. The play's success allowed Browne to give up journalism.

The Holly and the Ivy is a complex and quietly handled domestic play about a family gathering at a Norfolk vicarage on Christmas Eve. From the start one knows that this family is a unity, rather than a huddle of ill-assorted types tossed together for stage effect. The play lacks the deadlier theatrical devices; it is the play's simple, unvarnished statement that is so moving. The vicar's family has grown up in the belief that a clergyman must not be worried; that he is meant for wrapping in cotton wool. More cutting truths must be concealed. Life with Father means keeping facts from Father, and at this Christmas season he does not realize immediately what matters are agitating his household. "As a parson," his son Mick says to him, "you've got a different attitude to life. You think a thing like this that's happened to Margaret is wrong. And what's more, you expect other people to look at it in that way too. Can't you see? How can parsons expect to be told the truth when one can't even talk to them like human beings?"

In an apparently untheatrical but most dramatic third act, written with a quiet realism, the vicar and his three children reach an understanding. There is nothing glutinous, no sugary contrivance; the piece preserves to the end the honesty with which it opens. When his daughter admits her doubts, her disbelief, the vicar has a fine speech: "It's not belief that's religion. That's not the primary thing at all. There's something else has to be there before that, long before that—something that's the root of all the religions in the world—a need. This feeling ye have—if you stick to it, if you go through with it, if you're honest about it—this need ye have to make sense of the world; that's the prime essential of all religion."

It is a veracious and civilized play, and it is likely to be durable. Neither of the two succeeding plays surpassed it, though in *A Question of Fact* (1953) Browne proved again that his work was not for any playgoer who demanded the facile twist, the purely theatrical irrelevance, the violent manipulation of plot and character for an effect solely ephemeral. In *A Question of Fact*, a young, newly married public schoolmaster, who was an adopted child, discovers that his real father was hanged for murder. He seeks his real mother in order to know why the truth about his father's death has been kept from him. How can his marriage and his career prosper if he cannot be sure of his past? This is not the peaceful Norfolk vicarage of *The Holly and the Ivy*. But, as in the earlier work, the characters develop logically. The narrative flows; the end is quiet and satisfying though it must have disappointed playgoers who expected the play to end with a big scene. Browne was never one to write big scenes, but Paul Scofield as the young schoolmaster and Gladys Cooper as his mother had confrontations of great sensitivity.

In *A Question of Fact* Browne is writing of various levels and phases of imagination. The murderer, dead long before the play begins, was too powerfully imaginative, a state which forced him into fraud and led him at the last to kill the woman who was determined to expose him to his wife. Coupled with this dangerous imagination was a feeling of insecurity: he never believed that he was loved; he feared that his wife would despise him if she knew the truth. The son, in one sense, has followed his father. He too is overcome by his imagination; he believes feverishly that if the facts about his parentage are known, he must resign his post, an "idiotic, destructive thing" that would be to him the equivalent of murder. A feeling of insecurity exists in the son as well: he fears that his wife may not understand, and he resolves that there must be no children of the marriage. His wife loves him deeply, but she has come also to be slightly fearful; behind everything (her own imagination at play) lurks a doubt that needs to be settled.

All is settled at last. In describing her husband, the schoolmaster's mother (who proves to be a wise, assured businesswoman, her experience gained the hard way) demonstrates that the real man must sometimes be clarified from the blurred image of a newspaper story. The third act is "theatre theatrical" in the best sense; it never deserts the theater of the mind. We may agree or disagree with its reasoning, but the dramatist's integrity and art are unflinching. It is a play of two splendid acts and a third to argue about, no pretensions, no divagations, no nonsense.

The Ring of Truth (1959) is a more conventional play and a more frail structure than the two previous works. In it Browne demonstrates how a minor domestic disaster—a wife's loss of her wedding ring—can snowball into something like an avalanche. Comic, yet nearly catastrophic, the episode is stretched by superior craftsmanship, albeit in a somewhat anachronistic mode, into a full-length work.

Browne quickly became unfashionable although *The Holly and the Ivy* had run for more than a year in the West End. He did not marry until 1948, when he wed Joan Margaret Yeaxlee, with whom he had one daughter. He was in intermittent ill health in his forties and died at Norwich at the age of fifty-two.

References:

W. A. Darlington, *Six Thousand and One Nights* (London: Harrap, 1960), pp. 226-227;

J. C. Trewin, *Dramatists of Today* (London: Staples, 1953), pp. 197-200, 228.

Agatha Christie
(15 September 1890-12 January 1976)

Arthur Nicholas Athanason
Michigan State University

PRODUCTIONS: *Black Coffee*, 8 December 1930, Embassy Theatre, London;

Ten Little Niggers, adapted from Christie's novel, 17 October 1943, St. James's Theatre, London; produced again as *Ten Little Indians*, 27 June 1944, Broadhurst Theatre, New York, 425 [performances];

Appointment with Death, adapted from Christie's novel, 31 March 1945, Piccadilly Theatre, London;

Murder on the Nile, adapted from Christie's *Death on the Nile*, 19 March 1946, Ambassadors' Theatre, London; produced again as *Hidden Horizon*, 19 September 1946, Plymouth Theatre, New York, 12;

The Hollow, adapted from Christie's novel, 7 June 1951, Fortune Theatre, London;

The Mousetrap, adapted from Christie's *Three Blind Mice*, 25 November 1952, Ambassadors' Theatre, London; 5 November 1960, Maidman Playhouse, New York;

Witness for the Prosecution, adapted from Christie's story, 28 October 1953, Winter Garden Theatre, London; 16 December 1954, Henry Miller's Theatre, New York, 645;

Spider's Web, 14 December 1954, Savoy Theatre,

London; 15 January 1974, Lolly's Theatre Club, New York;

Towards Zero, adapted by Christie and Gerald Verner from Christie's novel, 4 September 1956, St. James's Theatre, London;

Verdict, 22 May 1958, Strand Theatre, London;

The Unexpected Guest, 12 August 1958, Duchess Theatre, London;

Go Back for Murder, adapted from Christie's *Five Little Pigs*, 23 March 1960, Duchess Theatre, London;

Rule of Three: Afternoon at the Seaside, The Patient, and *The Rats*, 20 December 1962, Duchess Theatre, London;

Fiddlers Three, 1971, Southsea; 1972, London;

Akhnaton and Nefertiti, 1979, New York.

SELECTED BOOKS: *The Mysterious Affair at Styles: A Detective Story* (London: Lane, 1920; New York: Dodd, Mead, 1927);

The Secret Adversary (London & New York: Lane, 1922; New York: Dodd, Mead, 1922);

Poirot Investigates (London: Lane, 1924; New York: Dodd, Mead, 1925);

The Secret of Chimneys (London: Lane, 1925; New York: Dodd, Mead, 1925);

Agatha Christie, circa 1950

The Murder of Roger Ackroyd (London: Collins, 1926; New York: Dodd, Mead, 1926);

Partners in Crime (London: Collins, 1929; New York: Dodd, Mead, 1929);

The Seven Dials Mystery (London: Collins, 1929; New York: Dodd, Mead, 1929);

The Murder at the Vicarage (New York: Dodd, Mead, 1930; London: Collins, 1935);

The Mysterious Mr. Quin (London: Collins, 1930; New York: Dodd, Mead, 1930);

The Thirteen Problems (London: Collins, 1932); republished as *The Tuesday Club Murders* (New York: Dodd, Mead, 1933);

Peril at End House (London: Collins, 1932; New York: Dodd, Mead, 1932);

The Hound of Death and Other Stories (London: Odhams Press, 1933);

Murder on the Orient Express (London: Collins, 1934); republished as *Murder in the Calais Coach* (New York: Dodd, Mead, 1934);

Black Coffee (London: Ashley, 1934);

The Listerdale Mystery and Other Stories (London: Collins, 1934);

Murder in Three Acts (New York: Dodd, Mead, 1934); republished as *Three Act Tragedy* (London: Collins, 1935);

Death in the Clouds (London: Collins, 1935); republished as *Death in the Air* (New York: Dodd, Mead, 1935);

The A.B.C. Murders: A New Poirot Mystery (London: Collins, 1936; New York: Dodd, Mead, 1936);

Cards on the Table (London: Collins, 1936; New York: Dodd, Mead, 1937);

Murder in Mesopotamia (London: Collins, 1936; New York: Dodd, Mead, 1936);

Murder in the Mews and Other Stories (London: Collins, 1937); republished as *Dead Man's Mirror and Other Stories* (New York: Dodd, Mead, 1937);

Death on the Nile (London: Collins, 1937; New York: Dodd, Mead, 1938);

Appointment with Death: A Poirot Mystery [novel] (London: Collins, 1938; New York: Dodd, Mead, 1938);

The Regatta Mystery and Other Stories (New York: Dodd, Mead, 1939);

Ten Little Niggers [novel] (London: Collins, 1939); republished as *And Then There Were None* (New York: Dodd, Mead, 1940);

One, Two, Buckle My Shoe (London: Collins, 1940); republished as *The Patriotic Murders* (New York: Dodd, Mead, 1941);

The Body in the Library (London & New York: Collins, 1942; New York: Dodd, Mead, 1942);

The Moving Finger (New York: Dodd, Mead, 1942; London: Collins, 1943);

Five Little Pigs (London: Collins, 1942); republished as *Murder in Retrospect* (New York: Dodd, Mead, 1942);

Towards Zero [novel] (London: Collins, 1944; New York: Dodd, Mead, 1944);

Ten Little Niggers [play] (London: French, 1945); republished as *Ten Little Indians* (New York & London: French, 1946);

Appointment with Death [play] (London: French, 1945);

The Hollow: A Hercule Poirot Mystery [novel] (London: Collins, 1946; New York: Dodd, Mead, 1946);

Murder on the Nile (New York: French, 1946; London: French, 1948);

The Labours of Hercules: Short Stories (London: Collins, 1947); republished as *Labors of Hercules: New Adventures in Crime by Hercule Poirot* (New York: Dodd, Mead, 1947);

Witness for the Prosecution and Other Stories (New York: Dodd, Mead, 1948);

A Murder Is Announced (London: Collins, 1950; New York: Dodd, Mead, 1950);

Three Blind Mice and Other Stories (New York: Dodd, Mead, 1950);

They Came to Baghdad (London: Collins, 1951; New York: Dodd, Mead, 1951);

They Do It with Mirrors (London: Collins, 1952); republished as *Murder with Mirrors* (New York: Dodd, Mead, 1952);

The Hollow [play] (London: French, 1952; New York: French, 1952);

Mrs. McGinty's Dead (London: Collins, 1952; New York: Dodd, Mead, 1952);

After the Funeral (London: Collins, 1953); republished as *Funerals Are Fatal* (New York: Dodd, Mead, 1953);

A Pocket Full of Rye (London: Collins, 1953; New York: Dodd, Mead, 1954);

The Mousetrap (New York: French, 1954; London: French, 1954);

Witness for the Prosecution [play] (London: French, 1954; New York: French, 1954);

Dead Man's Folly (London: Collins, 1956; New York: Dodd, Mead, 1956);

Spider's Web (London: French, 1957; New York: French, 1957);

4:50 from Paddington (London: Collins, 1957); republished as *What Mrs. McGillicuddy Saw!* (New York: Dodd, Mead, 1957);

Towards Zero [play], by Christie and Gerald Verner (New York: Dramatists Play Service, 1957; London: French, 1958);

Verdict (London: French, 1958);

The Unexpected Guest (London: French, 1958);

Cat among the Pigeons (London: Collins, 1959; New York: Dodd, Mead, 1960);

Go Back for Murder (London: French, 1960);

The Mirror Crack'd from Side to Side (London: Collins, 1962); republished as *The Mirror Crack'd* (New York: Dodd, Mead, 1963);

Rule of Three: Afternoon at the Seaside, The Patient, The Rats, 3 volumes (London: French, 1963);

The Caribbean Mystery (London: Collins, 1964; New York: Dodd, Mead, 1965);

At Bertram's Hotel (London: Collins, 1965; New York: Dodd, Mead, 1965);

Third Girl (London: Collins, 1966; New York: Dodd, Mead, 1967);

13 Clues for Miss Marple: A Collection of Mystery Stories (New York: Dodd, Mead, 1966);

By the Pricking of My Thumbs (London: Collins, 1968; New York: Dodd, Mead, 1968);

The Golden Ball and Other Stories (New York: Dodd, Mead, 1971);

Nemesis (London: Collins, 1971; New York: Dodd, Mead, 1971);

Fiddlers Three (London: French, 1972);

Akhnaton (London: Collins, 1973; New York: Dodd, Mead, 1973);

Hercule Poirot's Early Cases (London: Collins, 1974; New York: Dodd, Mead, 1974);

Miss Marple's Final Cases and Others (London: Collins, 1974);

Curtain: Hercule Poirot's Last Case (London: Collins, 1975; New York: Dodd, Mead, 1975);

Sleeping Murder (London: Collins, 1976; New York: Dodd, Mead, 1976);

An Autobiography (London: Collins, 1977; New York: Dodd, Mead, 1977).

Internationally acclaimed as one of the foremost mystery writers of our time, Agatha Christie was also a popular playwright of distinction and the author of such theatrical successes as *Ten Little Indians* (first produced in 1943 as *Ten Little Niggers*), *Witness for the Prosecution* (1953), and London's longest running play, *The Mousetrap* (1952). Christie, the undisputed Queen of Crime—or, as she preferred, the Duchess of Death—wrote, in all, sixty-six novels of mystery and detection, sixteen collections of detective stories, six novels of romance and suspense (under the pseudonym Mary Westmacott), fifteen stage plays, two radio plays, a book of travel reminiscences, two volumes of verse, a collection of children's stories, and *An Autobiography* (published posthumously in November 1977) which offers an intimate self-portrait of the author as woman, wife, and mother.

Agatha Mary Clarissa Miller Christie was born in Torquay, Devonshire, in 1890, the youngest of three children of Frederick Alvah and Clarissa Boehmer Miller. In Christie's *Autobiography* (1977), she recalls events in vivid detail from her life and career up to her seventy-fifth year. She describes her childhood in Devonshire, her late-Victorian upbringing under the tutelage of her mother until she was sixteen, her early writing efforts, and her formal training in Paris in piano and voice. She writes of her marriage to Colonel Archibald Christie on 24 December 1914, which ended in divorce in 1928, the birth of her only child, Rosalind, her World War I Red Cross Volunteer work, and her modest success in 1921 with her first published detective novel, *The Mysterious Affair at Styles* (which introduced the debonair Belgian detective, Hercule Poirot). Christie goes on to recount her travels in the Middle East, her meeting there with archaeologist Max Edgar Lucien Mallowan, their subsequent marriage on 11 September 1930, and her work with him at various digs in the Middle East, and her repeated successes from the 1940s on with her novels and plays and with films adapted by others from her works. What her autobiography does not disclose is possibly the most baffling mystery in Christie's entire career—her ten-day disappearance in 1926.

Christie's love of drama—particularly melodrama, which is possibly one of the key sources of her art—dates back to her childhood in Torquay, South Devon, when her father took the family once a week to the theater. During her life she went frequently to the theater and had a great respect for theater that amuses. She first tried playwriting in 1930 with *Black Coffee*, which she described as a "conventional spy thriller," and in 1937 with *Akhnaton*, an ambitious historical drama which was not published until 1973 and not produced until 1979 in New York as *Akhnaton and Nefertiti*. *Black Coffee*, which featured Hercule Poirot and his Watsonian Captain Hastings in pursuit of a secret formula for a new explosive, was first produced in London in 1930 and ran for approximately five months; when it was revived (with minor revisions) in repertory more than twenty years later, it proved more successful. *Akhnaton*, on the other hand, which concerns the ill-fated attempts of the young King Akhnaton to re-

place the old religion of ancient Egypt with a new religion of love, was an entirely new, if not very successful, dramatic departure for Christie, who had become interested in her subject after a visit to Luxor where she met Howard Carter, who with the earl of Carnarvon discovered Tutankhamen's tomb.

It was not until the 1940s, however, that Christie turned to playwriting with any serious intent. Annoyed by people's adapting her detective novels and stories for the stage in a way she disliked, she decided to adapt her critically acclaimed novel, *Ten Little Niggers* (1939), into a play. She believed that many of the previous stage adaptations of her novels had failed mainly because they had stuck too closely to the original work. To Christie, "A detective story is particularly unlike a play, and so is far more difficult to adapt than an ordinary book. It has such an intricate plot, and usually so many characters and false clues, that the thing is bound to become confusing and overladen. What is wanted is *simplification*." She recalled the challenge she faced in writing the novel which she would then adapt for the stage: "I had written the book *Ten Little Niggers* (entitled *Ten Little Indians* in America) because it was so difficult to do that the idea had fascinated me. Ten people had to die without it becoming ridiculous or the murderer being obvious. I wrote the book after a tremendous amount of planning, and I was pleased with what I had made of it. It was clear, straightforward, baffling, and yet had a perfectly reasonable explanation; in fact it had to have an epilogue in order to explain it. It was well received and reviewed, but the person who was really pleased with it was myself, for I knew better than any critic how difficult it had been." Christie's ensuing adaptation of *Ten Little Niggers* was equally as successful with the critics as the novel on which it was based. In fact, the New York production of *Ten Little Indians* proved one of the outstanding successes of the 1944-1945 season and ran for a total of 425 performances. Like the novel, the play specifically concerns ten people who have been mysteriously invited to a small island off the Devonshire coast. When they have gathered together, an equally mysterious phonograph blares forth the news that each of them is known to have been associated with the death of one or more persons at some previous time and that each is here to meet his proper fate. There is no escape. A storm has isolated the island and put the telephone out of commission. In accordance with the macabre nursery rhyme, "Ten Little Niggers" (in the United States, "Ten Little Indians"), they are each murdered one by one. However, unlike the original novel, the last two selected victims (the romantic interest) manage to solve the mystery and effect their own escape.

The great success of her first stage adaptation prompted Christie to decide that in the future only she would adapt her novels. True to her plan, she set to work and adapted three more plays from her fiction: *Appointment with Death* (1945), *Murder on the Nile* (1946), and *The Hollow* (1951). Each enjoyed moderate stage success, but it was not until *The Mousetrap* (1952) that Christie would enjoy a theatrical success comparable to that of *Ten Little Indians*.

The Mousetrap holds the unique distinction in the Christie canon of being, in its initial version, a royally commissioned work. When the late Queen Mary was approaching her eightieth birthday, she was asked by the British Broadcasting Company what in theater—anything from Shakespeare to opera—she would like for celebration of the event. The queen replied that she would like "an Agatha Christie play," and in three weeks time, Christie wrote a thirty-minute radio play entitled *Three Blind*

Mice, which was broadcast by the BBC on 30 May 1947. The play found immediate royal and popular favor, and at the encouragement of her agent Edmund Cork, Christie later adapted it into a novella also entitled *Three Blind Mice* (1950) and then, in 1951, into a play, *The Mousetrap*, which producer Peter Saunders brought to the West End the following year with Sheila Sim and her husband Richard Attenborough in the two leading roles for a supposed short run. When *The Mousetrap* opened at the Ambassadors' Theatre on 25 November 1952, the *Daily Telegraph* acclaimed it the "cleverest murder mystery of the British theatre," and the *Observer* pronounced it as being "deservedly a classic among murder thrillers." With the exception of the *Spectator* and the *Manchester Guardian*, *The Mousetrap* was accorded respectful attention and coverage on its London opening that had rarely before been lavished on mystery thrillers and other such theatrical entertainments. The production, which was admirably staged by Peter Cotes, has been playing to full houses ever since.

Christie said that the formula for writing a

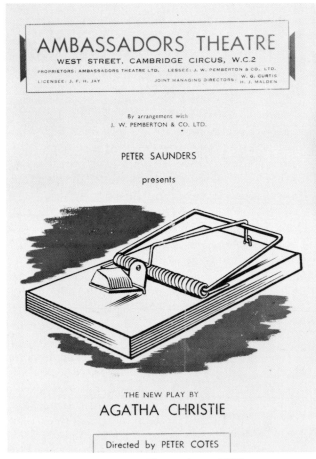

First and post-1958 program covers for Christie's record-breaking play

successful mystery play is to make every character a suspect and then to show how none of them could have possibly committed the crime before revealing the real culprit. *The Mousetrap* follows this formula. Its plot is derived from a familiar dramatic device in Christie's plays: the locked-room puzzle, for which Christie owes a historical debt to Edgar Allan Poe's "The Murders in the Rue Morgue" (1841) and a specific debt to Gaston Leroux's *The Mystery of the Yellow Room* (1908), a work of detective fiction which she greatly admired. *The Mousetrap* concerns a group of predominantly middle-class strangers— one of whom is a killer—stranded in an isolated English manor house during severely inclement weather and cut off from all communication with the outside world. Specifically, in *The Mousetrap*, the strangers are lodgers at a snowbound Berkshire guest house bearing the Gothically appropriate name of Monkswell Manor. The killer, an escaped psychopath whose signature tune is the macabre nursery rhyme, "Three Blind Mice," has strangled his first victim in London on the previous day and has now come to Monkswell Manor in pursuit of his remaining two victims. Somewhat reminiscent of Bernard Shaw's *Heartbreak House* (1920), which dramatized the plight of modern England foundering on the rocks of pre-World War I disillusionment, futility, pessimism, and decay, *The Mousetrap* can also be seen without too much taxing of one's imagination as another depiction of a dying England. Monkswell Manor, which Christie describes as a manor house that "looks not so much a period piece but a house which has been lived in by generations of the same family with dwindling resources," is in fact a museumlike repository of pre-World War II England in which the artifacts, remnants, and dispossessed character types of the last glory of the dying empire have been preserved for the predominantly middle-class English audiences of the 1950s. It is perhaps no coincidence that the psychopathic killer of *The Mousetrap* is revealed as a member of the working class. He is quickly pegged by his cockney accent and working-class manner as a social inferior who has had the effrontery—no doubt attributable to his psychological derangement—to forget his place and trespass into a world where he does not belong and to perpetrate the ultimate upper-middle-class social offenses: murder and chaos. He is appropriately punished for his arrogant presumptuousness by being sent not to a penitentiary but to a home for the criminally insane.

In 1953, Christie wrote what many consider to be her finest mystery play, *Witness for the Prosecution*, which she adapted from her short story of the same title. It is unquestionably one of her most ambitious dramatic ventures, for a considerable portion of its action takes place during a murder trial at the Old Bailey which is presented with great accuracy of detail. Sir Wilfred Robarts, Q.C., agrees to defend Leonard Vole, a young man who is being sought by the police for questioning in connection with the murder of his benefactress who recently changed her will in his favor. The defendant's wife, Romaine Vole, a German refugee who has cause to be grateful to Vole for marrying her, chooses instead to give evidence against him. However, unbeknown to Sir Wilfred, Leonard Vole, and the court, Romaine Vole has carefully prepared a plan by means of which Vole is made to appear innocent and his wife an unsympathetic character repaying with hatred all her husband's tenderness. *Witness for the Prosecution* has considerable suspense and a surprise ending that contains not one but three extremely clever twists that might be criticized on the grounds of probability had Christie not been so skillful in the handling of her material. When it opened in the West End on 28 October 1953, it received enthusiastic responses from both the *Times* and the *Spectator*, and J. C. Trewin, drama critic of the *Illustrated London News*, found the play "so essentially, so delightedly, a piece of the Theatre Theatrical [that] lives solely on the stage." *Witness for the Prosecution* opened in New York the following year, ran for a total of 645 performances, and received the New York Drama Critics Circle Award for best foreign play of 1955. *New York Times* critic Brooks Atkinson thought the play "skillfully written, neatly directed, and extremely well acted, by Francis L. Sullivan and Patricia Jessel in particular." *New York Herald Tribune* critic Walter Kerr remarked that "Christie's prose is not immortal, but she knows how to shape a scene, how to make a silence explode like a time bomb, how to make customers sit up and take intriguing nonsense for nourishment." In 1957, the play was adapted by Billy Wilder and Harry Kurnitz into a highly successful film directed by Wilder and starring Charles Laughton, Marlene Dietrich, and Tyrone Power.

Christie followed *Witness for the Prosecution* with a delightful, original comedy thriller, *Spider's Web* (1954), which concerns the discovery of a body in a country house. When suspicion falls on a neurotic schoolgirl, her stepmother, in attempting to shield the child, is in turn suspected. The situation is further complicated by various involved family relationships, drug peddling, and the like. As for the corpse itself, so much humor is attached to its disposal, that it is difficult to take the criminal

SAVOY THEATRE, STRAND, W.C.2
Box Office Phone TEMple Bar 8888

Dec 14' 54

PETER SAUNDERS presents

Margaret Lockwood

in

Agatha Christie's

SPIDER'S WEB

Directed by WALLACE DOUGLAS   Decor by MICHAEL WEIGHT

"SPIDER'S WEB"
BY AGATHA CHRISTIE

Characters in order of appearance :

Sir Rowland Delahaye	FELIX AYLMER
Hugo Birch	HAROLD SCOTT
Jeremy Warrender	MYLES EASON
Clarissa Hailsham-Brown	MARGARET LOCKWOOD
Pippa Hailsham-Brown	MARGARET BARTON
Mildred Peake	JUDITH FURSE
Elgin	SIDNEY MONCKTON
Oliver Costello	CHARLES MORGAN
Henry Hailsham-Brown	JOHN WARWICK
Inspector Lord	CAMPBELL SINGER
Constable Jones	DESMOND LLEWELYN

The Play is directed by WALLACE DOUGLAS

Décor by MICHAEL WEIGHT

Program cover and cast list for the first production of Christie's comic mystery play

STRAND THEATRE
LONDON

Proprietors - - - SEND MANOR TRUST LTD.
President - - - - LIONEL L. FALCK
Licensee and Managing Director - - R. L. WELLS, F.C.A.

MONDAY TO FRIDAY EVENINGS AT 7.30
MATINEE: WEDNESDAY 2.40   SATURDAYS AT 5.30 & 8.30

BY ARRANGEMENT WITH SEND MANOR TRUST LTD.

PETER SAUNDERS

presents

VERDICT

BY

AGATHA CHRISTIE

First Performance at this Theatre Thursday, May 22nd 1958

PROGRAMME - SIXPENCE

VERDICT
by AGATHA CHRISTIE

Characters in order of their appearance :

Lester Cole	GEORGE ROUBICEK
Mrs. Roper	GRETCHEN FRANKLIN
Lisa Koletzky	PATRICIA JESSEL
Professor Karl Hendryk	GERARD HEINZ
Dr. Stoner	DEREK OLDHAM
Anja Hendryk	VIOLA KEATS
Helen Rollander	MOIRA REDMOND
Sir William Rollander	NORMAN CLARIDGE
Detective Inspector Ogden	MICHAEL GOLDEN
Sergeant Pearce	GERALD SIM

Directed by CHARLES HICKMAN

Décor by JOAN JEFFERSON FARJEON

Program cover and cast list for the first production of Christie's original play depicting a troubled marriage

proceedings too seriously. Much of the success of *Spider's Web* has been attributed to the brilliant comic performance of Margaret Lockwood in the leading role of Clarissa Hailsham-Brown.

On 4 September 1956, *Towards Zero*, a stage adaptation by Christie and Gerald Verner of Christie's novel, opened in London. Containing mystery, suspense, murder, and an effective twist ending, *Towards Zero* proved only moderately successful with the critics. It has fared better in recent revivals. It was followed two years later with *Verdict* (1958), an original play whose depiction of a troubled marital situation had great personal significance for Christie, but which the London critics found quite disappointing because it was not a simon-pure mystery play like they had come to expect from her. Undaunted, Christie completed work on a mystery play, *The Unexpected Guest*, which opened with considerable success in London less than three months after the disappointing premiere of *Verdict*. In this original play, a stranger walks into a country house to find a woman with a gun standing before her husband's corpse which is slumped in a wheelchair. Although the woman is dazed, she admits the killing. The stranger is not convinced however, and he decides to help her blame the murder on an intruder. Matters are further complicated when the police find clues implicating a man who died two years earlier. Then, just as the murder seems solved, there is an unexpected twist.

After *The Unexpected Guest*, Christie wrote only three more dramatic works: *Go Back for Murder* (1960), *Rule of Three* (1962), and *Fiddlers Three* (1971), but none of these efforts came anywhere near touching the success she had achieved with *Ten Little Indians*, *The Mousetrap*, and *Witness for the Prosecution*. *Go Back for Murder* is in fact a very effective adaptation of her novel *Five Little Pigs* (1942), and *Rule of Three* is a collection of three one-act plays entitled *The Rats*, *The Patient*, and *Afternoon at the Seaside*. In *The Rats*, a married woman and her lover are enticed to a sunny Hampstead flat and trapped there with the body of the woman's husband lying in a large chest. Like rats in a trap, the woman and her lover can find no way of escape. *The Patient* is a suspense thriller which deals with the attempt to discover the name of the assailant of a woman who, as a result of the attack, is completely paralyzed and unable to speak. Christie's ingenious use of an electrical apparatus by means of which the patient is able to communicate with the police inspector provides a tension that is relieved only at the very end of the play, when the would-be murderer is unmasked onstage. *Afternoon at the Seaside* is a lighthearted

comedy-mystery that concerns the theft of an emerald necklace from a large house and its discovery on the beach at a quiet little seaside resort. *Fiddlers Three*, Christie's last play, underwent many revisions and reworkings, but none of them proved ultimately successful.

Believing as she did in the theater of entertainment and escape, Christie's objective in her plays was neither to move us profoundly nor to open our eyes to the ills of English society but merely to delight and entertain, which she did for more than forty years. Her stage entertainments are for those viewers who prefer the old-fashioned whodunit in the classical deductive vein, in which the unraveling of the crime is more important than the unpleasant aspects of the actual murder itself. She, in fact, defined her work as "halfway between a crossword puzzle and a hunt in which you can pursue the trail sitting comfortably" in a theater seat. She invariably wrote about what she knew: upper-middle-class professional life in London and in the country; hospitals; the delights and the doldrums of foreign travel; and the scholarly world of her husband, Sir Max Mallowan. It is this evocation of a very English world (both through locales and dramatis personae) of mannerly decorum and respectability that brings readers and audiences back

Agatha Christie, early 1970s

repeatedly to Christie novels and plays, for they have been assured from experience with the Christie canon of the precise world into which they will be entering. It is this world of seemingly cozy upper-middle-class English gentility—consciously devoid of the gruesome and the sordid—that so many of her plays, especially *The Mousetrap*, depict so charmingly and so invitingly. Vicarious participation in this world produces much of her plays' appeal for audiences—be those audiences English or not. *Ten Little Indians*, *The Mousetrap*, and *Witness for the Prosecution* are essentially English, and that characteristic—more than their clever surprise endings—provides much of the basis for their lasting attraction in England and abroad.

Christie's career was highlighted by numerous awards and honors. She received the Mystery Writers of America Grand Master Award in 1954 and a Litt.D. from the University of Exeter in 1961. In 1950, she was honored as a Fellow of the Royal Society of Literature, and in 1956, she was also honored with the title of C.B.E. (Commander, Order of the British Empire). In 1971, however, the ultimate honor of D.B.E. (Dame Commander, Order of the British Empire) was conferred upon her by Queen Elizabeth.

Christie died on Monday, 12 January 1976, at her home in Wallingford, Oxfordshire. She was eighty-five years old. On the day of her death, *The Mousetrap* gave its 9,612th performance, and London theaters dimmed their lights in tribute to her.

References:

Arthur N. Athanason, "*The Mousetrap* Phenomenon," *Armchair Detective*, 12 (Spring 1979): 152-157;

Robert Barnard, *A Talent to Deceive: An Appreciation of Agatha Christie* (New York: Dodd, Mead, 1980);

Frank Behre, *Studies in Agatha Christie's Writing* (Göteborg: Universitetet, 1967);

Ritchie Calder, "Agatha and I," *New Statesman* (30 January 1976);

Jeffrey Feinman, *The Mysterious World of Agatha Christie* (New York: Award Books, 1975);

Hubert Gregg, *Agatha Christie and All That Mousetrap* (London: Kimber, 1980);

H. R. F. Keating, ed., *Agatha Christie: First Lady of Crime* (London: Weidenfeld & Nicolson, 1977);

Clifford H. B. Kitchin, "Five Writers in One: The Versatility of Agatha Christie," *Times Literary Supplement*, 25 February 1955;

Derrick Murdoch, *The Agatha Christie Mystery* (New York & Toronto: Pagurian Press, 1976);

Gordon C. Ramsey, *Agatha Christie: Mistress of Mystery* (New York: Dodd, Mead, 1967);

Gwen Robyns, *The Mystery of Agatha Christie* (Garden City: Doubleday, 1978);

Randall Toye, comp., *The Agatha Christie Who's Who* (New York: Holt, Rinehart & Winston, 1980);

Nancy Blue Wynne, *An Agatha Christie Chronology* (New York: Ace, 1976).

Caryl Churchill

(3 September 1938-   )

Erica Beth Weintraub
Music Educators National Conference

PRODUCTIONS: *Downstairs*, 1958, Oxford University, Oxford; 1959, London;

Having a Wonderful Time, 1960, Oxford University, Oxford; 1960, London;

Easy Death, 1962, Oxford University, Oxford;

Owners, 22 November 1972, Royal Court Theatre Upstairs, London, 11 [performances];

Schreber's Nervous Illness, 1972, broadcast; 6 December 1972, King's Head Lunchtime Theatre, London;

Perfect Happiness, 10 March 1974, Soho Poly Lunchtime Theatre, London;

Objections to Sex and Violence, 2 January 1975, Royal Court Theatre, London, 27;

Moving Clocks Go Slow, 2 June 1975, Royal Court Theatre Upstairs, London;

Light Shining in Buckinghamshire, July 1976, Traverse Theatre, Edinburgh; 27 September 1976, Royal Court Theatre Upstairs, London, 20;

Vinegar Tom, 7 September 1976, Hull Arts Centre, Hull;

Traps, 27 January 1977, Royal Court Theatre Upstairs, London;

Caryl Churchill

Floorshow, by Churchill, Bryony Lavery, Michelene Wandor, and David Bradford, October 1977, North London Poly Theatre, London;

Cloud Nine, 29 March 1979, Royal Court Theatre, London, 26; 18 May 1981, Lucille Lortel's Theatre de Lys, New York;

Three More Sleepless Nights, 10 June 1980, Soho Poly Theatre, (transferred 5 August 1980 to the Royal Court Theatre Upstairs), London, 30.

BOOKS: *Owners* (London: Eyre Methuen, 1973);

Vinegar Tom (London: Theatre Quarterly Publications, 1977);

Light Shining in Buckinghamshire (London: Pluto Press, 1977);

Traps (London: Pluto Press, 1978);

Cloud Nine (London: Pluto Press, 1979).

Although it was obvious from her early radio play *The Ants* (1962) that Caryl Churchill could write good dialogue, she had difficulty translating that talent to a stage where she would be noticed. Nevertheless, Churchill has been writing plays—for radio, television, and the legitimate theater—since her college years. Churchill was born in London, where she spent the war years. She was educated from 1948 to 1955, at the Trafalgar School in Montreal, Canada. She returned to England and enrolled at Lady Margaret Hall, Oxford, in 1957, receiving a B.A. degree in English in 1960. It was there that her first plays were produced.

Her father was a cartoonist, but it was only well along in her career that she began to realize the impact of his work on her own. "Cartoons are really so much like plays. An image with somebody saying something. I grew up with his cartoons of the war—of Goebbels and Mussolini." Her mother, who left school at fourteen, was a secretary, model, and minor film actress, and show business came to young Caryl early. Pantomimes, especially Christmas pantomimes, are a large part of the English tradition, and she used to put on pantomimes as a child, "leaving the bear out front to entertain my parents while I changed the scenery."

Churchill began writing short stories as a schoolgirl, and spent one summer helping to paint sets for a summer theater. She did not "put the two things together"—writing and the stage—until her English studies at Oxford, her first play inspired by the need of a friend for something to direct. "It was a turning point. I realized I preferred things as plays. It has something to do with . . . liking things actually *happening*." Looking back, she now sees the relative paucity of women playwrights as related to the upbringing of girls, who are taught to avoid conflict, to be introspective rather than active. "That way of being lends itself much more readily to the letter, the diary—to the reflective form," she believes.

Marriage to David Harter in 1961 and the births of their three sons did not deflect her from playwriting, and a steady output of plays, at first most successfully for radio, kept Churchill busy. Yet while working away from the mainstream, she later said, "I didn't really feel a part of what was happening in the sixties. During that time I felt isolated. I had small children and was having miscarriages. It was an extremely solitary life. What politicised me was being discontent with my own way of life—of being a barrister's wife and just being at home. . . ." The event which turned her life around was an act of her husband's. Radical in politics, he left private practice to work for a legal aid group in 1972. "We did not want to shore up a capitalist system we did not like," she insisted, claiming that the decision was a joint one.

One radical choice led to others. After another miscarriage, she convinced her husband to take a six months' leave from his job—three months in Africa and three on Dartmoor, where she wrote *Objections to Sex and Violence* (1975). Here was her opportunity for self-expression, and she had become more feminist than Socialist after college years in which her work had developed leftist tendencies. The radio plays, said Churchill, "tended to be about bourgeois middle-class life and the destruction of it." One was *Identical Twins* (1968), played by the same radio "voice," in which one of the characters was a villainous landlord. *Not Without Oxygen*, an ecology-focused play set in the future, involved several young people who, in desperation, planned to set fire to themselves, an idea born from the more extreme Vietnam protests. The most successful of the radio plays was *The Ants*, which has since been published. The central character, she explains, is a young boy who is living with his grandmother because his parents have separated. At the beginning he plays with, and identifies with, some ants, but by the end of the play he wants to exterminate them by setting them on fire with gasoline. "It was really

about war, and about how one is ready to bomb people, to distance oneself from them." Churchill called *The Judge's Wife* (1972), a television play, "the last of the self-destructing plays, because I was self-destructing reality by then and it wasn't necessary to do it in the plays." One play written for radio, *Schreber's Nervous Illness* (broadcast in 1972), later was adapted by Churchill into a stage play for the King's Head Lunchtime Theatre. Based on a Freud case history, it dealt with a schizophrenic who "wrote these amazingly intelligent memoirs about his illness—talking about being a woman and that God was using him for an alien purpose." Radio and television were her initial media "because there was a better market" there for her work. "There wasn't anywhere near the number of fringe and lunchtime theaters, and the radio was an accessible way of having your plays done. The producers were also very good, very accommodating. If your play was seventeen minutes long, they wouldn't ask you to make it thirteen."

Owners, her first major stage play, was performed in 1972 at the Royal Court Theatre Upstairs. "I wrote it in three days," she said. "I'd just come out of the hospital after a particularly gruesome late miscarriage, still quite groggy and my arm ached because they'd given me an injection that didn't work. Into [the play] went for the first time a lot of things that had been building up in me over a long time, political attitudes as well as personal ones." The central character was a female property speculator growing more and more independent of her coarse husband, a butcher. Other characters included property owners and tenants, and possession is dramatized in both its material and its sexual connotations, with an angry accent upon the dramatically sordid—the butcher selling spoiled meat, a young mother signing her baby away to the childless female landlord to stave off eviction, the young man disconnecting his mother from hospital life-support tubing.

Churchill's next play to be produced was *Objections to Sex and Violence*, staged by the Royal Court Theatre in 1975. *Objections to Sex and Violence* marked the appearance of Churchill's emerging feminism in her work. Here a middle-class woman attempts to come to terms with her awakened political consciousness by taking a janitorial job and involving herself with terrorists committed to indiscriminate civilian bombings. Her family and former friends try without success to reclaim her, while through other episodes repressive sexuality is equated with violence, and there are scenes involving flashing, masturbating, pornography, and other by-products of repression and frustration. Critic Ronald Hayman noted that the play failed to come alive, calling it "a theme for wordy variations," and he blamed in part the Royal Court's entrusting the direction to a radio producer. The real problem, however, may have been Churchill's inability to discipline her social anger.

What was established instead [by Cromwell] was an authoritarian parliament, the massacre of the Irish, the development of capitalism.... The simple 'Cavaliers' and 'Roundheads' history taught at school hides the complexity of the aims and conflicts of those to the left of Parliament. We are told of a step toward today's democracy but not of a revolu-

Paul Seed and Rosemary McHale in the 1975 Royal Court Theatre production of Objections to Sex and Violence

Light Shining in Buckinghamshire, produced in 1976 by the Royal Court Theatre Upstairs, was written for the experimental workshop group, Joint Stock. The play's inspiration came from ideas about the religious nature of revolutionary feelings. "We had debates in the workshops ... about specific historical characters. We read a lot and talked about moments of amazing change and extraordinariness in our own lives, things turned upside down. We got ourselves fluent with the Bible, so the whole area was opened up and everybody knew what it was about." The result was a play set in the Cromwellian period, tracing the lives of six working-class people who rise against the system which has economically disenfranchised them. They revolt out of religious mission. "Soldiers fought the king in the belief that Christ would come and establish heaven on earth.

tion that didn't happen; we are told of Charles and Cromwell, but not of the thousands of men and women who tried to change their lives. Though nobody now expects Christ to make heaven on earth, their voices are surprisingly close to us."

Another seventeenth-century setting attracted the committed feminist in Churchill. In association with a women's theater workshop named Monstrous Regiment (after a sixteenth-century pamphlet by Scots reformer John Knox titled "The First Blast of the Trumpet Against the Monstrous Regiment of Women"), Churchill wrote *Vinegar Tom* (1976) about the dark side of witchcraft. "Quite consciously," she has said, "in a very perverse manner, we decided to break the [play] form completely apart by putting songs between the scenes. And though the rest of the play was set in the 1640's, performers appeared in their own contemporary clothes for the songs, which were really very aggressive and extremely difficult to communicate. We didn't want to allow the audience to ever get completely immersed in the stories of the women in the play. We wanted to make them continually aware of our presence, of our relationship to the material, which was combative, anguished. The songs had to contain what we sensed as a connection between the past of the play and our present experience."

Churchill's witches are legitimate healers who are made scapegoats of poverty, victims of religious persecution, superstition, and sexual repression, dramatized in a series of vignettes about frustrated male lechery, female frigidity, bungled abortion, and parentally compelled marriage. Witchcraft, in the distorted view of the community, is the villain. One woman's herbal home-pharmacy is in actuality a community health service; she is, however, hanged for performing her healing magic. A lecherous witch-hunter, Mr. Packer, probes women's private parts with a sharp metal prod to look for the "devil's mark," and is assisted in the torture by a woman who commits the treason to her sex for the good wages. In this way she manages to survive, the

play being about survival as a woman, whatever the century. While the audience may not condone her actions, they understand the difficulties she faced.

Returning to the present, and again writing for the Royal Court Theatre Upstairs, Churchill went to Harold Pinter for her inspiration for *Traps*, (1977), about the personal relationships of a group of six people in a room—first set in the city, then in the country, in the past, in the present. Everything apparently is "real while it happened," but the play questions perceptions of reality, Churchill comparing it to a painting by Dutch artist M. C. Escher where objects exist in permutations which would be impossible in life.

In 1978-1979, already having served as the Royal Court's first resident woman dramatist, Churchill became tutor to the theater's Young Writers' Group, and continued to work with other experimental organizations. With Joint Stock's workshop sessions as the catalyst, she developed what would become her most successful play to date, *Cloud Nine* (1979), which was not only premiered at the Royal Court's main theater but was afterwards revived for a second run. *Cloud Nine* became Churchill's ticket to success in the United

Scene from the 1979 Royal Court Theatre production of Cloud Nine

States, as the play opened Off-Broadway in New York at the Theatre de Lys in May 1981 to positive reviews, enthusiastic audiences, and a long run. Critic Rex Reed of the *New York Times* called the play "the most rewarding surprise of the theatrical season," while Jack Kroll of *Newsweek* called it "a riotously humane farce. . . . The audiences love it." Clive Barnes in the *New York Post* noted that it is "a play that has something to say about kindness, affection, perversion and most of all love."

"One of the things I wanted very much to do in *Cloud 9*," says Churchill, "was to write a play about sexual politics that would *not* just be a woman's thing. I felt there were quite a few women's groups doing plays from that point of view. And gay groups. . . . There was nothing involving straight men. Max [Stafford Clark], the director, even said, at the beginning, 'Well, shouldn't you be doing this with a woman director?' He didn't see that it was his subject—that it was his subject as well."

The first act of *Cloud Nine* is set in colonial Africa in the Victorian period, but the time is deliberately imprecise. Restless natives chafe at imperial rule, symbolically reflected through the experiences of a single colonial family. The second act is set in a London park in the present, using the same characters (and introducing a few new ones). Playing with time, Churchill makes the family only twenty-five years older even though a full hundred years have passed. Also, in act 2, each of the actors from the first act plays a new role. Further toying with appearance and reality, as she had done in *Traps*, she has a man play the mother in the first act, a rag doll her daughter, a girl her son, and a white the black servant. In the second act an adult man plays a little girl, to expose more grotesquely (and comically) sexual double standards. In act 1 Clive, the empire-building governor and rigidly authoritarian husband and father, keeps his wife, Betty, subjected while he pants for a neighboring lady of independent means. Meanwhile the quiet wife pines romantically for the heroic explorer Harry Bagley, who is actually a closet homosexual involved with the native servant, and for Clive and Betty's son, a gentle youth prodded to manliness by Clive. To protect his own reputation, Bagley marries the son's governess, who is actually a closet lesbian in love with Betty. These and other sexual undercurrents surface in the second act, and in the final moments the mother of the first act and the mother of the second meet and embrace.

"I had the image," Churchill observed, "of the black man aspiring to white values and literally being a white negro. And the idea of a woman who has taken on men's values, a sort of man-made woman who has no sense of herself as a woman." The play intended to invoke images equating sexual repression and sexual imperialism with economic repression and political imperialism. It also tried to raise disturbing questions about role conditioning. "For the first time," said Churchill, "I brought together two preoccupations of mine—people's internal states of being and the external political structures which affect them, which make them insane." Francis King, reviewing the opening in the *Sunday Telegraph*, found the "basic joke" in the contrast of "the hypocritical protestations of a group of Victorian stereotypes in Africa with their actual behaviour (adultery, pederasty, sapphism, flagellation, etc.). Lytton Strachey did this kind of thing [in *Eminent Victorians*] with greater finesse." Finding amusement in the grotesquerie of casting, King then added, "Once all this has been exhausted, all the uses of this sex-obsessed, two-dimensional world begin to become weary, stale and flat." John Barber in the *Daily Telegraph* thought better of the play, seeing it as "cheerfully entangling itself in the problems of fitting complex human instincts into workable social patterns." Perceiving it as "a very moral play" despite the explicit language and undecorous scenes, Barber concluded that the first act, with the straightlaced family "revealed as a nest of Tartuffes," is far funnier than the clinically observed second act about "who did what, and with which, and to whom." Still, he found that *Cloud Nine* "explodes myths and shines a curious torch into dark erotic corners with honesty and an all-saving sense of humour. . . . A fascinating evening, but emphatically not one for prudes."

Three More Sleepless Nights, produced in 1980, enhanced Churchill's reputation as "a sexually subversive playwright," as she has been described by critic Ned Chaillet. Her newest play, Chaillet commented in the (London) *Times*, "is enough to dissuade any emotionally wounded lover from returning to the comforts of a double bed. It is exactly that distance that remains between two people, even in bed, that she is examining, and if what she presents has the truthfulness of a clinical study, it [also] has the passionate edge of despair in what it shows. . . . Mercifully, it also has humour. . . ." The three sleepless nights are three scenes in a bed, the first with an argumentative couple in their tenth year of marital warfare, the second with a muted second couple, the wife grieving and suicidal, the husband alienated and unresponsive. For the third night, the playwright shuffles her four characters to expose the obsessively jealous wife of the first scene bedded with the husband of the second, until both find their paths back to their more familiar torments.

Like *Cloud Nine*, it is an energetic play not for prudes or idealists. Churchill has never written for prudes, but her audiences are less limited by that aspect of her work than by her inability thus far, even in her more comic plays, to give the medium priority over the message. Despite that, however, Churchill remains one of the most imaginative talents working for the theater in her generation.

Other:

The Ants, in *Penguin New Dramatists 12* (Har-

mondsworth, U.K.: Penguin, 1968).

References:

Richard Findlater, ed., *At the Royal Court* (New York: Grove Press, 1981), pp. 154-155ff;

Catherine Itzin, *Stages in the Revolution* (London: Eyre Methuen, 1980), pp. 62ff;

Judith Thurman, "Caryl Churchill: The Playwright Who Makes You Laugh About Orgasm, Racism, Class Struggle, Homophobia, Woman-Hating, the British Empire, and the Irrepressible Strangeness of the Human Heart," *MS* (May 1972): 51-54, 57.

Giles Cooper
(9 August 1918-2 December 1966)

Albert E. Kalson
Purdue University

PRODUCTIONS: *Never Get Out*, 30 May 1950, Gateway Theatre, London; 7 December 1954, Arts Theatre, London;

Haddocks' Eyes, 6 July 1950, New Lindsay Theatre, London;

Mathry Beacon, 18 June 1956, BBC Third Programme, London; 1968, Edinburgh Festival, Edinburgh;

Everything in the Garden, 13 March 1962, Arts Theatre (transferred 16 May 1962 to Duke of York's Theatre), London, 37 [performances];

Out of the Crocodile, 29 October 1963, Phoenix Theatre, London, 100;

The Spies Are Singing, 27 April 1966, Nottingham Playhouse, Nottingham;

Happy Family, 10 May 1966, Hampstead Theatre Club, London; 9 March 1967, St. Martin's Theatre, London, 36.

BOOKS: *Everything in the Garden* (London & New York: Evans, 1963);

The Other Man [novel] (St. Albans, U. K.: Panther Books, 1964);

Out of the Crocodile (London: Evans, 1964);

Six Plays for Radio (London: BBC Publication, 1966)—includes *Mathry Beacon*; *The Disagreeable Oyster*; *Without the Grail*; *Under the Loofah Tree*; *Unman, Wittering and Zigo*; and *Before the Monday*.

In 1961 when a *Times* correspondent wrote, "It is possible that Mr. Cooper is the busiest of British dramatists," Giles Cooper was unknown to British theatergoers. Only a small but loyal band of radio listeners knew him then as the gifted and witty creator of wickedly comic private worlds, each a sinister microcosm of a larger contemporary society, lost, embittered, half-crazed. Cooper would soon extend his enclosed worlds from disembodied radio to the peopled stage in three underrated, nearly forgotten plays of striking originality— *Everything in the Garden* (1962), *Out of the Crocodile* (1963), and *Happy Family* (1966)—which never attracted the audience that a fellow dramatist with similar strengths, Harold Pinter, was beginning to command. When Cooper, eventually the author of nearly fifty original pieces for radio and television and a dozen plays for the stage, was named best writer in 1961 by the Guild of Television Producers and Directors, ironically the works for which he was honored were adaptations rather than original plays. The recognition came for a successful three-year television series based on the Maigret detective novels of Georges Simenon, and this work may even have contributed to his being awarded the Order of the British Empire in 1960. Characteristically, Cooper claimed that such adaptations "are done with the part of the mind you do *The Times* crossword with."

Giles Stannus Cooper, born near Dublin in 1918, was the son of Commander Guy Edward Cooper, R.N., an Anglo-Irish colonial judge who fully expected him to join the colonial service, and Winifred Annette Warren. Reared in London, Cooper attended Lancing College in Sussex and studied languages at Grenoble University in preparation for the consular career for which his military bearing suited him. While continuing his Spanish studies in San Sebastian, he was slightly wounded when he got in the way of "a stray Civil War bullet," which may have convinced him that an actor's life was safer and surely more satisfying. He returned home to enroll in the Webber-Douglas School of Drama but was conscripted in August 1939 at the outbreak of World War II. Four of his seven years in the army were spent with the West Yorkshire Regiment in Burma. Once out of the army, he was drawn again to the theater, where he had little success as an actor but met aspiring actress Gwyneth Mary Lewis, whom he married in 1947. In London he played such undistinguished roles as Mullins in a 1949 production of James M. Barrie's *Peter Pan* and appeared among the guards and

Giles Cooper

senators in Orson Welles's 1951 production of *Othello*.

Still pursuing an acting career, Cooper began to write for the stage. *Never Get Out*, the first play he later cared to remember, is a two-character study of loneliness and alienation in which a man and a woman meet in an abandoned house in a chilling landscape marked for destruction in a military bombing practice. Miraculously surviving, the two attempt to inhabit the scarred world together but soon realize they must go their separate ways. Performed in a small London theater and at the Edinburgh Festival in 1950, the play attracted some interest, which Cooper felt was diminished by "a perfectly abominable" second play, *Haddocks' Eyes*, actually written earlier than *Never Get Out*. *Haddocks' Eyes* curiously foreshadows Cooper's own schizophrenic career as a writer supporting himself with hackwork for the popular media of radio and television while longing to make a mark in the theater. Old Joss, the protagonist, is actually both John Toddington, author of serious artistic novels, and Jonathan Trump, writer of "Thrilling Stories for Boys." Like Cooper himself, Joss comes to understand that either style holds the promise of satisfaction for the writer who will rise to any challenge. Soon meeting the challenge of radio drama, Cooper would lift the genre to the level of art, with his plays for radio far surpassing his early work for the more highly regarded legitimate stage.

Drawn to radio in the early 1950s by economic necessity (the BBC produces some 500 plays a year and actively encourages writers of talent), Cooper was soon engaged in a fruitful alliance with BBC producer-director Donald McWhinnie. He would help Cooper win his battles with the staid organization's higher-ups, who were disconcerted by the writer and producer's unconventional experiments as they explored the possibilities of the medium to its limits throughout the decade. Eventually, McWhinnie, director of Pinter's *Caretaker*, would guide the mature plays of Cooper to the stage.

Abandoning his wayward acting career, Cooper remained wary of the radio writer's reputation built on the ephemeral word. "We are those whose names are writ in air," he said, and always planned to return to the theater which he considered to be freer of fads and cliques. Nonetheless, Cooper's work is cited most frequently in references to the BBC's golden age of radio drama in the 1950s. If the radio plays *The Disagreeable Oyster* (1957) and *Under the Loofah Tree* (1958)—the former with its single protagonist played by two actors, and the latter with its imaginative retelling of a life by a hero sitting in his bath—are more obviously unconventional, the seemingly naturalistic radio dramas, *Mathry Beacon* (1956) and *Unman, Wittering and Zigo* (1958), are Cooper's more haunting and original works, the masterpieces which anticipate the style and tone of his comic nightmares for the stage. In both, Cooper ensnares the listener in an enclosed world where events may be implausible, but as critic Mervyn Jones states, "A writer of quality creates his own probability." These works, and the later plays for the stage, do not enter the world of fantasy as many critics have claimed. Instead, Cooper carries a perverse logic to a terrifying but actual possibility, as a handful of characters, a segment of a greater whole, mirrors the violence of today's irrational world.

In *Mathry Beacon* some army personnel, three men and two women, volunteer to join an officer in guarding a deflector, a machine which serves no practical purpose, in a remote part of coastal Wales. Lulled by the deflector's hypnotic whine, they enter a strange yet real utopian existence, farming the land, rearing children, unmindful that the war has come to an end. Their lives become a series of rituals with a useless machine that has become like a god to them at the center of their universe. Eventually they turn on one another for the very reasons of greed and power for which men wage wars in a less idyllic world, and the survivors are lured back to that world by the promise of material gain. The play has a rhythm of growing intensity and an economy which radio makes possible, qualities which Cooper would adapt to his later work.

Unman, Wittering and Zigo illustrates how Cooper's works begin as ideas. While adapting William Golding's novel *Lord of the Flies* (1955) for radio, he was intrigued by the concept that "evil might be imposed and not natural" and attempted to embody it in a play about soldiers. However, he finally set the work in a boys' school, where he focused on a single form of students, who terrorize a new master by informing him that they have murdered his predecessor. "When an idea associates itself with the wrong story," Cooper found as he abandoned the army setting, "it is usually . . . a story that treats it too directly." In *The Object* (1964), which won the Czech International Prize for Radio Drama in 1966, materialism and aggression on the grand scale of warring nations steeped in technology are contrasted with the petty quarrels of illiterate beings at the lowest rung of society who dismantle a space rocket to flog its parts on the Common.

Television did not stimulate Cooper to the extent that radio did, but some of his plays for the medium in the 1960s are memorable. These include *The Other Man* (1964), a "what-if" play about an England capitulating early in the war, and *The Long House* (1965), in which the residents of connecting houses tear down their walls to form a communal society.

In 1962 when the Royal Shakespeare Company introduced a season of experimental offerings at London's Arts Theatre with *Everything in the Garden*, an audience familiar with Cooper's works for radio and television might have been surprised to find the play beginning as a conventional comedy of manners: a suburban housewife enters a well-appointed sitting room through French windows which lead to the garden, where her husband is cutting the grass. When he joins her to discuss the placement of the flowers, their inconsequential but casually witty banter has the comforting ring of familiarity, but an ominous note enters: there is no money for a greenhouse, let alone a "four-stroke" mower. Cooper's first play for the stage in over a decade takes up the inexorable logic of the radio plays. How the Actons manage to keep afloat in suburbia with the aid of the wife's discreet afternoon prostitution is the subject of a chilling comedy with a devastating denouement which moves from innocence to acquiescence—"The more you get used to things the better you get . . . at . . . getting used to things." *Everything in the Garden*'s pattern, like that of the radio plays, is the gradual acceptance of horror if horror harbors material gain, of learning to live with anything in the garden—even the body of a neighbor who had inadvertently discovered the source of the Actons' sudden wealth. Accommodation is all in Cooper's wry immoral fable.

In the play's first production the audience accepted what Kenneth Tynan called its modulation "from the key of minor N. F. Simpson into that of major Dürrenmatt." They were unable, however, to accept "a second, and less persuasive, change of key: from Dürrenmatt to Pirandello" at the conclusion as the husband stepped out of character to denounce the cynical work as well as the audience willing to be entertained by it, only to be pulled back within the play's frame to be beaten by three other husbands whose wives are also engaged in the oldest profession. When the play transferred to the West End, Cooper devised a more conventional but no less disturbing ending. Yet the damage had been done by the earlier set of reviews, and the play quickly closed.

In 1967 American playwright Edward Albee adapted *Everything in the Garden* for a Broadway audience by sentimentalizing the family relationships, thus dulling the play's bitter tone, at the same time that he belabored some obvious satire. His turning the neighbor into a chorus who comments on the action, even after his death, further confused the adaptation, which suffered the same fate as the original version.

Out of the Crocodile safely avoids the mistakes of the more heartlessly effective *Everything in the Garden*, and, with the popular Celia Johnson and Kenneth More in the cast, enjoyed a moderate run of 100 performances in the West End in 1963. The play can be taken at a literal level—and probably was

having paid no bills in years, thanks to Peter's scheme, are so wrapped up in the little rituals of their daily lives that they have not even noticed. Complications arise when the couple skip their Brighton weekend; suddenly they are face to face with their intruding savior.

Beneath the comic surface, Cooper again explores the vacuum of routine existence dictated by a sterile society. Should the audience be tempted to applaud the Hampsters' opting out of the rat race, the realization that the couple is just as bored as they would otherwise be must give them pause.

Geraldine McEwan and Derek Godfrey in the 1962 London production of Everything in the Garden

by most of its audience—as a broad comedy about a ne'er-do-well, Peter Pounce, who straightens out a befuddled couple's lives, unbeknownst to them, by inhabiting their London flat during the weekends when they are in Brighton, and taking over the Brighton flat when they are in London. According to Peter's Theory of Ultimate Responsibility, "the world is run by girls," secretaries who do the bidding of landlords, bank managers, company directors, and the like. Should the girls be wooed with a little romance, due bills and overdrafts could find their way to the back of the files. The Hampsters,

Life in London means afternoon tea, followed by gin for Helen and whisky for Henry, and an evening of stupefaction in front of the television. Brighton offers the routine of brisk walks along the Front, which the Hampsters accept as a break from routine. Yet Peter is no better off. Keeping assorted secretaries interested in him but not too demanding of him has become his own tedious full-time job. Finally, he must resort to a monetary bribe for Julia, who knows too much, presumably the very tactic employed by more experienced practitioners in the world of commerce. That he has managed to credit the Hampsters' account with £9,000,000 makes a life of perpetual idleness a possibility for the four of them. Tired of the game, however, once the couple recognize their dependence upon him, Peter leaves them in the midst of their own version of a sack race, with cushion covers over their heads, a perfect emblem for "nullities with names" who can achieve happiness only by blinding themselves to a situation with which they cannot cope.

The characters of *Out of the Crocodile* may read about acts of horror in the newspapers, but they perpetrate no such actions themselves. Life as they live it, however, is horror enough. That they evoke the audience's laughter is the result of Peter's coldly logical manipulation of Helen and Henry, forcing them into the roles of indulgent parents or loyal retainers, which, with unthinking gratitude, they play to the hilt.

Whereas the Hampsters are bewildered by the adult world which they inhabit, the characters of *Happy Family*, threatened by it, actively flee it. Although Susan, Mark, and Deborah (siblings whose ages range from forty-three to thirty-five) live in various parts of England, they meet as often as they can to engage in the safe rituals of childhood—games, private jokes, an invented language. While Deborah, the youngest, hardly ventures outdoors, Susan and Mark live outwardly normal lives but have no real contact with the people they move among. Mark comments on his club, "nobody there at all and the whole damned place overcrowded." Susan has become engaged to a man who has told her he is a solicitor, even though he has frequently waited on her at the grocer's, where she has been oblivious to his existence. When she brings Gregory to meet the others at Deborah's cottage in Huntingdonshire, tensions mount. Mark is jealous of another male in his private domain; Deborah is perplexed by the first stirrings of her own sexuality; and Susan, counting on Gregory as a means of entry into an adult world, realizes how unwisely she has chosen him when her fiance, after attempting first to rape Deborah, then to electrocute her for humiliating him, reveals his own dangerously arrested emotional development and retreats in confusion. At last Deborah must face the fact that she, Susan, and Mark are the nobodies the three of them have mocked all their lives. In the second of Cooper's two endings for the play, Deborah's dawning awareness that life holds neither punishments nor rewards does not signal emotional maturation. Instead, the three, more dependent upon one another than ever before, sit down to the ritual of a nursery tea.

All of Cooper's plays present contained worlds, and his mastery here of his most tightly encased world makes the improbable nightmarishly believable. The audience accepts Mark's fear of the dark even though he has demonstrated by means of a phone call that as a stockbroker he can in fact cope with the intricacies of the world of finance. He is more at home, however, with the complexities of his Meccano erector set. Deborah's total innocence concerning sex seems no more extraordinary than her ignorance about electricity and fuse boxes and enables Cooper to imply that for Susan and Gregory, who are at least aware of the facts of life, it is love rather than sex that seems to be grotesquely comic. Once again a darkened image of the contemporary world develops with an uncanny logic that turns the eccentric into the seemingly commonplace as Cooper in his finest work for the stage reveals the frightened child within us all.

With cruel irony, between the promising first performance of *Happy Family* at the Hampstead Theatre Club in May 1966 and its unsuccessful West End production in March 1967, Cooper himself met the fate which Mark reports for his deceased parents: "A railway accident. Absurd." Returning by train to his home in Oatcroft, Sussex, after a dramatists' dinner in London on 2 December, Cooper "may have mistaken the carriage door for one leading to the corridor," the coroner stated at the inquest. He fell from the fast-moving train near Surbiton in Surrey. "Death by misadventure" was the verdict.

Although success in the theater sadly eluded him, his posthumous reputation as Britain's foremost radio dramatist was strengthened by the establishment in 1978 of the annual Giles Cooper Awards, jointly sponsored by the BBC and the publisher Eyre Methuen, for the year's best radio plays. Even without an annual reminder, however, he is assured of that position by the occasional rebroadcast of his indelible work, which Donald McWhinnie, including in his estimate the plays for the stage, calls "a chronicle of the sickness of society, the old evils, always with us: selfishness and cruelty behind the smile, violence hidden in the handshake, savagery always around the corner . . . this unflattering view of humanity . . . cloaked in wit and prodigious comic invention."

Television Scripts:
The No-Man, Associated Rediffusion, 1955;
General Confusion, Associated Rediffusion, 1955;
Liberty Hall, BBC, 1958;
Where the Party Ended, BBC, 1960;

Point of Honour, ATV, 1960;
Love and Penguins, ATV, 1961;
The Power of Zero, ATV, 1962;
The Lonesome Road, ATV, 1962;
The Freewheelers, ATV, 1963;
True Love and Limbeck, Associated Rediffusion, 1963;
The Double Doll, ATV, 1963;
Loop, ATV, 1963;
A Wicked World, ATV, 1964;
The Other Man, Granada, 1964;
Carried by Storm, BBC 2, 1964;
Seek Her Out, BBC, 1965;
The Long House, BBC 2, 1965;
I Am Osango, ABC, 1967;
Kittens Are Brave, BBC 2, 1967;
To the Frontier, BBC 2, 1968.

Radio Scripts:

Thieves Rush In, BBC Home Service, 1950;
The Forgotten Rotten Borough, BBC Home Service, 1950;
The Timbimbo Craze, or New Games for Old, BBC Home Service, 1950;
Small Fortune, BBC Home Service, 1951;
The Private Line, BBC Home Service, 1951;
The Owl and the Pussycat, BBC Light Programme, 1953;
The Sound of Cymbals, BBC Light Programme, 1955;
The Volunteer, BBC Home Service, 1956;
Mathry Beacon, BBC Third Programme, 1956;
The Disagreeable Oyster, BBC Third Programme, 1957;
Without the Grail, BBC Home Service, 1958;
Dangerous Word, BBC Home Service, 1958;
Under the Loofah Tree, BBC Third Programme, 1958;
All for Three Days: a Story of the Hungarian Revolution, BBC Home Service, 1958;
Unman, Wittering and Zigo, BBC Third Programme, 1958;
Part of the View, BBC Home Service, 1959;

Caretaker, BBC Home Service, 1959;
Before the Monday, BBC Third Programme, 1959;
A Crown of Gold, BBC Light Programme, 1959;
The Return of General Forefinger, BBC Third Programme, 1960;
Pig in the Middle, BBC Third Programme, 1960;
A Perfectly Ghastly Joke, BBC Home Service, 1962;
I Gotta Universe, BBC Home Service, 1963;
All the Way Home, BBC Third Programme, 1963;
The Object, BBC Third Programme, 1964;
Something from the Sea, Baden-Baden Sudvestfunk, Germany, 1965.

Other:

Happy Family, in *New English Dramatists 11* (Harmondsworth, U. K.: Penguin, 1967), pp. 19-95;
The Object, in *New English Dramatists 12: Radio Plays* (Harmondsworth, U. K.: Penguin, 1968), pp. 23-47.

References:

Michael Bakewell, "Giles Cooper: *Dangerous Word*," *From the Fifties: BBC Sound Radio Drama Series*, edited by Bakewell and Eric Ewens (London: BBC Publication, 1961), pp. 71-73;
"Busiest of British Dramatists," *Times*, 12 October 1961, p. 18;
Louise Cleveland, "Theatre Checklist No. 4: Giles Cooper," *Theatrefacts*, 1 (November 1974-January 1975): 13-14, 45;
Cleveland, "Trials in the Soundscape: Achievements of the Experimental British Radio Play," Ph.D. dissertation, University of Wisconsin, 1973;
Donald McWhinnie, *The Art of Radio Drama* (London: Faber & Faber, 1959);
McWhinnie, "Comic Mask, Cruel World: The Plays of Giles Cooper," *Theatre Quarterly*, 4 (November 1974-January 1975): 51-54;
John Russell Taylor, *Anger and After* (London: Eyre Methuen, 1977), pp. 26-28.

David Cregan
(30 September 1931-   )

Timothy J. Kidd
Trinity College, Cambridge

PRODUCTIONS: *Miniatures*, 25 April 1965, Royal Court Theatre, London, 2 [performances];

Transcending and *The Dancers*, 23 January 1966, Royal Court Theatre, London, 1;

Three Men for Colverton, 21 September 1966, Royal Court Theatre, London, 26;

The Houses by the Green, 2 October 1968, Royal Court Theatre, London, 19;

A Comedy of the Changing Years, 24 February 1969, Royal Court Theatre Upstairs, London, 18;

Tipper, 28 November 1969, Oxford Union Chamber, Oxford;

Liebestraum and *The Problem*, 11 December 1970, Studio Theatre, Birmingham, 4;

Jack in the Box and *If You Don't Laugh, You Cry*, 26 March 1971, Studio Theatre, Birmingham, 4;

How We Held the Square, 14 October 1971, Studio Theatre, Birmingham, 28;

The Daffodil and *Sentimental Value*, 1 November 1971, Ambiance Lunch Hour Theatre, London;

The Land of Palms, 14 November 1972, Barn Theatre, Dartington;

George Reborn, 2 February 1973, Orange Tree Theatre, Richmond, 15;

Cast Off, 7 April 1973, Crucible Studio Theatre, Sheffield, 28;

Pater Noster, in *Mixed Blessings*, 12 September 1973, Capitol Theatre, Horsham, 12;

The King, 24 May 1974, Shaw Theatre, London, 21;

Tina, 24 October 1975, Orange Tree Theatre, Richmond, 21;

Poor Tom, 29 October 1976, Orange Tree Theatre, Richmond, 21;

Tigers, 22 September 1978, Orange Tree Theatre, Richmond, 26;

Young Sir, 22 June 1979, Orange Tree Theatre, Richmond, 13;

Little Red Riding Hood, 28 November 1979, Victoria Theatre, Stoke on Trent, 38;

Getting It Right, 7 July 1980, Campus West Theatre, Welwyn.

BOOKS: *Ronald Rossiter* (London: Hutchinson, 1959);

Transcending and The Dancers (London: Methuen, 1967);

Three Men for Colverton (London: Methuen, 1967);

The Houses by the Green (London: Methuen, 1969);

Miniatures (London: Methuen, 1970);

The Land of Palms and Other Plays (London: Eyre Methuen, 1973)—includes *The Land of Palms, Liebestraum, The Problem, Jack in the Box, If You Don't Laugh, You Cry*, and *George Reborn*;

How We Held the Square (London: Eyre Methuen, 1973);

Poor Tom and Tina (London: Eyre Methuen, 1976).

David Cregan is a playwright who shows the externally inspired ideas and moral compulsions of modern people in conflict with instinct and reality.

130

Even though the spectacle of the collision is invariably comic, its result is often painful or violent. Cregan employs a rapid, episodic style, presenting characters in absurd situations, often of their own making. His work is literate, intelligent, but lacks resolution, appropriately perhaps for the dilemmas which he presents. He does not offer definite conclusions in his work; most of the issues are left open or are subsumed in cathartic violence.

David Appleton Quartus Cregan was born in the elegant Georgian spa of Buxton in Derbyshire. He was the fourth and youngest son of James Grattan Cregan, a prosperous shirt manufacturer of Ulster descent, and Gertrude Isabella Martha Fraser Cregan. Both of his parents were from a Congregationalist background; his father in particular instilled in him an indelible social and moral conscience. Cregan had a traditional education at the Leys School, Cambridge, and Clare College, Cambridge, graduating with a degree in English in 1955. During the 1940s he had discovered theater—with a particular interest in Ibsen and in farce—and while at Cambridge he was active in the Footlights Club, which has produced many English comedians. After graduating he spent 1955 to 1957 teaching at a private school in Palm Beach, Florida, but neither this nor his national service experience as an acting corporal in the Royal Air Force from 1950 to 1952 had any discernible impact on his plays, all of which are set in contemporary English society, either suburban or provincial. In 1957 he returned to Britain and for the next ten years earned his living by teaching English and drama; in 1958 he moved "from being an unhappy teacher in Manchester to being a happy one in Hatfield," where he has lived ever since. In 1960 he married Ailsa Mary Wynne Willson; they have three sons and an adopted daughter.

Cregan's first work was a novel, *Ronald Rossiter* (1959), of which both the landscape and the social context are drawn from his own childhood in Derbyshire. The unhappy circumstances of the central character, a young boy, are contrasted with scenes of pleasant family life drawn from Cregan's own memories. In the novel an emotionally deprived boy kills a small girl and then himself. *Ronald Rossiter* introduces many of the themes which recur in the plays: the effect of an unhappy childhood, sexual repression, sudden violence, and original sin. But the earnestness of moral search in the novel is not lightened by comedy, as it is in Cregan's drama.

His first play, *Miniatures* (1965), was produced at the Royal Court Theatre with a cast that included Nicol Williamson, George Devine, and Lindsay An-

derson. It is a wry comedy of school life based on Cregan's own experience. The central figure is a music teacher who tries to subvert the school by wrecking the gramophone, stealing from the pupils, and attempting unsuccessfully to hang himself in public. There are deft sketches of common-room types: the robust science teacher, the repressed spinster, the nubile gym-mistress, the anxiously progressive headmaster. Comic intrigues involve the efforts of two conservative teachers to raise the academic tone by introducing the wearing of gowns, and the inexplicable determination of a pretty but dim schoolgirl to become a teacher herself.

The problems of a young girl on the threshold of life form the subject of his next play, *Transcending* (1966). In this play a young girl suffers the attentions of two would-be lovers and an ineffectual father before escaping the farcical complications by becoming a nun: "You'll remember that I'm not a great success at facts, although I *am* hardworking, I *have* a conscience, and I'm devoted." This play, together with Cregan's *The Dancers* (1966), won the Charles Henry Foyle award for new drama in 1966. Both works were produced at the Royal Court Theatre. *The Dancers* is a slighter work, which takes the form of a dance in which four of the five characters eventually pair off, leaving the last as the odd man out. The character left without a partner is the first in Cregan's long line of anguished liberals, torn between sermonizing and lust, wanting "the mind of a revolutionary," but lacking any such conviction.

The themes of sex and religion were taken up again in Cregan's next play, *Three Men for Colverton*, produced at the Royal Court Theatre in 1966. It is set in a small ancient town bypassed by the motorway. Three West Country evangelists arrive with a call from God, but they are opposed by a worldly Anglo-Catholic clergyman with a portable confessional ("the nesting-box," he calls it) and by an earnest modern, liberal clergyman ("I'm a South Bank man, and we don't cheat."). The townsfolk continue with their wonted activities: saloon-bar drinking, cultural self-improvement, tea parties, seduction of schoolgirls in hayfields. The action centers on a struggle for power between the chief evangelist and the town's dominating woman; each of these two forceful characters is undermined by the fleshly weakness of their followers. The two junior evangelists succumb to the temptations of barroom and bed, while the two clergyman fail to come to the aid of orthodoxy, either through prurience or inner doubt. The play concludes with the death of the

Program cover for the 1966 Royal Court Theatre production of Cregan's third play

woman, the passing on of talismanic power in the form of her husband's ashes, and with a literal leap of faith by the youngest evangelist from the church tower. His conviction that his body will be lowered by angels to the ground proves disastrously mistaken, which shatters the belief of the chief evangelist ("I've been made a fool of!"). The play is written in a loose elliptical style, in which the characters follow their private or public obsessions, intersecting at times with comic inappropriateness. The texture is humorous, but the inner concerns are serious ones; as the playwright notes: "contemporary moral problems can be seen at the centre of the church's moral wrestling." Cregan is one of the few modern dramatists who takes traditional religion seriously enough to joke about it. The play was well received critically, and it remains his most original work.

Father Pym
(Richard Simpson)

Hester
(Natasha Pyne)

Ched
(Richard O'Callaghan)

Dorman
(John Shepherd)

Mrs Harrison)
(Margery Mason)

Miss Fisher
(Mary MacLeod)

Roofless
(Lennard Pearce)

Mr Milend
(Peter Wyatt)

Deaf
(Joe Greig)

Sheepskin
(Jean Boht)

Edward
(Malcolm Tierney)

Mrs Carnock
(Sylvia Coleridge)

Mr. Dole
(Leonard Sachs)

Rev. Swan
(Julian Curry)

Cast for the 1966 production of Three Men for Colverton

Cregan's association with the Royal Court Theatre continued with *The Houses by the Green* (1968) which, like the previous play and much of his subsequent work, is concerned in part with the theme of environmental conservation—in this case not the preservation of an old town but of a pleasant pair of houses by a village green, which are threatened by developers and in a sense by the modern world. The action is based on the traditional commedia dell'arte formula: a pair of young lovers, a heavy father, two elderly lovers, a resourceful servant, and a good-time girl, presented together with disguises, intrigues, and rapid reversals of fortune. With fine economy Cregan uses only four characters in various disguises and a single set. His next and last play for the Royal Court was *A Comedy of the Changing Years* (1969), which inaugurated the new Theatre Upstairs.

In 1967, Cregan gave up his teaching post and since then has subsisted largely on his own writing and on occasional grants from the Arts Council. He lives in a council house and writes in a small but comfortable wooden shed in the garden. His wife supplements the family income by teaching mentally handicapped children. He has worked with publicly funded arts bodies such as the Royal Court Studio (1964, 1968), the Royal Shakespeare Company Studio (1971), the Midlands Arts Centre (1971), and the West Midlands Arts Association (1972-1975). The British Council has sent him to Rumania and to Hungary, where he encountered the Squat Theatre, who formed the subject of his sole critical article after they became artistic refugees in 1977. He has also written several plays for radio and television. All of his works have been performed in subsidized theaters, except for the sketch *Pater Noster* (1973). With this exception, none have been seen on the commercial stage or in the West End; none have appeared in America except for an occasional university campus production.

In the early 1970s, the locus of Cregan's work shifted to the Midlands. He began an association

ROYAL COURT THEATRE
October 2nd to 19th

the HOUSES BY THE GREEN

BY DAVID CREGAN

THE COMPANY

Oliver	TOM CHADBON
The Commander	JOHN NORMINGTON
Mervyn Molyneux	BOB GRANT
Susan	YVONNE ANTROBUS

THERE WILL BE ONE INTERVAL

The Management reserve the right to refuse admission and to make any change in the cast necessitated by illness or other unavoidable causes.

Patrons are reminded that smoking is not permitted in the auditorium.

In accordance with the requirements of the Greater London Council:

(i) The public may leave at the end of the performance of exhibition by all doors and such doors must at that time be open.

(ii) All gangways, corridors, staircases and external passageways intended for exit shall be kept entirely free from obstruction whether permanent or temporary.

(iii) Persons shall not be permitted to stand or sit in any of the gangways intersecting the seating or in any of the other gangways. If standing be permitted in the gangways at the sides and rear of the seating, it shall be limited to the numbers indicated in the notices exhibited in those positions.

(iv) The safety curtain must be lowered and raised in the presence of such audience.
First-aid facilities in this theatre by The British Red Cross Society, Chelsea Division members, who give their services voluntarily.

Program cover and cast list for Cregan's 1968 comedy

with the director Philip Hedley and continued to develop an interest in improvisation, in the use of music, and in experimental dramatic technique. (He acknowledges a debt to the director Keith Johnstone and to his book *Impro*, published in 1979.) His work began to display increasing social and political concern. In *Tipper* (1969), a Labour politician is kidnapped by a group of grotesque poverty-stricken gypsies and excreted upon by their hugely fat female leader. His response is to lament that "I have failed to reach a member of my constituency. Someone my government is trying to help."

In *How We Held the Square* (1971), a socialist propaganda play for children, a group of local people hold off an attempt by a committee of corrupt Conservative councillors, acting at the behest of the Whip and his sinister team of cardboard boxes, to develop their village square. The locals are led by a grandmother enraged because the taxpayers will not build her a free bathroom; the locals build barricades in the square and shout "Lenin fights again!" Although the message of the play is conventional leftist propaganda, its style is free-flowing and improvisatory.

In *Cast Off* (1973) a group of social derelicts are threatened with eviction from the rubble-strewn common where they live by a variety of forces, including property speculators, forward-looking industrialists, and corrupt Conservative councillors. They are befriended by a rich girl, slumming for the sake of her conscience, and the play ends with their burning of the local council offices. In *Poor Tom* (1976) a group of tenants threatened with eviction are led by Tom, the downtrodden caretaker, in a fight against their landlord, a chorus of the upright bourgeoisie, and a judge. The caretaker murders the landlord in the belief that this will save their home. The judge, in sentencing him to life imprisonment, observes that "it is the weak, the timid, who go to the wall," but also that poor Tom only "asked all the world to dance." There was a vogue for this type of play in the subsidized theater of the 1970s. British society was presented as corrupt and authoritarian; anarchist violence or Communist revolution was proposed as the solution. Cregan's work avoids the totalitarian if not the paranoid features of the genre.

One rich vein of comedy in all of Cregan's plays is his characteristically English concentration on social class. In *Tina* (1975) the heroine is a repressed thirty-year-old teacher who believes that the experience of real life is to be found among the smelly proletariat; in the pursuit of such experience she dresses in stained jeans and leather jacket and

befriends a ten-year-old prostitute named Dawn. Tina cherishes the view that "the system has given her no one to love." Nostalgia for the proletarian way of life can also be traced in Sarah, the rich girl in *Cast Off*, who befriends the derelicts and even has her baby while she is living among them. She cries out to a God in whose existence she does not believe: "Are you listening? I've made a stand for these lousey stinking people and I must go on. But secretly I want to back out and wear clean clothes. Am I bourgeois after all?" Middle-class masochism is carried even further by the politician in *Tipper*; he allows himself to be jailed for life for a murder committed by his kidnappers because he wants to "know and understand others, others completely different from ourselves."

The activist characters in Cregan's work never examine the validity of their beliefs; the liberals seldom do anything else. Most of the liberals are paralyzed by social guilt; their dilemma is both painful and comic. This social guilt can be traced in the progressive headmaster of *Miniatures*, in the modern clergyman, Swan, of *Three Men for Colverton*, in Sarah's ineffectual boyfriend Maurice, an accountant with scruples, and in Tina's headmaster and fiance, who finally asserts himself by renouncing paperwork and teaching the children to sing instead.

Another recurring theme in Cregan's work is the liberating influence of sex. There is even a certain alarm at the nature of female sexual voracity and its allied instinct for motherhood. In several plays, real feeling is contrasted with the falsity of modern "open relationships." Cregan is expert at pinning down the self-awareness of modern couples who have read all the relevant paperbacks. As one such character glibly puts it: "Instincts, we have always felt, have little place in this, except the refined instincts of romantic sex, expensive homemaking, good food, and the Left Wing." Feminine sensuality is opposed to puritan or repressive forces.

The Land of Palms (1972) shows a peaceful oasis commune invaded by the last British survivors of the French Foreign Legion. These militaristic figures are all gradually absorbed and conquered in their turn, except for one vengeful victim of an unhappy childhood, who kills himself. In *Tigers* (1978) a garage owner interested solely in profit hires a willing young girl to offer free sex with the purchase of eight gallons of petrol. After a series of farcical complications with customers, gangsters, and the police, the garage is seized by its two mechanics and turned into a workers' cooperative.

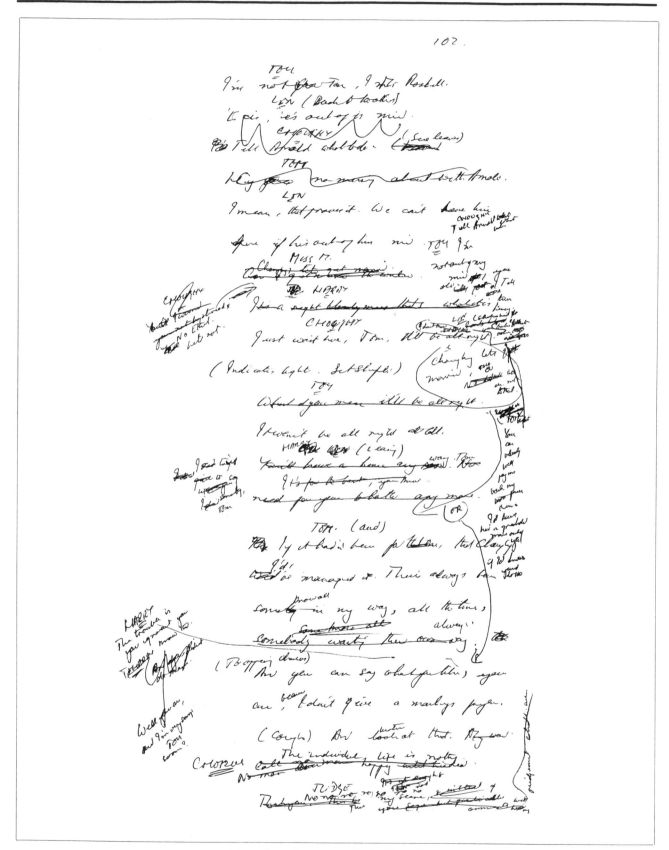

A page from the manuscript for Poor Tom

The elder mechanic is an old-fashioned socialist who explains with simple dignity to the girl that "what we're doing is taking responsibility for our lives and our working days." The girl, however, is mainly interested in sex, and when she tries to undo his overalls he kills her with a wrench.

Violence is characteristic of the repressive mentality in these plays. Sometimes this is self-directed, as in Cregan's latest play, *Getting It Right* (1980). Here a young architect is freed from his inhibitions by a sensual girl friend, only to be plunged back into atavistic guilt by the death of his father, which he has secretly desired. The warden of the local old people's home tries to secure his aid: "There's nothing like guilt, and he'll atone in public service for all his awful sins." The corpse of the father returns to sing a song about the wishes of the dead living on "and you can't ever get away." The young man declares his intention of being self-sacrificing and moral in the future, but he finds the impulse difficult to sustain. In the end he allows himself to be tracked down and killed by agents of the establishment, which, as one of them points out, has at least saved him from "a painful life of intro-version and uncertainty."

Critical reception of Cregan's work has on the whole been favorable, especially among the more intellectual critics. However, some have objected to his treating serious themes in a flippant manner; others have noted an inconsistency in his social attitude since, while he endorses in theory the struggle of the lower classes to capture power, he is repelled by the form which that struggle takes in practice. Like many contemporary English dramatists, Cregan has benefited from the policy of public subsidy for new plays. A dramatist of his ability has little difficulty in getting a new work performed; but subsequent productions have been much rarer, and he has yet to achieve transfers of his work to the commercial theater. His work has not been staged in central London since 1969, which has necessarily limited the amount of critical attention that has been paid to him, both in the press and in critical studies of the modern theater. Since the mid-1970s much of his work has been performed at the Orange Tree Theatre, Richmond; under the supervision of director Sam Walters, eleven of Cregan's plays have been produced there. The Orange Tree is a small theatre-in-the-round, and both playwright and director have sought to develop a spare, flexible style of playing to match the immediacy and unpredictability of the drama. Cregan's plays are less strident than those of his younger contemporaries; and he lacks the polish of a Tom Stoppard or a Simon Gray. In his book *The Second Wave* (1978) critic John Russell Taylor associates Cregan as a "farceur" with Alan Ayckbourn and Gray, but this is surely misconceived. The farcical pace of Cregan's work need not distract from an inner uncertainty that borders on moral anguish. It is perhaps this sense of irresolution that has prevented Cregan from achieving work of major importance.

Television Scripts:
That Time of Life, BBC, 1972;
George Reborn, BBC, 1973;
I Want to Marry Your Son, BBC, 1973.

Radio Script:
The Latter Days of Lucy Trenchard, BBC, 1974.

Other:
Arthur, in *Playbill One*, edited by Alan Durband (London: Hutchinson Educational, 1969).

Periodical Publications:
"New Voice at the Court," *Prompt*, no. 8 (Autumn 1966): 6-8;
"Pig Child Fire: Squat Theatre," *Plays and Players*, 24 (June 1977): 33.

References:
Robert Brustein, "The Land of Palms," *Observer*, 3 December 1972, p. 22;
Michael Coveney, "Tigers," *Financial Times*, 25 September 1978, p. 19;
Coveney, "Tina," *Financial Times*, 27 October 1975, p. 19;
Harold Hobson, "Three Men for Colverton," *Sunday Times*, 25 September 1966, p. 38;
John Holmstrom, "Three Men for Colverton," *Plays and Players*, 14 (November 1966): 16-18;
Charles Lewsen, "The King," *Times*, 25 May 1974, p. 9;
John Russell Taylor, "British Dramatists: Alan Ayckbourn & David Cregan," *Plays and Players*, 18 (December 1970): 14-16;
Taylor, "David Cregan," in *The Second Wave* (London: Methuen, 1971), pp. 162-169;
Simon Trussler, "Becoming a Dramatist," *Plays and Players*, 13 (January 1966): 52-55;
Irving Wardle, "Cast Off," *Times*, 30 January 1978, p. 6;
Wardle, "The Land of Palms," *Times*, 26 March 1976, p. 11.

Shelagh Delaney

(25 November 1939-   )

Susan Whitehead

PRODUCTIONS: *A Taste of Honey*, 27 May 1958, Theatre Royal, Stratford, London; 10 February 1959, Wyndham's Theatre (transferred 8 June 1959 to Criterion Theatre), London; 4 October 1960, Lyceum Theatre, New York, 376 [performances];

The Lion in Love, 5 September 1960, Belgrade Theatre, Coventry; 29 December 1960, Royal Court Theatre, London; 25 April 1963, One Sheridan Square, New York, 6.

BOOKS: *A Taste of Honey* (London: Methuen, 1959; New York: Grove, 1959);

The Lion in Love (London: Methuen, 1961; New York: Grove, 1961);

Sweetly Sings the Donkey (New York: Putnam's, 1963; London: Methuen, 1964).

After seeing the first production of Shelagh Delaney's *A Taste of Honey* in May 1958, Lindsay Anderson said of the play in *Encore*: "To talk as we do about new working-class audiences, about plays that will interpret the common experiences of today—all this is one thing and a good thing too. But how much better even, how much more exciting, to find such theatre suddenly here, suddenly sprung up under our feet!" He went on to call *A Taste of Honey* "A work of complete, exhilarating originality," which "has all the strength and none of the weaknesses of a pronounced, authentic local accent" and proclaimed it "a real escape from the middle-brow, middle-class vacuum of the West End." His view was shared by many critics, and although Delaney's second and only other stage play was later pronounced a flop, it was generally accepted that this tall, poised Salford girl, scarcely out of her teens, brought to the English theater a badly needed influx of new ideas from the provinces.

Of Irish heritage, Shelagh Delaney is the daughter of Elsie Delaney and Joseph Delaney, a bus-inspector. She was born and brought up in the industrial town of Salford, Lancashire. Her father, who died a few months after the first performance of *A Taste of Honey*, is remembered by Delaney as a great reader and storyteller. Delaney's formal education was patchy: she attended three primary schools, apparently enjoying the change from one to another and, after failing the eleven-plus examination to qualify for grammar school, she moved on to Broughton Secondary School. However, she proved a late developer and finally transferred to the local grammar school, where she had a record of fair achievement. In spite of this move, she seems to have lost any academic ambition she may have had and left school at seventeen for a succession of jobs, which included working as a shop assistant, milk-depot clerk, and usherette.

Even so, Delaney's school experience had left her with confidence in her literary ability and, between "enjoying myself, going out dancing," she began work on *A Taste of Honey* as a novel. At eighteen, she was already considering transforming her work-in-progess into a play when she saw Margaret Leighton in Terence Rattigan's *Variation on a Theme*. She told one interviewer: "It seemed a sort of parade ground for the star. . . . I think Miss Margaret Leighton is a great actress and I felt she was wasting her time. I just went home and started work." *A Taste of Honey* was written in a fortnight, while Delaney was taking time off from her latest job as a photographer's assistant in the research department of a large local firm. The young author sent her script to Joan Littlewood's Theatre Workshop in London's East End for criticism, and two weeks later the play went into rehearsal.

In *A Taste of Honey* two women—Helen, a "semi-whore," and her worldly-wise schoolgirl daughter Jo—move into the latest in a series of cheerless rented rooms. Helen has taken up with a faded roue, Peter, who promises marriage and whisks her away in the first act. Jo, left alone, spends Christmas with a black sailor from Cardiff. In the second act, he has disappeared, presumably gone back to the navy, and Jo, expecting his baby, has taken a job, and is living alone in the flat. Geof, a homosexual art student, moves in, and the pair become mutually dependent on each other until Helen, returning after a row with her boyfriend, bustles back to her carelessly discarded maternal role and shoos Geof away. In summary, the plot sounds unwholesome and uninteresting, yet the

Shelagh Delaney

play itself is a tart, humorous, sensitive study alive with pungent Lancashire dialogue. Delaney reveals an impeccable ear for contemporary speech and the language of her native Salford and a gift for re-creating what she has heard in warm and natural dialogue; she also demonstrates an acute eye for character and local mores and a generous measure of confidence, tact, and theatrical sense.

John Russell Taylor, who has compared Delaney's original manuscript with the version finally produced and published, notes that all these virtues are the playwright's own, but the whole play is the better for the imprint of its first director, Joan Littlewood, whose method it was to develop an

original playscript through improvisation, adaptation, and elaboration. It was probably sheer coincidence that led Delaney to send her script to Stratford: she remembers reading a newspaper report of conflict between Theatre Workshop and the Lord Chamberlain, and she also may have known of Theatre Workshop's origins with a group of radicals in nearby Manchester. But the decision was a lucky one: Littlewood's group eradicated several major weaknesses in the work without destroying the play's special character. The dialogue was pruned and tightened and some Brechtian and music-hall devices brought out elements of popular theater already present in the play. The "larger-

Stage design for the first New York production of A Taste of Honey

than-life" presentation characteristic of the play's director proved ideal for *A Taste of Honey* and served to heighten its strangely delicate atmosphere where, in the midst of squalid realism, the action seems almost a dream spun by the adolescent Jo, through whose eyes the audience sees events unfold. But, according to Taylor, the play as we know it was largely present in the original manuscript and the central character of Jo already fully formed and delightfully recognizable.

While some critics denied Delaney any credit for her play's success, attributing it instead to the Littlewood touch alone, others went too far in the opposite direction, extolling the young playwright for achievements which must have been largely unintentional—her creation of a distinctly English accent, entirely free from American and Continental influence, and her appreciation of the fresh subject matter to be found in the lives of ordinary working people. For, along with popular culture, Delaney had absorbed the speech patterns and essential character of her home town and had discovered her ready-made subject area at just the right time—when the English theater, after many years

of genteel drawing-room pieces by gentlemen playwrights, was undergoing a class revolution. Moreover, it would have been strange if Delaney, imperfectly educated and still in her teens, had shown in her first work the influences of foreign dramatists. But it would be wrong to suggest that she was totally screened from theatrical experience—she remembers seeing her first play, *Othello*, in a school production and was encouraged by Miss Leek, a perceptive teacher at Broughton Secondary, who recognized her literary ability: Delaney remembers that Miss Leek understood what she wrote, "and she didn't harp so much as others on rigid English. I write as people talk. . . . I had strong ideas about what I wanted to see in the theatre. We used to object to plays where factory workers come cap in hand and call the boss 'Sir.' Usually North Country people are shown as gormless, whereas in actual fact they are very alive and cynical." Apart from touring companies and school productions there were the cinema and pantomime. Her absorption of popular traditions dating back to the music hall proved one of the most exciting new aspects of *A Taste of Honey*, where actors break down the theatrical illusion by addressing the audience directly, keep up a steady patter of insult jokes, and frequently break into song or a form of comic routine—all stage devices yet all in character, since Helen has sung and played in a pub, Jo thinks of taking up the same line, and Peter has cast himself as the life and soul of the party.

The play won several awards, which included the Charles Henry Foyle Award for best new drama of 1958 and the New York Drama Critics Circle Award for best foreign play of 1961. Delaney received an Arts Council bursary in 1959. After the huge success of *A Taste of Honey*, critics waited eagerly to see what Delaney would produce next—some, no doubt, anxious to denounce her first play as beginner's luck, no more indeed than "the best play ever written by a 19 year old photographer's assistant." In fact, her next work, *The Lion in Love* (1960), was a commercial and critical failure, although in it Delaney took up many of the themes of *A Taste of Honey* and developed them with greater maturity. First produced in Coventry by Wolf Mankowitz, this play did not receive the Theatre Workshop treatment, although Littlewood's influence on director and playwright alike was evident in its music-hall inheritance—the constant flow of

movement across the stage, the dances, the conscious joking, and the loose style. But this effect contributed to the play's general lack of purpose and only served to underline Delaney's failure to resolve her various themes into a focal point of dramatic interest. Like *A Taste of Honey*, the play dealt simply with the lives of a few people subsisting on the edges of urban society, but it lacked the charm and briskness which enabled the earlier play to succeed. Moreover, the drama is often too uncomfortably like life—slightly boring, humdrum, and lacking a sense of beginning and end.

The Lion in Love deals with a loosely assembled family dependent for its income on selling tawdry wares from a peddler's tray. The action is framed by the son Banner's casual arrival after two year's absence and his equally casual departure for Australia. Meanwhile his sister Peg meets and may go to London with a Glaswegian dress designer, but it is a symptom of the play's general dramatic shapelessness that neither brother nor sister is an adequately developed character. In fact, the central position in *The Lion in Love* is taken by their parents, the long-suffering Frank and his alcoholic wife, Kit. Throughout the play Frank struggles to escape his worn-out marriage but finally lacks the conviction

Angela Lansbury and Joan Plowright in the first New York production of A Taste of Honey

to break away and join his mistress. Oddly, it is his wife, continually in court on charges of drunken and disorderly behavior, who emerges as the more sympathetic character, and her live-for-today philosophy finally dominates the play:

KIT: I can't be bothered with things that might happen. I'll face 'em when they comes and not before. Now lend me some money and I'll get going—
FRANK: It's as easy as that, isn't it?
KIT: Look, Frank, don't expect me to start thinking twenty years ahead of myself because I'm not going to do it. It's a waste of time. It does no good at all, and if you won't lend me half a dollar I'll just have to go and find someone who will, won't I?

By creating two successful adult characters in the husband and wife, Delaney proved that she was capable of more than the recreation of a young girl's dream, and *The Lion in Love* bears witness to Delaney's development as a writer, being more dramatically complex than *A Taste of Honey*, with a larger cast and more diffuse action. Her gift for dialogue reveals itself in flashes but she seems to have lost her instinct for selecting from everyday conversation in order to recreate speech for the stage—here the audience is often presented with banal dialogue dulled by cliches.

After *The Lion in Love*, many critics wrote *A Taste of Honey* off as a freak success and expected no more from Delaney. Others, however, among them Kenneth Tynan and John Russell Taylor, saw in the second play a promise of greater things to come. But although Delaney has continued to support herself through writing, she has produced nothing more for the stage. Now living in London with her teenaged daughter, she has written three screenplays which include an adaptation with Tony Richardson of *A Taste of Honey* (1962), *Charlie Bubbles* (1968), and "The White Bus," which has never been released, a number of radio plays and television plays, one of which she adapted for an Off-Off-Broadway production entitled "The House That Jack Built," and a collection of partially fictionalized autobiographical reminiscences, *Sweetly Sings the Donkey* (1963).

Coming in on the wave of new drama which hit London in the 1950s, Delaney can hardly escape comparison with John Osborne and his angry young contemporaries. Like the other young playwrights, she dealt with seamy reality, her characters spoke the slangy, colorful speech of their class and time, and she included, with complete acceptance, a Negro and a homosexual in the dramatis personae of her first play. It was not only

her plays which tended to ally her with the new realism—she was active in the movement for nuclear disarmament and, in 1961, she was arrested, along with John Osborne and actress Vanessa Redgrave, at a Committee of 100 demonstration. On the other hand, a program note for *A Taste of Honey* maintained she was different from the other new dramatists because she knew what to be angry about. But anger of any kind is not an emotion which underlies her writing. Instead, Delaney has created characters like Helen and Jo, Kit and Peg, who, while struggling against each other, ultimately accept their lives. There is plenty to complain about in their world, and both plays implicitly condemn social problems like poor housing and lack of opportunity. But despite flashes of rebellion her characters accept their lot in life without rancor and sometimes with a kind of unquenchable optimism. Even Frank seems oppressed by a sense of circumstance and twice fails to leave his wife. Delaney seems to write from an urge to communicate direct experience rather than from any sociopolitical standpoint. Nevertheless, it was as part of the general dramatic upheaval signalled by the arrival of the "angry young men" that Delaney had her importance, and it is there that we must ultimately place her.

Screenplays:
A Taste of Honey, by Delaney and Tony Richardson, Woodfall Films, 1962;
Charlie Bubbles, Memorial Enterprises/Universal Films, 1968.

References:
Lindsay Anderson, "*A Taste of Honey*," *Encore*, 5 (July-August 1958): 42-43;
W. A. Armstrong, ed., *Experimental Drama* (London: Bell, 1963), pp. 186-203;
Laurence Kitchin, *Mid-Century Drama* (London: Faber & Faber, 1960), pp. 175-177;
Colin MacInnes, "A Taste of Reality," *Encounter*, 12 (April 1959): 70-71;
Jacques Noël, "Some Aspects of Shelagh Delaney's Use of Language in *A Taste of Honey*," *Revue des Langues Vivantes*, 26, no. 4 (1960): 284-290;
Arthur K. Oberg, "*A Taste of Honey* and the Popular Play," *Wisconsin Studies in Contemporary Literature*, 7 (Summer 1966): 160-167;
John Russell Taylor, *Anger and After: A Guide to the New British Drama* (London: Methuen, 1962), pp. 109-118;
George Wellwarth, *The Theatre of Protest and Paradox* (London: McGibbon & Kee, 1965), pp. 250-253.

Nigel Dennis

(16 January 1912-   )

Ruth Milberg-Kaye
Herbert H. Lehman College, CUNY

PRODUCTIONS: *Cards of Identity*, adapted from Dennis's novel, 26 June 1956, Royal Court Theatre, London;

The Making of Moo: A History of Religion in Three Acts, 25 June 1957, Royal Court Theatre, London;

August for the People, 4 September 1961, Lyceum Theatre, Edinburgh; 12 September 1961, Royal Court Theatre, London.

BOOKS: *Boys and Girls Come Out to Play* (London: Eyre & Spottiswoode, 1949); republished as *A Sea Change* (Boston: Houghton Mifflin, 1949);

Cards of Identity [novel] (London: Weidenfeld & Nicolson, 1955; New York: Vanguard, 1955);

Two Plays and a Preface (London: Weidenfeld & Nicolson, 1958; New York: Vanguard, 1958—includes *Cards of Identity* and *The Making of Moo: A History of Religion in Three Acts*;

August for the People (London: French, 1961);

Dramatic Essays (London: Weidenfeld & Nicolson, 1962);

Jonathan Swift: A Short Character (New York: Macmillan, 1964; London: Weidenfeld & Nicolson, 1965);

A House in Order (London: Weidenfeld & Nicolson, 1966; New York: Vanguard, 1966);

Exotics: Poems of the Mediterranean and Middle East (London: Weidenfeld & Nicolson, 1970; New York: Vanguard, 1970);

An Essay on Malta (London: Murray, 1972; New York: Vanguard, 1974).

Nigel Dennis came to prominence as a playwright in 1956 at the same time as John Osborne. In fact, George Devine, director of the Royal Court Theatre, in summing up the successes of his first season, named Dennis and Osborne as the two important writers the company had discovered and brought to the stage. Perhaps because of these circumstances, the names of these playwrights were for some time linked; Dennis has even been labeled, quite incorrectly, as one of the Angry Young Men. Dennis's play *Cards of Identity* (1956) may have suffered from the great popular success of Osborne's *Look Back in Anger*, which preceded it in 1956, and Laurence Olivier's acting triumph in Osborne's *The*

Nigel Dennis

Entertainer, which succeeded it in 1957. Osborne, the better playwright, has had a career in the theater; Dennis has not. Nonetheless, *Cards of Identity* and, to a lesser degree, *August for the People* (1961) rest on their own merits.

Born in Bletchingley, Surrey, Nigel Forbes Dennis is the son of Louise Bosanquet Dennis and Lieutenant Colonel Michael Frederic Beauchamp Dennis, a member of a Scottish regiment of the British army. After the death of his father in World War I, his family moved to Africa, and he attended the Plumtree School in Southern Rhodesia. When he was fifteen, he joined his uncle A. E. Forbes Dennis and Forbes's wife, writer Phyllis Bottome, in Austria. Then he continued his education at the Odenwaldschule in Germany. In 1934 he moved to the United States, where he lived for the next fifteen years. He is the father of two daughters from his first marriage to Mary-Madeleine Massias; he subsequently married Beatrice Ann Hewart in 1959. Dennis recalls that while living in New York as a young man of twenty-three, he was paid by Alfred Adler, the expatriate Austrian psychologist, to translate some of his works. Dennis came to know Adler, then in the last years of his life, and remembers him with great affection. Indeed, he calls Adler his "master or 'father' " and feels that *Cards of Identity* was "merely repeating in paraphrase" Adler's views. During his fifteen years in the United States Dennis was secretary of the National Board of Review of Motion Pictures (1935-1936), assistant editor and book reviewer of the *New Republic* (1937-1938), and staff book reviewer for *Time* from 1940 to 1949; he continued to contribute reviews to *Time* through the London office through 1958.

Certainly some of these experiences and situations—that he was a citizen of the world with a strong sense of an international milieu and that he was a journalist—provided material for his first novel, *Boys and Girls Come Out to Play* (1949), published in the United States as *A Sea Change* (1949). The central character of the novel, Max Divver, is an American journalist and foreign correspondent who is an editor of a weekly progressive magazine, positions which were familiar to Dennis. The novel was favorably reviewed in England and America; one of its early and enthusiastic readers was Flannery O'Connor, who described it as a "wonderful" novel. *A Sea Change* won the Houghton Mifflin-Eyre and Spottiswoode Prize for fiction in 1950.

When Dennis returned to England, he continued his work as a reviewer and writer of fiction. His best-known novel, *Cards of Identity*, hailed by some critics as epoch-making, was published in 1955. In a review of the book W. H. Auden said that he had read *Cards of Identity* with "greater pleasure and admiration" than any other novel in the last fifteen years. The work is in marked contrast to *Boys and Girls Come Out to Play*, which employs an essentially realistic treatment of subject. In *Cards of Iden-*

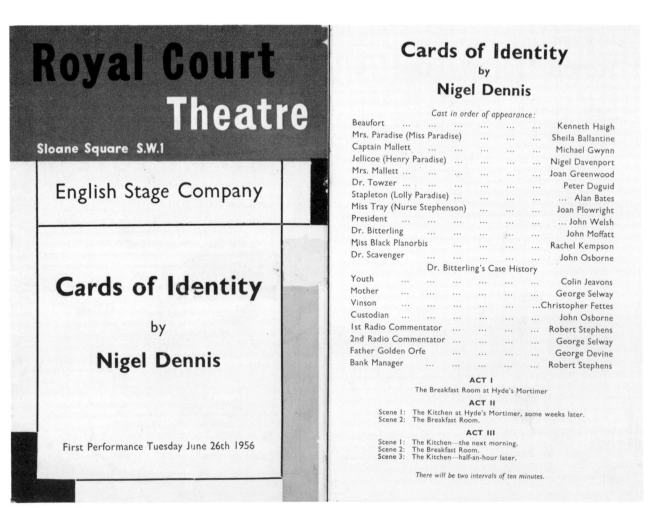

Program cover and cast list for the first production of Dennis's play adapted from his Adlerian novel

tity Dennis uses an absurdist plot and makes satiric attacks on society, religion, psychiatry, and role models. George Devine, who read the novel and recognized its potential as a play, discussed with Dennis the possibility of dramatizing it. Dennis admitted that he was interested in drama but had not worked directly in the field. Nonetheless, he prepared *Cards of Identity* for the stage, and it was produced in 1956 by the Royal Court Theatre, with a scheduled run of six weeks.

Dennis's involvement with the theater was most intense in the period between the middle 1950s and the early 1960s when he wrote his three plays. From 1960 to 1963 he was drama critic for *Encounter*, and a collection of his theater reviews, *Dramatic Essays*, was published in 1962.

The three plays show certain characteristic attitudes and techniques. Each has an audacious and irreverent theme—that people's identities can be changed at will (*Cards of Identity*); that a religion can be made by man in a few years of concentrated effort (*The Making of Moo*, 1957); and that "democracy is a disgusting thing" (*August for the People*). The plays are witty and ironic; the dialogue is repartee. Dennis is not interested in realistic portrayal of intimate or familial relationships but in satiric attacks on social attitudes, group behavior, religion, and psychiatry.

Cards of Identity is his best known and most successful effort as a dramatist. The title is based on Dennis's conceit that people have so little sense of their identity that they must carry cards with their names inscribed on them or they will not know who they are. In the play, a sinister trio—Captain Mallet, Mrs. Mallet, and a younger man—take over an empty great house and proceed to turn local townspeople—a middle-aged brother and sister, a nurse, a doctor—into their servants by creating new identities for them. The house, Hyde's Mortimer, chosen for its distance from London, is to be the setting of the Identity Club's annual meeting, at which time the members, who seem to be engaged in some kind of psychoanalysis, present "autobiographical" case histories. In the course of this meeting the old president, whose usefulness to the club has passed, is assassinated by the newest member of the club. Captain Mallet, who has been grooming himself for the role, assumes the presidency, and the club decamps for London, leaving the "servants" to foot the bills and face the charges of murder.

In moving from novel to play, *Cards of Identity* gained a greater cohesiveness and sense of unity. Tangential issues were excised—notably a play in the manner of Shakespeare performed by the "servants"; one of the case histories was dropped, and the two Dennis retained were considerably shortened. However, some of the zaniness and exuberance of the novel was lost in the process. Also, the play's strong connection with the mistaken identities and general mayhem of *A Midsummer Night's Dream* was muted in the conversion.

The play centers around the Identity Club, whose members adhere to the "Great Theory of Identity"—the belief that "identity is the answer to everything, that there is nothing that cannot be explained by means of the only primary question: Who am I?" Dennis's theories of identity are based on Adler's concept of "the style of life," that is, all of the forces that contribute to the creation of one's personality: behavior, sexual orientation, manners, mannerisms. For Dennis, the word "identity" is a "fictitious disguise." He credits Adler with carrying "the idea that every personality is a self-constructed 'fiction' farther than anyone" and showing "better than anyone what marvellous ingenuity went into the fabrications of selves." Dennis uses the club to elaborate on his views of how identities are built up, destroyed, and reconstructed. He pokes fun not only at psychiatrists and therapy of all sorts, and at the psychology of groups, but also at politics and, most importantly, religion. The two case histories are broad lampoons—the first, of two young men who worship an imaginary badger: "I feel like quite another person—[*very reverently*]—now I've found *him* [the badger] . . ." and the second, of a whiskey priest (played by George Devine) who starts his tirade with "*I stink: therefore, I am.*"

The controversy which resulted from the attacks on religion and class was exacerbated by the fact that the audience had difficulty in understanding what the play was about. Some reviewers felt that a few of the performers were almost as much in the dark as the viewers. In addition, the critics sensed that, for all the wit and sparkling dialogue, the play was a series of set pieces—a revue and not a unified drama. Some suggested that it would read better than it played.

In his next play, *The Making of Moo: A History of Religion in Three Acts*, Dennis appeared to overcompensate for the lack of cohesiveness of *Cards of Identity* by allowing a single and limited theme to dominate the work. *The Making of Moo* proposes that all religions emerge from the practice of barbarous rites, evolve and develop humanist concerns, and do not wish to acknowledge their primitive past. However, Dennis was not able to dramatize this idea effectively; it remains a thin scheme.

In the play, which is set in an unspecified col-

The Making of Moo

by

Nigel Dennis

Cast in order of appearance:

1st native	Anthony Creighton
2nd native	Robert Stephens
3rd native	John Wood
Frederick Compton, a Civil Engineer	George Devine
Donald Blake, his secretary	John Osborne
Constable	James Villiers
Elizabeth Compton	Joan Plowright
William, the Butler	Martin Miller
Sergeant	Nicholas Brady
Fairbrother } lawyers	John Moffatt
Willis	Stephen Dartnell
Mr. Fosdick	Robert Stephens
Walter	John Wood

ACT 1: "First Draught"
    Scene 1: A Colonial Drawing Room.
    Scene 2: Two days later.

Interval Ten Minutes

ACT 2: "Buckets of Blood"
Two years later.

Interval Ten Minutes

ACT 3: "Tea Time"
Many, many years later

Cast list for the 1957 Royal Court Theatre production of Dennis's "History of Religion in Three Acts"

ony, Frederick Compton, a civil engineer, has built a dam and in the process unknowingly "killed" the natives' river god, Ega. Fearful that without their god the natives will know no restraint, Compton is determined to make a god to replace Ega. He, his wife, and his secretary are so caught up in this missionary fervor that they emerge, in the second act, as the high priests of the god Moo, committed to human sacrifice. By the third act, fifty years later, a "well-established, respectable, Moovian community" has evolved, and the Comptons' son is about to set out to discover Moo's roots; the play has come full circle. While there is some humor in the first act, with Compton making the law, his wife writing the bible, and his musically talented secretary composing the hymns, the second act, with its human sacrifice and pails of blood, fails completely. The play is neither funny nor shocking, just silly, a view many of the first-night critics voiced, although Kenneth Tynan welcomed the "full gaiety of blasphemy" it

brought to the stage. Dennis's very concentration—the severe limitation of theme and the lack of characters with any humanity—is fatal.

In his next work, *August for the People*, perhaps in response to some of the concerns expressed by the critics, Dennis created Sir Augustus Thwaites, played by Rex Harrison in the Edinburgh Festival presentation and in the Royal Court production, both in 1961. Sir Augustus, the elderly "baronet of Nova Scotia," is chairman of the Open Homes Association, an organization of landlords who show their homes to the public during the month of August. In the prologue to the play, he stuns the meeting with a condemnation of democracy. Instead of losing paying guests as the association feared, Sir Augustus draws the public to his home in droves to hear his acerbic attacks upon them. He becomes so abusive that his butler of twenty-five years, his mistress, and his daughter who later commits suicide, leave him.

Martin Miller, George Devine, Joan Plowright, Robert Stephens, and John Wood in a scene from The Making of Moo

The play Dennis seemed to turn to for his inspiration is *Coriolanus*, about which he had written in "The Vigorous Fancy" (collected in *Dramatic Essays*, 1962): "here is a hard, remorseless blow at plebeian standards, made up entirely of direct hits, and couched most deliberately in a short, masculine language that fills one with respectful admiration." Sir Augustus, however, is a Coriolanus without sympathies and one for whom the audience can feel no sympathy, except in the early stages of the play. Sir Augustus's targets are all too obvious; his bitter feelings seem gratuitous. After he states publicly that people who show their houses are whores, his surprise that reporters wish to exploit his notoriety seems naive. Opening-night reviewers recognized the author's indebtedness to Bernard Shaw in Dennis's use of the metaphor of prostitution and in his dialogue which, at its best, is witty and wicked. But they were disturbed by what they sensed, legitimately, was an uncertainty about Dennis's appraisal of Augustus Thwaites's behavior. Tynan suggests that the "disingenuous" program notes describing the play, apparently written by Dennis, added to the confusion.

Dennis's satiric bent and his concern with character and identity also found expression in his interest in Jonathan Swift, about whom he wrote a biographical and critical study published in 1964. The work received the Royal Society of Literature Award in 1965. It is a sympathetic, astute, and moving account of Swift's life and works, with a lively comparison of Swift and Daniel Defoe. Dennis has served as a staff book reviewer for the *Sunday Telegraph* since 1961, and he was joint editor of *Encounter* from 1967 to 1970. In 1966 he received the Heinemann Award for nonfiction and became a Fellow of the Royal Society of Literature.

From the middle 1960s on, the style and tone of Dennis's work seems to have changed. His novel *A House in Order* (1966), which was generally well received, departs markedly from *Cards of Identity*. It is a short account of an unnamed and cowardly prisoner of an unspecified enemy in an unknown war, who winters in a greenhouse and, like the plants he nurses through the cold, is liberated in the spring as a hero. Gone are Dennis's high spirits, brilliance, and wit. The novel, an allegory, is a more private work reflecting, among other things, the writer's interest in horticulture and gardening. Dennis is also the author of a book of poems, *Exotics: Poems of the Mediterranean and Middle East* (1970), which includes his translations of the works of the Italian poet Giuseppe Giusti. In 1972 *An Essay on Malta* appeared.

Although Harold Pinter was most likely impressed by the dialogue and role playing of *Cards of Identity*, Dennis seems to have had relatively little influence on other contemporary dramatists. His plays, despite their witty repartee, seem eclectic and derivative. They are rarely performed, not easily available, and therefore unfamiliar to the theatergoing public.

Periodical Publications:

FICTION:

"Poor Signora!," *New Yorker* (13 May 1961): 157-165;

"A Blocked Feed," *Harper's*, 223 (December 1961): 79-83.

NONFICTION:

"Alfred Adler and the Style of Life," *Encounter*, 35 (August 1970): 5-11.

References:

Kenneth Allsop, *The Angry Decade* (London: Peter Owen, 1958), pp. 139-145;

George Devine, "The Royal Court Theatre: Phase One," *International Theatre Annual*, 2 (1957): 152-162;

Kenneth Tynan, *Curtains* (New York: Atheneum, 1961), pp. 138-140, 183-185;

Tynan, Review of *August for the People*, *Observer*, 10 September 1961, p. 23;

George Wellwarth, *The Theatre of Protest and Paradox* (New York: New York University Press, 1964), pp. 261-267.

Ronald Duncan

(6 August 1914-3 June 1982)

Eric Salmon
University of Guelph

PRODUCTIONS: *Birth*, 1937, London;

This Way to the Tomb, 11 October 1945, Mercury Theatre, London, 201 [performances];

The Eagle Has Two Heads, translated and adapted from Jean Cocteau's play, 1946, London;

Ora Pro Nobis, January 1946, St. Thomas's Church, Regent Street, London;

Stratton, 31 October 1949, Theatre Royal, Brighton, 24; 30 May 1950, London;

The Typewriter, translated and adapted from Cocteau's play, 1950, London;

Nothing Up My Sleeve, 8 December 1950, Watergate Theatre, London, 16;

Our Lady's Tumbler, 5 June 1951, Salisbury Cathedral, Salisbury, 8;

Don Juan, 13 July 1953, Palace Theatre, Bideford; 1956, London;

The Death of Satan, 5 August 1954, Palace Theatre, Bideford; 1956, London;

A Man Named Judas, adapted from C. A. Puget and Pierre Bost's play, 1956, Edinburgh;

The Cardinal, adapted by Duncan and Hans Keuls from Harold Brett's play, 1957, Cambridge;

The Apollo de Bellac, translated and adapted from Jean Giraudoux's play, 1957, London;

The Catalyst, 1958, London; revised as *Ménage à Trois*, 19 March 1963, Lyric Theatre, London, 38;

Abelard and Heloise, 24 October 1960, Arts Theatre Club, London, 24;

The Rabbit Race, translated and adapted from Martin Walser's play, September 1963, Edinburgh International Festival, Edinburgh;

$O\text{-}B\text{-}A\text{-}F\text{-}G {\Large\langle} \genfrac{}{}{0pt}{}{K\text{-}M}{R\text{-}N} \atop S$, 1963, Barnstaple High School, Barnstaple;

The Trojan Women, adapted from Jean-Paul Sartre's play based on the play by Euripides, 1967, Edinburgh;

The Seven Deadly Virtues, 19 May 1968, Criterion Theatre, London, 1;

The Gift, 1968, Exeter.

SELECTED BOOKS: *The Dull Ass's Hoof* (London: Fortune Press, 1940)—includes *The Unburied Dead*, *Pimp, Skunk and Profiteer*, and *Ora Pro Nobis*;

Postcards to Pulcinella (London: Fortune Press, 1940);

This Way to the Tomb: A Masque and Anti-Masque (London: Faber & Faber, 1946);

Stratton (London: Faber & Faber, 1950);

The Mongrel and Other Poems (London: Faber & Faber, 1950);

Our Lady's Tumbler (London: Faber & Faber, 1951);

The Last Adam (London: Dobson, 1952);

The Rape of Lucretia, opera by Benjamin Britten, libretto by Duncan, adapted from André Obey's play (London: Faber & Faber, 1953);

Don Juan (London: Faber & Faber, 1954);

The Death of Satan (London: Faber & Faber, 1955);

Judas (London: Blond, 1960);

The Solitudes (London: Faber & Faber, 1961);

St. Spiv [novel] (London: Dobson, 1961);

Abelard and Heloise: A Correspondence for the Stage (Bideford: Rebel Press, 1961);

All Men are Islands (London: Rupert Hart-Davis, 1964);

The Catalyst: A Comedy in Two Acts (Bideford: Rebel Press, 1964);

$O\text{-}B\text{-}A\text{-}F\text{-}G {\Large\langle} \genfrac{}{}{0pt}{}{K\text{-}M}{R\text{-}N} \atop S$ (London: Rebel Press, 1964);

How to make Enemies (London: Rupert Hart-Davis, 1968);

Unpopular Poems (London: Rupert Hart-Davis, 1969);

The Perfect Mistress and Other Stories (London: Rupert Hart-Davis, 1969);

Man, volumes 1-5 (London: Rebel Press, 1970-1974);

A Kettle of Fish (London & New York: Allen, 1971);

Collected Plays (London: Rupert Hart-Davis, 1971)—includes *St. Spiv*, *The Seven Deadly Virtues*, *The Gift*, *The Rehearsal*, *This Way to the Tomb*, *Our Lady's Tumbler*, and $O\text{-}B\text{-}A\text{-}F\text{-}G {\Large\langle} \genfrac{}{}{0pt}{}{K\text{-}M}{R\text{-}N} \atop S$

Obsessed (London: Rupert Hart-Davis, 1977).

Ronald Duncan, associated with various thoughtful and progressive theater movements in England in the period immediately following World War II, wrote a number of distinguished verse plays, the best known of which are *This Way to the Tomb* (1945), *Our Lady's Tumbler* (1951), *Don Juan* (1953), and *The Death of Satan* (1954). He became, along with Norman Nicholson, Christopher Fry, and Lawrence Durrell, a part of the "second wave" of British verse dramatists (the first had consisted of T. S. Eliot, W. H. Auden, Stephen Spender, and Louis MacNeice) whose work was at the time seen as the main hope for the rejuvenation of the British

theater. The fact that the theater, responding to large social pressures which it could not have foreseen and which it only partly understood, suddenly veered in another direction in the late 1950s does not detract from the quality or the ultimate value of the verse dramatists' plays, Duncan's included, even though it has had the incidental effect of driving them from the repertory a good deal sooner than would otherwise have been the case. It is fair to say that the twentieth-century British verse-drama movement did not produce a really major work (even Eliot's *Murder in the Cathedral*, first performed in 1935, is scarcely that) but did produce a number of very fine plays which reflected and celebrated experience in a lively and honest way and were entirely free from the pompous solemnity and cultural posturing that was, by and large, the hallmark of nineteenth-century verse drama. Among the twentieth-century verse plays which deserve to be remembered (and deserve more frequently to be acted) are several of those by Ronald Duncan.

Ronald Frederick Henry Duncan was born in Salisbury, Rhodesia, on 6 August 1914. His parents, Reginald John and Ethel Cannon Dunkelsbühler, had gone there from England immediately after their marriage in 1913. His father had intended to study farming in Rhodesia, but shortly after the outbreak of World War I he was interned as an enemy alien because of his German surname. He was, in fact, a British subject, though born in Germany of German parents. The family had moved to England when Duncan's father was a small child, and the boy had been brought up wholly in England, had attended Cambridge University, and spoke no German. Just before his internment, having some inkling of the way things might go, Duncan's father had sent his wife and small son back to England; so Duncan spent his early childhood in London. His father remained in internment for the whole of the war and then, late in 1918, volunteered his assistance in fighting an epidemic of influenza among local black residents, caught the disease himself, and died. Duncan's mother, therefore, never saw her husband again after the first year of their marriage and many of Duncan's early memories were of pain and loss: this had considerable significance with regard to his writing. It had an equally obvious connection with the fact that Duncan was one of the founders, in the 1930s, of the pacifist organization called the Peace Pledge Union (of which the most famous member was the Rev. H. R. L. Sheppard, author of *We Say 'No'*). In *All Men are Islands* (1964), the first of four volumes of autobiography, Duncan refers to the far-reaching effects of those childhood experiences:

> My mother was helped to her room. I followed her an hour or two later. . . . Between her tears I asked her what influenza was.
> "An infection."
> "What is an infection?"
> "Something that comes from flies." I promptly left the room ran down the stairs to the kitchen and managed to reach for a tumbler from the dresser. Then I ran out into the garden and sat and waited. I wonder if there has ever been more hatred in a small heart. Eventually I saw a blow-fly on a plant. I pounced and had it beneath the glass. This was the creature that had caused my mother's grief. I did not think anything of my father. He never meant anything to me but what he meant to her. I sat in front of the tumbler watching the fly go round and round the glass and I began to curse. I have been cursing ever since.

Both the strengths and the weaknesses of his future poetry and drama are foreshadowed in the small boy's responses—the intensity, the imaginative perception, the self-absorption and self-pity, the intellectual naivete.

Duncan was sent to school first in Yorkshire and later in Switzerland. When he was seventeen he was told of the family legacy which would make it possible for him to live the whole of his future life without "working for a living," and this might well be reckoned the second main influence on his future as an artist—though not by any means only in the sense of ensuring his freedom to pursue the arts unmolested by money worries. He continued his education at Downing College, Cambridge, where two major influences made themselves felt—Ezra Pound and F. R. Leavis. Duncan received an M.A. degree in 1936 from Cambridge. In 1939 he bought a farm in Devon and lived and worked there as a farmer until his death in 1982. In 1941 he married Rose Marie Theresa Hansom; they had one son and one daughter.

He had begun to write plays and film scripts while still at Cambridge, but his first play of any real consequence was *This Way to the Tomb*, written when he was thirty-one. The verse of the play, stripped and supple, is strongly reminiscent of Eliot:

> You have already heard how Antony
> Fasted, on the small island of Zante,
> Alone, during the fourteenth century;

> And how by meditating on his fears
> And on desire he came to shed those fears
> Till his own pride revealed, brought him to
>   tears
> And made him cry to Christ for Mercy,
> Which was confession of humility
> A new strength found in his own frailty;
> And how with this last prayer and effort
> He climbed from sin to Christ's own comfort.

The play, in the form of a masque and antimasque, seeks to explore the nature of religious faith. The masque presents the simple story of Saint Antony fasting on the island of Zante. He is attended by three novitiates, one of whom symbolically represents his bodily needs, one his artistic sense and sensual appetite (which are, curiously, equated), and one his pride. Fasting is shown to be part of pride and is, in true humility, finally rejected. The saint abandons his martyr's course and returns to live humbly with his lesser brethren. In the antimasque, a group of people making a television program in a series about faith visits the island and attempts, rationally and scientifically, to examine the saint's life there. The irony and satire of the antimasque now appear both heavy-handed and embarrassingly naive. They aim at targets which would be difficult to miss but they do so with arrows that do not pierce very deeply: the total effect is rather childish, though it seemed impressive enough in 1946 when it held the stage at the tiny Mercury Theatre for almost a year.

Stratton, first performed in 1949, is an altogether more considerable piece of work. Though not so well known as three or four of Duncan's others, it is probably his best play. Its one weakness is that it is overwritten, laden with an excess of themes and symbols which tend to blur its outlines and impede its forward movement. But its dramatic core, the central dichotomy which both determines its shape and gives it artistic energy, is sound and is of sufficient proportions to make the play important as well as interesting. Stratton, the central character, is a judge who, in his secret heart, dreams—as all sensitive men do—of a perfect, absolute justice; yet imagines himself committing every sort of crime and every sort of sin, including the strangling of his much-loved wife and the lusting after his young and beautiful daughter-in-law. The energizing dichotomy at the center of the play is one which subdivides, so to speak, into several parallel confrontations: animal reality versus spiritual reality; nature versus civilization; self versus altruism. The central symbol of the play is the river which runs through the Stratton estates and which, in spite of all efforts to control and contain it, bursts its banks every few years and ravages the surrounding countryside. Associated with this central dichotomy is an ancillary theme of human and cultural tradition, represented by Stratton's passing on to his son the family estate, the great house, and even the profession of barrister. This develops a number of fascinating sidelights on the central

concerns a group of cockney characters, people of little culture or refinement but great vitality. Horace, the central figure, is a hopelessly incompetent petty criminal, so innocent in his naive self-confidence as to be downright appealing. Among his other little tricks, he invents the idea of selling pill boxes containing sand to the crowds at a race track, pretending that the boxes have a miraculously curative medicament in them. When he is

Illustrated manuscript of a poem by Ronald Duncan

issue, but it is also the source of some of the most serious overelaboration in the play: it is here that a certain degree of artistic restraint would have improved the shape of the work and the clarity of the vision. Duncan said in an interview that this was the one play he had written which he would like to have revised. Even in its present form, however, the play is both profound and powerful, and its verse is among the best that Duncan wrote.

Nothing Up My Sleeve (1950), the play whose production followed almost immediately after *Stratton*, had in fact been written, under a different title, before *Stratton*. Originally called *St. Spiv*, it

caught and brought to justice, his vulnerability and humbled state restores her speech to Penny, the girl who quite literally has been struck dumb by Horace's having been hailed previously as a saint and healer. It is a pleasant play, designed to demonstrate that society's scale of values is always false, that fashionable morality is not only hypocritical but also valueless. The play's first London production in 1950 was directed by Kenneth Tynan. Duncan later turned the play, which was written wholly in prose, into a novel, entitled *St. Spiv* (1961).

Like *St. Spiv*, many of Duncan's plays have, by implication at least, a religious theme or base; some of them, however, deal explicitly with religious subjects. This is true of his next work, *Our Lady's Tumbler*, written at the request of the Salisbury and District Society of Arts specifically for performance in Salisbury Cathedral in connection with the 1951 Festival of Britain. In simple undecorated verse, the play tells the story, taken from a French legend called *Le Jongleur de Notre Dame*, of the monk who was once a clown and who, having no gift to offer to Our Lady, offers his skill as a juggler and tumbler; but even those abilities he has partially lost, being old now and clumsy. So he dances one last desperate childish dance before the statue of Our Lady and at the dance's end falls dead at the statue's feet. The statue lets fall from its hands onto his body the rose which had been the gift of one of the other monks.

Our Lady's Tumbler was followed by *Don Juan* and *The Death of Satan*, two plays of greater importance and more substance, which are connected to each other by subject matter—not precisely sequels one to the other, but interrelated nevertheless. In both plays Don Juan is the central character, and the central sense of each work attempts to link sensuous experience with spiritual experience—in particular, to establish some kind of living link between human love and the love of God. Along with *Stratton*, these two plays rank as Duncan's most accomplished work. The earlier of the two, *Don Juan*, is set in the traditional period and place of the original legend but treats Don Juan not as a rake and libertine but as a man deeply in love who searches for perfection in his relationship with Doña Ana. The second play is set in modern times and has Don Juan sent by Satan back to earth from hell to find out why people now settle in Hell so comfortably and find it so pleasant. The character of the Don is essentially the same in both plays, and the second play is thematically a continuation of the first. There is, in the last scene of *Don Juan*, a short passage which can be taken as a summary of the main thrust of both plays:

THE STATUE: Nothing can undo the past but. . .
DON JUAN: But what?
THE STATUE: Something beyond your reach.
DON JUAN: Nothing's beyond my reach.
THE STATUE: Redemption is. For that a man must kneel.
DON JUAN: Then I will kneel.
THE STATUE: To what? To God?
DON JUAN: No. To her. Her look is more gentle than love,
    Her love is more tender than passion.
THE STATUE: You dare blaspheme even in your last moment?
DON JUAN: She was the nearest thing to God I knew.
    By loving her I might in time have loved Him too.

This declaration is given a sardonic twist at the end of the second play, when Don Juan returns to Hell to give his report to Satan:

SATAN: But didn't Doña Ana love you?
DON JUAN: Yes, but for me, it was not enough.
    She lacked what I had admired.
    Only those women who know the spiritual side of life
      Are capable of great physical passion.
    The rest rehearse what they can't perform, and take
    What they cannot give. The paradox is
    I, who was an amorist, now know
    There's nothing in the flesh to love.
    I, who was an atheist,
    Discovered it was her soul which I adored.
SATAN: This is appalling!
    But what of my mission?
    Why don't people suffer in Hell any more?
    That's what I want to know.
DON JUAN: As I say: because they no longer love, as I have loved.
    Because they no longer believe, as she believed.
    Their heaven is comfort; their hell is lack of comfort.
    And universal comfort is the aim of all.
SATAN: But have they no god?
DON JUAN: Yes, their god is Man.
SATAN: Have they no spiritual aspirations?
DON JUAN: They have material ambitions.
SATAN: Do they not experience remorse
    Or sorrow?
DON JUAN: Some are frustrated, some are inhibited.
    All are disappointed, but none know sorrow.
SATAN: This is worse than I had feared;
    Worse than I had planned. . . .

The Hell of this play is like a comfortable club, where drinks are served twenty-four hours a day and where Oscar Wilde, Bernard Shaw, Lord Byron, and a bishop sit endlessly whiling away the time by playing cards and capping each other's epigrams. Newcomers arriving from earth feel at home immediately.

Because Duncan, as well as being a dramatist, was actively several other things—poet, novelist, translator, librettist, farmer, and editor—and because he periodically got both frustrated and furious with the theater, there were several longish gaps in his playwriting. Only one original Duncan play was written between 1954 and 1960 and this one was banned by the Lord Chamberlain. This was *The Catalyst*, which, because of the censor's ban, was given a brief "club" production in 1958 and then not seen again until 1963, when the ban was lifted. So the next of his plays after *The Death of Satan* to be publicly produced was *Abelard and Heloise* in 1960. Duncan claimed that it was his favorite of all the plays he had written. It is a generally straightforward rendering of part of the anguished correspondence between twelfth-century philosopher and theologian Pierre Abélard and his lover Héloïse. Duncan put the texts of the letters into striking, distinguished English verse, which is spoken by the two writers, the play's only characters. There is no dialogue, as such, and no "dramatization." The result is utterly simple and extremely moving.

When *The Catalyst* was performed publicly in 1963, it was produced as *Ménage à Trois*, the triangle consisting of two women and a man—but it is the wife, not the husband, who is in love with the "other woman." The *Times* (20 March 1963) said of it: "His characters more often discuss emotion than convince us that they experience it. . . . the moment at which the women realize the truth of matters is, in spite of a lot of clever preparation, too small a moment. Mr. Duncan's cleverness is never in doubt. But it is not, in spite of the careful planning of his play, theatrical cleverness. It looks at but not deeply into his people." The same reviewer had this comment on the two actresses (Phyllis Calvert and Elizabeth Shepherd) who played the wife and the secretary. "Their essential achievement is that they convince us that their future will not be utterly disastrous but that Thérèse and Leone are capable of creating a relationship of value into which the infinitely malleable Charles will fit himself."

In the same year in which *The Catalyst* was publicly produced, *The Rabbit Race* was presented at the Edinburgh International Festival. Adapted from Martin Walser's German play *Eiche and Angorra*, *The Rabbit Race* has as its central character another example of one of Duncan's favorite figures—the holy fool. Alois Grubel is a simpleminded man. He has been made the subject of medical experiments in a concentration camp during World War II and has been rendered sexually impotent. The action of the play begins in the last days of the war, in a small German town imminently threatened by the French advance; but Alois feels at home only with his rabbits and refuses to take any part in the defense of the town. Throughout the play, the same pattern continues: Alois, supposedly "cured," relapses repeatedly into that attitude of mind in which he finds it more congenial to reject the human race and turn to creatures who are innocent, guileless, and always beautiful. In the same

year, Duncan also wrote a brief play with a curious title:

$$O\text{-}B\text{-}A\text{-}F\text{-}G \Big\langle \begin{matrix} K\text{-}M \\ | \\ S \end{matrix} R\text{-}N$$

The title represents the elements of the sun and its planets. The play is performed without actors, using recorded voices only, in a completely darkened auditorium—except that at one point "a statue of a man similar to the figure of Perseus is revealed." The technique is interesting—music and vocal noises other than words are used as well as the speaking of recorded verse—and the subject is nothing less than Life itself:

> In other words, in other worlds when the first
> light
> fell on the earth's warm envelope of water
> the ultraviolet rays disassociated the ions
> H+ ,CH-,
> till the semiliquid colloidal gels
> developed into protein
> till the protein became plankton
> and the plankton nourished the whole
> and the cruel sea became busy with cruelty.

In 1968, Duncan returned to one of his old themes in a play called *The Seven Deadly Virtues*. The plan of the play is as simple—and as simplistic—as the title suggests. Duncan claimed that he set out to write seven scenes showing seven virtues and seven showing seven vices, with the conventional sins being seen as virtuous in certain circumstances and conventional virtues seen as sins. The play rather unpromisingly begins thus: "DR. SATAN *is seated at his desk in hell. He appears extremely bored.*" Benedict Nightingale, away from his usual desk at the *New Statesman*, wrote in the *Times* of 20 May 1968: "Ronald Duncan's new play deserves rather more than the one-night showing it got at the Criterion yesterday; but it is not the achievement we have the right, I think, to expect of him. Mr. Duncan has still not fulfilled the promise of his *Don Juan* and *The Death of Satan*, both first performed 12 long years ago." At the end of his review, Nightingale—who is one of the most perceptive of contemporary theater critics—makes an observation which acutely sums up, both positively and negatively, not only *The Seven Deadly Virtues* but a good deal of Duncan's drama: "In fact, he has only substituted one simplification for another. Women are rarely as straight-forwardly self-sacrificial as his Lavinia, men rarely as priggish as Christopher. The nature

Bust of Ronald Duncan by Jacob Epstein

of good and evil is a much more complex subject than Mr. Duncan, with his simple didactic purpose in mind, is ready to allow. But he still has his theatrically effective moments. He has a real feeling for the cutting sentence, the heated interchange. . . ."

This same kind of rather naive satire is also evident in the last of Duncan's plays, a one-act piece called *The Gift* (1968), written for amateur players. The gift of the title is a deep freeze, given by his family to an aging bank clerk as a means of guaranteeing his immortality: they recommend that he step into the freezer and thereby preserve himself. Seeing their eagerness to get rid of him, he complies with their request.

Duncan at his best was capable of transcending his own didactic intentions and of producing works of genuine poetic power, complexity, and intensity.

Unfortunately, he was not always at his best. The reasons for this lay partly in his self-regarding and self-pity, which are rarely far from the surface of his writing, and partly in his prolixity. He surely wrote too much, too quickly, in too many different genres, for the quality to remain consistently high. His constant desire to teach and demonstrate was, too, an artistic weakness, though in itself laudable and unquestionably sincere. But the best of his plays deserve revival in the theater and ought also to be much more widely known to the reading public. This applies particularly to *Stratton*, *Don Juan*, and *The Death of Satan*, none of which has yet had a full-scale, major London production. His frequent return to Christian themes and his constant attempts to revitalize religious faith and belief by translating it into real terms in the modern world and relating it to living experience were significant and moving. They had, however, an ambivalent effect upon his work as a dramatist: sometimes they were a source of strength and aesthetic illumination; on other occasions they tended to increase his rather arrogant stance of "different-ness" ("My God, I thank Thee that I am not as other men are") and his overreadiness to teach and moralize. His best plays, nevertheless, are important works; and the others are never less than interesting.

Television Scripts:

The Portrait, BBC, 1954;
The Janitor, BBC, 1955;
Preface to America, BBC, 1959;
The Urchin, BBC, 1959;
Not All The Dead Are Buried, BBC, 1960;
An Act of Charity, BBC, 1971;
Mandala, BBC, 1972.

Other:

Songs and Satires of John Wilmot, 2nd Earl of Rochester, edited by Duncan (London: Forge Press, 1948);
Selected Writings of Mahatma Gandhi, edited by Duncan (London: Collins, 1951);
The Rabbit Race, adapted from Martin Walser's play, in *Plays, Volume 1*, by Walser (London: Calder, 1963);
The Encyclopaedia of Ignorance, edited by Duncan and Miranda Weston-Smith (London: Pergamon Press, 1977).

Translations:

Jean Cocteau, *The Eagle Has Two Heads* (London: Vision Press, 1947; New York: Funk & Wagnalls, 1948);
Cocteau, *The Typewriter* (London: Dobson, 1947);
Jean Giraudoux, *The Apollo de Bellac* (London: French, 1957).

References:

"Broadway Postscript," *Saturday Review* (30 April 1960): 26-27;
"Dramatic Licence," *Times Literary Supplement*, 27 May 1955, p. 289;
Haueter, Max, *Ronald Duncan: The Metaphysical Content of his Plays* (London: Rebel Press, 1969);
Review of *The Death of Satan*, *Times* (London), 6 August 1954, p. 9;
Review of *Stratton*, *Times* (London), 31 May 1950, p. 6;
Review of *This Way to the Tomb*, *Times* (London), 23 October 1943;
Review of *This Way to the Tomb*, *New English Weekly*, 25 October 1945;
"Stage Lovers," *Irish Times*, 2 September 1961, p. 8;
William V. Spanos, *The Christian Tradition in Modern Verse Drama: The Poetics of Sacramental Time* (New Brunswick, N.J.: Rutgers University Press, 1967), pp. 282-293;
"Theatre Intellectual Strip-Tease," *Spectator* (4 April 1958): 428-429;
William B. Wahl, *A Lone Wolf Howling: The Thematic Content of Duncan's Plays* (Salzburg: Institute for English Language and Literature, 1973);
Wahl, *Ronald Duncan: Verse Dramatist and Poet Interviewed* (Salzburg: Institute for English Language and Literature, 1973).

Charles Dyer
(17 July 1928-)

Moylan C. Mills
Pennsylvania State University

PRODUCTIONS: *Clubs Are Sometimes Trumps*, 12 April 1948, Hippodrome Theatre, Staffordshire;

Wanted–One Body, April 1948, Hippodrome Theatre, Wednesbury, Staffordshire;

Who on Earth!, 24 July 1951, Q Theatre, London;

Turtle in the Soup, 14 December 1953, Intimate Theatre, London;

The Jovial Parasite, 6 December 1954, Intimate Theatre, London;

Single Ticket Mars, 12 December 1955, New Theatre, Bromley;

Time, Murderer, Please, 15 October 1956, King's Theatre, Portsmouth;

Poison in Jest, July 1957, Playhouse, Oxford;

Prelude to Fury, 23 November 1959, Intimate Theatre, London;

Red Cabbages and Kings, as R. Kraselchik, July 1960, King's Theatre, Southsea;

Rattle of a Simple Man, 19 September 1962, Garrick Theatre, London, 377 [performances];

Gorillas Drink Milk, adapted from John Murphy's play, 1964, Coventry;

Staircase, 2 November 1966, Aldwych Theatre, London, 104;

Mother Adam, 30 November 1971, Arts Theatre, London;

A Hot Godly Wind, 1975, Manchester.

BOOKS: *Wanted–One Body* (London: English Theatre Guild, 1961);

Time, Murderer, Please (London: English Theatre Guild, 1962);

Rattle of a Simple Man [play] (London & New York: French, 1963);

Rattle of a Simple Man [novel] (London: Elek, 1964);

Staircase [play] (Harmondsworth & Baltimore: Penguin, 1966; New York: Grove Press, 1968);

Staircase; or Charlie Always Told Harry Almost Everything (London: Allen, 1969); republished as *Staircase* (Garden City: Doubleday, 1969);

Mother Adam (London: Davis-Poynter, 1972).

Charles Dyer—actor, novelist, director, and playwright—is best known for two comedy-dramas

Charles Dyer

Rattle of a Simple Man (1962) and *Staircase* (1966). Produced internationally during the 1960s and 1970s to considerable critical acclaim, both plays deal compassionately with lonely humans reaching out to each other for love and understanding.

Born in Shrewsbury, Shropshire, Charles Raymond Dyer is the son of Florence Stretton Dyer and James Sydney Dyer, an actor. Dyer was educated at the Highlands Boys' School in Ilford, Essex, and at Queen Elizabeth's School in Barnet, Hertfordshire. In 1938 he became a callboy at the Hippodrome Theatre, Manchester. He served in the Royal Air Force from 1943 to 1947 and attained

157

the rank of Flying Officer Navigator. On 7 July 1959, Dyer married Fiona Jean Thomson, an actress. They have three sons.

Dyer made his acting debut in 1947 as Lord Harpenden in Terence Rattigan's *While the Sun Shines* in Crewe, Cheshire. He has subsequently acted in more than 250 plays, often appearing in productions touring the English provinces. Dyer's roles have included Digger in John Patrick's *The Hasty Heart* on tour during 1950, Flash Harry in John Chapman's *Dry Rot* in London and on tour during 1958, and Shylock in *The Merchant of Venice* in Bromley, Kent, during 1959.

Under the name C. Raymond Dyer, he had his first play, *Clubs Are Sometimes Trumps*, produced in Staffordshire on 12 April 1948. Between 1951 and 1960, Dyer had eight plays presented either in London or on tour. His earliest plays were experimental in nature and varied between stark tragedy and satire. It was in 1960, with *Red Cabbages and Kings*, a political comedy, that Dyer began to touch upon the theme of individual isolation and loneliness that would become the basic concern of his later works.

Dyer's first major success was *Rattle of a Simple Man*, which opened at the Garrick Theatre in London's West End in 1962. Essentially a two-character play, *Rattle of a Simple Man* focuses on the relationship between a timid middle-aged man from the provinces and a tarty London prostitute. The virginal Percy, in the city with his buddies to attend a rugby match, picks up Cyrenne on a bet and goes back to her flat. Percy pretends to social and sexual experiences that he has never had; Cyrenne disguises her insecurities by assuming upper-class airs. As the play progresses, Percy and Cyrenne force each other to reveal the loneliness and isolation that haunt their lives. Although at the conclusion of the play it is not certain whether a serious relationship will develop between them, it is clear that Percy and Cyrenne have each genuinely connected with another human being, perhaps for the first time.

Dyer's other international success, *Staircase*, was first presented by the Royal Shakespeare Company with Paul Scofield and Patrick Magee in the leading roles during its 1966-1967 season at the Aldwych Theatre. In this work, Dyer again deals with social outcasts. Harry and Charlie, aging homosexuals, alternately attack and comfort each other through a long night in the barber shop that they jointly operate. Harry, the older of the two, is anxiously awaiting a visit from the daughter he has not seen for twenty years. Charlie, a former second-rate actor, has been arrested for appearing in public in drag and is facing a court hearing.

Although both Harry and Charlie threaten to break off their longstanding affair, it is apparent that, despite its torments, their relationship is the one enriching element in their pathetic lives. Without each other, Harry and Charlie would be even more lost than they already are; they must go on bravely together, providing each other with fleeting moments of love and tenderness.

Rattle of a Simple Man and *Staircase*, dealing openly with prostitution and homosexuality, respectively, probably could not have been produced if John Osborne and his successors in the late 1950s had not gained greater freedom for their fellow dramatists. Dyer has used this freedom to deal in a nonexploitive way with once-forbidden subjects. Even so, the Lord Chamberlain, prior to the abolition of his office, made twenty-six cuts in *Staircase* before it was allowed onstage.

Both plays were presented in New York following their London productions. Although they received excellent critical notices, they did not catch on with the public and closed after several months. *Rattle of a Simple Man* was included in *The Best Plays of 1962-63*, and *Staircase* was published in *The Best Plays of 1967-68*. In addition, *Rattle of a Simple Man* was chosen for the 1962-1963 volume of the *Plays of the Year* series. Both plays have been translated into more than twenty languages and have been performed throughout the world.

With *Rattle of a Simple Man* and *Staircase*, *Mother Adam* formed Dyer's "trilogy of loneliness." Presented for short runs in 1971 at the Arts Theatre Club and in 1973 at the Hampstead Theatre Club and at the Royal Shakespeare Theatre in Stratford-upon-Avon, *Mother Adam* has not yet been accorded a full-scale West End production. *Sunday Times* critic Harold Hobson has called the play a masterpiece that is "one of the few real tragedies of our time." The drama details the love-hate relationship between a young man and his paralyzed mother. If Adam deserts his mother to gain his freedom, her life is ruined; if Adam stays to care for his tyrannical mother, his life is destroyed.

Dyer has pointed out, "man's disease is loneliness." However, in these three plays depicting confrontations between lonely, often physically or psychically handicapped people, the characters never succumb to the malady. They courageously confront their lonely lot, and, by clinging together, they often find temporary surcease from their travail. The trilogy has at times been called thin in terms of character development and repetitious with respect to plot narrative. On the other hand, Dyer has been praised for his fine ear for idiomatic

Paul Scofield and Patrick MaGee in a scene from the first production of The Staircase

language and for his skillful treatment of the homely details of his mise-en-scene. D. A. N. Jones has lauded the "depth and surprise" of Dyer's narrative. According to most critics, however, Dyer's strength lies in the tender and perceptive treatment of his characters. As one reviewer noted, Dyer "gives us pictures of human beings who are not particularly good or bad but are alive." Henry Hewes has noted that Dyer's audiences are "unflaggingly entertained" and "feel richer for the experience" of having been brought into contact with his characters. Harold Hobson has written the most

perceptive assessment of Dyer's work. He points out the similarities between Dyer and Jean Anouilh, noting that Anouilh "discovers the sordidness of purity," while Dyer "comes upon purity in sordidness." Hobson adds that "Against dispiriting odds, [Dyer's] people are capable of behaving unexpectedly well. This is one reason why Dyer's work is so much more exhilarating than that of most of even his most distinguished contemporaries."

Among his other activities, Dyer has written novels based on *Rattle of a Simple Man* and *Staircase*. He has also written screenplays for the film productions of both plays. Besides directing many of his own plays, as well as those of other playwrights, Dyer has written the incidental music for several of his own works. He has acted in a number of films, including *The Loneliness of the Long Distance Runner* (1962), *The Knack* (1964), and *Rattle of a Simple Man* (1964). In 1965 he appeared in the television series *Hugh and I*. More recently, he has been chairman and artistic director of Stage Seventy Productions, Ltd. Dyer continues to be active in the theater and television. His current projects include an adaptation of Arthur Schnitzler's *Reigen*, commissioned by the Schnitzler estate, and several original plays and television scripts.

Except for *Rattle of a Simple Man* and *Staircase*, Dyer's dramatic work has gone largely unnoticed. However, the emotional impact of these two plays stems from his deep respect for social outcasts. Dyer finds humor and pathos in the stunted lives of his characters, communicating his genuine compassion to his audiences. He has become in Britain the spokesman for the lonely and the lost as playwright Tennessee Williams has in the United States. Dyer has said, "I write about loneliness." He will no doubt pursue this overriding concern in his future dramatic work.

Screenplays:
Rattle of a Simple Man, Sydney Box, 1964;
Staircase, Twentieth Century-Fox, 1969.

Other:
A Hot Godly Wind, in *Second Playbill 3*, edited by Alan Durband (London: Hutchinson, 1973).

References:
Clive Barnes, "Theatre: Two Character 'Staircase,'" *New York Times*, 11 January 1968, p. 41;
"Comfortable Message in a Witty Study," *Times* (London), 3 November 1966, p. 7;
Brendan Gill, "Silk Purse," *New Yorker* (20 January 1968): 82;
Henry Hewes, "Kings, Queens, and Commoners," *Saturday Review* (27 January 1968): 41;
D. A. N. Jones, "Dyer's Hand," *New Statesman*, 11 November 1966, pp. 715-716;
John Simon, "More from London," *Commonweal* (16 February 1968): 592;
"Stamina and Skill for a Thin Theme," *Times* (London), 20 September 1962, p. 16;
Howard Taubman, "The Theatre: Rattle of a Simple Man," *New York Times*, 18 April 1963, p. 39.

David Edgar
(26 February 1948-)

Stanley Weintraub
Pennsylvania State University

PRODUCTIONS: *Two Kinds of Angel*, July 1970, Bradford University Theatre, Bradford; February 1971, Basement Theatre, London;
A Truer Shade of Blue, August 1970, Bradford University Theatre, Bradford;
Bloody Rosa, September 1970, Bradford University Theatre, Bradford; August 1971, Edinburgh Festival, Edinburgh;
Still Life: Man in Bed, May 1971, Pool Theatre, Edinburgh; July 1972, Little Theatre, London;
Acid, July 1971, Bradford University Theatre, Bradford; August 1971, Edinburgh Festival, Edinburgh;
The National Interest, August 1971, General Will, on tour;

Conversation in Paradise, October 1971, Edinburgh University Theatre, Edinburgh;
Tedderella, December 1971, Pool Theatre, Edinburgh; 10 January 1973, Bush Theatre, London;
The Rupert Show, January 1972, General Will, on tour;
The End, March 1972, Bradford University Theatre, Bradford;
Excuses Excuses, May 1972, Belgrade Theatre Studio, Coventry; July 1973, Open Space Theatre, London; produced again as *Fired*, January 1975, Second City Theatre Company, on tour;
Rent or Caught in the Act, May 1972, General Will, on tour; June 1972, Unity Theatre, London;

David Edgar

State of Emergency, August 1972, General Will, on tour; October 1972, Edinburgh Festival, Edinburgh; 7 November 1972, Royal Court Theatre Upstairs, London;

England's Ireland, by Edgar, Tony Bicât, Howard Brenton, Brian Clark, Francis Fuchs, David Hare, and Snoo Wilson, September 1972, Mickery Theatre, Amsterdam; 2 October 1972, Round House Theatre, London;

Road to Hanoi, October 1972, Paradise Foundry, on tour;

Not With a Bang But a Whimper, November 1972, Leeds Polytechnic Theatre, Leeds;

Death Story, November 1972, Birmingham Repertory Studio Theatre, Birmingham; March 1975, Manhattan Theatre Club, New York;

A Fart for Europe, by Edgar and Howard Brenton, 18 January 1973, Royal Court Theatre Upstairs, London;

Up Spaghetti Junction, by Edgar and others, February 1973, Birmingham Repertory Studio Theatre, Birmingham;

Gangsters, 13 February 1973, Soho Polytechnic Lunchtime Theatre, London;

Baby Love, 16 March 1973, Leeds Playhouse, Leeds;

28 May 1973, Soho Polytechnic Lunchtime Theatre, London;

Liberated Zone, June 1973, Bingley College of Education, Bingley;

The Case of the Workers' Plane, June 1973, Bristol New Vic, Bristol; revised as *Concorde Cabaret*, January 1975, Avon Touring Company, on tour;

Operation Iskra, 4 September 1973, Paradise Foundry, on tour;

The Eagle Has Landed, November 1973, Liverpool University, Liverpool;

The Dunkirk Spirit, January 1974, General Will, on tour;

Dick Deterred, 25 February 1974, Bush Theatre, London;

The All-Singing All-Talking Golden Oldie Rock Revival Ho Chi Minh Peace Love and Revolution Show, March 1974, Bingley College of Education, Bingley;

Man Only Dines, June 1974, Leeds Polytechnic Theatre, Leeds;

O Fair Jerusalem, May 1975, Birmingham Repertory Studio Theatre, Birmingham;

Summer Sports, July 1975, Birmingham Arts Lab,

Birmingham; 7 August 1975, Bankside Globe
Theatre, London; produced again as *Blood
Sports*, 28 June 1976, Bush Theatre, London;
The National Theatre, 14 October 1975, Open Space
Theatre, London;
Events Following the Closure of a Motorcycle Factory,
February 1976, Birmingham Repertory Stu-
dio Theatre, Birmingham;
Saigon Rose, July 1976, Traverse Theatre, Edin-
burgh;
Destiny, 22 September 1976, Other Place, Stratford;
12 May 1977, Aldwych Theatre, London;
The Perils of Bardfrod, November 1976, Theatre in
the Mill, Bradford University, Bradford;
Wreckers, 10 February 1977, 7:84 Theatre Com-
pany, Exeter; 19 April 1977, Half Moon
Theatre, London;
Our Own People, November 1977, Pirate Jenny, on
tour; 9 January 1978, Royal Court Theatre,
London;
The Jail Diary of Albie Sachs, 16 June 1978,
Warehouse Theatre, London; November
1979, Manhattan Theatre Club, New York;
Mary Barnes, 31 August 1978, Birmingham Reper-
tory Studio Theatre, Birmingham; 10 January
1979, Royal Court Theatre, London;
Teendreams, 26 January 1979, Vandyck Theatre,
Bristol;
Nicholas Nickleby, adapted from Charles Dickens's
novel, 21 June 1980, Aldwych Theatre, Lon-
don; 5 October 1981, Plymouth Theatre, New
York.

BOOKS: *Dick Deterred* (New York & London:
Monthly Review Press, 1974);
Destiny (London: Eyre Methuen, 1976);
Wreckers (London: Eyre Methuen, 1977);
The Jail Diary of Albie Sachs (London: Collings,
1978);
Ball Boys (London: Pluto Press, 1978);
Mary Barnes (London: Eyre Methuen, 1979);
Teendreams (London: Eyre Methuen, 1979);
Nicholas Nickleby (New York: Dramatists Play Ser-
vice, 1982).

Although now known for his gargantuan yet
compelling play crafted for the Royal Shakespeare
Theatre from Charles Dickens's *Nicholas Nickleby*,
David Edgar as playwright and political activist
grew up with the New Left political theater of the
1970s. Son of a Midlands television producer, Barrie Edgar, and his wife, Joan Burman Edgar, a
former radio announcer and actress, David Edgar
was born in Birmingham and attended Oundle

public school (1961-1965). In 1966 he taught for a
term at a preparatory school and then entered
Manchester University, where he received an honors B.A. in 1969. Several years as a political journalist in Bradford on the *Telegraph and Argus*, followed, during which he wrote short plays in his
spare time. Several were produced at the University
of Bradford during 1970-1971 and others in 1971
in Edinburgh, one of which was mounted at the
Edinburgh Festival. The visibility earned him ap-
pointments as Yorkshire Arts Association Fellow in
Creative Writing at the Leeds Polytechnic (1972-
1974) and Thames Television resident playwright
at the Birmingham Repertory Theatre (1974-
1975); and Edgar seized upon the opportunities to
churn out more polemical plays, often at the rate of
several per year. Some had titles suggesting his
counterculture contempt for the contemporary
scene, others suggested political urgency. A full-
length play about the German Communist agitator
Rosa Luxembourg, murdered by rightists early in
1919, *Bloody Rosa*, was not only produced in September 1970 by Bradford University but was also
performed at the Edinburgh Festival.

Much of his early work was produced by the
General Will, a political theater company which—
following Joan Littlewood's example—turned collective improvisation into revised scripts. His first
play for the General Will was *The National Interest*, a
semidocumentary in "cartoon" style and agitprop
tradition about the first year of the new conservative
government. In the play, which was on tour in August 1971, Tory officials were depicted as Chicago
gangsters raiding the workers inside their factories,
and a "Dole Beast" high-jumped over unemployment figures against a background of an Olympic
announcer's commentary. The plays developed
from company discussion, after which, Edgar recalled, "I would go away and write the scene, bring it
back, [they would] look into it and discuss that. . . .
We were presenting our view of the world in
memorable images. I think we thought we were
presenting a political image; in fact we were presenting an economic one."

The Rupert Show, taken on tour by the General
Will in 1972, attempted to transfer the agitprop
style to the problems of pornography and sexual
politics. The play purported to be a dramatized
church service. The songs were hymns and the
sketches the lesson, the sermon the credo. At the
close, riot police would raid the hippie service,
bashing heads. *Rent or Caught in the Act*, also presented on tour by the General Will in 1972, was
political theater played to tenants' groups to explain

the Housing Finance Act. "I mean," said Edgar in explanation, "how many working people have time to sit down and read an Act of Parliament? Providing information is an act of political theatre." In this case the form was that of Victorian melodrama, with music-hall acts. "Not because it was a popular cultural form," said Edgar, "but because it was funny." He was on his way, without knowing it, to *Nicholas Nickleby*. Thus there was a family called the Hard-Done-Bys—Joshua, Lydia, and Honest Tom—who, along with Lydia's fiance, were evicted from their home. There was a scheming lawyer named Devious, of the firm of Devious, Devious, and Downright Dishonest, as well as villains called Paynorm, Hiveoff, and Sir Jasper Pricestroke. Edgar thought the Dickensian characterization worked. "We put them through private landlords, public landlords, a squatting scene and then into a high-rise flat in Camden. Honest Tom became the borough councillor and sold out. And Lydia's long-lost brother

returned at the end to become a tenants' activist. It was quite funny."

State of Emergency (1972) was another agitprop cartoon in 1930s living-newspaper style, while *Operation Iskra*, a 1973 play set in a futuristic 1977, dated itself quickly into oblivion and deserved little better. A documentary set in the future, and indebted in the writing to contemporary espionage films, it dealt with legal inhibitions to liberty in England and included a stage demonstration of how to make your own bomb. Political terrorism, handled largely sympathetically if unconvincingly, sets the play apart as Edgar's most extreme work.

The Dunkirk Spirit, which toured the provinces until the 1974 general election, was a full-length play in Brechtian epic style on postwar Britain, opening in 1945 and following two demobilized sailors through economic vicissitudes into the 1970s. Through the General Will, Edgar's plays reached student groups, community theaters, and

Indira Joshi and Chrissie Cotteril in the 1978 Royal Court Theatre production of Our Own People

miners' welfare centers. However Edgar left the group when there was a dispute over what kind of material should be played. "My feeling was that we should remain very slick and almost arrogant in our relationship with the audience. The group's feeling was [for] . . . a relationship with the audience in the sense of popular culture." After Edgar's departure a new management changed direction radically and took on a gay emphasis, ending the group's relationship with its original audiences in any case.

Edgar by then had established a bond with the Royal Court Theatre in London, still the chief stage for experimental (and leftist) playwrights. His *State of Emergency* was produced there in 1972 as was his collaboration with Howard Brenton, the one-act, anti-EEC (European Economic Community), *A Fart for Europe*, in 1973. He had also begun writing for conventional theater and television. His *Death Story*

(1972) was a modernized *Romeo and Juliet* set in Northern Ireland, and *Excuses Excuses* (1972) was about a Yorkshire arsonist and involved a play-within-the-play about actors doing a documentary drama. Two plays performed at the Soho Polytechnic Lunchtime Theatre in 1973, *Gangsters* and *Baby Love*, further mined the vein of documentary drama. *Baby Love* explored, through the psychiatrists and probation officers who attempt to help her, the background of a young mother who batters her baby to death, while *Gangsters* concerned three 1970s bank robbers whose 1940s methods are out of date in the new technology. Two other plays dealt with well-known politicians—*Tedderella* (1971) satirized Edward Heath and the Common Market, while *Dick Deterred* (1974) told the Watergate-Nixon story through a parody of *Richard III*. Edgar also wrote a 1974 television play about Richard Nixon, *I*

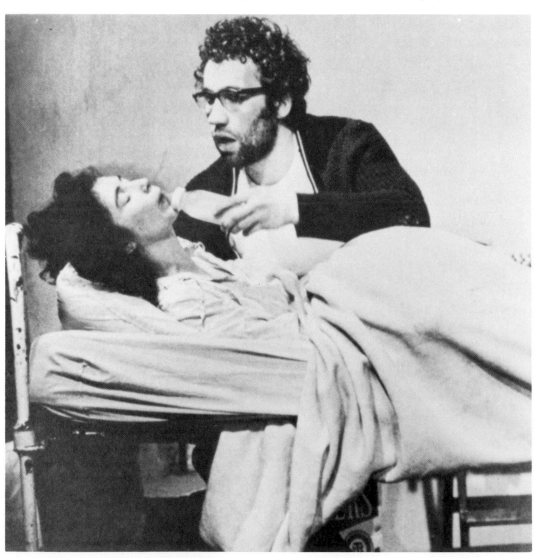

Patti Love and Simon Callow in the 1979 Royal Court Theatre production of Mary Barnes

Know What I Meant, in which a guilt-ridden president, played by Nicol Williamson, confronts the problem of the incriminating tapes.

As serious political theater, Edgar realized, these plays did not work—"They did not even work on the cartoon level of providing images that people retain." Yet he continued to turn out agitprop pseudodocumentaries, such as *The Case of the Workers' Plane* (1973), on the building of the *Concorde*, and the forty-one-scene *Events Following the Closure of a Motorcycle Factory* (1976), on the collapse of competitive British industry, specifically about an attempt to close a motorcycle factory in Coventry. Politics entered into everything Edgar was writing, and his pen seemed active without letup. In his *The National Theatre*, produced in 1975, just before the production of *Events Following the Closure of a Motorcycle Factory*, the setting is a dressing room backstage in which three actresses seem to be preparing to play Chekhov's *The Three Sisters*. Soon it is clear through exploration of their personal relationships that they are in a striptease show which mocks their aspirations to play Chekhov: they are earning a living by offering what the consumers of "culture" want. A final sequence even introduces a parody of the political rhetoric of Labour Prime Minister Harold Wilson when a character previously assumed to be an assistant stage manager talks into a microphone, appealing to the nation for austerity and restraint: "Not a year for self, but for Britain." The speech is counterpointed by a vulgar striptease the audience enjoys, suggesting the level of British creative energy and national commitment. Edgar also experimented with a medieval epic, in the style of Bertolt Brecht, about the Black Death, *O Fair Jerusalem* (1975), and succeeded with a polemical epic of postempire Britain (beginning in India in 1947), *Destiny* (1976). Edgar has confessed that he finds revolutionary ideas hard to dramatize. "I mean Marx's *Capital* is extraordinarily badly written, but even if it were well written, the ideas Marx expresses are difficult ideas. So you have two alternatives. You can make things ridiculously simple and partisan—in the sense of getting people to support socialism in the same way as they support [the] Leeds United [football team], on a straight, tribal basis. . . . Or you have to struggle to find a way of presenting extremely complex, difficult, precise ideas . . . in an accessible form."

Destiny, which received the Arts Council's John Whiting Award, focuses upon the rise of the Nation Forward Party, a political group like that organized by British Fascist leader Sir Oswald Mosley, in the industrial Midlands as a reaction to the influx of Asians after the relinquishing of India in 1947. The play follows the fortunes of a small shopkeeper attracted to the new party in what he conceives as self-defense, only to discover that Right is not only not right but suicidal for his interests. As Catherine Itzin writes in her study of the 1970s left-wing political theater in England, *Stages in the Revolution* (1980), "There were powerful scenes in the play: the meeting in the pub to celebrate Hitler's birthday; violence on the picket line and the confrontation of two former friends, one of whom had joined the Nation Forward Party, the other going the way of the left; the news received by the former Indian army officer of the death of his son in Northern Ireland, and how this fuelled his energies for the fascist party; the elections themselves . . . and the final invocation of Hitler." After first planning to set the play in the Mosley period, the 1930s, Edgar changed his mind, for he was writing political theater, not merely a play. "I soon realized that the only way to alert people was to do a play based on real fascist parties operating in Britain now. . . . I was determined from the start to show the British middle class was just as susceptible to fascism, potentially, as the German middle class had been. . . ."

Indeed, the play does demonstrate the way in which disparate grievances can be cobbled together into a powerful force by a party that locates appropriate scapegoats and appeals to a variety of self-interests. Everyone, Edgar suggests alarmingly, is a cryptofascist under the skin:

KERSHAW: I'm sorry, Lewis. Just can't see it in those terms.
ROLFE: Why not?
KERSHAW: I suppose—a basic faith in people's reason.
ROLFE: Reason?
KERSHAW: Loyalty.
ROLFE: To what?
KERSHAW: To Britain. No, that's meaningless. The National Interest.
ROLFE: Whose? Whose loyalty? (*Slight pause.*) Come on, whose loyalty? The miners? Dockers? Students? Irish? Blacks?
KERSHAW: Now, Lewis—
ROLFE: I will tell you. Whose commitment to the National Interest matters. Whose loyalty is both vital and, now, under strain.
KERSHAW: Yes, well?
ROLFE: The lower middle classes.
KERSHAW: Continue.
ROLFE: Whose loyalty is bought. By giving them the independence property affords. A social status, noses just above the Joneses. And the feeling that they're part of something wider, nation, if you like, its destiny. All right?
KERSHAW: Right.

ROLFE: (*Increasingly emotional as the speech goes on*): And, on all counts, they've been betrayed. Their property no longer secure. Their status, in our age, increasingly irrelevant. And in the place of national destiny, we've given them. . . . You see, Frank, it's not true we've lost an Empire, haven't found a role. We have a role. As Europe's whipping boy. The one who's far worse off than you are. Kind of—awful warning system of the West. And to play that role, we must become more shoddy, threadbare, second-rate. Not even charming. Quite unlovable. And for those—the people that I come from—that is a betrayal.

One effective scene in *Destiny*, according to Ronald Hayman in *British Theatre Since 1955* (1979), suggests how indebted Edgar may be to Brecht. Hayman sees reminders of Brecht's *The Resistible Rise of Arturo Ui* (1958) in a scene in which Clifton, the Hitler character, is coached in oratory—rehearsed for his major election speech. The suggestion is logical, as Edgar attempted for more than a decade to be the Brecht of his time and place, and like Brecht, often sacrificed characterization for editorializing. His own kind of theater, Edgar wrote in 1976, prior to the production of *Destiny*, "must be serious in content, but accessible in form. It must be popular without being populist. It must be orientated towards a working-class audience. It must be temporary, immediate, specific, functional. It must get out of theatre buildings. It must be ideological, and proud of it. It must be celebratory. . . . It must not be escapist; it must take our times by the throat. . . . The central artistic problem is portraying people's behaviour as a function of their social nexus rather than individual psychology."

The statement, although Edgar must have believed it when he wrote it, is a bundle of paradoxes. Although it explains the ephemeral nature of so many of his plays and is highly Brechtian in its thrust, it neither explains the success of Brecht's best plays in the conventional commercial theater, nor does it explain Edgar's own move in that direction immediately afterward with *Destiny*. Four years in the making, unlike most of his hastily turned-out plays, it received Royal Shakespeare Company attention, with productions at Stratford and the Aldwych Theatre in London, as well as a television showing. The Royal Shakespeare Company was not a working-class theater.

In the meantime, Edgar continued with his more documentary dramas. The 7:84 Theatre Company, a left-wing touring group, took his *Wreckers*, about a 1972 dock strike, on tour around England in early 1977. Also another Brecht-inspired company calling itself Pirate Jenny toured Edgar's *Our Own People* (1977), a play in the form of a "Committee of Inquiry into a dispute between [Asian] employees of the Darley Park Mills Company . . . and their employers."

Under no illusions that his political drama would revolutionize England, Edgar said, "You know the old joke about the man who was sentenced to 999 years and said to the judge, 'I can't possibly serve all that' and the judge said, 'Well, do as much as you can.' Well, one does as much as one can." In that spirit he wrote *Mary Barnes*, given a major production at the Royal Court Theatre in 1979 after an initial run the year before in Birmingham. The play is about a schizophrenic patient who undergoes the radical therapy of being treated as a human being in a community "therapeutic center" instead of being confined to a conventional mental hospital. Mary Barnes, a real nurse with artistic aspirations, had chronicled her own breakdown in a memoir which Edgar used, documentary fashion, to explore not only what constitutes madness by societal standards but also whether or not society is guilty of complicity in the maladjustment of a talented human being, whether or not the mind's potential is wasted in order to seize easy solutions for controlling a "mad" person, and whether or not one can even talk of sanity in a less-than-sane society.

A few weeks after *Mary Barnes* was moved from Birmingham to London, the prolific Edgar produced, with the feminist Monstrous Regiment company, *Teendreams* (1979) at the Vandyck Theatre in Bristol. It was a look back at the previous decade of women's liberation activism in many episodes—short scenes punctuated by blackouts—ranging from portrayals of university sit-ins and street demonstrations to marital discord among the wiser but no happier activists. Although commercially unsuccessful, the production, with *Mary Barnes*, Eric Shorter wrote in the *Daily Telegraph* (27 January 1979), "confirms Mr. Edgar's reputation as an entertainingly intelligent guide to various social, political and medical issues." However, the work that would most confirm Edgar's stage reputation was then in preparation for the Royal Shakespeare Company—his two-part treatment of *Nicholas Nickleby*, three hundred typescript pages in length. Dickens's social conscience and inherent theatricality could not have helped but attract Edgar; nonetheless, it was theatricality which overwhelmed social conscience in the script as produced, creating one of the company's greatest box-office successes. That this happened was no accident. As Edgar

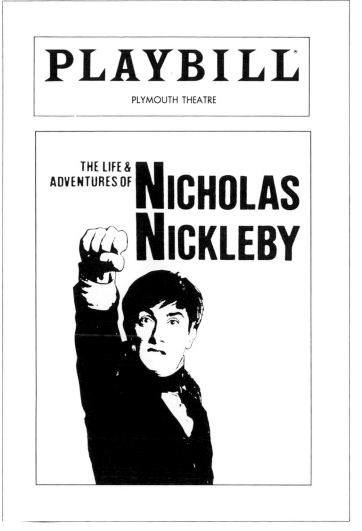

Program cover for the first New York production of Edgar's faithful adaptation of Dickens's novel

explaincd, "Almost everything academic that came out of the late 'sixties has been undermined. Laing has been undermined, since it is now much clearer that there is a chemical causative effect to schizophrenia. Chomsky has been undermined. Marcuse's theories have been shown just not to have been true, and the Black Power Movement has withered on the vine. The generation that was never going to be assimilated *has* been assimilated."

Nicholas Nickleby opened at the Aldwych Theatre in London on 21 June 1980, as the first lengthy play of a two-part production. It was "so faithful" to Dickens, *Times* critic Ned Chaillet wrote, "that David Edgar's credit as the adaptor seems superfluous. For the first quarter of eight and a half hours of performance, in two parts, there is nothing of the text [of the play] that is not simple editing [of the novel]." The remark made the crafting of a

dazzling theatrical achievement from Dickens's novel seem like a small thing; however, from the arrival of young Nicholas Nickleby in London with his mother and sister to cast themselves upon the mercy of their rich and remote uncle, Ralph Nickleby, the story is colorfully alive onstage—something Dickens himself, with all his love of the theater, was unable to accomplish in numerous adaptations of his own fiction.

Nicholas is sent off as a teacher to a vicious and corrupt Yorkshire school; his sister and mother remain and are abused by the mean uncle. Later Nicholas encounters the traveling theatrical troupe of Mr. Crummles, with whom he allies himself as actor and playwright; and while young Kate Nickleby is facing assaults upon her virtue in London, events with the troupe are neatly interwoven. Forty-two performers share more than 150 roles,

"The Life and Adventures of Nicholas Nickleby"
is set in England in the first half of the Nineteenth Century.

CAST

(in order of appearance)

THE NICKLEBY FAMILY

Nicholas Nickleby .... ROGER REES
Kate Nickleby .... EMILY RICHARD
Ralph Nickleby .... JOHN WOODVINE
Mrs. Nickleby .... PRISCILLA MORGAN

LONDON

Newman Noggs .... EDWARD PETHERBRIDGE
Hanna .... HILARY TOWNLEY
Miss La Creevy...................................... CATHERINE BRANDON
Sir Matthew Pupker .... DAVID LLOYD MEREDITH
Mr. Bonney .... ANDREW HAWKINS
Irate Gentleman .... PATRICK GODFREY
Flunkey .... TIMOTHY KIGHTLEY
Mr. Snawley .... WILLIAM MAXWELL
Srawley Major .... JANET DALE
Snawley Minor .... HILARY TOWNLEY
Belling .... STEPHEN RASHBROOK
William .... JOHN McENERY
Waitresses .... SHARON BOWER, SALLY NESBITT
Coachman .... CLYDE POLLITT
Mr. Mantalini .... JOHN McENERY
Madame Mantalini .... THELMA WHITELEY
Flunkey .... RICHARD SIMPSON
Miss Knag .... JANET DALE
Rich Ladies .... SHARON BOWER, SHIRLEY KING
Milliners .... SUZANNE BERTISH, SHARON BOWER, LUCY GUTTERIDGE,
CATHRYN HARRISON, IAN EAST, WILLIAM MAXWELL,
SALLY NESBITT, STEPHEN RASHBROOK, HILARY TOWNLEY

YORKSHIRE

Mr. Squeers .... ALUN ARMSTRONG
Mrs. Squeers .... LILA KAYF
Smike .... DAVID THRELFALL
Phib .... SALLY NESBITT
Fanny Squeers .... SUZANNE BERTISH
Young Wackford Squeers .... IAN McNEICE
John Browdie .... BOB PECK
Tilda Price .... CATHRYN HARRISON
Boys
Tomkins .... WILLIAM MAXWELL
Coates .... ANDREW HAWKINS
Graymarsh .... ALAN GILL
Jennings .... PATRICK GODFREY
Mobbs .... CHRISTOPHER RAVENSCROFT
Bolder .... MARK TANDY
Pitcher .... SHARON BOWER
Jackson .... NICHOLAS GECKS
Cobbey .... JOHN McENERY
Peters .... TEDDY KEMPNER
Sprouter .... LUCY GUTTERIDGE
Roberts .... IAN EAST

LONDON AGAIN

Mr. Kenwigs .... PATRICK GODFREY
Mrs. Kenwigs .... SHIRLEY KING
Morleena Kenwigs .... HILARY TOWNLEY
Mr. Lillyvick .... TIMOTHY KIGHTLEY
Miss Petowker .... CATHRYN HARRISON
Mr. Crowl .... IAN EAST
George .... ALAN GILL
Mr. Cutler .... JEFFERY DENCH
Mrs. Cutler .... JANET DALE
Mrs. Kenwigs' Sister .... SHARON BOWER
Lady From Downstairs .... CATHERINE BRANDON
Miss Green .... PRISCILLA MORGAN
Benjamin .... TEDDY KEMPNER
Pugstyles .... RODERICK HORN
Old Lord .... RICHARD SIMPSON
Young Fiancée .... LUCY GUTTERIDGE
Landlord .... JEFFERY DENCH

PORTSMOUTH

Mr. Vincent Crummles .... CHRISTOPHER BENJAMIN
Mrs. Crummles .... LILA KAYE
The Infant Phenomenon .... HILARY TOWNLEY
Master Percy Crummles .... TEDDY KEMPNER
Master Crummles .... MARK TANDY
Mrs. Grudden .... CATHERINE BRANDON
Miss Snevelicci .... SUZANNE BERTISH
Mr. Folair .... CLYDE POLLITT
Mr. Lenville .... CHRISTOPHER RAVENSCROFT
Miss Ledrock .... LUCY GUTTERIDGE
Miss Bravassa .... SHARON BOWER
Mr. Wagstaff .... ALUN ARMSTRONG
Mr. Blightey .... JEFFERY DENCH
Miss Belvawney .... JANET DALE
Miss Gazingi .... SALLY NESBITT
Mr. Pailey .... WILLIAM MAXWELL

Cast list for the first New York production of Nicholas Nickleby

Mr. Hetherington	ANDREW HAWKINS
Mr. Bane	STEPHEN RASHBROOK
Mr. Fluggers	RICHARD SIMPSON
Mrs. Lenville	SHIRLEY KING
Mr. Curdle	HUBERT REES
Mrs. Curdle	EMILY RICHARD
Mr. Snevellicci	JOHN McENERY
Mrs. Snevellicci	THELMA WHITELEY

LONDON AGAIN

Scaley	IAN McNEICE
Tix	TEDDY KEMPNER
Sir Mulberry Hawk	BOB PECK
Lord Frederick Verisopht	NICHOLAS GECKS
Mr. Pluck	TEDDY KEMPNER
Mr. Pyke	MARK TANDY
Mr. Snobb	CHRISTOPHER RAVENSCROFT
Colonel Chowser	TIMOTHY KIGHTLEY
Brooker	CLYDE POLLITT
Mr. Wititterley	RODERICK HORN
Mrs. Wititterley	JANET DALE
Alphonse	STEPHEN RASHBROOK
Opera Singers	SHARON BOWER, ANDREW HAWKINS, JOHN WOODVINE
Charles Cheeryble	DAVID LLOYD MEREDITH
Ned Cheeryble	HUBERT REES
Tim Linkinwater	RICHARD SIMPSON
The Man Next Door	PATRICK GODFREY
Keeper	ALAN GILL
Frank Cheeryble	CHRISTOPHER RAVENSCROFT
Nurse	THELMA WHITELEY
Arthur Gride	JEFFERY DENCH
Madeline Bray	LUCY GUTTERIDGE
Walter Bray	CHRISTOPHER BENJAMIN
Peg Sliderskew	SUZANNE BERTISH
Hawk's Rival	EDWARD PETHERBRIDGE
Captain Adams	ANDREW HAWKINS
Westwood	ALAN GILL
Croupier	IAN McNEICE
Casino Proprietor	PATRICK GODFREY
Surgeon	TIMOTHY KIGHTLEY
Umpire	RODERICK HORN
Policemen	ANDREW HAWKINS, MARK TANDY
Mrs. Snawley	JANET DALE
Young Woman	HILARY TOWNLEY

UNDERSTUDIES

Understudies never substitute for listed players unless a specific announcement
for the appearance is made at the time of the performance.

Wilfred Grove, Katharine Levy, Joyce Worsley

MUSICIANS

Donald Johnston — *Musical Conductor/Piano*
Mel Rodnon — *Flute*
Seymour Press — *Clarinet*
Ethan Bauch — *Bassoon*
Lowell Hershey — *Trumpet*
Robert Zittola — *Trumpet*
Christine Snyder — *French Horn*
Daniel Repole — *Trombone*
Sandra Billingslea — *Violin*
Karen Ritscher — *Viola*
Doc Solomon — *Bass*
Bruce Yuchitel — *Banjo*
Jack Jenrings — *Percussion*

Wedding Anthem sung by Choristers from St. Paul's Cathedral. Master of the Choir: Barry Rose.

PLEASE NOTE:

Part One is approximately 4 hours in length with one intermission of 15 minutes.
Part Two is approximately 4¾ hours in length with two intermissions of 12 minutes.

On Wednesdays, Saturdays and Sundays,
there is a 55-minute dinner break between parts I and II.

WHO'S WHO in the CAST

THE COMPANY

As this production has a large cast and
program space is limited, the following
biographies are necessarily brief. They
represent only a very small percentage of
the work of each artist: in most cases just
a few credits from each of the fields of the
performing arts.

ALUN ARMSTRONG

THEATRE: Yescanab in *The Sons of
Light* (Repertory), Billy Spencer in *The
Changing Room* (Royal Court), Azdak in
The Caucasian Chalk Circle, Dogberry in
Much Ado About Nothing, Alun in *Bas-
tard Angel* (RSC).
TELEVISION: "Days of Hope," "The
Stars Look Down," "Hard Day Out,"
"Measure for Measure," "One in a Thou-
sand."
FILM: *Get Carter, The Duellists*.

CHRISTOPHER BENJAMIN

THEATRE: Pozzo in *Waiting For Godot*,
Max in *The Homecoming* (Repertory),
Reader in *Nashville* (King's Head), Jim
Broadbent in *John Bull's Other Island*
(Greenwich), Stagg in *The Hang of the
Gaol* (RSC).
TELEVISION: numerous appearances in-
clude "Dick Turpin," "Donkey's Years,"
"We the Accused," "Spy at Evening."

SUZANNE BERTISH

THEATRE: Title role in *The Duchess of
Malfi*, Lady Macbeth in *Macbeth*, Nurse
in *Romeo and Juliet* (Glasgow Citizens'),
Sparrowfall (London), *Devil's Island*
(Joint Stock), Ophelia in *Hamlet*, Octavia
in *All for Love* (Prospect), Masha in *Three
Sisters*, Dionyza/Diana in *Pericles*, Desde-
mona in *Othello* (RSC).
TELEVISION: includes "Play of the

John Woodvine, Roger Rees, and Emily Richard in a scene from the first New York production of Nicholas Nickleby

with only Nicholas and Smike, the wretched boy who becomes Nickleby's faithful companion, permitted roles in which no doubling-up is possible.

With the help of director Trevor Nunn and a cast which suggests that it is unlikely that the lavish combination of pageant and morality play will be mounted soon again by another company, Edgar captured the feel of Dickensian London. As Bernard Levin wrote in the *Times* (8 July 1980), the production was "a celebration of love and justice that is true to the spirit of Dickens's belief that those are the fulcrums on which the universe is moved, and the consequence is that we come out not merely delighted but strengthened, not just entertained but uplifted, not only affected but changed." Peter Keating in the *Times Literary Supplement* (27 June 1980) observed that "given the shapelessness of *Nicholas Nickleby*, there is no convincing reason why, long as it is, it shouldn't be twice as long, or half or a third or a quarter as long, or any length that artistic ingenuity can maintain." Given that initial problem, Edgar managed his adaptation adroitly, retaining the scope of the original and challenging his audiences. The overwhelming success of the production—it could have run far longer but at the cost of the Royal Shakespeare Company's repertory

system—led the company to a fourteen-week season at the Plymouth Theatre in New York beginning 5 October 1981. Again, despite a huge price for the pairing—$100 regardless of location—the play was a critical and commercial success, although Frank Rich in the *New York Times* (6 October 1981) called it "an outsized event that sometimes seems in search of a shape." The fact that the ticket price made it chic to be a patron, and eliminated Dickens's natural audience entirely, was the ultimate irony for the playwright, who had begun his career with morality plays for the underprivileged. But Edgar's message had not changed—only the medium was different.

Television Scripts:
The Eagle Has Landed, Granada Television, 1973;
Sanctuary, adapted from Edgar's *Gangsters*, Scottish Television, 1973;
I Know What I Meant, Granada Television, 1974;
Baby Love, BBC, 1974;
Concorde Cabaret, adapted from Edgar's *The Case of the Workers' Plane*, Harlech Television, 1975;
Censors, by Edgar, Robert Muller, and Hugh Whitemore, BBC, 1975;
The Midas Connection, BBC, 1975;

Destiny, BBC, 1978.

Radio Scripts:
Ecclesiastes, BBC Radio 4, 1977;
Saigon Rose, BBC Radio 3, 1979.

Other:
Two Kinds of Angel, in *The London Fringe Theatre*, edited by V. E. Mitchell (London: Burnham House, 1975);
"Socialist Theatre and the Bourgeois Author," in *Workers and Writers*, edited by Wilfried van der Will (Birmingham: Department of German, Birmingham University, 1975);
Comment in *Contemporary Dramatists*, second edition, edited by James Vinson (London: St. James Press, 1977), pp. 236-237.

Periodical Publications:
"Something Rotten in the State of Drama," *Month in Yorkshire* (February 1972);
"Against the General Will," *Plays and Players*, 20 (May 1973): 14-15;

"Residence Permits," *Plays and Players*, 22 (July 1975): 16-17;
"Return to Base," *New Edinburgh Review*, 30 (August 1975): 2-3;
"Political Theatre: Part One," *Socialist Review* (April 1978);
"Political Theatre: Part Two," *Socialist Review* (May 1978);
"Ten Years of Political Theatre," *Theatre Quarterly*, 32 (Winter 1979): 25-33.

Interview:
"A Drama of Dynamic Ambiguities," in *New Theatre. Voices of the the Seventies*, edited by Simon Trussler (London: Eyre Methuen, 1981), pp. 156-171.

References:
Ronald Hayman, *British Theatre Since 1955* (London: Oxford University Press, 1979), pp. 107-113;
Catherine Itzin, *Stages in the Revolution* (London: Eyre Methuen, 1980).

Michael Frayn

(8 September 1933-   )

Mark Fritz

PRODUCTIONS: *Zounds!*, by Frayn and John Edwards, music by Keith Statham, May 1957, Cambridge;
The Two of Us, 30 July 1970, Garrick Theatre, London;
The Sandboy, 16 September 1971, Greenwich Theatre, London;
Alphabetical Order, 11 March 1975, Hampstead Theatre Club (transferred 8 April 1975 to the Mayfair Theatre), London;
Donkeys' Years, 15 July 1976, Globe Theatre, London;
Clouds, 16 August 1976, Hampstead Theatre Club, London; 1 November 1978, Duke of York's Theatre, London;
Liberty Hall, 24 January 1980, Greenwich Theatre, London;
Make and Break, 18 March 1980, Lyric Theatre, Hammersmith (transferred 24 April 1980 to

Theatre Royal, Haymarket), London;
Noises Off, 11 February 1982, Lyric Theatre, Hammersmith (transferred 31 March 1982 to Savoy Theatre), London.

BOOKS: *The Day of the Dog* (London: Collins, 1962; Garden City: Doubleday, 1963);
The Book of Fub (London: Collins, 1963); republished as *Never Put Off to Gomorrah* (New York: Pantheon, 1964);
On the Outskirts (London: Collins, 1964);
The Tin Men (London: Collins, 1965; Boston: Little, Brown, 1966);
The Russian Interpreter (London: Collins, 1966; New York: Viking, 1966);
At Bay in Gear Street (London: Fontana, 1967);
Towards the End of the Morning (London: Collins, 1967); republished as *Against Entropy* (New York: Viking, 1967);

A Very Private Life (London: Collins, 1968; New
    York: Viking, 1968);
The Two of Us (London: Fontana, 1970);
Sweet Dreams (London: Collins, 1973; New York:
    Viking, 1974);
Constructions (London: Wildwood House, 1974);
Alphabetical Order and Donkeys' Years (London: Eyre
    Methuen, 1977);
Clouds (London: Eyre Methuen, 1977; London &
    New York: French, 1977);
Make and Break (London: Eyre Methuen, 1980).

Michael Frayn is a satirist who has moved from
newspaper columns to novels to television productions to stage plays. Judging from the critical responses, he seems to have conquered each medium.
His plays have been popular with audiences who are
attracted to their humor and with critics who have
noticed the underlying social commentary and the
influence of Wittgensteinian philosophy.

Frayn was born above a liquor store in Mill
Hall on the northwestern edge of London. His
father, Thomas Allen Frayn, was a sales representative for an asbestos company; his mother, Violet
Alice Lawson Frayn, had been a shop assistant. Soon
after his birth, his parents moved to Ewell on the
southern fringe of London. Frayn believes his sense
of humor began to develop during his years at
Kingston Grammar School where, to the delight of
his classmates, he practiced the "techniques of
mockery" on his teachers. Referring to this early
practice of making jokes at the expense of others,
Frayn says, "I sometimes wonder if this isn't an
embarrassingly exact paradigm of much that I've
done since."

After leaving school in 1952, Frayn was conscripted into the Royal Army and sent to a Russian
interpretership course at Cambridge. He also
studied in Moscow for several weeks, returning with
the opinion that the so-called Cold War was ridiculous. East/West relations would later become a
subject of satire in many of his works. Eventually
Frayn was commissioned as an officer in the intelligence corps. His second novel *The Russian Interpreter*
(1966) was partially influenced by his experiences
during this time. Discharged from the army in
1954, he returned to Cambridge to study philosophy at Emmanuel College. Frayn recalls, "the
philosopher who entirely dominated the way that
philosophy was done and taught at Cambridge, and
who had the greatest possible influence on me and
everything I've written was Wittgenstein." An Austrian expatriate who spent most of his life in England, Ludwig Wittgenstein is a leading figure in

Michael Frayn, 1981

twentieth-century philosophy. He studied logic
under Bertrand Russell at Cambridge and later
taught philosophy there himself until 1947.
Wittgenstein's work deals primarily with the nature
and limits of language. He discussed the limits of
language as a means of interpersonal communication and as a means of representing reality. Words,
he said, present a picture of reality but not reality
itself. Another subject of philosophical scrutiny for
Wittgenstein was how the expression of concepts is
linked to human actions and reactions.

At Cambridge, Frayn wrote humorous articles
for the undergraduate newspaper. He also collaborated with John Edwards on a musical comedy,
Zounds!, which was performed in 1957 by the Cambridge theatrical club, the Footlights. After graduation in 1957, Frayn worked for the Manchester
Guardian, where he was a reporter from 1957 to
1959 and a columnist from 1959 to 1962. His columns of social satire for the *Guardian* soon became
very popular and have been collected in two books,
The Day of the Dog (1962) and *The Book of Fub* (1963).
In 1962 he moved to the *Observer* in London where

he continued writing humorous columns until 1968. His work for the *Observer* has also been collected as *On the Outskirts* (1964) and *At Bay in Gear Street* (1967). In 1969 he married Gillian Palmer. With their three daughters they live near Blackheath in southeast London.

Frayn's columns are social spoofs, often written in dialogue form and with a cast of fictional characters. The pieces usually take a popular trend or human foible and stretch it to ludicrous proportions. His wit, sophistication, and imagination are like that of American humorist S. J. Perelman, but his satire is sharper. Like most satirists, Frayn has favorite targets for his barbs. Among his pet peeves are liberal-minded hypocrisy, middle-class convention, and class snobbery.

Frayn's first novel, *The Tin Men* (1965), won the Somerset Maugham Award for fiction. The work satirizes computers and automation. His second novel, *The Russian Interpreter*, a spy story which deals more with the deceit between individuals than between nations, was awarded the Hawthornden Prize. During the following two years, Frayn completed two more novels. *Towards the End of the Morning* (1967) is similar to *Alphabetical Order* (1975), a play Frayn would write eight years later. Both the novel and play are satires set in a newspaper office. Like the newspaper in the play, the one in *Towards the End of the Morning* is stagnating (a condition reflected by the title of the American edition of the novel, *Against Entropy*). *A Very Private Life* (1968) is a futuristic fable satirizing the penchant for privacy held by the upper class.

Frayn's first dramatic work was a television play, *Jamie, On a Flying Visit*, aired by the BBC on 17 January 1968. The drama focuses upon a casual reunion of two college sweethearts. Lois has settled down with her three children and her unmoneyed schoolmaster husband. Jamie arrives at Lois's modest bungalow in his sports car and with his new girl friend. Jamie has not changed—he is still wild, rich, energetic, and freewheeling. His life-style contrasts sharply with that of Lois, and she envies him. But as novelist Anthony Burgess commented in the *Listener*, "There is nothing for anybody to do except make social noises, put the lid on resentment, note the lack of that common language called money." Because of the play's serious nature, it was not well received by those who were expecting a comedy with the wit of Frayn's columns.

The following year on 12 February the BBC produced *Birthday*, which is also about a visit. At her apartment, Liz is celebrating her twenty-seventh birthday with her boyfriend and other guests when Jess, her older married sister, drops by. Jess is pregnant, and in the midst of Liz's birthday party, she creates another birthday by bearing her child. The sisters are drawn together emotionally by the experience but then drift apart again. *Guardian* critic Stanley Reynolds said, "We had seen [Frayn's] people touch upon real life, feel it, and then recoil back into their shells and assumed identities. It was some play for a humorist." Also impressed by *Birthday* was theatrical producer Michael Codron, who according to Frayn, "kept nagging at me to do something for the theatre."

Codron's prodding led to *The Two of Us*, Frayn's first stage play, which opened in the West End on 30 July 1970. It is actually four separate short plays strung tenuously together in the manner of Neil Simon's *Plaza Suite* (1968). In its premiere, Richard Briers and Lynn Redgrave played all eleven roles, which required very creative staging and some contrived exits. *Black and Silver* is the curtain raiser of the quartet. In it a couple's second honeymoon is humorously complicated by the presence of their new baby. The second playlet, *The New Quixote*, shows a young woman's reaction when her casual lover decides to move in. She discovers that he is a neurotic mama's boy who wants to play the stereo constantly. At first she tries to get rid of him but eventually accepts his presence. *Mr. Foot*, the third playlet, is about a suburban housewife who is being driven mad by her demanding but boring husband and his weird habits. When the husband insists that she make a good impression on his prospective employer, she spouts out her grievances instead. In the final skit, *Chinamen*, a host and hostess of a dinner party try frantically to keep a husband separated from his estranged wife and her boyfriend. The many contrived exits and entrances partially explain why London *Times* reviewer Irving Wardle said that Frayn uses "characters as comic machines." According to Wardle, the characters have no sense of humanity. That lack of humanity is one of the themes of the play, however. Frayn is satirizing people who deal with one another not as their humanness dictates but as social convention dictates.

Although Frayn was working primarily in the theater in 1970, he also contributed occasional humorous articles to the *Observer* and other newspapers. Those contributions won him the National Press Award that year.

Frayn's second play, *The Sandboy*, opened the next year at the Greenwich Theatre. Its central character is a city planner who is so successful that a documentary film is being made about him. In the

Richard Briers and Lynn Redgrave in each of the four parts of The Two of Us

play the actors speak to the audience as if it is an imaginary film crew which is present to record a day in the life of Phil Schaffer, city planner. This unusual dramatic framework was declared ingenious by one critic; another called it "notoriously unworkable." In any event, it places Phil and his wife in the position of having to present a social facade and yet appear natural at the same time. It is a play of ironic contrasts between what the liberal, intellectual Phil announces to the camera and what he actually does. Essentially, it is a play about one man's self-delusions. Critic Melvyn Jones felt the play goes beyond this level, examining fundamental questions about the very nature of reality. He said it raises questions like those raised by the philosopher Wittgenstein: What is the reality signified by what people say? Do the words people use signify what they really mean—do they themselves know what they mean and what reality is? What is real and what is merely a representation of what is real?

During the three and a half years between *The Sandboy* and Frayn's next play, he wrote two books and contributed to a weekly BBC comedy series called *Beyond a Joke*, which began in April 1972 and ran for six weeks. Frayn collaborated with the series's star Eleanor Bron on the assorted offbeat sketches which comprised the show. The novel *Sweet Dreams*, a satirical fantasy about a typical middle-aged Londoner's experiences in heaven, was published in 1973, and *Constructions*, a collection of dense philosophical aphorisms, appeared the next year.

Frayn's next play, *Alphabetical Order* (1975), is perhaps his most successful attempt at blending serious social comment with comedy. As the play begins, a stern young woman is taking up her new position as an assistant in the clippings library of a provincial newspaper. Before her arrival the library was haphazardly organized but functional. By the second act she has transformed it into a model of order and efficiency. But somehow the humanness is gone. The young woman then proceeds to reorganize the personal lives of the other characters as well. She is not a total villain, however. In a way, the newspaper staff needs her: without a strong-willed person to manipulate them, weak-willed people often stagnate. At the heart of the play is the question: which is better, order or chaos? Frayn leaves it up to the audience to decide. Frayn personally believes there must be a middle ground. When asked in an interview about the theme of *Alphabetical Order*, Frayn said, "You have to structure your life, otherwise it's impossible. But when the structure takes over you have to think again." Among the

critics impressed with *Alphabetical Order* was Clive Barnes. Reviewing its American premiere in 1976 at the Long Wharf Theatre in New Haven, Connecticut, he praised the "heightened simplicity" of the play's dialogue and called it "the best play to be written about newspapers since *Front Page*." In London *Alphabetical Order* won the *Evening Standard* Drama Award for best comedy of the year.

Frayn returned to work for the BBC in 1975, again writing a comedy series for actress Eleanor Bron. *Making Faces* was six short situation comedies chronicling the varied career of a multifaceted woman named Zoya. According to the *Guardian* critic, Zoya's facets are actually "rather a ragbag of the last 16 years' trendiness." The first episode aired on 25 September 1975.

Frayn began in 1975 a series of four documentary films for the BBC. The first, *Imagine a City Called Berlin*, was completed and broadcast that year, and the second, *Vienna: The Mask of Gold*, was completed and aired in 1977. The third, *Three Streets in the Country* (1979), is about the suburbs of London, and the last of the series, *The Long Straight* (1980), is about Australia. Frayn describes these documentaries as "kind of filmed essays, really, with a lot of history in them."

London's Globe Theatre staged Frayn's next play, *Donkeys' Years*, in 1976. The play's characters meet at "one of the lesser Colleges, at one of the older Universities" for their twenty-year reunion and proceed to get drunk and reminisce. The wife of the Master was well known to them all—quite intimately—when they were undergraduates, the audience learns when she drops by to say hello. They all pursue her amorously, making for frantic stage action as the nine characters dart in and out of dormitory doors with "Feydeau-like abandon," as Clive Barnes phrased it. A witty and ironic farce, *Donkeys' Years* is also a serious character study. Each man is looking back on his life and trying to convince the others (and himself) that it has gone as he wished, that he is successful in his profession and happy in his marriage. Of course, none of them really is.

Donkeys' Years was named best comedy of the year by the Society of West End Theatre. In a London *Times* interview Frayn described the difficulties of writing this play: "I've totally lost count of the number of drafts of *Donkeys' Years* that I wrote. I just couldn't finish it. It went on for years. At one point I decided to turn it into a television play and rewrote it for the BBC. But I knew they weren't ever going to do it, so I got the script back and began it again as a stage play. When it ran for 18 months I felt as

Billie Whitelaw, Bernard Gallagher, June Ellis, and A. J. Brown in the first production of Alphabetical Order

though I'd earned the royalties."

In the summer of 1976, only a month after the debut of *Donkeys' Years*, Frayn's fifth play opened at the Hampstead Theatre Club in London. *Clouds*, as the title implies, is a philosophical and enigmatic, yet amusing, play. Later produced in 1978 in the West End, the play received generally favorable reviews. It begins in the British embassy in Cuba. There Owen, a professional journalist, and Mara, a novelist, meet and discover that they have similar assignments with rival newspapers. Along with an American professor, they are given a driving tour of the island by a government official. Flirtatious affairs develop between Mara and each of the three men. Mara—at first a prim, withdrawn woman who has spent her life cloistered inside her quaint English cottage—eventually blossoms, as Irving Wardle said, "into a formidable tease." The play examines relationships, the way they are constantly forming and changing like the clouds in the sky. It also deals with the divergence of human perceptions. Again clouds serve as a metaphor: every per-

son sees life differently, the same way different people perceive different images in cloud forms. *Clouds* is constructed in short scenes like a film. In fact, like its predecessor, it started out as a television play. But the television executives, frightened by the cost of shooting on location in Cuba or Spain, turned it down. Thus Frayn decided to rewrite it for the theater and to stage it very abstractly with just six chairs and a blue backdrop.

Throughout his work, from his columns to novels like *The Russian Interpreter* to plays like *Clouds* and the next one, *Liberty Hall* (1980), Frayn has been commenting on the ridiculous schism between Soviet Russia and the so-called free world. *Liberty Hall* is based on the hypothetical question: what if the 1917 revolution had occurred in England instead of Russia? The play is set in Balmoral Castle, which, since the fictional revolution, has been a home for state-supported writers. The year is 1937 and residing at Balmoral are Godfrey Winn, Enid Blyton, John McNab, Warwick Deeping, and Hugh Walpole. The action gets underway when Walpole mysteriously disappears just as an official inspector arrives and demands to see him. Believing Walpole to have been kidnapped, several of the writers try to cover up the disappearance by impersonating Walpole. A series of cases of mistaken identity follows, and eventually it turns out that Walpole has died of a heart attack. Then follows a series of humorous attempts to hide the body from the inspector, who is finally revealed to be a reporter from the capitalist state of Russia. As in Frayn's other farces, *Liberty Hall* contains lots of slapstick and frantic action. The play was generally well received by the critics.

Make and Break (1980), which followed *Liberty Hall* by about two months, is a portrait of super-salesman John Garrard. At first Garrard seems to be a hyperactive fanatic who never stops selling, like an actor who cannot step out of a role. But later as Frayn delves deeper into the character, the audience realizes that Garrard is not just a fanatic—he is like an automaton, devoid of human emotions.

The action takes place in Frankfurt in a hotel suite which has been converted to a display room. As the play begins, three of Garrard's employees are demonstrating their line of movable walls to potential customers. The walls open and close at the touch of a switch, and the audience catches bits of the ongoing sales pitches as each of the three customer-salesman pairs appears and then disappears behind the walls. These movable walls are not merely partitions, the salesmen say, but something indistinguishable from real walls. This statement is part of a Wittgenstein-inspired theme that runs throughout the play—what is not real is indistinguishable from what is real. By the end of the play, the audience wonders too if Garrard is a real human being. He looks like one, but there are some intangible emotional elements missing in his character. Garrard is unable to communicate with other people on a human, emotional level. Even when he makes love to the company secretary, it is very much

DONKEYS' YEARS
a new comedy by MICHAEL FRAYN

GLOBE THEATRE

DONKEYS' YEARS

by MICHAEL FRAYN

COLLEGE NOTES:—

MR. S. BIRKETT, Head Porter, completes fifty years' service with the College this October	A. J. BROWN
C. D. P. B. HEADINGLEY, M.A., M.P., is Parliamentary Under-Secretary of State at the Department of Education and Science	PETER BARKWORTH
D. J. BUCKLE, M.B., M.R.C.S., is assistant chief surgeon in the Department of Urology, Royal Wessex Hospital, Southampton	PETER JEFFREY
K. SNELL, M.A. is engaged in research in parasitology at British Alkalis (Pharmaceutical Division), Rotherham	ANDREW ROBERTSON
A. V. QUINE, B.A., is now in the grade of Assistant Secretary at the Department of Education and Science	JULIAN CURRY
THE REV. R. D. SAINSBURY, M.A., is Curate in Charge of St. Columba's, Small Heath, Birmingham	HAROLD INNOCENT
N. O. P. TATE, M.A., has recently published 'The Complete Home Encyclopaedia of Japanese Flower Arrangement' and 'A Boys' and Girls' Guide to Overseas Development'	JEFFRY WICKHAM
W. R. TAYLOR, M.A., Ph.D., Research Fellow and College Lecturer in English, has published 'Mythopoeic Structures in the Metonymy of Two Jacobean Children's Rhymes' (*Revue des Etudes Semiologiques*, Toulouse)	JOHN HARDING
LADY DRIVER, M.A., The Master's wife (formerly Rosemary Gilbert), has been appointed a member of the Royal Commission on Obesity	PENELOPE KEITH

Directed by MICHAEL RUDMAN

One of the smaller quadrangles, in one of the lesser Colleges, at one of the older Universities.

The play is in three Acts with ONE INTERVAL of fifteen minutes between Acts II and III.

Program cover and cast list for the first production of Frayn's 1976 award-winning farce

like a business transaction. *Make and Break* is a relentless, darkly comical character study.

Many critics believe that *Make and Break* is Frayn's best work thus far. Reviewers have frequently commented that Frayn's characters lack depth. Frayn, they say, avoids human emotions in favor of cold intellectual witticisms. *Make and Break*, however, seems to have outdistanced that sort of criticism. *Times* critic Ned Chaillet said, "There are glorious signs in *Make and Break* that Mr. Frayn is willing to embrace a more dazzling stagecraft, and with his usual display of wit he now offers sharp, kaleidoscopic insights into feelings and even attempts an interior look at the moment of dying."

Michael Frayn's latest farce, *Noises Off* (1982), is a play about the production of a play. A fictitious provincial touring company is shown preparing a ludicrous farce which is finally performed with disastrous and therefore humorous consequences. Alcoholism and sexual intrigue are rampant among the cast. While these problems make rehearsals run less than smoothly, they also create the comedy. In the first act of *Noises Off* the audience witnesses the first act of the players' farce, a parody of the plays of Ben Travers, during a last-minute, combined dress and technical rehearsal. The first act of *Noises Off* is expository, introducing the characters, their peculiarities, and their complicated personal problems. In the second act of *Noises Off*, the first act of the Travers parody is repeated (the company is making its next road appearance), but it is played offstage so that the audience only hears it; what they see is the "backstage" activity. As the play goes on, relationships between cast members deteriorate, and the business of performing the show becomes subordinate to the business of solving personal problems. As a result, theatrical chaos reigns: an actress barricades herself in her dressing room and refuses to perform, the leading man gets more and more intoxicated, practical jokes are pulled, scenery collapses, and props explode. This humorous pandemonium was appreciated by the critics; the reviewer for *Punch*, for example, said, "there are bigger laughs in *Noises Off* than I have heard in years."

Although one cannot say that Michael Frayn's plays revolutionized the British stage during the 1970s, they certainly helped to enliven it. Frayn contributed a string of lively, witty comedies with some serious philosophical questions lurking beneath the surfaces. Like many other playwrights of the era, Frayn experimented with dramatic structures borrowed from film and television—perhaps more a natural result of having started his dramatic writing career in television than an attempt to find new methods of expression.

Television Scripts:
Jamie, On a Flying Visit, BBC, 1968;
Birthday, BBC, 1969;
Making Faces, BBC, 1975;
Imagine a City Called Berlin, BBC, 1975;
Vienna: The Mask of Gold, BBC, 1977;
Three Streets in the Country, BBC, 1979;
The Long Straight, BBC, 1980.

References:
Ian Jack, "Frayn, Philosopher of the Suburbs," *Sunday Times*, 13 April 1975, pp. 43;
"Playwrights on Parade," *Sunday Times Magazine*, 26 November 1978, p. 71.

Brian Friel
(9 January 1929-   )

June Schlueter
Lafayette College

PRODUCTIONS: *A Doubtful Paradise*, 1959, Group Theatre, Belfast;

The Enemy Within, 6 August 1962, Abbey Theatre, Dublin; 9 September 1963, Lyric Players Theatre, Belfast;

The Blind Mice, 19 February 1963, Eblana Theatre, Dublin;

Philadelphia, Here I Come!, 28 September 1964, Gaiety Theatre, Dublin; 16 February 1966, Helen Hayes Theatre, New York, 326 [performances]; 20 September 1967, Lyric Theatre, Hammersmith, London;

The Loves of Cass McGuire, 6 October 1966, Helen Hayes Theatre, New York; 24 September 1967, Abbey Theatre, Dublin; 20 May 1968, Grove Theatre, Belfast; 8 November 1970, Hans Crescent British Council Theatre, London;

Lovers: *Part One: Winners*; *Part Two: Losers*, 18 July 1967, Gate Theatre, Dublin; 25 June 1968, Vivian Beaumont Theatre, New York; 25 August 1969, Fortune Theatre, London;

Crystal and Fox, 12 November 1968, Gaiety Theatre, Dublin; February 1969, Mark Taper Forum, Los Angeles; 23 March 1973, McAlpin Rooftop Theatre, New York, 24;

The Mundy Scheme, 11 June 1969, Olympia Theatre, Dublin; 11 December 1969, Royale Theatre, New York, 4;

The Gentle Island, 30 November 1971, Olympia Theatre, Dublin;

The Freedom of the City, 20 February 1973, Abbey Theatre, Dublin; 27 February 1973, Royal Court Theatre, London; 17 February 1974, Alvin Theatre, New York, 37;

Volunteers, 5 March 1975, Abbey Theatre, Dublin; 20 May 1982, Westbeth Theatre Center, New York;

Living Quarters, 24 March 1977, Abbey Theatre, Dublin;

Aristocrats, 8 March 1979, Abbey Theatre, Dublin;

Faith Healer, 5 April 1979, Longacre Theatre, New York; September 1980, Abbey Theatre, Dublin; 2 March 1981, Royal Court Theatre, London;

Translations, 16 September 1980, Guild Hall, Londonderry; 6 October 1980, Gate Theatre, Dublin; 12 May 1981, Hampstead Theatre, London.

BOOKS: *The Saucer of Larks* (London: Gollancz, 1962; Garden City: Doubleday, 1962);

Philadelphia, Here I Come! (London: Faber & Faber, 1965; New York: Farrar, Straus & Giroux, 1966);

The Gold in the Sea (London: Gollancz, 1966; Garden City: Doubleday, 1966);

The Loves of Cass McGuire (London: Faber & Faber, 1967; New York: Farrar, Straus & Giroux, 1967);

Lovers: Part One: Winners; Part Two: Losers (New York: Farrar, Straus & Giroux, 1968; London: Faber & Faber, 1969);

The Saucer of Larks: Stories of Ireland (London: Arrow, 1969);

Two Plays: Crystal and Fox and The Mundy Scheme (London: Faber & Faber, 1970; New York: Farrar, Straus & Giroux, 1970);

The Mundy Scheme (London: Faber & Faber, 1970; New York: Farrar, Straus & Giroux, 1970);

The Gentle Island (London: Davis-Poynter, 1973);

The Freedom of the City (London: Faber & Faber, 1974);

Living Quarters (London: Faber & Faber, 1978);

Volunteers (London: Faber & Faber, 1979);

Selected Stories (Dublin: Gallery Press, 1979);

Faith Healer (London: Faber & Faber, 1980);

Aristocrats (Dublin: Gallery Press, 1980);

Translations (London: Faber & Faber, 1981).

Over the past two decades, Brian Friel has become one of Ireland's best-known playwrights. Following the example of William Butler Yeats, John Millington Synge, Sean O'Casey, and others who were part of the flourishing literary movement at the turn of the century, and encouraged by the annual Dublin Theatre Festival, Friel has produced drama that is clearly indigenous to Ireland. In each of Friel's stage plays, Ireland not only provides the canvas upon which his largely rural characters are portrayed but also acts as a character itself. Friel's canon characterizes not only individuals but an entire people, whose hopes and disappointments play themselves out against a menacing undercurrent of violence and death. In nearly all his plays, the interplay of reality, memory, and dream suggests the spiritual flux of a people whose sense of tradition and place is frequently at war with contemporary realities. Yet even as Friel creates his cameos of Irish life, his themes acquire an elasticity stretching beyond the private lives of his characters to the unlocalized realm of the human spirit.

Throughout his work, Friel handles his characters with affection and compassion, reflecting an extraordinary sensitivity to human nature. Outwardly simple, the characters are inwardly complex, and the emotional battle of each is kept free of sentimentality by Friel's skillful use of language. The combination of intelligence and emotion in Friel's characters succeeds in conveying a strong sense of the inadequacies of human nature while affirming the continuum of life.

A Catholic native of Northern Ireland, presently living in Muff, County Donegal, Friel was born outside the town of Omagh, County Tyrone, to Patrick and Christina MacLoone Friel. The family moved to Londonderry when he was ten so his father could take the principalship at Long Tower School. Friel attended St. Columb's College in Londonderry from 1941 to 1946. He entered St. Patrick's College, a seminary in Maynooth, in 1946 and received a B.A. degree in 1948. Having abandoned his plans for the priesthood, he studied at St. Joseph's Teacher Training School in Belfast in 1949-1950. In 1954 he married Anne Morrison, with whom he has five children. For the ten years following his graduation from St. Joseph's, Friel taught school in Londonderry, but in 1960, encouraged by the *New Yorker*'s regular publication of his stories, he left the profession to write full time.

Between 1958 and 1962, Friel wrote several short stories, two radio plays (*A Sort of Freedom*, 1958, and *To This Hard House*, 1958), and three stage plays. Produced in 1959, *A Doubtful Paradise* (originally "The Francophile") deals with the family and job problems of Willie Logue, a Derry post office employee; *The Enemy Within* (1962) dramatizes the conflict of a sixth-century scholar-priest (later canonized as Saint Columba), who is as attracted to the secular life as to the religious; and *The Blind Mice* (1963) follows the fate of Chris Carroll, a priest who renounces his faith following five years' imprisonment in Communist China. Despite Friel's dismissal of these early plays, *The Enemy Within* brought Friel recognition in Ireland.

Stimulated by Ireland's encouragement of young dramatists and by a sense of his own deficiency in theatrical knowledge, Friel spent several months in 1963 at the Tyrone Guthrie Theatre in Minneapolis, Minnesota, an experience that undoubtedly helped him to win the Irish Arts Council McAuley Fellowship. In 1964, the Dublin Theatre Festival produced the play that was to establish Friel's critical reputation not only in Dublin but, within a few years, in New York and London as well.

Philadelphia, Here I Come! (1964) is a "memory play" in which Gar O'Donnell, age twenty-seven, lives through his last hours in Ireland before boarding a plane for Philadelphia. Friel expresses Gar's conflict, and that of several generations of young Irish emigrants, with extraordinary compassion and a somewhat unconventional device: Gar is split into his public and private selves, played by two actors, who interact with one another as the public Gar interacts with others. In Gar's relationships with his widowered father, his sweetheart, and his friends, he cannot articulate his feelings. The young man sees in his old schoolmaster an image of what he might become if he too continues in this provincial existence. Yet Gar's attachment to life in County Donegal is a

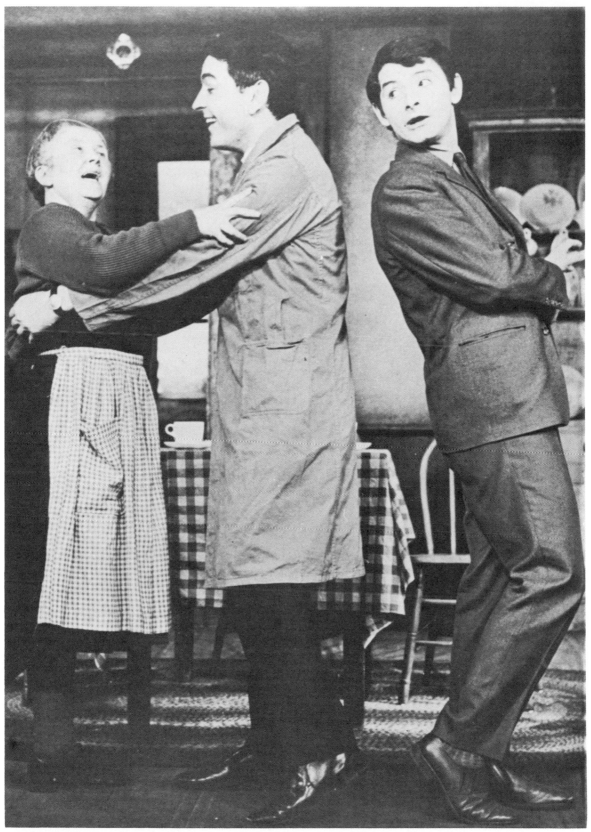

Mairin O'Sullivan, Patrick Bedford, and Donal Donelly in a scene from the 1966 first American production of
Philadelphia, Here I Come!

strong one, and as he comes to realize this, his initial excitement defers to a contemplative sadness and to the understanding that the American city to which he looks for redemption is "only another place to live."

Philadelphia, Here I Come! enjoyed 326 performances at the Helen Hayes Theatre, making it the longest running Irish play on Broadway. A *Time* reviewer called the play "honest, lyrical, unaffected and affecting," and Henry Hewes of the *Saturday Review* praised the play for its assessments of "two unsatisfactory civilizations: inhibited and materially impoverished Ireland and its opposite, America." The *New Yorker*'s reviewer wrote that "in the dimness of the current theatrical season, [*Philadelphia, Here I Come!*] burns at least part of the time with an almost gemlike flame."

The warm reception the American theater community gave Friel was exemplified by the production of his next play, *The Loves of Cass McGuire* (1966), which was staged in New York even before its production in Dublin. In that play, an eighty-nine-year-old woman returns to her native Ireland after a thirty-four-year stay in America, only to have her brother and his wife, who have accepted her financial support for years even though they did not need it, relegate Cass to a rest home. Surrounded by uncaring relatives, a patronizing maid, and senile companions, the disillusioned woman establishes a relationship with the audience as a last effort to sustain human contact. Unable to come to terms with her own bleak reality, she turns finally to the past, embellishing it until she creates the illusion of a remembered love. Friel calls the composition a concerto and Cass the soloist, counterpointing the old woman's memories with the magnificent love story of Tristan and Isolde.

Reviews of *The Loves of Cass McGuire* were mixed, with *Time* regretting that "the bitter beauty of human existence that irradiated . . . *Philadelphia, Here I Come!* last season nowhere shines in this play." Others felt the play too fragmented in its construction; critic John McCarten found the play "too loosely wrought to amount to much dramatically." The production's chief problem, however, may have been in its casting, for, as nearly every reviewer remarked, the inability of Ruth Gordon as Cass to master the Irish idiom robbed the play of its essential character. As Henry Hewes noted, "Miss Gordon seems as Irish as Levy's Rye Bread."

Despite this obvious error in casting, tender handling of characterization is evident in the text of *The Loves of Cass McGuire* and is recreated in *Lovers* (1967), two one-act plays united not by common characters or a continuing plot but by a shared sense of the loss occasioned by the passage from innocence into experience. In *Winners*, Meg, a young pregnant woman, and her friend Joe picnic on a hillside, studying for final exams and looking forward to their marriage. As two narrators dispassionately, almost clinically, tell of the circumstances that led to the couple's mysterious drowning, Meg and Joe reenact the conversations that occupied the final moments of their lives. The irony becomes pervasive as the audience learns that these two children on the brink of adulthood, who so innocently celebrate life, meet death instead, yet Friel calls them "winners."

In the companion piece, *Losers*, Andy and Hanna are a middle-aged couple whose passion is tempered by the constant presence of Hanna's puritanical mother, who summons her daughter with a bell whenever she suspects the couple is kissing. Andy attempts to outwit the old woman by reciting Thomas Gray's "Elegy Written in a Country Churchyard" while making love to his wife. The optimism that characterizes Meg and Joe's vision of their future is transformed here into the disillusionment of mature love, as Andy, who is also the play's narrator, succumbs to the will of the old woman.

In the season following the production of *Lovers*, *Crystal and Fox* (1968) premiered at Dublin's Gaiety Theatre. In this play, Fox Melarkey, an aging showman, heads a troupe of less than talented itinerant players. Wearied by third-rate performances and infatuated by a romanticized past, Fox intentionally mistreats his dwindling company. His desire to return to the happier and simpler time when he and his wife, Crystal, first met and he was at the top of his form proves to be a death wish, foreshadowed by his poisoning of the troupe's dancing dog. The play's poignant climax reveals the intensity of Fox's need to destroy his own vitality. The troupe disbanded, he tells his wife he was responsible for their son's arrest for the beating of an old woman, knowing this act of betrayal will alienate even Crystal. Friel's play gently yet inexorably digs beneath the surface of a man driven by a passion he does not understand.

The next year, the Olympia Theatre produced *The Mundy Scheme*, a satire on Irish politics in which the ailing Irish economy desperately needs revitalization. Unwilling to sacrifice Cork and Galway to an American nuclear submarine base, Prime Minister F. X. Ryan consents instead to Texas entrepreneur Homer Mundy's proposal to turn western Ireland into an international graveyard. As the world applauds the scheme, the heads of state pursue the enterprise with more than national interests at heart. Friel handles the spoof lightheartedly, successfully satirizing the plight of the emerging nation, the corruption of its officials, and the morbidity of its people, but he does not sufficiently develop his characters or dramatize their moral conflicts to make his only attempt at satire a successful play. The play's inadequacies were confirmed by its unhappy reception on Broadway six months later, where it closed after only four performances.

Friel began the second decade of his full-time writing career with a play that looks back to this political satire and also looks ahead to a more disturbing contemporary problem. Though not explicitly political, *The Gentle Island* (1971) exposes the fundamental nature of a family of Irish islanders, suggesting that their attraction to violence is both an individual tendency and a part of the Irish national character as well. Friel's setting is Inishkeen, an island off the coast of County Donegal, his focus its sole remaining inhabitants, the family of Manus Sweeney. Two homosexual travelers arrive, causing the undercurrents of the "gentle island" to erupt and turning the seemingly idyllic setting into a hell of brutality and revenge from which Joe, one of the two sons, manages to escape.

In *The Freedom of the City* (1973), an overtly political play with clear allusions to Northern Ireland's Bloody Sunday, three characters are less fortunate than Joe. The play follows the events of a February day in 1970 when British troops killed three Irish civil-rights demonstrators in Londonderry. It moves freely through time, intercutting scenes from the tribunal of inquiry, a priest's eulogy, and the events leading to the deaths of the demonstrators, and counterpointing the action with snippets from an American sociologist's unimpassioned lecture on poverty. Chance brings the three who are eventually killed—Michael, a pacifist; Skinner, an unemployed intellectual; and Lily, a mother of eleven—to the Derry Mayor's Parlor in search of safety from British tear gas, and official and public misinterpretation of their intent transforms them first into terrorists and then into dead heroes. More than a political play, however, the drama examines the psychology behind people's commitments, the ways in which perceptions distort truth, the accidental nature of life and death.

Like all of Friel's plays since *Philadelphia, Here I Come!*, with the exception of *The Gentle Island*, *The Freedom of the City* was produced in the United States, where Friel had by this time established a solid, if uneven, reputation. In recognition of Friel's

dramatic achievement, Bucknell University Press published D. E. S. Maxwell's critical study in 1973, and in 1974 Rosary College in Chicago awarded Friel an honorary degree.

Since the appearance of Maxwell's book, Friel has written five additional plays. The first of these, *Volunteers*, was produced in 1975 at Dublin's Abbey Theatre. The play is set at an archaeological site in the center of an Irish city, where a crew of seven is completing its excavations. Five of the workers are political prisoners who have volunteered for public service but must now return to their cells. All are intelligent, aware men whose crime was passionate commitment and whose running commentary reflects on the irony of their own fate, which, they learn, will be death at the hands of their fellow inmates. During their five months' work, the group has extracted a wealth of artifacts from the huge crater, including 593 pieces of a skeleton that they have reassembled and now symbolically bury.

In *Living Quarters* (1977), a character named Sir serves as "ultimate arbiter," director, and guardian of the ledger containing the Butler fam-

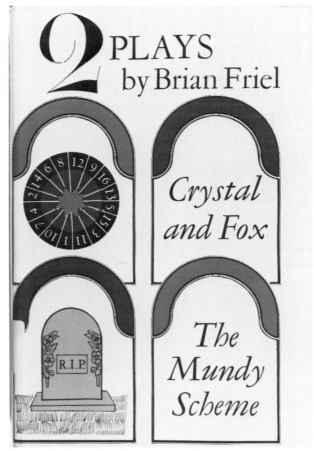

Dust jacket for the first American publication of two plays that express Friel's perception of the dilemma of Irish life

ily's story. The play is a reenactment of the last hours preceding Commandant Frank Butler's suicide. The Irish army officer returns home to his four children and a hero's welcome, only to discover his young wife and son Ben have shared an infidelity. Violating conventional dramatic expectations, Friel interrupts the play's action with Sir's introduction of characters and with individual characters' attempts to alter the truth by denying dramatic events. Despite their resistance, however, the family, like the Ancient Mariner, is doomed to retell—and reenact—its story.

Faith Healer (1979) presents a sequence of four monologues, spoken successively by Frank; his wife, Grace; their friend Teddy; and Frank again. Frank is a professional mountebank, a faith healer who claims an extraordinary capacity to restore others' health. Dramatic tension grows as both Grace and Teddy doubt the faith healer's story and power, until the final monologue reveals that Frank is indeed a miracle worker. Yet Frank, unable to bear the burden of his own mysterious gift, refuses to perform the cure that will save his life. Friel's identification of the faith healer with the artist extends the play's concern with the nature of the imagination into a concern with the nature of fiction as well. In Friel's other 1979 play, *Aristocrats*, Joe Brennan, a radio-television repairman, discovers that his neighbors, the Hogans, are living in squalor in a Catholic big house. But so that he can continue to endure his own difficult life, he refuses to believe the Hogans' misery.

Recently, Friel and actor Stephen Rea have formed the Field Day, a theater company dedicated to bringing professional theater to cities throughout the island. Friel's play, *Translations* (1980), the Field Day's first production, is set in Donegal in 1833, when the English succeeded in closing Gaelic hedge schools and opening English language schools, despite native resistance. The contemporary struggle in Northern Ireland resonates in Friel's sensitive treatment of the collision between the English and the Irish. As London *Times* critic Irving Wardle remarked, in *Translations* Friel "voices the tragedy of his country more eloquently than any play . . . since *The Plough and the Stars*."

The American reception of Friel's plays has not been uniformly enthusiastic. The *Time* critic reviewing *Lovers*, for example, complained that Friel's "lace-curtained Irish dramas could easily have been written three decades ago." Nonetheless, Friel's writing over the last two decades has been characterized by a willingness to experiment with different ways of dramatizing essential truths of the Irish character and of human nature and existence. If his plays are not consistently superior works of art, this may be explained on two grounds. First, Friel's sense of dramatic action falls considerably short of his ability to create character and deprives his plays of a feeling of inevitable movement. Second, Friel's sense of drama in general does not match his sense of narrative, and the intrusion of his fondness for storytelling upon his drama frequently creates the feeling that the writer is working in the wrong medium. Friel himself admits he is more comfortable writing short stories than plays, and his numerous stories (collected in *The Saucer of Larks*, 1962; *The Gold in the Sea*, 1966; *The Saucer of Larks: Stories of Ireland*, 1969; and *Selected Stories*, 1979) attest to his skill in that genre. Nonetheless, the essential strengths of Friel's writing—sensitivity of characterization, authenticity of language, and an overall perceptivity—would surface in any medium. These, coupled with his enduring commitment to dramatizing the Irish national character and dilemma, are responsible for Friel's deserved place among Ireland's most important contemporary playwrights.

Radio Scripts:
A Sort of Freedom, BBC, 1958;
To This Hard House, BBC, 1958;
The Founder Members, BBC, 1964.

Other:
"Plays Peasant and Unpeasant," *Times Literary Supplement*, 17 March 1972, pp. 305-306;
The Enemy Within, in *Journal of Irish Literature*, 4, no. 2 (1975): 3-64;
Peter Luke, ed., *Enter Certain Players: Edwards-MacLiammóir and the Gate, 1928-1978*, includes an essay by Friel (Dublin: Dolmen, 1978), pp. 21-22.

References:
James Coakley, "Chekov in Ireland: Brief Notes on Friel's *Philadelphia*," *Comparative Drama*, 7 (1973): 191-197;
Séamus Deane, "Brian Friel," *Ireland Today*, no. 978 (July-August 1981): 7-10;
Robert Hogan, *After the Irish Renaissance: A Critical History of the Irish Drama since "The Plough and the Stars"* (Minneapolis: University of Minnesota Press, 1967), pp. 195-197;

Reinhardt Küsgen, "Brian Friel: *Philadelphia, Here I Come!*," in *Das englische Drama der Gegenwart: Interpretationen*, edited by Horst Oppel (Berlin: Erich Schmidt, 1976), pp. 95-106;

Milton Levin, "Brian Friel: An Introduction," *Éire*, 7, no. 2 (1972): 132-136;

D. E. S. Maxwell, *Brian Friel* (Lewisburg, Pa.: Bucknell University Press, 1973);

Walter R. Rix, "Beispiele gegenwärtiger anglo-irischer Dramatik: Brian Friel und John B. Keane," *Literatur in Wissenschaft und Unterricht*, 11 (1978): 19-37.

Christopher Fry

(18 December 1907-   )

Audrey Williamson

PRODUCTIONS: *Psalm in C*, libretto by Fry and Michael Tippett, 1930;

Youth and the Peregrines, 1 May 1934, Tunbridge Wells Repertory Players at the Pump Room, Tunbridge Wells, Kent, 5 [performances];

She Shall Have Music, by Fry, F. Eyton, and M. Crick, 1935, London;

To Sea in a Sieve, as Christopher Harris, 1935, Reading;

Open Door, 1936, London;

The Boy With a Cart, 1938, Coleman's Hatch, Sussex; 16 January 1950, Lyric Theatre, Hammersmith, London;

Robert of Sicily: Opera for Children, libretto by Fry, music by Tippett, 1938;

Seven at a Stroke: A Play for Children, libretto by Fry, music by Tippett, 1939;

The Tower [pageant], 18 July 1939, Tewkesbury Festival, Tewkesbury;

Thursday's Child [pageant], music by Martin Shaw, 1939, London;

A Phoenix Too Frequent, 25 April 1946, Mercury Theatre, London; 20 November 1946, Arts Theatre, London;

The Lady's Not for Burning, 10 March 1948, Arts Theatre, London; 11 May 1949, Globe Theatre, London, 294; 8 November 1950, Royale Theatre, New York, 151;

Thor, With Angels, June 1948, Chapter House, Canterbury; 27 September 1951, Lyric Theatre, Hammersmith, London;

The Firstborn, 6 September 1948, Gateway Theatre, Edinburgh; 29 January 1952, Winter Garden Theatre, London, 46; 30 April 1958, Coronet Theatre, New York, 38;

Venus Observed, 18 January 1950, St. James's Theatre, London, 230; 13 February 1952, Century Theatre, New York, 86;

Ring Round the Moon, adapted from Jean Anouilh's *L'Invitation au château*, 26 January 1950, Globe Theatre, London, 682; 23 November 1950, Martin Beck Theatre, New York, 68;

A Winter's Tale, music by Fry, arranged by Leslie Bridgewater, 1951, London;

A Sleep of Prisoners, 23 April 1951, University Church, Oxford; 15 May 1951, St. Thomas's Church, Regent Street, London; 16 October 1951, St. James's Church, New York, 31;

The Dark Is Light Enough, 30 April 1954, Aldwych Theatre, London, 242; 23 February 1955, ANTA Theatre, New York, 69;

The Lark, adapted from Anouilh's play, 11 May 1955, Lyric Theatre, Hammersmith, London; 17 November 1955, Longacre Theatre, New York, 229;

Tiger at the Gates, adapted from Jean Giraudoux's play, 2 June 1955, Apollo Theatre, London; 3 October 1955, Plymouth Theatre, New York, 217;

Crown of the Year [cantata], libretto by Fry, music by Tippett, 1958;

Duel of Angels, adapted from Giraudoux's *Pour Lucrèce*, 22 April 1958, Apollo Theatre, London; 19 April 1960, Helen Hayes Theatre, New York, 51;

Curtmantle, 1 March 1961, Stadsschouwburg, Tilburg, Holland; produced in English, 4 September 1962, Edinburgh Festival, Edinburgh; 6 October 1962, Aldwych Theatre, London;

Judith, adapted from Giraudoux's play, 20 June 1962, Her Majesty's Theatre, London;

Peer Gynt, based on Johan Fillinger's translation of

Christopher Fry, 1947

Henrik Ibsen's play, 13 May 1970, Chichester Festival Theatre, Chichester;

A Yard of Sun, 11 July 1970, Nottingham Playhouse, Nottingham, 17; 10 August 1970, Old Vic Theatre, London, 8;

Cyrano de Bergerac, translated from Edmond Rostand's play, 14 May 1975, Chichester Festival Theatre, Chichester.

BOOKS: *The Boy With a Cart* (London: Oxford University Press, 1939; New York: Oxford University Press, 1951);

A Phoenix Too Frequent (London: Hollis & Carter, 1946; New York: Oxford University Press, 1949);

The Firstborn (Cambridge: Cambridge University Press, 1946; London & New York: Oxford University Press, 1950);

Thor, With Angels (Canterbury: H. J. Goulden, 1948; London: Oxford University Press, 1949);

The Lady's Not for Burning (London & New York: Oxford University Press, 1949; revised, 1973);

Venus Observed (London & New York: Oxford University Press, 1949);

Ring Round the Moon, adapted from Jean Anouilh's *L'Invitation au château* (London: Methuen, 1950; New York: Oxford University Press, 1950);

A Sleep of Prisoners (London & New York: Oxford University Press, 1951);

The Dark Is Light Enough (London & New York: Oxford University Press, 1954);

The Lark, adapted from Anouilh's play (London: Methuen, 1955; New York: Oxford University Press, 1956);

Tiger at the Gates, adapted from Jean Giraudoux's play (London: Methuen, 1955; New York: Oxford University Press, 1956);

Duel of Angels, adapted from Giraudoux's *Pour Lucrèce* (London: Methuen, 1958; New York: Oxford University Press, 1959);

Curtmantle (London & New York: Oxford University Press, 1961);

Judith, adapted from Giraudoux's play (London: Methuen, 1962);

The Boat that Mooed (New York: Macmillan, 1966);

A Yard of Sun (London & New York: Oxford University Press, 1970);

Peer Gynt, based on Johan Fillinger's translation of Henrik Ibsen's play (London & New York: Oxford University Press, 1970);

Cyrano de Bergerac, adapted from Edmond Rostand's play (London & New York: Oxford University Press, 1975);

Memoirs: Can You Find Me: A Family History (London: Oxford University Press, 1978);

Death Is a Kind of Love, with drawings by Charles E. Wadsworth (Cranberry Isles, Maine: Tidal Press, 1979).

Born in Bristol, Christopher Fry is the son of Charles John Harris, an architect who later became a church lay reader, and Emma Marguerite Fry Hammond Harris. Fry attended Bedford Modern School in Bedford from 1918 to 1926. He became a schoolmaster, teaching at Bedford Froebel Kindergarten in 1926-1927 and Hazelwood School in Limpsfield, Surrey, from 1928 to 1931. From 1932 to 1935 he served as a founding director of the Tunbridge Wells Repertory Players, where a play he had written as a schoolboy, *The Peregrines*, was produced in a revised form, as curtain raiser to the English premiere of Bernard Shaw's "comediettina for two voices in three conversations," *Village Wooing*. He also wrote the music for a musical comedy, *She Shall Have Music* (1935), and a play on the life of British social reformer Dr. Thomas John Barnardo, which was performed in aid of Dr. Barnardo's Homes for Children.

These works he considers outside his serious professional career, which began in 1938 with *The Boy With a Cart*, a slight but charming play about the young Saint Cuthman. It was written in verse, as all his later plays would be, and already showed characteristic qualities of humor in both word and characterization as well as a religious theme. It was staged in Sussex but was not professionally performed until 1950, when it achieved a London production notable for the emergence of the young actor Richard Burton, who, in his first leading part, played Cuthman.

By 1938 Fry's creative impulse had remarkably flowered, and the next twelve years were to see a glittering succession of plays and a poetic revival in the theater in which he and T. S. Eliot shared. Fry's rise in the theater had begun in 1946 with *A Phoenix Too Frequent*, a comedy based upon Petronius's tale of the Ephesian widow—the false heroics of Dynamene's mourning of her husband in his tomb, and her reawakening to the joy of life by a handsome officer who enters the tomb to rest on a course

of duty. The play showed Fry's characteristic turn of wit and also that vein of lyricism, based on the clamoring calls of nature and of love, found in most of his later work. It also had the distinction of giving his first London part to Paul Scofield, a young actor destined to become the most distinguished classical actor on the English stage after the older John Gielgud and Laurence Olivier, both of whom played outstanding parts in later plays by Fry: *The Lady's Not for Burning* and *Venus Observed*, respectively.

"Death is a kind of love," the young officer's cry in *A Phoenix Too Frequent*, crystallizes a facet of Fry's imagination in which life and death are both part of the radiant and mysterious fabric of living and in which human love is a sustaining thread. This facet recurs in *The Lady's Not for Burning*, which was first staged in 1948 at the Arts Theatre in London and produced in 1949 in the West End for a run of 294 performances, and which made the author, for the first time, a major and recognized figure in British drama. It is the story of a young soldier of fortune disillusioned with life and seeking death and of a young woman equally passionately trying to keep the one and evade the other. She is a medieval alchemist's daughter on the verge of arrest for witchcraft, beating symbolic wings against superstition and eventually drawing the man into love and life, almost against his will. Yet it is a cunning element of Fry's design that one comes to realize how much of the soldier's attitude had been deliberately assumed in an effort to distract attention and save the girl. He is a misanthrope caught up in magic, like John Tanner magnetized by the Shavian Life Force.

Fry's wit scintillates in his verse. The first of a quartet of plays on the seasons, *The Lady's Not for Burning* is a lyric of spring: it has an April shimmer, like the dust of pollination shot by sunlight. There is a kind of golden haze about it that is penetrated by the occasional bawdiness of the humor: for Fry has combined the robustness of the Elizabethans with touches of the cheerful blasphemy that mingled with piety in the medieval morality play. But the sense of the abundance, mystery, and poetry of life is unimpaired.

In *The Lady's Not for Burning* Fry demonstrates he has a sharp eye for characterization, not only of his leading but also of his minor figures. The lute-playing Chaplain, mildly expostulating that legal matters "Are Greek to me, except, of course / That I understand Greek," is neatly placed beside the fussy Mayor, harried by draughts and unexpectedly knotting red tape, and the sarcastic, obese Judge.

Of his following plays, *The Firstborn* (1948),

Venus Observed (1950), and *The Dark Is Light Enough* (1954) most clearly show Fry's stature and maturity, although *Thor, With Angels* (1948), set on a Jutish farm, and *A Sleep of Prisoners* (1951), in which wartime captive soldiers sleep and dream in a church (the play was performed in churches), had some originality. *The Firstborn*, produced the same year as *The Lady's Not for Burning*, was a darker play: a play of Egypt in the throes of a threatening conflict between master and slave, with Moses throwing off his privileges as an Egyptian-reared soldier and finding a new range and responsibility as a leader of his people. The domestic issues—the mutual attachment of Pharoah's young son and Moses; the wavering Miriam; her son, Shendi, who becomes, in office, more Egyptian than the Egyptians—are dramatically woven into a political tapestry with echoes of Nazi domination, and the plagues seem a harrowing succession of natural disasters until

Moses lets loose the forces of destruction on Egypt's firstborn sons, and too late faces the death of the boy Rameses in the holocaust. It is a more dramatic play than most of Fry's, tragic in its implications and in Moses' final dilemma. The part of Moses indeed is almost Shakespearean in scale.

With *Venus Observed* Fry returned to a lighter theme. It is a play of autumn, the second of the quartet on the seasons. Here Fry materializes his vision of solar space, his sense of the mysterious universe, in the character of the amorous Duke with a penchant for watching the stars in his observatory. The play begins with an eclipse of the sun and is heavy with the mists and mellow fruitfulness of autumn: the middle-aged Duke preparing for his approaching winter by searching for a wife (to be chosen impartially by his son from the Duke's three earlier mistresses) is the human representation of the allegory. It is not necessary to pursue the young

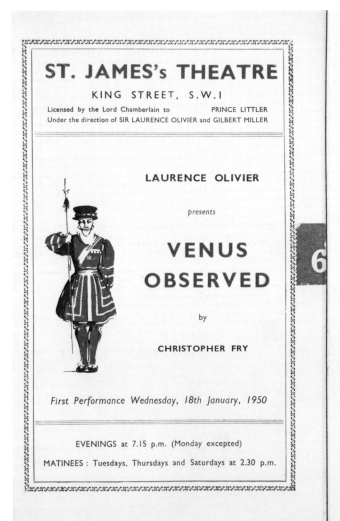
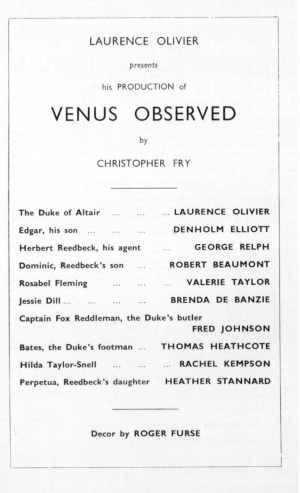

Program cover and cast list for the first London production of the autumn play in Fry's quartet of the seasons

heroine Perpetua's symbolism of Venus (Perpetua, the perpetual) too closely because the play is, on the surface, a sophisticated amorous comedy, though its wit and quality of mind penetrate well below that surface. Fry's verbal dexterity is as great as ever, including a sentence (given to Perpetua) of heroic length and ingenious construction; but only in the last act, and in particular in the final tableau of the Duke and his half-sleeping agent alone in the October night, does it deeply strike at the heart. Here wisdom becomes merged with the wonder of nature, subduing the Duke's pain in a new heart's ease.

It is a play, partly, about loneliness, but the aging Duke's disappointment in losing the young Perpetua to his son does not cut deep: he does, in fact, look forward to solace with Rosabel, the former love whose passionate resentment of his lack of humanity has caused her to set fire to his house and observatory, destroying both. The irony is that in fact the Duke's human consideration for others has led him to overlook for years the systematic cheating of his agent, Reedbeck, and to employ an ex-burglar on his staff. Reedbeck himself, dreaming of the philanthropies possible through wealth, however illegally acquired, is an amiable character, and the old laggards in the Duke's employment and the ladies themselves are lovingly as well as sharply delineated. It is a play about human beings with an autumnal shading: "The landscape's all in tune, in a falling cadence, / All decaying. . . ." In spite of this quality, there is a well-sustained tension, as Rosabel is driven toward her destructive fire, and the Duke and Perpetua are drawn together in the potential trap of the observatory.

"A sad tale's best for Winter"; yet, although Fry's play of winter, *The Dark Is Light Enough*, ends in a death, it is brightened by an introductory quotation from Jean Henri Fabre, the French naturalist, on a butterfly undeterred by storm and the night: "So well it directs its tortuous flight that, in spite of all the obstacles to be evaded, it arrives in a state of perfect freshness, its great wings intact. . . . The darkness is light enough. . . ."

Fry sets his play in a countess's mansion near the Hungarian border in the "year of revolutions," 1848. The indomitable countess, Rosmarin, has taken a lonely sleigh ride to rescue a revolutionary ne'er-do-well, once her son-in-law, from the Hungarians he has deserted and who plan to execute him. His fierce, dark, rebellious spirit and fear of death are placed beside a quiet portrait of the liberal new son-in-law who, though a Hungarian patriot, has taken the more conciliatory role of diplomat and representative in the Austrian capital.

But this work is not primarily a political play, nor is Fry primarily a political writer. His theme once again concentrates on human characters in conflict and, above all, on the infinite variety of the countess herself, a woman of wit, courage, and distinction who feels, as she puts it, a "disenchantment of the body." The viewer senses a summer radiance on which winter has set its feathered touch, light and cold as the snowflakes descending outside the window. Yet her spirit bounds on, unconquered in upheaval, while the Hungarians invade her house. The deserter, Richard Gettner, is to her, if to few others, someone with a half-hidden quality she can discern and admire. She is a woman of principle who loves life; he is a man without principles who dislikes it yet fears to lose it. She will not give him up to the Hungarians, and, after sustaining her battle against man's inhumanity to man, only relinquishes her fragile hold on life when he has escaped. Yet her spirit has entered him. He returns and, conquered by her will in death, finds the courage to stay and face his pursuers.

Fry adapts his verse to his theme, conveying wisdom and a new verbal austerity. It makes for a play of dramatic tension and fascination, and if Gettner, the rootless intellectual, is not, one feels, quite fully explored, the countess's spirit permeates the play and gives it a wintry radiance.

It was eight years before Fry produced another play of this scale. *Curtmantle* (produced in English in 1962) is one of several plays by notable dramatists this century to concentrate on Henry II of England and his conflict with Thomas à Becket. Here Henry is a vigorous figure, rightly a lawgiver to whom England owes much; but the dramatic conflict is in the king's relationship with his obstreperous and warring sons, and the clash with Becket (except for its repercussions) only concerns the first half of the play. Perhaps, in the end, the play takes too wide a canvas, trying to encompass a reign of enormous length and variety in states of peace and war. The analogy is with the Shakespearean chronicle play; but although T. S. Eliot admired its "real thought and real care for the English language," *Curtmantle* is not quite on the imaginative level of the previous major plays.

Extraordinarily active and diverse in his writing activities, Fry wrote several major film scripts, as well as some very successful English adaptations of foreign plays, in particular, works by Jean Anouilh and Jean Giraudoux. He has also composed music and has written television and radio plays (specifically for the BBC's Children's Hour Series in 1939-1940) as well as pageants. There was, however,

Peter Hall, Stuart Burge, Farrah, and Fry at rehearsal of Curtmantle, *1962*

another eight-year gap between *Curtmantle* and *A Yard of Sun* (1970), an absorbing play with volatile Italian characters, set just after World War II at the time of the famous annual horse race, known as the Palio, in the streets of Siena. Again, there is little of Fry's earlier iridescence, but rather a concentrated glow of language, pared to a new, more austere structure. The Italianate characterization is vivid and varied, and the story line taut and gripping. *A Yard of Sun* was the play of summer, long promised, to complete the quartet of spring (*The Lady's Not for Burning*), autumn (*Venus Observed*), and winter (*The Dark Is Light Enough*). It is Fry's latest original full-length play.

Fry and his wife, Phyllis Marjorie Hart Fry,

live near Chichester, Sussex, where there is an annual theater festival at which a number of his plays have been produced, including, in 1970, his lively and sensitive adaptation of Henrik Ibsen's *Peer Gynt*, and in 1975 his adaptation of Edmond Rostand's *Cyrano de Bergerac*.

Fry's philosophy can be summed up in his comment made on BBC Radio's Third Programme in 1950: "A playwright's view of the contemporary theatre is one with his view of the contemporary world, and his view of the contemporary world is one with his view of all time. He is exploring for the truth of the human creature, his truth in comedy or his truth in tragedy, because over and above the drama of his actions and conflicts and everyday

Frank Middlemass, Cherith Mellor, John Shrapnel, and Eilhue Dunne in the 1970 London production of A Yard of Sun

predicaments is the fundamental drama of his ever existing at all." Fry went on to say, "The inescapable dramatic situation for us all is that we have no idea what our situation is. . . . We are plunged into an existence fantastic to the point of nightmare, and however hard we rationalise, or however firm our religious faith, however closely we dog the heels of science or wheel among the stars of mysticism, we cannot really make head or tail of it."

In Fry's hands the English theater turned, for an elegantly creative period, away from prosaic reality and explored both the poetry and the mystery of life.

Screenplays:

The Beggar's Opera, adapted by Fry and Denis Cannan from John Gay's play, British Lion, 1953;

The Queen Is Crowned, documentary by Fry, Universal, 1953;

Barabbas, adapted from Pär Lagerkvist's novel, Columbia, 1962;

The Bible: In the Beginning, by Fry, Jonathan Griffin, Ivo Perilli, and Vittorio Bonicelli, Twentieth Century-Fox, 1966.

Television Scripts:

The Canary, BBC, 1950;

The Tenant of Wildfell Hall, BBC, 1968;
The Brontës of Haworth, BBC, 1973;
The Best of Enemies, BBC, 1976;
Sister Dora, BBC, 1977;
Star Over Bethlehem, BBC, 1981.

Other:
An Experience of Critics, in *The Experience of Critics and The Approach to Dramatic Criticism*, edited by Kaye Webb (London: Perpetua Press, 1952);
Colette, *The Boy and the Magic*, translated by Fry (London: Dobson, 1964).

Periodical Publications:
"How Lost, How Amazed, How Miraculous We Are," *Theatre Arts* (August 1952);
"Why I Write in Verse," *Plays and Players*, 1 (December 1954).

References:
Alec Clunes, "Christopher Fry," *Drama* (Summer 1949);
Harold Hobson, "Christopher Fry's Other World," *Drama* (Spring 1979);
Hobson, *Theatre* (London: Longmans, Green, 1948), p. 29;
Hobson, *The Theatre Now* (London: Longmans, Green, 1953), pp. 5ff;
Hobson, *Theatre 2* (London: Longmans, Green, 1950), pp. 31ff;
Hobson, *Verdict at Midnight* (London: Longmans, Green, 1952), pp. 181-183;
Emil Roy, *Christopher Fry* (Carbondale: Southern Illinois University Press, 1969);
Heiner M. Schnelling, *Christopher Fry's Seasonal Comedies* (Frankfurt: Verlag Peter Lang, 1981);
Derek Stanford, ed., *Christopher Fry Album* (London: Peter Nevill, 1952);
Stanford, *Christopher Fry: An Appreciation* (London: Peter Nevill, 1951);
J. C. Trewin, *The Theatre Since 1900* (London: Andrew Dakers, 1951), pp. viii, 276, 290-295;
Kenneth Tynan, *Curtains* (London: Longmans, Green, 1961), pp. 68-70, 72-73, 96-98;
John Whiting, Review of *Curtmantle*, in *John Whiting on Theatre* (London: Alan Ross/London Magazine Editions, 1966), pp. 52-56;
Audrey Williamson and Charles Landstone, *The Bristol Old Vic: The First Ten Years* (London: J. Garnet Miller, 1957), pp. 87-88, 102, 112;
Williamson, *Contemporary Theatre, 1953-1956* (London: Rockliff, 1956);
Williamson, *Theatre of Two Decades* (London: Rockliff, 1951).

Pam Gems
(1 August 1925-)

Rodelle Weintraub
State College, Pennsylvania

PRODUCTIONS: *Betty's Wonderful Christmas*, December 1972, Cockpit Theatre, London, 18 [performances];
My Warren, May 1973, Almost Free Theatre, London, 18;
After Birthday, May 1973, Almost Free Theatre, London, 18;
The Amiable Courtship of Miz Venus and Wild Bill, September 1973, Almost Free Theatre, London, 18;
Go West, Young Woman, May 1974, Round House Theatre, London, 6;
Up in Sweden, November 1975, Haymarket Theatre, Leicester, 11;
The Rivers and Forests, translated from Marguerite Duras's play, March 1976, Soho Poly Theatre, London, 12;
My Name is Rosa Luxemburg, translated from Marianne Auricoste's play, March 1976, Soho Poly Theatre, London, 12;
The Project, May 1976, Soho Poly Theatre, London, 12;
Dead Fish, August 1976, Edinburgh Festival, Edinburgh, 18; expanded as *Dusa, Fish, Stas and Vi*, 6 December 1976, Hampstead Theatre Club (transferred February 1977 to Mayfair Theatre), London;
Guinevere, August 1976, Edinburgh Festival, Edin-

burgh, 18; September 1976, Soho Poly Theatre, London, 12;

Queen Christina, 9 September 1977, Other Place, London, 27;

Franz into April, November 1977, Institute of Contemporary Arts, London, 12;

Piaf, 11 October 1978, Other Place (transferred to Warehouse Theatre; to Aldwych Theatre; to Wyndham's Theatre; to Piccadilly Theatre), London, 119; 5 February 1981, Plymouth Theatre, New York;

Sandra, April 1979, King's Head Theatre, London, 12;

Ladybird, Ladybird, April 1979, King's Head Theatre, London, 12;

Uncle Vanya, adapted from Anton Chekhov's play, November 1979, Hampstead Theatre Club, London, 42; 18 May 1982, National Theatre, London;

A Doll's House, adapted from Henrik Ibsen's play, January 1980, Tyne-Wear Theatre, Newcastle;

The Treat, 10 February 1982, Institute of Contemporary Arts, London, 12;

Aunt Mary, 3 June 1982, Warehouse Theatre, London.

Pam Gems

BOOKS: *Piaf* (London: Amber Lane Press, 1979);

Anton Chekov: Uncle Vanya, A New Version (London: Eyre Methuen, 1979);

Dusa, Fish, Stas and Vi (New York: Dramatists Play Service, 1977; London: French, 1978).

Pam Gems, perhaps the most prolific contemporary English-language woman playwright, was virtually unrecognized by London critics before her 1976 West End success, *Dusa, Fish, Stas, and Vi.* Described two years later by John Barber as a rarity who celebrates womanhood better than anyone else, and selected by John Walker as one of the British theater's top playwrights, Gems did not seriously turn to playwriting until after her fortieth birthday. She had earlier written three television scripts. Born in New Forest, Dorset, Gems had her first play produced when she was seven and classmates in Miss Collin's class in the New Forest school performed in it. The confluence of personal tragedy, her move to London, and her immersion in the feminist movement returned Gems to serious efforts at playwriting.

The daughter of working-class parents, Pam Price Gems was brought up in a female household. Both of her grandmothers had been widowed in World War I, and her own mother, Elsie Mabel Price, was widowed when her twenty-six-year-old husband, Jim Price, died in the workhouse. Left with Pam, who was only four at the time of her father's death, and her two younger brothers, Derrick Brian and Michael Cedric Dewys, Mrs. Price reared her children alone. Gems became even more acutely aware of women's need for men and the variety of sexual experience women alone enjoy and suffer when, during World War II, she lived on the south coast of England: it was "all sex and high adrenalin. We knew . . . these men we were with were probably going to get killed. The adrenalin made them more, not less sexual. . . . Some of the women in my hometown had the time of their lives—nothing has been so good since." Although Gems had won a scholarship to grammar school, her education was interrupted by the war. She joined the Women's Royal Naval Service (WRENS) and served in the armed forces through the war. After her military service, she attended Manchester University (1946-1949) as an ex-service student. There she read psychology because, she claims, the line for registering for a place in psychology was shorter than the line for those wishing to learn to teach English. She earned her psychology degree in 1949 but has never held a position as a psychologist. Her formal education, however, along with her acute observations of women alone were, two decades later, to come together in the plays she writes.

In September 1949, shortly after her graduation from Manchester University, she married Keith Gems. The young model manufacturer, formerly an architect, and his bride settled down to an idyllic 1950s marriage. Keith Gems's work took them to Paris during the 1950s and then to the Isle of Wight, where they remained until moving to London in 1979. She held odd jobs and threw herself into motherhood. (Jonathan, born in 1952, has followed his mother into playwriting. In 1979 his play *The Tax Exile* earned him the George Devine Award for Most Promising Playwright. Daughter Sara, born in 1954, is working in genetics and son David, born in 1960, is studying biology.) After the births of her first two children, Gems returned to London to work for the BBC, for which she had worked briefly before her marriage. While working for Audience Research, she lived in a "house which turned out to be a brothel" and wrote three plays for television. Although all were accepted, only *A Builder by Trade* (1961) was aired by Associated Television. In 1965 the dream shattered when the Gemses' youngest daughter, Lala, was born. Lala was severely afflicted with Down's syndrome. The need to provide Lala with greater opportunities for education motivated the Gems family to leave the Isle of Wight for London.

The strain and isolation of rearing a severely mentally handicapped child propelled Gems back to playwriting, and the time and freedom afforded when Lala attended nursery school permitted Gems to become involved in London's lunchtime theater and the feminist movement. Through the movement she increased her awareness of the many levels of women's experience with men and the range of their responses, from hostility through lesbianism. She became even more sensitive to the needs of the women who most concern her and about whom her most powerful plays are written: women who have been damaged by men and men's society. When commissioned by Almost Free, a London feminist group, to do what they described as "some sexy pieces," Gems wrote *My Warren* (1973) and *After Birthday* (1973). Whatever Almost Free may have intended by "sexy," they got two plays which examine the desperate circumstances in which some women find themselves. *My Warren* is about a girl who kills her baby, disposing of it in the toilet. *After Birthday* is about an older woman who lives alone in a one-room apartment and who, as a mean joke, is sent a vibrator. To Gems, "these two women were tough survivors."

Although involved in and helped by the feminist movement, Gems rejects some of the movement's hostility toward men. She feels that women, despite the damage they suffer and their sexual oppression, need men, and children need two parents. While recognizing the need for feminist theater, she insists that "an all-women theatre wouldn't work. It would be chauvinistic and boring." Nevertheless, her first play to reach the West End, *Dusa, Fish, Stas and Vi*, grew out of the feminist theater and has an all-female cast.

Written for the Women's Company, *Dusa, Fish, Stas and Vi*, originally entitled *Dead Fish*, had been intended for five characters rather than four. Economics forced the reduction to four and, as a result, the many parallels to Harold Pinter's *No Man's Land* (1975) are reinforced. Both plays deal with sexual oppression: Pinter's about men who sexually oppress each other; Gems's about women oppressed by men. Both works have four characters; both take place in one claustrophobic set. Both might well be titled *No Man's Land*. *Dead Fish* (a shorter version of the later play) had eighteen performances at the Edinburgh Festival before moving as *Dusa, Fish, Stas and Vi* to London in December 1976, first appearing at the Hampstead Theatre Club for forty-two performances and then moving in February 1977 to the Mayfair Theatre, where it ran for eight months. Critical acceptance of Gems's first commercial success was overwhelming. The *Sunday Times* critic said it "pulsates with humanity. The writing has both warmth and uncompromising toughness; a humour which can be both zany and lethal; and a sense of character which captures the nuances of self-deception, exhilaration or misery." According to the Manchester *Guardian* reviewer, "the cumulative fury and force of the play and the wit discovered on the journey there make this a joyful occasion." The *Evening Standard* critic said Gems "viewed with an ironic sense of detachment the inconsistencies and uncertainties of women trying to find their own road to self-fulfillment." Another reviewer expressed surprise and pleasure that Gems could put on the stage four women who could be funny, supportive of each other, and not bitchy. In Pinter's *No Man's Land*, the four male characters are not in the least supportive of each other and are excessively bitchy.

Gems wrote this play, she said, because she "wanted to write about . . . women in their twenties who would almost certainly be mothers but for the pill. . . . I wanted to show some women as they are now, against mechanised, urban backgrounds, isolated in eyries, breeding sometimes, more often divorced from their mothers, reacting against modern commercial brutality by becoming anorexic—a female disease which is a rejection of sexuality. Women who are the pathfinders of the new breed, trying to live the revolution with their fellers, and so often getting knocked back in what is still so inexorably a man's world."

The catalyst which brings the four women together, and which holds them together, is their mistreatment by men, and the plot is moved forward by the women's attempts to recover Dusa's children, who have been kidnapped by her former husband. Fish appears, at first, to be the strongest of the four, a young woman described by the author as having "all the natural authority and self-confidence of the upper-middle classes." Active in revolutionary politics, she seems to be the source of stability in a volatile situation. Apparently able to solve the others' problems, to coordinate their activities, and to make the contacts and employ the public relations necessary to create an atmosphere in which the children can be regained, she lacks any power to control her own life. As the other characters grow stronger, she becomes utterly consumed by her former lover's rejection and increasingly schizophrenic. Dusa, the overprotected child-wife,

mother of two, has been sheltered and protected by her husband until he unexpectedly divorces her and, not gaining custody of their children, kidnaps them. Stas spends her days as a physiotherapist in a London hospital, working with brain-damaged children and mentally disturbed adults. She spends her nights as a highly paid prostitute, and spends her energies dreaming about, and saves her money for, a future as a marine biologist. Vi, the youngest and apparently most helpless of the four, in the first act is an anorexic, 1970s dropout from society, experimenting with drugs, vegetarianism, and yoga and reacting with acute depression to the abortion she claims to have had. Typical of "the vast numbers of working class adolescents who are bright, restless or maladjusted," she, in the second act, with the help of antidepression drugs and amphetamines, becomes as manic as she was depressed in the first act. All victims, the women support each other, fight each other, and work toward what seems to be their common goal, the reuniting of Dusa and her children. The play's happy ending, the return of the children, is shattered by the suicide of Fish, who has become more deranged and weak as Vi has moved toward sanity and strength.

Having gained the critics' attention in 1976,

Sheila Allen in the first production of Queen Christina

Gems has had one or more plays noted by critics every season through 1982. Following the success of *Dusa, Fish, Stas and Vi*, the Royal Shakespeare Company presented *Queen Christina* (1977), Gems's play about the Queen of Sweden who, forced to play a man's role in a woman's body, fails as man and woman. Before the Royal Shakespeare Company accepted *Queen Christina*, the Royal Court Theatre had rejected it because it "was too sprawly, too expensive to do and any way it would appeal more to women," exactly the attitude in society against which Gems's pen was wielded. When the play opened at the RSC's the Other Place in September 1977, John Peter of the *Sunday Times* described Gems's Christina as "a sensitive misfit in a stultifying society which . . . brought her up as a man. . . ." He viewed Christina as "a sensual and emotional woman" who "is trapped in a sexual no man's land. . . . She is burdened with inquisitive intelligence . . . [and] in the jungle of a male world she's finally constrained by her feminine conscience." Although the play has thirty-two characters, only the role of Christina is fully developed. Peter, who described *Dusa, Fish, Stas and Vi* as excellent, would have preferred that Gems had "stuck to what really interested her, which is this woman's heart and mind, instead of writing a diffuse history play." Still he finds Gems's play about Christina better than August Strindberg's "because the Swede was, as usual, being both vindictive and soppy about women, whereas she writes with humour, compassion and intelligence." *Queen Christina* also played at Stratford-on-Avon in 1979 and was revived for the 1982 season by the Tricycle Theatre. Also produced during the 1977-1978 season, *Franz into April*, a "powerfully comic" one-act play about Franz, director of a mental-health farm, and April, a repressed Englishwoman, played at London's Institute of Contemporary Arts. The play is dedicated to Fritz Perls, the founder of gestalt theory of psychotherapy.

The next season the Royal Shakespeare Company produced what has been, so far, Gems's biggest hit, *Piaf*. After its premiere in October 1978 at the Other Place, the play transferred to the Warehouse Theatre, the Aldwych Theatre, Wyndham's Theatre, and the Piccadilly Theatre. Despite being moved from theater to theater, *Piaf* played to sold-out houses throughout its run. Gems's first play to cross the Atlantic, it opened on Broadway in February 1981. Based on the life of Edith Piaf, the popular French singer who rose from her slum background and life as a prostitute to success as a cabaret star but who never allowed her success and her wealth to make her "respectable," *Piaf* telescopes the life of the Little Sparrow into an intense narrative. When Gems described *Piaf* as "a bit rude," Pauline Peters, in the *Sunday Times*, corrected, "it's not 'a bit rude'—it's filthy. It's also funny and desperate, being the blunt bits of Edith Piaf's life from prostitution to cantankerous stardom and morphine addiction. At the end, respectable elderly ladies stand and applaud . . . proving that Pam Gems has the rare talent to push the boundaries of acceptability." Reviewers in the United States were not so sure *Piaf* would be as well received by respectable, elderly ladies and warned that the play was not one to which to take one's elderly aunt from Kansas City. Still it played to sold-out houses in Philadelphia before opening in New York, where it was not as well received. The producers tried to make the play more acceptable by removing some of its vulgar language but still, because of dwindling audiences, had to schedule the end of its limited run for early May. On the evening before the last scheduled performance, Jane Lapotaire was awarded a Tony for her performance as the Little Sparrow. The run was extended, and CBS arranged to film the play for presentation on cable television. Lapotaire commented, "It was like knowing you were to be executed and then to be reprieved just at the last moment. The trouble was that the Americans couldn't cope with the vulgarity of the language—then suddenly we got the good housekeeping seal of approval." It was not just the vulgarity of language, however, with which some American audiences and American critics could not cope. Some did not like the play's form. Barbara Garson in a review more about Piaf's life than the play, described *Piaf* as "a pastiche of scenes from Piaf's adult life . . . nothing is discernible onstage but bright splotches and meaningless lines." Garson wanted more than the drama of Piaf's life or a presentation on stage of another woman survivor. She felt that Piaf's "life was a mess but her art was magnificent" and that the play should have concentrated on the art instead of the life.

Piaf is actually Gems's first full-length play, having been written in 1973, before the writing of *Dusa, Fish, Stas and Vi*. Like both *Dusa, Fish, Stas and Vi* and *Queen Christina*, *Piaf* depicts a woman's struggle, according to Irving Wardle, to "achieve full humanity against the obstacles of her sex and birth." Piaf had to struggle against brutalizing poverty, the four women in *Dusa, Fish, Stas and Vi* against the variety of problems imposed by middle-class life, and Queen Christina against the burdens of sovereignty. All have had to struggle against the

Jane Lapotaire in the London production of Piaf

special burdens imposed by womanhood. In Piaf, as earlier in Stas, Gems portrays the businesslike young prostitute, whom she had numerous opportunities to observe during her stay in Soho in the late 1950s. Irving Wardle recognizes in *Piaf* a feminist documentary which Gems has written "for the theatre precisely to avoid arid feminist polemics." John Barber credits her for being "that rarity, an unboring feminist" who "writes like an angel if and when her dramaturgy is maladroit. She also creates gorgeous acting roles.... In *Piaf* one hears the unique voice of Pam Gems, with her pity and awe for female talent embattled in a man's world."

During the run of *Piaf*, Gems's Chekhov adaptation, *Uncle Vanya* (1979), the first of her adaptations of the plays by founders of modern drama, was produced. It was followed, in January 1980, by her adaptation of Henrik Ibsen's *A Doll's House*. Also during that season, her second television play, *We Never Do What They Want* (1979), was aired on Thames Television.

The Treat (1982), a play about how men view and abuse women sexually, played at the Institute of Contemporary Arts for a ten-day lunchtime theater

run. *The Treat* takes place in a French brothel. In a day's work the prostitutes experience more and more savage treatment from their customers while fulfilling the men's many fantasies. Reviewer Ann McFerran describes the play as a "compelling, graphic morality tale which smartly takes the lid off the glamour of commercial sex." Ned Chaillet, in the *Times*, describes the production as one which "captures the grotesque atmosphere of an exercise by a feminist Marquis de Sade.... The cruelty of the imagery is regularly leavened by jokes, and a strained communication between the women allows them to develop as characters." Both he and Charles Spencer, of the *Evening Standard*, expressed concern that the play's portrait of victimized women was likely to appeal to exactly the kind of men Gems so ruthlessly caricatured.

Aunt Mary (1982), which premiered at the Warehouse Theatre, is unusual for Gems in that it is not about a woman. Aunt Mary is a man who has an exotic imagination and lives out his fantasies. The play is described as a comedy of ambition, sex, and marriage. Also on the boards for the 1982 summer season in London were revivals of Gems's *Uncle*

Vanya, *Queen Christina*, and *Sandra* (1979). Works in progress include an expansion of *Guinevere* (1976) into a full-length play and an expansion of *Franz into April*, which is "very rude indeed," into a full-length play.

In just one decade, Gems has produced a considerable canon which examines the human condition, especially the plight of women in western society. For a theater which has traditionally had few roles for women and even fewer roles for realistic women rather than stereotypes derived from male fears and fantasies, Gems has produced a great many nonstereotypic roles which are also, to repeat John Barber, "gorgeous acting roles." She has forcefully examined the roles western society has imposed not only upon actresses but upon all women and, in the tradition of Bernard Shaw, has done so with humor, understanding, extraordinary insight, and her own razor-sharp scalpel.

Television Scripts:
A Builder by Trade, Associated Television, 1961;
We Never Do What They Want, Thames Television, 1979.

Interviews:
"Goings On: Late Edition," *Sunday Times*, 23 January 1977, p. 37;
Pauline Peters, "Pam Gems, Piaf and domesticity," *Sunday Times*, 3 February 1980, p. 36.

References:
John Barber, "Arresting tribute to an heroic urchin," *Daily Telegraph*, 15 June 1979, p. 15;
Ned Chaillet, *"Dusa, Fish, Stas and Vi,"* *Times*, 10 December 1976, p. 11;
Chaillet, "The Treat," *Times*, 16 February 1982;
James Fenton, "RSC: A company of all the talents," *Sunday Times*, 20 January 1980, p. 39;
Barbara Garson, "Piaf—Her Own Best Impersonator," *MS*, 9 (May 1981): 72-74;
Catherine Itzin, *Stages in the Revolution: Political Theatre in Britain Since 1968* (London: Eyre Methuen, 1980), pp. 209-291;
Bernard Levin, "The rough side of her tongue," *Sunday Times*, 11 December 1977, p. 37;
Ann McFerran, "The Treat," *Time Out*, 12 February 1982;
John Peter, "A woman's face," *Sunday Times*, 18 September 1977, p. 35;
Peter, *Sunday Times*, 12 December 1976, p. 35;
"Piaf's reprieve," *Observer*, 21 June 1981;
Victoria Radin, "Honest Gems," *Observer*, 15 October 1978, p. 31;
Charles Spencer, "A bruising kind of love," *Evening Standard*, 12 February 1982;
Irving Wardle, "Four drop-outs from the cat race *Dusa, Fish, Stas and Vi*," *Times*, 11 February 1977, p. 9;
Wardle, "Jane Lapotaire: *Piaf*," *Times*, 12 October 1978, p. 16;
Wardle, "Powerfully comic: *Franz into April*," *Times*, 6 December 1977, p. 7.

Simon Gray

(21 October 1936-   )

Anthony Stephenson
York University

PRODUCTIONS: *Wise Child*, 10 October 1967, Wyndham's Theatre, London;

Spoiled, 1968, BBC Television, London; 4 February 1970, Close Theatre Club, Glasgow; 1971, Haymarket Theatre, London; 31 October 1972, Morosco Theatre, New York, 135 [performances];

Dutch Uncle, 3 March 1969, Theatre Royal, Brighton; 1969, Old Vic, London;

The Idiot, adapted from Dostoevsky's novel, 15 July 1970, Old Vic, London;

Butley, 7 July 1971, Oxford Playhouse, Oxford; 14 July 1971, Criterion Theatre, London;

Otherwise Engaged, 30 July 1975, Queen's Theatre, London;

Dog Days, 26 October 1976, Oxford Playhouse, Oxford;

Molly, 23 November 1977, Palace Theatre, Watford;

The Rear Column, 23 February 1978, Globe Theatre, London;

Close of Play, 24 May 1979, Lyttleton Theatre (National Theatre), London;

Stage Struck, 21 November 1979, Vaudeville Theatre, London;

Quartermaine's Terms, 28 July 1981, Queen's Theatre, London.

BOOKS: *Colmain* (London: Faber & Faber, 1963);
Simple People (London: Faber & Faber, 1965);

Simon Gray

199

Little Portia (London: Faber & Faber, 1967);
Sleeping Dog (London: Faber & Faber, 1968);
Wise Child (London: Faber & Faber, 1968; New York: French, 1974);
A Comeback for Stark, as Hamish Reade (London: Faber & Faber, 1969);
Dutch Uncle (London: Faber & Faber, 1969);
Spoiled (London: Methuen, 1971);
Butley (London: Methuen, 1971; New York: Viking, 1972);
The Idiot, adapted from Dostoevsky's novel (London: Methuen, 1972);
Otherwise Engaged (London: French, 1976);
Otherwise Engaged and Other Plays (London: Eyre Methuen, 1976; New York: Viking, 1976)—includes *Otherwise Engaged*, *Two Sundays*, and *Plaintiffs and Defendants*;
Dog Days (London: Eyre Methuen, 1977);
The Rear Column and Other Plays (London: Eyre Methuen, 1978; New York: Viking, 1979)—includes *The Rear Column*, *Molly*, and *Man in a Side-Car*;
Close of Play and Pig in a Poke (London: Eyre Methuen, 1979);
Molly (London: French, 1979);
Stage Struck (London: Eyre Methuen, 1979);
Quartermaine's Terms (London: Eyre Methuen, 1981).

An American theater critic observed recently that the British theater has traditionally been a theater of language rather than a theater of emotion and spectacle. The comment, though patently less than a half-truth, was made to illustrate the special qualities and weaknesses of the American stage, and in that light it does seem that British playwrights, actors, and, indeed, audiences have felt more comfortable with highly literate dialogue than their American counterparts. Certainly, since John Osborne's *Look Back in Anger* (1956), the modern British playgoer has been reminded of the potent possibilities of words handled with vigor and intelligence. Simon Gray belongs to a group of English playwrights, among whom might be numbered Tom Stoppard and Christopher Hampton, who have not been afraid of putting on stage the kind of literate conversation that might more usually be heard in a faculty club or senior common room.

Born on Hayling Island in Hampshire, Simon Gray is the son of James Davidson Gray, a pathologist, and Barbara Celia Mary Holliday Gray. His father was a first-generation Canadian, and when World War II began, Gray was evacuated to the home of his Scottish grandparents in Montreal. He

returned to England after the war ended and was educated at Westminster School in London, but by 1954 was again in Canada, attending Dalhousie University. In 1958, with a B.A. degree with honors in English from Dalhousie, he moved back across the Atlantic to France, settling in Clermont-Ferrand as a lecturer at the university. In 1959 he moved from France to Cambridge University to take a second degree in English. Cambridge at that time was something of a forcing house for talent, and undergraduates who aspired to careers in theater, journalism, politics, or as poets and novelists were fiercely competing for what Cambridge novelist Frederic Raphael has called "the glittering prizes." Among Gray's contemporaries were Peter Cook, who contributed to the satirical revue *Beyond the Fringe* (1959), Christopher Booker, one of the founders of *Private Eye* magazine, Margaret Drabble, Derek Jacobi, and David Frost. Sylvia Plath, though not an undergraduate, was living in Cambridge, and director John Barton was a don at King's College. Many of these people were already beginning to make their mark in the world at large while still pursuing their studies. Gray was no exception.

In 1963, after earning his second honors B.A. in English, but while still a research fellow at Trinity College, he had his first novel, *Colmain*, published. The novel made use of his Canadian experiences, and in the following year he returned to Canada, this time as a lecturer in English at the University of British Columbia. During Gray's stay in Canada, John Hobday of the Canadian Broadcasting Corporation commissioned a radio adaptation of *Colmain* (produced as *Up in Pigeon Lake*) and a number of other radio scripts. These were Gray's first experiences of professional playwriting. He returned to Trinity College, Cambridge, as supervisor in English after a year in Canada and remained in that position until 1966. On 20 August 1964 he married Beryl Mary Kevern, a picture researcher, with whom he has two children. In 1966, he moved to Queen Mary College, London University, as lecturer in English, and has taught there ever since. His first stage play was presented in 1967. Since then he has divided his time between teaching and writing for stage, screen, and television.

Gray claims that he first discovered his ability to write plays when, as a young teacher, he was writing novels and short stories. One of the short stories was mostly dialogue, and he was able to sell it as the basis for a television script. He then found he could make more money from writing the television adaptation than he was being paid for the original story. That adaptation, *The Caramel Crisis*, was televised in 1966. *Death of a Teddy Bear* and *A Way with the Ladies* followed in 1967. The same year, his fourth television play, *Sleeping Dog*, made a considerable impact. *Sleeping Dog* is a fable about a retired colonial administrator, Sir Hubert, who entraps and enslaves Claud, an intelligent, homosexual, black bartender, and reduces him to the status of a domestic animal, chained up in the basement of Sir Hubert's country house. The themes of domination and submission, the probing of the sickness and guilt that have made the British "the beggars of Europe" (as a character in one of his later plays says), and the element of ambiguous sexuality are preoccupations that tend to recur throughout Gray's work.

Gray's first stage play, *Wise Child* (1967), was written originally for television but at the time was considered too bizarre for home viewing. When Gray began writing the play, he conceived the central character as a woman, but gradually the character evolved into a man dressed as a woman. The character, Mrs. Artminster (played in the original production at Wyndham's Theatre by Alec Guinness), is in fact a male criminal wearing women's clothing to evade the police, who want him for a brutal mail robbery. He is staying with his young accomplice, Jerry, who poses as Mrs. Artminster's son, at a shabby provincial hotel run by a homosexual. The curious interdependence of the pair reaches its climax when, after murdering the homosexual landlord, Jerry dresses in the maid's clothes and Mrs. Artminster reverts to his male attire. Again, in this play, a black character (the maid) is used, reviled, and humiliated by the other characters. *Wise Child* and the play that followed it, *Dutch Uncle*, have been compared to the work of Joe Orton, but Gray's *bizarrerie* seems forced compared

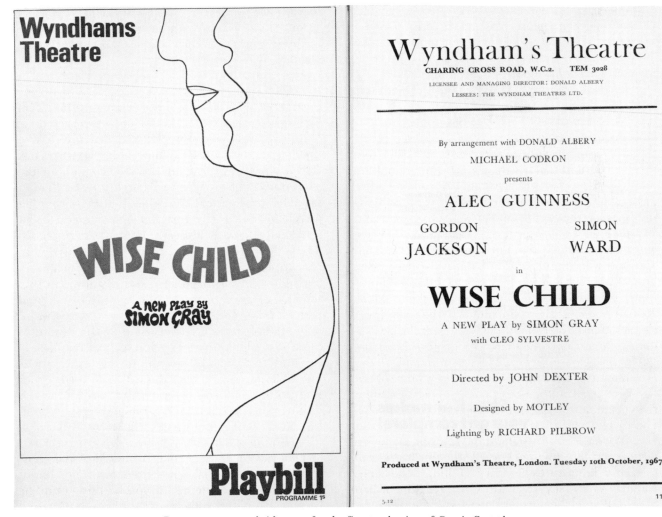

Program cover and title page for the first production of Gray's first play

to the manic extravagance of Orton, and the idiosyncratic dialogue of Gray's lower-class characters does not have the peculiar conviction of Orton's characters' conversations.

Dutch Uncle, which was presented by the Royal Shakespeare Company at the Old Vic in 1969, is a black farce about attempted wife murder. Mr. Godboy, the central character, is an impotent, failed chiropodist whose lifelong ambition is to bring himself to the attention of Inspector "Manly" Hawkins, whom he has admired since Godboy was a special constable during World War II. The murder of Godboy's wife is the device by which he hopes to get the inspector to pursue him. The underlying implication of homosexual obsession is apparent. His sexually frustrated and domineering wife, May, easily and unconsciously evades his fumbling attempts to lock her in a wardrobe and gas her. The final irony is that the inspector's attention is drawn to the household not by Godboy, but by his upstairs tenant, Eric Hoyden, who proves to be the "Merritt St. rapist." The play is clearly suggested by the case of Reginald Christie, an ex-special constable who murdered a number of women, including his wife and the wife of his upstairs tenant, and walled them up in his kitchen. Christie, too, was impotent, except with corpses. Christie's tenant, Timothy Evans, was originally convicted of the crime.

The verbal idiosyncrasies in the play, such as Godboy's repetitive "I merely said," seem imposed rather than natural to the characters, and the mechanics of the farcical action seem too coldly manufactured. The play was rewritten several times during the pre-London tour, and Gray himself has said that "a comedy that covered the audience in a vast shroud of depression" was turned into "a farce as witless as it was macabre that would goad the audience into an irritated restlessness." He has since described the London opening as "the worst night in the British theatre." What Gray still seems not to have understood about the play is that British audiences were still too close to the sickening realities of the Christie case to find it a possible subject for mirth.

This resounding failure with macabre farce seems to have driven Gray to the opposite extreme for his next dramatic work. Originally presented as a television play in 1968, *Spoiled* was staged at the Haymarket Theatre in 1971. A realistic domestic drama, it presents what is essentially a triangular relationship between Howarth, a high-school teacher, a teenage male student, and Howarth's pregnant wife. The teacher, in the course of giving the boy extra French lessons, probes relentlessly into his private life and sexual feelings and finally seduces him. Howarth's sin is the sin of too much involvement, just as in a later play, *Otherwise Engaged* (1975), the central character's sin is too much detachment. *Spoiled* has been criticized for naively attempting to shock the viewer and not facing up to the serious issue it raises. These criticisms, based on the assumption that the play is chiefly about homosexuality, miss the point. *Spoiled* is, in fact, a careful, honest play about the unthinking abuse of trust and power. It is significant that Gray takes teaching very seriously, believes education is more important than politics, and sees himself as a teacher first and a writer second. That *Spoiled* is not wholly successful is perhaps due to Gray's over-scrupulous adherence to a pedestrian realism which shunned both the grotesque characters and bizarre incident that his earlier plays displayed and the verbal pyrotechnics which he proved himself capable of in his later work.

Butley (1971), in fact, which opened within a few months of *Spoiled*, and which was his first major success, is a good example of the increasing reliance in Gray's work on highly expressive dialogue. Comparing *Butley* with Tom Stoppard's *Jumpers* (1972), Stanley Kauffman said: "Stoppard's dialogue has some sheen and a degree of donnish wit, but it is . . . much less surgical than Simon Gray's in *Butley*." It was also the first of his plays to be directed by Harold Pinter. Seeing Pinter's *The Homecoming* (1965) had given Gray the impetus for his own early attempts at playwriting, and the association of Gray and Pinter as playwright and director has continued for almost a decade. Gray says of Pinter: "His great gift is to realize the text. He is a man of great scrupulousness and integrity. I don't want a magnificently inventive director magnificently inventing for my play." The combined talents of Pinter, Gray, and Alan Bates, who played Ben Butley and subsequently the leads in several of Gray's stage and television plays, made *Butley* an immensely satisfying piece of theater. *Butley* is a play that is almost plotless in the conventional sense, revolving as it does around one day in the working life of a self-indulgent, arrogant, and viper-tongued teacher of English at London University. In the course of the day, he causes problems for his students, his wife, his office-mate with whom he seems to have a quasi-homosexual relationship, his office-mate's lover, and an aging female faculty member. His technique is to put them in the wrong by demonstrating through satire the woolliness of their thinking and the insincerity of their motives. In striking out at everyone around him, he reveals the

Anna Massey, Jeremy Kemp, and Simon Ward in the first London stage production of Spoiled

emptiness and hollowness of his own life. The play is tightly structured and at times almost seems to parody the techniques of the neoclassical theater. Butley himself remarks: "We're preserving the unities. The use of messengers has been quite skillful."

The themes which recur throughout Gray's work are all present in *Butley*: the games of dominance and submission, ambiguous sexuality, the sense of a declining culture, and (as in *Spoiled*) the metaphor of the corrupt teacher as a symbol of the abuse of trust and power. Joey, Butley's office-mate, clearly states the last of those themes when he says: "But those were in the days when you still taught. Now you spread futility." Butley not only abuses his intellectual gifts by using them to humiliate others,

but he also fritters them away on the pseudoscholarly study of the children's stories of Beatrix Potter and of middle-class nursery poems when he is supposed to be writing a critical work on T. S. Eliot. Commenting on the play, Harold Clurman wrote that it is "more devastatingly nihilistic" than John Osborne's *West of Suez* (1971), and that it has "little dramatic core" being essentially "a pen portrait of a college professor." He goes on to say, "But there is a certain relief from spiritual depression in *Butley*. Its protagonist makes inconsequentiality, disinterestedness, deliberate folly appear acceptable through laughter—and not only acceptable but somehow darned clever."

After a four-year gap, during which time he

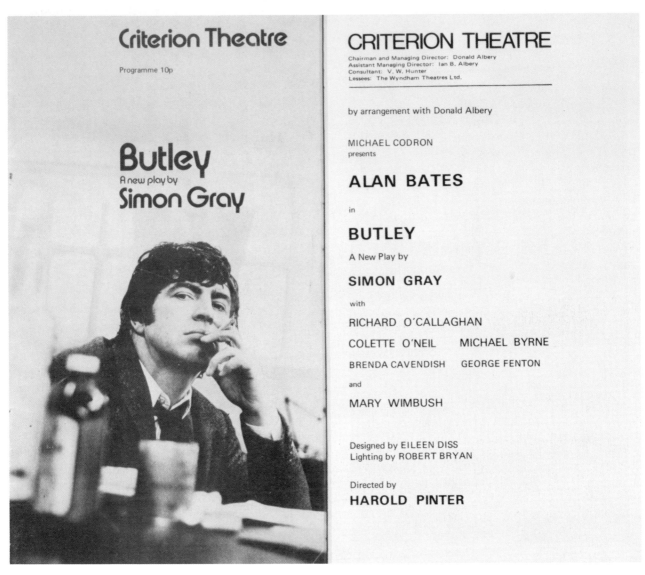

Program cover and title page for the first London production of Gray's first play directed by Harold Pinter

was working on the screenplay of *Butley* (which was filmed in 1974) and other projects, Gray returned to the West End stage in 1975 with *Otherwise Engaged*. Simon Hench, the central figure of the play, belongs to a world with which Gray has become increasingly concerned—the world of writers, publishers, and academics. The play is cleverly structured. Essentially the idea is to present a character preoccupied with a single, simple activity and have the activity delayed by a series of increasingly dramatic interruptions. The activity, Gray has said, could have been anything—watching football on television, for instance—though, as he admits, the activity chosen would necessarily affect his approach to the character. In fact, Hench, a successful publisher, is at home trying to listen to a recording of Richard Wagner's opera *Parsifal*. He is interrupted by his brother, who is anxious about his prospects of becoming a deputy headmaster; by Jeff, a literary critic, who, like Butley, launches a series of verbal attacks on a variety of targets; by Jeff's mistress, who tries to seduce him; by Wood, a failure, who at one time had attended a private boarding school, reveals Hench's homosexual activities as a schoolboy and accuses Hench of seducing his fiancee; by his wife, who tells him she is pregnant by either Hench or her lover, Ned; by his tenant Dave, who denounces him as a complacent fake liberal and moves squatters into Hench's house; and by a telephoned suicide message from Wood, which Hench switches off in mid-sentence. He is finally moved to take some action when his friend, Jeff, returns and falsely accuses Hench of reporting him to the police as a drunk driver. Hench then throws a glass of whiskey in his friend's face, saying: "What sort of man do you think I am?" The play ends with the two men sitting together and listening to Wagner.

Otherwise Engaged is, in effect, a series of encounters with an almost immovable object. Things happen, lives change all around Hench, and he remains curiously, inhumanly detached until he is accused of a trivial betrayal. It is a study which can be interpreted either as a portrait of emotional nullity or as an examination of a man whose sensibility is so acute that he has to hide it behind a shell of imperviousness. As Walter Kerr says, the hero of *Otherwise Engaged* has "the tough resilient reserve of a boxer who has sworn never to fight again; his most intense desire was to offend no one, cause no scenes,

stir no exacerbating emotions." Kerr comments further, "There is a most contrary sense—cunningly fostered by the playwright Gray—in which the folk who badger Simon [Hench] are not only working to define themselves by the fire they can draw from Simon, they are also working to define Simon, to kindle a blaze in him that will warm him back to what the rest of us call life."

The source of *Otherwise Engaged*, as well as two television plays produced the same year (*Plaintiffs and Defendants* and *Two Sundays*), was *Dog Days*, a play written earlier but staged later. In *Dog Days* the Hench figure, Peter, is less interesting precisely because he is less mysterious, and the structure of the play is looser and less satisfying. Gray, indeed, was reluctant to have it staged and refused several times to give permission before it was finally presented at the Oxford Playhouse in 1976. *Molly* (1977), the

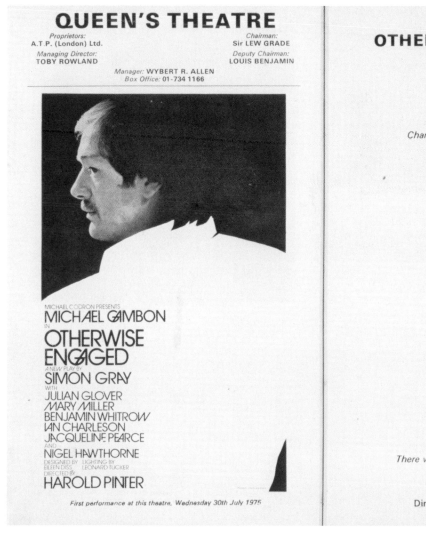
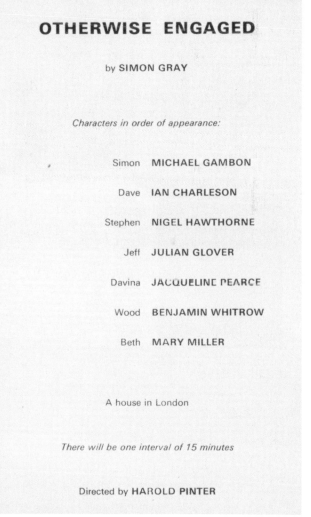

Program cover and cast list for the first London production of Gray's 1975 play, marking his return to the theater after a four-year interval

play which followed the production of *Dog Days*, was essentially a rewriting of Gray's television play, *Death of a Teddy Bear* (1967), based on the celebrated murder trial of Alma Rattenbury, a subject which also provided the material for Terence Rattigan's *Cause Célèbre* (1977). *Molly* is neatly constructed and quite gripping but a much more conventional piece of West End fare than any of Gray's other works, with the exception of *Stage Struck* (1979).

With *The Rear Column* in 1978, Gray returned to the theme of Britain's guilty colonial past, which he had exploited in *Sleeping Dog*. As in *Molly* and *Dutch Uncle*, the material of the play is derived from a real event. In *The Rear Column*, however, the event is not used as a springboard for brutal farce as in *Dutch Uncle* or as an excuse for rehashing an old scandal as in *Molly*. The play tells the story of some members of H. M. Stanley's expedition to the Congo in 1887 who are left behind to guard supplies and to wait for native reinforcements, who are being recruited by Tippu-Tib, a local chieftain. The main focus is on the deterioration of the men and the cruelty they inflict on the natives. The action revolves around the half-mad Major Barttelot whose insistence on following Stanley's instructions to the letter results eventually in disaster. In many ways, this is one of Gray's most impressive works, and in the character of Jameson, a civilian scientist, Gray shows the ultimate horror of intellectual curiosity and emotional detachment. Jameson, on the surface a kind, patient, and sympathetic figure, is shown to have allowed his scientific fervor to lead him to a particularly ghastly extreme. He buys a native girl so that he can resell her to the cannibals in order to make sketches of the process of cannibalism. Jameson seems to be a combination of Simon Hench of *Otherwise Engaged* and Sir Hubert of *Sleeping Dog*, and the play's exploration of the essential inscrutability of evil has some of the force of Conrad's *Heart of Darkness* and Golding's *Lord of the Flies*.

With his next work, *Close of Play* (1979), Gray returned to the familiar milieu of contemporary middle-class academics and intellectuals. Structurally the play is based on a device similar to that used in *Otherwise Engaged*. The action revolves around an elderly retired academic, Jasper (played in the National Theatre production by Michael Redgrave), who sits mutely until the last moments of the play, while his silly, desperate second wife (portrayed by Peggy Ashcroft), his children and their spouses, and his grandchildren pour out a stream of terrible revelations about their lives. They seem not to know or to care whether he can hear them, for their object is

not to communicate with others but to purge themselves of the poisons that are killing them. At the end of the play, Jasper struggles half out of his chair and says, "The door is open . . . ," echoing half of the Eliotic chant the other characters have spoken in unison a little earlier. His wife, who has not noticed his previous silence, does not notice that he has broken it and continues her self-absorbed chatter as the play ends. It is the first of Gray's plays, apart from television plays like *Plaintiffs and Defendants* (1975) and *Two Sundays* (1975), in which relationships between parents and children play almost as important a part as relationships between husbands and wives, or lovers. Gray's picture of this aspect of life is rigorously unsentimental and chillingly convincing.

Gray's recent plays, *Stage Struck* (1979) and *Quartermaine's Terms* (1981) are disappointing. *Stage Struck*, a thriller on the model of Anthony Shaffer's *Sleuth* (1979) or Ira Levin's *Deathtrap* (1978), seems to have been hastily written and marks no real advance either dramaturgically or philosophically. *Quartermaine's Terms* is more interesting but still a failure. The central character, Quartermaine, is an ineffectual upper-class Englishman, more than a little reminiscent of P. G. Wodehouse's Bertie Wooster, who is employed to teach English to foreign students, a job which he does with a notable lack of success. Unfortunately, he does not function well as a central character. Where Butley and Hench were strong focal figures for whom the other characters were foils, Quartermaine is a foil to all the other characters. He is used by them, patronized by them, and finally rejected by them. This generates an effect of mild pathos but little more. Both *Stage Struck* and *Quartermaine's Terms* seem like apprentice works compared to the mature achievements of *Butley*, *Otherwise Engaged*, *The Rear Column*, and *Close of Play*.

Gray, like Pinter, would deny that he sets out to convey a message in his plays. He claims that he has no particular philosophy to promote, nor any program to propose about politics, sex, ethics, or the future of mankind. What he does seem to be interested in, however, is the mystery of character. As a teacher of English, his area of specialty is the study of Charles Dickens, and he would name Dickens, along with Pinter, as an important influence on his work. This effect is easier to see in the grotesques of Gray's earlier plays: Sir Hubert, Mrs. Artminster, Godboy, "Manly" Hawkins, all of whom display obsessive character traits that remind one of what E. M. Forster called Dickens's "flat" characters. It is harder to see in the later plays, though Gray main-

6‐7

James: I shan't be able to manage anything tonight, I'm afraid. I've got a College Committee coming up.

Amanda: Oh. What on?

James: Port.

Amanda: Port?

James: Yes. It's the wine Committee. I'm the chairman this term. There's an auction of various ports ~~coming up~~. Feelings are bound to run high ~~as~~ about our bidding. It'll ~~go~~ on for ever. (Pause) But if I do get away at a reasonable time I'll give you a ring, shall I?

Amanda: (brightly brave) No, don't do that. We've been seeing a lot of each other. Perhaps a trifle too much. Let's have a rest.

James: ~~If~x~that's~x~what~~ (carefully, warmly) ~~If that's what you'd like.~~ ~~But of cou~~rse I'll give you a ring ~~you soon~~ *tomorrow are bidiers evz.*

Amanda: in you want.
And cut to:

Int. James's car. Evening.

Approaching the drive. It is about eight. The light just beginning to turn to dusk. Goes down the drive, and as he does, slows, looks at the house. There is an atmosphere of silence. Of desertion even. There is a ladder against the roof, one section of tiles still to be laid. He looks up at thw windows. There is the suggestion of a face, surrounded by a

A revised page from the filmscript for Moths

tains that his interest in sexual ambiguity is prefigured in the work of Dickens, specifically in the "women who are almost men," like Sarah Gamp, the disreputable nurse in *Martin Chuzzlewit*. The characters of his later plays are largely from the world he knows best, the world of middle-aged, educated, intelligent men, who work in jobs where literacy is important, who are often sardonic and unhappily married. The characters, he says, are "defined by their professions." In his own life, this seems to be true also. "I went to university when I was seventeen," he says, "and I never left."

Gray's technique as a playwright bears some resemblance to Pinter's. Both claim that they write instinctively and are not clear what a play is about until it is finished. Pinter tends to begin with a picture in his head, but Gray says that he "starts with a line of dialogue and then asks himself, who said it?" This is not to say that he is not conscious of structure. *Butley*, *Otherwise Engaged*, which went through thirty-five drafts, and *Close of Play* are clearly not the work of a writer with no plan or direction. The pity is that, for so intelligent and gifted a playwright, he has not been more innovative. Apart from his earlier flights of fancy and some hints of poetic resonance in *The Rear Column* and *Close of Play*, his work has been not only literate but literal. Younger British playwrights have generally been more daring with form and more challenging in content.

It may be that *Stage Struck* marks the beginning of a phase in which Gray will content himself with being a successful, competent West End playwright—a sort of latter-day Rattigan—but the tart brilliance of *Butley*, the Conradian complexity of *The Rear Column*, and the bitter candor of *Close of Play* suggest that there are resources yet untapped by Gray.

Screenplay:
Butley, American Film Theatre, 1974.

References:
Mel Gussow, "Teaching is My Bloody Life," *New York Times*, 9 February 1977, p. C12;
Ian Hamilton, "Simon Gray," *New Review*, 3 (January/February 1977): 39-46;
Oleg Kerensky, "Laughter in Court: Alan Ayckbourn, Simon Gray, Tom Stoppard," in his *The New British Drama* (London: Hamish Hamilton, 1977), pp. 132-144;
John Russell Taylor, "Three Farceurs," in his *The Second Wave* (London: Methuen, 1971), pp. 169-171.

Graham Greene
(2 October 1904-   )

Kathleen B. Hindman
Mansfield State College

PRODUCTIONS: *The Living Room*, 16 April 1953, Wyndham's Theatre, London;
The Potting Shed, 29 January 1957, Bijou Theatre, New York, 143 [performances]; 5 February 1958, Globe Theatre, London;
The Complaisant Lover, 18 June 1959, Globe Theatre, London; 1 November 1961, Ethel Barrymore Theatre, New York, 101;
Carving a Statue, 17 September 1964, Haymarket Theatre, London; 30 April 1968, Gramercy Arts Theatre, New York, 16;
The Return of A. J. Raffles, 4 December 1975, Aldwych Theatre, London;
Yes and No and *For Whom the Bell Chimes*, 20 March 1980, Haymarket Studio, Leicester.

SELECTED BOOKS: *The Man Within* (London: Heinemann, 1929; Garden City: Doubleday, Doran, 1929);
Brighton Rock (New York: Viking, 1938; London & Toronto: Heinemann, 1938);
The Lawless Roads (London, New York & Toronto: Longmans, Green, 1939); republished as *Another Mexico* (New York: Viking, 1939);
The Labyrinthine Ways (New York: Viking, 1940); published simultaneously as *The Power and the Glory* (London & Toronto: Heinemann, 1940);
British Dramatists (London: Collins, 1942);
The Little Train, illustrated by Dorothy Craigie (Norwich: Jarrold, 1946; New York: Lothrop, Lee & Shepard, 1958);

Graham Greene

The Heart of the Matter (London: Heinemann, 1948; New York: Viking, 1948);

The End of the Affair (Melbourne, London & Toronto: Heinemann, 1951; New York: Viking, 1951);

The Living Room: A Play in Two Acts (Melbourne, London & Toronto: Heinemann, 1953; New York: Viking, 1954);

Loser Takes All (Melbourne, London & Toronto: Heinemann, 1955; New York: Viking, 1957);

The Quiet American (Melbourne, London & Toronto: Heinemann, 1955; New York: Viking, 1956);

The Spy's Bedside Book, edited by Graham Greene and Hugh Greene (London: Hart-Davis, 1957);

The Potting Shed: A Play in Three Acts (New York: Viking, 1957; London, Melbourne & Toronto: Heinemann, 1958);

Our Man in Havana (New York: Viking, 1958; London, Melbourne & Toronto: Heinemann, 1958);

The Complaisant Lover: A Comedy (London, Melbourne & Toronto: Heinemann, 1959; New York: Viking, 1961);

A Burnt-Out Case (London, Melbourne & Toronto:

Heinemann, 1961; New York: Viking, 1961);

Carving a Statue: A Play (London: Bodley Head, 1964);

The Comedians (New York: Viking, 1966; London: Bodley Head, 1966);

Modern Film Scripts The Third Man: A Film by Graham Greene and Carol Reed (London: Lorrimer, 1968; New York: Simon & Schuster, 1969);

Collected Essays (London, Sydney & Toronto: Bodley Head, 1969; New York: Viking, 1969);

Travels with My Aunt (London, Sydney & Toronto: Bodley Head, 1969; New York: Viking, 1970);

A Sort of Life (New York: Simon & Schuster, 1971; London, Sydney & Toronto: Bodley Head, 1971);

Collected Stories (London: Bodley Head & Heinemann, 1972; New York: Viking, 1973);

The Pleasure-Dome: The Collected Film Criticism 1935-40, edited by John Russell Taylor (London: Secker & Warburg, 1972); republished as *Graham Greene on Film: Collected Film Criticism 1935-1940*, edited by Taylor (New York: Simon & Schuster, 1972);

The Honorary Consul (New York: Simon & Schuster, 1973; London, Sydney & Toronto: Bodley Head, 1973);

The Return of A. J. Raffles: An Edwardian Comedy in Three Acts Based Somewhat Loosely on E. W. Hornung's Characters in the Amateur Cracksman (London, Sydney & Toronto: Bodley Head, 1975; New York: Simon & Schuster, 1976);

Doctor Fischer of Geneva or the Bomb Party (New York: Simon & Schuster, 1980; London: Bodley Head, 1980);

Ways of Escape (London: Bodley Head, 1980; New York: Simon & Schuster, 1981);

Monsignor Quixote (London: Bodley Head, 1982; New York: Simon & Schuster, 1982).

Graham Greene is a novelist, short-story writer, dramatist, screenplay writer, film critic, news correspondent, author of children's books, biographer, editor, essayist, and world traveler. Born in Berkhamstead, Hertfordshire, he is the fourth of six children of Marion Raymond Greene and Charles Henry Greene, the headmaster at Berkhamstead School. Greene received his elementary education at his father's school. From 1922 to 1925 he attended Balliol College, Oxford, where he edited the *Oxford Outlook* and won an exhibition in modern history. After serving a brief apprenticeship in journalism in Nottingham, he was hired in 1926 as a subeditor for the London *Times* in the letters department. In 1926 Greene converted to

Catholicism. The next year he married Vivien Dayrell-Browning. After his first novel, *The Man Within*, was published in 1929, he left the *Times* and has lived mainly by his writing ever since. Greene's first play, *The Living Room*, was not produced or published until 1953, but he writes that he was not a complete novice at that time: "My life as a writer is littered with discarded plays, as it is littered with discarded novels." Since 1953 he has written and seen produced six more plays, one a twenty-minute curtain raiser written to provide more length to the production of another play (according to Greene, length has consistently given him problems). His plays have sparked the same wide range of critical praise and condemnation as have his novels, but have also, again like his novels, enjoyed considerable popular approval, with most of his stage plays proving successful. Greene has also written nine screenplays since 1939, the last six without collaborators.

The Living Room, Greene's first play to be produced, enjoyed a two-month run in London in 1953. By this time he had already had published fourteen book-length fictions, two volumes of short stories, two travel books, two volumes of essays, and had written five film scripts. He had also suffered through the frustration, semipoverty, and near despair of writing two unsuccessful novels following the modest success of *The Man Within*. Through trial and error, he had found that his personal mode of novel involved a contemporary setting, melodrama, and a religious dimension. He had received the Hawthornden Prize in 1941 for *The Power and the Glory* (1940), the James Tait Black Memorial Prize in 1949 for *The Heart of the Matter* (1948), and the Catholic Literary Award in 1952 for *The End of the Affair* (1951). He had traveled to Liberia for a walking tour through the jungle, to Mexico for a strenuous journey through the jungles and mountains of Tabasco and Chiapas to observe the effects of the government's efforts to wipe out the Catholic church, to West Africa as a member of the Foreign Office during World War II, and to Malaya, Czechoslovakia, Vienna, and Indochina. The success enjoyed by *The Living Room* in 1953, Greene writes, "was more than a success. I needed a rest from novels. I disliked the drudgery of film-writing. I had discovered what was in effect a new drink just at that period when life seemed to have been going on for far too many years." Like his youthful experiments with Russian roulette and his continual travel throughout his adult life, Greene's turning at times to drama seems to have been partly motivated

by his personal demon, boredom, and the welcome challenge of a new form.

Moreover, the direction *The Heart of the Matter* and *The End of the Affair* had taken led naturally to the dramatic form of *The Living Room*. As Philip Stratford observed, "The limiting of action, the deepening of insight into character, the domestication of setting and atmosphere, the increase in quantity and flexibility of dialogue all point to the challenge of the three unities, to an action single and complete and of a certain magnitude, and to the author alive only in his characters." Besides, Greene "felt he had reached the end of a cycle in his fiction" with *The End of the Affair* and was in a "slack period."

While *The Living Room* is Greene's first original dramatic script, he actually began to write plays at the age of sixteen. These early efforts as well as attempts twenty years later had not worked out. His first real step into the theater was an adaptation of his novel *The Heart of the Matter* for the stage in 1950. Although backed by Richard Rodgers and Oscar Hammerstein and produced by Basil Dean, the play closed in Boston without getting to New York. Even with his fifth screenplay, *The Third Man* (1949), Greene found it necessary to write the story first in novel form before translating it into script form. In *The Living Room*, Greene was finally able to convey his characteristic melodrama satisfactorily through dialogue.

In his 1942 study, *British Dramatists*, Greene discusses some of the characteristics that would later appear in *The Living Room* and his future plays. (Kenneth Allott and Miriam Farris in their 1951 study of Greene also describe Greene's method of constructing a novel as a variation of the poetic dramatist.) Greene praises the medieval morality play, "the bones without the flesh," as superior to much of twentieth-century drama with its individualized characters, "the flesh without the bones," and he describes Shakespeare's genius as being indebted to both the morality play and to the character play, as achieving a near-perfect balance between the two. He deplores the fact that after Shakespeare the universals of religion and morality were largely ignored and that during the Restoration drama became a class art rather than a popular art. At the same time he acknowledges the tremendous technical improvements which have taken place in drama and the modern attention to realism. In Greene's drama, then, the viewer might expect to find some of the "bones" of metaphysics and morality as well as the "flesh" of the individual character, and he should anticipate the popular appeal of melodrama because, as Samuel Hynes has written, melodrama provides Greene's world "with the texture of violence, terror, and cruelty that he finds in life." These characteristics are also present in Greene's novels and reflected in his plays.

In *The Living Room*, Greene centers the plot on a love triangle as he had often done in his novels. Young and innocent Rose Pemberton is in love with a family friend, Michael Dennis, twice her age and

the ineffectual priest, Father James Browne, here symbolically confined to a wheelchair; the pious and self-righteous Christian, critical of others and oblivious to personal errors, Miss Helen Browne, who unsympathetically manipulates the destruction of the "sinful" triangle while ignoring her own quite unchristian terror of death; the middle-aged psychiatrist, Michael Dennis, worldly-wise and world-weary, drawn to the younger, more naive

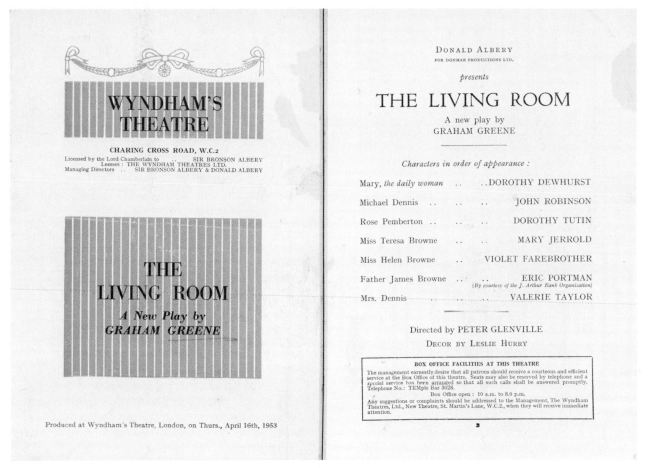

Program cover and cast list for the first production of Greene's first play

unhappily married to the neurotic, emotionally distraught, dependent Mrs. Dennis. As usual, the triangle creates all kinds of melodramatic complications and confrontations. The end result, as in *The Heart of the Matter*, is suicide—Rose kills herself. The consequence of the suicide, again similar to the events of *The Heart of the Matter*, is an intense consideration of the meaning of faith and justice on the part of all the living characters.

Most of the characters in *The Living Room* are already familiar to the reader of Greene's fiction:

woman, yet constantly guilt-ridden; the dependent, helpless wife, Marion Dennis, who is incapable of giving any kind of love but that of the spoiled sickly child; and the still innocent, blindly optimistic, simplistic child-woman, Rose Pemberton, dangerous to all those around her because of her ignorance and dangerous to herself when she is abruptly forced to face the complexity and cruelty of life.

Thematically, *The Living Room* is concerned with the complexity of life, with the impossibility of finding clear-cut answers, and with the inevitable

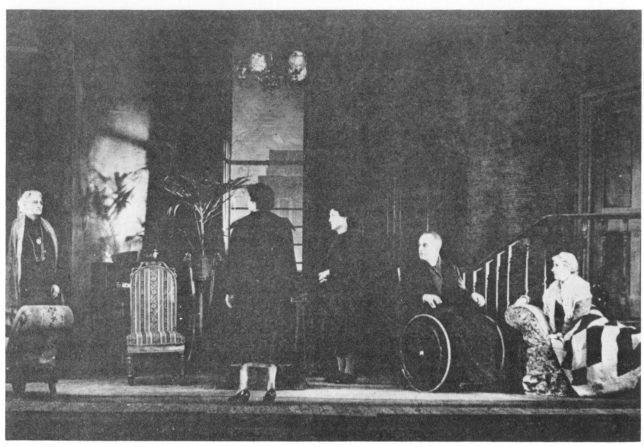

A scene from the first London production of The Living Room

result for the sincerely charitable person of finding what Greene felt were the hallmarks of a Christian civilization—"the divided mind, the uneasy conscience, the sense of personal failure." Father Browne labors under these characteristics from the beginning, Rose confronts them too painfully to be able to cope with them, and Michael simply denies them. The title of the play directs the viewer to the central symbol of the play. The place in which we live contains pain and death. To deny these qualities, as Helen has done, is to deny life. The only escape, as Rose demonstrates, is death. As is so often the case in Greene's fiction, it is the representative of the church, Father Browne, who has the last word and who, like Shakespeare's figure of authority at the end of his plays, reestablishes order. The primary characteristic of this order is that it is God's and not man's. Rose has committed suicide, which the church considers eternally damning, but Father Browne insists upon the inability of any man to penetrate another person's mind or heart. The state of Rose's soul is known only to God, and she will be dealt with justly, with understanding and love, by

Him, regardless of human judgment. *The Living Room* suggests that it should be the goal of human beings, and it is often the goal of Greene's art, to understand even those individuals who repel us and to learn through compassionate understanding how to love them. It is the shock of Rose's suicide which gives Father Browne the religious assurance to accept truly his role of priest and insist that Helen also must stop hiding from reality. This revitalization of Helen psychologically and of Father Browne spiritually attests to the possibility of Rose's final grace in spite of her suicide, as well as to the feeling that there is indeed some divine plan underlying the apparently disjointed events of life.

New York Times reviewer Brooks Atkinson described the play as "vague and shadowy," like T. S. Eliot's *The Cocktail Party*, with "a certain Puritanical distaste for human beings," the latter comment a chord frequently struck by critics of Greene's novels, in spite of his insistence upon the saving power of love. It is not so much that Greene finds human beings distasteful as that he finds them sinful and in need of love and mercy, an orthodox

212

Christian view of human nature. The "vagueness" Greene would probably call the "abstractness" or "bones" necessarily underlying any serious drama. The indefinite allows for universality in a way that the very particular does not. Many critics have been tempted to compare Greene and Eliot. (David Higham parodies Eliot and Greene at the same time in his play *The Confidential Cleric or The Land Below the Waistline*, published in his book *Literary Gent*, 1978.) While no critic has given *The Living Room* unqualified praise, the play has received favorable comment on its symbolism and the depth attained through its tragic implications. The most frequent criticism is aimed at its tendency to slip away from the tragic into the pathetic.

Greene's second play, *The Potting Shed*, was produced four years later in 1957. Since the production of his first play, Greene had published another volume of short stories, a novel, and *Loser Takes All* (1955), which he called an "entertainment," his term for a book-length fictional work emphasizing plot rather than theme. He made a third trip to Indochina as correspondent for the *Sunday Times* and *Figaro*, a trip to Poland as correspondent for the *Sunday Times*, and trips to Kenya, Haiti, China, Russia, and Cuba. He adapted for film *Loser Takes All* in 1956 and Bernard Shaw's *Saint Joan* in 1957. *The Potting Shed* continues the interest in religion, but it was not an inspired play. It was written deliberately from one of Greene's abandoned novels. Produced first in New York with a rewritten last scene constructed at rehearsals and produced later in London in the original version, the play has never completely satisfied Greene, who concludes that he drew a better "hollow man" in the novel *A Burnt-Out Case* (1961).

The plot of *The Potting Shed* turns upon a "miracle," which some critics have found unclearly handled and hence detrimental to the play. Even so, this melodramatic miracle provides the mystery and suspense of the play and is a key factor in the formation of the play's characters. How these characters are shaped by the event depends upon how they perceive the event. Because their perceptions vary, the audience is never really certain about the true nature of the miracle, an uncertainty which could be viewed as a contribution to the reality of the play, since most miracles must be encountered as unsubstantiated hearsay.

The miracle occurs thirty years prior to the time of the play. Desperately torn between the Catholicism of his beloved uncle who is a priest and the confirmed and rationalistic atheism of his father, the teenager James Callifer commits suicide,

hanging himself in the gardener's potting shed. Found dead by the gardener who is soon joined by the grief-stricken Father William Callifer, James is apparently miraculously revived by his uncle while the gardener is absent fetching a doctor. The entire episode is unremembered by James, and his parents and older brother refuse to tell James anything about the experience while carefully excluding the uncle from their lives, because they are unwilling to accept the possibility of any occurrence which would destroy their entire atheistic philosophical structure. The consequence of such a hidden past is a hollow man, the emotionless, unmotivated James, an adult unable to understand himself, constantly in psychotherapy but making no progress.

The occasion of the first act of the play is the approaching death of the father, of which James and Father Callifer are purposely not notified by the family. But James's thirteen-year-old niece, Anne, sends him a telegram, the first of her many efforts as a child sleuth which result in James's finally finding out his history and the history of the potting shed. A climactic scene occurs between James and his uncle, which many critics view as the most powerful scene in the play. As the two men relive that fateful day in the potting shed, they are both brought to the conviction that a God does indeed exist. James's emotions and will are revitalized. The alcoholic and unbelieving Father Callifer reaffirms his faith. For, like Scobie in *The Heart of the Matter* and Sarah in *The End of the Affair*, Father Callifer had unwittingly struck a bargain with God. He had offered up his faith for the life of his nephew, but when James reopened his eyes Father Callifer apparently failed to understand the significance of the event. The real impact of the event only comes to Father Callifer thirty years later when he recognizes the significance of the last thirty faithless years; he realizes that his loss of faith is the only completely convincing evidence for the miracle that could have been given. His loss of faith therefore becomes sufficient cause for a powerful reaffirmation of that faith.

Although the play has been described as Ibsenian by Jacob H. Adler because it is a problem play, because of the nature of the characters and the events, and because of the use of objects as symbols—especially the potting shed, the place wherein one is shaped by the master potter—the religious dimension is characteristic of Greene's work. Once again, as in *The Living Room*, the danger of ignorance (for James as for Rose) and the more eternally dangerous denial of a truth (for the Callifers as for the Brownes) are presented, and the power of love is demonstrated. Once the truth is in the open, the potting shed—the world—sheds its aura of fear and dread. All of the characters are better able to cope with life. Unfortunately, however, this positive change in the characters is presented in a very "talky" third act. Still, *The Potting Shed* is a play with particular religious appeal and was produced for ten performances by the Chapel Players at the Broadway Congregational Church in New York about six months after its original run.

In 1958 one of Greene's funniest entertainments, *Our Man in Havana*, was published. The following year, Greene's third play, *The Complaisant Lover*, which also demonstrates his hilarious, if rather bizarre, humor was produced. Greene says he wrote the play as an escape from the confinement of novel writing just as he has often produced his entertainments. He found the play easy to write and a satisfying blend of his manic and depressive moods. It was well received by the public, its lack of explicit religion welcomed with relief by some critics. The play was even adapted for the French stage by Jean Anouilh. Most critics describe *The Complaisant Lover* as good theater but more shallow than Greene's earlier plays, suggesting what Philip Stratford considers a shift from Greene's early aim of popular universal drama toward bourgeois, domestic comedy. Actually, *The Complaisant Lover* probably bears a relationship to the earlier plays similar to the relationship of Greene's entertainments to his novels. The themes of the plays are similar, but in this play, as in the entertainments, theme is presented less emphatically, while more emphasis is given to plot.

The play again deals with three characters involved in a triangular relationship: Victor Rhodes, fortyish, a practical joker, a dentist, apparently insensitive and totally unromantic; Mary Rhodes, also fortyish, a capable mother and housewife, dedicated to fulfilling her husband's and children's needs, but long separated sexually and romantically from her husband; and Clive Root, an antiquarian bookstore owner, in his thirties, who habitually falls in love with older married women only to lose out each time to the husband—Mary is his latest romantic attachment. The play ends with the unexpected but successful efforts of the husband to fulfill his wife's wish to have both her husband and her lover so that she will not be forced into an impossible choice between the two. Although he is persuaded by the husband to accept this arrangement for Mary's happiness, the lover Clive is reluctant because his experience tells him that he will once again be the loser.

The Complaisant Lover connects thematically with the earlier plays and with the novels by way of audience sympathy. Even though Mary is the sinner of the play, the audience is inclined to cheer her on. She is seen as loving in her relationships with her son, her husband, and her lover. Her rationale for taking on a lover is, in part, that this relationship will take nothing from her husband and therefore will not hurt him. So long as her husband remains as she perceives him—dense, insensitive, and a little helpless—the audience's sympathy is not engaged for him. However, by the end of the play, after the husband has explained that his cessation of sexual activity was a result of realizing he no longer gave his wife pleasure and has gone to such great lengths to keep his wife under any terms, it becomes clear why she married him and why Clive will once again be deserted after a time. Victor is willing to endure considerable pain himself if it is necessary in order to give his wife pleasure, even the pleasure of illusions. Clive is never portrayed as possessing such an unselfish and complete love, so that his future suffering seems just. Greene's definition of love, even in this lighter play, goes beyond sex and self toward a definition of agape with its qualities of inclusion and unlimited forgiveness. Victor's love is finally perceived as much the same as that of Father James Browne in *The Living Room* and Father William Callifer in *The Potting Shed*—compassionate, understanding, merciful.

Between 1959 and 1964 Greene had published another novel, a travel book, and a volume of short stories and had edited the four-volume *The Bodley Head Ford Madox Ford* (1962, 1963). He also wrote a screenplay of his entertainment *Our Man in Havana*, produced by Columbia Pictures in 1959. Greene traveled to Cuba, the Belgian Congo, Russia, Brazil, Tunis, Rumania, Berlin, East Germany, and Haiti. In 1964 *Carving a Statue* was produced in the West End. The play returns to the notion of a morality play with a cast of five characters, only one of whom is named. It is the story of two people: a man obsessed, to the exclusion of wife and son and all else, with one goal—creating a statue of God the Father—and the sculptor's neglected adolescent son who is struggling to encounter and understand life. There are some echoes of Harold Pinter and Samuel Beckett in the dialogue, but *New York Times* reviewer B. A. Young declared that Greene had lost his "theatrical cunning" in this work, which has not been a successful play. Greene acknowledges the difficulty he had in writing the play, but he denies that *Carving a Statue* depends heavily on symbols or is concerned with theology. Instead, he insists that it is a farce and that farce and tragedy are closely allied. He compares this play to *The Complaisant Lover*. But in *Carving a Statue* it is difficult to experience the humor to be found in the father's intimacy with his son's first girl friend or in the death of the young deaf and dumb second girl friend, struck by a car and killed while trying to escape the embraces of the father's doctor. The pain of the son, twice betrayed, weighs more heavily than the ridiculousness of the father's obsession even though the obsession is given material form in the huge and ugly feet which dominate the stage. Perhaps it is the omnipresence of religion, however perverted by the father's obsession, which engages the sympathy of the audience instead of allowing them to view the events as farce, or perhaps it is a consequence of the apparent guiltlessness of the betrayed son, unlike the more obvious imperfections of the betrayed Victor Rhodes or Clive Root in *The Complaisant Lover*.

Greene did not write another play for eleven years. Instead, he traveled to Sierra Leone, Istanbul, Paraguay, Argentina, and Chile, and he produced a variety of literary works: one screenplay, two novels, a volume of short stories, a biography, a volume of essays, the introduction to a collection of his film criticism, an autobiography, and a book-length edition of an interview with Dottoressa Moor

Hugh Beaumont, Peter Wood, and Greene during rehearsal for the London production of Carving a Statue

of Capri, whose style and enthusiasm gave him the character Augusta in the novel *Travels with My Aunt* (1969).

In December 1975 *The Return of A. J. Raffles* opened in the West End. The idea for the play came to Greene after viewing the 1974 Royal Shakespeare Company production of *Sherlock Holmes*. Because Greene is an expert in Victorian and Edwardian crime fiction, the material for this play was familiar to him. The critics responded to *The Return of A. J. Raffles*, which contains homosexuality, adultery, and nudity, with comments that ranged from "clumsy plot" and "sniggering lechery" by London *Times* reviewer Harold Hobson to "delightful entertainment" by Martin Esslin. Perhaps the fact that the play was produced as a Christmas play contributed to the outrage of some of the critics. Although unconventional sexual behavior is certainly a part of the play, Greene has never found such acts to be nearly so dangerous as being self-righteous and having a lack of sympathy. Like *The Complaisant Lover*, this play seems to be a theatrical entertainment rather than serious drama. The audience is more concerned with untangling the complicated plot than it is with any thematic statement.

The supposedly dead (and therefore safe from the law) A. J. Raffles, a clever cricketer and burglar (the literary creation of E. W. Hornung some seventy years before the play's production), returns to his old quarters and his associate, Bunny. At the request of Bunny's new friend from prison, Lord Alfred (Bosie) Douglas, the notorious lover of Oscar Wilde, Raffles, who is also a homosexual, agrees to steal money from Lord Alfred's father, the Marquess of Queensberry, as retribution for the marquess's making public his son's illegal homosexual relationship with Wilde and then using this affair as an excuse to deny his son money. Entangled with this plot by coincidence of time and place and an immediate attraction to Raffles is the Prince of Wales, who is using the marquess's home as a rendezvous point with his mistress, Alice. The affair has been discovered by the prince's ambitious German cousin Willy, who has sent a spy to steal and publish the prince's love letters to Alice. In spite of the many potential disasters, the ending is happy. No one is imprisoned or loses reputation, although the marquess does lose his money to his son who then flees to France to find Wilde.

Thematically, the play has been described as a presentation of the gentle crook or as a comment on the shortcomings of the modern world while laughing at the follies of another age. But this play is concerned with the same "bones" and "flesh" as the earlier plays. The audience's conventional moral instincts are once again proved wrong by the particular characters and events presented in the play. The adulterous prince and the homosexual burglar Raffles come out ahead of the law-abiding marquess, who turns in his own son and righteously denies him money, and ahead of the dutiful Inspector Mackenzie, obsessed with capturing lawbreakers, especially the clever Raffles. In spite of the prince's and Raffles's faults, these men are capable of love and understanding in a way that the marquess and Inspector Mackenzie are not. The sinners here, as elsewhere in Greene's work, come closer to sainthood than the righteous or the legalistic. Because one of the play's sinners, the prince, holds political power, he is able to control the denouement of events to the satisfaction of the audience in favor of himself and Raffles.

Greene's latest play, *For Whom the Bell Chimes*, and its accompanying curtain raiser *Yes and No* were produced at the Haymarket Studio in Leicester in March 1980, following the publication of two more novels. Both of these plays have been described as Pinteresque. *For Whom the Bell Chimes* is about a man who has killed his unattractive girl friend and finally succeeds in persuading a visiting con-man into trading clothes with him for his escape from the police. The characters include a transvestite police officer and a lascivious Scotsman. The plot incorporates all kinds of theatrical tricks such as the corpse hidden in the folding bed which keeps falling down onstage. *Yes and No* is a satire on the theater in which a director attempts to show a beginning actor the proper way to convey his bit part, which consists of only two words, *yes* and *no*. The fact that the actor uses only those two words in any situation adds to the fun. Although the reviewers admitted that neither play is substantial dramatic literature, both plays were found by most of them to be hilarious comedy excellently presented by the Leicester company. Sally Aire, however, calls the play "mechanical, embarrassing farce, . . . a piece lacking in basic stagecraft," and the curtain raiser "a little piece of icing sugar . . . which confirms all lay prejudices about how theatrical performances are and are not arrived at."

Although critics generally agree that Greene's drama is not equal to his fiction, he continues to gain in facility, and his writing in one genre contributes to his growth in another. He is considered a significant modern religious dramatist. While in his later plays he has moved away from the more direct presentation of his religious obsession, he continues to approach it tangentially by dramatizing the uncertainty of human judgment, by casting doubt on conventional morality, and by insisting upon the importance of Christian charity. If melodrama is inescapable for Greene—it seems to be his most characteristic perception of life—it nevertheless operates effectively in his plays as a method for popularizing his religious and intellectual concerns.

Screenplays:

Twenty-One Days, by Greene and Basil Dean, Columbia, 1939;

The Green Cockatoo, by Greene and E. O. Berkman, New World, 1940;

Brighton Rock, adapted by Greene and Terence Rattigan from Greene's novel, Associated British Picture Corporation, 1947;

The Fallen Idol, London Film Productions, 1948;

The Third Man, London Film Productions, 1949;

Loser Takes All, J. Arthur Rank Productions, 1956;

Saint Joan, adapted from Bernard Shaw's play, Wheel Productions, 1957;

Our Man in Havana, Columbia, 1959;

The Comedians, MGM, 1967.

Other:

The Bodley Head Ford Madox Ford, 4 volumes, edited by Greene (London: Bodley Head, 1962, 1963).

Periodical Publications:

"A Stranger in the Theatre," *Picture Post*, 59 (18 April 1953): 19-20;

"The Potting Shed," *Theatre Arts*, 42 (March 1958): 24-48;

Letter to the editor, *Times*, 23 December 1960, p. 9.

Bibliography:

R. A. Wobbe, *Graham Greene: A Bibliography and Guide to Research* (New York: Garland, 1979).

References:

Kenneth Allott and Miriam Farris, *The Art of Graham Greene* (London: Hamish Hamilton, 1951);

John D. Boyd, "Earth Imagery in Graham Greene's *The Potting Shed*," *Modern Drama*, 16 (June 1973): 69-80;

Martin E. Browne, "Graham Greene: Theatre's Gain," *Theatre Arts*, 45 (November 1961): 20-24;

Beekman W. Cottrell, "Second Time Charm: The Theatre of Graham Greene," *Modern Fiction Studies*, special Greene issue, 3 (Autumn 1957): 249-255;

Fred D. Crawford, "Graham Greene: Heaps of Broken Images," in his *Mixing Memory and Desire. The Waste Land and British Novels* (University Park: Pennsylvania State University Press, 1982), pp. 103-123;

Robert O. Evans, ed., *Graham Greene: Some Critical Considerations* (Lexington: University of Kentucky Press, 1963);

Graham Greene: A Collection of Critical Essays, edited by Samuel L. Hynes (Englewood Cliffs, N.J.: Prentice-Hall, 1973);

Henry Hewes, "Resurrection Will Out—Broadway Postscript," *Saturday Review*, 40 (16 February 1957): 26-27;

John P. Murphy, "*The Potting Shed*—Dogmatic and Dramatic Effects," *Renascence*, special Greene issue, 12 (Fall 1959): 43-49;

Philip Stratford, "The Novelist as Playwright," *Faith and Fiction: Creative Process in Greene and Mauriac* (Notre Dame: University of Notre Dame Press, 1964), pp. 243-282.

Papers:

The Humanities Research Center, University of Texas, Austin, contains a large collection of Greene's manuscripts, letters, diaries, and other relevant materials. The British Broadcasting Corporation has his broadcast scripts.

Trevor Griffiths

(4 April 1935-   )

Max Le Blond
National University of Singapore

PRODUCTIONS: *The Wages of Thin*, 13 November 1969, Stables Theatre Club, Manchester; December 1970, QUIPU Basement Theatre, London;

The Big House, 10 December 1969, BBC Radio 4, London; 15 January 1975, University Theatre, Newcastle-upon-Tyne;

Occupations, 28 October 1970, Stables Theatre Club, Manchester; 13 October 1971, Place Theatre, London;

Apricots, 28 June 1971, QUIPU Basement Theatre, London;

Lay By, by Griffiths, Howard Brenton, Brian Clark, David Hare, Stephen Poliakoff, Hugh Stoddart, and Snoo Wilson, 24 August 1971, Traverse Theatre Club, Edinburgh; 26 September 1971, Royal Court Theatre, London;

Thermidor, 25 August 1971, Cranston Street Hall, Edinburgh;

Sam, Sam, 9 February 1972, Open Space Theatre, London;

Gun, Spring 1973, Pool Theatre, Edinburgh;

The Party, 20 December 1973, Old Vic, London;

All Good Men, 31 January 1974, BBC Television, London; 13 May 1975, Young Vic Studio, London;

Comedians, 20 February 1975, Nottingham Playhouse, Nottingham; 24 September 1975, Old Vic, London;

The Cherry Orchard, adapted from Helen Rappaport's translation of Anton Chekhov's play, 1977, Nottingham Playhouse, Nottingham;

Deeds, by Griffiths, Brenton, Ken Campbell, and Hare, 8 March 1978, Nottingham Playhouse, Nottingham;

Oi for England, 7 June 1982, Royal Court Theatre Upstairs, London.

BOOKS: *Occupations and The Big House* (London: Calder & Boyars, 1972); revised as *Occupations* (London: Faber & Faber, 1980);

Lay By, by Griffiths, Howard Brenton, Brian Clark, David Hare, Stephen Poliakoff, Hugh Stoddart, and Snoo Wilson (London: Calder & Boyars, 1972);

Tip's Lot (London: Macmillan, 1972);

The Party (London: Faber & Faber, 1974);

Comedians (London: Faber & Faber, 1976; New York: Grove Press, 1976; revised edition, London: Faber & Faber, 1979);

All Good Men and Absolute Beginners: Two Plays for Television (London: Faber & Faber, 1977);

Through the Night and Such Impossibilities: Two Plays for Television (London: Faber & Faber, 1977);

Apricots and Thermidor (London: Pluto Press, 1978);

The Cherry Orchard, adapted from Helen Rappaport's translation of Anton Chekhov's play (London: Pluto Press, 1978);

Country: "A Tory Story" (London: Faber & Faber, 1981);

Oi for England (London: Faber & Faber, 1982).

Trevor Griffiths has noted of his own work: "nearly everything I write is political in one way or another." He is, in fact, a classic example of the dramatist engagé, passionately Marxist in his political convictions and profoundly committed in his plays to an exploration of the possibilities of and obstacles to a radical transformation of British society, which he has described in its present state as "corrupt and sliding." In terms of the general development of British drama since World War II, Griffiths is something of a curiosity. His violent opposition to the existing social system in Britain, and in particular the Marxist radicalism of his politics tend characteristically to be associated with a younger generation of dramatists such as David Hare, Stephen Poliakoff, Snoo Wilson, and Howard Barker, all born after World War II. Yet, born in 1935, Griffiths is in fact a member of the first generation of postwar British playwrights, coming to maturity in the decade after the war; and he may be seen as a transitional figure between the writers of John Osborne's generation, whose satiric indictments of social evils in Britain were generally cast in apolitical terms (even Arnold Wesker's socialism is ultimately a profound humanistic faith in man), and the dramatists of the second generation, whose attacks on society are generally rooted in the premises of hardline left-wing politics.

Born in Manchester, Griffiths is the son of Ernest and Ann Connor Griffiths. His early family background provided little in the way of shaping political influences. He has noted, in this connection: "There was no political background on either side, except that I discovered later that one of my mother's brothers had been a shop steward in an engineering factory, and had been called a Communist, though he wasn't. There was no political background at all. There was a lot of cynicism around in the house, about politics and politicians." Griffiths, however, was an avid reader, and in his middle teens he spent much of his time at the Manchester Central Reference Library, where he read, in addition to works by Ben Jonson and James Joyce, volume one of Karl Marx's *Das Kapital* (1867). Between the ages of seventeen and twenty, he still found time to write "about 200 poems."

Griffiths studied at St. Bede's College in Manchester from 1945 until 1952, when he entered Manchester University. He received a B. A. honors degree in English language and literature in 1955. On leaving the university, Griffiths completed his National Service, serving as an infantryman in the Manchester Regiment between 1955 and 1957. From his brother, who had fought in Kenya with the First Battalion Lancashire Fusiliers during the Mau Mau uprisings, Griffiths received what he described as "maybe . . . the first real politicisation I had." His brother's descriptions of British interrogation techniques during the insurgency convinced Griffiths of the British capacity for political repression.

On leaving the army, Griffiths worked for four years as an English teacher in a private school, where he met Janice Elaine Stansfield, a sociology student whom he married in 1960. Through his involvement at this time with Stansfield, he was introduced to new friends who shaped his politics: sociologists, anthropologists, and workers in the fields of social and community medicine. Gradually, Griffiths's own involvement in politics deepened: around 1960-1961 he became chairman of the Manchester Left Club and, shortly afterward, was appointed acting editor of the Labor newspaper, *Northern Voice*.

It is against this background of deepening political involvement that Griffiths's writing took shape. His early work in dramatic form included two "fairly dreadful" pieces, one dealing with the army and the other concerning a homosexual. A third play, dealing with people whom Griffiths describes as resembling his brother and himself, was entitled "The Daft Un." All three plays, Griffiths claims, have been "lost." The plays were written while Griffiths was working as an Education Officer with the British Broadcasting Corporation, from 1965 to 1972. It was also at this time that Griffiths received his first payments for creative work. "The Love Maniac," a television play with the relationship between a teacher and his pupils as its central theme, was adapted for radio by Griffiths and broadcast as *Jake's Brigade* on BBC Radio Four on 11 December 1971.

It is significant that some of Griffiths's early efforts were works for radio and television: for he has expressed the conviction that the theater is "incapable, as a social institution, of reaching, let alone *mobilising*, large popular audiences, at least in what is more and more desperately referred to as the Free World." This interest in reaching out to and mobilizing a mass audience is consonant with Griffiths's central thematic interests: the search for a viable mode of Marxist social revolution and the creation of a politicized mass consciousness which will provide effective resistance against the capitalist system. Expressed in these terms, the subjects of Griffiths's work seem forbiddingly remote and doctrinaire. But the great achievement of Griffiths's drama is that, notwithstanding his hardline politics, his characters and their dramatic situations live in the memory. The plays, far from being structures of bloodless Marxist abstractions or lukewarm propaganda pieces, are compelling theatrical experiences. If there are great theoretical debates, the dialectic comes alive, because it is seen to stem from and give expression to fully realized dramatic characters who are interesting in themselves.

Although there is little in Griffiths's canon which fails to excite interest, the solidity of his reputation as a dramatist writing for the stage may be said to rest on three plays: *Occupations* (1970), *The Party* (1973), and *Comedians* (1975). Griffiths himself has described *The Wages of Thin*, an earlier work for the stage which was given three late-night performances at the Stables Theatre in Manchester in 1969, as "an exercise play." *Occupations* was Griffiths's next play to be presented at the same theater and is the first major work of his career. The play is set in Turin, Italy, in 1920, and deals with the crisis in Italian history when labor unrest led to the Fiat motor strike and the Italian workers' final occupation of the factories before the Fascist backlash. The dramatic core of the play resides in the confrontation between Gramsci, the brilliant Marxist intellectual, leader of the local Communists, and Kabak, a Soviet agent. Griffiths uses the contrast between these two personalities to illuminate conflicting modes of political commitment. Gramsci is passionately devoted to the revolutionary cause, but he also loves the workers as individuals rather than statistics to buttress Marxist theory. Kabak on the other hand is cold, ruthless, and utterly devoid of any concern for human complexity. Because the Italian workers are obstacles to Soviet interests, they must be manipulated and sacrificed. It is a testament to Griffiths's honesty that *Occupations* demonstrates an awareness that revolutionary politics may be as dehumanizing a force as the capitalist system which it seeks to destroy.

Occupations was followed by *Apricots* and *Thermidor*, two short plays written and produced in 1971, by *Lay By*, a collaborative work with several other playwrights, including Howard Brenton and David Hare, which was staged in 1971, and by the full-length play *Sam, Sam* (1972). While *Sam, Sam* focuses on the lives of two working-class brothers, one of whom marries into a wealthy family, to illustrate the conviction that capitalism may dehumanize individuals at either end of the ladder of social status and opportunity, *Apricots* uses the sexual relationship of a couple, Sam and Anna, as an emblem of the destructive forces at work in their external world. *Thermidor*—the title recalls the French revolution—returns to the direct treatment of political issues; set in Moscow in 1937, it is an attack upon and warning against the Stalinist impulse in revolutionary politics, the tendency to sacrifice humanity and compassion on the altar of an abstract political creed.

The Party, first produced in late 1973, marks in dramatic terms a development in Griffiths's political vision. It is a work rooted in the assumption that the British social democratic process has failed in the task of creating a viable socialist society to replace capitalism. *The Party*, however, marks a deepening disillusion which takes the viewer beyond this conviction, because it evokes an atmosphere of stalemate and failure, of compromise and hypocrisy on the part of individuals supposedly committed to revolution. Griffiths has noted that he tried in this play "to square the circle of how do you become a full-time revolutionary in a part-time society, where you have to make temporal commitments to counter-productive processes. Like being a television producer or an education officer, as I was, or a teacher inside an education system which is supportive of bourgeois values--and all the rest of it."

The action of *The Party* takes place against the background of the *événements*—the student demonstrations in Paris which threatened the De Gaulle administration in May 1968. While the demonstrations are taking place, representatives of various left-wing organizations in Britain gather in the fashionable Southwest London apartment of television producer Joe Shawcross to discuss the way ahead for British revolutionary socialism. A focal point of the meeting is a lengthy analysis of the existing political situation from the lecturer, Andrew Ford, and the Glaswegian Trotskyite John Tagg. Gradually, and with a great deal of subtlety, those who gather at the Shawcross apartment are worked into a microcosm of the revolutionary left-wing movement in Britain, the collective hope in Britain of a better society. As the action develops, however, it becomes clear that the individuals present are, in their varying ways, compromised, ineffectual, self-hating, or paralyzed by a sense of failure. Shawcross and his friend, playwright Malcolm Sloman, for example, are embittered and paralyzed by the awareness that they are successes in a bourgeois world which their political convictions have taught them to despise, and Griffiths, in fact, works Shawcross's sexual failure with his wife into a symbol of his wider spiritual failure as an individual and as a social being. Other characters, such as the academic Ford, are seen to be hypocritical, self-seeking, or puerile. Only Tagg embodies the force

A scene from the first production of The Party. *Laurence Olivier is at the extreme left.*

of character needed to keep hope in the revolution alive; significantly, Tagg is dying of cancer—his approaching death the symbol of the fading hopes of the bright socialist future.

    In dialogue, characterization, and symbolic strategy, *The Party* is a triumph of dramatic writing. The theoretical debate, rooted as it is within the context of commanding characterizations, is invested with vigor and passion; minor characters such as "Grease" Ball, the North London anarchist working in street theater, are vividly drawn. The result is that Griffiths achieves in this play a complex and powerful statement of the exhaustion of contemporary British society. In the words of Michael Billington, *The Party* is a drama which is "complex, gritty, intellectually fascinating."

    Comedians, first presented in Nottingham in February 1975, and subsequently given its first London production in September 1975, is further testimony to the richness of Griffiths's dramatic tal-

ent. In a run-down Manchester schoolroom, six aspiring comedians gather for a final coaching session under the tutelage of Eddie Waters, once a stand-up comedian of great eminence. All six are shortly to appear at a local bingo club where talent scout Bert Challenor will be on hand to select the more promising comics for future engagements. The play focuses upon the coaching session, the subsequent performances at the bingo hall, and the eventual fortunes of the six aspirants, placing particular stress upon the relationship between the old pro Waters and his most talented protege, Gethin Price.

    Commentators have interpreted the play as an exploration into the nature and the processes—psychological, emotional, instinctive—of a comic performer. Peter Ansorge, for example, has seen it as "a beautiful, multi-layered and unforgettable account of the comic art." This is a concern which Griffiths himself has admitted is central to the play. He has pointed out that "the characteristic of the

1

Act One.

A classroom in a secondary school, ~~built just built around~~
in Manchester, about three miles east of the centre, on the way
~~towards~~ Ashton-under-Lyne and the hills of east Lancashire. ~~The~~
~~school was built in 1947.~~ Built 1947 in the now disappearing but
still familiar two-storey style, the school doubles as evening
centre for the area, and will fill, as the evening progresses, with
the followers of yoga, karate, cordon bleu cookery, 'O' level
English, secretarial prelims, do-it-yourself, small investments
and antique furniture. Adults will return to school, and
the school will do its sullen best to accommodate them.

This room, on the ground floor, is smallish,
about a dozen chipped and fraying desks, two dozen
chairs set out in rows facing the small dais
~~on which stands~~ the teacher's desk, with green blackboard unwiped
from the day's last stand beyond. Two starkish lights on the
window side of the room, ~~on~~ are on, finishing, don't afford of it.
~~the room with thirty reluctances.~~ A clock, over the
board says 7.27. ~~[It's a real clock, keeping real time~~
~~for the evening].~~ Cupboards of haphazard heights
and styles line the walls, ~~below~~ above which the tired
dogged maps, charts, tables, illustrations and notices
warp, fray, tear, curl and droop their way to limbo.
Windows on the left wall show the night dark and
wet.

→   Gethin Price arrives, in wet raincoat, ~~braces~~
~~three or four inches above~~ carrying a long canvas bag and
a pint mug of hot water. He puts down bag and mug
by a desk, ~~returns to switch on the remaining lights,~~
~~returns to the desk,~~ removes coats and shirt, & takes
shaving tackle from the bag and sits, in his
greying vest, to shave in the tiny mirror he has propped

The caretaker finishes, descends, catches sight of Price, almost falls the final step to the floor.

> **Caretaker**
> Are you in here?

Price looks round, behind, about, with strange, clown-like timing, the foam gleaming like a mask, brush poised.

> **Price** [finally]
> Yeah.

The caretaker sniffs, looks for his clipboard and list of classes; scans it.

> **Caretaker**
> I don't see it.

> **Price**
> Been here since ~~Septem~~ January.
> [Pause] Mr. Waters.....

> **Caretaker**
> Waters. Oh, him [~~St~~ Studying
> Price at his ablutions]. What is it,
> Gents' Hairdressing?

> **Price**
> Yeah. Somet like that.

> **Caretaker**
> I thought you practised on balloons.
> I saw it once in a film . . .

He stumps out, carrying the ladder, ~~Price~~ pins Phil Murray to the door as they pass.
~~Yeah, but that was before the raw materials market~~

play is to set up something as funny and then take a look at it and say 'Well, that's not really so funny' and this could become increasingly disturbing for audiences. If the play works at all, by the end the audience should be making some very conscious evaluations about what they laugh at."

Yet *Comedians* is more than a study of the dynamics of comic art. A principal source of the play's energy, tension, and conflict is in Griffiths's depiction of the relationship between Eddie Waters and Gethin Price. Waters is fascinated by Price because he sees his own past embodied in the younger man, whose comic routine is by implication a masterly and terrifying indictment of social injustice in contemporary Britain. The older man's own greatness as a stand-up comic was similarly rooted in his rage against the evils of British society; but at the time of the play's action, Waters is drained of his former anger, and significantly, the wellsprings of his talent have dried up. Waters and Price represent in fact polarized responses to the evils of British society: the former clothes his despair and his impotence in an appeal to compassion, while the latter suggests an extreme of violent negation. Neither response is adequate, and the play closes on a note of futility and defeat.

Through the group of comedians, therefore, Griffiths establishes a brilliant microcosmic symbol of the range of possible responses to the corruption of the contemporary social system. Some of the group, like Sammy Samuels and Phil Murray, compromise their art to achieve success (defined here in terms of the approval of the talent scout Challenor); they are absorbed and defeated by commercialism, just as Shawcross and Sloman in *The Party* are sucked into a bourgeois world whose values they despise. Waters and Price, on the other hand, do not compromise in this fashion. But again, we sense the pessimism of Griffiths's vision, the deepening uncertainty of his hopes for Britain. Waters's compassion is, ultimately, a collapse into silence. Price possesses the energy but not the leadership to create the revolution, and can only wait for a leader.

Comedians is a somber, complex, and fascinating play, even more subtle in its symbolism than *The Party*. It testifies to a growing maturity on Griffiths's part in his ability to dramatize political themes without a cheapening in the human texture of his writing; he never allows his interest in pushing a political thesis to loosen his grasp on the human complexity of his chosen dramatic situations. *Comedians* fully justifies Catherine Itzin's contention that Griffiths is "one of the most important Marxist playwrights of the seventies," while the overall achievement of *Occupations*, *The Party*, and *Comedians* lends more than ample substance to Peter Ansorge's claim

Jonathan Pryce in a scene from the first London production of The Comedians

that Griffiths is British drama's "most capable explorer of the dilemmas which confront the radical imagination."

In the meantime, Griffiths continues in his conviction that the television drama is his proper medium, by its very nature being able to attract the audiences whom he hopes to reach. Indeed, Griffiths has done honorable work in this medium. Television plays such as *All Good Men* (1974), *Through the Night* (1975), and the unproduced *Such Impossibilities* (published in 1977) display Griffiths's gifts for poignant and compelling characterization to the full. Edward Waite, the protagonist of *All Good Men*, is a splendid creation, a Manchester working-class figure who rose from the position of a simple miner to high Trade Union and cabinet offices. His progress is a paradigm of the achievements of the working class in the twentieth century, and at the same time a reminder (in the painful details of his professional and personal lives) of the spiritual and emotional compromises necessary for success within the system. *Through the Night* focuses upon a twenty-nine-year-old woman, Christine Potts, who enters a National Health hospital for the examination of a lump in her breast which is revealed to be cancerous. At the center of the play's conflict is the unwillingness of the authorities, who have Christine's breast removed, to treat her as a human being possessed of the intelligence and responsibility to confront a problem of this nature. The satiric point of the play resides in the impersonality of bureaucracy and in the dehumanizing effects of the system which the hospital represents.

Griffiths's work in the medium of television drama certainly does no damage to his reputation as a writer, and his work as coauthor with Warren Beatty of the screenplay of *Reds* (1981), is formidable proof of his screenwriting talents. Nevertheless, his achievement in television seems somewhat thin in comparison with the stage plays. The television plays are informed by their author's characteristic humanity, his grasp of character, and his feeling for telling detail; but the stage plays possess a resonance, a symbolic richness and complexity which render them superior works of art. It would be a pity if Griffiths should turn his attention entirely to television: that medium would gain a competent craftsman, but the stage would lose a provocative and original artist.

Screenplay:

Reds, by Griffiths and Warren Beatty, Paramount, 1981.

Television Scripts:

The Silver Mask, adapted from Horace Walpole's short story, London Weekend Television, 1973;

Occupations, Granada, 1974;

All Good Men, BBC, 1974;

Absolute Beginners, BBC, 1974;

Through the Night, BBC, 1975;

Bill Brand, Thames Television, 1976;

Comedians, BBC, 1980;

Sons and Lovers, adapted from D. H. Lawrence's novel, BBC, 1981;

The Cherry Orchard, adapted from Helen Rappaport's translation of Anton Chekhov's play, BBC, 1981;

Country: "A Tory Story," BBC, 1981.

Radio Scripts:

The Big House, BBC Radio 4, 1969;

Jake's Brigade, BBC Radio 4, 1971.

Periodical Publications:

Sam, Sam, Plays and Players, 19 (April 1972);

Letter to the editor, *Plays and Players*, 21 (October 1974): 6.

Interviews:

Nigel Andrews, "A Play Postscript," *Plays and Players*, 19 (April 1972): 82-83;

Robert Cushman, "Towards the Mountain Top," *Plays and Players*, 21 (August 1974): 14-19;

Catherine Itzin and Simon Trussler, "Transforming the Husk of Capitalism," *Theatre Quarterly*, 6 (Summer 1976): 25-46;

Pat Silburn, "*Gambit* Interview: Pat Silburn Talks to Trevor Griffiths," *Gambit*, 8, no. 29 (1976): 30-36;

Alison Summers, "Trevor Griffiths: Politics and Populist Culture," *Canadian Theatre Review* (Summer 1980): 22-29;

John Wyver, "Countering Consent," in his *Ah! Mischief—The Writer and Television* (London: Faber & Faber, 1982).

References:

Peter Ansorge, *Disrupting the Spectacle* (London: Pitman, 1975), pp. 63-66;

Stephen Dixon, "Joking Apart," *Guardian*, 19 February 1975, p. 10;

Malcolm Hay, "Theatre Checklist No. 9: Trevor Griffiths," *Theatrefacts*, 3, no. 1 (1976): 2-8, 36;

Albert Hunt, "A Theatre of Ideas," *New Society*, 16 January 1975, pp. 138-140.

Christopher Hampton
(26 January 1946-)

Brian F. Tyson
University of Lethbridge

PRODUCTIONS: *When Did You Last See My Mother?*, 5 June 1966, Royal Court Theatre (transferred 4 July 1966 to Comedy Theatre), London, 26 [performances]; 4 January 1967, Young People's Repertory Theatre, New York;

Marya, adapted from Michael Glenny and Harold Shukman's translation of Isaac Babel's play, 19 October 1967, Royal Court Theatre, London, 25;

Total Eclipse, 11 September 1968, Royal Court Theatre, London, 19;

Uncle Vanya, adapted from Nina Froud's translation of Anton Chekhov's play, 24 February 1970, Royal Court Theatre, London, 45;

Hedda Gabler, adapted from Henrik Ibsen's play, 10 June 1970, National Theatre, Stratford, Ontario, 22;

The Philanthropist, 3 August 1970, Royal Court Theatre (transferred 7 September 1970 to Mayfair Theatre), London, 1,114; 15 March 1971, Ethel Barrymore Theatre, New York, 72;

Don Juan, translated and adapted from Molière's play, 1970, BBC Radio 3, London; 24 May 1972, Theatre Royal, Bristol;

A Doll's House, adapted from Hélène Gregoire's translation of Ibsen's play, 13 January 1971, Playhouse Theatre, New York, 89;

Savages, 5 April 1973, Royal Court Theatre (transferred 20 June 1973 to Comedy Theatre), London, 32;

Treats, 4 February 1976, Royal Court Theatre (transferred 6 March 1976 to Mayfair Theatre), London;

Tales from the Vienna Woods, adapted from Ödön von Horvath's play, 21 January 1977, Olivier Theatre (National Theatre), London;

Don Juan Comes Back from the War, adapted from von Horvath's play, 18 April 1978, Cottesloe Theatre (National Theatre), London;

Ghosts, adapted from Ibsen's play, 25 September 1978, Key Theatre, Peterborough;

The Wild Duck, adapted from Ibsen's play, 13 December 1979, Olivier Theatre (National Theatre), London;

The Portage to San Cristobal of A. H., adapted from George Steiner's novel, 17 February 1982, Mermaid Theatre, London;

Tales of Hollywood, 25 March 1982, Mark Taper Forum, Los Angeles.

BOOKS: *When Did You Last See My Mother?* (London: Faber & Faber, 1967; New York: Grove, 1967);

Total Eclipse (London: Faber & Faber, 1969; New York: French, 1972);

The Philanthropist (London: Faber & Faber, 1970; New York: French, 1971);

Hedda Gabler, adapted from Henrik Ibsen's play (London & New York: French, 1972);

A Doll's House, adapted from Hélène Gregoire's translation of Ibsen's play (London & New York: French, 1972);

Don Juan, adapted from Molière's play (London: Faber & Faber, 1974);

Savages (London: Faber & Faber, 1974; revised edition, London: French, 1977);

Treats (London: Faber & Faber, 1976; New York & London: French, 1976);

Tales from the Vienna Woods, adapted from Ödön von Horvath's play (London: Faber & Faber, 1977);

Don Juan Comes Back from the War, adapted from von Horvath's play (London: Faber & Faber, 1978);

Able's Will (London: Faber & Faber, 1979).

Just as John Osborne burst onto the contemporary stage in 1956 with *Look Back in Anger*, so, a decade later, at the same theater, Christopher Hampton made his debut to similar acclaim with *When Did You Last See My Mother?*. Comparison between the two dramatists is inevitable: both write in a style of modified realism; both deal with the problem of the social misfit; both portray characters who are ferociously articulate; and in much of the work of both there is a powerful political subtext. Yet Hampton is markedly of a different generation: one whose anger is under better control than that of Osborne's generation. Hampton's work is witty, intelligent, and carefully structured, and he has al-

Christopher Hampton

ready provided a memorable body of plays.

Born at Faial in the Azores, Christopher James Hampton is the son of Bernard Patrick Hampton, a marine telecommunications engineer, and Dorothy Patience Herrington Hampton. He went to school in Aden and Alexandria, Egypt, before being repatriated from Suez in 1956 to a boys' preparatory school in Reigate, England. In 1959 he won a scholarship to Lancing College in Sussex, where he boarded for three years, visiting his parents abroad once a year during the holidays. He was accepted at New College, Oxford, to read German and French, but first came to London, where he did odd jobs and in the evenings wrote his first play, *When Did You Last See My Mother?*. He was eighteen at the time, and he wrote the play because "the entire plot came to me in 15 minutes when I was sitting in a pub." It took him only six weeks to write the play, but two years passed before it was produced. Submitted during his second year at Oxford to an undergraduate play festival, the work was chosen three weeks before the opening night when one of the two previously selected plays failed in rehearsal. Since the remaining entry also collapsed, Hampton's play, starring its author, was the only work to be presented. The performance was favorably reviewed by the *Manchester Guardian*. Faber and Faber asked to see the manuscript, which they published the following year. Hampton was advised by Elizabeth Sweeting of the Oxford Playhouse to send the play to theatrical agent Margaret Ramsay, who arranged with the Royal Court Theatre for the play's first professional production on 5 June 1966. Hampton's career as a dramatist was launched.

Julian Holloway, Lucy Fleming, and Victor Henry in a scene from the first London production of
When Did You Last See My Mother?

When Did You Last See My Mother? concerns two young men, Ian and Jimmy, who share a bedroom-sitting room in London while waiting to go to the university. Both are shedding the comfortably familiar homosexuality of their youth spent in a single-sex school and taking their first steps into a heterosexual world. After a fierce row, Jimmy storms out and returns to live with his parents. His mother visits Ian to discover the cause of the dispute between the two boys, is clearly attracted to him, and they make love. When she returns to apologize for her behavior, Ian brutally tells her that he only made love to her because she reminded him of her son. Later, Jimmy informs Ian of his mother's death in a car crash that followed a row at home, and Ian cannot bring himself to confess his affair with her. Only after Jimmy has left does Ian remark that, even after having seduced the mother and indirectly caused her death, he will probably make love to her son again.

For a first effort, *When Did You Last See My Mother?* is a remarkable play. Technically, it is marked by an almost Mozartean economy of line;

for together with Hampton's strong sense of structure, evident in his use of parallel scenes and leitmotiv, there is an emotional intensity locked beneath the lines sufficient to overcome even the melodramatic car crash, perhaps the one revelation of the apprentice hand. The portrait of youthful despair is well done, but the major themes are touched on rather than explored: the search among the young for love and self-realization; the want of understanding between generations; and the tragedies that these problems can lead to. Described by the *Times* as "an astonishing first play" and by the *London Magazine* as "one that speaks firmly and decisively with the voice of a new generation," *When Did You Last See My Mother?* had two performances at the Royal Court Theatre and then began a three-week run at the Comedy Theatre in July 1966. Six months later, on 4 January 1967, it opened at the Young People's Repertory Theatre Off Broadway.

In 1967, Hampton took a year off from Oxford to improve his German and joined the Schauspielhaus in Hamburg, where his job was to read

English plays and write reports on them in German. This association lasted for six weeks, following which he traveled first to Munich, then to Brussels, and finally to Paris, where he made money translating lectures on James Joyce and began researching his next play, *Total Eclipse* (1968), a historical drama about two French poets. He finished writing the play in Paris and, returning to Oxford, took a First Class degree in 1968. There was some possibility of his continuing his studies toward a doctorate, but William Gaskill, director at the Royal Court Theatre, wishing to keep contact with Hampton, created for him there the position of resident dramatist.

Evidently, Hampton's first play had been a working draft for his second. *Total Eclipse* concerns the sixteen-year-old French poet Arthur Rimbaud and the older poet Paul Verlaine, ten years Rimbaud's senior. Their tempestuous two-year relationship, climaxed by Verlaine's shooting Rimbaud, is clearly Hampton's primary concern in this play; but a secondary theme is the contrast between their attitudes toward their art. For Rimbaud, poetry was a godlike activity; for Verlaine it was

merely a craft to be plied. Consequently, when Rimbaud discovered that his work did not have a transforming effect upon society, he simply stopped writing poetry altogether after the age of twenty. Verlaine persisted, although both he and his poetry were in decline for many years. No doubt the need to dramatize a sequence of historical facts prevented Hampton from more fully developing this theme. *Total Eclipse* opened in September 1968, and was a success, although many reviewers devoted more time to discussing the poets than the play itself. Martin Esslin, however, believed that Hampton had succeeded in portraying the characters as men of genius. Esslin went on to say, "His dialogue is witty and lyrical in turn; the characters emerge as real people; the language creates a credible atmosphere of French people. . . ."

During this time Hampton also tried his hand at adaptation, writing versions of Isaac Babel's *Marya*, produced in 1967, Anton Chekhov's *Uncle Vanya*, produced in 1970, and Henrik Ibsen's *Hedda Gabler*, produced in 1970 in Stratford, Ontario. Hampton's special interest in Molière (which had led to his translating *Don Juan*, broadcast in 1970

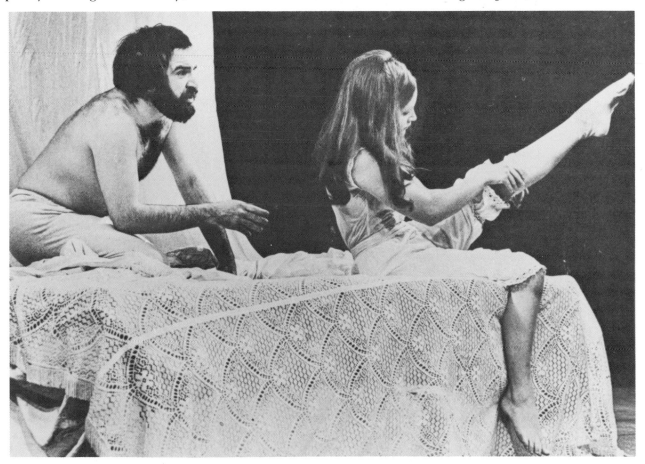

John Grillo and Michele Dotrice in the first London production of Total Eclipse

and staged in 1972) also blossomed into his own successful comedy *The Philanthropist* (1970), which he conceived as a "riposte to *Le Misanthrope*." The action of Hampton's play takes place in the quiet of a bachelor don's rooms at a university, but the play begins with a spectacular coup de théâtre. A young man holds a revolver as he faces two companions. He takes a passionate leave of them, holds the revolver to his head, and says "Bang." He is an author reading aloud the conclusion of his play. One of the men, Don, criticizes the suicide ending as improbable; and Philip, a philologist who enjoys all words uncritically, infuriates the young author even more by his bland approval. The author believes the play's conclusion by suicide could be quite powerful. To prove it, he again holds the revolver to his head, this time blowing his brains out.

Philip, the philanthropist, is the converse of Alceste in *Le Misanthrope*: condemning society's hypocritical behavior, Alceste vows to speak and act with complete honesty; Philip, on the other hand, is unable to see faults in people. Paradoxically, this characteristic in Philip produces the same effect as if he were misanthropic. We see the disastrous consequences of his benign responses to numerous acquaintances including a seductress, an episode which brings about the collapse of his engagement to another girl, and the play ends with Philip in despair but too indecisive to commit suicide, except symbolically by taking up smoking again. Hampton has matched Molière's play with parallel themes and incidents; but in addition *The Philanthropist* examines the contrast between the worlds of action and contemplation, stressing the violence of the former (numerous prominent figures are reported to have been assassinated in offstage action), and the utter ineffectuality of the latter, as seen in the character of Philip. *The Philanthropist* is impressive in its combination of wit and passion; in the development of the play's other themes, loneliness

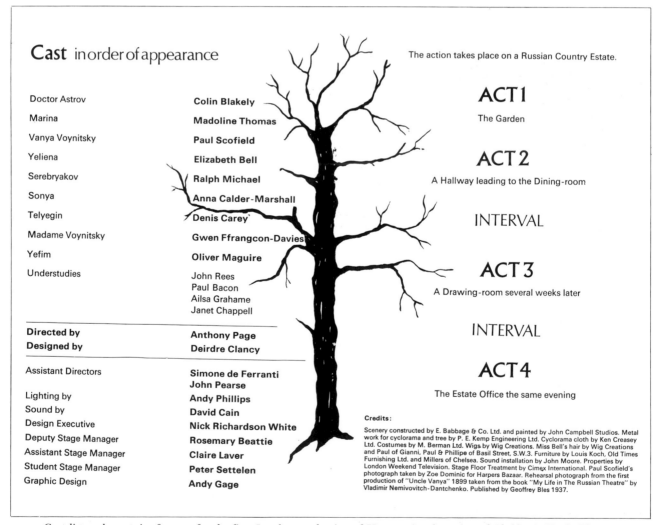

Cast in order of appearance

Doctor Astrov — **Colin Blakely**
Marina — **Madoline Thomas**
Vanya Voynitsky — **Paul Scofield**
Yeliena — **Elizabeth Bell**
Serebryakov — **Ralph Michael**
Sonya — **Anna Calder-Marshall**
Telyegin — **Denis Carey**
Madame Voynitsky — **Gwen Ffrangcon-Davies**
Yefim — **Oliver Maguire**
Understudies — John Rees
Paul Bacon
Ailsa Grahame
Janet Chappell

Directed by — **Anthony Page**
Designed by — **Deirdre Clancy**

Assistant Directors — **Simone de Ferranti**
John Pearse
Lighting by — **Andy Phillips**
Sound by — **David Cain**
Design Executive — **Nick Richardson White**
Deputy Stage Manager — **Rosemary Beattie**
Assistant Stage Manager — **Claire Laver**
Student Stage Manager — **Peter Settelen**
Graphic Design — **Andy Gage**

The action takes place on a Russian Country Estate.

ACT 1
The Garden

ACT 2
A Hallway leading to the Dining-room

INTERVAL

ACT 3
A Drawing-room several weeks later

INTERVAL

ACT 4
The Estate Office the same evening

Credits:
Scenery constructed by E. Babbage & Co. Ltd. and painted by John Campbell Studios. Metal work for cyclorama and tree by P. E. Kemp Engineering Ltd. Cyclorama cloth by Ken Creasey Ltd. Costumes by M. Berman Ltd. Wigs by Wig Creations. Miss Bell's hair by Wig Creations and Paul of Gianni, Paul & Phillipe of Basil Street, S.W.3. Furniture by Louis Koch, Old Times Furnishing Ltd. and Millers of Chelsea. Sound installation by John Moore. Properties by London Weekend Television. Stage Floor Treatment by Cimex International. Paul Scofield's photograph taken by Zoe Dominic for Harpers Bazaar. Rehearsal photograph from the first production of "Uncle Vanya" 1899 taken from the book "My Life in The Russian Theatre" by Vladimir Nemivovitch-Dantchenko. Published by Geoffrey Bles 1937.

Cast list and synopsis of scenes for the first London production of Hampton's adaptation of Chekhov's Uncle Vanya

Program cover and title page for the first London production of Hampton's "riposte to Le Misanthrope"

and incompatibility; and in the contrast between those who succeed on the world's terms and Philip, who fails on his own.

When the play opened in August 1970, it was described by Irving Wardle in the *Times* as a "gently mocking comedy of academic manners," while for *Nation* critic Harold Clurman its strength lay in the creation of Philip, a character "usually accounted undramatically flaccid and which Hampton has nevertheless made entirely worth concern." Transferred in September to the Mayfair Theatre, *The Philanthropist* was still running at year's end, and was voted best new play of 1970 by the London theater critics in the poll conducted by *Plays and Players* magazine. It also won in 1970 the *Evening Standard* Drama Award for best comedy. Its first production

had coincided with the expiration of Hampton's two-year term as resident dramatist at the Royal Court Theatre, a period during which he had clearly learned much about the practical aspects of the theater.

In 1970, Hampton married Laura de Holesch, a social worker; and in September of that year he was commissioned by Hillard Elkins to adapt Ibsen's *A Doll's House* for production in New York. The play opened at the Playhouse Theatre in January 1971 and was favorably received, with Clive Barnes claiming that it had "the freshness of a new play about it." *The Philanthropist*, which opened at New York's Ethel Barrymore Theatre on 15 March, was also well received by the critics, the chorus of praise being loud enough for Hampton to be voted Most

Promising Playwright (1971) by *Variety*'s poll of the New York drama critics. By this time *The Philanthropist* had also played successfully in Germany (winning wide acclaim at the annual Berlin Theater Review), and in Sweden, just as later it enjoyed a successful premiere in French at the Europalia Festival in Brussels.

The inspiration for Hampton's next play, *Savages* (1973), came from Norman Lewis's article "Genocide," published in the *Sunday Times Magazine* in 1966, which told of the genocide being practiced on Brazilian Indians by both rich landowners and the Brazilian government. Hampton began to write the play in London but felt he had to visit Brazil before continuing. When the authorities discouraged his stay there, Hampton resumed his research in London and, in the interest of authenticity, had his script checked by Lewis and the production itself supervised by an anthropologist.

Savages concerns the kidnapping of a British diplomat (appropriately named West) in Brazil by members of a revolutionary movement. Scenes of West's conversation with his captors alternate with scenes depicting the Indian death/rebirth ritual known as the Quarup and flashbacks which constitute a series of revelations about the destruction of the Indian tribes. The climax of the play is the bombing of the Indian village during the Quarup, which coincides with the shooting of West by his captors. The play is more overtly political than Hampton's previous ones, but it shares their prevailing concerns. The diplomat possesses the same kind of benevolent impotence as the philanthropist; again, as in *Total Eclipse*, a confrontation between contemplation and commitment occurs. In *Savages* this confrontation is better managed dramatically, the violence of the world of action being brought into collision with the powerlessness of the contemplative world by means of the hostage-taking device.

The play premiered at the Royal Court Theatre in April 1973 to mixed reviews. Interestingly, on its transfer to the Comedy Theatre on 20 June, the reviews warmed up considerably, and by December *Savages* shared with Athol Fugard's *Sizwe Bansi is Dead* the honor of being voted best new play of 1973 by the London theater critics in the annual poll conducted by *Plays and Players*.

Savages was performed in Hamburg during the 1973-1974 season and received its premiere in French in Brussels a year later. On 15 August 1974, the play opened at the Mark Taper Forum in Los Angeles, Hampton having flown to the United States to make changes in his original text. The critics praised the play highly, and Hampton was awarded the Los Angeles Drama Critics Circle Playwriting Award for distinguished theatrical productions and performances in Los Angeles during the 1974-1975 season.

In an interview in late 1973, Hampton said he was working on "a play of a more personal nature—with three characters." This project was *Treats*, first performed in 1976. The play presents a love triangle in which Ann has to choose between Dave, an amusing but aggressive journalist, and Patrick, a rather dull companion from the office. The play is little more than a jeu d'esprit and is full of echoes of Hampton's dramatic past. Patrick is the familiar portrait of indecision, literal-mindedness, and general helplessness, traits found in Philip (and to some extent in West), while the Irish protests about the home secretary (mere offstage noises in *Treats*) are reminders of the ghoulish offstage assassinations in *The Philanthropist*. Thematically, the play is slight, perhaps functioning best as an illustration of Don's theory in *The Philanthropist* that "we're only capable of loving people who are fundamentally incompatible with us."

Hampton himself said that he found *Treats* an unsatisfactory experience, and for the next four years he devoted himself to adaptation and to writing for television and the cinema, a medium he has always loved. He had previously completed four screenplays, so far not filmed: "When Did You Last See My Mother?" (written in 1966), "The Tenant" (written in 1972 and based on Roland Topor's novel), "A Temporary Life" (written in 1974 and based on David Storey's novel), and "The Moon and Sixpence" (written in 1975 and based on W. Somerset Maugham's novel). His next three filmscripts, "Carrington" (written in 1978 and based on Michael Holroyd's biography of Lytton Strachey), "The Last Secret" (written in 1979 and based on Nicholas Bethell's book), and "The Honorary Consul" (written in 1980 and based on a novel by Graham Greene), also remain unproduced. Two others did reach the screen: *A Doll's House*, directed by Patrick Garland, released in 1974, and *Geschichten aus dem Wiener-Wald*, (Tales from the Vienna Woods), written in collaboration with and directed by Maximilian Schell, released in 1979.

Also produced during this period was Hampton's first original television play, *Able's Will* (1977). It concerns a rich writer who is dying and who, inexplicably, has not written for thirty years. Those unfamiliar with Hampton's literary activity

Jane Asher, James Bolam, and Stephen Moore in the first London production of Treats

from 1976-1980 might be forgiven for seeing in this reprise of Rimbaud's problem personal significance for a writer whose stage activity at this time was confined to adaptations of works by Ödön von Horvath and Ibsen. Moreover, Hampton's successful television adaptation in 1981 of Malcolm Bradbury's *The History Man*, with its strong satire on the academy, is a resumption of his prime concern in *The Philanthropist*.

Hampton returned to stage plays in the 1980s: *Tales of Hollywood*, which concerns expatriate European intellectuals in Hollywood during World War II, and *The Portage to San Cristobal of A. H.*, based upon a novel by George Steiner, in which a ninety-year-old Hitler is captured in the Brazilian jungles by vengeful Israelis. This play disturbingly returns to the political paradoxes evident in *Savages* and was controversial when first produced in February 1982.

Screenplays:
A Doll's House, adapted from Henrik Ibsen's play, E.M.I., 1974;

Geschichten aus dem Wiener-Wald, by Hampton and Maximilian Schell, Constantin Films, 1979.

Television Script:
The History Man, adapted from Malcolm Bradbury's novel, BBC, 1981.

Radio Script:
Don Juan, BBC Radio 3, 1970.

Other:
Isaac Babel, *Marya*, adapted by Hampton from Michael Glenny and Harold Shukman's translation, in *Plays of the Year 35* (London: Elek, 1969);
Anton Chekhov, *Uncle Vanya*, adapted by Hampton from Nina Froud's translation, in *Plays of the Year 39* (London: Elek, 1971).

Interviews:
"Christopher Hampton interviewed by Brendan Hennessy," *Transatlantic Review*, 31 (Winter 1968-1969): 90-96;
"Hampton's Court, W. Stephen Gilbert talks to the

author of *Savages*," *Plays and Players*, 20 (May 1973): 36-38;

"Hampton on his Early Plays," *Theatre Quarterly III* (October/December 1973): 62-67;

"The Art of Finding English for Ibsen; Hampton interviewed by John Higgins," *New York Times*, 12 December 1979, p. C11.

References:

Jules Aaron, Review of *Savages*, *Educational Theatre Journal*, 27 (March 1975): 117;

Harold Clurman, Review of *Total Eclipse*, *Nation*, 218 (16 March 1974): 348-349;

Martin Esslin, "Document of A Passion," review of *Total Eclipse*, *Plays and Players*, 16 (November 1968): 18-19;

Esslin, "In Search of 'Savages,'" *Theatre Quarterly III*, (October/December 1973): 79-83;

Brendan Gill, "Troubled Don," review of *The Philanthropist*, *New Yorker*, 47 (27 March 1971): 83;

John Hall, "Bona fide boy wonder," *Times Educa-tional Supplement Review*, 6 April 1973, p. 23;

Peter Holland, "The Director Intervenes: Christopher Hampton's *Savages*," *Comparative Drama*, 13 (Summer 1979): 142-149;

John Holmstrom, "Crippled Gadfly," review of *When Did You Last See My Mother?*, *Plays and Players*, 13 (September 1966): 23, 66;

J. W. Lambert, Review of *Treats*, *Drama*, no. 121 (Summer 1976): 45-47;

Frank Marcus, "A New Voice," *London Magazine*, new series, 6 (September 1966): 99-100;

Jonathan Rice, "All the School's a Stage," *Daily Telegraph Magazine*, 9 August 1974, pp. 22-23, 25-26;

Ruth Morris Schneider, "The Interpolated Narrative in Modern Drama," Ph.D. dissertation, State University of New York, 1973;

Irving Wardle, "Maladies of Youth," review of *When Did You Last See My Mother?*, *Times* (London), 12 August 1970, p. 10;

Wardle, "With respect," review of *The Philanthropist*, *Times* (London), 4 August 1970, p. 10.

David Hare
(5 June 1947-)

Roger N. Cornish
Pennsylvania State University

PRODUCTIONS: *Inside Out*, adapted by Hare and Tony Bicât from Kafka's diaries, 1968, Portable Theatre, London;

How Brophy Made Good, 1969, Brighton Combination Theatre, Brighton;

Slag, 2 April 1970, Hampstead Theatre Club, London; 21 February 1971, Public Theatre, New York; 24 May 1971, Royal Court Theatre, London;

What Happened to Blake, 28 September 1970, Royal Court Theatre Upstairs, London;

The Rules of the Game, adapted by Hare and Robert Rietty from Luigi Pirandello's *Il giuoco delle parti*, 15 June 1971, New Theatre, London;

Lay By, by Hare, Howard Brenton, Brian Clark, Trevor Griffiths, Steven Poliakoff, Hugh Stoddart, and Snoo Wilson, 24 August 1971, Traverse Theatre, Edinburgh; 26 September 1971, Royal Court Theatre, London;

Deathsheads, 1971, Edinburgh Festival, Edinburgh;

The Great Exhibition, 28 February 1972, Hampstead Theatre Club, London;

England's Ireland, by Hare, Bicât, Brenton, Clark, David Edgar, Francis Fuchs, and Wilson, September 1972, Mickery Theatre, Amsterdam; 2 October 1972, Round House Theatre, London;

Brassneck, by Hare and Brenton, 10 September 1973, Nottingham Playhouse, Nottingham;

Knuckle, 29 January 1974, Oxford Playhouse, Oxford; 4 March 1974, Comedy Theatre, London; 23 January 1975, Playhouse II, New York;

Fanshen, adapted from William Hinton's *Fanshen: A Documentary of Revolution in a Chinese Village*, 10 March 1975, Institute of Contemporary Arts Terrace Theatre, London;

Teeth 'n' Smiles, music by Nick Bicât and Tony Bicât,

David Hare, 1977

2 September 1975, Royal Court Theatre
(transferred 24 May 1976 to Wyndham's
Theatre), London; 4 April 1980, Folger
Theatre, Washington, D. C.;

Deeds, by Hare, Brenton, Ken Campbell, and Griffiths, 8 March 1978, Nottingham Playhouse,
Nottingham;

Plenty, 12 April 1978, Lyttelton Theatre (National
Theatre), London; 4 April 1980, Arena Stage,
Washington, D. C.

BOOKS: *Slag* (London: Faber & Faber, 1971);

Lay By, by Hare, Howard Brenton, Brian Clark,
Trevor Griffiths, Steven Poliakoff, Hugh
Stoddart, and Snoo Wilson (London: Calder &
Boyars, 1972);

The Great Exhibition (London: Faber & Faber, 1972);

Brassneck, by Hare and Brenton (London: Eyre
Methuen, 1974);

Knuckle (London: Faber & Faber, 1974; London &
New York: French, 1974);

Fanshen, adapted from William Hinton's *Fanshen: A
Documentary of Revolution in a Chinese Village*
(London: Faber & Faber, 1976);

Teeth 'n' Smiles (London: Faber & Faber, 1976);

Licking Hitler (London: Faber & Faber, 1978);

Plenty (London & Boston: Faber & Faber, 1978);

Dreams of Leaving (London: Faber & Faber, 1980).

David Hare stands as a leader in the generation of young British dramatists who came to the
fore in the 1970s, a group that includes David
Edgar, Trevor Griffiths, Steven Poliakoff, and the
so-called "wild bunch," Howard Brenton, Snoo Wilson, Howard Barker, and Hare himself. He is dou-
bly important because he has assisted the others as a
founder of fringe companies that first mounted
their work and as the director of some of their first
productions. For example, he is credited with com-
missioning and then directing one of Howard
Brenton's first important plays, *Christie in Love*
(1969). At the Royal Court Theatre, he directed
Snoo Wilson's *The Pleasure Principle* (1973) and
Tony Bicât's *Devil's Island* (1977). At the National
Theatre, he directed Brenton's *Weapons of Happiness*
(1976), and for the BBC he directed his own teleplay, *Dreams of Leaving* (1980). So total a man of the
theater is he that his productivity is the more
remarkable.

Born in Sussex, Hare was educated at Lancing
College and at Jesus College, Cambridge, where he
earned an honors M.A. in English. There he began
directing plays and formed a friendship with Tony
Bicât, with whom, after Cambridge, he collaborated
on a play and formed the Portable Theatre Company, a peripatetic experimental group which performed wherever it could find a house and an audience. Hare wrote his first three plays for the Portable Theatre and established it as one of the forces
in England's fringe theater movement, a loose collection of small semiprofessional groups that might
be likened to New York's Off-Off-Broadway. He
served as a Portable Theatre director from its
founding in 1968 until 1971 while simultaneously
serving as literary manager of the Royal Court
Theatre from 1969 to 1970 and as Royal Court
resident dramatist from 1970 to 1971.

Hare is a self-declared political playwright
who also writes about romantic love. His politics are
decidedly left wing, but Hare's plays are not crudely
polemical. His concern is to hold up for examination the history of postwar England, which his plays
suggest is dominated by lies, corruption, and the
inability to change toward a more rational mode of
politics. Often there lies at the heart of a Hare play a
romantic relationship which is somehow poisoned
by the larger world of English decay.

In both the political and the private story, lies
tend to dominate. Hare has said that the theater is at
its best when portraying lies, and he believes that the
moment when the audience sees the ironic contrast
between what is professed and what is done is one of
the most exciting in the theater. By this criterion, his

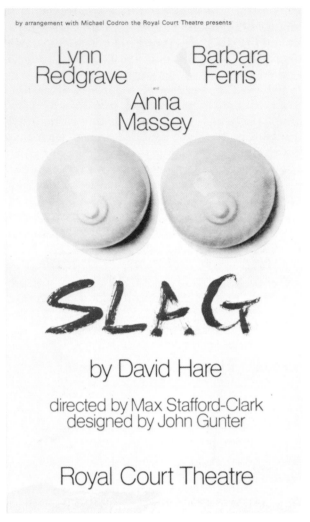

by arrangement with Michael Codron the Royal Court Theatre presents

Lynn
Redgrave

Barbara
Ferris

and

Anna
Massey

SLAG

by David Hare

directed by Max Stafford-Clark
designed by John Gunter

Royal Court Theatre

*Program cover for the 1971 Royal Court Theatre production
of Hare's first major play, a farce about
three neurotic school mistresses*

plays have many moments of excitement; lies are everywhere. In *Brassneck* (1973), the war hero never fought. In *Slag* (1970), Elise's pregnancy turns out to be gas. At the climax of *Teeth 'n' Smiles* (1975) Maggie, the lead singer, accepts the lie that she and not her fellow band members should be arrested for narcotics possession. Beyond lies and perhaps because of lies, the inability to change dominates Hare's plays. Only in *Fanshen* (1975), set in the People's Republic of China, does political (or even personal) life lead to new forms of thinking and acting. In the other plays, the action is a wheel that turns from frustration to frustration. As Maud says in *The Great Exhibition* (1972), "If we haven't the chance to change our lives . . . there's no particular point, is there?"

Although he eschews the surreal visual effects of such contemporaries as Brenton, Hare tests his audience's limits by constantly employing the tough language of his increasingly impolite generation. He is also willing to assault his audience visually, calling as he does for male nudity in *Plenty* (1978) or for anarchic physical destruction in *Teeth 'n' Smiles*. But the outstanding stylistic feature of his work is his cinematic handling of time and space. Hare became a movie buff during his Cambridge days and has expressed regret that the film has not offered much of a welcome to writers of his stamp because his narratives would lend themselves to film treatment. Indeed, his plays generally begin from a relatively early point of the story and present many incidents taken from many moments in time. By this choice of approach he allies himself with the cinematic tendency to show the march of events as opposed to the Ibsenian theatrical tendency to show only a narrow present and describe a lengthy past.

Hare's first major play was *Slag*, a three-woman farce in which, under the leadership of its three neurotic mistresses, the student body of Brackenhurst School declines over a year's time from eleven girls (all unseen) to none. Ann, the headmistress, is keen and incurably optimistic; Elise is frantically libidinous; and Joanne, the feminist left-wing virgin, drives the girls away with her inane teaching of such subjects as masturbation. There is little linear plot development. Instead, the play is best seen as presenting a revolutionary conflict in which conservative England (represented by Ann) competes with Maoist radicalism (Joanne) for the loyalty of the common masses (Elise). At the finale, Elise's hysterical pregnancy expires "like a great wet fart," and, when Joanne appears to gun down Ann, her submachine gun turns out to be a toy. The three women and their school will go blundering on despite the absence of students; the revolutionary struggle has changed nothing.

If the action solves nothing, it is nonetheless packed with humor, game playing, public-school rituals turned on their heads, and a constant emotional intensity which gives the play an expressionistic tone within a primarily realistic frame. After opening at the Hampstead Theatre Club in April 1970, *Slag* was produced the next year at New York's Public Theatre, where, despite a short run, it drew high praise from such critics as Clive Barnes and John Simon. In 1970 Hare was awarded the *Evening Standard* Drama Award for most promising playwright.

Like *Slag*, Hare's next major play was a rueful farce which deprecated British ineffectuality. Charlie Hammet, the protagonist of *The Great Exhibition*, gives this play its title by displaying his privates in a public park after his wife, Maud, has left him for an Australian drug freak and he has been expelled from Parliament for nonperformance. He is picked up in a park, where he spends his evenings "flashing," by Catriona, an old friend of his wife, but their affair proves to be only a mask for Catriona's true interest, which is Maud. By the end of the play, Maud has returned to Charlie, but the reunion is not joyous, merely a wistful surrender to the old boring pattern of life. Both Hammet and Maud have rebelled to no purpose.

Hare's divided political vision is clearly realized in Charlie Hammet, a socialist politician who has no drive to action. He entered politics in order to impress Maud with leftist speeches and even quoted *Das Kapital* in his marriage proposal. Having acted a leftist to no real effect, he now acts as

exhibitionist with similar results. The problem with Hammet and Maud, the audience is given to understand, is that they have personalities ("am") but lack conviction ("do"). As Maud puts it, "my am is superb, my does is non-existent."

Despite its obvious relevance to contemporary English life, both public and private, *The Great Exhibition* is much less satisfying than *Slag*. Hare claimed that the play was a deliberate parody of "Royal Court plays emphasizing characters who suffer," but a lack of solid results combined with a perhaps too insistent wisecrackery vitiates the play. *Plays and Players* stated that the play "darts uncertainly between tragi-comedy and farce, unable to resist taking a pot shot at any target which crosses the author's sights."

Hare's next major efforts, *Brassneck* and

Chairman and
Managing Director
Donald Albery

Assistant Managing
Director
Ian B Albery

New Theatre
St Martin's Lane London WC2

Consultant
V W Hunter

Lessees
The Wyndham Theatres
Ltd

by arrangement with
Donald Albery

The National Theatre
presents

English version by
David Hare
and by
Robert Rietty

THE RULES OF THE GAME

(Il giuoco delle parti)
by Luigi Pirandello

First performance at the New Theatre
15 June 1971

The Rules of the Game

Leone Gala	Paul Scofield
Silia, his wife	Joan Plowright
Guido Venanzi	Edward Hardwicke
Dr Spiga	Paul Curran
Filippo, Leone's servant	Tom Baker
Barelli	Frank Barrie
Marquis Miglioriti	Howard Southern
First drunken gentleman	Tom Georgeson
Second drunken gentleman	Lionel Guyett
Third drunken gentleman	Michael Edgar
Clara, Silia's maid	Judy Wilson
Neighbours	Gillian Barge
	Tom Dickinson
	Alan Dudley
	Barry James
	Jo Maxwell-Muller

Production by Anthony Page

Designed by Enrico Job
Lighting by Andy Phillips
Assistant to the producer: Misha Williams
Stage Manager: Richard Mangan
Deputy Stage Manager: Jason Barnes
Assistant Stage Manager: Elizabeth Markham

Act one: Silia's apartment

Act two: Leone's house

Act three: The same

The action takes place in any Italian town. 1918

There will be one interval of eighteen minutes between the first and the second act

Program title page and cast list for the first production of Hare and Robert Rietty's adaptation of Pirandello's play

Edward Fox and Leonard Kavanagh in the first London production of Knuckle

Knuckle (1974), were to be far more sure-handed and would establish him with critics, if not with the ticket-buying public, as an important playwright. In 1973 Hare served as resident dramatist at the Nottingham Playhouse for which, in close collaboration with Howard Brenton, he wrote *Brassneck*. A mammoth play whose technical requirements—multiple locales and thirty parts—may have prevented its moving to London despite its Nottingham success, *Brassneck* (which is Midlands slang for "criminal nerve") traces the thirty-year rise, fall, and rise of the Bagley family, whose patriarch gets his start by murdering his wife during the blitzkrieg so that he can become a slumlord on her insurance. Roderick, Bagley's nephew, becomes rich through rigged building contracts and goes to jail because he is stupid enough to leave records of the bribes. The third-generation Bagley, Roderick's son, becomes a nightclub owner and heroin entrepreneur. Throughout, the business community and upper classes connive at the Bagley success because of fear or greed. As Bagley's lawyer puts it, "I could take all my clothes off . . . greed would be blazoned across my bum."

The decay of Britain and British politics dominates the play, in which incompetence proves as great a force as criminality. Roderick Bagley, for example, goes to jail because his prefabricated building stress system cracks in the rain. Not one character is even half good, least of all the two

Labourite politicians who sell out socialism for the perquisites of the establishment. One of them, Browne, who had been a leftist postal worker in the 1940s, says, "I was a communist in my youth. Now I'm looking for revenge . . . on everything I believed in."

Commenting on *Brassneck*'s failure to achieve a London production, Oleg Kerensky says the play was perhaps "too large scale for the commercial theatre." Still, Michael Coveny described it as a watershed event that proved the large audience appeal of the group of dramatists to which Hare and Brenton belong.

After an Oxford Playhouse premiere, *Knuckle* finally brought Hare to the West End. The play was produced at the Comedy Theatre in March 1974. *Knuckle* is a much more solidly structured work than Hare's earlier efforts. *Knuckle* adheres closely to the model of the intrigue film while at the same time subtly parodying it. Its Bogart-like hero, Curly, is a cynical international arms dealer who returns to England to solve the disappearance of his sister. In the process he encounters a good woman, Jenny, and a series of sordid truths about British business ethics that prompts him to place blame for his sister's apparent suicide on his father. At this point the play veers away from its model; instead of demanding justice, Curly yields to his criminal father and so loses Jenny, who knows the truth, including the last revealed fact, that sister Sarah, repelled by her father's machinations, has not committed suicide but only decamped to the Continent. Curly is doomed to the meaninglessness he might have escaped by one forthright act.

Knuckle has the flow as well as the plot of a film: its seventeen scenes move rapidly through time and space like the major sequences of a film while retaining the surface patina of tough-guy realism. Its picture of contemporary England is bleak; only Jenny possesses a real ethical sense, and the other characters will do anything for greed. Patrick, Curly's upper-class father; Max, a journalist; and the working-class Malloy all conspire to the commitment of Malloy's mother in order to profit from the sale of her property. The play is half tragedy in the sense that Curly shows the promise for positive action while he is seeking the truth but succumbs to epidemic cynicism once he has found it. *Knuckle* is at once a virtuoso rendering of the tough-guy style and a serious look at moral fecklessness. Although it received mixed reviews in London and New York, *Knuckle*'s quality was affirmed by the award of the John Llewellyn Rhys Prize for 1974 and its designation in the *Times Literary Supplement* as one of the best

political plays of the new generation.

Hare's first four major plays all demonstrate the failure of post-World War II English people to change for the better or accomplish anything of value. With *Fanshen*, produced in London in 1975, Hare set out to demonstrate that in another culture, in another system, positive change might be a real possibility. In an Oxford lecture, Hare described European society as unbudgeable and suggested that he was attracted to William Hinton's *Fanshen: A Documentary of Revolution in a Chinese Village* (1967) precisely because it offered the possibility of dramatizing another, riper society in which the historical dialectic might actually work; humans and political structures could work on and modify each other. *Fanshen* is a sweeping portrait of a Chinese village in the years immediately following the Maoist victory over the Kuomintang in the late 1940s. The thirty-odd characters (to be portrayed by seven actors and two actresses) struggle through the process of revolutionary change. The village peasants learn to stand up for their new rights, acquire political consciousness and the habits of group criticism and discussion, develop indigenous cadres, redistribute wealth, abuse their powers, and correct themselves. No individual protagonist emerges. Instead, the revolutionary process itself dominates the stage. To each of the twelve episodes Hare gives a title or slogan which, in the Brechtian fashion, may be displayed in order to alert the audience to the logical meaning of the scene it is about to see. This tactic is especially appropriate because in *Fanshen* Hare comes closer than before to emulating Brecht in the depiction of positive revolutionary change.

Harold Hobson praised the play but warned that "those who demand easy messages will be baffled." And, indeed, the play often takes an ambiguous stance toward the revolution it depicts. For example, in one scene, the peasants are rewarded materially for the vigor with which they denounce landlords and other antisocial elements, suggesting that here lie the seeds of another repressive state. In spring 1980, *Fanshen* was given a staged reading by twenty-two Asian-American actors of New York's Public Theatre.

Hare next collaborated with the Bicât brothers, composer Nick and lyricist Tony, who wrote six songs to go with Hare's *Teeth 'n' Smiles*, which Hare has called "absolutely my only autobiographical play." *Teeth 'n' Smiles* concerns a rock group of the sort Hare remembered from his Cambridge days. During a university concert, the group falls apart under the strain of its own excesses, foremost

A scene from the first production of Fanshen

among which is singer Maggie's neurotic drinking and self-destructive sexual promiscuity. During the course of the evening, the band does half a dozen numbers, sets fire to the auditorium, and plants drugs in Maggie's bag so that when the police come she is arrested.

Full of song, humor, music and drug jargon, and physical high jinks, the play is constantly lively. At the same time, Hare suffuses it with emptiness. The characters are mindless, destructively selfish, or both; everyone is a victim of someone else's greed. The play ends with a musical finale, "Last Order," a tough ballad about the sinking of the *Titanic*, in which the singer vows to survive at the expense of others.

J. W. Lambert greeted the play's opening at the Royal Court with high praise, calling it "an exhilarating start to the English Stage Company's new artistic direction." When the play transferred to the West End's Wyndham's Theatre in 1976, Harold Hobson hailed it as "a play of quality," and, writing in the *New York Times*, Charles Marowitz promoted Hare to the highest rank of the new dramatists.

In the usual British pattern, Hare's increased recognition as a stage writer led to television offers. In 1978, the BBC produced a Hare teleplay which exemplifies well the concerns that inform all of his writing. *Licking Hitler* (1978) deals with the manufacture of "black" material—false information—by a group of British propagandists during World War II. On a country estate where the group produces fake German radio broadcasts designed to demoralize German troops, Anna, a naive upper-class girl, goes to work for MacLean, a hard-drinking Scots journalist who initiates her both professionally and sexually. Like Curly, MacLean has no ideals but goes about his assignment with frightening efficiency. His great coup is a series of broadcasts designed to convince German fighting men that the blood plasma on which their lives depend is taken from tainted, diseased prisoners. Perhaps to keep Anna's innocence from being totally destroyed, perhaps because he loves her (although the script is not explicit on that point), MacLean drives her from the organization with a false accusation that she has attempted to seduce him. Thirty years later, Anna is still in love with MacLean though she has never received from him a word of affection.

Leaving the audience to choose between the strong arguments for and against the lies by which its characters live and work, the play goes to the heart of Hare's preoccupations. Not only does MacLean lie about Anna, and not only is the daily

Hugh Fraser and Helen Mirren in a scene from the first production of Teeth 'n' Smiles

round of the station the generation of bigger and better lies, but even Anna's innocence is grounded in lies. With the barely forgivable naivete of the young rich, she arrives at the station thinking that electricity is something delivered free to rich and poor alike. Hare's contention that private relationships are not to be separated from public life is borne out with the utmost clarity. The play is subtle in plot and language, and Hare, as one would expect considering his already cinematic stage style, seems very much at home with the freedom of the teleplay form. Dennis Potter described *Licking Hitler* as "dangerous and subversive good writing."

Hare continues to exploit World War II in his most recent and best major play, *Plenty*, which premiered on the National Theatre's Lyttelton stage in 1978 and appeared at Washington, D.C.'s Arena

Stage in 1980. Flashing backward and forward in time with a flexibility suitable to a teleplay, *Plenty* deals with twenty years in the life of Susan, a woman who experiences the best part of her life as a terrified courier to the French resistance in 1942. From that point forward, her life worsens. Never adjusting to the banalities of postwar life, she suffers frequent breakdowns, destroys the career of her foreign service husband, and, in an attempt to find meaning by bearing a child by Mick, a brainless teddy boy, fails to conceive.

A series of vignettes with almost no causal connection beyond the assumptions the audience makes about Susan's disappointed hopes, the play is held together well by her intensity and mystery. Fine dialogue abounds, and the play reaches a high point during the Suez crisis when Susan stylishly

Julie Covington in a scene from the first production of Plenty

demolishes her husband's foreign service superior for the Eden government's lack of principle. Since the ambassador himself has protested the Suez policy to the length of his ability, Susan's attack is in large part unreasonable and increases the audience's puzzlement about her judgment. In the end, her idealism, expressed as it is through extreme behavior, ruins her husband, and the audience is left to ponder a woman of the best potential achieving only the worst. Mel Gussow, who reviewed both the London and the Washington productions, saw Susan as a modern Hedda Gabler, stifled by the inability of a barren society to offer her either challenge or meaning.

According to Charles Marowitz, "Hare has always been obsessed with John Osborne," both despising his politics and hoping to duplicate his success. In bringing *Plenty* to a climax built around the Suez crisis, Hare was perhaps making a specific reference to Osborne, in whose *The Entertainer* (1957) the Suez affair leads to the moment of greatest suffering. *Plenty* has been deservedly

praised by many critics, Ronald Hayman, in particular, calling it Hare's best work.

In his next work, the BBC teleplay *Dreams of Leaving* (1980), Hare studies another lost English woman, Caroline. The audience observes her through the eyes of an innocent young journalist, William, who offers her devotion but cannot solve the mystery of her erratic behavior. Like *Plenty*'s Susan, Caroline finds no emotional anchor in contemporary English life; she possesses neither a moral nor a professional goal worthy of serious pursuit. Unlike Susan, she follows a course of promiscuity and self-indulgence to actual madness—at the end of the play she is in a mental institution. Caroline is not to be understood, but the theme of wasted English talent is clear.

With the achievement of several fine plays behind him, Hare may be expected to have an outstanding career as a dramatist ahead of him. However, he is also much in demand as a stage director, and the pressures of that occupation may slow his output. This would be a loss, for his virtues as a writer are many. He is one of the most literate of the younger generation of British dramatists; perhaps only Tom Stoppard and Edward Bond surpass him in that area. But neither Stoppard nor Bond has taken dead aim, as has Hare, at the recent history of England, the angst associated with national decline and senescence.

Beyond his wit, polish, and cool detachment, Hare is to be admired for his variety; his major plays are all different from one another. *Slag*, though a serious statement about failed revolutions, is a knockabout farce full of sexual humor and outrageous games. *Knuckle* is an excellent imitation of the tough-guy flick. *Fanshen* is a reasonable English version of Brechtian epic theater; *Teeth 'n' Smiles* a pocket musical; and *Plenty*, his most compassionate play, a truly engrossing character study. Hare's political vision has yet to become a fully informing influence on his work. His dissatisfaction with postwar England is a strong constant, but he has yet to develop a positive vision of change in England that might give a forward thrust to either his politics or his drama.

Television Scripts:
Man Above Men, BBC, 1973;
Licking Hitler, BBC, 1978;
Dreams of Leaving, BBC, 1980.

Other:
"Time of Unease," in *At the Royal Court*, edited by

Richard Findlater (New York: Grove, 1981), pp. 139-142.

Periodical Publication:

"From Portable Theatre to Joint Stock . . . via Shaftesbury Avenue," *Theatre Quarterly*, 5 (December 1975): 108-115.

References:

Peter Ansorge, "Underground Explorations No. 1: Portable Playwrights," *Plays and Players*, 19 (February 1972);

Michael Coveny, "Beyond the Fringe," *Sunday Times Magazine*, 26 November 1978, p. 73;

Ronald Hayman, *British Theatre Since 1955* (London: Oxford University Press, 1979);

Catherine Itzin, *Stages in the Revolution* (London: Eyre Methuen, 1980);

Oleg Kerensky, *The New British Drama* (New York: Taplinger, 1977);

Colin Ludlow, "Hare and Others," *London Magazine*, 18 (July 1978): 76-81;

John Peter, "Meet the Wild Bunch," *Sunday Times*, 11 July 1976, p. 31.

Ronald Harwood

(9 November 1934-)

Richard B. Gidez

Pennsylvania State University

PRODUCTIONS: *Country Matters*, 16 October 1969, University Theatre, Manchester;

The Good Companions, adapted from J. B. Priestley's novel, libretto by Harwood, music by André Previn, lyrics by Johnny Mercer, 11 July 1974, Her Majesty's Theatre, London, 250 [performances];

The Ordeal of Gilbert Pinfold, adapted from Evelyn Waugh's novel, 15 September 1977, Royal Exchange Theatre, Manchester; 14 February 1979, Round House Theatre, London, 33;

A Family, 6 July 1978, Theatre Royal, Haymarket, London, 92;

The Dresser, 6 March 1980, Royal Exchange Theatre, Manchester; 30 April 1980, Queen's Theatre, London, 274; 9 November 1981, Brooks Atkinson Theatre, New York.

BOOKS: *All The Same Shadows* (London: Cape, 1961); republished as *George Washington September, Sir!* (New York: Farrar, Straus & Cudahy, 1961);

The Guilt Merchants (London: Cape, 1963; New York: Holt, Rinehart & Winston, 1969);

The Girl in Melanie Klein (London: Secker & Warburg, 1969; New York: Holt, Rinehart & Winston, 1969);

Sir Donald Wolfit C. B. E. His Life and Work in the Unfashionable Theatre (London: Secker & Warburg, 1971; New York: St. Martin's, 1971);

Articles of Faith (London: Secker & Warburg, 1973; New York: Holt, Rinehart & Winston, 1974);

The Genoa Ferry (London: Secker & Warburg, 1976; New York: Mason/Charter, 1977);

One. Interior. Day. Adventures in the Film Trade (London: Secker & Warburg, 1978);

César and Augusta (London: Secker & Warburg, 1978; Boston: Little, Brown, 1980);

A Family (London: Heinemann, 1978);

The Dresser (London: Amber Lane Press, 1980; New York: Grove, 1981).

Ronald Harwood has written several favorably reviewed novels, a well-received biography, and many television plays, film scripts, and stage plays. But not until the success of his 1980 play *The Dresser*, winner of the New Standard and Drama Critics Award for best play of 1980, did he reach a wide audience and become well known in theatrical circles in London and New York.

Born Ronald Horwitz in Cape Town, South Africa, in 1934, the son of Isaac Horwitz and his wife, Isobel Pepper Horwitz, Harwood went to England in 1951 where he spent a year studying at the Royal Academy of Dramatic Art. Having obtained an introduction to Shakespearean actor Donald Wolfit, he became a student-member of his company at King's Theatre, Hammersmith, in 1953. From 1953 to 1958 he worked and toured for Wolfit as understudy, actor, dresser, and finally business manager. As he writes in the introduction to his biography of Wolfit, "He was, by far, the most important influence on my early adult life."

In 1959 he married Natasha Riehle. The same year he began a season as actor with the 59 Theatre Company at the Lyric Theatre, Hammersmith. The change from actor to writer resulted from an occurrence in his native South Africa. He recalled no violence at home as a youth. But a bloody incident in early 1960 in Sharpeville where a black was shot in the back served as a catalyst for Harwood's first novel, *All The Same Shadows* (1961, published in the United States as *George Washington September, Sir!*), the story of a few days in the life of a young Cape Town Zulu.

Over the next twenty years, five other novels as well as a collection of short stories on the film industry appeared. The subject matter of these books ranges from the adventures of the inhabitants of a luxury London asylum in *The Girl in Melanie Klein* (1969) to the saga of a South African family in *Articles of Faith* (1973, winner of the Winifred Holtby Memorial Prize), to the love life of composer César Franck in *César and Augusta* (1978), perhaps his best work of fiction.

During the years that he was writing novels, he was also busy turning out television scripts. His first television play, *The Barber of Stamford Hill* (1960), deals with a Jewish barber who considers marrying a widow with two children. Directed by Casper Wrede, it was turned into a motion picture in 1962 with Harwood providing the screenplay. Wrede continued to work with Harwood, directing more of his television plays, films, and stage plays and collaborating with him on *Private Potter* (1961), about a soldier in Cyprus during World War I who cries out at a vision of God and spoils an army operation. Both the television play and the subsequent film (1962), again with Harwood as screenwriter, starred Tom Courtenay, who was to appear in Harwood's film adaptation of Aleksandr Solzhenitsyn's *One Day in the Life of Ivan Denisovich* (1971) as well as the London and New York productions of *The Dresser*.

Harwood's best television play is *The Guests* (1972), a one-character drama that starred Margaret Leighton as an old woman who believes there are guests at her dinner table. Not only are they not there, but also at no time have they ever existed. The play is a striking study in loneliness. Other notable television scripts include *The New Assistant* (1967), a drama about an alcoholic trying to mend his ways; *A Sense of Loss* (1978), written with John Selwyn, a documentary on novelist Evelyn Waugh; and *Evita Peron* (1981), a splashy, sympathetic

Ronald Harwood

treatment of the Argentine dictator's controversial wife, starring Faye Dunaway.

As a screenwriter Harwood has written or collaborated on several films, ranging from *Drop Dead, Darling* (1966, presented in the United States as *Arrivederci, Baby!*), a comedy, to *Eyewitness* (1970, released in the United States as *Sudden Terror*), a suspense thriller. In addition to the Solzhenitsyn novel, he also adapted for film Richard Hughes's 1929 novel, *A High Wind in Jamaica* (1965).

When Sir Donald Wolfit died in 1968, he left Harwood fifty pounds "with the hope that he will undertake . . . some form of biography of my work in the theatre." Three years later, *Sir Donald Wolfit C. B. E. His Life and Work in the Unfashionable Theatre* was published. Harwood defines "unfashionable theatre" as "that section of the theatrical profession, actors in particular, who are regarded by their fellow men with a mixture of grudging admiration, disdain, and often amusement." Actors may be unfashionable because they are born out of their time, "not necessarily too late, perhaps too soon." The biography is not only a critical but also a sympathetic portrait of a much-loved and much-hated actor who could be inspiring and exasperating, irrational and endearing, friend and foe. It is also a history of a kind of acting mode, that of the virtuoso performer, that has gone out of style and a history of the acting company that took Shakespeare's plays, in the words of the aging Shakespearean actor in *The Dresser*, "to every corner of our beloved island," the kind of company that likewise no longer exists.

Country Matters, Harwood's first performed stage play, opened in Manchester in October 1969. Set in an empty country house in Wiltshire, it concerns a church committee, run by an opinionated aristocrat, which has come to survey the property with the idea of turning it into a home for refugees. The catalyst for the action is a female refugee who becomes the object of affection for the committee's lesbian secretary and for a novelist who is working on a book on the committee's years of achievement; and an object of lust for the aristocratic chairman. The chairman rapes the refugee, the committee closes ranks and returns to town, and the novelist destroys his manuscript. Michael Billington of the *Times* found the characters hardly credible and had trouble believing the committee could run anything. *Country Matters* never opened in London.

Harwood's only musical, *The Good Companions*, based on J. B. Priestley's 1929 novel, premiered in London in July 1974. With music by André Previn, lyrics by Johnny Mercer, and a libretto by Harwood, it tells how three outsiders come to the rescue of an ailing concert park and in the process find their own happiness. Harwood's book found praise, but the music was dismissed as bland and the lyrics as unintelligible. Starring John Mills, *The Good Companions* had not found too many admirers among theater audiences before it closed in February 1975.

The new Royal Exchange Theatre in Manchester was the stage in 1977 for Harwood's next play, a dramatization of Evelyn Waugh's 1957 autobiographical novel, *The Ordeal of Gilbert Pinfold*. Both novel and play recount the experiences of a middle-aged novelist who, because he takes drugs for insomnia and pain, suffers from tormenting hallucinations. Through his inner strength and with the help of his commonsense wife, he is able to overcome these visions. The adaptation succeeded beyond all expectations of *Times* critic Irving Wardle, who felt that Harwood's going outside the novel to Waugh's own life for material strengthened the play.

Before *The Ordeal of Gilbert Pinfold* made it to London, another Harwood play, *A Family*, had preceded it in July 1978. Starring Paul Scofield and Harry Andrews and directed by Casper Wrede, it

depicts a family whose members are, ironically, tearing the clan apart with their protestations of loyalty. Three generations of the Kilner family are dominated by the loving tyranny of its patriarch, Ivan, who strongly believes that if only one member rebels against that tyranny, the family as a unit will be threatened. "I will not allow the circle to be broken. Not by anyone." Thirty-three years before, Ivan had parachuted into the Italian war zone to bring Freddie, his son, home. An escapee from a prisoner-of-war camp, Freddie, then fighting with the Italian partisans and planning to marry an Italian girl, did not want to return. But Ivan would not be denied. Too weak to stand up to Ivan, Freddie returned to England and the girl tried to kill herself. Now the family has another rebellion to face as Paula, Freddie's niece, attempts suicide, feeling the pincers of family loyalty "coming together to squeeze blood blisters out of us." To Ivan, individual freedom endangers the power of the family. He sees family only. "That's what we built. That's what we made. We will be remembered for nothing else." To Freddie and Paula, "Families make good prisons." Paula is young and strong enough to find a balance between herself and family. But for Freddie, the trauma of the past is still unresolved. She makes him see that perhaps he really wanted Ivan to fetch him home. At the play's end, Freddie envies Paula's freedom to feel what she likes; he can only grieve and mourn.

Harwood has said that if there is one theme that links his work, it is individuals facing up to themselves. In *A Family* he has hold of a valid theme, but unfortunately he has not satisfactorily dramatized it. Of the major characters, only Ivan is strongly drawn. Paula and Freddie are earnest but not particularly believable or interesting. The play closed in September 1978, less than four months after it had opened.

Harwood's most successful play, *The Dresser*, opened in Manchester in March 1980 and moved to London in April. It is set backstage in an English provincial theater during World War II. Sir—he is given no other name—is the last of the great but dying breed of English actor-managers, but tonight he is in no shape to go on as Lear. Through the valiant efforts of Norman, his personal servant, confidant, and dresser, who combines tender sympathy, nannylike severity, and bitchy connivance, Sir does make it onstage and through the performance. The appearance is his last, for backstage after the play, Sir dies, leaving his faithful dresser alone.

In the foreword to the published edition of the

play, Harwood notes some of the similarities between Sir and Sir Donald Wolfit, but denies that Sir is Wolfit. He does not deny, however, that his memory "of what took place night after night in Wolfit's dressing room is part of the inspiration of the play." If Sir is not Wolfit, neither does Norman represent Harwood. "He, like Sir, is an amalgam of three or four men I met who served leading actors as professional dressers," says Harwood, disclaiming that Norman's relationship with Sir is "mine with Wolfit."

Because *The Dresser* is essentially a backstage drama, the audience is able to observe the rites and rituals actors go through before a performance, overhear the tired jokes and gossipy conversations of actors in the wings awaiting their entrances, and learn the secrets of stage effects, in this case, the creation of the storm scene in *King Lear*. Most of all the audience witnesses the magic that happens when the theater's lights darken. When Sir first appears, he is an exhausted, dying man who cannot remember his first line although he has performed the role 226 times (in the New York production he is said to have performed it 426 times) and who is in a catatonic state before his first entrance (he comes to himself only upon hearing there is a full house). Once he sets foot onstage, however, Sir is transformed. The audience has every reason to believe his Lear is a fine portrayal. (Harwood wisely shows them none of the performance.) "I thought tonight I caught sight of [Lear]," Sir tells his wife. Despite a company that consists, according to Sir, of "old men, cripples and Nancy-boys," he can exclaim at the end of the performance, "We've done it, Will, we've done it."

Even the tight-lipped, seemingly emotionless, often cynical Norman becomes a new man when he must get in front of the curtain and announce a delay in the performance because of an air raid. Despite a slip of the tongue ("Will those who wish to live—will those who wish to leave do so as quietly as possible"), he bubbles with childlike excitement at the experience, seeking approval. "Was I all right? . . . I was ever so nervous. . . . Was I really all right?" Such is the transformation the theater can effect.

The play is not without flaws. Harwood tries to explore too many relationships, Sir's with Madge, the stage manager, being the least satisfactorily developed (especially in the New York production where many of her lines were cut). For the most part, Harwood keeps the parallels between Lear's story and Sir's discreetly in the background. But

occasionally he presses the similarities too hard, as in the closing scene where Norman sings the Fool's song, "The Wind and the Rain," over Sir's body. At this point, Robert Brustein suggests, it becomes clear how presumptuous Harwood is in drawing a correspondence between Shakespeare's unremitting tragedy and his own affectionate, nostalgic, comic tribute to the shabby provincial touring companies of a bygone day in England. Finally, Sir's death right after he has given his best performance is too melodramatic, but it affords Norman the opportunity to speak both harsh and loving words about Sir. Yet they are unnecessary words for they tell the audience nothing about Norman's relationship with Sir that they do not already know. Better to have ended the play with the company, Sir included, leaving the theater empty—just as the theater in which the audience is sitting will soon be empty—awaiting, as Frank Rich has put it, "the promise . . . of transfiguration, of a make-believe world ablaze with light and finery" that will come with the next performance.

If Harwood often settles for the easy laugh and if the play is predictable at times, it is still a wonderful piece of theater, brilliantly acted by Tom Courtenay (Norman) and Freddie Jones (Sir) in London and by Courtenay and Paul Rogers in New York.

Harwood's best works, his biography of Wolfit and *The Dresser*, have been concerned with the theater. How much more ore can be successfully mined from that lode remains to be seen. It is interesting and encouraging to note, however, that Harwood, now a Fellow of the Royal Society of Literature, is currently writing a thirteen-part history of the theater, *All the World's a Stage*, for BBC/Time-Life, which will be presented in 1983.

Screenplays:
The Barber of Stamford Hill, British Lion Film, 1962;
Private Potter, MGM, 1962;
A High Wind in Jamaica, adapted by Harwood, Stanley Mann, and Dennis Cannan from Richard Hughes's novel, Twentieth Century-Fox, 1965;
Drop Dead, Darling, by Harwood and Ken Hughes, Seven Arts, 1966; released in the United States as *Arrivederci, Baby!*, Paramount, 1966;
Eyewitness, adapted from Mark Hebden's novel, Irving Allen Associate British Production, 1970; released in the United States as *Sudden Terror*, National General Pictures, 1971;

One Day in the Life of Ivan Denisovich, adapted from Aleksandr Solzhenitsyn's novel, Cinerama Releasing Group W, 1971;

Operation Daybreak, adapted from Alan Burgess's novel, American Allied, 1975.

Television Scripts:

Private Potter, by Harwood and Casper Wrede, ITA, 1961;

Take a Fellow Like Me, ITA, 1961;

The New Assistant, ATV, 1967;

The Guests, ATV, 1972;

A Sense of Loss, by Harwood and John Selwyn, BBC 2, 1978;

Evita Peron, NBC, 1981.

Other:

New Stories 3: An Arts Council Anthology, edited by Harwood and Francis King (London: Hutchinson, 1978).

Reference:

Ion Trewin, "Ronald Harwood: A Multiple Life," *Times*, 18 March 1978, p. 9.

William Douglas Home
(3 June 1912-   )

Michael J. Mendelsohn
University of Tampa

PRODUCTIONS: *Great Possessions*, 8 February 1937, Duke of York's Theatre, London;

Passing By, 29 April 1940, Q Theatre, London;

Now Barabbas, 11 February 1947, Boltons Theatre, Kensington (transferred 7 March 1947 to Vaudeville Theatre), London;

The Chiltern Hundreds, 26 August 1947, Vaudeville Theatre, London, 651 [performances]; produced again as *Yes, M'Lord*, 4 October 1949, Booth Theatre, New York, 87;

Ambassador Extraordinary, 30 June 1948, Aldwych Theatre, London;

The Thistle and the Rose, 6 September 1949, Boltons Theatre, Kensington, London; 15 May 1951, Vaudeville Theatre, London;

Master of Arts, 7 September 1949, Strand Theatre, London;

The Bad Samaritan, 2 September 1952, New Theatre, Bromley, Kent; 24 June 1953, Criterion Theatre, London;

Caro William, 22 October 1952, Embassy Theatre, London;

The Manor of Northstead, 28 April 1954, Duchess Theatre, London, 307;

The Reluctant Debutante, May 1955, Theatre Royal, Brighton; 24 May 1955, Cambridge Theatre, London, 752; 10 October 1956, Henry Miller's Theatre, New York, 134;

William Douglas Home

The Iron Duchess, 14 March 1957, Cambridge Theatre, London;

Aunt Edwina, 3 November 1959, Fortune Theatre, London;

The Bad Soldier Smith, 14 June 1961, Westminster Theatre, London;

The Cigarette Girl, 19 June 1962, Duke of York's Theatre, London;

The Drawing Room Tragedy, 1963, Salisbury Theatre, Salisbury;

The Reluctant Peer, 15 January 1964, Duchess Theatre, London, 475;

Two Accounts Rendered (*The Home Secretary* and *Lady J P 2*), 15 September 1964, Comedy Theatre, London;

Betzi, 23 March 1965, Salisbury Playhouse, Salisbury; revised version, 29 October 1975, Haymarket Theatre, London;

A Friend Indeed, 27 April 1966, Cambridge Theatre, London;

The Queen's Highland Servant, 2 May 1968, Savoy Theatre, London;

The Secretary Bird, 16 October 1968, Savoy Theatre, London, 1,463;

The Grouse Moor Image, 1968, Plymouth;

The Jockey Club Stakes, 30 September 1970, Vaudeville Theatre, London, 396; 24 January 1973, Cort Theatre, New York, 69;

The Douglas Cause, 10 November 1971, Duke of York's Theatre, London;

Lady Boothroyd of the By-Pass, 1 February 1972, Boston; produced again as *Lloyd George Knew My Father*, 4 July 1972, Savoy Theatre, London, 637;

At the End of the Day, 3 October 1973, Savoy Theatre, London;

The Dame of Sark, 17 October 1974, Wyndham's Theatre, London;

The Lord's Lieutenant, 13 November 1974, Redgrave Theatre, Farnham, Surrey;

The Bank Manager, 1975; produced again as *In the Red*, 25 March 1977, Whitehall Theatre, London;

The Kingfisher, 4 May 1977, Lyric Theater, Hammersmith, London; 6 December 1978, Biltmore Theatre, New York, 170;

Rolls Hyphen Royce, 11 May 1977, Shaftesbury Theatre, London.

BOOKS: *Home Truths* (London: Lane, 1939);
Now Barabbas (London: Longmans, Green, 1947);
The Chiltern Hundreds (London: French, 1949);
Half-Term Report (London: Longmans, Green, 1954);

The Bad Samaritan (London: Evans, 1954);
The Manor of Northstead (London: French, 1956);
The Reluctant Debutante (London: Evans, 1956; New York: French, 1957);
The Iron Duchess (London: Evans, 1958);
The Plays of William Douglas Home (London: Heinemann, 1958)—includes *Now Barabbas*, *The Chiltern Hundreds*, *The Thistle and the Rose*, *The Bad Samaritan*, and *The Reluctant Debutante*;
Aunt Edwina (London: French, 1960);
The Bad Soldier Smith (London: Evans, 1962);
The Reluctant Peer (London: Evans, 1964; New York: French, 1965);
A Friend Indeed (London & New York: French, 1966);
The Bishop and the Actress (London & New York: French, 1969);
The Secretary Bird (London & New York: French, 1969);
The Jockey Club Stakes (London & New York: French, 1971);
Lloyd George Knew My Father (London & New York: French, 1973);
The Dame of Sark (London & New York: French, 1976);
Betzi (London & New York: French, 1977);
In the Red (London & New York: French, 1978);
Mr. Home Pronounced Hume (London: Collins, 1979).

William Douglas Home, scion of an old, aristocratic Scottish family, has written a substantial body of plays for the English stage. His versatility is manifest, and the quality of his plays, while uneven, is generally high. Three or four of his best plays are likely to remain in the permanent repertoire for summer stock, as well as for London revivals. A few of his later works, most notably *The Kingfisher* (1977), have also been extremely successful in New York and on tour in the United States.

Home was born in Edinburgh, fifth child of a prominent Scottish family. His father was the thirteenth earl of Home and his mother, Lilian Lambton Home, was the daughter of the fourth earl of Durham. Upon his father's death in 1951 the title fell to William's elder brother Alec, who was British prime minister in the Conservative government during 1963-1964 and foreign secretary for several years. William Douglas Home himself has always taken an active interest in politics, running unsuccessfully for a seat in Parliament on several occasions. In 1951 Home courted and married Rachel Brand. They have four children, three daughters and a son.

Home's autobiography (1979) reveals a proud, somewhat defensive man, living under the shadow of his more famous brother and, like many British artists of today, excessively concerned with creditors and taxes. While Home has always practiced his profession and has supported his wife and four children comfortably on his royalties, he has apparently found himself frequently in need of cash and has branched off into a variety of business interests such as ownership of race horses.

Home grew to manhood in a wealthy, highly protected environment, in one or another of his family's estate homes. As a young man he attended Eton (1927-1932) and subsequently earned a degree in history at New College, Oxford, in 1935. While still a student at Eton, Home began to dabble in writing plays, but nothing of his prewar writing is notable. After graduation from Oxford, Home studied at the Royal Academy of Dramatic Art from 1935 to 1937 and through the help of friends in

London was cast in some bit parts. Acting opportunities soon dried up, however, and Home turned to playwriting in an attempt to fill up time.

The approach of World War II became the turning point in his career and his life, as it was for most of his generation. Although he reluctantly enlisted in 1940 and successfully went through the officer candidate training course, Home, an early vocal opponent of the war on philosophical grounds, became angered with the Churchill-Roosevelt policy of unconditional surrender. Refusing to mask his antiwar feelings, he ran for Parliament for Glasgow as an independent. In the middle of the war, and in uniform, Home startled many friends by almost winning his election as an antigovernment candidate.

For Home the major event of the war involved an episode in France, not politics. He was an acting captain with the advancing British army. At Le Havre, the German commander, realizing the des-

*Marjorie Fielding, Leora Dana, Peter Coke, A. E. Matthews, and Michael Shepley
in the first production of* The Chiltern Hundreds

perate situation, requested permission to evacuate the French citizens through British lines, apparently in order to avoid needless bloodshed. Home fully expected that the British commander would agree to this request, in the name of humaneness and common sense. When the evacuation request was ignored, Home became enraged and thereupon refused to participate in the assault on the city. Thousands of casualties among the civilians of Le Havre resulted from the ensuing battle.

British army authorities were seemingly willing to allow the incident to pass, but Home, still angered over the unnecessary loss of life, wrote a letter to an English newspaper exposing the entire episode. He was court-martialed and was sentenced to one year at hard labor. Thus, Home spent his thirty-third birthday in prison—a cashiered officer, generally in disgrace, without prospects for a career.

Still determined to try writing as a career, Home emerged from prison after the war, lived for a time with his parents, but soon headed for London. In his suitcase he carried the finished scripts of two plays, *Now Barabbas* and *The Chiltern Hundreds*, written immediately after the war. Through Lady Astor, then M.P. for Plymouth, Home met Bernard Shaw late in 1946. Shaw was ninety. Lady Astor introduced him to Shaw bluntly with, "William writes plays. No one wants to put them on, and quite rightly!" Shaw considered the matter, and then advised, "Go on writing, my boy. One of these fine days, one of those London managers will go into his office one Monday morning and say to his secretary, 'Is there a play from Shaw this morning?' And when she says, 'No, sir,' he'll say, 'Well, we'll have to start on the rubbish.' And there's your chance, my boy."

Critics, once Home found his metier, have largely agreed with Shaw's prophecy, but Home has been able to laugh all the way to the bank. *Now Barabbas* (1947), a serious play about prison life, was Home's first postwar work to be staged. It met generally favorable audiences and critical reaction, with one critic suggesting that the new playwright was in the mold of John Galsworthy. A narrative play in thirteen brief scenes, *Now Barabbas* focuses on a convicted murderer, Tufnell, building suspense over his appeal. Most of the play, however, centers on the empty, boring routine of the desperate inmates of an English prison. Compared to more recent scenes depicting prison conditions in many parts of the world, these scenes are fairly mild.

Now Barabbas, however, was not the appropriate beginning for Home. With his second play, *The Chiltern Hundreds* (1947), he found his true voice.

This amusing comedy, in the tone of several of Home's later successes, established him as a clever, witty writer. *The Chiltern Hundreds* deals with a rather preposterous situation. It is 1945, and the son of an old, landed family is standing for Parliament, a safe seat held by his family and the Tories for some 200 years. When the results are announced, he has lost the election, an event accepted with equanimity by his family, but not by the family butler. This worthy, Beecham, cannot easily accept the thought of a Labour victory. Through a series of barely credible plot twists, Beecham enters a by-election and defeats his young master, by now opportunistically running as a Labour candidate. With a few assorted love affairs mixed in, the play moves quickly to its denouement with the old order restored to its comfortable aristocratic routine.

Much of the fun in this first successful play comes with the character of the father, Lord Lister. He is a caricature, to be sure, but Home draws him with charm and warmth. Home later acknowledged that the character was inspired by his own father, and even the plot grew from an election loss of Alec Home's. Upon seeing the successful London production of *The Chiltern Hundreds*, Lord Home thought briefly about the characterization of the aristocratic father. Then he pronounced his judgment: "Dear old man. He knew what's important in life and what isn't."

A fallow period of several years followed the production of *The Chiltern Hundreds*. Although earning a living by writing film scripts, Home was unsure of his profession and was writing nothing of great interest to London producers. The situation changed substantially in 1955 with the production of *The Reluctant Debutante*. At least from a literary perspective, *The Reluctant Debutante* must be considered the best of Home's work. Home wrote this play in a burst of energy while recovering from a mild illness. He filled several notebooks with dialogue for the situation, ran into a writer's block concerning the ending, and thereupon put the entire play out of his mind for more than a year. The Homes had meanwhile moved to Drayton House in Hampshire, where they finally settled permanently in 1953. With his family growing and with still very meager royalties coming from his early plays, Home was faced with the necessity of abandoning his chosen profession or coming up with a major success.

Pulling out the unfinished play for the first time since he had written it, Home read it to his wife, Rachel, one evening. She not only loved the play but also solved the problem of the ending. The inheritance of a title by young David Hoylake-Johnston, which permits the clever denouement of the play, was Rachel Home's inspired suggestion to her husband.

The Reluctant Debutante involves a young girl (the part created by Anna Massey in her first role) who is brought to London for the "season." A modern version of William Wycherley's country girl, Jane is straightforward and unpretentious. London's social conventions are exceptionally distasteful and demeaning to her. She dislikes the entire game being played by her mother, a social climber who, beneath the thin veneer of cultivation, is a flesh peddler at heart. Jane finds a helpful ally in her father, the delightful Jimmy Broadbent. Jimmy supplies the money for his wife's socializing and escapades and also provides much of the comedy for the play. When Jane finally manages to find a young man to her taste, predictably he is not what her mother was hoping for; moreover, he has a reputation of being a rake, having allegedly been involved in a rather sordid sexual encounter at a country estate the previous year.

The action takes place in a tightly knit twenty-four-hour period at the Broadbents' London flat. The situation makes *The Reluctant Debutante* reminiscent of the plays of Richard Sheridan and Oliver Goldsmith, and the sharp, though not harsh, parody of Mrs. Broadbent frequently invokes memories of Restoration comedy. While Sheila Broadbent is not a grotesque, she is a neatly satirized modern mother.

Home cleverly employs the telephone throughout the play as a device for Sheila to use in her various arrangements for her daughter. Thus the ending, which so troubled the playwright, is a natural. David, the much-maligned suitor, has learned that his great-uncle has died, and David has now inherited a title. Jimmy slyly suggests that the appropriate dinner partner for his daughter might be the new Duke of Positano. Sheila falls neatly into the trap and phones "the Duke" at his club to extend the invitation, not knowing that it is the detested David on the other end of the line. Predictably for the comedy, it is clear at the final curtain that young

Jane Downs, Terence Longdon, Judith Arthy, and Kenneth More in a scene from the first production of The Secretary Bird

Wensley Pithey, Hazel Bainbridge, Alastair Sim, Christina Gray and Ernest Clark

Geoffrey Sumner, Barry Walker and Alastair Sim

THE JOCKEY CLUB STAKES

Characters in order of appearance:

The Marquis of Candover	ALASTAIR SIM
Lord Coverley de Beaumont	GEOFFREY SUMNER
Colonel Sir Robert Richardson	ROBERT COOTE
Captain Trevor Jones	TERENCE SKELTON
Miss Hills	CHRISTINA GRAY
P. Brown	TERENCE MORAN
Lady Ursula Itchin	JULIA LOCKWOOD
Lord Green	WENSLEY PITHEY
Tom Glass	ALAN WHITE
Charlie Wisden	BRIAN HAYES
Perch Graham	BARRY WALKER
Sir Dymock Blackburn, Q.C.	ERNEST CLARK
Lady Green	HAZEL BAINBRIDGE

The Scene is laid throughout in the Jockey Club Rooms

Act 1	Scene I	A Summer Morning
	Scene II	The Following Morning
		INTERVAL
Act 2	Scene I	Two weeks later
		A few days after the Warwick Meeting
	Scene II	It is not yet 2.30 p.m. the same day

OVERTURE AND ENTR'ACTE MUSIC PLAYED BY
ROBB STEWART

Scenes and cast list from the program for the first production of Home's comedy about upper-class high jinks

love has triumphed, that Jimmy has put one over on his oppressively social-climbing wife, and that Sheila—faced finally with a fait accompli and a wealthy and titled young man—will suppress her own concerns about David for the sake of her daughter. In the true Wycherley to Sheridan tradition, the younger generation's romanticism has won out over the older generation's snobbery and materialism; moreover, while it is not an absolute requirement that the young suitor be wealthy, it certainly helps.

Between *The Reluctant Debutante* and *The Secretary Bird* (1968) came another period filled with rejection letters and frequent discouragement. During this time the main theatrical event for Home was the production of his ill-fated play, *Aunt Edwina*, in 1959. A comedy based on the theme of sex change, *Aunt Edwina* proved to be too much for London critics. There resulted a public battle and outcry over the play, with Home unsuccessfully committing his energy and his money in a prolonged battle with the critics. As is normally the result of such arguments, the author did not win his fight. While the play hardly seems vile or dangerous to today's reader, it lacks the spark and wit of a successful comedy. It remains of interest more for the argument it aroused than for its merit, and it is certainly not among Home's better plays.

The Secretary Bird, which played during 1967 in various cities and then arrived in London in the fall of 1968, proved to be Home's longest running play. The plot involves the shaky marriage of Hugh and Liz Walford and the events of a weekend at their country home. Hugh, an intellectual firmly dedicated to an indirect approach to love games, bides his time in a clever plot to hold onto his wife, even to the point of inviting her lover for a weekend stay. The fourth member of this intriguing quartet is Hugh's attractive secretary, Molly. While the play is heavily reliant on sexual innuendo, Home manages to keep the comedy at a level of sophisticated dialogue and characterization. Though it takes Liz a while to understand the rules, it is clear that Hugh is engineering a brilliant mating game between Molly and Liz's lover, John. Hugh is a well-drawn character, witty and civilized at all times, and it is easy to sympathize with him. Although the outcome of this quadrangular affair is hardly in doubt, Home keeps the audience in suspense by careful plot manipulation. Like many of his drawing-room comedies, this is a trivial play, but one well designed to amuse audiences, as the play's run of more than 1,400 performances in London demonstrates.

Lloyd George Knew My Father and *The Dame of Sark*, plays of the mid-1970s, were both successful on stage and were departures from Home's traditional mode of drawing-room comedy. *Lloyd George Knew My Father*, originally produced as *Lady Boothroyd of the By-Pass* (1972), presents a central figure who convinces her family (and the newspapers) that she intends to commit suicide at precisely 8:00 A.M. on a Monday morning. The reason for her somewhat overstated symbolic gesture is the taking of part of the family land for a new highway. Boothroyd Park is a major estate; her husband, General Sir William Boothroyd, is a rather antique member of a noble family; her son is a member of Parliament; therefore, there is a general assumption that Lady Sheila Boothroyd will triumph in her battle against progress and bureaucracy. However, like Anton Chekhov's decaying aristocrats, the Boothroyd family is facing a new and unsentimental society. Like the cherry orchard, a corner of Boothroyd Park must give way to progress.

While all this is plausible thematically, the play is hampered by frequently wooden dialogue and generally unsympathetic characterization. The scenes with the vicar, ineptly trying to convince Lady Boothroyd that suicide is an unwise and unchristian approach to the problem, are the most

Peggy Ashcroft (at the piano) and Ralph Richardson (far right) in a scene from the first London production of
Lloyd George Knew My Father

pleasant and amusing in the play. Sir William, slightly dotty and hard-of-hearing, provides obvious comedy. The ending is sentimental and insufficiently prepared by the playwright: none of the characters is a match for Lady Sheila; and therefore the audience is increasingly aware that the denouement will necessarily come down to the question of what she decides to do. The tone of *Lloyd George Knew My Father* is light, but the idea is plodding in its execution.

The Dame of Sark is an even further departure from Home's most successful work. This is a serious play in six scenes, developing chronologically historical incidents of World War II. Sibyl Hathaway, titular ruler of Sark, one of the Channel Islands, wrote her story soon after the war. When Home read her book, he determined to use the material for a drama. In 1974, writing one scene per day for six consecutive days, he worked out the play for an Oxford festival and specifically for actress Celia Johnson. Although the events cover a five-year period, the play, perhaps because of Home's determined method of tight composition, displays an effective unity. Essentially *The Dame of Sark* traces the battle of wills between a tough-minded English lady and the forces of Nazi evil. Symbolically it is clear that the real battle is civilization versus anarchy, chaos, and darkness. Since the audience knows the outcome of World War II, the real suspense rests with the battle of wills, the minor skirmishes, the small victories that the Dame manages during an unwelcome period of occupation by a small German force.

Home, however, invests the play with an intriguing added dimension that was not part of his source. The German commandant, Colonel von Schmettau, is humanized; though diligent and demanding, he is not a stereotyped, grotesque Nazi. Furthermore, Muller, a youthful German guard, is portrayed in enormously sympathetic tones. Home's basic theme becomes the senselessness of war, suggested by the bonds of all mankind.

It is intriguing to note that the Dame herself, reading Home's draft, told the playwright that he was distorting her work by building in sympathy for young Muller. At the play's conclusion, when the island is liberated by English soldiers and the young German is killed accidentally, the Dame demonstrates her sympathy for Muller, an effective dramatic touch. But the ever-crotchety real Dame, writing to Home in 1974, told him that in fact there were two German soldiers blown up in the accident in the harbor, and furthermore that she was not in the least bit sorry.

The Kingfisher is a romp involving the rejuvenation of love in a pair of golden-agers who presumably ought to know better. Almost all critics saw the play for what it is—a piece of fluff but a great vehicle for its three-person cast. *The Kingfisher* did extremely well on Broadway, owing heavily to the efforts of a superb cast, Claudette Colbert, Rex Harrison, and George Rose, and then played with equal success in a national American tour. Although it shows no particular progress for the playwright, it does suggest that he is still capable of writing clever situation comedy and effective, if implausible, dialogue.

Thus Home has written plays with admirable durability and frequent success over a period of forty years. Although reasonably successful as a playwright both in England and abroad, Home has found the critics frequently difficult to deal with. They have often pilloried him for what they perceive as upper-class attitudes and have attacked him for writing what he really writes best—drawing-room comedy. With the rise of the angry young playwrights in England, championed vocally by Kenneth Tynan and other prominent drama critics, Home suffered a series of difficulties in having his plays produced. Typical of the attitude for a long time was Tynan's glib line, "Mr. Home (pronounced Hume), made me foam (pronounced fume)." Turning the other cheek, Home later preempted Tynan's line and used it as the title of his autobiography.

Other critics, notably Harold Hobson of the *Times*, have been kinder. While conceding that Home's plays suffer from unevenness, Hobson has suggested that there is a large measure of talent beneath the whipped cream. In his review of Home's autobiography, Hobson admitted that class bias was often a factor in his colleagues' and his own damning reviews of several of Home's plays: "We do really find it hard to forgive a man who can write plays which run for hundreds of nights (something that none of us could do to save our lives), and who at the same time has the effrontery to be the son of an Earl and the brother of a Prime Minister." This may yet be the fairest comment with which to conclude an appraisal of Home's plays.

Screenplays:
Now Barabbas, De Grunwald, 1949;
The Chiltern Hundreds, Rank, 1949;
The Colditz Story, by Guy Hamilton and Ivan Foxwell with additional dialogue by Home, Republic, 1957;
The Reluctant Debutante, MGM, 1958.

Ann Jellicoe
(15 July 1927-   )

Barbara J. Small
Montclair State College

PRODUCTIONS: *Rosmersholm*, translated and adapted from Henrik Ibsen's play, 1952, Cockpit Theatre Club, London, 38 [performances]; revised version, 18 November 1959, Royal Court Theatre (transferred 5 January 1960 to Comedy Theatre), London, 86;

The Sport of My Mad Mother, 25 February 1958, Royal Court Theatre, London;

The Lady from the Sea, translated and adapted from Ibsen's play, 15 March 1961, Queen's Theatre, London, 93;

The Knack, 9 October 1961, Cambridge Arts Theatre, Cambridge; 27 March 1962, Royal Court Theatre, London, 30; 27 May 1964, New Theatre, New York, 685;

Der Freischütz, translated from Friedrich Kind's libretto, music by Karl Maria von Weber, 12 September 1963, Sadler's Wells, London;

The Seagull, adapted by Jellicoe from Adriadne Nicolaeff's translation of Anton Chekhov's play, 12 March 1964, Queen's Theatre, London, 93;

Shelley; or The Idealist, 18 October 1965, Royal Court Theatre, London;

The Rising Generation, 23 July 1967, Royal Court Theatre, London;

The Giveaway, 1968, Edinburgh; 8 April 1969, Garrick Theatre, London;

You'll Never Guess, 19 May 1973, Arts Theatre, London;

Clever Elsie, Smiling John, Silent Peter and *A Good Thing or a Bad Thing*, 29 January 1974, Royal Court Theatre Upstairs, London;

The Reckoning, 13 December 1978, Woodroffe School Hall, Lyme Regis.

SELECTED BOOKS: *The Knack* (London: Encore, 1962; New York: French, 1962);

The Sport of My Mad Mother, revised version (London: Faber & Faber, 1964);

Shelley; or The Idealist (London: Faber & Faber, 1966; New York: Grove Press, 1966);

Some Unconscious Influences in the Theatre (London & New York: Cambridge University Press, 1967);

The Giveaway (London: Faber & Faber, 1970);

The Seagull, adapted by Jellicoe from Adriadne Nicolaeff's translation of Anton Chekhov's play (New York: Avon, 1975);

Three Jelliplays (London: Faber & Faber, 1975)—includes *You'll Never Guess, Clever Elsie, Smiling John, Silent Peter*, and *A Good Thing or a Bad Thing*;

Devon, by Jellicoe and Roger Mayne (London: Faber & Faber, 1975).

Ann Jellicoe, who is one of a group of young playwrights who have made their names with the

English Stage Company at the Royal Court Theatre, is both a dramatic writer and director. She prefers to direct her own plays because, for her, the writing, casting, and directing are inextricable parts of the same creative expression. Born in Middlesbrough, Yorkshire, she is the daughter of John and Andrea Jellicoe. She was educated at Polam Hall School in Darlington, County Durham, and Queen Margaret's School in Castle Howard, Yorkshire. Originally desiring to act, she studied at London's Central School of Speech and Drama from 1944 to 1947, where she discovered herself as a director and where she was awarded the Elsie Fogerty prize in 1947. She then worked in repertory as an actress, stage manager, and director, and traveled abroad to learn languages and study theater architecture. In 1950 Jellicoe married C. E. Knight-Clarke. The marriage ended in divorce in 1961, and the following year she married Roger Mayne. She has two children.

In 1951 Jellicoe founded the Cockpit Theatre Club in London to experiment with the open stage. Deriving basically from the Elizabethan platform stage, an open-stage theater has the acting platform, or stage, against one wall of the auditorium with the audience on three sides. Like theater-in-the-round, where the audience is on all four sides, the open-stage theater calls for adjustments in acting, staging, setting, and lighting, for those accustomed to the proscenium-arch theater. During the two years that she ran the club, which involved doing everything from painting scenery to running the box office, she directed a number of productions including *The Confederacy*, *The Frogs*, *Miss Julie*, *Saint's Day*, *Rosmersholm*, *The Comedy of Errors*, and *Olympia*. As a result of her study of theater architecture and her practical experience at the Cockpit Theatre, she strongly favors the open stage, a preference reflected in her plays.

Returning to the Central School in 1953 as an

Wendy Craig in the first production of The Sport of My Mad Mother

acting teacher, Jellicoe was responsible for many student productions. Since leaving in 1955 she has returned frequently to direct student productions, mainly of plays by modern English writers.

In 1956, wanting to break into professional theater as a director and deciding to provide herself with the means, she wrote *The Sport of My Mad Mother*, beginning, she explains, with a fragment she had written "in which youngsters cavorted around a college-bred American teasing, tormenting, losing control and finally, as their ecstasy rose to a climax, passing out with hysteria: the words they used were meaningless sounds to release emotion." From this fragment she built the symbolic characters and ritualistic situations of the play. *The Sport of My Mad Mother* is anti-intellectual in both form and content. The action, which includes a birth and a death, arises from irrational forces and urges. The content is conveyed directly to the audience's senses by rhythm, noise, gesture, and music. Jellicoe wanted to get at the audience primarily through their emotions, bypassing their intellect. The play has been compared to Antonin Artaud's plays in its use of ritual and to T. S. Eliot's *Sweeney Agonistes* (1933) in its verbal style. "In an ideal production," critic Kenneth Tynan has written, "it would have the effect of spontaneous improvisation, or of a vocal *danse macabre* that makes up its own rules as it goes along." Jellicoe's *The Sport of My Mad Mother* shared third prize with Richard Benyon's *The Shifting Heart* and N. F. Simpson's *A Resounding Tinkle* in the 1956 London *Observer* play competition. Jellicoe's play was selected for production by the English Stage Company at the Royal Court Theatre in 1958; Jellicoe served as codirector with George Devine, who had formed the company in 1956 to discover and promote new writing talent. Along with John Osborne, whose play *Look Back in Anger* was produced during the first season, Jellicoe, Simpson, Arnold Wesker, John Arden, David Storey, Charles Wood, and Edward Bond are among the playwrights who have made their names at the Royal Court Theatre. Though a complete commercial disaster, *The Sport of My Mad Mother* introduced Jellicoe as an experimental playwright.

Shortly after the production of *The Sport of My Mad Mother*, the Girl Guides Association commissioned Jellicoe to write a pageant commemorating the fiftieth anniversary of the organization in Great Britain for performance at the Empire Pool in Wembley. Why the traditional Guides would commission the avant-garde Jellicoe is still a mystery, but Jellicoe was intrigued by the idea of a cast of 800 girls, 100 boys, and some adults, and a nightly audi-

Lobby poster for the first London production of Jellicoe's best-known play

Philip Locke and Rita Tushingham in the first London production of The Knack

ence of 7,000. *The Rising Generation*, which was rejected by the Guides even after a complete, conventionalized rewriting, is an imaginative projection of childhood free association in large-scale theatrical terms in which a regiment of women headed by a monstrous mother-figure try to dominate the world and exterminate men. The original version was produced successfully at the Royal Court Theatre in 1967 with a cast cut down to 150 school children and a few adults.

Before the staging of her next original play, Jellicoe's translations and adaptations of two of Henrik Ibsen's plays were produced: *Rosmersholm*, revised since its 1952 production, was staged at the Royal Court Theatre in 1959 starring Peggy Ashcroft as Rebecca West, and *The Lady from the Sea* was produced at the Queen's Theatre in 1961 starring Margaret Leighton as Ellida. Both productions were extremely well received, as was her later adaptation of Anton Chekhov's *The Seagull*, produced in 1964 at the Royal Court Theatre starring Peggy Ashcroft as Irina and Vanessa Redgrave as Nina. Jellicoe finds that in Chekhov's plays, as in her own, the words form a pattern of sound which may reveal or hide the feelings of the characters, but which does not directly state them.

With Keith Johnson she codirected her next play for production at the Royal Court Theatre in 1962. *The Knack*, first produced in 1961 in Cambridge, is easily her best known and most popular work, partly due to the film *The Knack . . . and How to Get It*, adapted by Charles Wood from her play, which won the best picture award at the 1965 Cannes Film Festival. The play has been produced successfully in Canada, the United States, Australia, and on the Continent. Essentially a comedy about human relationships, *The Knack* is good entertainment. Indeed Jellicoe wrote the play, she explains, "for the same reason Shaw wrote *You Never Can Tell* (1898) and Ibsen *Love's Comedy* (1862): to make sure of getting a play produced after an early one had failed. So *The Knack* is a comedy with four characters and one set, but I wrote it mainly because I wanted to explore comedy, to write a play that should be full of joy, innocence and zest." She chose its subject—sex—because she feels that sex is the key to how people treat each other; the "knack" referred to in the title is the knack of getting girls.

Dandy Nichols, Gawn Granger, Margaret Nolan, and Roy Hudd in a scene from the first London production of The Giveaway

There exists a darker side to the comedy, however, a hint of the contagiousness of cruelty and the nature of sadism, which has been compared to the style of Harold Pinter. Some critics have found political overtones, seeing a parallel to international relations in the interpersonal relationships of the characters; although a parallel might be implied, the play is not an allegory.

In *The Knack* Jellicoe continues to develop the principle that action is not narrated; what happens is not what is said. Like in *The Sport of My Mad Mother*, Jellicoe creates a musical form through the verbal rhythms of speech and accompanying percussive sounds to convey content directly to the senses of the audience. The improvisational nature of the work was enhanced by Mike Nichols's direction of the New York production, which ran for 685 performances. *The Knack* has been most successful commercially when the comedy is stressed and the darker side softened as in the New York production, Desmond O'Donovan's revival at the Royal Court Theatre in 1966, and in the film version.

Shelley; or The Idealist (1965), a documentary melodrama of the poet's life, was a calculated departure from the use of vocal rhythms as an integral part of characterization and situation but a continuation of Jellicoe's experimentation with theatrical form. She tries to strip away all theatrical pretense and catch the audience's imagination in the simplest way possible with a narrative. Her preface betrays some creative and experimental ideas which she rejected at the time as being too theatrical. Afraid of being stereotyped after the success of *The Knack*, she seemed to be denying her natural tendencies as a writer and indulging in an intellectual exercise. Neither *Shelley* nor her experiment with farce in *The Giveaway* (1968) had the spontaneity or success of her earlier works.

Jellicoe is one of several British playwrights who came to prominence after 1956 but have now receded in critical estimation. Jellicoe's *The Sport of My Mad Mother* and *The Knack*, her two early plays which explore the conflict that arises from the basic hostilities between people, are generally considered her best. Most of her plays involve some improvisation; she believes, as a director and dramatist, in leaving a great deal open for the actors themselves to interpret. In each of her plays she has sought to

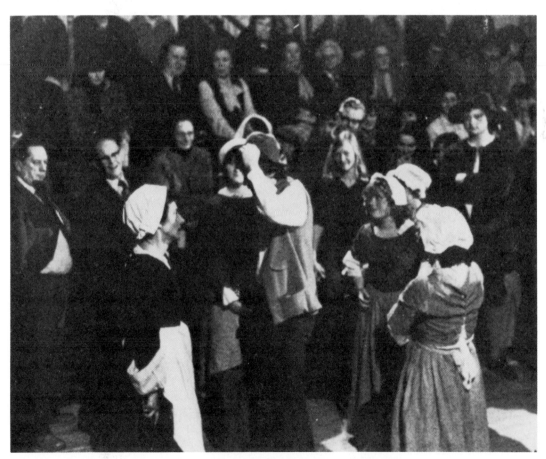

A scene from the first production of The Reckoning

First page of the manuscript for "Flora and the Bandits"

work out a different problem or question of dramatic form.

During the 1970s, Jellicoe served as literary manager of the Royal Court Theatre (1973-1974) and continued her work with improvisation and open staging by writing and directing three plays for children: *You'll Never Guess* (1973), a variation on the Rumpelstiltskin story; *Clever Elsie, Smiling John and Silent Peter* (1974), based on a Brothers Grimm folk tale; and *A Good Thing or a Bad Thing* (1974), an original play on how to deal with a monster. *The Reckoning*, her most recent project, is a piece of community art which deals with a brief period in the history of Lyme Regis. The production in 1978 involved more than two hundred people in a remarkable collaboration between professionals and a large section of the population of Lyme Regis. Jellicoe directed the action on three stages, with the audience in the middle and often involved in the crowd scenes. An intensely theatrical piece, it represents Jellicoe at her experimental best.

Other:

The Sport of My Mad Mother, in *The Observer Plays* (London: Faber & Faber, 1958);

The Rising Generation, in *Playbill 2*, edited by Alan Durband (London: Hutchinson Educational, 1970);

"The Writers' Group," in *At the Royal Court: 25 Years of the English Stage Company*, edited by Richard Findlater (New York: Grove, 1981), pp. 52-56.

Interviews:

"Theatre People Reply to Our Inquiry," *World Theatre*, 14 (January-February 1965): 44-53;

Robert Rubens, "Ann Jellicoe, Interviewed by Robert Rubens," *Transatlantic Review*, 12 (Spring 1963): 27-34.

Bibliography:

Kimball King, *Twenty Modern British Playwrights, A Bibliography* (New York & London: Garland, 1977), pp. 65-68.

References:

Harold Clurman, *The Naked Image: Observations on the Modern Theatre* (New York: Macmillan, 1966), pp. 88-89;

Richard Findlater, ed., *At the Royal Court: 25 Years of the English Stage Company* (New York: Grove, 1982);

Martin Gottfried, *A Theater Divided: The Postwar American Stage* (Boston: Little, Brown, 1967), pp. 218-225;

F. M. Kuna, "Current Literature 1970—II: New Writing," *English Studies*, 52 (December 1971): 565-573;

Frederick Lumley, *New Trends in 20th Century Drama* (New York: Oxford University Press, 1967), pp. 311-312;

Marie-Claire Pasquier, Nicole Rougier, and Bernard Brugiére, *Le Nouveau Théâtre Anglais* (Paris: Librairie Armand Colin, 1969), pp. 229-233;

Review of *The Giveaway*, *Times*, 9 April 1969, p. 6;

Review of *The Knack*, *New York Times*, 28 May 1964, p. 42;

Review of *The Knack*, *Times*, 28 March 1962, p. 15;

Review of *The Reckoning*, *Plays and Players*, 26 February 1979, p. 29;

Review of *The Rising Generation*, *Times*, 24 July 1967, p. 6;

Review of *Shelley; or The Idealist*, *Times*, 19 October 1965, p. 16;

Review of *The Sport of My Mad Mother*, *Times*, 26 February 1958, p. 3;

John Russell Taylor, *The Angry Theatre* (New York: Hill & Wang, 1962), pp. 64-71.

John B. Keane
(21 July 1928-   )

Christopher Murray
University College, Dublin

PRODUCTIONS: *Sive*, 2 February 1959, Walsh's Ballroom, Listowel; 29 June 1959, Father Matthew Hall, Cork, 50 [performances]; 1959, Olympia Theatre, Dublin;

Sharon's Grave, 1 February 1960, Father Matthew Hall, Cork, 32; 8 November 1961, Maidman Playhouse, New York, 6;

The Highest House on the Mountain, 14 September 1960, Gas Company Theatre, Dun Laoghaire, County Dublin, 10;

Many Young Men of Twenty, 5 July 1961, Father Matthew Hall, Cork, 48; 28 August 1961, Olympia Theatre, Dublin, 7;

No More in Dust, 12 September 1961, Gas Company Theatre, Dun Laoghaire, County Dublin, 11;

The Man from Clare, 1 July 1962, Father Matthew Hall, Cork, 46; 5 August 1963, Queen's Theatre, Dublin, 41;

The Year of the Hiker, 17 July 1962, Father Matthew Hall, Cork, 42; 18 August 1964, Gate Theatre, Dublin, 28;

Hut 42, 12 November 1962, Queen's Theatre, Dublin, 24;

The Field, 1 November 1965, Olympia Theatre, Dublin, 18; 1976, Irish Rebel Theatre, New York;

The Roses of Tralee, 29 November 1965, Opera House, Cork, 28; 12 April 1966, Gaiety Theatre, Dublin, 13;

The Rain at the End of Summer, 19 June 1967, Gaiety Theatre, Dublin, 14;

Big Maggie, 20 January 1969, Opera House, Cork; 10 February 1969, Olympia Theatre, Dublin, 42; 24 May 1979, Seton Hall University/ Irish-American Cultural Institute, South Orange, New Jersey, 8;

Faoiseamh, October 1970, Damer Hall, Dublin;

The Change in Mame Fadden, 10 May 1971, Opera House, Cork; 24 May 1971, Olympia Theatre, Dublin, 24;

Moll, 1 July 1971, Abbey Theatre, Killarney, 5; 26 July 1971, Opera House, Cork, 18; 4 October 1971, Olympia Theatre, Dublin, 28;

The One-Way Ticket, March 1972, Plaza Theatre, Listowel;

Values (*The Spraying of John O'Dorey*, *Backwater*, and *The Pure of Heart*), 25 April 1973, Group Theatre, Cork, 18;

The Crazy Wall, 27 June 1973, Theatre Royal, Waterford, 4; 23 July 1973, Opera House, Cork; 6 May 1974, Gaiety Theatre, Dublin, 35;

The Good Thing, 1 March 1976, City Theatre, Limerick, 6; 19 April 1976, Eblana Theatre, Dublin, 48;

The Buds of Ballybunion, 7 July 1978, White Memorial Theatre, Clonmel, 3; 24 July 1978, Olympia Theatre, Dublin, 32;

The Chastitute, 3 June 1980, Opera House, Cork, 11; 16 June 1980, Olympia Theatre, Dublin, 12.

SELECTED BOOKS: *Sive* (Dublin: Progress House, 1959);

Sharon's Grave: A Folk Play (Dublin: Progress House, 1960; Minneapolis: University of Minnesota Press, 1967);

The Highest House on the Mountain (Dublin: Progress House, 1961);

Many Young Men of Twenty (Dublin: Progress House, 1961; Minneapolis: University of Minnesota Press, 1967);

The Street and Other Poems (Dublin: Progress House, 1961);

The Man from Clare (Cork: Mercier Press, 1962);

The Year of the Hiker (Cork: Mercier Press, 1963);

Self-Portrait (Cork: Mercier Press, 1964);

The Field (Cork: Mercier Press, 1966);

Letters of a Successful T. D. (Cork: Mercier Press, 1967);

Hut 42 (Dixon, Cal.: Proscenium Press, 1968);

The Rain at the End of Summer (Dublin: Progress House, 1968);

Big Maggie (Cork: Mercier Press, 1969);

Letters of an Irish Parish Priest (Cork: Mercier Press, 1970);

Moll (Cork: Mercier Press, 1971);

The One-Way Ticket (Barrington, Ill.: Performance Publishing, 1972);

Values (Dublin & Cork: Mercier Press, 1973)— includes *The Spraying of John O'Dorey*, *Backwater*, and *The Pure of Heart*;

The Change in Mame Fadden (Cork & Dublin: Mercier Press, 1973);

The Gentle Art of Matchmaking (Cork: Mercier Press, 1973);

The Crazy Wall (Dublin & Cork: Mercier Press, 1974);

Letters of a Love-Hungry Farmer (Dublin & Cork: Mercier Press, 1974);

Letters of an Irish Publican (Dublin & Cork: Mercier Press, 1974);

Letters of a Matchmaker (Cork & Dublin: Mercier Press, 1975);

Death Be Not Proud and Other Stories (Dublin & Cork: Mercier Press, 1976);

Letters of a Civic Guard (Dublin & Cork: Mercier Press, 1976);

Strong Tea (Cork: Mercier Press, 1976);

Letters of a Country Postman (Dublin & Cork: Mercier Press, 1977);

The Good Thing (Newark, Del.: Proscenium Press, 1978);

Unlawful Sex and Other Testy Matters (Dublin & Cork: Mercier Press, 1978);

Letters of an Irish Minister of State (Dublin & Cork: Mercier Press, 1978);

The Buds of Ballybunion (Dublin & Cork: Mercier Press, 1979);

Stories from a Kerry Fireside (Cork & Dublin: Mercier Press, 1980);

The Chastitute (Dublin & Cork: Mercier Press, 1981).

John B. Keane is a regional dramatist. He writes of the people and culture of County Kerry, an area of Ireland which both John Millington Synge and Brendan Behan admired as possessing imaginative richness but which Keane, as a native, is able to study more intimately. His earliest plays seem to come from another era, having a haunting sense of remoteness and even barbarity in their tales of mountain folk, matchmakers, and lonely farm people. Their power stems mainly from the characterization, which may strike modern urban audiences as exotic or melodramatic but which is true to the colorful locale of the plays. The language is a second reason for Keane's power and popularity. While he does not rival Synge for beauty of phrasing, he is a true son of George Fitzmaurice (also a Kerry dramatist) inasmuch as he uses a racy, idiomatic speech, at times highly lyrical or explosive. The later plays tend to be more realistic than the earlier, grappling with the problems of rural people facing social and moral changes in modern Ireland. In general terms, Keane's plays are noted for their entertainment value rather than for artistic merit. He is a popular dramatist, in the purest sense of the word, authentically mirroring and articulating the passions and shortcomings of ordinary people. Because he deals with nonurban, nontechnological man, in a style fundamentally realistic, Keane appears old-fashioned and unsophisticated; but his work possesses qualities of authenticity and honesty which entitle him to be regarded as the principal spokesman in the theater for Ireland's modern provincial society.

John Brendan Keane, born on Church Street in Listowel, County Kerry, is the son of a schoolteacher father, William B. Keane, and a patriotic mother, Hannah Purtill Keane. The young Keane attended school locally, graduating from St. Michael's College in 1947. He then became apprenticed to a pharmacist in Listowel until January 1952 when he immigrated to Northampton, England, where he held a variety of jobs, from chemist's assistant to road sweeper, and began to write poetry and fiction seriously. The plight of the Irish immigrant in England struck him forcibly, with two effects: he was to write two plays on the topic ten years later, and he abandoned England for Ireland in 1954, working again as a chemist's assistant in Listowel before marrying a local girl, Mary O'Connor, on 5 January 1955. Keane bought a public house at 37 William Street at this time and settled into the business of operating a tavern for a living, which has remained part of his career. Some time in the late 1950s he saw the Listowel Drama Group's production of Joseph Tomelty's tragedy *All Souls' Night*, first performed by the Abbey Theatre, and felt inspired to write for the stage. *Sive*, Keane's first play, was performed by the same group of amateurs on 2 February 1959, and Keane was launched as a significant new Irish dramatist. A professional company, the Southern Theatre Group, headed by actor James N. Healy, took an immediate interest in Keane, acquired the rights to *Sive*, and thereafter Keane had a Cork-based company to write for. Nineteen more produced plays followed, up to 1980, usually premiering in the provinces and later going to Dublin.

The major themes of Keane's plays were largely determined by his having derived from the amateur drama movement, which was very strong in Ireland in the 1950s. During this time many small towns competed in regional drama festivals, aiming to reach the major event, the all-Ireland Drama Festival held in Athlone every spring. Keane's *Sive* won this all-Ireland competition in April 1959, and his subsequent plays have featured significantly in it. Amateur drama in Ireland in the 1950s reflected the style and standards of the Abbey Theatre, and, accordingly, realistic or kitchen drama dominated the repertory. Keane followed the Abbey tradition, but wrote more forceful works than were then in fashion at the Abbey Theatre, which rejected *Sive* when Keane submitted it for performance. Ironically, as time went on, Keane, more than any other playwright, carried on the Abbey Theatre's time-honored themes, that is, the land, emigration, and the trials of love in a rural environment.

Sive caused immense excitement with its first appearance on the festival circuit, and, after the Southern Theatre Group produced it professionally in Cork in 1959, it ran another six months in Dublin and other cities. It has frequently been revived and to date has amassed almost 500 performances. The play itself is melodramatic, which is the obvious but inadequate criticism to make. Undoubtedly, the structure is faulty, especially in the use of a letter which goes astray and a suicide which seems sensational, though explicable. What is striking about the play, however, is the impression it conveys of fierce poverty in its degrading, humanly destructive aspects.

The eponymous Sive is a young orphan girl who lives with her uncle Mike Glavin and his harsh and childless wife, Mena; against Mike's better judgment, Mena virtually sells the young girl into marriage with a lecherous old farmer, and Sive kills herself. The plot is not original, but the handling is given theatrical power through the use of two

James N. Healy, Mairin Morrish, Michael Twomey, and Eddie Hayes in the first professional production of Sive

traveling beggars or tinkers, Pats Bocock and his son, whose songs comment satirically on the intrigues of the older people and whose manipulation of a *bodhrán* (traditional percussion instrument) and staff forms a menacing drumbeat effect.

Sharon's Grave: A Folk Play (produced and published in 1960) is in a mode similar to that of *Sive*. Set in a small farmhouse in an isolated part of the southwest of Ireland, it is peopled by hard, obsessed, and, at times, abnormal individuals. The most striking character is a deformed cripple, Dinzie Conlee, who is carried on the back of his brother, Jack, which gives his presence a monstrous effect. Dinzie demonically terrorizes his cousin Trassie in an effort to force her to abandon house and farm to him so that he can perhaps offer some attractions to a woman, any woman, to satisfy his sexual craving. He is opposed by a traveling thatcher, Peadar Minogue, who, rather like the Tramp in Synge's *In the Shadow of the Glen* (1903), takes the side of the abused woman. The ending is violent, as perhaps befits the primitive atmosphere which permeates the play. Trassie's idiot brother, Neelus, runs off with Dinzie on his back and plunges into a whirlpool known as Sharon's grave, in the insane belief that he is appeasing the anguish of the mythological prin-

cess Sharon. With the elimination of the Heathcliffian figure from the landscape, a normal sexual relationship, between Trassie and Peadar, becomes possible.

The Highest House on the Mountain was premiered at Dun Laoghaire at the Dublin Theatre Festival in 1960, an event which annually offers a showcase of international and Irish theater. In this testing ground Keane's play, directed by Barry Cassin for Orion Productions, did very well, being the longest runner of the festival. As with the former two plays, violence, sex, and passion for the land loom large thematically, but the form of *The Highest House on the Mountain* is less of a folk play and more realistic. Yet there is symbolism suggested in the title, which refers to the abode of Sonny, the sensitive and haunted uncle of the two main contending brothers; Sonny emerges as a sort of savior figure, who brings the ex-prostitute Julie away from the scene of violence on the farm to his own place on the mountain. There is perhaps too much material in the play, some of it comic, to the detriment of characterization. Where subtle psychological study seems called for, skimpy outlines are provided; but the plot, on the whole, is effective.

More successful in its handling of narrative

was *Many Young Men of Twenty* (1961), a play with songs. Here Keane writes a thesis play against the prevalence of emigration from Ireland in the 1950s and 1960s. The theme had been handled already by Abbey dramatists, notably M. J. Molloy, but Keane's voice is distinctive on this topic. Avoiding mawkishness, he indicates the hemorrhagelike effect of emigration on a rural area, where whole families of young people depart to earn their living in England and elsewhere. To some extent *Many Young Men of Twenty* is an angry play, but it is also entertaining in its use of songs (such as the theme song, "Many Young Men of Twenty Said Goodbye") and its presentation of stereotyped but colorful local characters.

Sive was presented for the Abbey Theatre by the amateur Listowel Drama Group after the play's victory at Athlone, thus initiating a practice observed by the competition winners ever since. In 1962 *Hut 42* was premiered by the Abbey Theatre Company at the Queen's Theatre (its home for fifteen years after the 1951 fire), marking Keane's arrival as a professional playwright. The drama, which continues the theme of emigration, is set in England, at a building site where Irish "buck navvies" work alongside their Welsh and English counterparts. The loneliness of the immigrant is well portrayed, although the plot is slight and no more than a vehicle for Keane's comments. That Keane feels strongly about the subject of emigration is borne out by *Self-Portrait* (1964), an autobiography in which he repeats some of the points already made in *Many Young Men of Twenty* and *Hut 42*. All three works make clear that Keane holds the Irish government responsible for its failure to provide for its population.

The Man from Clare, first produced in Cork in 1962, began its Dublin run during Horse Show Week (first week in August), a time when only the most popular plays are acceptable. It opened on 5 August 1963, playing on alternate nights with Bernard Shaw's *The Devil's Disciple*, which may have been the Abbey Theatre's cautious means of hedging its bets. But by 12 August *The Man from Clare* had proved itself sufficiently popular to be run every night, until 31 August, when James Plunkett's *The Risen People* came into the repertory on alternate nights. From 9 September to 28 September Keane's play again ran on its own and was revived in mid-October to run on alternate nights with Federico García Lorca's *The House of Bernarda Alba*; it subsequently appeared as the Abbey Theatre's contribution to the Dublin Theatre Festival for 1963. The *Evening Herald* reviewer remarked: "A few more comedies like this each year from Mr. Keane might help solve some of the Abbey's financial problems." (The Abbey company was then, from 1951 to 1966, playing at the over-large Queen's Theatre.)

The Man from Clare is a character study of an aging Gaelic footballer who is forced to yield to the new "god," the younger footballer. The theme is interesting, and the character of the footballer, Padraic O'Dea, the man from Clare, is well drawn. Immature at age thirty-three, O'Dea comes to see that his mentor, Daigan, trainer of the team, feeds off his youth and wants to deprive him of marriage and his normal process of development. The play, then, is an attempt to probe the problem of the erosion of a public role by time. The footballer is the image of the public hero, and although he is a parochial figure he is well chosen; Keane's forte is the clarification of the sociological interdependence of personality and community on the parochial level, the nexus that binds individual to community, the arena within which people must work out their lives. But the ending, with O'Dea about to marry Nellie Brick, could be called contrived, given the rapid transitions through which the feelings of the characters are required to go in a single night.

After *The Man from Clare*, Keane focuses even more on character study, leaving aside the tendency to crowd his plots with incident. *The Year of the Hiker* (1962) offers a seldom-considered figure in Irish life, the man who takes to the roads, deserting wife and family because of a flaw in the marital situation. Earlier Irish plays, such as Padraic Colum's *The Fiddler's House* (1907), had treated the wanderlust figure, usually as an artist in search of an audience. Lacey, Keane's hiker, is no artist; his identity is defined solely by his absence from home. He returns after twenty years, suffering from a terminal disease. His return throws the family into disorder, but Keane shows the gradual acceptance of the emigrant, who draws out the love long buried in his family. There is some sentimentality and also some melodrama in this tale of conflict and reconciliation, but it is a simple play, where simple feelings are appropriate. Working well within his limitations, and depicting the details of Irish country life with great accuracy, Keane achieves a moving study of a man beloved by two sisters, whose rivalry drove him away from home.

The Field (1965) is a stronger, more violent play, often regarded as Keane's best. Keane seems always to be aware of the violence that lurks behind the pastoral exterior of Irish life. Here he tells the story of a murder, based on an actual case which occurred in Kerry in 1958. Thady "Bull" McCabe considers he has a right to a widow's field which he has leased for several years; when she puts it up for auction he intimidates all except William Dee, an emigrant anxious to return and build up an industry in Kerry. Bull and his loutish son Tadhg attack Dee at night to drive him off, and Dee dies of his injuries. Nobody in the locality will offer evidence against Bull. The bishop of Kerry comes to the village to chastise the people for their silence (a

brutal murder is offset by the Irish veneration for marital purity. The theme that silence signifies assent to violence is also found effectively expressed in Keane's radio play *The War Crime* (1976).

The Field made a powerful impact when staged in Dublin in 1965, largely through the much-praised performance of Ray McAnally as Bull McCabe. The play was several times revived during the later 1960s, and on 31 January 1980 it was staged at the Abbey Theatre (for 27 performances),

James N. Healy and Mairin Morrish in the first production of The Year of the Hiker

detail drawn from the actual, unsolved murder case) but to no avail. The play ends with Bull in possession of the field, mourning the fact that he alone will remember the stranger Dee forever. The problem Keane sets himself in the play is to provide a balance between the murderer's cruelty and his burning passion for the land (set against the intention of Dee to use the field as a factory site). In this regard, the field is representative, standing for the cause for which the Irish are often prepared to kill; the people's silence in the face of the killing may be construed as a traditional form of collusion. *The Field* may be compared with the one-act play, *The Pure of Heart* (contained in *Values*, 1973), where a

with Joe Lynch in the role of Bull. In a program note, Micheál Ó hAodha compared *The Field* with George Shiels's *The Rugged Path*, a big Abbey Theatre success in 1940; Keane had now taken his rightful place among traditionalist Abbey dramatists.

Four years were to pass before Keane wrote anything comparable with *The Field*. In the meantime, he wrote another musical drama, *The Roses of Tralee* (1965), which, like *No More in Dust* (1961), remains among his unpublished plays; it was a satire on the annual festival held in Tralee to select a beauty queen. He also wrote *The Rain at the End of Summer* (1967), an unusual attempt to break out of

Amharclann na Mainistreach

ABBEY THEATRE

The National Theatre Society Limited

Directors
Micheál O hAodha
Chairman

Peadar Lamb   *Artistic Director*
Tomás MacAnna   Joe Dowling
Charles McCarthy
Thomas Murphy   *Manager*
Margaret O Dalaigh   Martin Fahy
Gabrielle Wilson

Thursday 31 January 1980

THE
FIELD
by
John B. Keane

*John B. Keane
b. Listowel 1928*

*The National Theatre Society acknowledges the
assistance of the Arts Council of Ireland.*

*Program cover for the 1980 Abbey Theatre production of Keane's highly acclaimed play, contrasting the violence
of Irish life with its pastoral tradition*

the peasant-play pattern. Set in a city, it describes the family problems of Joss O'Brien, a widower whose two sons and daughter deny him the possibility of marriage with his housekeeper, Kate. The action takes place outdoors, in a suburban garden, and the rain signifies storm rather than renewal; the style is reminiscent of Tennessee Williams, a writer Keane admires, but there are too many family problems raised, and Joss, though strongly drawn, is not of sufficient stature to hold the play together. Yet, as the critic for the *Irish Times*, the late Seamus Kelly, remarked, "Keane has always something worthwhile to say, if only he would take more trouble in the saying of it."

Big Maggie (1969) returns to rural concerns and stands as one of Keane's most popular and successful plays. The plot is slight, allowing Keane to concentrate on the depiction of Big Maggie Polpin, a role first created by Marie Kean and subsequently played by many other outstanding Irish actresses. The outspoken Maggie, the widow who refuses to bend to the marital plans of her two daughters and the hopes of her ambitious sons, defies many conventions of Irish life. After a marriage to a philanderer, she wants her own way, that is, full control of the family business and full possession of all property; she will not speak well of the dead and she will not be manipulated into the role of a "good" providing mother. The blistering honesty, crude though it is, of Maggie Polpin makes her cruelty to her children entirely acceptable to audiences. As Phyllis Ryan, cofounder of Gemini Productions (responsible for many Keane productions in Dublin), has put it: "No play I can remember in a life spent in theatre made such a powerful impact on the Irish playgoer. In terms of business, any previous records were broken all over the country. In terms of emotive response from audiences, it seemed they could not get enough of this play, and large numbers of people from every walk of life went four or five times to see it." When *Big Maggie* was staged in the United States in 1979, Marie Kean won the State of New Jersey best actress award.

Keane next undertook the subject of menopause and the stresses it can cause in an unsympathetic family in *The Change in Mame Fadden* (1971). As in *The Rain at the End of Summer*, Keane combines the urban play and the problem play. The play suggests, indeed, that Keane is trying to deal with complex emotional problems in simple terms. The crass lack of understanding shown by Mame's husband, Edward, when she takes to roaming the streets at night and the equally self-centered responses of her two married sons make the charac-

terization seem thin and the plot (leading to Mame's suicide) contrived. Yet there are some fine scenes of confrontation in the play, and the role of Mame is original in Irish drama.

Keane, who at this time had begun his highly successful publications in the epistolary mode and was writing a weekly column for the *Evening Herald* and the *Limerick Leader*, seems to have overextended himself. He was involved in the initiation of Listowel Writers' Week in 1970, an annual occasion of book publication, writers' workshops, and public readings, and has been closely associated with it ever since (he is currently president of the Writers' Week Committee). Also, in 1973 he became president of the Irish Consultative Council of P. E. N. As a result of all of this activity his writing for the stage suffered. He continued to write plays, but where new advances were expected he disappointed with several lightweight and uneven pieces. *Moll* (1971), for example, is a comedy illustrating the effect of Moll Kettle, a new housekeeper, on three priests. She feeds the canon well and starves the two curates, imposing her will on the running of the parish as a result, until her success leads to promotion for the canon to another parish and the elevation of one of the curates to parish priest. Moll then coddles the latter, her former enemy, giving him privileged diet in order to secure her own future. Although shrewdly enough written and highly popular with some audiences, *Moll* is slight in content.

A few one-act plays, *The One-Way Ticket* (1972) and *Values* (1973), also appeared at this time. *The One-Way Ticket* concerns a reluctant lover whose best friend persuades him to break off the affair and then marries the girl himself. *Values* is a set of three plays: *The Spraying of John O'Dorey*, a futuristic look at the question of pollution; *Backwater*, something of a paean to the values of rural over urban life; and *The Pure of Heart*, a black farce wherein adultery is presented as a worse crime than murder. Keane handles the one-act form as he does the short story, as anecdote on which to erect a surprising finale. *Death Be Not Proud*, a short story collection published in 1976, demonstrates this technique. *Faoiseamh* (1970), which means "release," is a one-act play in Irish. It tells of an Irish emigrant in London who has taken a mistress while continuing to send home weekly remittances to wife and family; suddenly his wife turns up, with the eldest boy in tow. The situation is explored with insight as well as humor, and to some extent Keane here anticipates Maeve Binchy's much-acclaimed television play, *Deeply Regretted By . . .* (1979).

The Crazy Wall (1973) is a strange, rather

rambling full-length play, which centers on the fecklessness of the head of a family, Michael Barnett, whose failings are symbolized in a garden wall he starts to build but never finishes. The play takes the form of a flashback, after Michael's funeral, as his sons recall the years of crisis, set ironically during World War II; the effect here is similar to the irony of Patrick Kavanagh's poem,"Epic" (1959). Although Keane captures the period well, the theme of the play remains blurred, and it made little impact on audiences. The criticism was made that Keane was wasting his powers and going for the easy laugh.

The Good Thing (1976) reveals Keane in the rather surprising role of advocate of sexual liberation. Keane had explored this theme to some extent in *Big Maggie*, but now he writes rather more in the vein of the later Sean O'Casey, by indicating that sexual relations in Ireland are guilt-ridden and needlessly inhibited. The "good thing" is a married woman, Maudie, whom men incorrectly see as a flirt; it is her "affliction" and Keane's comic device that she be constantly misunderstood. Her marriage is both happy and prolific, however, and is used to show up the deficiencies of the marriages of her two sisters, Leslie and Eva, when all three meet in a hotel for a wedding reception. Through the introduction of Leslie's old flame, John Barrow (once rejected, in Ibsenian fashion, because he was socially inferior), and a series of farcical episodes involving Eva's oversexed husband; Maudie; her drunken-but-true husband, Mickey; and the hotel porter, sex is given pretty solid promotion. Reminiscent of the works of Ibsen and Feydeau, the play requires the audience suddenly to stop laughing and to acknowledge that there is a bit of a good thing in everybody; or so one may understand what Leslie and Eva mean by "the formula"—sexual liberation within marriage—they claim to have learned for a happy marriage at the end of the play. This risque thesis was developed in Keane's fiction at this time also, for example, in *Letters of a Matchmaker* (1975), which was successfully adapted to the stage as *The Matchmaker* (1975) by actor Ray McAnally and director Barry Cassin. *Letters of a Matchmaker* and Keane's other Letters volumes have a Rabelaisian bawdiness and an honest vulgarity reminiscent of Tobias Smollett. It is a vein of comic humor which Keane now, after *The Good Thing*, apparently intends to mine further and find serious elements therein, as is shown in his latest play, *The Chastitute* (1980), based on his *Letters of a Love-Hungry Farmer* (1974).

Prior to *The Chastitute*, Keane wrote *The Buds of Ballybunion* (1978), a nostalgic musical play, rather a slight piece paying tribute to the "buds" (from the Irish *bodaire*, a rough country person) who visited the Kerry seaside resort of Ballybunion in the 1940s. The play describes the demise of the boardinghouse they frequented and made their "cultural" center; it is a lament for a vanished part of tradition, comparable perhaps with M. J. Molloy's *The Visiting House* (1946). One Dublin reviewer called *The Buds of Ballybunion* "Not so much a play, more an entertainment," and this is a fair description.

The Chastitute has its entertaining qualities too; indeed, it is broadly comic in its depiction of the efforts of the lonely hero/narrator, John Bosco McLaine, to rid himself of his virginity at age fifty-three. He is, however, a "chastitute," one who suffers from the effects of chronic sexual abstemiousness, as the liberal Father Kimmerley tells him when he tries to confess his miserable attempts to have sex. In line with Keane's earlier attacks on emigration, the point is made here that those countrymen left at home, with aged parents to care for, fell victim to repressive and puritanical forces in Irish life. At the end of the play, John Bosco, haunted by two Catholic priests whose sermons on hell fire permanently inhibited his sexual nature, pledges himself to a slow form of suicide through alcoholism. Although the play keeps up a flippant tone right to the end, Keane wishes the tragic plight of John Bosco finally to shock the audience. (An earlier manuscript version of the ending had John Bosco reach for the shotgun in a more obvious suicidal gesture.)

The reviews of Keane's best plays have been enthusiastic, but at times Irish reviewers seem exasperated with him. It may be that his work for the theater is marred by flaws of dramaturgy likely to disturb the professional critic; many of the plays give the impression that they would benefit from rewriting. Yet the fact remains that for more than twenty years audiences have been entertained by Keane's plays, actors and actresses have found great scope for their talents in his plays, and directors have found sure-fire theater in his plays. It is perhaps up to the critic, after Keane's record is considered, to come to terms with it and find appropriate means for its assessment and evaluation: this has not yet happened in Ireland, and Keane's work is little known on the stage outside of Ireland.

From *Sive* and *Sharon's Grave* to *The Good Thing* and *The Chastitute* marks a definite development in

Program cover for the first Dublin production of Keane's comedy about a reluctant male virgin

Keane's playwriting, away from the romantic and florid style toward a far greater degree of realism and social criticism. He himself has commented: "I'd say my ideal play now would be a kind of a cross between *The Summer of the Seventeenth Doll* and *Streetcar* [*A Streetcar Named Desire*]. My aim is to eviscerate the weaknesses, foibles and essential dignity of my characters. I try to give the full human picture in all its starkness, and I never make any apologies for [bad] language." It is a commonplace criticism that Keane writes too much and too quickly; besides his plays, he produces numerous prose works and little volumes of humorous and highly popular essays (based on his journalism). He has also written five plays for radio between 1959 and 1980, and these, too, comic and wise in their exploration of Irish life, deserve study. Keane's development, it might be said in conclusion, has not been steady, but fitful and wayward; the "evisceration" he speaks of is sometimes fatal to his own characters, given the speed of the surgeon. He believes that he will write his best work in his fifties, and it remains to be seen if this will be so. But already he has established himself as not only a major entertainer in Ireland but also a shrewd chronicler for, analyst of, and commentator on a changing Irish society.

Radio Scripts:

Barbara Shearing, RTE, 1959;
A Clutch of Duckeggs, RTE, 1970;
The War Crime, BBC, 1976;
The Talk Specific, RTE, 1979;
The Battle of Ballybooley, RTE, 1980.

References:

John M. Feehan, ed., *Fifty Years Young: A Tribute to John B. Keane* (Dublin & Cork: Mercier Press, 1979);

J. Anthony Gaughan, *Listowel and its Vicinity* (Cork: Mercier Press, 1073), pp. 469-470;

Elgy Gillespie, "The Saturday Interview: John B. Keane," *Irish Times*, 19 June 1976, p. 5;

Joanna L. Henderson, "Four Kerry Writers: Fitzmaurice, Walsh, MacMahon, Keane, a Checklist," *Journal of Irish Literature*, 1 (May 1977): 118-119;

Robert Hogan, *After the Irish Renaissance: A Critical History of the Irish Drama since The Plough and the Stars* (London & Melbourne: Macmillan, 1968), pp. 208-220;

Hogan, ed., *Dictionary of Irish Literature* (London: Macmillan, 1980), pp. 345-348;

Gus Smith, *Festival Glory in Athlone* (Aherlow Publishers, 1977), pp. 9-42.

Barrie Keeffe
(1945-   )

H. Lloyd Goodall, Jr.
University of Alabama in Huntsville

SELECTED PRODUCTIONS: *Only a Game*, March 1973, Shaw Theatre, London;

Gem, 7 July 1975, Soho Poly Theatre, London; produced again in *Gimme Shelter*, 31 January 1977, Soho Poly Theatre, London; 23 March 1977, Royal Court Theatre, London; 1978, Brooklyn Academy of Music, New York;

A Sight of Glory, August 1975, Cockpit Theatre, London;

My Girl, 15 September 1975, Soho Poly Theatre, London;

Gotcha, 17 May 1976, Soho Poly Theatre, London; produced again in *Gimme Shelter*, 31 January 1977, Soho Poly Theatre, London; 23 March 1977, Royal Court Theatre, London; 1978, Brooklyn Academy of Music, New York;

Here Comes the Sun, August 1976, Jeannetta Cochrane Theatre, London;

Abide With Me, 28 September 1976, Soho Poly Theatre, London; produced again in *Barbarians*, 28 August 1977, Soho Poly Theatre, London; 28 September 1977, Greenwich Theatre, London;

Scribes, October 1976, Greenwich Theatre, London; 1977, Phoenix Theatre, London;

Gimme Shelter (*Gem*, *Gotcha*, and *Getaway*), 31 January 1977, Soho Poly Theatre, London; 23 March 1977, Royal Court Theatre, London; 1978, Brooklyn Academy of Music, New York;

A Mad World, My Masters, 28 April 1977, Young Vic

(transferred to Roadhouse Theatre), London;

Barbarians (*Killing Time*, *Abide With Me*, and *In the City*), 28 August 1977, Soho Poly Theatre, London; 28 September 1977, Greenwich Theatre, London;

Up the Truncheon, August 1977, Shaw Theatre, London;

Frozen Assets, 9 January 1978, Warehouse Theatre, London;

Sus, 1979, Soho Poly Theatre, London; 1979, Royal Court Theatre, London;

Bastard Angel, January 1980, Warehouse Theatre, London;

She's So Modern, 1980, Queen's Theatre, London;

Chorus Girls, 1981, Theatre Royal, Stratford East.

BOOKS: *Gadabout* (Harlow: Longman, 1969);

Gimme Shelter (London: Eyre Methuen, 1977; New York: Grove, 1979)—includes *Gem*, *Gotcha*, and *Getaway*;

A Mad World, My Masters (London: Eyre Methuen, 1977; New York: Eyre Methuen, 1981);

Barbarians (London: Eyre Methuen, 1977; New York: Eyre Methuen, 1981)—includes *Killing Time*, *Abide with Me*, and *In the City*;

Frozen Assets (London: Eyre Methuen, 1979; New York: Eyre Methuen, 1981);

Sus (London: Eyre Methuen, 1980; New York: Eyre Methuen, 1981);

Bastard Angel (London: Eyre Methuen, 1980; New York: Eyre Methuen, 1981);

Heaven Scent (London: Eyre Methuen, 1980);

The Long Good Friday (London: Magnum, 1981).

Barrie Keeffe's plays are alive with the music, the violence, the talk, the passions, and the pursuits of the life he has known since his birth in East Ham, London, in 1945. Since the production of *Only a Game* in 1973, Keeffe, the only son of Edward Thomas Keeffe, a post office employee, and Constance Marsh Keeffe, a Women's Voluntary Service worker, has risen steadily in professional stature. In 1977, the television adaptation of his play *Scribes* won the Thames Television Award; in 1978, Keeffe won the French Theatre Critics Prix Revelation for *Gotcha*; and his 1980 radio play *Heaven Scent* won the Giles Cooper Award.

Unlike many of his contemporaries, Keeffe did not attend a university to gain training as a writer. After leaving grammar school he held a variety of odd jobs, some of which, such as work in journalism, provided material for his plays. He did not give up regular wages as a reporter for the East London weekly, the *Stratford Express*, until June 1976. Since then he has made his living with his depictions of contemporary working-class London, completing more than a dozen stage plays, eight original television plays, five radio scripts produced for the BBC, and a screenplay.

Keeffe began his writing career not as a dramatist but as a novelist. *Gadabout*, a novel written when he was eighteen and published in 1969, was his first attempt to draw on the experiences of his youth. "Mercifully," he said to a London *Times* reporter in 1977, "it's out of print. I've bought up piles of them when I've seen them on remainder at railway stations. I've spent a fortune buying up the bloody things." A second novel, the story of three generations of cockneys, and a quarter of a million words in length, was responsible for his turn to the theater: the first draft of the book, Keeffe's only copy, was taken from his car by vandals who stole the car's racing seats, wheels, and a bag in which the manuscript and a few other things were stored. "I went really crazy for quite a long time. It had been nearly three years' work. I couldn't even think about re-writing it. That's when the idea came of taking one strand of it and making it into a play. It never occurred to me to write a play before then. Now I'm sort of grateful to the thief. I've taken about three plays directly from the novel."

Keeffe's first memory of theater is a play called *High Street China*, performed by Joan Littlewood's Theatre Workshop. He attended it on a school outing, and, although the play has not survived as part of the Theatre Workshop's repertoire, he has never forgotten it. "It was an amazing experience because it was the first time I confronted people living a life I recognized." The influence of that experience can readily be found in his work.

His characters are customarily drawn from East Ham people he has known or seen, people "alienated within the British class system and rendered impotent by it." His plays are not intended for the wealthier, more traditional West End audiences because his goal in life is "to attract to my plays people who would not be seen dead in a theatre." He fears dying "before completing the work I want to do, or even worse, to have my plays studied for the purposes of examinations." In this vein, Keeffe claims no literary heroes or associations; his heroes are songwriters and musicians Mick Jagger, Keith Richards, and Raymond Douglas Davies, the soccer player Bobby Moore, and the boxer Muhammad Ali.

Keeffe's tastes are carefully worked into his plays. He is one of the first playwrights to incorporate rock music, street violence, and the language of the East End into his plays, having used Rolling Stones, Beatles, Clash, Van Morrison, and Beach Boys soundtracks in his productions. At least two of his works have been banned by the BBC for violence and harsh language. His work has almost universally been praised or panned on the same four grounds: humor, sex, violence, and rebellion.

Keeffe's first four plays (*Only a Game*, 1973; *A Sight of Glory*, 1975; *My Girl*, 1975; and *Here Comes the Sun*, 1976) were early attempts to adapt his unique street-gang style to the theater form. The major themes are youth, sport, violence, and rebellion. In *Scribes* (1976), Keeffe produced an account of life in the offices of a suburban London newspaper that was compared unfavorably by Kenneth Hurren to Michael Frayn's *Alphabetical Order* (1975). Most other reviewers gave better accounts of the work, finding it amusing, even acute in its depiction of the slow, boorish, hierarchical malaise of second-class, second-rate journalism. The play may well have been Keeffe's not-so-fond farewell to the life he had been leading as a reporter, and, oddly enough, it was welcomed most by those who shared similar lives. With *Scribes* Keeffe developed his talents for verisimilitude and at the same time identified his primary audience, one which would not include the highbrow, West End tastes of Kenneth Hurren.

In 1977, Keeffe wrote four stage plays, two television plays, and a radio script. The same year he served as resident dramatist at the Shaw Theatre. Two of the stage plays revealed a major new development in Keeffe's dramatic style—construction of the trilogy. In the much praised *Gimme Shelter* (1977) and the less formidable *Barbarians* (1977), Keeffe's sharp satirical wit, open anger at the class system, and ability to use variety in achieving his effects coalesce to transform the street-gang ideology into penetrating social statements.

In *Gimme Shelter* (a title borrowed from a Rolling Stones' record), three short plays are linked by a frustration common to life's human worms—the inability to gain entrance to a life of self-worth, if not substance, represented by the middle classes. The dramatic tension in the plays is revealed in the emotional dialogue of the characters, individuals who are at once attracted to and repelled by the way they will never be. In the trilogy, Ronald Hayman observes, Keeffe emerges "as a sturdy champion of the semi-literate" and cannot "be accused, as Eliot and Pinter could, of treating uneducated speech with critical condescension." Keeffe's dramatic language, rather, shows his characters to be victims "of a system that has not taught [them] how to communicate." In *Gem*, the first of these short plays (produced separately in 1975), the focus is on Kev, a rebel from the marginal security represented by his marginal job. The scene is a view from just outside a cricket match played on August Bank Monday—a holiday. As the match is played, Kev vents his anger at the university lads who always seem to get the girls, and at his boss, who has all the style Kev lacks. Through a series of dialogues with his friends, Kev complains of the humiliations and small defeats that could be remedied, he fantasizes, by a worker's revolution, led by Clive Jenkins. While the match goes on, Kev's social inaction contrasts sharply with the efforts of his contemporaries on the playing field, and he loses a girl, a friend, and any chance to overcome his frustrations. In the end, after his impotent dream dissolves, he catches his friend post-coitus with his girl. When he objects to this treatment, the girl tells him, "Why don't you crawl in a hole." He responds, "I can't find one big enough."

The second play of the trilogy, *Gotcha* (first produced in 1976), presents an antihero named only Kid. Sixteen, the Kid is about to leave comprehensive school with a report card that sums up his aptitude for the labor exchange—"weak . . . lazy . . . very poor." This damning report was composed by teachers who hardly recall the Kid's name, including the headmaster, who signed the report. The Kid realizes that his life will be shaped by this report, prepared by unsympathetic, middle-class bureaucrats. His chance for revenge comes when he stumbles upon two of his teachers making love in the school stockroom, where he parked his motorcycle. He dangles lit cigarettes over the gas tank, threatening to blow them all up. As the cigarettes burn down, he increases his demands, and, in a brilliant series of comic ironies, Keeffe shows the desperate futility of the Kid's dreams: he forces the overweight, flabby male teacher to do exercises beyond his flagging capacities; he extracts unobtainable middle-class promises from the headmaster, including the Kid's playing ball for the West End and becoming a brain surgeon. When he hears these false promises, the same lies that have plagued generations of East End youth, he is enraged. He sees, in one moment of clarity, the impossible connection between the realities of his life and the empty dreams inspired by his compulsory education. Even his single act of rebellion is suddenly understood for what it is—a flash in the pan, signifying nothing. The pseudosympathetic female teacher seizes this moment of confusion to tempt him with the offer of a dance. With his guard down, the Kid is overpowered by the male teacher and the headmaster. He is brutally beaten, kicked, and left with the echo of the female teacher's last words ringing in his ears: "It's important that you can . . . believe someone."

The final play of the trilogy, *Getaway*, has the loser Kev, from *Gem*, meet the Kid, now a gardener. Kev believes the Kid to be a revolutionary hero. The Kid, who has "paid his debt to society" for his act of stockroom terrorism, will have none of the praise. He sees the act as a "mistake" and is glad he is now "straight," with "self-respect and a future." Kev, who has been promoted to a mid-level management position, will not admit he "has gone over to the other side." The Kid laughs at Kev's treatment of his private nightmare. The trilogy ends with Kev watching the end of a cricket match, cheering his team on to victory. *Gimme Shelter* established Keeffe's reputation as a maturing dramatist, and critical acclaim helped bring the trilogy to New York's Academy of Music in 1978.

A Mad World, My Masters (1977) enlarges the theme of class struggle with Jacobean bawdiness and wit, complete with a title borrowed from Thomas Middleton. Billed as a "happy comic strip," this play concerns the attempts of a Hackney family to claim £20,000 insurance from the bourgeois villain, Horace Claughton. Both parties are corrupt, and the interplay of wit and insult make the play memorable for its caricature of high and low society. The superintendent of police dresses like Prime Minister Margaret Thatcher, Claughton appears at a palace party dressed as a goose, and the Queen offers a dirty handshake with the words, "Don't worry, it's only horseshit." The only character who escapes this comedy of greed and error is a musician, a likely testimony to Keeffe's belief in the purity of artists in this world.

Up the Truncheon (1977) is about the Soho constabulary's attempts to arrest "Vicious Bert, a Great Train Robber," and a record pusher's exploitation of a talented but unknown rock group. The play is a 1960s period piece, complete with "wisecracks in the style of the Beatles' films," and music by the Kinks, the Rolling Stones, and the Who. Again, Keeffe shows himself to be a master of the art of caricature—and irony—in creating a vicar who impersonates Mick Jagger, a policeman who struggles with his loyalty to his criminal family, and a sad young girl from Liverpool who is seduced and betrayed by a rock star. Most reviewers did not find this work to be of the quality of Keeffe's previous plays, but with a cast of seventy actors, musicians, and singers, *Up the Truncheon* was an ambitious attempt to reveal the impact of the psychedelic era.

Since that minor setback, Keeffe has con-

tinued to produce quality plays capable of gaining both critical and popular acclaim. The best of his work to date, *Gimme Shelter*, has found new and appreciative audiences in the United States and France. He continues to draw on his knowledge of working-class London, but he has also expanded this base with a recent entry into the world of rock superstardom, *Bastard Angel* (1980). In this play, the tale of a female lead vocalist for a band that resembles Debby Harry's Blondie, with overtures to Bette Midler's version of Janis Joplin's career in the film *The Rose* (1980), Keeffe reveals the inner and outer worlds of his generation's most persistent fantasy—rags-to-riches with rock and roll. Music, always a major element in his plays, becomes the theme of *Bastard Angel*, supported by the usual associations of international fame—drugs, sex, glitter, and personal gloom.

If Keeffe's work can be seen as a strong attempt to identify, and to express, the real and imagined lives of his young working-class audiences, then his dramatic chronicles of the post-World War II generation must be judged a triumph. He has begun to do for the stage what his rock counterparts have done for music: to use the form to embody the process of change. Hence the necessity of human dialogue and human violence, the two agents of change common to everyday experience and the two interlocking forces found everywhere in Keeffe's art.

From his comic-strip plays to his ambitious trilogies, he has channeled his special awareness of the contradictions within the individual in a changing social world to stage, television, and radio productions that are truly alive. He writes well about what he knows best—the people, the places, the music, and the general malaise of the working class. If his work caricatures his generation, it also informs it; if his dramatic vision is compelling, it also tells us, shows us, how a language of rage, alienation, despair, and rock and roll, born on the back streets of London's East End, can be successfully transformed to powerful stories for the contemporary stage, to be played at full volume, with much passion, compassion, and skill.

Screenplay:
The Long Good Friday, Black Lion Films, 1980.

Television Scripts:
Substitute, Granada Television, 1972;
Gotcha, BBC, 1977;
Not Quite Cricket, Thames Television, 1977;

Scribes, BBC, 1977;
Nipper, BBC, 1978;
Hanging Around, BBC, 1978;
Champions, Granada Television, 1978;
Waterloo Sunset, BBC, 1980.

Radio Scripts:
Uncle Jack, BBC, 1975;
Pigeon Skyline, BBC, 1975;
Only a Game, BBC, 1976;

Self Portrait, BBC, 1977;
Heaven Scent, BBC, 1980.

References:
Ned Chaillet, "Barrie Keeffe: The Play's the Thing," *Times Saturday Review*, 26 March 1977, p. 10;
Ronald Hayman, *British Theatre Since 1955* (London: Oxford University Press), pp. 28-29, 133, 142.

Bernard Kops
(September 1926?-)

Philip Klass
Pennsylvania State University

SELECTED PRODUCTIONS: *The Hamlet of Stepney Green*, 19 May 1958, Playhouse, Oxford; 15 July 1958, Lyric Opera House, Hammersmith, London; 13 November 1958, Cricket Theatre, New York;
Goodbye, World, 2 February 1959, Guildford Theatre, Guildford;
Change for the Angel, 1 March 1960, Arts Theatre, London;
The Dream of Peter Mann, 5 September 1960, Lyceum Theatre, Edinburgh;
Stray Cats and Empty Bottles, 5 May 1961, A.D.C. Theatre, Cambridge;
Enter Solly Gold, 10 September 1962, Centre 42, Wellingborough; 1969, Mermaid Theatre, London;
Ezra, 14 May 1981, New Half Moon Theatre, London.

SELECTED BOOKS: *The Hamlet of Stepney Green* (London: Evans, 1959);
The Dream of Peter Mann (Harmondsworth, U.K. & Baltimore: Penguin, 1960);
The World is a Wedding (London: MacGibbon & Kee, 1963; New York: Coward-McCann, 1963);
On Margate Sands (London: Secker & Warburg, 1978).

Bernard Kops

Bernard Kops belongs to that group of playwrights (Arnold Wesker is another notable example) whose work began appearing in the late 1950s and whose statements of generalized protest against life as they found it and politics as they saw it were drawn largely from backgrounds in poverty and lower-class Jewish family life in England. Kops uses the idiom of this background with great sensitivity, mixing it with humor and fantasy, to achieve, in several of his plays, telling effects. Directly or indirectly, his work shows the influences of a wide group of predecessors: Sean O'Casey, Bertolt Brecht, Shalom Aleichem, Brendan Behan, and even Karel Capek and Samuel Beckett. He is a peculiarly controversial figure among critics in that there is as yet little agreement as to his proper stature as an artist or upon the precise category of drama to which his work belongs.

Remarkably enough for a living playwright, there is even disagreement as to the year of his birth. Frederick Lumley and John Russell Taylor give it as 1928; however, 1926 seems to be the correct date, if we are to go by the author's own words in his autobiography: "Nearly thirteen years old, when I should have been studying and practising for my Bar Mitzvah, I found myself in Buckinghamshire in a church hall at that. . . . So there we were, September the first 1939, Friday night, when we should have been having lockshen soup, waiting to be billeted on a family who wanted us about as much as we wanted them."

This experience, on the eve of Britain's entry into World War II, for Kops was the first important one of that larger, gentile England, so different from the cultural hothouse of London's East End in which he had been born and reared. The peculiar nature of the Stepney culture in which he grew up infuses so many of the characters in his best plays. His family was large and desperately poor, but not working class, as most of the upper-class Britishers who write about him insist—not working class, at least, in the way that gentile equivalents of his relatives definitely are. Though his father was a leather worker and he himself was trained as a waiter, a barber, and a cook, Kops's family and neighbors were *luftmensch* oriented: they essentially lived by the economic traditions of their starveling but ingenious East European Jewish ancestors—willing to turn their hands and minds to almost any enterprise, preferably speculative ones, that offered the possibility of large returns for small investments as well as an independent and mobile way of life. Shalom Aleichem wrote of this tradition in Yiddish, developing it in terms of one of his most colorful characters: Menachem Mendel—matchmaker, stockbroker, or what-have-you. Kops himself has been a wandering actor, a peddler ("on the knock"), and the proprietor of a tiny bookstall ("next to the jellied eel and the flower stall"). He shows much more understanding in his plays of the exact social position and social relevance of a herring-seller, for example, than he does of the religion in which he

was raised or of the left-wing politics he later espoused. Nor is this to be regretted. There have been many—almost too many—literary exponents of Judaism and socialism; there have been remarkably few good poets and playwrights who have left us pictures of the talk and attitudes and aspirations of Seven Dials and Commercial Road and the slums of Stepney.

The Hamlet of Stepney Green (written in 1956, produced in 1958) was Kops's first professional play. Several critics feel it is also his best. He began the play after an unsuccessful first marriage and terrible experiences with drugs and a psychiatric hospital, after a harrowing trip through France and Spain with an impecunious theatrical troupe and a subsequent, government-subsidized return from grisly living conditions in North Africa as a "distressed British subject." *The Hamlet of Stepney Green* suggests that Kops had gone back to that part of his life which made most sense to him. Although his personal world had been chaotic in the years since he had left Stepney Green, there was an understanding of the novel richness of the material to which memory gave him access. Also, involved by this time in a happier marriage, he was able to reconsider the family life against which he had rebelled. Finally, he looked through Shakespeare at Stepney Green.

His Hamlet is not a young prince but a would-be crooner, who is probably meant to represent the adolescent Kops's rather romantic and garish notions of life as a bohemian cafe poet. The father, Sam Levy, is not the erstwhile king of Denmark, slain suddenly in his sleep by his wife's lover, but a rather warm though neurotic pickled-herring peddler who, dying, decides he has been poisoned by his life—or, perhaps he should say, by his wife? The play is full of such word games; occasionally they become song numbers ("Dance, sing, love, and laugh," the insurance salesmen carol, "We'll make up your epitaph. The second time is so much nicer; I DIED OF LOVE TODAY.") that at their best suggest Brechtian equivalents or bits from Brendan Behan's *The Hostage* (1958).

Here, the father's ghost is not at all asking for the revenge that young David Levy is all too ready to take: on the contrary, he is quite willing to have his widow remarry, especially since a good prospect, a neighbor by the name of Mr. Segal, is available; he even pushes his son most determinedly in the direction of Mr. Segal's daughter, the Kopsian Ophelia. To his son's Hamlet-like question, "What is the purpose in life? It seems senseless to me," the ghost of Sam Levy replies, "The purpose in life is to be aware

Lyric Opera House
Hammersmith

Lessees: Associated Theatre
Seasons Ltd.
Licensee: J. Baxter Somerville
Box Office Riv 4432 & 6000

JAMES H. LAWRIE (for Gleneagles Productions Ltd.)

presents

The Oxford Playhouse Production

The Hamlet of Stepney Green

by **BERNARD KOPS**

The Characters in order of appearance :

The Children	**Linda Blackledge**
	Janet Derry
	Dione Ewin
Hava Segal	**Ruth Meyers**
Mr. Segal	**John Barrard**
Sam Levy	**Harold Lang**
David Levy	**John Fraser**
Bessie Levy	**Thelma Ruby**
Mr. Stone	**George Selway**
Mrs. Stone	**Pat Keen**
Mr. Green	**Christopher Hancock**
Mr. Black	**Gilbert Vernon**
Mr. White	**Robert Bernal**

Directed by	**Frank Hauser**

Designed by	**Michael Richardson**
Accordionist	**Leon Rosselson**

The Songs are set to traditional Jewish melodies

Cast list, synopsis of scenes, and credits for the first London production of Kops's first professional play, an attempt to set the themes of Hamlet in a modern Jewish idiom

SYNOPSIS OF SCENES :

The action takes place at Sam Levy's house in Stepney Green

ACT I

An afternoon in June

ACT II

Scene 1. The next day

Scene 2. A week later

ACT III

The following year in May

There will be two intervals of ten minutes each

First performance at the Oxford Playhouse May 19th, 1958

First performance at this theatre Tuesday, July 15th, 1958

JOHN FRASER appears by permission of Associated British Picture Corporation Ltd.

scenery built by	Brunskill & Loveday
scenery painted by	Alick Johnstone
Miss Thelma Ruby's clothes by	Marks & Spencer
furniture by	Old Times
wigs by	Wig Creations
nylon stockings by	Kayser
Olivier cigarettes by	Benson & Hedges
electrical equipment by	Strand Electric
wardrobe care by	Lux
spectacles by	Negretti and Zambra
cigars by	King Six

PHOTOGRAPHS OF THIS PRODUCTION by KENNY PARKER of OXFORD

Management Advisers	⎫	MICHAEL CODRON LTD.
Stage Manager	⎪ For	.. .. DAVID BUXTON
Deputy Stage Manager ..	⎬ Gleneagles	.. MICHAEL SIMPSON
Assistant Stage Managers ..	⎪ Productions	.. .. JANET DERRY
	⎪ Ltd.	.. .. .. DIONE EWIN
Wardrobe Mistress	⎭	. JANE GREENWOOD
Press Representatives	PHILIP RIDGEWAY ASSOCIATES LTD. Tel.: Cov 0333	

The Management reserve the right to make alterations to the items or the cast without warning.

General Manager	⎫	REGINALD CORNISH
Assistant Manager	⎪	.. JACK BROWN
Secretary	⎪ For	.. .. GILLIAN LINDO
Artistic Adviser	⎬ Lyric Opera House	.. .. DISLEY JONES
Resident Stage Manager ..	⎪ Hammersmith	.. .. .. PAT FEARON
Chief Electrician	⎪	.. .. .. JOE ENGLISH
Assistant Electrician	⎪	.. .. JACK BARCLAY
Property Master	⎭	. .. SAM INGRAM

BOX OFFICE (Mrs. Vera Murray) open from 10 a.m. to 8 p.m. .. RIV 4432 & 6000

SMOKING IS NOT PERMITTED IN THE AUDITORIUM

that that question exists." It is not just that Sam is a traditional good Jewish father rather than a stern and vengeful Danish one; he is more believable to a modern audience because he is so weary and old and yet full of love for everything left alive.

The play fails, however, chiefly in its attempt to parallel Shakespeare's *Hamlet*. E. Martin Browne suggests, "The link between the crooner-son and Hamlet the Dane is rather tenuous; it is the author's link, not the character's . . . ," and there are passages, as John Russell Taylor points out, that "are sometimes embarrassingly self-conscious." Certainly the son's happy ending speech ("I'll sell herrings and croon at the same time. . . . I'll be the first singing herring salesman in history—") compares miserably to Shakespeare's last-act majesty. Even the knowledge that Kops was translating *Hamlet* validly and honestly for the East End audience he understood, even gay throwaway lines like Sam's at the end ("Well, Davey, it's all over. Hamlet is dead and may flights of angels sing him down the stairs") cannot quite cover the disquieting similarity between *The Hamlet of Stepney Green* and the kind of burlesque of a masterwork that might be done by any ethnic group in the privacy of its Saturday-night social hall.

Nevertheless, the play is remarkably strong in just that ethnic content and swagger. "Family life, family life is the measure, is all," it announces to dead kings and adulterous wives and dueling princes; "The world is a wedding," it sums up, prefiguring the title of Kops's 1963 autobiography. Its gaiety is the infectious, slightly drunken gaiety of the lowest-level Eastern European Jew, now living in London and no longer quite clear about things like the Talmud and Torah, remembering Yiddish lullabies incorrectly but with great nostalgia, sure only of the need for the pound note and of the taste of pickled herring. Weak as it may be in intellectual content, *The Hamlet of Stepney Green* blazes in setting and speech. The first-act stretch of dialogue between Sam Levy and Mr. Segal on Rasputin and Stalin and Bakunin and Trotsky is funny and magnificent, and it evokes the peculiar radicalism of the East End Jew—something that has more to do with mother's milk remembered than with manifestos read.

Kops's two subsequent plays, *Goodbye, World* (1959) and *Change for the Angel* (1960), lack this kind of homey radicalism and full-blooded joy, although family relationships are crucial to both. In the first, the hero, a criminal escaped from prison, hides in a room near where his mother has recently died, determined to give her a respectable funeral. He has long, long conversations with various inarticulate but more or less colorful people paralyzed by hopeless inertia and wonders whether his mother had any message for him other than the one she left, fingered in the dust on her bedroom mirror— "Goodbye, World." He finally surrenders to the police.

The family in *Change for the Angel*—another proletarian drama—is falling apart; it dissolves into a bunch of drunkards, criminals, and sexual problem cases. The father, once a decent and competent baker, has become a drunkard in response to the attack on his craft from machines and the big bread manufacturers: he even turns—rather incredibly

Harold Lang and John Fraser in The Hamlet of Stepney Green

for such a gentle, pathetic man—into a would-be rapist. The dramatic conflict of the play has to do with the father's desire for his youngest son, Paul, to be an engineer—a ruler of machines, rather than their victim—and the son's desire to be a writer. *Change for the Angel* carries its argument—the son's personal protest—closer to the surface than does *The Hamlet of Stepney Green*, and the themes of the play—alienation, estrangement from loved ones, and loss of pride in the modern world—are more interestingly developed. There are occasional scenes, especially those having to do with violence, madness, desperation, that are genuinely terrifying. But *Change for the Angel* failed, the *Times* critic commenting that when Kops dealt with working-class types the dialogue was theatrical, but that when he attempted to make "superior" sensibilities talk, the language was lifeless. Like *The Hamlet of Stepney Green*, *Change for the Angel* was derivative (but less successful in the transition). Like D. H. Lawrence's Paul Morel in *Sons and Lovers* (1913), Paul clashes with his working-class parents over his occupational aspirations, has an Oedipal relationship with his mother, and experiences an unsatisfactory love affair; he then goes out as a defiant writer (Paul Morel is an artist) into a hostile world.

The Dream of Peter Mann (first produced at the Edinburgh Festival in 1960) moves further away from family issues and individual protests. It picks up the note of criminality from *Goodbye, World* and couples it with the objection to big business and modern times in *Change for the Angel* to produce an apocalyptic drama rather reminiscent of European theater of the 1920s and most particularly the plays of Karel Capek. Peter Mann is knocked unconscious when a safe falls on him while he is stealing his mother's savings. Thereupon he begins a dream, which takes up most of the play, about running away with Penny, his old sweetheart, and Alex, a tramp, to prospect for uranium. When the three return twelve years later, they find that everyone in their old neighborhood is now searching for uranium. Peter talks them into working for him and becomes very rich and powerful making the only worthwhile commodity in a world dominated by the Bomb—shrouds. The Bomb falls, and though Peter has a shelter to hide in, his mother appears to him as the Angel of Death and lets him know, through a song from his childhood, that he must be killed along with everyone else. He wakes up, marries Penny (rather than another girl he had been in love with before the dream), and is able to round out a perfectly happy ending with the discovery that the tramp Alex is really his father. In contrast to Sam

Levy's provocative point about purpose and life in *The Hamlet of Stepney Green*, we are told here: "A great opportunity never to be repeated—a unique bargain—going—going—so make the most of it before it's gone!" East End barrel-thumping does not mix at all well with philosophy in *The Dream of Peter Mann*, and the political message barely survives its crude packaging mixture of Bomb, shrouds, and everyone's-out-for-what-they-can-get. Yet once more there is much power in several scenes, and Kops is at his best and most comfortable when using material dealing with life in the kinds of streets in which he grew up: children's songs, for example, and the kind of business dealings that *luftmenschen* can appreciate. The *Times* reviewer was scornful, calling it "a rather poor specimen of the proletarian drama. . . . People have to stand about in silence for too long [while others speak] and inevitably what is meant to effervesce goes flat."

Kops's one-act play, *Stray Cats and Empty Bottles* (1961), is the one that suggests Beckett—with a heavy admixture of Saroyan. It is a charming piece about a couple of derelicts trying to help a third, somewhat more upper-class derelict to marry for money. The scheme fails because the lady in question has no money after all. The fantasy succeeds, despite skinned cats and similar unpleasantness, and the songs, mime, and dialogue bubble delightfully in the junkyard universe. Jack of the cats and Iris of the bottle-collecting, however, are still distillates of the world Kops knows and can depict best, the scrabbling-for-a-shilling East End.

"I sometimes bought a book for a few coppers," Kops says in his autobiography, "and a little way along the street tried to sell it for sixpence. Then I would buy something for sixpence and try selling it for a shilling. Often I lost the lot and would be left with one useless flat-iron, or an ugly plaster dog or a few volumes of the Waverley Novels." This East End come to judgment, this scrabbling world with its smile utterly gone, these poor, ignorant Jews turned rich and ignorant and like everyone else, provide the setting and the theme of Kops's most ambitious play, *Enter Solly Gold*. It was the inaugural production of Arnold Wesker's Center 42 during Wellingborough's Trades Union Festival in September 1962 and was then staged in many other places throughout England.

The play is one long suspiration of hatred for the Jews (whom Kops loved so tenderly, if a bit wickedly, when they were poor), for the people of his blood and boundaries who have made it out of the Depression 1930s into the comfortable and inflationary 1960s—and beyond. Solly Gold is a con

Esta Charkham, Stella Moray, Pamela Manson, and David Lander in the first London production of Enter Solly Gold

man, a *luftmensch* superman. He can change into any character at a moment's notice, so long as there is something—money, position, a good meal—to be made out of it. And he will swindle anybody available—prostitutes, tailors, old ladies—but he prefers Jewish millionaires. Posing as the least likely rabbi of all time ("Well then, you surely must know that seven years ago the American Reform Orthodox Proxy Rabbi's Association proclaimed this Chicken Sunday. In the old days it used to be a great Hasidic feast. Don't you remember?"), he announces that Morry Swartz, a gullible Jewish millionaire with the right kind of family, is the Messiah. He convinces Morry, and has almost reached his

goal of taking over Morry's assets and the shoe business which is the basis of Morry's millions, when he goes too far and is exposed. Losing not only the money but also the control he has developed over the entire Swartz family, Solly Gold picks up a cigar butt at the end and mutters: "One thing I'm sure of, I'm not going to work. No, work's too much like an occupation—work's alright for the working class, but for me—it's got to be something better." Kops seems to minimize Solly's importance at the curtain, suggesting that Solly is the thread of the play, not the issue.

The Swartz family is the issue. The name itself is notable: it is meant to vibrate with evil, as Peter

Mann's name in the earlier play was meant to vibrate with universality. Every member of the Swartz family, members by birth, by marriage, by acquaintance, members young and old, male and female, short and tall—all are savagely ridiculed by Kops. He makes fun of their religion and of their lack of it, their nouveau riche pretensions and their old baggage of sentimentality, their hopes, their understandings, and their relationships with each other. Most of all, he makes fun of what they own and spend money on. It is the poor boy's revenge on rich relatives; more, perhaps, it is a ghost's revenge: Kops is the Hamlet of Stepney Green come back to haunt himself for what he no longer is. The tenderness found in Kops's first play is gone completely.

These are faults, no doubt. Even worse are the faults of what must be taken for ignorance: a Judaic mumbo jumbo that seems not to be deliberate satire because it is built on nothing substantial in the culture or the religion. But the play as a whole is crafted with certainty; the characters, if not round, are brilliant in their posterlike flat colors.

John Russell Taylor calls *Enter Solly Gold* "a very patchy play," but adds, "there are enough good patches to make it on the whole one of Kops's most fetching works." George Wellwarth feels that "the gay and witty *Enter Solly Gold*" is a far more mature piece of work than either *The Hamlet of Stepney Green* or *The Dream of Peter Mann*. Wellwarth believes that critics tend to ignore Kops as not being serious enough and particularly deplores the fact that the "latest round up of 'new dramatists' [in *Twentieth Century*, February 1961] does not even mention Kops." Kops seemed to be aware of this growing coldness toward him from the established critics: in a 1961 article, "The Young Writer and the Theatre," for *Jewish Quarterly*, he announced somewhat belligerently that "theatre in England is no longer the precious sanctum for the precious few."

Many of what must be considered Kops's minor pieces have been highly praised and a definite audience for his work can be said to exist. Not only was his one-act *Stray Cats and Empty Bottles* well received but so were his two radio plays, *Home Sweet Honeycomb* (1962) and *Lemmings* (1963), both science fiction and both dealing with nightmare futures much more clearly realized than the one in *The Dream of Peter Mann*. John Russell Taylor says: "A work of intense gloom and despondency, *Home Sweet Honeycomb* still suggests that Kops is, or will be, a more considerable dramatist than we have up to now had cause to take him for." Although ignored by most critics, Kops has received an Arts Council

award of £500, has been resident dramatist with the Bristol Old Vic, and even supervised the production of *Stray Cats and Empty Bottles*.

During a fallow period in his writing for the stage, Kops produced not only radio plays but poetry and fiction, returning to the British theater, finally, with *Ezra*. Produced in London in May 1981, the play was a revelation of new, matured talent. "Birdie no sing in cage," Ezra Pound had replied after his imprisonment in Italy in 1945 to the queries of a journalist; and his vow of silence remained little broken even after he gained his freedom years later. "*Ezra* takes place in the battlefield of Pound's mind," *Times* critic Irving Wardle writes, "from the time of his capture by the Allies to his release from the Washington lunatic asylum in 1958. To this daunting subject Kops brings his established concern with the mechanics of mental collapse and a capacity for evolving fluid forms that mirror the experience of inner reality. From the opening scene, with Pound pacing his six-foot metal cage, the writing achieves a jagged synthesis of past and present, actuality and dream, fully compatible with the splintering intelligence that produced the *Pisan Cantos*." The setting is largely surreal, with a background of rusting girders, scrap lumber, and petrified rope suggesting the debris of a life, and at one point Kops strikingly juxtaposes past and present voices when Pound's notorious anti-Semitic, anti-American broadcasts from Rome in the early 1940s are balanced by his crackling contemporary voice.

"A powerful collage portrait takes shape," Wardle observes. "Never more so than in the scene of his final return to Italy, where he leads his wife into a Jewish quarter to prove he has friends there; and calls out to them, and stands vainly waiting in the empty street." The play was criticized for not evoking Pound's poetry; however the copyrighted poetry was rigidly controlled by the poet's estate, and Kops in any case was evoking the wreck of the man. The play proved equally moving when broadcast on BBC Radio 3 for which it had been commissioned.

The verdict on Kops cannot yet be brought in, and it is not clear in which direction his fully realized powers will take him: toward the apocalyptic, in which the individual is inevitably dwarfed, or back to his basic folk material, where his pitfalls have been the merely jolly or the dreadfully spiteful. But his control has been growing visibly in both directions and his potential range remains enormous. *Enter Solly Gold*, with all its possible faults, may still be the most remarkable. That play, and *Ezra*, make one hope, still, for something very large indeed from Kops.

Other:

Enter Solly Gold, in *Satan, Socialites and Solly Gold* (New York: Coward-McCann, 1961).

Periodical Publications:

"English Theatre Today: III. Back Toward the Epic," *International Theatre Annual*, 3 (1957-1958): 150-160;

"The Young Writer and the Theatre," *Jewish Quar-*

terly, 8 (1961): 19-22.

References:

Ruby Cohn, *Modern Shakespeare Offshoots* (Princeton: Princeton University Press, 1975), pp. 190-194, 217, 231, 391;

Frederick Lumley, *New Trends in 20th-Century Drama* (New York: Oxford University Press, 1972), pp. 240-243;

John Russell Taylor, *The Angry Theatre: New British Drama* (New York: Hill & Wang, 1969);

George Wellwarth, *The Theatre of Protest and Paradox: Developments in the Avant-Garde Drama* (New York: New York University Press, 1964).

Hugh Leonard
(John Keyes Byrne)
(9 November 1926-)

Heinz Kosok
University of Wuppertal

PRODUCTIONS: *The Italian Road*, 1954, Dublin;

The Big Birthday, 23 January 1956, Abbey Theatre, Dublin;

A Leap in the Dark, 21 January 1957, Abbey Theatre, Dublin;

Madigan's Lock, March 1958, Globe Theatre, Dublin; 1963, London;

A Walk on the Water, 1960, Eblana Theatre, Dublin;

The Passion of Peter Ginty, adapted from Henrik Ibsen's *Peer Gynt*, 1961, Gate Theatre, Dublin;

Stephen D.: A Play in Two Acts, adapted from James Joyce's *A Portrait of the Artist as a Young Man*, 24 September 1962, Gate Theatre, Dublin; 12 February 1963, St. Martin's Theatre, London; 24 September 1967, East 74th Street Theatre, New York, 56 [performances]; 18 May 1978, Abbey Theatre, Dublin;

Dublin One, adapted from Joyce's *Dubliners*, 1963, Dublin Theatre Festival, Dublin;

The Poker Session: A Play, 23 September 1963, Gate Theatre, Dublin; 11 February 1964, Globe Theatre, London; 19 September 1967, Martinique Theatre, New York, 16;

The Family Way, adapted from Eugène Marin Labiche's play, August 1964, Dublin; 1966, London;

Hugh Leonard

When the Saints Go Cycling In, adapted from Flann O'Brien's *The Dalkey Archive*, 1965, Dublin Theatre Festival, Dublin;

Mick and Mick, 1966, Dublin Theatre Festival, Dublin; produced again as *All the Nice People*, 3 August 1976, Olney, Maryland, 21;

The Quick, and The Dead, 1967, Dublin;

The Au Pair Man, 1968, Dublin Theatre Festival, Dublin; 1969, Duchess Theatre, London; 27 December 1973, Vivian Beaumont Theatre, New York, 37;

The Barracks, 1969, Dublin;

The Patrick Pearse Motel: A Comedy, 15 March 1971, Olympia Theatre, Dublin; 17 June 1971, Queen's Theatre, London;

Da: A Play in Two Acts, 7 August 1973, Olney, Maryland, 21; 8 October 1973, Olympia Theatre, Dublin; 8 March 1978, Hudson Guild Theatre, New York, 24; 1 May 1978, Morosco Theatre, New York, 36;

Summer: A Play, 6 August 1974, Olney, Maryland, 21; 7 October 1974, Olympia Theatre, Dublin; 31 May 1979, Watford Palace Theatre, London;

Irishmen, 5 August 1975, Olney, Maryland, 21; 1975, Dublin;

Some of My Best Friends Are Husbands, adapted from Labiche's play, 1976, London;

Liam Liar, adapted from Keith Waterhouse and Willis Hall's *Billy Liar*, 1976, Dublin;

Time Was, 21 December 1976, Abbey Theatre, Dublin;

A Life, 4 October 1979, Abbey Theatre, Dublin; 2 November 1980, Morosco Theatre, New York.

BOOKS. *The Poker Session· A Play* (London: Evans, 1964);

Stephen D.: A Play in Two Acts, adapted from James Joyce's *A Portrait of the Artist as a Young Man* (London & New York: Evans, 1964);

The Late Arrival of the Incoming Aircraft (London: Evans, 1968);

The Patrick Pearse Motel: A Comedy (London: French, 1971);

The Au Pair Man (New York: French, 1974);

Da: A Play in Two Acts (Newark, Del.: Proscenium Press, 1975; revised edition, London: French, 1978);

Leonard's Last Book (Enniskerry: Egotist Press, 1978);

Home Before Night (London: Deutsch, 1979; New York: Atheneum, 1980);

A Peculiar People and Other Foibles (Enniskerry: Tansy Books, 1979);

Summer: A Play (London: French, 1979);

Time Was (London: French, 1980);

Da, Time Was, and A Life (Harmondsworth, U.K.: Penguin, 1981).

Hugh Leonard was born in Dublin. As he records in his autobiographical volume, *Home Before Night* (1979), his name was originally John Byrne, but he was adopted soon after his birth and later on called himself John Keyes Byrne, using the name of his adoptive father as his middle name. He grew up in the vicinity of Dublin, won a scholarship in 1941 to Presentation College Glasthule, and in 1945 joined the Irish civil service. *Home Before Night* is a moving account of his early life in a working-class family that, despite his adoptive parents' conflicting characters, provided an atmosphere of warmth and shelter. During his time as a civil servant in the land commission, he became involved in amateur theatricals and began to write for as well as about the stage. The second play he submitted to the Abbey Theatre, *The Big Birthday* (originally called "Nightingale in the Branches"), was accepted for production in 1956. When he sent in this play he used the pseudonym Hugh Leonard, ironically choosing the name of a character in *The Italian Road* (1954), his play that the Abbey had rejected earlier.

After two more of his plays, *A Leap in the Dark* (1957) and *Madigan's Lock* (1958) had been performed in Dublin, Leonard saw a chance to realize his lifelong ambition to become a professional writer. In 1959, four years after he had married Paule Jacquet, a Belgian by birth, he left the civil service, at first supporting himself by writing serials for sponsored radio. Ever since, Leonard has been successful at combining the career of a serious dramatist with the breadwinning activities of a commercial writer. In 1961 he joined Granada Television in Manchester as a script editor, and from 1963 to 1970 he worked as a free-lance writer in London, adapting novels for television, writing film scripts and television serials. In 1967 he received the Italia Award for one of his television plays.

In the meantime, Leonard had had a number of successes on the Dublin stage. Almost from the start he was associated with the Dublin Theatre Festival. Nearly every year since 1960 a play of his has been produced during the festival. Some of these plays are adaptations of well-known literary works, such as *The Passion of Peter Ginty* (1961), a modernized and Dublinized version of Henrik Ibsen's *Peer Gynt*. *Stephen D.*, which became Leonard's first great international success, premiered at the

1962 festival. The play went on from Dublin to London, Hamburg, New York, and many other cities and eventually was even produced at the Abbey Theatre. *Stephen D.* is a curious work to have made Leonard famous, because, as he himself emphasized repeatedly, it was written in a few weeks and hardly contains a word of his. It is based on James Joyce's *A Portrait of the Artist as a Young Man* (1916), with additional material taken from *Stephen Hero*, Joyce's first draft for *A Portrait of the Artist as a Young Man*, wherever the former did not yield sufficient plot or dialogue. Leonard decided to use Joyce's words, and made only an occasional change of tense or pronoun. However, the praise *Stephen D.* elicited everywhere may be attributed in large part to Leonard's craftsmanship, his wealth of experience as an adaptor, and his excellent sense of stage effectiveness.

After *Stephen D.*, roughly one third of Leonard's output for the stage consisted of adaptations. He took up Joyce again when in 1963 he dramatized *Dubliners* (1914) as *Dublin One*. It was followed by *The Family Way* (1964), adapted from a play by Eugene Marin Labiche. The 1965 festival saw *When the Saints Go Cycling In* from Flann O'Brien's novel *The Dalkey Archive* (1964). Later, he wrote *Some of My Best Friends Are Husbands* (1976)

from another Labiche play, and *Liam Liar* (1976) from *Billy Liar* (1960), a play by Keith Waterhouse and Willis Hall. However, to state that Leonard is a successful adaptor is not to say that he is not an original playwright. In addition to his adaptations, he has written almost twenty original plays, at least five of which—*The Poker Session* (1963), *The Au Pair Man* (1968), *The Patrick Pearse Motel* (1971), *Da* (1973), and *Summer* (1974)—merit detailed attention.

Typical of Leonard's plays, *The Poker Session* is witty, clever, brittle, and skillfully constructed, with an ingenious twist that will surprise even the wariest theatergoer. First staged at the 1963 Dublin Theatre Festival, *The Poker Session* is representative of the kind of plays that became fashionable in the early 1960s. Assembled around a table are a group of people whose seeming respectability is stripped off layer by layer. This type of play requires little stage action because it merely displays a situation, the result of past events that are being rediscovered in analytical technique. In *The Poker Session*, the Beavis family meet for a game of poker to celebrate Billy Beavis's discharge from a mental asylum. Billy appears to be cured; he has learned to face his own situation with ruthless frankness and applies the same attitude to his relations as well. With the help

Jerry Sullivan, Martin Dempsey, and Maureen Toal in a scene from the 1966 Dublin Theatre Festival production of Mick and Mick

of Teddy, his roommate from the institution, Billy succeeds in stripping their characters to the bare bones of egotism and self-interest. There remains only one mystery nearly to the end: why did his brother-in-law Des fail to turn up for the poker session? It is solved with the final curtain when one suddenly realizes that Billy has killed Des just before the play began, thus confirming his own madness and perhaps involving in it his relations, whom he seems now to resemble in sanity. The play is witty in a cruel sense, reflecting on the near-identity of madness and sanity. It is also critical, in a fairly conventional way, of bourgeois respectability. And it has some of the makings of a tragedy of character, the tragic aspect consisting of Billy's insight into his own situation without the power to change it. Leonard himself, in his production note, sees in *The Poker Session* elements of a detective play, a comedy, a thriller, a tragedy, an allegory, and a black farce. In other words, the play is rich in meanings to the point of meaninglessness; where any interpretation is possible, taken together they tend to cancel each other out. Its effect on an audience is therefore paradoxical, its very fullness of conflicting meanings resulting in a sensation of emptiness.

The Poker Session is Irish only in the sense that it happens to take place in the suburbs of Dublin. In some of his subsequent plays, Leonard was much more clearly concerned with Ireland and her specific social and historical conditions. *The Au Pair Man*, it is true, is set in London, but the Irishness of one of its two characters is essential to its deeper meaning. Superficially, the play shows the confrontation between Mrs. Rogers, a grass widow of nebulous aristocratic origin who never leaves her dilapidated house, and Eugene, a raw young man, insecure and undereducated, whom Mrs. Rogers takes in as an au pair man, that is, an unpaid companion-cum-servant. Eugene receives an education in fashionable behavior and finally breaks away to take a job with a firm of estate agents. He comes back to turn Mrs. Rogers out of a derelict house, which is about to be demolished, but to his dismay discovers that the girl whom he intends to marry is Mrs. Rogers's niece, which makes him as dependent on the grass widow as ever. On this level, the play is as Pinteresque as anything Leonard has written: a theater-of-the-absurd situation composed of minute fragments of closely observed reality that becomes grotesque—simultaneously comic and frightening—through an unusual arrangement of the fragments. Yet the play contains (as Pinter's works do not) certain fairly obvious hints at an allegorical meaning. Mrs. Rogers, whose

Joan Greenwood and Donal McCann in the first London production of The Au Pair Man

doorbell plays the British national anthem and whose clock chimes "Land of Hope and Glory," becomes the personification of a decaying empire, while Eugene is obviously Irish in more than an individual sense. Once such a context of political allegory has been established, even small details take on an added significance: when Mrs. Rogers repeatedly borrows Eugene's fountain pen, this can be seen as a reference to the role of Irish writers in English literature, and the wall unit that separates Eugene's room from the rest of the flat becomes reminiscent of another border in the North of Ireland. The play is funny and effective even without these allegorical associations, but it reveals a wealth of additional ideas once the subterranean meaning has been grasped.

The Au Pair Man had been preceded by *The Late Arrival of the Incoming Aircraft*, televised in Britain in 1964, *Mick and Mick* (originally called *All the Nice People* and produced under this title in 1976), a Dublin Theatre Festival production in 1966, and *The Quick, and The Dead* (1967), a double bill of two short plays. *The Barracks* (1969) and *The Patrick*

Pearse Motel (1971) followed *The Au Pair Man*. *The Barracks* was the last of Leonard's plays to be written in London, because early in 1970 he decided to terminate his semi-exile and return to Dublin. Although Leonard rejects the idea that he ever was self-exiled, his subsequent plays show an increased awareness of specific problems of Ireland and contemporary Irish society.

The Patrick Pearse Motel is a particularly interesting example because it deals with a dominant theme of modern Irish literature: Ireland's relationship to her immediate past and the discrepancy between the Irish people's professed hero worship and their actual materialism. The Patrick Pearse Motel is a commercial venture about to be opened on the edge of the Wicklow Mountains. Each of the rooms, complete with full-length portrait, is named after one of the heroes of Irish history, and the restaurant ("best steaks in Ireland") is in the Famine Room. The owners have even succeeded in engaging as caretaker a participant in the 1916 Easter Rising against the British. This patriotic setting becomes the scene of a farcical action in the

A scene from the first London production of The Patrick Pearse Motel

best tradition of English stage farce, with characters playing hide-and-seek in the bedrooms, always missing each other or meeting the wrong person. The accretion of improbabilities is such that it precludes any semblance of reality. The characters—two married couples, who own the motel, the future manageress, and a television personality—are exaggerated in the tradition of farce, with one dominant characteristic that monopolizes the personality of each. They all become mere counters in a turbulent charade, all the more hilarious because they bear the names of figures from Irish mythology, such as Dermod, Grainne, Niamh, and Usheen (Ossean). It is Leonard's specific achievement that the farcical situations of his play add up to a bitter satire on present-day Irish society, its superficiality, materialism, hypocrisy, lack of values, neglect of the past, and cynical attitude toward religion. As one character remarks, "After all, it's the same God we all disbelieve in."

Up to the early 1970s, Leonard's writings had been remarkably impersonal and objective. However personal some of his plays may appear to Leonard himself, such relations are hidden behind a glazing of irony, sarcasm, and detachment. In his choice of plot and characters, too, he had seemed determined to keep out any reference to his own life. This approach was changed completely with *Da*, and perhaps this play's resonant international success was due to the fact that Leonard here touched upon very personal matters and showed himself emotionally more vulnerable than one would have thought possible. *Da*, the story of Leonard's relationship with his adoptive father, is one of the most decidedly autobiographical plays of the modern stage. The term *story* is not misapplied, because in its technique the play owes a great deal to the epic tradition of the international theater. Essentially a play of memories, *Da* utilizes material that Leonard was to use again for his autobiography *Home Before Night*. A successful middle-aged writer has come back from London to the small Dublin corporation house of his youth for the funeral of his adoptive father. When he sits in the house alone at night, burning the last papers and trying to break with the past, Da steps out of the shadows, and the two reenact those scenes from the past, significant and insignificant, that the writer will never be able to forget. He realizes that Da's infuriating foibles, worn-out jokes, his stubbornness, ignorance, and naiveté are all part of his life, and when finally the son sets out for London, Da is ready to go with him because, as Da says, "you can't get rid of a bad thing." The play, for all its gruff abruptness and

understatement, is a deeply moving account of a man's attempt to come to terms with his past, to reappraise, in the moment of ultimate loss, what he has always taken for granted, and to understand a love that has never been put into words. Technically, *Da* is a remarkable achievement. It is reminiscent in part of Arthur Miller's *Death of a Salesman* (1949), but Leonard succeeds, even better than Miller, in completely fusing the past and the present. When *Da* eventually reached Broadway in 1978, on being transferred from the Hudson Guild Theatre to the Morosco Theatre, it received both the New York Drama Critics Circle Award and the Antoinette Perry Award for the best play of the 1977-1978 season.

The first American production of *Da*, in 1973, marked the beginning of Leonard's close relationship with the theater group at Olney, Maryland, where several of his subsequent plays were produced for the first time and others had their American premiere. *Summer*, his next play, like *Da*, had its world premiere at Olney. The play is an analysis of the problems of bourgeois middle age, a theme that Edward Albee had made fashionable with *Who's Afraid of Virginia Woolf?* (1962). Three well-to-do married couples meet for a picnic on the hills above Dublin city. Leonard brilliantly copies the small talk of conventionalized conversation: witty, ironical, daring up to a point where it will shock nobody, and carefully avoiding the pitfalls of genuine emotion and those facts that one does not talk about. But Leonard just as clearly reveals the underlying frustrations, the failure to keep up financially with the rest, the emptiness of a pro forma marriage, the secret desires, the heartbreak occasioned by a desperate attempt to find a more meaningful relationship, the inconveniences caused by the necessity to hush up an affair, the fear of disease and death. When, in act 2, the couples meet again after a six-year interval, the impression one has formed of them in act 1 is confirmed, but the resignation, the frustration, the fear are deepened. Only Myra, who is naively happy in her religious belief, is an exception. She blunders into an exposure of the affair between Richard and Jan that everybody has preferred to ignore, but the others "save" the situation, and to the end they continue to uphold social conventions. Nevertheless the external conditions have worsened; the picnic spot, at one time a place for contact with nature, is now encroached upon by commercial building projects, and the old stone cross, the symbol of an intact relationship with the past, has been removed. What is worse, the two youngsters who in act 1

A scene from the first London production of Summer

embodied the hope for a different, if utopian, future have been caught in the net of social conventions and bourgeois morality. Leonard's view is, therefore, deeply pessimistic, despite an occasional outburst of altruism or spontaneous feeling.

Leonard returned to the milieu of *Da* with *A Life*, his 1979 contribution to the Dublin Theatre Festival that was subsequently transferred to the London Old Vic. The play is about the life of Mr. Drumm, a civil servant with whom the young John Keyes Byrne seems to have had a love-hate relationship ever since Drumm helped him to get into the land commission, where he became Byrne's immediate superior. Drumm, as he appears in *Home Before Night*, was bitterly sarcastic and disillusioned. *A Life* shows how he may have reached this stage, with Drumm, who is dying of cancer, looking back on the many missed opportunities of his youth. *A Life* is an exercise in the bittersweet mood that seems

to have become dominant in Leonard's recent plays.

For the past few years, Leonard has been program director of the Dublin Theatre Festival and as such has been partly responsible for the excellence of the festival and its emphasis on new plays and new playwrights, which entails a great deal of risk. In 1976-1977 he was also literary editor of the Abbey Theatre. To the average Irishman, he is perhaps even better known for his weekly column in *Hibernia* (1973-1976) and the *Sunday Independent* (since 1977) that is in the best tradition of Irish satirical and polemical writing. Some of these columns have been collected in *Leonard's Last Book* (1978) and *A Peculiar People and Other Foibles* (1979).

The adjective most frequently used to characterize Leonard's dramatic work is *professional*, a description that carries connotations of criticism as well as admiration. Leonard is highly conscious of a play's effectiveness onstage, and not infrequently he seems to employ effects for their own sake rather than out of any deeper necessity. He is well aware of changing fashions in modern drama, and he follows these fashions rather than creating them. Leonard is professional also in the mastery of technical requirements and in the sheer quantity of his output. But in comic invention and witty dialogue he is comparable to the best of those Irish writers who have had such a large share in the history of English stage comedy, and the underlying seriousness of his themes, as well as the variety of genres he employs to express them, ranks him with Brian Friel as one of the two most important living playwrights of Ireland.

Screenplays:

Great Catherine, adapted from Bernard Shaw's play, Warner Brothers, 1968;

Interlude, by Leonard and Lee Langley, Columbia, 1968;

Percy, Anglo EMI, 1971;

Our Miss Fred, EMI, 1972.

Periodical Publications:

"Half the Agony," *Plays and Players*, 10 (March 1963): 18-19;

All the Nice People, *Plays and Players*, 14 (December 1966).

Benn Wolfe Levy

(7 March 1900-7 December 1973)

Susan Rusinko
Bloomsburg State College

See also the Levy entry in *DLB Yearbook: 1981*.

PRODUCTIONS: *This Woman Business*, 18 October 1925, Royalty Theatre, London; 15 April 1926, Haymarket Theatre, London, 187 [performances]; 7 December 1926, Ritz Theatre, New York, 63;

A Man with Red Hair, adapted from Hugh Walpole's novel, 27 February 1928, Little Theatre, London; 8 November 1928, Garrick Theatre, New York, 19;

Mud and Treacle, or The Course of True Love, 9 May 1928, Globe Theatre, London;

Mrs. Moonlight: A Piece of Pastiche, 5 December 1928, Kingsway Theatre, London; 29 September 1930, Charles Hopkins Theatre, New York, 294;

Art and Mrs. Bottle, or The Return of the Puritan, 21 October 1929, Empire Theatre, Southampton; 12 November 1929, Criterion Theatre, London;

The Devil: A Religious Comedy, 12 January 1930, Arts Theatre, London; produced again as *The Devil Passes*, 4 January 1932, Selwyn Theatre, New York, 97;

Topaze, adapted from Marcel Pagnol's play, 8 October 1930, New Theatre, London; 12 February 1930, Music Box Theatre, New York, 159;

Ever Green, book by Levy, music and lyrics by Richard Rodgers and Lorenz Hart, 3 December 1930, Adelphi Theatre, London, 254;

The Church Mouse, adapted from Siegfried Geyer and Ladislaus Fodor's play, 16 April 1931, Playhouse Theatre, London;

Hollywood Holiday: An Extravagant Comedy, by Levy and John van Druten, 15 October 1931, New Theatre, London;

Springtime for Henry, 9 December 1931, Bijou Theatre, New York, 198; 8 November 1932, Apollo Theatre, London, 104;

Young Madame Conti: A Melodrama, adapted by Levy and Hubert Griffith from Bruno Frank's play, 19 November 1936, Savoy Theatre, London; 31 March 1937, Music Box Theatre, New York, 22;

Madame Bovary, Levy's adaptation of Gaston Baty's play adapted from Flaubert's novel, 16 November 1937, Broadhurst Theatre, New York;

The Poet's Heart: A Life of Don Juan, 1937, Bristol University, Bristol;

Benn Wolfe Levy

If I Were You, by Levy and Paul Hervey Fox, 24 January 1938, Mansfield Theatre, New York, 8;

The Jealous God, 1 March 1939, Lyric Theatre, London;

Clutterbuck: An Artificial Comedy, 14 August 1946, Wyndham's Theatre, London, 366; 3 December 1949, Biltmore Theatre, New York, 218;

Return to Tyassi, 29 November 1950, Duke of York's Theatre, London;

Cupid and Psyche, 31 March 1952, King's Theatre, Edinburgh;

The Rape of the Belt, 12 December 1957, Piccadilly Theatre, London; 5 November 1960, Martin Beck Theatre, New York, 9;

The Tumbler, 24 February 1960, Helen Hayes Theatre, New York, 5;

Public and Confidential, 17 August 1966, Duke of York's Theatre, London.

SELECTED BOOKS: *This Woman Business* (London: Benn, 1925; New York: French, 1925);

A Man with Red Hair, adapted from Hugh Walpole's novel (London: Macmillan, 1928);

Mud and Treacle, or The Course of True Love (London: Gollancz, 1928);

Mrs. Moonlight: A Piece of Pastiche (London: Gollancz, 1929);

Art and Mrs. Bottle, or The Return of the Puritan (London: Secker, 1929; New York: French, 1931);

The Devil: A Religious Comedy (London: Secker, 1930); republished as *The Devil Passes* (New York: French, 1932);

Hollywood Holiday, by Levy and John van Druten (London: Secker, 1931);

Springtime for Henry (New York & London: French, 1932; London: Secker, 1932);

The Poet's Heart: A Life of Don Juan (London: Cresset Press, 1937);

Young Madame Conti: A Melodrama, adapted by Levy

and Hubert Griffith from Bruno Frank's play (London: French, 1938);

The Jealous God (London: Secker & Warburg, 1939);

Clutterbuck: An Artificial Comedy (London: Heinemann, 1947; New York: Dramatists Play Service, 1950);

Return to Tyassi (London: Gollancz, 1951);

Cupid and Psyche (London: Gollancz, 1952);

The Great Healer (London: French, 1954);

The Island of Cipango (London: French, 1954);

The Rape of the Belt (London: MacGibbon & Kee, 1957);

Britain and the Bomb: The Fallacy of Nuclear Defense (London: Campaign for Nuclear Disarmament, 1959);

The Member for Gaza (London: Evans, 1968).

Benn Wolfe Levy's first play, *This Woman Business*, produced in 1925, began a career in the British theater that spanned the turbulent middle years of the twentieth century. Working in a variety of dramatic styles, he wrote comedies, farces, Gothic and psychological melodramas, thesis plays, fantasy dramas, and a musical. Adaptations of works by other authors such as Hugh Walpole, Gustave Flaubert, Marcel Pagnol, Bruno Frank; collaborations with Richard Rodgers, Lorenz Hart, Hubert Griffith, Paul Hervey Fox; and reworking of legends such as the Don Juan and the Antiope-Hippolyta stories illustrate the varied nature of his work. Levy was frequently mistaken for an American because some of his plays were given American premieres and were enormously successful in the United States. One of these, *Springtime for Henry* (1931), provided almost an entire acting career for the well-known American actor Edward Everett Horton, who toured in the title role for eighteen years and then brought it to Broadway.

In addition to *Springtime for Henry*, Levy's most popular successes were the musical, *Ever Green* (1930, with Rodgers and Hart), and *Clutterbuck* (1946), a geometrically designed situation comedy similar to Noel Coward's *Private Lives*. His most critically successful plays were among his post–World War II group. *The Rape of the Belt*, first produced in 1957 with an impeccable cast headed by Constance Cummings, Kay Hammond, John Clements and Richard Attenborough, was acclaimed by such critics as T. C. Worsley of the *New Statesman* for its splendid comic reversal and for its adult and civilized comedy. Whatever Levy's subject matter, his dramas are characterized by a literate, Shavian-style wit, by pleas for a rational humanism, and by a

craftsmanship which became increasingly sophisticated.

Born in London to Octave and Nannie Joseph Levy, Levy was the grandson of the Honorable J. Levy of New South Wales. Educated at Repton and, after World War I, at University College, Oxford, Levy took a job in publishing after leaving Oxford and later became managing director of Jarrolds.

Levy's first play, *This Woman Business*, produced in 1925, concerns a group of misogynists who retreat to the country to be free from female distractions. As the group discusses their common bond, their objections diminish until they prove to be little more than lies or self-deceptions, and when a female thief intrudes on them she proves herself indispensable to the inhabitants. Because the play has much talk and little action the plot seems like a "Chekhovian design to pack the story between the lines," as a reviewer of the 1926 New York production noted in the *New York Times*. The lively dialogue of this feminist play emphasizes character. Throughout Levy's career female roles in his plays become increasingly strong and sympathetic.

Levy's second play, *A Man with Red Hair*, produced in 1928, was adapted from Hugh Walpole's Gothic novel. Crispin, the central character, is an obsessive sadist who talks endlessly to two other men and a female prisoner about pain and the necessity and benefits of enduring it. Levy's emphasis on the psychological aspects of the lead character is a departure from the conventions of the Gothic play. The *Times* reviewer praised Charles Laughton's portrayal of Crispin, saying that he created a "fanatic who has raised a lust for the infliction of pain to the level of a faith." Various aspects of Crispin's grotesquerie recur in Levy's later plays.

Indeed, his next play, *Mud and Treacle, or The Course of True Love*, also produced in 1928, opens in a similarly grotesque manner, with a description of a dead woman's body hanging over a chair, an opening that reveals to the audience the eventual fate of the main character, Polly Andrews (her name is a pun on *polyandrous*). In this melodrama set in the Victorian period Polly, bored by men of her own class, falls in love with an idealist and a misfit, a former clergyman named Solomon, who has actively espoused socialism. Although Polly invites Solomon to kiss her, he strangles her instead, realizing that Polly may be intrigued with the mud, but she must also have her treacle.

Levy's third play to be produced in 1928, *Mrs. Moonlight: A Piece of Pastiche*, is a variation of the legend of Tithonus, a handsome young Trojan who was granted his wish for eternal life but who forgot to ask for eternal youth and beauty. Instead of asking to live forever, Mrs. Moonlight asks to be beautiful for her whole normal life span, but after her wish is fulfilled, she becomes increasingly fearful that men will continue to desire her long after her desire for them has died. Comparing *Mrs. Moonlight* to James M. Barrie's plays, reviewers praised the play and the acting of Leon Quartermaine and Joan Barry in London and Leo G. Carroll in New York.

Art and Mrs. Bottle, or The Return of the Puritan, produced in 1929, deals with another sort of illusion. Irene Vanbrugh returned to the London stage to play Mrs. Bottle, a woman who has left her husband, a sanitary engineer. Mrs. Bottle's daughter is in love with an artist who was once Mrs. Bottle's lover, and her son wants to become an artist. Eventually Mrs. Bottle returns to her husband, convinces her daughter to give up the artist, and persuades her son to seek a different career. The play's witty dialogue is increasingly overshadowed by disquisitions about art that emphasize the play's ironic message.

The Devil, produced in 1930, presents a host and his guests, who, at the suggestion of the young Reverend Nicholas Lucy, play the game Truths, in which each person confesses what he most wishes to do or be. The game culminates with the Reverend Messiter's admission that he wants to reveal "God to be the mad, malignant bully that he is." Nicholas Lucy (his name a play on "Old Nick" and Lucifer) is the representative of the devil, but he unwittingly does God's work, as the "good in man far outweighs the evil." As in earlier plays, wit eventually reveals a serious theme. *Topaze*, also produced in 1930, is Levy's adaptation of a play by Marcel Pagnol. A character study of a schoolmaster who has been too innocent to be aware of the world's corruption, the play reveals the stupidity of such innocence and shows how it leads him into a life of crime. As a criminal he gains the security, respect, and love previously denied him.

In contrast to earlier, more moralistic thesis plays, three of Levy's next four plays are pure entertainments. *Ever Green*, with Levy's book, Richard Rodgers's music, and Lorenz Hart's lyrics, was produced by C. B. Cochran in 1930. Jessie Matthews, a star of Britain's musical comedy stage, enjoyed her greatest success in this musical, whose flapper-heroine is said to have been based in part on American Fannie Ward. The *Evening Standard*'s judgment that the play was "superb entertainment" was a typical comment.

The second of these entertainments is *The Church Mouse*, produced in 1931. An adaptation of a Viennese play by Siegfried Geyer and Ladislaus Fodor, the play focuses on a mousy secretary who gradually convinces a rakish baron, president of the universal bank, that despite his firm convictions otherwise romance and business may be allowed to mix. The play's opening comic mode is not sustained, a charge that could not be leveled against *Hollywood Holiday*, also produced in 1931. A farce about the American film industry, the play was described by W. A. Darlington as "the best laugh I have had for months."

Levy's most successful play of 1931 was *Springtime for Henry*, written in the polished farcical style of Restoration comedy. The hero, Henry Dewlip, has been cuckolding his best friend, Jelliwell, but soon Dewlip's amorous activities are diverted by his new, apparently virtuous, secretary. One day, however, after she has successfully reformed Dewlip's rakish gambling and drinking habits, she innocently remarks that she has a daughter. When asked by her "reformed rake" about the whereabouts of her husband, she replies with equal innocence, "I shot him." Meantime Dewlip learns that Jelliwell's carburetor business has not been doing well and that Jelliwell's domestic tranquillity has suffered because of his wife's unhappiness at being squeezed out by the moralistic secretary. Brought to his senses, Dewlip resumes his cuckoldry, and the old patterns of relationships are once more in place. Dewlip and Jelliwell are variations of the soldier-braggart comic character, miles gloriosus, that dates back to Plautus.

After its initial success in New York in 1931, the Broadway production of *Springtime for Henry* was transferred to the London stage in 1932. Although favorably received, the play did not fare as well as it had in New York, possibly because Leslie Banks had been replaced in the role of Dewlip. However, the play had renewed success when Edward Everett Horton starred in a new production in 1933 and toured with the play for eighteen years before he brought it back to Broadway in 1951. Critics and audiences once more greeted it enthusiastically. Brooks Atkinson contended that one would have "to go back in history for the kind of irresponsibility that is crackbrained and uproarious" as Levy's. After twenty years, he said, the play was still "the most skillful farce written in English for many years."

The action of the play, sophisticated farce at its best, represents Levy's cockeyed world at its most comically logical. Once the amoral premises are activated, the working out of the complications is inevitable. Much of the farce stems from the manner

PROGRAMME

ADELPHI THEATRE

Sole Proprietors .. .. J. & R. GATTI
Lessees .. .. MUSICAL PLAYS, LTD.

CHARLES B. COCHRAN'S
PRODUCTION

"EVER GREEN"

A Musical Show

Book by BENN W. LEVY   Lyrics by LORENZ HART
Music by RICHARD RODGERS   Staged by FRANK COLLINS
Dances and Ensembles by BUDDY BRADLEY and BILLY PIERCE
The Whole Production under the personal direction of CHARLES B. COCHRAN

ACT I.

Scene 1.—The Albert Hall, London
THE BEAUTY COMPETITION

The Chairman	EDWARD IRWIN
Mary Tucket (Harriet Green's Publicity and Business Manager)	JOYCE BARBOUR
Harriet Green	JESSIE MATTHEWS
Miss Lindfield, Sussex	IRIS BROWNE
Miss Cheltenham	MADELINE GIBSON

Scene 2.—(a) At the Seaside
(b) Mrs. Platter's Boarding Establishment (Evening of the same day)

Mrs. Platter	JEAN CADELL
Major Sack	AUBREY DEXTER
Mr. Openshaw	W. E. C. JENKINS
Mrs. Openshaw	FLORENCE WOOD
Mrs. Sack	CHRISTINE JENSEN
Mr. Tolley	CLAUDE NEWMAN
A Flapper	JEAN BAMBERGER
Eric Merivale	ALBERT BURDON
Tommy Thompson	SONNIE HALE
Harriet Green	JESSIE MATTHEWS
Mary Tucket	JOYCE BARBOUR
A Chauffeur	CYRIL WELLS

Scene 3.—(a) Exterior of the Casino des Folies, Paris
(b) A Rehearsal at the Casino des Folies, Paris (A few days later)

Saint-Didier (The Actor-Producer)	LEON MORTON
Albert (His Stage Manager)	AUBREY DEXTER
Harriet Green	JESSIE MATTHEWS
Mrs. Platter	JEAN CADELL
Dolly	KAY HAMMOND
Esme	W. E. C. JENKINS
Nero	GEORGE CHILD
Mary Tucket	JOYCE BARBOUR
Tommy Thompson	SONNIE HALE
Eric Merivale	ALBERT BURDON

Scene 4.—Interior of a Tent at Neuilly Fair, Paris (Three weeks later)

Scene 5.—Exterior of the Tent (The same evening)

Scene 6.—Neuilly Fair

Scene 7.—(a) Exterior of the Casino des Folies, Paris—at night (The next night)
(b) During the Performance at the Casino des Folies

La Commère	MABEL COUPER
Le Compère	W. E. C. JENKINS
Song—"Quand notre Vieux Monde était Tout neuf" (When the Old World was New)	MABEL COUPER

(c) The New Master
(d) The Finale "La Synthèse De La Belle De Soixante Ans"
CARLOS and CHITA with CO.

ACT II.

Scene 1.—Catalonia, Spain (A year later)
Festa Major
(Music arranged by PEDRO MORALES)

Scene 2.—Harriet Green's Bedroom and Bathroom in her Hotel in Paris (The following night)

Scene 3.—At the Cabaret de l'Abbaye (The following night)

Scene 4.—Harriet Green's Dressing Room at the Casino des Folies (Some weeks later)

Scene 5.—(a) Exterior of the Casino des Folies—at Night
(b) Finale of a Revue at the Casino des Folies—" The Moon and the Stars "
(c) Behind the Curtain

The Orchestra under the Direction of Richard Crean

General Stage Director .. .. FRANK COLLINS

Title credits and synopsis of scenes for the first production of Levy's popular musical

in which "well-bred Englishmen can insult each other with a perfect sense of decorum and without any sign of human emotion. It is a high art that has to be studied industriously." Levy's farcical manipulation of situations seems at its most ingenious in a play with four main characters. Sets of entangled relationships, similar to those in *Springtime for Henry*, characterize a number of Levy's most successful plays, including *Clutterbuck* and *The Rape of the Belt*.

ried American-born actress Constance Cummings, who performed to frequent acclaim in most of Levy's later plays, beginning with *Young Madame Conti* (1936).

A courtroom drama, which Levy and Hubert Griffith adapted from a play by Bruno Frank, the play is subtitled *A Melodrama*. Yet only the prologue and epilogue are conventionally melodramatic. Overhearing a conversation in which her lover admits that he is interested only in her money,

A scene from the first London production of Ever Green

Beginning in 1929, Levy was also at work on screenplays. His first, the script for Alfred Hitchcock's *Blackmail* (1929), which he wrote with Charles Bennett, is generally considered England's first talking cinema. In the 1930s he wrote such screenplays as *The Gay Diplomat* (1931); *Lord Camber's Ladies* (1932); *The Old Dark House* (1932), with R. C. Sherriff; *The Devil and the Deep* (1932); and *Loves of a Dictator* (1935); and by 1932, with *The Devil* (retitled *The Devil Passes*) and *Springtime for Henry* running concurrently in New York, Levy's involvement in directing had increased, and he was spending much time in New York. In 1933 he mar-

Madame Nella Conti, a prostitute, shoots him and then admits her crime. The mood of the play is hard, in spite of the judges' sympathetic treatment of Madame Conti.

Another flawed but sympathetic female character is Emma Bovary in Levy's 1937 adaptation of Gaston Baty's dramatization of Flaubert's *Madame Bovary*. Combining the weaknesses as well as the appealing romantic fantasies of Flaubert's Madame Bovary, Levy's Emma becomes a character of cameo daintiness, who, while more like Flaubert's than Baty's Emma in her "romantic stupidity," was, according to some critics, lacking the Flaubertian deadly balance of the two characteristics. Constance Cummings as Emma and Eric Portman as Rodolphe received praise for their outstanding performances.

The familiar hero-as-rake and the equally familiar theme of disillusionment are the subjects of Levy's *The Poet's Heart: A Life of Don Juan*, produced in 1937 by the University of Bristol theater. The influence of Shaw is present; yet the play overall evokes more the bittersweet irony of Arthur Schnitzler's *La Ronde*, which, like Levy's play, is structured in a succession of scenes that move circularly, leaving the audience with a sense of emptiness.

If I Were You, by Levy and Paul Hervey Fox, premiered in Princeton, New Jersey, before its short New York run in January 1938. Based on an idea expressed in a novel by Thorne Smith, it is a fantasy about a chemist and his wife, whose bodies have been interchanged by a servant girl, and who desperately attempt to return to their proper bodies. Brooks Atkinson complained that the sound farcical idea of the play lacked the "real invention" necessary to develop that idea.

Levy's last play of the 1930s, *The Jealous God*, opened in London in 1939, with Constance Cummings and Irene Vanbrugh playing the lead roles. Throughout the play, four principal characters—an idealistic woman, her uncomplicated husband, her lover, and an artist who is a conscientious objector to military service—find that their liberal attitudes lead to indecisiveness about how they are to live their lives. In the last act, with her husband now dead, Kate Settle finds the other two men more disillusioned but still holding on to their liberal principles. Similar to Terence Rattigan's *After the Dance*, also produced in 1939, Levy's comedy is permeated with a bleakness that reflects the era in which it was written. On the basis of *The Jealous God*, F. Majdalany called Levy an angry playwright.

After serving as a sublieutenant in the Royal Navy during World War II and being wounded in the Adriatic, Levy was awarded the order of MBE in 1944. Earlier in the war he had worked for British Intelligence and had been based in a hotel in mid-Manhattan, where he and other well-known theatrical personalities, including Noel Coward, worked on a project to shake public belief in the invincibility of Adolf Hitler.

Elected to parliament on the Labour ticket in 1945, Levy represented the Eton and Slough constituency for five years. An active supporter of liberal causes such as antinuclear proliferation, Levy also served as an executive council member of the Arts Council (1953-1961) and as chairman of the

executive committee of the League of Dramatists (1946-1947, 1949-1952). Consequently, after 1939 he wrote approximately one-third the number of plays that he wrote before World War II.

The only Levy play of the 1940s, *Clutterbuck*, produced in 1946, deals with two married couples who find themselves on board an ocean liner with a third couple, Clutterbuck and Melissa. In the series of revelations that follow they discover that Clutterbuck has been the lover of both wives and Melissa the mistress of both husbands. Ironic reversals, repetitions, secrets disclosed, and witty dialogue sustained the stylized, artificial comedy throughout, assuring it long runs and frequent revivals in the 1940s and 1950s.

No more plays by Levy were produced until he left parliament in 1950. *Return to Tyassi* (1950) focuses on the troubled conscience of a woman who seeks romance outside marriage. She finally becomes reconciled to life with a husband who does not love her. The play explores the conflict between so-called civilized and natural virtues, becoming what the *Manchester Guardian* critic called a "penetrating study" of the central character's dilemma. Directed by her husband, Constance Cummings again received high praise for her performance. *Return to Tyassi* is Levy's serious look at his generation, while *Cupid and Psyche*, produced in 1952, is a comic look at a younger generation familiar with the latest Freudian jargon. The play premiered in Edinburgh and did not go on to London or New York.

Themes from Levy's earlier plays recur in *The Rape of the Belt*, a feminist thesis comedy that draws on the legend of the Amazons. The low-keyed satire is built on the amorous complications of two Amazon queens, Antiope and Hippolyta, with Heracles and Theseus. Levy's Amazons have become a peace-loving culture, who, nevertheless, select the finest male infants to rear for reproductive purposes and drown the others at birth. They argue that men make war while women have created a peaceful civilization. The situation changes, however, when Hera, the meddling goddess, enters the body of Hippolyta and causes her to resume the warring practices of men. *The Rape of the Belt* is a sophisticated working out of Levy's feminist and, ultimately, humanist principles of human behavior. Kenneth Tynan found the play "squarely in the great tradition of Shaw and Giraudoux" as a "playful philosophic debate," while T. C. Worsley praised it as adult, civilized comedy. Other reviewers noted similarities between *The Rape of the Belt* and Giraudoux's *Amphitryon 38* (1929). With Constance Cummings and Kay Hammond in the lead roles the play was a resounding success, running in London for eleven months.

In 1960 *The Tumbler*, a verse drama about a daughter's return home and her brief liaison with her stepfather, was far less successful. Starring Rosemary Harris and Charlton Heston and directed by Laurence Olivier, the play received mostly unfavorable notices and closed shortly after its New York opening.

Public and Confidential, produced in 1966 and published in 1968 as *The Member for Gaza*, is a penetrating character study of a politician, Malkin, who risks his impeccable reputation to expose a scandal within his party, which includes cover-ups, covert actions, Communist scare tactics, blackmail, and secret taping of conversations. Critics described the play as absorbing, intelligent, and civilized.

Levy died in 1973 and is survived by his wife and their adopted children, Jonathan and Jemima. Constance Cummings continues to be active in the theater. Among the plays that remain unproduced and unpublished are "The Auction," "Anniversary," "The Curtains Are Blowing," "How to Be Nobody," "The Marriage," "Safari," "A Seat by the Fire," and a trilogy of short plays entitled "A Tap on the Door."

Levy once said that he "sometimes allowed reason to lead, under the delusion that it could strengthen illumination instead of dimming it. To a rationalist and a convinced partisan like myself neutrality seemed a double betrayal." Perhaps in some of his plays rationality wins too easily over feeling. His rational turn of mind served him well, however, in his farces, melodramas, and thesis plays, which, once the premises are established, continue to their inevitable conclusions.

Levy was sometimes criticized for writing conventional well-made plays that lacked the originality of both their great predecessors and modern ex-perimental drama, but Levy countered the accusation that his plays were merely well-made by saying, "*Waiting for Godot* is a superbly well-made play. So are the plays of Pinter. *Saint Joan* could not carry the weight of its discursiveness nor *The Three Sisters* its burden of inertia nor *Lear* its narrative puerilities nor *Hamlet* its exploratory diffuseness, if their authors had not been by inalienable instinct master-mechanics of the theatre."

Writing in the traditions of James M. Barrie, Noel Coward, T. S. Eliot, George Bernard Shaw, Jean Giraudoux, and Restoration comedy, Levy was most notably an observer of human foibles. Many of his dramas continue to enjoy substantial popularity in England and the United States.

Screenplays:

Blackmail, by Levy and Charles Bennett, BIP, 1929;

The Gay Diplomat, RKO, 1931;

Lord Camber's Ladies, RKO, 1932;

The Old Dark House, by Levy and R. C. Sherriff, Universal, 1932;

The Devil and the Deep, Paramount, 1932;

Loves of a Dictator, Ludovico Toeplitz, 1935.

Television Script:

Triple Bill: The Great Healer, The Island of Cipango, The Truth About the Truth, BBC, 14 September 1952.

Radio Script:

Anniversary, or The Rebirth of Venus, BBC, 1941.

References:

Barrett H. Clark and George Freedley, *A History of Modern Drama* (New York: Appleton-Century, 1947), pp. 196-208;

Robert Burns Mantle, *The Best Plays of 1931-32* (New York: Dodd, Mead, 1932), p. ix.

Joan Littlewood
(1914-   )

Ronald Hayman

PRODUCTIONS: *Alice in Wonderland*, adapted from Lewis Carroll's *Alice's Adventures in Wonderland* and *Through the Looking Glass*, 2 January 1950, Grand Theatre, Llandudno, Wales;

The Long Shift, by Littlewood and Gerry Raffles, 21 October 1951, Ystrad-Mynach;

A Christmas Carol, adapted from Charles Dickens's story, 8 December 1953, Theatre Royal, Stratford, London;

Treasure Island, adapted from Robert Louis Stevenson's novel, 26 December 1953, Theatre Royal, Stratford, London;

Cruel Daughters, adapted from Honoré de Balzac's novel, 19 October 1954, Theatre Royal, Stratford, London;

The Chimes, adapted from Dickens's story, 30 November 1954, Theatre Royal, Stratford, London;

The Quare Fellow, after Brendan Behan's play, 24 May 1956, Theatre Royal, Stratford, London;

You Won't Always Be On Top, after Henry Chapman's play, 9 October 1956, Theatre Royal, Stratford, London;

A Taste of Honey, after Shelagh Delaney's play, 27 May 1958, Theatre Royal, Stratford, London;

The Hostage, after Behan's play, 14 October 1958, Theatre Royal, Stratford, London;

Fings Ain't Wot They Used T'Be, after Frank Norman's play, 17 February 1959, Theatre Royal, Stratford, London;

Make Me an Offer, adapted from Wolf Mankowitz's novel, 19 October 1959, Theatre Royal, Stratford, London;

Sparrers Can't Sing, after Stephen Lewis's play, 24 August 1960, Theatre Royal, Stratford, London;

Oh, What a Lovely War!, inspired by Charles Chilton's *A Long, Long Trail*, 19 March 1963, Theatre Royal, Stratford, London;

Mrs. Wilson's Diary, after John Wells and Richard Ingrams's play, 21 September 1967, Theatre Royal, Stratford, London.

Perhaps playmaker would be a better word than playwright or dramatist to describe Joan

Joan Littlewood

Littlewood, but certainly the word director is not adequate. In the cinema it is taken for granted that often the director not only collaborates with the writer but originates some of the crucial ideas and molds the film in such a way that the script, instead of determining the shape, must be accommodated in the spaces that are left for it. In the post-World War II theater, some directors, such as Mike Leigh, have evolved ways of working with actors which make the script into a by-product of improvisational rehearsal with professional performance being the main product, while other directors, such as Jerzy Grotowski and Tadeusz Kantor, have yoked the creativity of actors to scenarios in which the stage picture is usually more imporant than the words.

299

Joan Littlewood has an important place in the growth of this theatrical counter tradition which has demoted the writer from having sole control over the spoken word.

On 24 May 1956, when Brendan Behan made a curtain speech after the first night of his play *The Quare Fellow*, he said: "Miss Littlewood's company has performed a better play than I wrote." Two years later when Theatre Workshop was preparing Shelagh Delaney's *A Taste of Honey* the script was largely rewritten in rehearsal. "We did a lot of improvisation," testifies Avis Bunnage, the actress who played the mother. "When we came to bits that didn't seem to work we ad-libbed round the ideas, made it up as we went along."

Many writers objected to Littlewood's rough handling of their scripts. In his book *Why Fings Went West* (1975), Frank Norman recalls Theatre Workshop's production of *Fings Ain't Wot They Used T'Be*, which opened on 17 February 1959. Norman complained that anarchic rehearsals ruined the script: "With every day that passed, my original conception of the play seemed to drift further and further away, until eventually I was hardly able to identify

with the antics on the stage at all. As the weeks went by more songs were added and once in a while I was called upon to write a few more pages of bad language." Other writers, such as John Wells, coauthor with Richard Ingrams of *Mrs. Wilson's Diary*, staged on 21 September 1967 with a script based on their long-running joke in the satirical magazine *Private Eye* about Prime Minister Harold Wilson's wife, admired Littlewood's skill in what she termed "taking the arse out of it." Her point was that what had been written while sitting in a chair could sometimes be brought to theatrical life only by dint of making changes that derived from actors who were not sitting down but moving about. But occasionally she sat down herself to rework part of a writer's script. Wolf Mankowitz, author of the musical *Make Me An Offer*, produced in October 1959, arrived at rehearsal one morning "to find that she'd been up all night, worrying herself into writing a completely new scene, which was so irrelevant and so bad, that one could hardly believe it was worth the loss of a night's sleep. There she was rehearsing the new scene. The actors were confused and I was utterly infuriated by the impossibility of getting to grips

Frances Cuka, Avis Bunnage, Joan Littlewood, and Murray Melvin during rehearsal for the 1959 Theatre Workshop production of A Taste of Honey

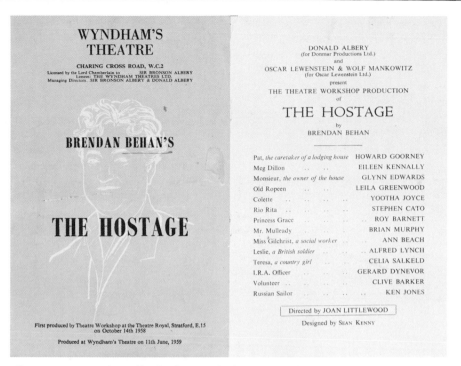

Program cover and cast list for the second Theatre Workshop production of The Hostage

with her intentions. I think Joan doesn't know what her intentions are until she acts them out on the stage."

Fundamentally Littlewood believed that teamwork produced better results than solitary cerebration. As she said in her first farewell to the stage, "A Goodbye Note from Joan," in the October 1961 issue of *Encore*:

> I do not believe in the supremacy of the director, designer, actor or even of the writer. It is through collaboration that this knockabout art of theatre survives and kicks. It was true at The Globe, The Curtain, The Crown, and in the "illustrious theatre" of Molière and it can work here today.
>
> No one mind or imagination can foresee what a play will become until all physical and intellectual stimuli, which are crystallised in the poetry of the author, have been understood by a company, and then tried out in terms of mime, discussion and the precise music of grammar; words and movement allied and integrated. The smallest contact between characters in a remote corner of the stage must become objectively true and relevant. The actor must be freed from the necessity of making effective generalisations.

> I could go on but you too know how the theatre must function if it is to reflect the genius of a people, in a complex day and age. Only a company of artists can do this. It is no use the critics proclaiming overnight the genius of the individual writer; these writers must graft in company with other artists if we are to get what we want and what our people need, a great theatre.

Littlewood was the first important director in England to allow actors to contribute creatively to a text. What she was doing, in effect, was importing into serious theater knockabout techniques derived from clowning and busking and from music hall, agitprop, and street theater. If her training at the Royal Academy of Dramatic Art (RADA) was important mainly as a negative influence, the early positive influence that was important came from Jimmy Miller (who later adopted the name Ewan MacColl). The son of an unemployed steel worker, he had left school at fourteen and soon become active in agitprop street theater. In 1930-1932 he worked with the Red Cops in Rochdale near Oldham and Salford near Manchester. Littlewood met him early in 1934 when they were both working for the BBC in Manchester.

Earlier, she had left RADA before the end of the course, seeing it only as an extension of the West

End theater she despised, to go to France, hoping to find work with director Gaston Baty. The times were bad for radical theater there too, and Littlewood soon returned, using the prize she had won for radio technique at RADA to secure work via BBC director Archie Harding, who had actually presented the medal. Offered a role in Manchester, she hitchhiked there, and remained afterwards as part of the company of the Rusholme Repertory Theatre.

Barely twenty, she was eager to learn and seized one opportunity when German expressionist playwright Ernst Toller produced, at Rusholme, his own *Draw the Fires*, a pacifist play about a German navy mutiny in World War I. Toller needed actors who could look convincing when stripped to the waist, shoveling coal into boilers. Littlewood suggested that he use MacColl and his friends, who knew how to wield a shovel. Her recommendation brought MacColl into the commercial theater. With a common interest in left-wing politics and in making physical movement bulk larger in theatrical performance, they founded a company called the Theatre of Action, working exclusively with recruits who had no theatrical experience, not even as amateurs. Taking some cues from Russian director and actor Vsevolod Meyerhold and from constructivism, they put on shows, using scripts but almost never leaving them intact—cutting dialogue out or reworking it or drastically reducing it.

The second company they formed together, a year later, was Theatre Union. Using Manchester as their base, they toured, playing to youthful working-class audiences and changing the script each week in order to keep pace with changing conditions and political situations. During World War II Littlewood was not only directing but also acting, mostly in radio documentaries, and writing scripts for such series as *Billy Welcome* and *Front-Line Family*. After the war ended they formed a new company, Theatre Workshop, and when auditioning actors for it, Littlewood asked them to improvise. The first production was a ballad opera by Ewan MacColl, *Johnny Noble*, based on research Littlewood had done in Hull during the war. The central character was a merchant seaman, and the background was unemployment during the 1930s, the Spanish Civil War, and World War II. MacColl's next play, *Uranium 235*, was provoked by the atom bombs dropped on Hiroshima and Nagasaki. He tried to recount the history of atomic energy in contrasting styles: "Energy as a gang boss in a Hollywood gangster movie, Max Planck and Niels Bohr explaining the quantum theory as a couple of knock-about comics with phony German accents. Einstein as a comic figure." Littlewood's 1963 production of *Oh, What a Lovely War!* was clearly influenced by *Uranium 235*.

In 1949, while the company was touring, Littlewood wrote an adaptation of Lewis Carroll's *Alice's Adventures in Wonderland* and *Through the Looking Glass*. The production was rehearsed in December and presented at the beginning of 1950. *Alice in Wonderland* was staged in Llandudno, Stratford, Hastings, and Weymouth, running one week in each location, but it was highly unsuccessful. In the autumn of 1951 she wrote with Gerry Raffles *The Long Shift*, a play about colliers in a Lancashire pit. In 1953 the company moved into the Theatre Royal at Stratford in East London, where Littlewood directed and rewrote plays until the mid-1960s. Working cooperatively with little money and scanty sets, the company under Littlewood's direction evolved its own style, improvising to solve elaborate technical problems cheaply and improvising in rehearsal. Most of the plays were classics, but two adaptations by Littlewood were staged in December 1953: Charles Dickens's *A Christmas Carol* and Robert Louis Stevenson's *Treasure Island*. In 1954 she did another adaptation from Dickens, *The Chimes*, which ran for three weeks, and one from Balzac, *Cruel Daughters*, which played for four weeks. Her 1955 production of Ben Jonson's *Volpone* kept the text intact but set the action in contemporary Italy, making the characters into spivs and street-sellers. Corbaccio wheeled himself about the stage in an invalid chair; Sir Politick Would-Be, wearing swimming trunks, carried a snorkel.

The company started work on Behan's *The Quare Fellow* in 1956 without being given scripts or knowing who would play which part. The actors improvised to create the feeling of prison life. Littlewood took them up to the theater's flat roof, where the grimy slate and stone helped them to imagine a prison yard. They formed a circle and trudged around. It became less like a game when they improvised washing out their cells, talking obsequiously to warders, conversing furtively, snatching drags at a cigarette. Knowing that the script would need to be cut and reshaped, Littlewood guided her company toward the necessary demolition and reconstruction without letting it see the text.

In the autumn of 1956 she directed another play which invited improvisation. Henry Chapman was a builder, and in *You Won't Always Be On Top* he wrote about a day in the life of workers on a building site. Opening on 9 October, the performance varied slightly from night to night as the actors ad-libbed, not without some obscenity, but the system then prevalent in the English theater was inimical not only to obscenity but to improvisation. According to the Theatres Act of 1843, public performances were legal only if they conformed to the script which had been submitted to the Lord Chamberlain and licensed; the management was fined £15 for presenting unlicensed dialogue.

In 1958, when *A Taste of Honey* was produced, Shelagh Delaney was nineteen, and at the first reading, the play lasted four and a half hours. Delaney came to rehearsals and, guided by Littlewood, rewrote dialogue after watching improvisations. It was not unusual at Theatre Workshop for the author to attend rehearsals and to join in the improvisations, as Frank Norman did during preparations for *Fings Ain't Wot They Used T'Be*. Littlewood made him test out passages of script, sometimes by playing one of the characters he had created, sometimes by improvising another character who entered into interaction with them. Lines he improvised were often incorporated. With his expert knowledge of criminal behavior, he could act out what a character would do in a given situation, and other actors could build on what he gave them. Authorship became partly collective, with the playwright serving as editor.

When Brendan Behan's second play, *The Hostage*, opened on 14 October 1958, audiences could have no notion of how much depended on Littlewood's masterful handling of material gleaned from improvisation or of how desperate she had become when the script for the second act remained unwritten. Behan loved telling stories and singing songs to the company, and the character Miss Gilchrist, the social worker, was an important addition, evolved out of anecdotes told in a pub, but the group's long drinking sessions made the production highly precarious. According to Avis Bunnage, "Brendan was going round the Covent Garden pubs in the morning, taking a kip in the afternoon and drinking again at night, so he wasn't taking too much notice of rehearsals. The actors were improvising a second act and Joan was getting desperate, so one night, Gerry sat Brendan down, pointed a gun at him and told him to write. It probably wasn't loaded, but it did the trick." The production, which was taken to Paris for the Théâtre des Nations in April 1959, was enormously

Brian Murphy and Murray Melvin in the 1963 Theatre Workshop production of Oh, What a Lovely War!

successful. In August 1960 Littlewood directed *Sparrers Can't Sing*, a play by Stephen Lewis, a former bricklayer, now an actor in the company. Lewis was already accustomed to her method of working and wrote his script knowing that dialogue would be tested, augmented, and remolded during rehearsals in which improvisation and ad-libbing would loom large.

One of Littlewood's biggest successes was *Oh, What a Lovely War!* (1963), which was based on her idea of depicting World War I through a Pierrot show. Charles Chilton had devised a radio program, *A Long, Long Trail*, based on songs from the war, and it was Gerry Raffles's idea to present a show based on the material. Two playwrights, Gwyn Thomas and Ted Allan, both produced scripts, but Allan afterwards complained that Littlewood "threw out my main plot, kept my peripheral scenes, rewriting most of them, took my name off the play in England, and gave writing credits to a few hundred people, to indicate that nobody wrote it." The only authorial credits on the program were to Charles Chilton and the company. Charles Chilton, an expert on music-hall productions, may have suggested more than how the songs could be used, and many of the best ideas derived, no doubt, from the actors, individually and collectively, in improvisation. The main concept for the production depended on Littlewood's dislike for the color khaki and her resolute refusal to let the actors appear in uniform. She used improvisation, but she also used historical facts and statistics, whisking the narrative dizzyingly between songs, fiction, facts, and figures. Behind the actors was a screen that ran the whole width of the stage. On the screen, picked out in moving lights, were the grim statistics—so many thousand lives lost, so many hundred yards gained—which counterpointed the clowning and the caricature in the foreground. In some sequences dialogue was replaced by disconnected nonsense. During bayonet practice the soldiers shouted gibberish, and the tycoons, while shooting at wildfowl, spoke surrealistically about using neutral trade routes for exporting arms to the enemy. Here, as in many other scenes, Littlewood arrived at forms of theatrical expression which no playwright could have evolved while sitting at his typewriter. The combination of farce and horror was seminal: without Littlewood's example, Joe Orton would probably never have written as he did.

In 1965-1966 Littlewood worked in Tunisia, running an international cultural center, and afterwards she was more interested in working with children than in directing plays. She did return to Stratford briefly, however, in 1967 and 1973. Her latest production there was *So You Want To Be in Pictures* by Peter Rankin. Though she has never directed for either the National Theatre or the Royal Shakespeare Company, neither of these institutions would be quite the same but for her pioneering achievement.

As the art of theater develops, relationships between director, actors, and script are becoming more fluid: like film directors who use the camera as a fountain pen (caméra-stylo), directors can write in stage pictures using the medium as a means of thinking and of making statements that could not have been made in any other way. Littlewood is a pioneer whose importance can be summed up by saying that she made it harder to put directors and playwrights into separate categories.

References:

Clive Goodwin and Tom Milne, "Working with Joan," *Encore*, 7 (July-August 1960);

Howard Goorney, *The Theatre Workshop Story* (New York & London: Eyre Methuen, 1981);

Ronald Hayman, *British Theatre since 1955* (Oxford & New York: Oxford University Press, 1979);

Ewan MacColl, "The Grass Roots of Theatre Workshop," *Theatre Quarterly*, 3 (January-March 1973).

Henry Livings
(20 September 1929-   )

Michael J. Weimer

SELECTED PRODUCTIONS: *Stop It, Whoever You Are*, 15 February 1961, Arts Theatre, London;

Big Soft Nellie, 18 September 1961, Playhouse Theatre, Oxford;

Nil Carborundum, 12 April 1962, Arts Theatre, London;

Kelly's Eye, 12 June 1963, Royal Court Theatre, London;

Eh?, 29 October 1964, Aldwych Theatre, London; 16 October 1966, Circle in the Square, New York, 232 [performances];

The Little Mrs. Foster Show, 8 November 1966, Playhouse Theatre, Liverpool; revised version, 27 March 1968, Playhouse Theatre, Nottingham;

Good Grief! (*After the Last Lamp*, *You're Free*, *Variable Lengths*, *Pie-Eating Contest*, *Does It Make Your Cheeks Ache?*, and *The Reasons for Flying*),18 July 1967, Library Theatre, Manchester;

Honour and Offer, 21 November 1968, Shelterhouse Theatre, Playhouse in the Park, Cincinnati; 12 May 1969, Fortune Theatre, London;

The Gamecock, October 1969, Library Theatre, Manchester;

Rattel, October 1969, Library Theatre, Manchester;

Conciliation, March 1970, Theatre Royal, Lincoln;

The Boggart, 1970, Birmingham;

Beewine, 1970, Birmingham;

The Rifle Volunteer, 1970, Birmingham;

The ffinest ffamily in the Land, 16 June 1970, Theatre Royal, Lincoln; 27 July 1972, Theatre Royal, London;

Tiddles, November 1970, Midland Arts Centre, Birmingham;

Mushrooms and Toadstools, 1970, London;

Brainscrew, 1971, Midlands Arts Centre, Birmingham;

This Jockey Drives Late Nights, adapted from Leo

Harry Livings [signature]

305

Tolstoy's *The Power of Darkness*, 27 January 1972, Midland Arts Centre, Birmingham;

The Rent Man, April 1972, Victoria Theatre, Stoke-on-Trent;

Cinderella, September 1972, Victoria Theatre, Stoke-on-Trent;

The Tailor's Britches, January 1973, Victoria Theatre, Stoke-on-Trent;

Jug, adapted from Heinrich von Kleist's *The Broken Jug*, November 1975, Playhouse Theatre, Nottingham;

Shuttlecock, May 1976, Thames Theatre, London;

Tom Thumb, December 1979, Unicorn Theatre, London.

SELECTED BOOKS: *Big Soft Nellie* (London: Methuen, 1961; New York: Hill & Wang, 1964);

Kelly's Eye (London: Methuen, 1963; New York: Hill & Wang, 1964);

Eh? (London: Methuen, 1965; New York: Hill & Wang, 1967);

Good Grief! (London: Methuen, 1968)—includes *After the Last Lamp*, *You're Free*, *Variable Lengths*, *Pie-Eating Contest*, *Does It Make Your Cheeks Ache?*, and *The Reasons for Flying*;

The Little Mrs. Foster Show (London: Methuen, 1969);

Honour and Offer (London: Methuen, 1969);

Pongo Plays 1-6: six short plays (London: Methuen, 1971; revised, 1976)—includes *The Gamecock*, *Rattel*, *Conciliation*, *The Boggart*, *Beewine*, and *The Rifle Volunteer*;

This Jockey Drives Late Nights: a play from The Power of Darkness by Leo Tolstoy (London: Eyre Methuen, 1972);

The ffinest ffamily in the Land (London: Eyre Methuen, 1973);

Six More Pongo Plays (Including Two for Children) (London: Eyre Methuen, 1974)—includes *Tiddles*, *The Rent Man*, *The Ink-Smeared Lady*, *The Tailor's Britches*, *Daft Sam*, and *Mushrooms and Toadstools*.

Although the controversy surrounding him has dwindled since his partial withdrawal from the London theatrical scene, Henry Livings remains one of the most misunderstood of the British playwrights who emerged during the 1950s. Often misrepresented by reviewers as a new Spike Milligan (scriptwriter for the popular *Goon Show*), Livings defies classification as either an absurdist or an "angry young man," the literary labels sometimes applied to him. With a dozen published titles to his credit and nearly as many produced but unpublished works, Livings merits attention as a voice in the contemporary British theater.

Livings's origins are relatively humble. He was born to working-class parents, George and Dorothy Buckley Livings, at Prestwick, Lancashire. He won a scholarship from the Stand Grammar School to Liverpool University but attended college for only two years, leaving in 1950 before receiving a degree. From there he went on to serve in the Royal Air Force (1950-1952), became an expert cook, and held a number of jobs before going into the theater. He married Judith Francis Carter on 2 April 1957, and they have two children.

Livings began his theatrical career as an actor, appearing with the Century Mobile Theatre, Hinckley, Leicestershire, in February 1954, as Curio and Sebastian in *Twelfth Night*. He made his first appearance on the London stage in May 1956 when he played Prisoner C in Brendan Behan's *The Quare Fellow*, produced by Joan Littlewood's Theatre Workshop. Littlewood had at that time a formative influence on Livings as both an actor and a writer, for he began writing plays while at her Theatre Workshop. His first play, *Jack's Horrible Luck*, was written in 1958 but went unproduced until 1961 when it was televised by the BBC.

Livings's first play to gain critical attention was *Stop It, Whoever You Are*, produced at London's Arts Theatre in 1961. The influence of Littlewood is apparent in Livings's description of his playwriting method: "I had entirely theatrical tools to use. I chose simple stories and corny situations because I didn't want to be wasting time going forward along a single track when I could see a way of covering St. Pancras Station. And I broke down the story into 'units' of about ten minutes each—about as long, I reckoned, as you can hold a new situation clearly and totally in mind." This description, with its emphasis on the sequence of events in a play, could be applied as well to Livings's later works.

Stop It, Whoever You Are consists of five scenes, each one a farcical skit in itself. The play as a whole is organized around the events surrounding the opening of a municipal library and arts complex. William Perkin Warbeck (the name derives from an unsuccessful pretender to the English throne) is a janitor in a factory near the new library, where Alderman Michael Oglethorpe is expecting the mayor to attend the dedication ceremony. His Excellency's natural indisposition creates a need for the lavatory in Warbeck's care; and the bald, inglorious old Warbeck uses this embarrassing situation to extract an increase in salary.

In the fifth scene, news of her husband's collapse at work reaches Rose Warbeck about the same time that a policeman delivers a summons for Warbeck's arrest for having molested fourteen-year-old Marilyn Harbuckle. Mrs. Warbeck expresses only contempt and bitterness when Warbeck arrives and drops dead. At this time the mystical Mrs. Harbuckle, played by the same actor as Warbeck, enters and allows Warbeck to speak to Rose from the beyond: "You can do whatever you've a fancy to do. I've been a nuisance all my life. To you, me, and everybody—and I haven't had much joy of it, I can tell you—But I might have gone down to the grave not knowing what a hairy old baboon I was. I didn't. I did it. I'm entirely dead now, and you can heap words on me. You can heap six foot of dirt on me, for that matter. But I shall have been entirely alive."

Mrs. Harbuckle is a medium for even the mechanical, clocklike sounds that Warbeck makes. The play's title emerges in Mrs. Warbeck's frantic curtain line: "I can't stand it! You're driving me out of my mind; it's enough! Shut up shut up shut up! Whoever you are, stop it!"

In the critical controversy that surrounded *Stop It, Whoever You Are* Kenneth Tynan's review was relatively encouraging: "Livings has a flavour of his own, a regional tang that comes to his rescue whenever pretentiousness impends. . . . Beneath the flaws, a vigorous young talent is flexing its mus-

cles." In 1961 Livings won the *Evening Standard*'s Drama Award for most promising playwright.

Big Soft Nellie (1961), originally entitled "Thacred Nit," attracted less attention when produced; but *Nil Carborundum*, based on Livings's experience in the Royal Air Force, was a noteworthy attraction of the Royal Shakespeare Company's experimental season at the Arts Theatre in 1962. Tynan described the play to American readers as a manic farce: "One imagines Livings crowing with glee as he taps out the words, each sentence treading on the heels of its predecessor, each page ripped from the typewriter and flung to the floor at random."

It was with the 1963 production of *Kelly's Eye* at the Royal Court Theatre that the place of Livings in the British theater became established. Because Livings was more serious in this play than most critics had expected him to be, controversy erupted. The play is a straightforward dramatization of a fugitive's escapade with a runaway ingenue. Kelly, originally played by Nicol Williamson, has killed a man three years before the action begins in August 1939. The first act depicts Kelly's first encounter with Anna Brierly (played by Sarah Miles) on the beach where he has been living like a hermit for most of the three years since the fatal shooting incident. After Anna's overprotective father appears,

A scene from the 1966 New York production of Eh?

Kelly succeeds in holding her affections, and the two leave for a coastal town in order to frustrate Mr. Brierly's efforts.

Act 2 is situated in the one-room apartment that the unmarried pair rent. Kelly admits to being a stupid man; but stupidity for him does not bring along bovine contentment, as he says: "I sometimes get a glassy feeling that there's too many people been at the words before I got round to needing them; a hammer with half the handle split off. Christ, I'm cooped up here." When Kelly is captured at the play's violent climax, the audience realizes his story will be obscured by the outbreak of a more famous fight—World War II—for it is now September 1939. Unlike any other play that Livings had written, *Kelly's Eye* caused the defection of Kenneth Tynan, who had touted the comedies. Tynan thought that Livings was losing his savage satirical

bite, but the play won Livings the *Encyclopaedia Britannica*'s award for playwrights in 1965.

Despite these achievements, Livings remained unknown in America until the 1966 Off-Broadway production of *Eh?*, originally produced by the Royal Shakespeare Company in 1964. This play represents Livings's return to his special brand of "serious farce." It is situated entirely in the boiler room where Valentine Brose, played by David Warner in London and by Dustin Hoffman in New York, is employed as an attendant. Like Livings's earlier plays in this genre, there is almost no consecutive plot. Brief gestures and a series of absurd confrontations create the play's essential interest. As John Russell Taylor observes, *Eh?* is not a farce of external action but one of character, the opposition of an obsessed and eccentric individual to the mechanism of a large factory. The machines become the an-

Maxwell Shaw and Clare Sutcliffe in the first London production of The ffinest ffamily in the Land

Pat Keer, Ursula Smith, and Jean Taylor-Smith in the first production of Jugs

tagonists of Val, who is more mindful of his hallucinogenic mushrooms than of his primary duties. Much of the drama is in the stage directions, such as the following routine in act 1: "The phone gives its regurgitative double gurk again. Val strolls to his seedboxes and looks into the top one, has a thought and goes back to gaze up at the steam gauge. As he looks it gives a brief hiss of steam; and the dial's finger moves tentatively round, then spins, then stops, quivering."

Val's frantic behavior is only accelerated in act 2 with his marriage to Betty Dorrick and the rapid growth of the mushrooms. It should be noted that Val does not deliberately obstruct the boiler works; but even with Betty's help his inner rhythm cannot be synchronized with the relentless demands of the machine. At the play's explosive conclusion, strikingly like that of *Stop It, Whoever You Are*, Val is enwrapped in a trancelike state and reciting a babyish bedtime story: "And once upon a time . . . (A prolonged reverberating boom from the boiler as it collapses, spewing its steam, smoke, soot and coal.) There was a boiler. Once upon a time." *Eh?* had its American premiere at the Cincinnati Playhouse in the Park in July 1966, moved to New York's Circle in the Square that October, and won the *Village Voice*'s Obie Award for the 1966-1967 season.

Since the resounding success of *Eh?*, Livings has written only three original full-length plays for the stage—*The Little Mrs. Foster Show* (1966), *Honour and Offer* (1968) and *The ffinest ffamily in the Land* (1970). The first of these is a loose-jointed revue vaguely related to imperialism in Africa. It can be read by interested students in the paperback edition. *Honour and Offer* centers on another eccentric, a beekeeping bachelor named Henry Cash, who is unfortunately much like Val in *Eh?*. The play premiered at Cincinnati with an American cast before having a short run in London. *The ffinest ffamily in the Land* was the most poorly received of Livings's recent plays. One reviewer compared its humor to that of a picture postcard and called the play "a splendid music hall sketch spoilt by inflation to conventional length."

Good Grief! (1967) is a selection of Livings's short works, including two one-act plays (*After the Last Lamp* and *You're Free*) and four sketches (*Variable Lengths*, *Pie-Eating Contest*, *Does It Make Your Cheeks Ache?*, and *The Reasons for Flying*). The production of these short plays continues the pattern of regional premieres that started with *The Little Mrs. Foster Show*. The twelve *Pongo Plays* have been produced mostly outside of London, for the movement away from the capital is wholly appropriate to the popular, accessible theater that Livings wants to promote. Sam Pongo, a simple weaver, is a folk hero of the wily servant type. He appears in all the plays but the twelfth and is characteristically pitted against blustering masters and military figures. The skits are farcical parables of the survival of Pongo's Sancho Panza-like common sense against all odds. This character has proved to be Henry Livings's most fertile creation.

During the 1970s, Livings adapted several classic and mythical stories. *This Jockey Drives Late Nights* (1972) is an interesting adaptation of Leo Tolstoy's play, *The Power of Darkness*, into an idiomatic British situation. The more recent *Jug* (1975) relocates Heinrich von Kleist's satirical comedy, *The Broken Jug*, to a rural Victorian setting. The remainder of the recent plays are mainly children's entertainments based on biblical and traditional stories and characters such as Jonah, the Braggart Soldier, Jack and the Beanstalk, Cinderella, and Tom Thumb. Occasionally a producer has devised a collective title for a theatrical presentation of short works by Livings, such as *The Cross-Buttock Show* at Leicester Polytechnic in July 1973.

It would be premature to state the ultimate importance of Livings's plays. However, certain tendencies are already apparent. His increasing identification with the regional theatrical scene, his development of a popular hero such as Pongo, his more recent treatment in *Jug* of ingrained social injustice as an aspect of English country life all mark a committed playwright whose characteristic voice is distinguishable from the tirades of a John Osborne. Livings has always tried to awaken his audiences through laughter rather than strident protest. He seems to be seeking out the audiences that he wants. Never satisfied with being a playwright for the critics, he is now living in his native Lancashire and is indifferent to success in the London theater. This indifference may have led to his neglect by major critics and scholars on both sides of the Atlantic.

Screenplay:

Work Is a Four-Letter Word, adapted from his play *Eh?*, Cavalcade Films-Universal, 1968.

Other:

Stop It, Whoever You Are, in *New English Dramatists 5* (Harmondsworth, U.K.: Penguin, 1962);

Nil Carborundum, in *New English Dramatists 6* (Harmondsworth, U.K.: Penguin, 1963);

Brainscrew, in *Second Playbill 3*, edited by Alan Durband (London: Hutchinson, 1973).

References:

Paul Ferris, "Finding Fresh Writers," *Observer* (London), 13 October 1963, p. 23;

Louis D. Giannetti, "Henry Livings: A Neglected Voice in the New Drama," *Modern Drama*, 12 (1969): 38-48;

William Glover, "No 'Protest' Plays: Dramatist Makes Points With Laughs," *Newark Sunday News*, 7 August 1966, VI: E4;

Benedict Nightingale, "Rough Justice," review of *Jug*, *New Statesman*, 21 November 1975, 651-652;

Robert Pasolli, "Non-Brooding Mr. Livings: The Eccentric Is the Real," *Village Voice*, 14 July 1966, pp. 19-20;

John Russell Taylor, *The Angry Theatre: New British Drama* (New York: Hill & Wang, 1969), pp. 286-300;

Taylor, "The Human Dilemma," *Plays and Players*, 10 (June 1963): 24-26;

Peter Thomson, "Henry Livings and the Accessible Theatre," *Western Popular Theatre*, edited by

David Mayer and Kenneth Richards (London: Methuen, 1977), pp. 187-202;

Kenneth Tynan, "A Farce that Draws Blood," review of *Stop It, Whoever You Are*, *Observer* (London), 19 February 1961, p. 30;

Tynan, "Killer at the Seaside," review of *Kelly's Eye*, *Observer* (London), 16 June 1963, p. 29;

Tynan, "Manic Farce on the R.A.F.," review of *Nil Carborundum*, *New York Herald Tribune*, 22 April 1962, IV: 2.

Peter Luke
(12 August 1919-)

Robert Coskren
Oklahoma State University

PRODUCTIONS: *Hadrian VII*, 9 May 1967, Birmingham Repertory Theatre, Birmingham; 18 April 1968, Mermaid Theatre, London; 8 January 1969, Helen Hayes Theatre, New York, 359 [performances];

Bloomsbury, 11 July 1974, Phoenix Theatre, London.

BOOKS: *The Play of Hadrian VII* (London: Deutsch, 1968; New York: Knopf, 1969);

Sisyphus and Reilly: An Autobiography (London: Deutsch, 1972);

Bloomsbury (London: French, 1976; New York: French, 1976);

Under the Moorish Wall: Adventures in Andalusia (Dublin: Dolmen, 1980);

Telling Tales: Collected Short Stories (Kildare: Goldsmith Press, 1981).

Peter Luke

Peter Luke did not write his first play until he was nearly forty and, after his one and only stage success, retired to free-lance writing in Spain. The son of Sir Harry Luke—a writer—and Joyce Fremlin Luke, Peter Ambrose Cyprian Luke was born in St. Albans in Hertfordshire and educated at Eton and the Byam Shaw school of art in London as well as the Atelier André Lhote in Paris. Before he could involve himself professionally in painting, World War II intervened, and he served from 1940 to 1946 with the Rifle Brigade in the Middle East, Italy, and the second front in France. After the war he worked briefly as a news subeditor for Reuters News Service (1946-1947), and then went into the wine trade for ten years. He married Carola Peyton-Jones. After her death, he married Lettice Crawshaw, with whom he had a son and daughter; the marriage ended in divorce. In 1963 Luke and actress June Tobin were married, and they have two sons and three daughters.

Luke became involved again in the writing trade as book critic for *Queen* magazine in 1957 and as story editor (then called drama editor) with commercial television from 1958 to 1960 and as drama producer with the BBC from 1963 to 1967.

In 1959 his first television play, *Small Fish Are Sweet*, starring Donald Pleasence and Katherine Blake, was produced, and Luke began writing short fiction as well as other television plays, including *Roll On, Bloomin' Death*. "I did not intend to become a playwright," he has written. "It happened by accident." And it was by accident that he landed the opportunity for the major dramatic success of his career. In 1959, director James Roose-Evans had set out to adapt two books for the stage, poet Laurie Lee's autobiography *Cider with Rosie* (1959) and Frederick Rolfe's *Hadrian the Seventh* (1904), a novel which has been described as Rolfe's attempt to compensate for his failure to become a priest after his conversion to Catholicism. Both works looked like difficult adaptation problems likely to take more time than Roose-Evans had available. Meeting Luke, who was then head of scripts for ABC (London) Armchair Theatre Television, Roose-Evans explained his dilemma. Luke in turn confided his interest in writing for the legitimate stage. Thus was set the scene for the making of Luke's *Hadrian VII* (1967). Roose-Evans said, "I realized I could not adapt two books simultaneously and invited him to choose the one that appealed to him and I would complete the one he did not choose."

"My father knew Rolfe," Luke said. "Rolfe invested him as Grand Master of the Order of Santissima Sophia. There were only ever three members!" Roose-Evans assigned Luke *Hadrian the Seventh*, and, as director of the Hampstead Theatre Club, he began working with Luke on the play in the summer of 1960. Four years later, however, the script was still going the rounds unsuccessfully. According to Alec McCowen, who later created the title role, "It was considered uncommercial and impractical, and the role of Hadrian considered unplayable." McCowen found out about the play in

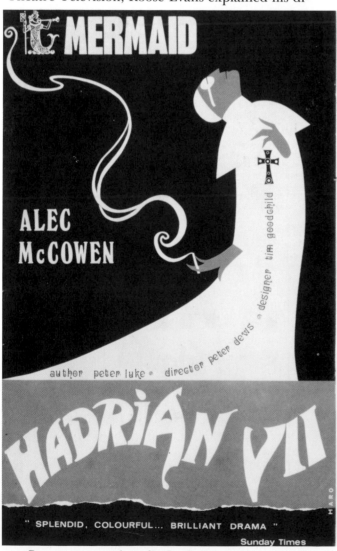

Cast

Fr. William Rolfe	*Alec McCowen*
Mrs. Crowe	*Margaret Courtenay*
Bailiffs:	*Alan MacNaughtan*
	Donald Eccles
Agnes	*Peggy Aitchison*
Dr. Talacryn, Bishop of Caerleon	*Alan MacNaughtan*
Dr. Courtleigh, Cardinal-Archbishop of Pimlico	*Donald Eccles*
Jeremiah Sant	*Patrick McAlinney*
The Cardinal-Archdeacon	*William Bond*
Father St. Albans, Prepositor-General of the Jesuits	*Brian Tully*
Cardinal Berstein	*Otto Diamant*
Cardinal Ragna	*Brian Coburn*
Rector of St. Andrew's College	*Aidan Turner*
George Arthur Rose	*Vivian Mackerrell*
Papal Chamberlain	*Patrick Marley*
Cardinals:	*Anthony King, Graham Leaman, Raymond Graham Jeffrey Sacks, John C. Wright*
Seminarists:	*Roger Clayton, Alan Helm, Laurence Terry*
Papal Guards:	*David Ralph, Edmund Thomas*
Swiss Guards:	*Roger Clayton, Alan Helm, Anthony King, Christopher Masters, Jeffrey Sacks, Laurence Terry*
Acolytes:	*Roger Clayton, Alan Helm, Christopher Masters, David Ralph, Laurence Terry, Edmund Thomas*

There will be one interval

9

Program cover and cast list for the first London production of Luke's play based on Frederick Rolfe's "unadaptable" novel

1964. It had, he decided, "a Cinderella theme. Poor persecuted Cinders achieves her dream, goes to the ball and marries Prince Charming. In Hadrian VII poor persecuted Freddy Rolfe achieves his dream, goes to the Vatican and becomes Pope." But like Cinderella, Luke's play first met rejection; and McCowen, reading the play for the first time, noted "A lot of it is totally undramatic and looks impossible."

Only several appearances in unsuccessful plays in the West End returned McCowen to his agent and subsequently to Luke's play. Reading it again, and enthralled with act 3, McCowen, faced with what seemed to him a dead act 2, suggested fashioning a two-act play. Most of the material in the second act would be cut and the remainder moved to the surviving acts. For Luke it was a painful procedure, but it meant a production, which opened on 9 May 1967 at the Birmingham Repertory Theatre. First-night critics, some of whom came up from London, were unimpressed. The novel, Irving Wardle concluded in the *Times*, was unadaptable, and the playwright's devices were unworkable: "Rolfe certainly has a lot in common with his hero; but for all his obsessive attachment to the Roman Catholic Church he never managed to enter the priesthood, let alone find himself elected Pope. Mr. Luke gets round this by transforming the novel into a fantasy which Rolfe [a bankrupt "George Rose" in the original novel] indulges while waiting for the bailiffs to seize his belongings—a trick which always strikes one as a cheat, and which belittles the artist into a mere daydreamer. *Hadrian the Seventh* may have been fired with wish-fulfillment, but Walter Mitty could not have written it." Still, logic aside, Wardle observed that the "leapfrog jumps" in which the hero ascends from indigent obscurity to St. Peter's throne in "a whirlwind of underdog eloquence," with Rolfe's "corrosive dialogue" utilized where possible by Luke, were "brilliantly speakable." Eric Shorter in the *Telegraph* thought the "dream pope" ought to have been brought to Rome more quickly; but whether *Hadrian VII* would now be brought to London was the real question, given the nearly empty houses of its Birmingham run.

The Mermaid Theatre, however, needed a new play, and before the transfer the next year, the acting script was shortened from 104 to 77 pages, indeed bringing Hadrian to Rome with more dispatch, while the motives of the villain, Jeremiah Sant, were strengthened. The play now opened with Rolfe's landlady knocking on the door of his nearly bare room, where Rolfe is writing at his book:

LANDLADY: "Mr. Rolfe! Mr. Rolfe!!"
ROLFE: "Tickle your arse with a feather!"
LANDLADY: "What's that?"
ROLFE: "Particularly nasty weather!"

London reviews in the papers the morning after the opening were enthusiastic. In the *Sunday Times* Harold Hobson wrote of "this splendid, colourful, recklessly melodramatic and vituperatively brilliant drama." The play sold out its scheduled six-week run and continued to the Helen Hayes Theatre in New York, where it opened 26 December 1968 for thirteen previews prior to the official opening on 8 January 1969. Again the play was a success. The play as a wish-fulfillment fantasy treatment of the novel had worked.

The first act takes Rolfe (no longer, as in the novel, disguised thinly as George Arthur Rose), in his fantasy, from penury to the papacy by the simple device of having the two bailiffs who come to seize Rolfe's possessions turn into Talacryn and Courtleigh, the two ecclesiastics whom Rolfe imagines as arriving to offer him ordination as a priest. Eventually—since as a priest he is eligible to become pope—he triumphs over his enemies in the church and is voted into the supreme office. The act closes with his response to the question, "Reverend Father, the Sacred College has elected thee to be the successor to St. Peter. Wilt thou accept pontificality?" Rolfe accepts, and becomes Hadrian VII.

In the second act, the new pope begins to reform the church, acquiring more enemies, in particular Jeremiah Sant, the Belfast Fenian who will eventually assassinate him. To a gathering of cardinals, Hadrian appeals, "Venerable Fathers, ask yourselves whether we are really as successful as we think we are, whether in fact we are not abject and lamentable failures in the eyes of God. We have added and added to the riches, pomp and power of the Church, and yet everywhere there is great wealth alongside dire poverty. . . . Let us now try the road to Apostolic simplicity. . . , the simplicity of Peter the fisherman. Let us at least try!" But the cardinals have no interest in permitting this threat to their style of living to survive and prosper. In the end, Luke has Rolfe stand at the side of the stage, smoking his inevitable cigarette and holding the manuscript of the novel, watching the funeral cortege of Hadrian. An epilogue (scene 8 of act two) returns us to Rolfe's bleak, bare London room as the bailiffs arrive with their warrant to remove all of Rolfe's possessions. He retains one item—a manuscript he has written about a man who made the mistake of living before his time. "Any value?" asks

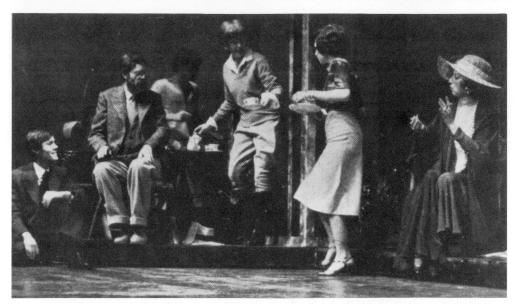

A scene from the first production of Bloomsbury

Penelope Wilton and Moyra Fraser in a scene from the first production of Bloomsbury

Alec McCowen as Hadrian VII

the first bailiff. "It's a masterpiece," says Rolfe, "and, therefore, probably not worth tuppence." The bailiffs are convinced, and one of them seizes it, too. After all, Rolfe might be right. And Rolfe is left alone in the cold, utterly bare, room.

After the success of *Hadrian VII*, Luke moved with his family to Spain, where he wrote several television plays and another stage work, *Bloomsbury* (1974), an effort to bring to theatrical life the Bloomsbury writers and artists in Virginia Woolf's circle. The narrator is Woolf herself, who soliloquizes but never interacts with the other Bloomsburyites. Woolf says, "I have conducted their gyrations, their rise and fall. I have orchestrated their movements like waves," but her isolation proves a weakness in the play's concept. Reviewing the production at the Phoenix Theatre in London, Irving Wardle noted that none of the action takes place in Bloomsbury and that the production itself takes place "in a bare cavern (the interior of Mrs. Woolf's head) animated with projected seascapes and trucked pieces which belong neither quite to reality nor to dream." The melange of melodramatic scenes failed to work. As Wardle put it, "See Virginia Woolf going mad. See Lytton Strachey in bed with two close friends. Hear armistice bells peal out their joyous message on the same morning that he gets his rave reviews. Or, by the same token, witness him struck down by a jealous rival at the moment war is declared." *Bloomsbury* was pat and false, both to history and to personality. The play failed to run, and Luke has since not offered the West End another.

Other:

Enter Certain Players: Edwards-MacLiammoir and the Gate, 1928-1978, edited by Luke (Dublin: Dolmen, 1978).

Periodical Publication:

"Peter Luke Used to Be a Television Producer. Then He Escaped," *Listener* (12 September 1968): 335-336.

Reference:

Alec McCowen, *Double Bill* (London: Elm Tree Books, 1980).

Contributors

Arthur Nicholas Athanason...*Michigan State University*
Deirdre Bair..*University of Pennsylvania*
Roger N. Cornish...*Pennsylvania State University*
Robert Coskren...*Oklahoma State University*
Bernard F. Dukore...*University of Hawaii at Manoa*
Mark Fritz...*Lafayette, Louisiana*
Richard B. Gidez...*Pennsylvania State University*
H. Lloyd Goodall, Jr....................................*University of Alabama in Huntsville*
Ronald Hayman..*London, England*
Kathleen B. Hindman...*Mansfield State College*
John R. Kaiser...*Pennsylvania State University*
Albert E. Kalson...*Purdue University*
Timothy J. Kidd..*Trinity College, Cambridge*
Philip Klass..*Pennsylvania State University*
Heinz Kosok...*University of Wuppertal*
Max Le Blond...*National University of Singapore*
Stanley Lourdeaux...*College of William and Mary*
Patrick A. McCarthy..*University of Miami*
Michael J. Mendelsohn..*University of Tampa*
Ruth Milberg-Kaye......................................*Herbert H. Lehman College-CUNY*
Moylan C. Mills...*Pennsylvania State University*
Christopher Murray...*University College, Dublin*
Andrew Parkin...*University of British Columbia*
Susan Rusinko..*Bloomsburg State College*
Eric Salmon...*University of Guelph*
June Schlueter..*Lafayette College*
Barbara J. Small...*Montclair State College*
Anthony Stephenson...*York University*
J. C. Trewin...*London, England*
Brian F. Tyson..*University of Lethbridge*
Michael J. Weimer..*Greenvale, New York*
Erica Beth Weintraub...*Arlington, Virginia*
Rodelle Weintraub...*State College, Pennsylvania*
Stanley Weintraub..*Pennsylvania State University*
Susan Whitehead...*London, England*
Audrey Williamson..*London, England*
Betsy Greenleaf Yarrison..*Rutgers University*

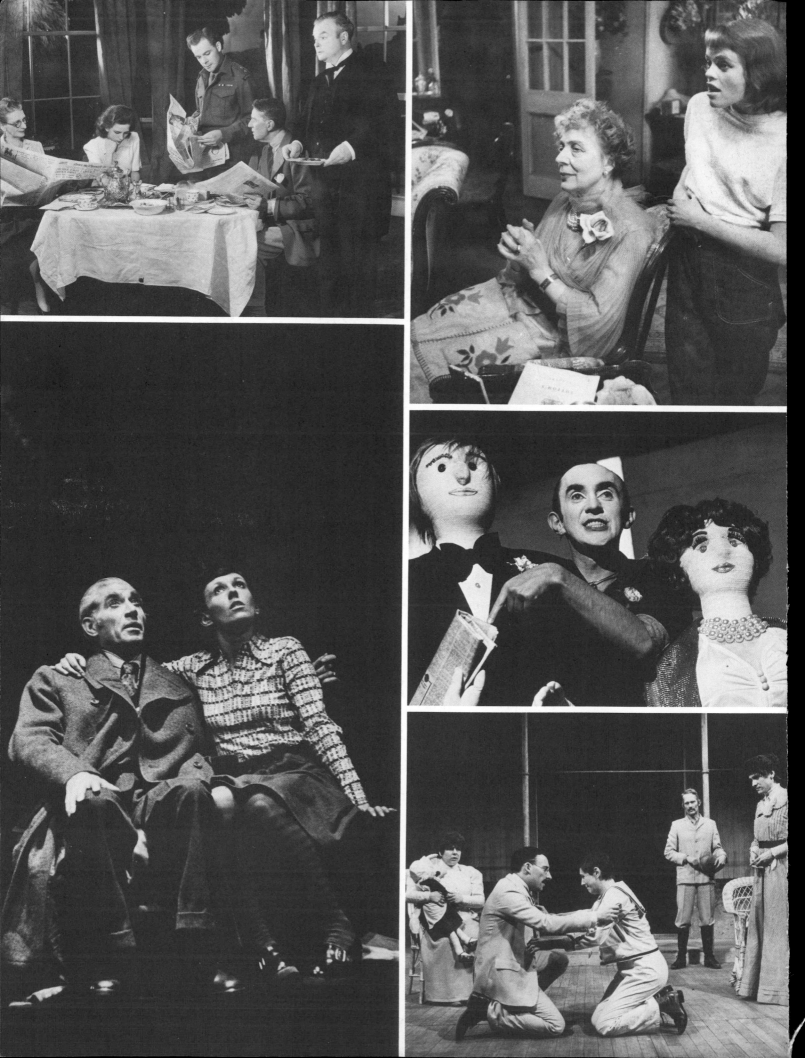